S0-BEA-922

Me MONEY EDUCATION

FUNDAMENTALS OF FINANCIAL PLANNING

THIRD EDITION

Michael A. Dalton
Joseph M. Gillice
James F. Dalton
Thomas P. Langdon

FUNDAMENTALS OF FINANCIAL PLANNING

THIRD EDITION

MONEY EDUCATION

115 JAMES DRIVE WEST
SUITE 140
ST. ROSE, LA 70087
888-295-6023

Copyright© 2013 by ME. All rights reserved.

No part of this publication may be reproduced or transmitted in any form or by any means, electronic or mechanical, including photocopy, recording, or any other information storage and retrieval system, without prior permission in writing from the publisher. Requests for permission to make copies of any part of the work should be mailed to: Permissions Department, ME, 115 James Drive West, Suite 140, St. Rose, LA 70087.

This publication is designed to provide accurate and authoritative information in regard to the subject matter covered. It is sold with the understanding that the publisher, authors, and contributors are not engaged in rendering legal, accounting, tax, financial planning, or other professional services. If legal advice, tax advice, or other professional assistance is required, the services of a competent professional should be sought.

CFP®, CERTIFIED FINANCIAL PLANNER™, and CFP (with flame logo)® are certification marks owned by Certified Financial Planner Board of Standards Inc. These marks are awarded to individuals who successfully complete CFP Board's initial and ongoing certification requirements.

Printed in the U.S.A.

ISBN-13: 978-1-936602-09-4
ISBN-13(S): 978-1-936602-10-0

Library of Congress Card Number: - 2012953338

ABOUT THE AUTHORS

Michael A. Dalton, Ph.D., JD, CFP®
- Former Chair of the Board of Dalton Publications, L.L.C.
- Associate professor of Accounting and Taxation at Loyola University in New Orleans, Louisiana
- Adjunct faculty in Financial Planning at Georgetown University in Washington, D.C.
- Former Senior Vice President, Education at BISYS Group
- Ph.D. in Accounting from Georgia State University
- J.D. from Louisiana State University in Baton Rouge, Louisiana
- MBA and BBA in Management and Accounting from Georgia State University
- Former board member of the CFP® Board's Board of Examiners, Board of Standards, and Board of Governors
- Former member (and chair) of the CFP® Board's Board of Examiners
- Member of the Financial Planning Association
- Member of the *Journal of Financial Planning* Editorial Advisory Board
- Member of the *Journal of Financial Planning* Editorial Review Board
- Member of the LSU Law School Board of Trustees (2000 - 2006)
- Author of *Dalton Review for the CFP® Certification Examination: Volume I – Outlines and Study Guides, Volume II – Problems and Solutions, Volume III - Case Exam Book, Mock Exams A-1 and A-2 (1st - 8th Editions)*
- Author of *Retirement Planning and Employee Benefits for Financial Planners (1st - 7th Editions)*
- Co-author of *Estate Planning for Financial Planners (1st - 6th Editions)*
- Co-author of *Income Tax Planning for Financial Planners (1st - 4th Editions)*
- Co-author of *Dalton CFA® Study Notes Volumes I and II (1st - 2nd Editions)*
- Co-author of *Dalton's Personal Financial Planning Series – Personal Financial Planning Theory and Practice (1st - 3rd Editions)*
- Co-author of *Dalton's Personal Financial Planning Series – Personal Financial Planning Cases and Applications (1st - 4th Editions)*
- Co-author of *Cost Accounting: Traditions and Innovations* published by West Publishing Company
- Co-author of the *ABCs of Managing Your Money* published by National Endowment for Financial Education

Joseph M. Gillice, MBA, CPA, CFP®
- President, Dalton Education, L.L.C.
- Former Director of University Programs for BISYS Education Services
- Former adjunct instructor in financial planning at Georgetown University in Washington, D.C.
- Former adjunct instructor in financial planning at Duke University in Durham, NC
- Instructor in live online financial planning programs for Rice University, New York University, and Northwestern University
- Author of *Financial Calculator Essentials*
- Co-author of *Fundamentals of Financial Planning (1st Editions)*
- Co-author of *Fundamentals of Financial Planning Insurance Supplement (1st - 2nd Editions)*
- Co-author of *The Dalton Review® Pre-Study Materials in Fundamentals of Financial Planning and Insurance*
- Co-author of *The Dalton Review® Pre-Study Materials in Investment Planning*

- Developed the Online Executive Certificate in Financial Planning program for New York University and Northwestern University
- MBA from Georgia State University
- BS in finance from Florida State University

James F. Dalton, MBA, MS, CPA/PFS, CFA®, CFP®

- Adjunct faculty member at Georgetown University
- Former Executive Vice President, Assessment Technologies Institute LLC
- Former Senior Vice President, Kaplan Professional
- Former President, Dalton Publications LLC
- Former Senior Manager of KPMG, LLP, concentrating in personal financial planning, investment planning, and litigation consulting
- MBA from Loyola University New Orleans
- Master of Accounting in Taxation from the University of New Orleans
- BS in accounting from Florida State University in Tallahassee, Florida
- Member of the CFP Board of Standards July 1996, Comprehensive CFP® Exam Pass Score Committee
- Member of the AICPA and the Louisiana Society of CPAs
- Member of the Financial Planning Association
- Member of the *Journal of Financial Planning* Editorial Review Board
- Member of the New Orleans Estate Planning Council
- Author of Kaplan Schweser's Personal Financial Planning Understanding Your Financial Calculator
- Author of Kaplan Schweser's Understanding Your Financial Calculator for the CFA® Exam
- Co-author of BISYS CFA® Study Notes Volumes I and II
- Co-author of Kaplan Schweser's Personal Financial Planning Cases and Applications
- Co-author of the Kaplan Schweser Review for the CFP® Certification Examination, Volumes I–VIII and Kaplan Schweser's Financial Planning Flashcards

Thomas P. Langdon, JD, LL.M.

- Professor of Business Law, Gabelli School of Business, Roger Williams University, Bristol, RI
- Principal, Langdon & Langdon Financial Services, LLC (Connecticut-based tax planning & preparation firm)
- Former Professor of Taxation at The American College, Bryn Mawr, PA.
- Former Adjunct Professor of Insurance and Economics at The University of Connecticut Center for Professional Development
- Former Member (and Chair) of the CFP Board's Board of Examiners
- Master of Laws (LL.M.) in Taxation from Villanova University School of Law
- Juris Doctor, from Western New England College School of Law
- Master of Science in Financial Services from The American College
- Master of Business Administration from The University of Connecticut
- Bachelor of Science in Finance from The University of Connecticut, Storrs, CT.

- Chartered Financial Analyst (CFA), Certified Financial Planner (CFP), Chartered Life Underwriter (CLU), Chartered Financial Consultant (ChFC), Accredited Estate Planner (AEP), Chartered Advisor in Philanthropy (CAP), Certified Employee Benefits Specialist (CEBS), Chartered Advisor in Senior Living (CASL), Registered Employee Benefits Consultant (REBC), Registered Health Underwriter (RHU), Associate in Life & Health Claims (ALHC), and Fellow of the Life Management Institute (FLMI)
- Associate Editor of the *Journal of Financial Services Professionals*
- Co-author of *Estate Planning for Financial Planners (1st - 6th Editions)*
- Co-author of *Income Tax Planning for Financial Planners (1st - 4th Editions)*
- Contributing of *Fundamentals of Financial Planning Insurance Supplement (1st - 2nd Editions)*
- Faculty member for National Tax Institute

ABOUT THE CONTRIBUTING AUTHOR

Randal R. Cangelosi, JD, MBA
- Practicing litigator throughout Louisiana, in business/commercial law and litigation, products liability litigation, wills and trust litigation, environmental law and litigation, medical malpractice defense, and insurance law and litigation
- Has successfully defended numerous corporations, businesses, and doctors in jury and judge trials
- Juris Doctorate from Loyola University New Orleans
- Masters of Business Administration from Loyola University New Orleans
- BS in Finance from Louisiana State University
- Member of the American & Federal Bar Associations
- Member of the Bar of the State of Louisiana
- Member of the New Orleans and Baton Rouge Bar Associations
- Board Member of the Baton Rouge Area Chapter of the American Red Cross
- Board Member of La Lupus Foundation
- Admitted to practice before US District Courts, Western, Eastern & Middle Districts of Louisiana
- Admitted to practice before the Federal 5th Circuit Court of Appeals
- Admitted to practice in USDC, Southern District of Iowa (Pro Hac Vice)
- Admitted to practice in Circuit Court of Wayne County, Mississippi (Pro Hac Vice)
- Admitted to practice in Circuit Court of Barbour County, Alabama (Pro Hac Vice)
- Admitted to practice in Court of Common Pleas, Darlington County, South Carolina (Pro Hac Vice)
- Admitted to practice in Los Angeles County Superior Court, California (Pro Hac Vice)
- Admitted to practice in Superior Court of New Jersey: Morris County (Pro Hac Vice)
- Admitted to practice in 17th Judicial Court, Broward County, Florida (Pro Hac Vice)
- Former Chairman of New Orleans Bar Association, Community Service Committee
- Former Chairman of New Orleans Bar Association, Food and Clothing Drives
- Co-author of *Personal Financial Planning: Theory and Practice (1st - 3rd Editions)*
- Co-author of *Professional Ethics for Financial Planners*

ABOUT THE REVIEWERS & CONTRIBUTORS

We owe a special thanks to several key professionals for their significant contribution of time and effort with this text. These reviewers provided meticulous editing, detailed calculation reviews, helpful suggestions for additional content, and other valuable comments, all of which have improved this edition.

Dr. James Coleman has over 15 years teaching experience, including undergraduate, graduate, and Executive MBA programs at Troy University, Mercer University, and Dalton State College. In addition, as Vice President of Market Results, a financial planning training and consulting firm, he has helped hundreds of candidates pass the Certified Financial Planner™ exam over the last decade. Prior to his academic career, Jim spent over a decade in public accounting and corporate management, concluding with the position of Managing Director of Public Relations at Federal Express, where he was responsible for the company's global public and investor relations activities. His degrees include a MS and Ph.D. from University of Alabama as well as BBA in accountancy from University of Mississippi.

Donna Dalton made a significant contribution to this textbook by her thoughtful and meticulous editing throughout the book. She provided many valuable improvements to both the textbook and instructor materials. We are extremely grateful for her contributions. This book would not have been possible without her extraordinary dedication, skill, and knowledge.

Phyllis Duhon made a significant contribution to this textbook by her thoughtful and meticulous reading, rewriting, and editing throughout the book. She provided many valuable suggestions and improvements to both the textbook and instructor materials that significantly improved this edition. We are extremely grateful for her contributions. Ms. Duhon is an attorney and received her J.D. from Loyola University New Orleans College of Law and a B.S. in Business Administration/Finance from the University of New Orleans. She is a contributor to *Estate Planning for Financial Planners, Retirement Planning and Employee Benefits for Financial Planners,* and *Income Tax Planning for Financial Planners* by Money Education.

Katheleen F. Oakley is the Academic Program Director for classroom and web-based CFP Certification Education programs in the Susanne M. Glasscock, School of Continuing Studies at Rice University. She is co-author of Money Education's Cases in Financial Planning, Analysis and Presentation, 1st edition textbook and instructor manual. Kathy is also former vice president and chief financial planning officer with Kanaly Trust Company (Houston, Texas), the former director of financial planning for the Houston office of Lincoln Financial Advisors, and a former board member of the Pearland Economic Development Corporation. She is a member of the Financial Planning Association. Kathy received her BS in Finance and an MBA from the University of New Orleans.

Randy Martinez is a personal financial planner specializing in personal financial planning, estate, and individual income tax planning. He teaches retirement planning, estate planning, and income tax planning through various CFP® Board-Registered Programs as well as comprehensive reviews for the CFP® certification.

Robin Meyer made a significant contribution to this textbook by organizing and directing the entire project. Developing a textbook that is aesthetically pleasing and easy to read is a difficult undertaking. Robin worked diligently with the authors and reviewers to manage the project, performed numerous reviews, and provided invaluable feedback throughout the entire project. This book would not have been possible without her extraordinary dedication, skill, and knowledge.

Dr. Moshe Shmuklarsky has a keen personal interest in the conceptual underpinning and practical knowledge related to business and personal finance as reflected by his Master of Business Administration from the John Hopkins School of Professional Studies and a Certificate in Personal Financial Planning from the Georgetown University. Dr. Shmuklarsky has more than 25 years experience in research and development of drugs and vaccines. Through the application of the Balanced Score Card, Dr. Shmuklarsky has transformed the Department of Clinical Trials at the Walter Reed Army Institute of Research in Washington DC to a center of excellence in clinical research.

Henry Spil is an adjunct faculty member at Oglethorpe University with 25 years of tax experience. He works for a financial planning firm in Atlanta, Georgia, is a CPA and a CFP® certificant. Mr. Spil is a graduate of Emory University with a Bachelor of Business Administration degree. He also has a Master of Science in Taxation from Florida International University.

Kristi Tafalla is an attorney and personal financial planner specializing in income tax and estate planning. She teaches estate planning, income tax planning and comprehensive case courses through various CFP® Board-Registered Programs as well as comprehensive reviews for the CFP® certification. She is a contributor to Money Education's Estate Planning for Financial Planners and Retirement Planning and Employee Benefits for Financial Planners.

Steve Wetzel is the President and founder of a financial planning firm in Pennsylvania. He is both the program director and adjunct professor for the financial planning program at New York University. Mr. Wetzel received his BA in Economics from State University of New York – Stony Brook. He also received his MBA in Finance and International Business from New York University along with his Advanced Professional Certificate in Accounting. Mr. Wetzel is also a CFP® certificant.

Bill Yurkovac has a private practice in Florida focusing on asset management and estate planning considerations for his clientele. Mr. Yurkovac holds a Master's Degree in Education, has more than twenty-five years experience in the financial services arena, and enjoys serving as an instructor for candidates preparing for the CFP® Certification Examination. Current community involvement includes assisting and counseling several nonprofit organizations and a chair on the local Estate Planning Council's Board of Directors.

ACKNOWLEDGEMENTS & SPECIAL THANKS

We are most appreciative for the tremendous support and encouragement we have received throughout this project. We are extremely grateful to the instructors and program directors of CFP® Board-Registered programs who provided valuable comments during the development stages of this text. We are fortunate to have dedicated, careful readers at several institutions who were willing to share their needs, expectations, and time with us.

A special thanks to several of Dr. Dalton's financial planning students at Georgetown University. The students reviewed numerous chapters of this textbook and provided valuable feedback regarding 1st edition improvements.

We would like to pay special thanks to Donna Dalton and Robin Meyer. It takes more than just the writer to produce a finished book and they are an essential element of our team. Thanks also goes out to Desktop Miracles for designing our new cover and chapter title artwork.

PREFACE

Fundamentals of Financial Planning is written for graduate and upperdivision undergraduate level students interested in acquiring an understanding of financial planning from a professional financial planning viewpoint. The text is intended to be used in a Fundamentals course as part of an overall curriculum in financial planning. The text is also intended to serve as a reference for practicing professional financial planners.

This text was designed to meet the educational requirements for a Fundamentals Course in a CFP® Board-Registered Program. Therefore, one of our goals is to assure CFP® Board-Registered Program Directors, instructors, students, and financial planners that we have addressed every relevant topic covered by the CFP® Board Exam Topic List and the most recent model curriculum syllabus for this course. The book will be updated, as needed, to keep current with any changes in the law, exam topic list, or model curriculum.

Special Features

A variety of tools and presentation methods are used throughout this text to assist the reader in the learning process. Some of the features in this text that are designed to enhance your understanding and learning process include:

- **Key Concepts** – At the beginning of each subsection are key concepts, or study objectives, each stated as a question. To be successful in this course, you should be able to answer these questions. So as you read, guide your learning by looking for the answers. When you find the answers, highlight or underline them. It is important that you actually highlight/underline and not just make a mental note, as the action of stopping and writing reinforces your learning. Watch for this symbol:

- **Quick Quizzes** – Following each subsection you will find a Quick Quiz, which checks and reinforces what you read. Circle the answer to each question and then check your answers against the correct answers supplied at the bottom of the quiz. If you missed any questions, flip back to the relevant section and review the material. Watch for this symbol:

- **Examples** – Examples are used frequently to illustrate the concepts being discussed and to help the reader understand and apply the concepts presented. Examples are identified in the margin with the following symbol:

EXAMPLE

- **Exhibits** – The written text is enhanced and simplified by using exhibits where appropriate to promote learning and application. Exhibits are identified with the following symbol:

EXHIBIT

- **Key Terms** – Key terms appear in **boldfaced type** throughout the text to assist in the identification of important concepts and terminology. A list of key terms with definitions appears at the end of each chapter.

- **End of Chapter Questions** – Each chapter contains a series of discussion and multiple-choice questions that highlight the major topics covered in the chapter. The questions test retention and understanding of important chapter material and can be used for review and classroom discussion.

- **Quick Quiz Explanations** – Each chapter concludes with the answers to the Quick Quizzes contained in that chapter, as well as explanation to the "false" statements in each Quick Quiz.

- **Glossary** – A compilation of the key terms identified throughout the text is located at the end of the book.

Additional Information Available on Money Education's Website (money-education.com)
- Time Value of Money Formulas
- CFP Job Knowledge Requirements
- Resourceful Websites
- Cost of Living Adjustments (COLA) Increases

**VISIT OUR WEBSITE AT
MONEY-EDUCATION.COM
FOR UPDATES TO THE TEXT**

This book is dedicated to
Donna Dalton & Robin Meyer
for their incredible ability to make miracles
happen against all odds. They truly went above
and beyond even their own high standards with
the publication of this book. They are the
embodiment of Money Education's spirit
and work ethic and we are honored to
have them on our team.

Table of Contents

Chapter 3 - Financial Planning Approaches: Analysis & Recommendations

Chapter 4 - Personal Financial Statements: Preparation and Analysis

Chapter 5 - Risk Management for the Individual Client

Chapter 6 - John & Mary Burke Case and Case Analysis

Chapter 7 - Time Value of Money

Chapter 8 - Education and Education Funding

Chapter 9 - Investments

Chapter 10 - David & Amy Rudolph Case and Case Analysis Part 1

Chapter 12 - Income Tax Planning

Chapter 13 - Business Entity Selection and Taxation

Chapter 14 - Estate Planning

Chapter 15 - Economics and the External Environment

Chapter 16 - Ethics & Standards of Professional Conduct

Chapter 17 - Planning for Special Circumstances

Chapter 18 - David & Amy Rudolph Case and Case Analysis Part 2

Appendix

Introduction to Financial Planning

LEARNING OBJECTIVES

After reading this chapter, you should be able to:

- Describe the personal financial planning process.
- Diagram the personal financial planning process as defined by the CFP Board's Job Task Domains and *Financial Planning Practice Standards*.*
- List the contents of a comprehensive financial plan.
- Describe the establishment and definition of the client relationship including the introductory meeting and engagement letter.
- Define the activities that are typically part of the scope of an engagement.
- Describe the client data gathering process including internal and external data.
- Understand what goes on in the analysis and evaluation of the client's financial status.
- Understand the development and presenting of financial plan recommendations.
- Understand the implementation of financial plan recommendations.
- Understand the monitoring of the plan.
- Describe the benefits from financial planning.
- Clearly delineate why clients use a professional financial plan.
- Have a broad understanding of the practice of financial planning.
- List and differentiate the various recognized certifications in financial planning.
- Have a broad view of the employment and job outlook for financial planners and the various means of compensation for financial planning services.

* CFP Board Resource Document - Student-Centered Learning Objectives based upon CFP Board Principal Topics.

INTRODUCTION

This textbook is a valuable resource for financial planning students and practitioners, including those with either limited or substantial experience, and those who are interested in improving their financial planning skills. The broad knowledge base required of a financial planner is covered in an introductory manner throughout this textbook, including the financial planning process from the initial contact with a client to the presentation of the plan itself. Case studies are included in the textbook that cover a range of scenarios from basic to more complex. Varied financial planning approaches are provided to ensure that the financial planner has the appropriate planning methodologies necessary to arrive at logical and substantiated planning recommendations. This textbook should remain an important reference tool for the financial planner seeking knowledge and assistance in the preparation of professional comprehensive personal financial plans.

PERSONAL FINANCIAL PLANNING

Personal financial planning (financial planning) is the process of formulating, implementing, and monitoring financial decisions into an integrated plan that guides an individual or a family to achieve their financial goals.

THE PROCESS

The **process of financial planning** includes, but is not limited to:

Establishing and defining the client relationship
- the introductory meeting
- identifying general goals and objectives
- formulating an engagement letter

Gathering client data
- gathering internal client data, including goals
- determining relevant external data

Analyzing and Evaluating Client's Financial Status
- preparing data analysis including an evaluation of the client's risk management portfolio, financial statement analysis, and the external economic environment
- establishing alternative options (plans) to achieve financial goals including time frames

Developing and Presenting Financial Plan Recommendations
- selecting one set of recommendations from the alternative options

Implementing Financial Plan Recommendations
- defining the planner's responsibilities separately from the client's responsibilities
- guiding the implementation of the plan

Monitoring the Plan
- setting a schedule for the periodic review and adjustment of the agreed to plan

Exhibit 1.1 provides a visual representation of the financial planning process.

EXHIBIT 1.1

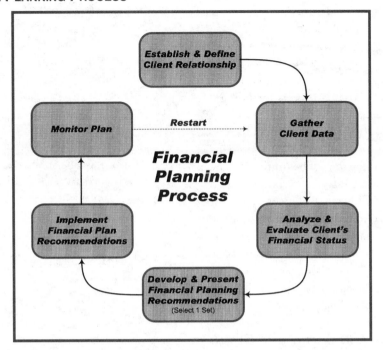

CONTENTS OF THE FINANCIAL PLAN

A **financial plan** is a written document that generally sets out a list of recommendations to achieve a set of goals and objectives based on an understanding of a client's current financial situation. A financial plan is the work product and result from the application of several financial planning concepts to a client's current and prospective financial situation. The application of the concepts (listed below) considers the client's financial goals and values (**internal data**) and the external environment (**external data**). The external environment includes current and expected future income, gift and estate taxes, investment returns, inflation and interest rates.

Financial planning concepts applied include:

- an evaluation of the client's risk management portfolio (includes risks retained and risks transferred through the use of insurance contracts)
- financial statement preparation and analysis including cash flow analysis and budgeting
- emergency fund and debt management (short-term goals)
- long-term goal planning including:
  - achieving financial security (retirement planning)
  - education planning for children's or grandchildren's college or private secondary education
  - planning for lump-sum purchases (major expenditures)
  - legacy planning (estate planning)
- income tax planning is integrated throughout all aspects of the plan
- the investment planning portfolio is used to fund many of the client's short and long-term goals

---

1. Abbreviated from the CFP Board's Financial Planning Practice Standards.

In order to apply each of these concepts to a client's current and prospective financial status, the financial planner uses tools such as financial statement preparation and analysis, cash flow analysis, and budgeting. This chapter introduces the first two steps in the financial planning process including: (1) establishing the relationship and (2) gathering client data. The chapter also provides information regarding the financial planning profession. The entire financial planning method is comprehensively reviewed in Chapter 3 (Financial Planning Approaches) and then applied to a case in detail in Chapter 6 (Burke Case). Two additional case studies in Chapters 10 and 18 (Rudolph Case Part 1 and 2) provide additional applications of and insights into the financial planning process.

Key Concepts

Underline/highlight the answers as you read.

1. Define the steps in the financial planning process.

2. Explain the difference between internal and external data collected as part of the financial planning process.

3. Identify the subject matter areas that are applied to a client's financial plan considering the client's profile, financial goals, and values.

4. Know what the financial planner should attempt to accomplish during the client introductory meeting.

ESTABLISH AND DEFINE THE CLIENT RELATIONSHIP

Communication with Client

The role of the financial planner is to educate the client, gather relevant information, analyze that information, and assist the client in preparing and implementing a financial plan that will achieve the client's financial goals within the desired time frame.

In order to educate the client and gather relevant information, the financial planner must be able to communicate effectively with the client. The planner must respect the client and establish a relationship of trust. The planner must be empathetic and assess the attitudes and values of the client as well as the client's risk tolerance and views regarding savings, spending, taxation, and financial discipline. Issues such as the importance of work versus leisure time, job security, community service, attitudes regarding children from previous marriages, former spouses, and the client's extended family all are important in understanding and assisting the client to achieve their goals.

How does a planner effectively communicate with a client? From the onset, the financial planner should address the client formally (Mr., Mrs., Dr., etc.) using the appropriate salutation. This formality can be relaxed later in the relationship if the client is more comfortable with first names. The planner should actively listen to the client and especially to the verbs the client uses. This often indicates the client's learning style. Use of phrases such as "see what I mean," "imagine that," and any other words that imply that the client is a visual learner suggests that the planner should use examples including charts, graphs, and other visual aids to make the client more comfortable. If the client appears to pay attention to every spoken word or is asking for an explanation of words, the client's learning style is likely that of a verbal learner and graphics may be supplemented with carefully selected words. There is some data that suggests that up to 65 percent of people are visual learners. A generous use of pictures, graphs, and charts is always helpful in the communication process.

Key Concepts

Underline/highlight the answers as you read.

1. List the elements of the financial planning engagement letter.

2. Describe the purpose of a financial planning client questionnaire.

3. Summarize the types of necessary quantitative and qualitative data that is collected from the client.

4. Provide examples of external environment data that a financial planner needs to know in order to properly analyze, evaluate, and make recommendations related to a comprehensive financial plan.

As a matter of professional courtesy, the financial planner should respect the client's time. This means being punctual, starting on time, ending on time, and telling the client how long each meeting will last. In order to establish a trusting relationship, the planner can generally share prior experiences. However, the planner must ensure that the client knows that client information is confidential by not identifying details about other clients.

The planner can show empathy by use of nonverbal pacing and showing a genuine interest in the hobbies, activities, vacations, and children of the client. To make communication effective, the financial planner can use restatement, paraphrasing, summarizing, open ended questions, and questions that show interest. This can assure minimal miscommunication allowing the planner to reach the pertinent details.

Introductory Meeting

If there has been little communication before the first meeting, the financial planner should at least provide the client with a list of documents and information that the client needs to provide for the first meeting (e.g., get to know each other, collect some data, answer questions, clarify goals, reduce fears). At the first meeting, the financial planner should assist the client with establishing defined goals and discuss how the client's values fit into those goals. There will also be a general discussion of the client's personal data and family data. Typically the planner will meet with either one, or preferably both spouses to get an overview of the family and extended family (e.g., ages, marital status, children, grandchildren, net worth, income, self employment). From this basic information the planner can make a preliminary assessment of the general risks and goals of the client.

The financial planner and client should mutually agree as to how they will communicate (e.g., email, office telephone, cell phone) and how often they will meet (e.g., 2 hours per week for 10 weeks). The client should be given a time frame for when the plan will be completed (e.g., 3 months). The financial planner should discuss the planning process, fees, and answer questions that the client is likely to have. The planner should effectively manage the client's expectations and have a remedy for instances when the client is dissatisfied. At the end of the introductory meeting an engagement letter should be prepared and sent to the client for approval.

Engagement Letter

An **engagement letter** is a legal agreement (a contract) between a professional organization and a client that defines their business relationship. The engagement letter should define the parties to the agreement, the specific services to be provided, the duration of the agreement, the methods of communication (email, meetings), and the expected frequency of contact. The letter should also specify the conditions under which the agreement can be terminated.

Elements of an engagement letter:
- define the parties to the agreement
- a description of the mutually agreed upon services (the scope of work)
- the time horizon for the work to be completed
- a description of the fees and costs
- the obligation and responsibilities of each party (planner/client) regarding:
  - defining goals, needs, and objectives
  - gathering data
  - projecting the result of no action
  - formulating alternative possibilities
  - selecting from those alternatives
  - establishing who is expected to implement which elements of the plan (this can be subject to revision at the implementation phase of the process)
  - defining who has monitoring responsibilities
  - delineating services that are not provided, such as legal documents or income, gift, or estate tax return preparation

In addition to the above, there should be a mutual understanding regarding the use of proprietary products and/or other professionals or entities in meeting any of the service obligations in the engagement agreement.

EXHIBIT 1.2

Sample Engagement Letter

Dear Client:

This letter will confirm the terms of our agreement regarding the financial planning services we will provide for you.

Engagement Objectives

The primary objective of our engagement is to review and analyze your personal financial situation and make recommendations for your financial plan. This review will identify your personal financial goals and objectives, and will include possible strategies to achieve them. Our analysis and recommendations are based on information provided by you that will be relied upon for representations.

Activities

The initial phase involves accumulating and organizing facts about your current financial status, identifying specific goals and objectives, and agreeing upon planning assumptions. This information will be obtained during an initial meeting or conversation with you and/or from the use of a financial planning data questionnaire. We will also review copies of pertinent documents, such as wills, company-provided fringe benefit booklets, prior tax returns, investment account statements, and insurance documents.

After the information has been received, the data will be analyzed and projections will be made. A subsequent meeting will be held to verify the accuracy of the data and will allow you to validate the assumptions used. Alternative courses of action to meet goals and address any issues will be comprehensively discussed.

The projections will then be updated for any required changes and a comprehensive financial planning report containing recommendations in all relevant areas of your financial situation will be presented. We will work with you to finalize the choice of strategies, to set time goals, and to establish responsibilities for your implementation of the plan.

The methods that you choose to follow for the implementation of the financial planning recommendations are at your discretion. You will be responsible for all decisions regarding implementation of the recommendations.

We are available, via a separate engagement, to assist you with implementation of your chosen strategies or to coordinate implementation with other financial professionals of your choosing. As part of this separate engagement, we can answer questions, monitor activities, or make new recommendations regarding your financial matters as circumstances change. In addition, we do not offer legal services such as will or trust preparation; however, we will be happy to refer you to a legal professional.

Your plan should be reviewed with us informally on a semiannual basis and more formally on an annual basis. These update sessions are essential so that adjustments can be made for changes in circumstances, economic conditions, and income, gift, or estate tax law revisions.

Fees

The fee for your Comprehensive Financial Plan has been determined by our mutual agreement and is $_____ which is due and payable upon return of this Engagement Letter. Please note that this fee is for the written financial plan alone and the plan shall contain all of our recommendations to you through the date of its delivery.

This agreement and fee does not provide for any product sales that may be offered at no obligation to you. This is a separate service that may be considered a conflict of interest because commissions and/or additional fees may be paid in connection with products purchased. We will inform you if there is any conflict of interest.

If additional conferences and interactions are beyond the scope of the services stated above, our fee for this service is based upon the time necessary to complete the additional agreed upon tasks. The agreed time allocated to accomplish additional tasks will be billed at our rate of $_____ per hour.

We reserve the right to discontinue services if billings are not paid when due.

If at any time you are dissatisfied with our services, you may terminate this agreement. If you do so within three business days of your acceptance, you will receive a full refund. Subsequently, any fees that you have paid to us in advance will be charged for the time and effort that has been devoted, up to that termination time, to prepare your written report and any remaining balance will be refunded.

We anticipate beginning the engagement immediately. If this letter meets with your approval, please sign the enclosed copy in the space provided and return it to us in the enclosed envelope.

We thank you for the opportunity to be of service, and we welcome you as a valued client.

Sincerely,

Financial Planner

I/We agree to the above terms & conditions:

Client Signature: _____   Date: _____

Client Signature: _____   Date: _____

The Scope of the Engagement

A financial planning engagement can be very narrow or fully comprehensive. Activities that are typically part of a comprehensive plan include:

- Preparation and analysis of personal financial statements;
- A review of all risk management policies (including life, health, disability, long-term care, property and liability insurance) and what to do about any uncovered areas of risk;
- An evaluation of short-term financial goals including the emergency fund and debt management;
- The establishment of long-term goals including retirement, education funding, lump-sum (major) expenditures, and legacy planning including documents;
- An evaluation of the current investment portfolio with the objective of creating a new investment approach that helps to achieve the client's goals within the risk tolerance of the client; and
- An examination and recommendation regarding any special needs situation of the client (divorce, elderly parent, special needs child). (See Special Needs chapter.)

Quick Quiz 1.1

Highlight the answer to these questions:

1. Personal financial planning is the comprehensive process of formulating, implementing, and monitoring financial decisions that guide the client to achieve financial goals.
   a. True
   b. False

2. Long-term goal planning includes emergency funding, financial security planning, education planning, lump-sum purchase planning, and legacy planning.
   a. True
   b. False

3. At the introductory meeting, the financial planner will collect data, come to understand the client's values and goals, establish the scope of the engagement, and discuss fees.
   a. True
   b. False

4. Examples of internal data include current interest rates, housing market status, job market status, local cost of living, and the expected inflation rate.
   a. True
   b. False

True, False, True, False.

GATHER CLIENT DATA

The Internal Data Collection Process

The planner must obtain sufficient information (both quantitative and qualitative) from the client in order to assess and analyze the client's financial situation. Quantitative information is measurable and includes the client's age, income, number of children, death benefit of life insurance policies, and much more. Qualitative information is how the client feels about something, or their attitude or belief, including working versus retiring and spending versus saving. The information includes client provided documents and may be obtained by the planner through the use of questionnaires and/or interviews. See Exhibit 1.3 for a basic sample of a client questionnaire. The planner will need to explore and evaluate the client's values, attitudes, expectations, and time horizons as they affect client goals, needs, and priorities.

Quantitative information collected must be complete, accurate, verifiable, and free from bias. The information to be collected will include:

- The family - list of members, their age, health, education, income, financial competence, and any special situations (e.g., special needs child, aging parents who are or may become dependents).
- The insurance portfolio - collect all insurance policies and a detailed description of any employer provided or sponsored insurance. Make sure to identify the premiums paid by the client (life, health, disability, long-term care, property including homeowners, flood, auto, boat, etc., and whether the client has a personal or professional liability policy).
- Banking and investment information - collect current statements on all bank accounts and investment accounts including qualified plans (IRAs, SEPs, SIMPLEs, 403(b)s, 457s). Obtain from the client any other investment information and their valuation, amount of debt and cash flows, such as rental property or business interests.
- Taxes - all income, gift and trust tax returns for the last five years if available.
- Retirement and Employee Benefits - all retirement information including Social Security statements or benefits (SSA 7004), employer sponsored retirement plans, and employee benefits (get a copy of the booklets and summary description of plan).
- Estate Planning - all wills, durable powers of attorney for health care decisions, all advance medical directives and any trust documents.
- All personal financial statements if available including any recently used to obtain debt (balance sheet and income statement) - a list of debt with original amount, date of inception, interest rate, term of repayment and current balance. Most clients will not have financial statements and either the planner or a CPA will have to prepare them.

The financial planner also needs to collect qualitative information from the client. Qualitative information includes the client's attitude and beliefs regarding:
- Education goals,
- Retirement goals,
- Employment goals,
- Savings goals,
- Risk tolerance,
- Charitable goals, and
- General attitude towards spending.

The financial planner will request that the client bring all of the above information to the first meeting. Frequently, the client will not have all the quantitative information (such as insurance policies and employee benefits brochures) and rarely do clients have properly prepared personal financial statements. The engagement letter may be modified to include an addendum of missing information needed for later meetings.

EXHIBIT 1.3

Sample of a Financial Planning Client Questionnaire*

General Information:	General Information:
Client 1 Full Name:	Client 2 Full Name:
Home Address:	Home Address
City, State, Zip:	City, State, Zip:
Home Phone:	Home Phone:
Work Phone:	Work Phone:
Mobile Phone:	Mobile Phone:
Occupation:	Occupation:
Employer:	Employer:
Annual Earned Income:	Annual Earned Income:
Fax:	Fax:
Email:	Email:
Social Security #:	Social Security #:
Birth date:	Birth date:
Prior Marriage(s):	Prior Marriage(s):

Family/Dependent Information:	Family/Dependent Information:
Name:	Name:
Relationship:	Relationship:
Date of Birth:	Date of Birth:
Social Security #:	Social Security #:
Dependent:	Dependent:
Resides:	Resides:

Assets:	Ownership: Client 1 or 2	Assets:	Ownership: Client 1 or 2
Bank Account:		**Bank Account:**	
Account Number & Type:		Account Number & Type:	
Average Balance:		Average Balance:	
CD – Held:		**CD – Held:**	
Maturity:		Maturity:	
Value:		Value:	
Primary Residence:		**Secondary Residence:**	
Value:		Value:	
Automobile 1:		**Automobile 2:**	
Value:		Value:	
Retirement Accounts:		**Retirement Accounts:**	
Type/Ownership:		Type/Ownership:	
Held by:		Held by:	
Account Number:		Account Number:	
Value:		Value:	
Other Account:		**Other Account:**	
Account Number & Type:		Account Number & Type:	
Value:		Value:	

Insurance:	Ownership: Client 1 or 2	Insurance:	Ownership: Client 1 or 2
Health/Company:		Health/Company:	
Coverage/Cost:		Coverage/Cost:	
Disability/Company:		Disability/Company:	
Coverage/Cost:		Coverage/Cost:	
Life/Company:		Life/Company:	
Type/Coverage/Cost:		Type/Coverage/Cost:	
Homeowners:		Homeowners:	
Type/Coverage/Cost:		Type/Coverage/Cost:	
Auto:		Auto:	
Type/Coverage/Cost:		Type/Coverage/Cost:	
Umbrella Liability:		Umbrella Liability:	
Type/Coverage/Cost:		Type/Coverage/Cost:	
Professional Liability		Professional Liability:	
Type/Coverage/Cost:		Type/Coverage/Cost:	
Long Term Care:		Long Term Care:	
Type/Coverage/Cost:		Type/Coverage/Cost:	

Liabilities:	Client 1 or 2	Liabilities:	Client 1 or 2
Credit Card:		Credit Card:	
Monthly Pmt. /Balance:		Monthly Pmt. /Balance:	
Residence Loan:		Residence Loan:	
Monthly Pmt. /Balance:		Monthly Pmt. /Balance:	
Auto Loan:		Auto Loan:	
Monthly Pmt. /Balance:		Monthly Pmt. /Balance:	
Other Debt:		Other Debt:	
Monthly Pmt. /Balance:		Monthly Pmt. /Balance:	

Estate Issues:	Client 1 or 2	Estate Issues:	Client 1 or 2
Current Will: Y N		Current Will: Y N	
Living Will: Y N		Living Will: Y N	
Medical Power of Attorney: Y N		Medical Power of Attorney: Y N	
General Power of Attorney: Y N		General Power of Attorney: Y N	

Items that may be needed:
Prior Year Tax Returns
Brokerage Account Statements
Trust account Statements
Retirement Plan Account Statements
Loan Documents
Insurance Policies
Legal Documents

Current Advisors:
Attorney: _____
Accountant: _____
Insurance Agent: _____
Stockbroker: _____

Comment on advice you are seeking:
_____
_____
_____

The External Data Collection Process

It is important that the planner is cognizant of the current external environmental data including the economic, legal, political, sociological, taxation and technological environment. This general knowledge may be obtained by taking various university courses, attending professional conferences, and reading professional and news related journals.

The financial planner should identify and document the following external information at the inception of the engagement:

- Interest rates
  - the current and prospective outlook including savings rates and mortgage rates
- Housing market - housing is a major asset but markets are local
  - what is the stock of available housing
  - is it a buyer's or seller's market
- Job market
  - what is the unemployment rate
- Investment market
  - current and prospective outlook
- Business cycle
  - peak, contraction, trough, expansion
  - where are we now
- Local insurance costs
  - housing, auto, liability
- Local cost of living
- Expected inflation rate, both short and long term
- Expected rate of increase in the prices of education and medical care
- Legislation that may impact certain industry sectors (e.g., healthcare)
- Current and expected income, gift, and estate tax rates

Analyzing and Evaluating the Client's Financial Status

Once the planner has collected internal and external data and mutually established the goals, needs, and priorities of the client, the planner will begin the analysis phase. This textbook goes into great detail using many financial planning approaches to analyze, evaluate, and make recommendations to the client. Specifically, Chapter 3 covers additional steps of the financial planning process including the analysis of the client's financial situation and the development and presentation of recommendations.

Developing and Presenting Financial Plan Recommendations

While developing and presenting the plan is discussed to some extent in Chapter 3, it is worth mentioning that this phase is one of the most critical steps in the financial planning process. This step comes after the analysis phase and the recommendations. Suggestions made by the financial planner must be based on:

- The scope of the engagement as set forth in the engagement letter
- The goals and objectives of the client
- The information gathered from the client by the planner
- An analysis of the economic environment, including the current and projected tax law environment
- The alternatives available to accomplish the client's goals

These recommendations should also be based on the expertise of the financial planner and may require input from other experts, such as attorneys, accountants, or actuaries.

This step in the process is generally an iterative one. Often, recommendations will be made and discussed with the client with further questions and investigation before an agreement on final plan recommendations can be made. In addition, there will always be alternative solutions that may work for a particular client and it will be part of the process that the alternative solutions are discussed and prioritized before the implementation of the plan.

EXAMPLE 1.1	Bob, who is a financial planner, advises his client to obtain a disability insurance policy. While a disability policy may be appropriate, there are choices to be made in terms of the elimination period and such choice or choices should be consistent with another choice regarding the emergency fund. Therefore, while the recommendation to cover the risk is sound, there may be alternative solutions in terms of what is ultimately chosen by the client.

The recommendations that are made by the advisor should be based on the criteria listed above and should be made independent of how the advisor is compensated. The advisor should make disclosures about how she is compensated and if there are any conflicts of interest. These disclosures should be made in writing if the planner is engaged in financial planning.

Implementing Financial Plan Recommendations

This phase of the financial planning process is initiated after there is agreement as to the recommendations as between the client and the planner. The client must agree that the recommendations made by the planner are appropriate and will further the achievement of her goals and objectives before implementation can begin.

Implementing the recommendations is the process of taking action on the recommendations. This is the part of the process where change actually occurs. However, there are several steps that may be necessary, including defining the necessary activities for implementation and determining which activities will be performed by the client and which ones will be performed by the planner.

In most cases, part of the implementation process will require the use of and coordination with other professionals. For example, advisors will generally work with attorneys to implement any estate planning or other necessary legal work (e.g. establishment of a family limited partnership). In the case that another professional is necessary as part of the implementation process, the planner or the client will need to coordinate with that professional.

In many cases, implementation will require the selection of financial services products, such as insurance or investment vehicles. Similarly, this may be accomplished directly with the planner or by working with other professionals.

Implementation is critical because without it the plans does not come alive. There are times when a plan will be created and agreed to by the client that does not get implemented. This outcome is unfortunate since the client will be unlikely to accomplish the goals that were the basis for the initial recommendations. However, when clients do follow through with implementation, they are often closer to accomplishing the goals they set out to achieve.

Monitoring the Plan

It is not uncommon to think that once the recommendations are implemented, that is the conclusion of the financial planning process and engagement. However, it is really the beginning of the process. Once the plan is implemented, the planner and the client must monitor the actual results of what was implemented relative to what was expected. For example, if a retirement plan was implemented and was based on specific savings amounts and earnings rates of return, it is important to evaluate periodically to ensure that progress is being made as was expected. If the actual results are different from what was anticipated, then adjustments to the plan may be required.

There are other reasons that require monitoring. For example, to the extent that tax laws change, such changes may positively or negatively impact the financial plan.

It is important as part of the engagement process to define who will be responsible for monitoring the plan and to define the specifics around monitoring if the planner will be responsible for it, including frequency, depth, and how the results of such monitoring will be communicated.

This process continues until such time as further analysis occurs.

FINANCIAL PLANNING PROFESSION

THE BENEFITS FROM FINANCIAL PLANNING

The planning process helps to identify risks and to establish and prioritize goals. The process helps to anticipate where financial needs exist (such as, education and retirement needs) and where new risks may arise (for example, long-term care insurance and property and liability insurance on newly acquired major assets).

The plan itself establishes benchmarks (metrics) within a finite time frame where a comparison with actual results creates an early warning system for deviations. It also helps to keep the client focused on achieving the objectives of the plan and provides for more efficient and effective resource utilization. The financial planning process provides the client with choices and alternatives to consider, enhancing the awareness of the opportunity costs of foregone options (see Chapter 15 on Economics for more information on opportunity costs) leading to better decisions. Perhaps the greatest benefit that comes from financial planning is the confidence that with clear direction the client can accomplish their financial goals.

WHY USE A PROFESSIONAL FINANCIAL PLANNER

Most clients do not know how to prepare a comprehensive financial plan and do not want to spend the time to learn how. Even where the client may have the knowledge, he typically lacks the confidence to undertake this process and is likely seeking confirmation of his own financial planning decisions.

An expert in financial planning (like any other expert) has probably spent 10,000 or more hours in financial planning over at least 10 years. The education of a competent financial planner generally consists of at least an undergraduate degree (4,000 hours) and additional financial planning related courses (1,000 hours). If the planner is a Certified Financial Planner™, the planner likely has passed a comprehensive exam requiring another 300 - 400 hours of study. A financial planner brings objectivity to an otherwise subjective world. The competent financial planner has knowledge about the following:

Key Concepts

Underline/highlight the answers as you read.

1. Describe the benefits of a client having a financial plan.

2. Explain why a client should consider using a professional financial planner.

3. Summarize the economic forecast for the practice of financial planning.

- mortality risk
- disability risk
- investment returns
- risks associated with various asset classes
- the cost of college education
- the cost of retirement
- the needed savings rate to drive various goals

A client rarely has knowledge of objective factors and instead perceives subjectively that he is fine (e.g., does not need life or disability insurance). One of the most important qualities a professional brings to the client/planner relationship is objectivity.

Finally, the financial planner brings experience from previous engagements with variously situated clients. The client seeks an initial plan that meets his objectives and the trusted, experienced practitioner is more likely to be able to create such a plan.

THE PRACTICE OF FINANCIAL PLANNING

The position of "financial planner" is largely unregulated. Neither the federal nor the state laws directly regulate the practice of financial planning. There are, however, licenses that must be obtained by those engaging in the sale of insurance products and securities. Financial planning is much broader than the sale of products or securities and is practiced by a wide variety of professionals. In addition to the planners who have earned the certifications listed below, other professionals such as bankers, brokers, accountants, lawyers, and insurance agents practice in the broad field of financial planning.

RECOGNIZED CERTIFICATIONS IN FINANCIAL PLANNING

In a newly emerging profession such as financial planning, there is an initial lack of regulation. The need for some form of self-regulation and the demand that a financial planner be competent and trustworthy have prompted several independent financial services organizations to introduce certifications and ethical standards. Those who meet the requirement of the certification process and subscribe to specific ethical standards are awarded a professional financial planning designation.

One of the oldest, best-known financial planning certification trademarks is the CERTIFIED FINANCIAL PLANNER™ certification, which has gained global recognition because of its standard setting activities and worldwide presence. The CFP® certification was first introduced in the United States in the early 1970s to meet the needs of consumers. The CFP Board, based in Washington, D.C., owns the CFP marks within the United States. The CFP® marks are owned outside the United States by the Financial Planning Standards Board, a nonprofit standards-setting body based in Denver, Colorado.

The CFP Board was founded in July 1985 as the International Board of Standards and Practices for Certified Financial Planners, Inc., (IBCFP) by the College for Financial Planning (College) and the Institute of Certified Financial Planners (ICFP). The IBCFP became the Certified Financial Planners Board of Standards Inc. (CFP Board) on February 1, 1994. As a professional regulatory organization acting in the public interest by fostering professional standards in personal financial planning, the CFP Board establishes and enforces education, examination, experience and ethics requirements for CFP® certificants. The CFP® service mark is promoted world-wide through member associations (such as the Financial Planning Association).

The Chartered Financial Consultant (ChFC) is another financial planning qualification, conferred by the American College. To date, more than 41,000 individuals have attained this distinction. This designation has also spread to Asia, where designees are found in countries like Singapore, Malaysia, Indonesia, China, and Hong Kong.

In Europe, the European Financial Planner (EFP) designation conferred by the European Financial Planners Association (EFPA) is gaining ground as a financial planning certification mark. The EFPA is the largest professional and educational organization for financial planners and financial advisors in Europe and is the only financial planning association created solely in the interest of European financial planning consumers and practitioners.

EMPLOYMENT AND JOB OUTLOOK

As of 2010, the United States Department of Labor[2] reports that personal financial planners hold 206,800 jobs across the country (projected to be 273,200 in 2020). Approximately 29 percent of the reported planners are self-employed and 63 percent work in the finance and insurance industries. With the rising number of baby boomer retirees over the next decade, the occupation is expected to grow by 32 percent (2010 to 2020). As both retirement savings

---

2. United States Department of Labor Bureau of Labor Statistics; Occupational Outlook Handbook, 2012-13 Edition; www.bls.gov/ooh/Business-and-Financial/Personal-financial-advisors.htm

options and the complexity of retirement plans increase, the need for skilled financial planners will grow. Those planners with a college degree, certification, and sales skills will likely be the most successful.

Earnings

Financial planners earn on average $64,750[3] annually. This average does not include bonuses or the wages of self-employed practitioners. The lowest 10 percent earned less than $32,660, and the top 10 percent earned more than $166,400. Financial planners earn compensation in the form of:

- An hourly rate or fee
- A flat fee
- A commission on investment and insurance products sold
- A percentage of the assets managed
- A combination of the above

Personal financial planners can be compensated from their client's for professional financial planning services in a variety of ways. For example, a planner can choose to charge based on an hourly rate or charge a flat fee for a comprehensive plan. The amount of the flat fee may vary based on the complexity of the plan. If the client desires only planning services for a particular issue, the planner can charge a flat fee for the particular module of a plan serviced. Many planners earn the predominant amount of their fees through commissions on the sale of investments and insurance products, having to rely on new client business or updated client plans in order to generate revenue. Others focus on a niche of high wealth clients and charge fees based on the percentage of assets they manage for those clients. In order to build and sustain a financial planning practice, financial planners can offer a variety of fee arrangements to fit the needs of their business and their clients.

---

3. United States Department of Labor Bureau of Labor Statistics; Occupational Outlook Handbook, 2012-13 Edition; www.bls.gov/ooh/Business-and-Financial/Personal-financial-advisors.htm

A 2009 survey of CFP® certificants by the College for Financial Planning[4] illustrates the array of compensation methods for financial planner provided services:

MEANS OF COMPENSATION FOR FINANCIAL PLANNING SERVICES, 2009

EXHIBIT 1.4

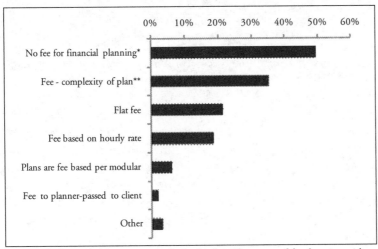

No fee for financial planning means no fee for the plan. The purpose of the plan was to either sell product or take assets under management.
** Fee - complexity of plan means the fee charged was determined by the complexity of the plan.*

Before entering into a relationship with a client, the financial planner should make certain that fee arrangements are in writing and clearly understood by the client. Financial planning is a valuable service, and fee arrangements must be unambiguous in order to manage the client's expectations regarding the cost of the service.

---

4. College for Financial Planning, *2009 Survey of Trends in the Financial Planning Industry*, www.cffpinfo.com/pdfs/2009SOT.pdf

Key Terms

Engagement Letter - A legal agreement between a professional organization and a client that defines their business relationship.

External Data – The external data, also known as the external environment includes the current economic, legal, political, sociological, tax, and technology environments. Examples of external data are the current interest rates, status of the housing, job, insurance and investment markets, the local cost of living, and the expected inflation rate.

Financial Plan - A written document that generally sets out a list of recommendations to achieve a set of goals and objections based on an understanding of a client's current financial situation.

Internal Data – The client's internal data has both quantitative and qualitative elements. Some quantitative data includes family specifics, insurance, banking, investment, tax, retirement, and estate planning information. Some qualitative data includes the client's values, attitudes, expectations, goals, needs, and priorities.

Personal Financial Planning – The process of formulating, implementing, and monitoring financial decisions integrated into a plan that guides an individual or a family to achieve their financial goals.

Process of Financial Planning – The process of financial planning includes: (1) establishing and defining the client relationship, (2) gathering client data, (3) analyzing and evaluating the client's financial status, (4) developing and presenting financial plan recommendations, (5) implementing financial plan recommendations, and (6) monitoring the plan.

DISCUSSION QUESTIONS

1. What is personal financial planning?

2. Define the process of financial planning.

3. What are examples of internal data items collected from the client as part of the "gather client data" part of the financial planning process?

4. What are examples of external data items required as part of the "gather client data" part of the financial planning process?

5. List some important elements of a financial planning engagement letter.

6. What are some of the benefits a client receives from choosing to use a professional financial planner?

7. What is the job and economic outlook for the financial planning profession?

1. Lisa Cooper recently came to your office for her second appointment after receiving your engagement letter. During the meeting you collect several documents from her including her prior year tax returns, estate planning documents, and investment statements and history. You also worked with her on identifying her goals and objectives. Which of the following is the next step in the financial planning process?

    a. Establish and define the client relationship.
    b. Analyze and evaluate the client's financial status.
    c. Implementing the financial plan recommendations.
    d. Developing and presenting the financial plan recommendations.

2. Your client, Jed, engaged you to help him with his financial situation. During the course of your meetings you sold Jed a $1,000,000 life insurance policy. Which part of the financial planning process were you engaged in?

    a. Analyze and evaluate the client's financial status.
    b. Monitoring the plan.
    c. Developing and presenting the financial plan recommendations.
    d. Implementing the financial plan recommendations.

3. After meeting with your new client, Sid, you prepared his current financial statements. Which part of the financial planning process were you engaged in?

    a. Monitoring the plan.
    b. Establish and define the client relationship.
    c. Analyze and evaluate the client's financial status.
    d. Developing and presenting the financial plan recommendations.

4. Reverend Lola Pak, a prospective client, came to your office for the first time today. Which is the most appropriate way to greet her?

    a. "Welcome to my office."
    b. "Welcome to my office, Ms. Pak."
    c. "Welcome to my office, Reverend Pak."
    d. "Welcome to my office, Lola."

5. Steve Stein, a local CFP® practitioner, recently met with one of his new clients, Merrell. During the course of the meeting Steve did the following things:

    1. Steve did not meet with Merrell until 10 minutes after the scheduled start time.

    2. In order to establish Merrell's confidence in him, Steve told Merrell the names of several well known clients that currently do business with him.

    3. Steve asked Merrell several questions regarding Merrell's family situation, hobbies, and activities.

    Which of these actions would be considered inappropriate?

    a. 3 only.
    b. 1 and 2.
    c. 2 and 3.
    d. 1, 2 and 3.

6. Roy Al Pain has been a client of yours for several years. During that time, Roy has been rude to both you and your staff on numerous occasions. He has used profanities in front of your staff and other clients, thrown things, and screamed at your staff. You have tired of working with Roy and want to terminate your relationship with him. Which of the following is true?

    a. You must continue the relationship since only clients can end the client/ planner relationship.
    b. You should consult your engagement letter to determine your rights to terminate the relationship.
    c. You should start to offer subpar services to Roy in hopes that he will tire of you and end your relationship.
    d. You should bad mouth Roy in the community and hope it gets back to him so he will decide not to work with you anymore.

7. Which of the following items of information is least likely to be obtained from your client during the data gathering portion of the client meeting?

    a. General attitude towards spending.
    b. The income tax bracket of your client's adult children.
    c. Employer sponsored employee benefits.
    d. Repayment term of outstanding debt.

8. Dustin Towns is a well-known financial planner in your area. His clients rave about how great he is and after meeting him you understand why. While describing him to your friend Jim, Jim wanted to know what was so great about financial planners in general. You responded with the following statement "One of the most important qualities a professional financial planner brings to the client/planner relationship is: _____."

    a. Subjectivity.
    b. Empathy.
    c. Objectivity.
    d. Sympathy.

9. You are a relatively new financial planner. You have been working for an investment firm in the United States and have decided that you would like to add more credibility to your practice. Which of the following professional credentials would provide you with the most credibility since it is the oldest and best known?

    a. CFP®.
    b. ChFC.
    c. EFP.
    d. ICFP.

Quick Quiz Explanation

Quick Quiz 1.1

1. True.
2. False. Emergency funding is considered a short-term goal, along with debt management. All of the other planning subjects are included in long-term goal planning.
3. True.
4. False. These items are external data information which can be obtained from education and professional reading. Internal data includes the client's pertinent family information, insurance portfolio, banking, investment, tax, retirement, and estate planning information.

Interpersonal Communication & Behavioral Finance

LEARNING OBJECTIVES

After reading this chapter, you should be able to:

- Explain the counseling theories and the schools of thought regarding communications.
- Explain the developmental, humanistic, and cognitive-behavioral schools of thought.
- Identify the elements of communication.
- Describe nonverbal behavior or body language.
- Differentiate between active listening and passive listening.
- Describe open and closed questions.
- Describe ways to clarify or restate a client's statement.
- Describe client data collection.
- Describe the concepts and theories behind behavioral finance.
- Discuss the assumptions and building blocks of traditional finance.
- Describe the issues and questions unanswered by traditional finance.
- Define behavioral finance.
- Identify the pyramid of assets and describe its mental accounting layers.
- Describe what makes investors "normal" instead of "rational."
- Describe patterns and types of cognitive biases.
- Define anchoring, confirmation bias, gambler's fallacy, herding, hindsight bias, overconfidence, overreaction, and prospect theory.
- Describe the Disposition Effect.
- Analyze a client's degree of risk and loss aversion and insure recommendations are consistent with a client's risk propensity, attitudes, capacity, knowledge, and needs.*
- Explain how a client's psychological profile, such as a Meyers-Briggs assessment, and learning style, and values impact the format of the plan produced and presented.*
- Evaluate how a client's values, including cultural and religious values and attitudes will affect his/her goals and a planner's recommendations.*

- Describe how behavioral psychology, such as a client's comfort zone, impacts a client's objectives, goals, understanding, decision making and actions.*
- Explain the applications of counseling theory to financial planning practice.*
- Demonstrate how a planner can develop a relationship of honesty and trust in client interaction.*

* CFP Board Resource Document - Student-Centered Learning Objectives based upon CFP Board Principal Topics.

INTRODUCTION

This chapter is organized into three main sections. The first section identifies theories and schools of thought for counselors. Knowing these schools of thought can place the advisor in a better position to communicate effectively with the client. The second section addresses communication tools and techniques for financial counselors. The third section discusses and examines the realm of what is referred to as "Behavioral Finance." Traditional or conventional wisdom about finance typically assumed that all investors participating in the market are "rational" machine-like beings. Yet, individuals are different, subject to errors in judgment and are guided or misguided by emotions. To put it simply, people are human. These two realms of financial knowledge will be compared and discussed.

COMMUNICATION WITH CLIENTS FROM A COUNSELING PERSPECTIVE: COUNSELING THEORIES AND SCHOOLS OF THOUGHT

Financial advisors serve to educate their clients on financial matters, identify financial goals or problems, make recommendations and monitor the client's progress. This relationship is that of counselor and client. As will be discussed later in this chapter, there has been a movement in recent times for the financial industry to be more in touch with psychology and sociology due to their effect and persuasiveness in financial matters. Therefore, when dealing with fundamentals of financial planning in the context of communication and counseling, a basic understanding of the different schools of counseling and therapy would benefit the advisor and, ultimately, the client. These counseling theories or schools of thought apply to the *advisor*, and what are the advisor's beliefs, strengths and style. For advisors to be effective, they must first understand from what perspective and school of thought they are most properly situated.

A number of theories and models have been developed, investigated and studied so as to account for various aspects of human development and behavior. There are hundreds of models of counseling and therapy and hundreds of different techniques that are linked to these models.[1] Rather than provide an entire course in this area, this chapter provides a general overview of these counseling theories which will assist the later evaluation of communication tools and techniques for the financial planning advisor with clients.[2]

---

1. MacCluskie, Acquiring Counseling Skills: Integrating Theory, Multiculturalism, and Self-Awareness, Chapter 7, p. 181-182 (Pearson 2009).
2. For a detailed look at the various theories and models in the subject of counseling and therapy, see text by MacCluskie. Id. at n.1 above.

As explained and summarized by Professor MacCluskie, there are three general and noteworthy schools of counseling:

1. Developmental;
2. Humanistic;
3. Cognitive-Behavioral.

These three areas emerged temporally in this same order and sequence in the 20th century.

The specific, numerous theories in each school of thought will not be discussed, however, the common elements of the theories that cluster within each school of thought will be briefly described. These general schools of thought can serve as a guide for the individual counselor's beliefs and style so as to aid the financial counselor in identifying a style that fits himself or herself and in developing and honing in on skills and techniques to make the planner a better counselor. Knowing these schools of thought may also help shape an understanding of client behavior and assist in defining the client's goals during the advisor-client relationship.

Key Concepts

Underline/highlight the answers as you read:

1. Identify the three general schools of counseling.

2. What is the fundamental belief of the Developmental School of Thought?

3. What is the nature of the relationship between advisor and client in the different Schools of Thought?

THE "DEVELOPMENTAL" SCHOOL OF THOUGHT

The Developmental school of thought, or the "**Developmental Paradigm**" as it will be referred to in this chapter, believes that human development occurs in stages over time. Relationships that are formed early in life become a template for establishing relationships in adulthood. As to emotions, the Developmental Paradigm assumes that all humans develop and progress in a predictable sequence. Disruptions, whether by trauma, incident or otherwise, at a particular stage of that individual's development will result in predictable problems, symptoms and behavior. Much of the Developmental approach has its origin in and was influenced by Freudian psychoanalytic theory. Counseling in the Developmental Paradigm has an overall aspiration to recount or correct earlier, disrupted development to foster change in the client or the client's behavior. Once the client can resolve those earlier conflicts or disruptions, there is more understanding and self-awareness, thus allowing the client to grow.

For some counselors who follow the Developmental Paradigm, questions could play a larger role in the counseling process than they do for counselors who follow the Humanistic Paradigm (discussed in the next subsection). Questions should be used in moderation for Developmental counselors especially if the counselor is seeking to increase a client's awareness of the developmental tasks or issues associated with a presenting problem. For instance, if a client has had issues in the past with debt accumulation and the advisor has noticed that the client has overspent on personal items to compensate for an event that occurred in that client's earlier stage of life, then the questioning process should be done in moderation.

THE "HUMANISTIC" SCHOOL OF THOUGHT

The **Humanistic Paradigm** is dominated by theorists whose models have their origins from a shared philosophical approach. Like the developmental approach, much of the Humanistic approach was influenced by Freudian psychoanalytic theory. For a client to grow, the relationship requires a transparent and genuine counselor. The advisor needs a philosophical stance that humankind is basically good and that people have the inherent capability of self-direction and growth under the right set of circumstances. A Humanistic counselor would define mental health as having congruent and aligned thoughts, feelings and behavior. Goals in treatment are centered on establishing congruence and acceptance of personal responsibility.

Part of achieving this "congruence" is that treatment emphasizes one's experience of the present moment, freedom of choice, and keeping in touch with oneself. It is therapeutic in and of itself to have an authentic, human relationship between the client and counselor. For example, if an advisor is more comfortable with a close, more friendly relationship with clients (as opposed to a more professional and distant relationship), then the advisor may be more inclined to operate under the Humanistic Paradigm. Indeed, the alliance between the counselor and client is extremely important for Humanistic counselors and is the basis of the treatment or plan of action.

The majority of the Humanistic theories view clients as experts on themselves. Accordingly, counselors who subscribe to the Humanistic Paradigm are disinclined to use questioning with any frequency. When questioning is used, the emphasis is likely to be more weighted on process and feelings rather than details or content. In fact, a humanistic counselor would help clients articulate for themselves what their questions are.

Applying the Humanistic Paradigm to the financial advisor-client relationship, the advisor may consider spending time with the client on discovering what goals will help the client achieve congruence, allow for self-growth and identify some of the client's feelings about money and tendencies to cognitive biases.

THE COGNITIVE-BEHAVIORAL SCHOOL OF THOUGHT

In the **Cognitive-Behavioral Paradigm**, humans are beings that are subject to the same learning principles that were established in animal research. The basic principles of classical and operant conditioning are assumed to account for an individuals' behavior and understandings throughout their lives. The quintessential example of "classical conditioning" is Ivan Pavlov's initial research conducted on dogs. Meanwhile, B.F. Skinner's related model on "operant conditioning" posited that all behavior is subject to the principles of reinforcement by environmental conditions that reinforce or fail to reinforce a given behavior. Self-talk, which refers to that ongoing internal conversation one has with oneself that can influence feelings, and behavior can be reinforced and persist. The counselor's challenge lies in performing a sound evaluation of how reinforcers are maintaining problematic self-talk and behaviors. The counselor is the expert in the Cognitive-Behavioral Paradigm, but the counselor and client have a working alliance where the client must be actively engaged.

For Cognitive-Behavioralists, the questioning process is most prevalent because the counseling process is considerably more directive than it is in either of the other two paradigms. The counselor in the Cognitive-Behavioral Paradigm must identify behavioral excesses and inadequacies, identify their source of reinforcement for these excesses and inadequacies, and try to manipulate these reinforcers to change the client's behavior and thought process. In short, a Cognitive-Behavioral counselor is searching for specific material and information from the client so as to design and implement a counseling intervention or plan that is consistent with Cognitive-Behavioral theory.

If the financial advisor is more attuned to the Cognitive-Behavioral Paradigm, then the advisor may discover goals of the client and point out during the relationship areas where the client has succeeded on certain financial issues. The advisor may spend more time on content and positive results that will reinforce the client's belief in the process, in the client's financial behavior, and in the client's trust in the advisor. Cognitive-Behavioral advisors would also want to reinforce positive financial feedback during the plan monitoring stage of the financial planning process which is after the recommendation stage.

Quick Quiz 2.1

Highlight the answer to these questions:

1. The nature of the relationship between advisor and client following the Cognitive-Behavioral approach is highly directed.
   a. True
   b. False

2. All of the counseling theories use active listening as a tool.
   a. True
   b. False

3. The Humanistic theory emphasizes accepting personal responsibility whereas the other two theories do not.
   a. True
   b. False

True, True, True.

EXHIBIT 2.1 COMPARISON OF COUNSELING PARADIGMS[3]

Theory Group	Nature of Relationship	Emphasis of Treatment (Prominent Themes)	Microskills Most Likely to be Used Frequently
Developmental	• Moderately directive. • Alliance is important. • Provides client a chance to resolve emotional needs not met during earlier development.	• Healthy development. • Focus on past experiences in family of origin and relationship to present difficulties. • Resolution of conflict. • Understanding and self-awareness.	• Active listening. • Client observation. • Paraphrasing. • Feeling reflection. • Supportive challenging. • Reflection of meaning.
Humanistic	• Varies from nondirective (person-centered, existential) to highly directive. • Alliance is extremely important; is the basis of the treatment (person-centered, existential).	• Experiencing present moment. • Accepting personal responsibility. • Emphasis on freedom of choice. • Authenticity, fully in touch with oneself.	• Active listening. • Client observation. • Feeling reflection. • Reflection of meaning. • Supportive challenging.
Cognitive-Behavioral	• Highly directive. • Alliance only important to extent client feels engaged to participate in assignments.	• Identification of behavioral excesses and inadequacies. • Identification of reinforcers. • Manipulation of the reinforcers to change the behavior and thought process.	• Active listening. • Questioning. • Reflection of meaning. • Supportive challenging.

In conclusion, the advisor can better serve the client by understanding what counseling school of thought is most suited to the advisor. Of course, there may be times that the client's style may necessitate a change to a different school of thought or combination of any two or all three. These are decisions that should be made by the advisor using his or her best judgment.

---

3. Id. at p. 156, Table 11.1. This chart was compiled and crafted by Professor MacCluskie in her textbook.

COMMUNICATION TOOLS AND TECHNIQUES FOR FINANCIAL COUNSELORS

Communication is the key factor in the financial advisor-client relationship. The advisor must determine the client's goals and craft a plan designed to reach those goal. The advisor must also educate the client so as to cause the client to act in a way consistent with the financial plan. Great advice can be given, but if the advice is not followed, then the client's best interests are not served. The advisor must get to know the client in a way that will foster a healthy relationship of trust, so that the correct information is gathered by the advisor and the best advice is followed by the client. While the advisor cannot do some or all of the actual tasks of implementation for the client, having a good relationship with effective communication can be persuasive to and positive for the client.

Financial counselors or advisors must establish and maintain the advisor-client relationship based on their ability to communicate. Proper and practical communication skills and techniques in financial counseling can aid the financial planning advisor. This section of this chapter will identify and discuss effective techniques and skills that will contribute to successful counseling strategies. These techniques and skills are vital to financial advisors' efforts to understand their clients and what their clients' perceptions of their own needs and objectives are.

Key Concepts

Underline/highlight the answers as you read:

1. What are the fundamental elements of communication?

2. Identify non-verbal gestures that substitute for or reinforce verbal expressions.

3. Identify situations where the non-verbal communication contradicts the verbal communication.

ELEMENTS OF COMMUNICATION

Human communications are comprised of fundamental elements. Societal groups use a system of signs in their communication process. A sign could be a word, object, gesture, tone, quality, image, substance or other reference according to a code of shared meaning among those who use that sign for communication purposes. While people consciously use language in one way, there are times when the language can be used subliminally or subconsciously. Language can be used to manipulate, conceal or withhold what is really meant or felt by the person speaking. While spoken words are signs used in communication, there are also nonverbal gestures, actions or other expressions that are not verbal but can substitute or reinforce verbal expressions.

A good example of a purely nonlinguistic but highly expressive system of sign communication is grief. Crying can be a sign of grief, but there are less common instances where it could be a sign of joy. Context is very important with verbal and nonverbal communication. People all experienced times when somebody is providing one signal verbally and their body language is providing a different signal. Such communications among people are complex and have a wide range.

While financial advisors obtain a lot of quantitative information from clients, including checkbooks, financial statements and other documents, the financial advisor should strive to build a rapport with the client, which may help to recognize more of the value or truth of information that clients communicate through verbal, nonverbal, or a combination of these messages.

NONVERBAL BEHAVIOR OR "BODY LANGUAGE"

Nonverbal cues, or body language, can communicate feelings and attitudes from the client to the financial advisor. **Nonverbal behaviors** are mainly provided from the body and the voice. Body position and body movement are important, while voice tone and voice pitch are also telling.[4] When observing nonverbal behavior, the literature stresses that the "observer" should try to notice the ways the body communicates and whether or not the body is in agreement with what is being said. The positioning of the client's body is an early sign for the advisor to observe.

For instance, good posture by the client may indicate positive self-esteem, whereas poor posture may signal a lack of self-esteem. Sitting comfortably can mean that one is relaxed. Leaning slightly forward is a sign of interested involvement. Slouching or slumping may indicate less interest or a lack of trust in the counselor. If arms are uncrossed, the client can be seen as relaxed and open, whereas crossed arms may indicate that the client is defensive, disinterested or closed-off.

The movements of the client's body could also indicate thoughts or emotions of the client. If the client frequently moves indicating a physical discomfort or perhaps emotional dislike, the counselor should take note of these movements to extrapolate those cues to information that may be learned at a later time. Verbal statements may indicate they are not nervous about something, while at the same time, they may be rocking back and forth or biting their nails. People are prone to say what they think is be expected, and all the while may not notice that they are actually communicating something quite different through their body language.

Gestures and facial expressions are also very important signs and cues for the listener. Eye contact is an indicator of one being engaged in a conversation where they are peering into the counselor's eyes with interest and openness. There may be times when a client's eyes are shifty and unable to remain on the counselor, and this could indicate distrust, fear, shyness, or even anxiety, something the counselor may wish to explore later on through questions.

As to voice communication, tone and pitch may also indicate feelings of the speaker that at times can be at odds with what is being said. Things can be said softer or louder, which can emphasize or de-emphasize a point. Of course, shouting very loudly could indicate anger or hostility, whereas fear, nervousness or shyness can be exuded through somebody who speaks very softly. When detecting a change in pitch in one's voice, the listener should observe and

---

4. An excellent article in this area of communication was authored by Professor Dale Johnson, entitled "Practical Communications Skills and Techniques in Financial Counseling Part I," The Financial Planner (July 1982), where Professor Johnson highlights the four types of nonverbal signs of meaning: body position, body movement, voice tone and voice pitch.

try to determine which vocal qualities are natural to a particular client so as to recognize the variations when they occur. These variations can be important clues of strong emotions that may affect the client's motivation, biases, goals or needs.

There can be times that what is being said is opposite to the tone, pitch or gestures being made or exuded by the speaker. When the indicators cross or are different, this is probably a time when the financial advisor should speak up. It is one thing if all behavior supports what is being said, but when they are at odds or give mixed signals, it is the responsibility of the advisor to ask more questions and to delve into the issues. If there is an incongruent statement with nonverbal behavior, it could be a sign of something else, something that went awry in the prior financial life or personal life of the client, and the planner or advisor ought to seek that out and get to the source of the issue. The advisor should investigate further through questions and learning more information in order to clarify how the advisor perceives one thing and hears another.

Even When Listening, You are a Speaker

Advisors must also be mindful of the verbal and nonverbal cues that they may communicate to the client. During the relationship, especially in the beginning, there will be times where the client is sizing up the advisor, checking the trust factor, deciding whether to heed the advice, and has other accompanying thoughts. These modes of communication will have their own effects on the client.

In short, one of the main responsibilities of the financial advisor is to extract the goals and desires of the client. This task is accomplished through verbal and nonverbal communication. The advisor must not only listen to the words, but to understand client and clients' conceptions of themselves, the advisor must diligently note the nonverbal cues and signs being exuded by the client during the counseling sessions and meetings.

Quick Quiz 2.2

Highlight the answer to these questions:

1. Gestures and facial expressions are important clues to communication for the listener.
   a. True
   b. False

2. Tone and pitch of voice can indicate congruence or incongruence with the words spoken.
   a. True
   b. False

3. Body language does not play an important role in understanding communications.
   a. True
   b. False

True, True, False.

ACTIVE LISTENING VERSUS PASSIVE LISTENING

 The financial advisor's relationship with the client should be one dominated by "active listening" on the part of the advisor, not passive listening.

Passive Listening

Passive listening is described as listening in the normal or usual conversation or conversational setting to which most people are accustomed at seminars, in class, at social gatherings, or at sermons. Passive listening is invoked when communication rests entirely on another person, and the person receiving the information sits back and listens. The effectiveness of the listening being accomplished by the passive listener is subject to many obstacles, such as interruptions, daydreaming, checks to one's personal handheld device, bathroom or refreshment breaks, and the like. There are numerous obstacles or opportunities to screen out information by the passive listener, depending on the listener's mood or depending on what is going on or where their interests lie. One of the most reported interruptions or disruptions in passive listening is when the listener is thinking about what he or she may say in response to what is being discussed while the listener should instead be listening.

Key Concepts

Underline/highlight the answers as you read:

1. Define passive listening.

2. Define active listening.

3. Define open and closed questions.

4. Explain how thinking of a response can hamper listening.

Active Listening

Active listening, on the other hand, requires the <u>listener's undivided attention.</u> Active listening involves concentration of what the speaker is saying. The listener must put aside irrelevant thoughts. The advisor should not think about "what to say next," but should be listening and observing the speaker's body language. The listening advisor should assume that the data and information conveyed is important, while sorting and sifting various items into categories. To reveal the listener's interest, the listener may nod occasionally, provide follow up comments with brief affirmative responses such as "yes," "I understand," or "go on," and smile or use other facial expressions.

The feedback provided during active listening should result in the speaker continuing to speak and provide information. The feedback should not interrupt the speaker. Active listening requires determination and concentration, so that basically everything the speaker says is relevant and interesting.

In short, advisors should strive to be active listeners throughout their sessions with clients. While it is best if the client is engaged in active listening when it comes time for input by the advisor and recommendations to the client, the advisor cannot control the actions of the client; the advisor can control his or her actions, though.

USING OPEN AND CLOSED QUESTIONS

During counseling sessions, the use of proper questions is vital for the relationship between the financial advisor and the client to succeed. The focus here is on the form and content of the questions. Questions are one of the best tools for the advisor.

An open question is one that will result in a person answering with a lengthy response, whereas a closed question seeks a response that is very specific and commonly involves an answer that can be accomplished with a single word or two. One may be inclined to think that, during a counseling session, open questions are better than closed questions because the client is talking. That may not necessarily be true. In some situations, closed questions are preferable or necessary. Closed questions are also called leading questions.

Open questions usually begin with words such as how, what, when, where, who and why. Closed questions lead with is, are, do, did, could, would, have, or "is it not true that..." Sometimes open questions result in a client continuing to talk and providing much material that may or may not be needed. Nonetheless, whether the questions are open or closed, asking questions is vital, and it directs a client into an area to which the advisor needs the counseling session to go or proceed. The advisor must assess the need for an open discussion on a subject, and if so, an open question is needed. However, if the point has been made and only a clarification needed, then a closed question is in order.

While the "why" questions are tempting and may help understand the client's motives, the "why" question may be ill-advised because it could have limited benefit for the client. It could place the client in a position of having to justify what was done, and that could put the client in a defensive posture.

<table>
<tr><td>

When a client comes in for an initial first session, it is necessary for the counselor to gather information. When establishing an advisor-client relationship, a few pointed well-phrased questions may aid in relationship development more than a lengthy series of questions. Here is an example of an opening that uses one well-phrased question.

ADVISOR: Thanks for coming in today. Let's start by talking about what brought you here to meet with me.

CLIENT: I found out that I have just inherited a portion of an estate. I am not sure what to do with it.

ADVISOR: I can help, but since you just received this information, can you tell me about what are some of your goals are with this?

</td><td>

EXAMPLE 2.1

</td></tr>
</table>

Overly open-ended questions are fine to set the client at ease, but they may lead to the client recounting what has happened in his or her life in the recent past. While that may be an intended result, the disadvantage is that overly open-ended questions may take the focus of discussion in a direction that does not really pertain to the tasks at hand.

In the alternative, an advisor can begin a session with a question that immediately focuses the client's attention in a relevant direction.

EXAMPLE 2.2

ADVISOR: Frank, at our last meeting, we focused on some things you could do to improve your debt elimination. Were you able to try any of them?

FRANK: Yes, I tried a few.

ADVISOR: Please tell me about that.

Open and closed questions are effective tools for the advisor. They can be used through the advisor-client relationship to improve communication. The advisor must learn which methods and questions to use.

CLARIFYING OR RESTATING A CLIENT'S STATEMENT

In the event that a client is trying to communicate a message that is not clear, then the advisor will want to clarify what the client is trying to communicate. It could also be that the client is exuding verbal or nonverbal behavior that is inconsistent with what is being said. If there is an ambiguous meaning, it is best to clarify the statement from the client to insure accuracy or to clear up the ambiguity. Clarifying a client's statement is part of the process of feedback under active listening.

Quick Quiz 2.3

Highlight the answer to these questions:

1. It is better not to make any gestures to the speaker when an advisor is practicing active listening.
   a. True
   b. False

2. Open-ended questions are answerable with lengthy responses.
   a. True
   b. False

False, True.

EXAMPLE 2.3

Frank, a client, indicates that he feels he could obtain a 20% return on some commodities that he frequently trades. When the advisor, Jeffery, hears this message, he denotes overconfidence from Frank. Jeffery attempts to understand the statement, but the body language of Frank shows that he is fidgeting, looking at the floor, and biting his nails. This seems inconsistent with overconfidence. This leaves Jeffery feeling that he should ask an open-ended question to allow Frank to elaborate on the remark.

The follow-up question from Jeffery would be something like: "That sounds to me like you are very confident in the commodities market." At that point, Jeffery can try to understand or clarify the message being conveyed by Frank. Frank's message may not be necessarily overconfidence in the commodities market, but he might be indicating that within a certain area of his portfolio, he is willing to take more risks. This could be a sign that Jeffery may consider his portfolio in different mental accounting layers and not as a whole. This could lead Jeffery to assess Frank's overall risk and returns in his portfolio and to check for proper diversification.[5]

This approach is just another way of determining the accuracy of advisor perceptions and getting more information to enhance understanding about the client. By paraphrasing, the advisor can help verify correctly an understanding of what the client is communicating. Some of the key tools to use when clarifying client statements include repeating a key word or phrase that was used by the client. Some authors in the literature advocate a direct method to clarify a statement or a more diplomatic method of asking questions that are pertinent to the statement. When asking relevant questions, the closed questions can help confirm some beliefs that the advisor has understood, whereas open questions may help the counselor obtain more information.

At times, a client will say something that is confusing to the advisor or it will seem to have ambiguous meaning. Where a paraphrase could be helpful, it is just easier and makes more sense to ask a question that clarifies what the client is trying to communicate.

EXAMPLE 2.4

CLIENT: Well, I was an investor in a joint venture with 3 other people. Things were not going so well, but we were breaking even. Then, suddenly 2 of the investors had a blow up. I was mad about the whole thing, and ended up losing $20,000.

ADVISOR: Do you mean that the joint venture fell apart because of this blow up?

CLIENT: No, we all decided it was not worth the effort and stress, so we mutually agreed to shut it down and limit our losses.

The advisor must assess the accuracy of his or her perception, and if needed, get more information to enhance his or her understanding. The optimal time for a clarification is *before* leaving a subject matter area during the session.

---

5. The mental accounting layers and principles of the Behavioral Portfolio Theory are discussed later in this chapter.

Proper questions can be effective in accomplishing clarification or checkout. Continuing with the dialogue example above and adding a question could assist in understanding or clarifying what was conveyed by the client.

| **EXAMPLE 2.5** | Continuing with the dialogue example from above: |

CLIENT: Well, I was an investor in a joint venture with 3 other people. Things were not going so well, but we were breaking even. Then, suddenly 2 of the investors had a blow up. I was mad about the whole thing, and ended up losing $20,000.

ADVISOR: Do you mean that the joint venture fell apart because of this blow up?

CLIENT: No, we all decided it was not worth the effort and stress, so we mutually agreed to shut it down and limit our losses.

ADVISOR: So basically, 2 of the other investors had a disagreement, not about you, and based on the fact of breaking even plus the internal problems, the whole group decided to shut it down and limit losses? Did I understand this correctly?

The advisor must also sharpen the counseling focus in a particular way as to content or on the process. In the dialogue above, the clarifying questions up to this point have focused on the content of the client's concerns and the details of the story. The questions sharpened the focus on the sequence of events. That same discussion about the client's concerns would go in a completely different direction had the advisor asked questions that emphasized the process rather than the content. Here is an example of how that might unfold:

| **EXAMPLE 2.6** | Continuing with the same dialogue example: |

CLIENT: Well, I was an investor in a joint venture with 3 other people. Things were not going so well, but we were breaking even. Then, suddenly 2 of the investors had a blow up. I was mad about the deal, and ended up losing $20,000.

ADVISOR: What specifically were you mad about at the time?

CLIENT: I was mad at myself for getting involved in the whole thing. I just did not want to stay in a venture where our chances at making a profit were limited and there was fighting.

ADVISOR: It seems like you wanted to rid yourself of a strained situation and limit your losses in terms of money and in terms of stress. I can understand that. Let's discuss what you believe would be a "good situation" in comparison to that one. Could that be helpful?

As seen in the latter part of the dialogue above, the advisor focused on more process questions than content. Either way, the clarifying or "checkout" type of questions aided in the fact gathering process and in learning about the client. For instance, it was learned that the client, Frank, was willing to limit his losses in the form of stress and money. This will help the advisor understand the client's goals and priorities later.

The above dialogue example also illustrates that the emotional underpinnings of many of the client's statements are very important. They not only help to identify priorities, needs and goals, but as will be discussed later in this chapter, they may shed light on some of the client's leanings, biases, thoughts and feelings towards money, the market and other relevant considerations. It is important for the advisor to be mindful of focusing on content and focusing on process when needed. As a result, by repeating or clarifying comments from a client, the financial advisor may be in a better position to understand and accurately capture the goals, priorities, emotions and needs of the client, and know what the client really wants.

CLIENT DATA COLLECTION

Collecting the client's data is more than just reviewing bank statements and papers. The advisor needs to learn about who the client is and what are the client's personal and financial goals, needs and priorities. These goals, needs and priorities are relevant and, in fact, are likely the very reason the client is consulting the advisor in the first place.

By way of example, the CFP Board's Financial Planning Practice Standards require that the CFP® designee explore the client's values, attitudes, expectations and time horizons as they affect the client's goals, needs and priorities. The process of mutually defining the client's goals, needs and priorities is essential in determining what activities may be necessary to proceed with the client engagement. Personal values and attitudes shape the client's goals and objectives, along with the priorities placed on them. Thus, it is very important for the advisor to be able to understand the client's values and attitudes along with the goals and objectives.

Do not be misguided by the word "data." It is not merely the client's net worth that needs to understood; it is the client's self-worth and goals that need to understood. During the data gathering process, there may be unrealistic goals and objectives that the client may have. If these goals and objectives are unrealistic, then the advisor must explain to the client how or why they are unrealistic. The information the advisor is gathering is not just numbers, statements and tax returns. It is also about the beliefs, attitudes and desires of the client. This type of data gathering is just as important, if not more important, than the gathering of quantitative information and documents.

When getting into personal information and personal goals, sometimes clients may be reluctant to share some information. Asking questions when entering such an area can either diminish the relationship or exacerbate the client's difficulty. For instance, if the advisor notices that the client has omitted some key details in a story or event, the advisor must carefully handle the issue. One way to handle the predicament is through trying a direct question of "What parts have you left out?" While this could be seen as confrontational, using the phrase "left out" provides the client an implied permission to admit to the information that he or she is reluctant to share. However, if the client denies that any information was omitted, the advisor must cease the small confrontation, accept the client's denial, and go on to the next subject matter area.

The quantitative stage of data acquisition is where the advisor receives relevant quantitative information and documents pertaining to the client's financial resources, obligations and personal situation. This is obtained directly from the client or other sources, such as interviews, questionnaires, client records, and other documents.[6] The advisor must communicate to the client a reliance on the completeness and accuracy of the information provided. This information will impact later on conclusions and recommendations.

Do Not Use Long Questionnaires

While there is a lot of information that needs to be provided by the client and extracted by the advisor, there is certainly a time for questionnaires to be filled out. Questionnaires provide quick and easy information, while they ensure that subject areas are not omitted or forgotten by the advisor. Questionnaires can be very thorough and cover many areas that must be identified during the acquisition of quantitative information from the client. However, especially in the early stages of the relationship including the initial meeting, long questionnaires are considered to be less desirable if the advisor does not know the client well. The reason is that, while getting acquainted and establishing the relationship with the client as a person, the advisor needs to get to know the client and understand the client's goals and desires.

If a prospect or new client must bring wills, trusts, tax returns and other financial statements to the initial meeting, the message sent may be that their belongings or their balance sheet is your main concern, and not the person that the advisor is counseling. The first, or initial, meetings should send a message to the client that the client is important - that the client *is* the subject matter. The relevant question throughout the relationship is how do we make a recommendation and plan for the client in a way that maximizes his or her best interests? The client must be reminded of this question throughout.

Of course, there can be some short questionnaires or questionnaires that touch on who the client is, what kind of goals do they have in life, and what are their feelings toward specific financial aspects of their lives. Personal checklists are excellent tools. A short survey or questionnaire is certainly appropriate prior to, or being provided at, the initial meeting. That provides a foundation from which the meeting can progress.

---

6. See Financial Planning Practitioner Standards for CFP Designees, Practice Standard 200-2: Obtaining Quantitative Information and Documents.

Notably, during the establishment of the financial advisor-client relationship and during the data gathering process, the counseling relationship inherently has an imbalance of power between the client and counselor. Counselors hold power in that they are being sought out for professional services. Financial advisors are in positions of trust and must be cautious not to inadvertently misuse their power and refrain from wielding a disproportionate amount of the power in interactions with clients. Instead, financial advisors must respect the client's position, hold the client's interest above that of the advisor, and try to communicate effectively to realize the client's goals and achieve desired results.

CONCEPTS AND THEORIES BEHIND BEHAVIORAL FINANCE

INTRODUCTION TO BEHAVIORAL FINANCE

Before understanding the relatively new area of finance termed "Behavioral Finance," there must first be an understanding of the more established conventional financial theory, which is known as "Traditional Finance." **Traditional Finance** is also described in the literature as "Modern Portfolio Theory," though some of the concepts of the theory are not necessarily modern and have been subject to much debate and change over recent decades.

Traditional Finance, or Modern Portfolio Theory, was created and developed during the 1950s and 1960s when a more objective and scientific view of economics and financial markets existed. The development of Traditional Finance provided focus and attention on relevant facts and information about markets, industries and companies, while having streamlined information that was useful and available for comparison.

More specifically, Traditional Finance extracted information from the markets and made the information narrow, objective and standardized. This was accomplished with much success through the introduction of scientific method into finance. This was a ground-breaking development, and it helped

Key Concepts

Underline/highlight the answers as you read:

1. Identify the building blocks of Traditional Finance.

2. Explain what Behavioral Finance assumes?

3. Compare what determines returns under Traditional Finance versus Behavioral Finance.

breathe life into financial market analysis and aided investors and those participating in the market at a time when some may have been intimidated by or felt ignorant of available market information or financial data. The concepts of Traditional Finance and the scientific calculations that developed with it helped synthesize a wealth of information. In an area where there was a vast amount of data, information and numbers, it aided investors with information akin to a proverbial financial assembly line. To explain this further, the four basic premises of Traditional Finance are discussed.

ASSUMPTIONS AND BUILDING BLOCKS OF TRADITIONAL FINANCE

Traditional Finance is premised on four basic premises:
1. Investors are Rational;
2. Markets are Efficient;
3. The Mean-Variance Portfolio Theory Governs;
4. Returns are Determined by Risk (Beta).

The Rational Investor

Merton Miller and Franco Modigilani (1961)[7] made some significant declarations or assumptions about investors - that they are "rational." The rational investor, it was assumed, preferred more wealth as compared to less wealth. It was also assumed that rational investors were never confused by the manner or form of wealth.

To provide an example of how rational investors are never confused by the form of wealth, a rational investor would be considered to be indifferent or uncaring if a profit is realized by a dividend declared by a company versus if the same profit is realized by selling the stock at a gain. The source of the wealth is not important to the rational investor. The thing that is important to the rational investor is that more value was obtained, or more money was realized or earned.

Efficient Markets

The second assumption in the Traditional Finance framework is that financial markets are considered to be "efficient."[8] This market theory has, at its core, the belief that, at any given time, a stock's share price in the market incorporates and reflects all relevant information about that stock. Stocks are deemed at all times to trade at their fair value on stock exchanges, thus preventing investors from buying undervalued stocks or selling overvalued stocks. In other words, there are no "mispricings" in an efficient market. If there are truly no mispricings, then it is impossible, as the theory goes, to "beat" or "outperform" the market. If it is true that outperforming the overall stock market is impossible, then investors are forced to acquire riskier investments in order to realize higher returns. The activity, inaction or interaction of all hypothetical rational investors combines into the market as a whole.

When combining all rational investors into the "marketplace," the market is then seen as a "rational market" where stock prices are equal to their intrinsic value. Intrinsic value is the underlying value of a security or stock when considering future cash flows and the riskiness of the security.[9] Intrinsic values, in an efficient market, would therefore be determined by an analysis of reasonable expected cash flows and of the risk associated with those cash flows. According to Traditional Finance proponents, most, if not all, of the other information about the market would be irrelevant or considered to be "noise." Noise aside, if a market is

---

7. Miller and Modigliani, "Dividend Policy, Growth, and the Valuation of Shares", Journal of Business, Vol. 34, No. 3 (October 1961), pp. 411-433.
8. Fama, "The Behavior of Stock Market Prices", Journal of Business, Vol. 38 (1965), pp. 34-105; Fama, "Random Walks in Stock Market Prices", Financial Analysts Journal, (September/October 1965), pp. 55-59; Fama, "Efficient Capital Markets: A Review of Theory and Empirical Work", Journal of Finance, Vol. 25 (1970), pp. 383-417.
9. See Chapter 9 of this textbook, *infra*, discussing intrinsic value in more detail.

truly efficient in that stock prices are equal to the fundamental or intrinsic value of the stock, then that market cannot be beaten.

Another view, though softer than pure market efficiency, is an "unbeatable" market. An unbeatable market may allow for the generation of excess returns, including times of temporary overvaluation or undervaluation (*i.e.,* mispricings). An overvaluation (*i.e.,* a "bubble") can occur, but such occurrences are rare and seen as anomalies that do not present consistent opportunities for excess returns. Without consistent excess returns, the market is considered "unbeatable," though not truly "efficient."

The Mean-Variance Portfolio Theory Governs

The third assumption essential to the realm of Traditional Finance is that investors, as computer-like as they are, follow the Mean-Variance Portfolio Theory faithfully and tailor their portfolios to comply with it constantly. Harry Markowitz is the father of the Mean-Variance Portfolio Theory, as seen in his works in 1952 and 1959,[10] which officially fostered in the process of scientific method into the world of finance. Hypotheses were made, vigorous number crunching and empirical studies would follow, and the scientific assembly line for finance was born. Each question or thought about a company or the economy would invoke a common retort by Traditional Finance proponents, with the retort simply questioning the company's asset price.

Mean-Variance Portfolio Theory spawned the introduction by William Sharpe in 1964 of the Capital Asset Pricing Model ("CAPM") (defined in the next section). Mean-Variance investors choose portfolios by viewing and evaluating mean (averages) and variance. Variance in this sense is the range of expected difference between a projected return and an actual return.

Risk Yields Expected Returns

The fourth and final assumption from Traditional Finance deals squarely with risk. Risk, in this decision-making process, is measured by "Beta." Beta is a concept borrowed from the CAPM. The CAPM calculates the relationship of risk and return for an individual security using Beta (ß) as its measure of risk. The CAPM is derived by combining a risk-free asset with risky assets from an efficient market. The CAPM is the basic theory that links return and risk for all assets. The inputs and results are used to construct the security market line. The difference between the return of the market (r_m) and the risk-free rate of return (r_f) is considered the risk premium ($r_m - r_f$). The risk premium is the increase in return an investor should be compensated to take on the risk of a market portfolio versus investing in a risk-free asset. The CAPM formula is as follows[11]:

$$r = r_f + Beta \, (r_m - r_f)$$

---

10. H.M. Markowitz, "Portfolio Selection", Journal of Finance, Vol. 7, No. 1 (March 1952), pp. 77-91; see also Portfolio Selection: Diversification of Investments, New York (John Wiley & Sons 1959).
11. For a more detailed look at the CAPM and investments, please see discussion *infra* in Chapter 9 of this textbook.

While leaving the investment specifics for a later chapter, suffice it to say that the Beta of a stock is a calculation representing the volatility of an asset in relation to the volatility of the overall market or a given representative index. Stated differently, Beta is the measure of an asset's risk in correlation to the market or to an alternative benchmark.

This inquiry into Beta and risk-return was the main goal of Traditional Finance. It focused on the asset risk in relation to the market.

Issues and Questions Unanswered by Traditional Finance

By introducing Modern Portfolio Theory, Mean-Variance Portfolio Theory, the Capital Asset Pricing Model, and Beta, financial analysts and investors were able to narrow the focus of the financial industry. The framers and proponents of Traditional Finance made many strides, but in this process and evolution, other theorists and observers believed that they ignored many relevant and justified questions and data. For instance, the October 19, 1987 stock market crash, also infamously known as "Black Monday," resulted in a twenty (20%) percent decrease in the stock market as a whole. However, no studies or evidence of a twenty (20%) percent drop in fundamental values across the nation has ever been uncovered or proven. As a result, many critics used this event and others to express their concern that markets are not efficient and investors are not rational. These recurring questions and massive shifts in markets provided much empirical data, the very data that was so vital to (and developed by) proponents of Traditional Finance, showing that not all investors are rational, not all markets are efficient, and not all expected returns are tied to risk alone.

BEHAVIORAL FINANCE

A relatively new and evolving area of finance is termed "Behavioral Finance." As will be seen in this chapter, **Behavioral Finance** does not fully reject Traditional Finance's views or methods. Instead, it contains much of the scientific framework and lessons learned from Traditional Finance, amends some of it with basic assumptions based on normal, more human-like behavior, and supplements other aspects of it with notions from psychology and sociology.

Behavioral Finance begins with an assumption - investors are normal people like you, your friends and family, and your neighbors, and some are not like you. Some are smart, but some are not. Some are driven by emotion or by societal beliefs, while some are not so driven. Investors are normal people who make errors and prove that decisions can be made when focused on things that are subjective, not necessarily objective.

In Traditional Finance, the rational investor focused on investments that had average outcomes in an efficient market. Behavioral Finance attempts to understand normal investors and how the action or inaction of these investors reflects collectively in the overall market. The four main premises or assumptions in the area of Behavioral Finance are discussed below.

Investors Are "Normal"

Unlike a rational, number-crunching automaton, proponents of Behavioral Finance theory assume first that investors are "normal," not rational. Normal investors have normal wants and desires, but may commit cognitive errors (through biases or otherwise). Normal investors may be misled by emotions while they are trying to achieve their wants.

The normal investor is considered to be a person with emotions and cognitive biases. However, it is significant to understand that money managers, mutual fund managers, professional traders and others in the market are normal, too. These are people that are subject to the same "normalcy" as all of us.

Markets Are Not Efficient
Behavioral Finance does not suppose that, at every given moment in time, the price of a stock is equal to its fundamental value. Instead, while markets can be difficult to beat, the key concept is that there can be deviations in price from fundamental value so that there are opportunities to buy at a discount or sell at a premium. Conversely, there are times when an investor buys at a premium and sells at a discount. As a result, markets can be tough to beat, but they are not efficient.

Part of the reasoning here is that the market is a collection of normal investors. These are investors who do not know the future, who may be smart or not, who may be informed or not, and who may be lead by emotion or not. For example, if a company's stock is popular and rising, investors take note and frequently join the craze. Sometimes it is profitable; sometimes it is not. Normal investors do not contribute necessarily to efficient markets. This does not mean that markets are "normal" in the same sense as used with investors. It simply illustrates that the market is not truly efficient.

The Behavioral Portfolio Theory Governs
Many proponents of Traditional Finance would consider it a mistake to neglect to look at one's portfolio as a whole. Our next premise, or assumption, in Behavioral Finance involves this relevant question: Would you accept a greater return with less risk if you looked at your portfolio overall instead of looking at your portfolio in layers? A rational investor would certainly choose greater return for less risk. A normal investor may accept a greater risk with less return, but then again, he or she may not. The main problem, however, for normal investors is that they may not even know the risk-return ratios of their portfolio as a whole.

The "Behavioral Portfolio Theory" was introduced by Shefrin and Statman (2000)[12] as a goal-based theory. Under this theory, investors segregate their money into various mental accounting layers. This mental process occurs when people "compartmentalize" certain goals to be accomplished in different categories based on risk. Behavioral Portfolio Theory can be explained by visualizing a pyramid with layers that correspond to certain goals. These goals could include food and shelter, a secure retirement, paying for college education, paying for children's expenses like weddings, or being rich enough to fulfill a lifelong dream or desire.

Investors in the Behavioral Portfolio Theory (hereinafter also referred to as "BPT") hence view their portfolios in distinct mental account layers in a pyramid of assets. This perspective

---

12. See Shefrin and Statman, "Behavioral Portfolio Theory", Journal of Financial and Quantitative Analysis, Vol. XXXV, No. 2 (June 2000), pp. 127-151.

is different from investors under the Mean-Variance Portfolio Theory who view their portfolios as a whole at all times.

As observed by Statman, these mental accounting layers are pigeonholed in the mind of the normal investor to correlate to specific goals. However, they also reflect attitudes or leanings of the investor towards risk from layer to layer.[13]

The following is an example of a pyramid for one who places different assets into different layers, categorized by goals:

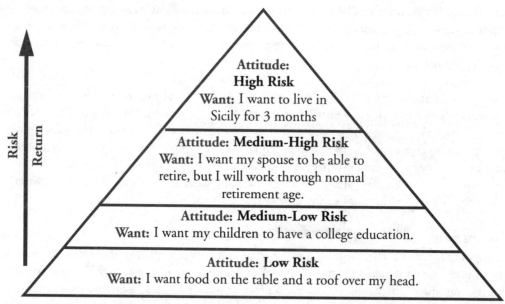

EXHIBIT 2.2   RISK/RETURN RELATIONSHIP

Risk
Return

**Attitude:
High Risk**
Want: I want to live in
Sicily for 3 months

Attitude: Medium-High Risk
Want: I want my spouse to be able to
retire, but I will work through normal
retirement age.

Attitude: Medium-Low Risk
Want: I want my children to have a college education.

Attitude: Low Risk
Want: I want food on the table and a roof over my head.

Much of the Behavioral Portfolio Theory has its roots dating back to observances by Friedman and Savage (1948), addressing the apparent contradiction of buying lottery tickets and insurance policies. Friedman and Savage studied people who bought lottery tickets and who also purchased insurance policies. They concluded that those who bought lottery tickets were risk-seeking through buying them, but were also averting risk by purchasing insurance. They reasoned that the lottery ticket purchase was to achieve higher social classes, yet the insurance protection safeguarded against dropping into lower social classes. While this could be seen as inconsistent behavior, it can be explained through the process of mental accounting that occurs when one places goals in separate layers with different degrees of risk on the pyramid.

There is one interesting common area between BPT and Modern Portfolio Theory (also referred to as "MPT").[14] Mean-Variance investors choose portfolios by evaluation and decisions based on mean and variance. Behavioral investors, instead, choose portfolios by evaluation and decisions based on expected wealth, desire for security, aspiration levels, and

13. Id. at pp. 141-142.
14. Id. at pp. 138-146.

probabilities of aspiration levels.[15] While these show that the two disciplines do not coincide, it does allow for a similar analysis if the investor has only one mental account or one mental layer. Some Behavioral investors may use a framework where there is only one mental account, such as having a desire for food and shelter only.

Such an investor under the BPT is referred to as "BPT-SA," the "SA" referring to a "single account" or just one layer. BPT-SA investors would integrate their portfolios into a single mental account, just as Mean-Variance or MPT investors do by considering covariance.[16] Covariance is the measure of how two securities change or move together when combined or of how the price movements between two securities are related to each other. Covariance is a measure of relative risk.[17] This integration is also called "diversification," the bedrock of Traditional Finance and Modern Portfolio Theory, and one of the most vital and accepted strategies in finance and investing.

The layers of mental accounting in the pyramid result in multiple mental accounts. Behavioral investors with several mental accounts, declared to be "BPT-MA" (with the "MA" referring to "multiple accounts"),[18] segregate their portfolios into mental accounts. Though risk is considered within each layer, behavioral investors in the BPT-MA category overlook or ignore covariance among these differing mental accounts.

Quick Quiz 2.4

Highlight the answer to these questions:

1. In Traditional Finance, investors are assumed to be rational.
    a. True
    b. False

2. Markets are assumed to be efficient in both Traditional and Behavioral Finance.
    a. True
    b. False

3. Returns are determined by risk (beta) in both Traditional and Behavioral Finance.
    a. True
    b. False

True, False, False.

A popular example with BPT-MA investors is that they may assign risky foreign stocks into one mental account and domestic accounts into another. While they may consider the foreign stocks in emerging or underdeveloped countries to be highly risky, they would in this instance overlook the covariant effect between such foreign and domestic stocks because the pyramid as a whole would not be evaluated in terms of risk and expected return of the portfolio and, hence, would not be viewed as an integrated single account.[19]

---

15. Id. at p. 128.
16. Id.
17. See discussion of variance and covariance later in Chapter 9 Investments of this textbook.
18. Shefrin and Statman, "Behavioral Portfolio Theory", *supra* note 8, at p. 128.
19. Id.

Risk Alone Does Not Determine Returns

The fourth and final assumption of Behavioral Finance is that expected returns are not measured by Beta or risk alone. While Traditional Finance has the Capital Asset Pricing Model, Behavioral Finance has the "Behavioral Asset Pricing Model." In its simplest form, the Capital Asset Pricing Model could be expressed in the following equation:

$$\text{Expected Return} = F \text{ (market factor)}$$

However, the Behavioral Asset Pricing Model reaches far beyond the simplicity of an objective risk calculation from the CAPM. The Behavioral Asset Pricing Model determines the expected return of a stock using Beta, book to market ratios, market capitalization ratios, stock "momentum," the investor's likes or dislikes about the stock or company, social responsibility factors, status factors, and more.[20]

In its simplest form, the Behavioral Asset Pricing Model is expressed in the following equation:

$$\text{Expected Return} = F \text{ (market factor, book to market ratio,}$$
$$\text{market capitalization, momentum, affect factor,}$$
$$\text{social responsibility factor, status factor, and more)}[21]$$

The realm of subjective risk is prevalent with the Behavioral Asset Pricing Model. As illustrated by the equation above, there are many more factors that are involved in Behavioral Finance, in contrast to the simpler and more pure pricing models of Traditional Finance. The next section will provide us with a brief look into what makes investors normal in this subjective realm.

WHAT MAKES INVESTORS NORMAL INSTEAD OF RATIONAL: COGNITIVE BIASES, ERRORS AND BEING HUMAN

What is the difference between a rational investor and a normal one? The answer is that normal investors are prone to making cognitive mistakes due to their beliefs or cognitive biases. Due the wealth of empirical and theoretical evidence showing that markets are not always "efficient" and investors are not "rational," a large amount of research from the field of psychology and sociology was injected into the financial industry in the last two to three decades.

A large number of psychologists and sociologists weighed in on thinking and the decision-making process that was applied to the financial industry. This spurned a lot of literature and studies in Behavioral Finance. With the disciplines of psychology and sociology on one side and the financial industry and planning on the other side, there is a vast amount of information and theories. The following is not an exhaustive list, but a list of the more commonly known biases or heuristics that have been observed or linked to normal investors.

---

20. See, Statman, "What is Behavioral Finance?", Behavioral Finance in Investment Management, Handbook of Finance Vol. II, Chap. 9, 2008 Wiley & Sons, Inc., at pp. 5-7)
21. Id. at p. 7.

A note on the word "heuristic." A heuristic is a tool used in the minds of people, also known as a "rule of thumb." The heuristic serves to basically shorten the decision-making process for the decision maker, or may make the process easier. However, when things change as they sometimes do, heuristics can lead to biases or can lead to investment decisions that are less than optimal. Some heuristics that are significant in the financial planning industry are the affect heuristic, availability heuristic, and similarity heuristic.

Affect Heuristic

The **affect heuristic** deals with judging something, whether it is good or bad. When stimuli occur, those stimuli cause the mind to have an effective response. This response occurs quickly and, in some cases, automatically and with or without consciousness. For instance, when the word "beautiful" is mentioned, feelings associated with that word are quickly sensed, just as the opposite occurs with the word "hideous." A similar sense of feelings is associated with the word hate versus the word treasure. Relying on these feelings is characterized by the affect heuristic.

Key Concepts

Underline/highlight the answers as you read:

1. Define heuristic.

2. Describe three common heuristics associated with financial decisions.

3. Explain how the month of October is associated with heuristic.

Numerous studies have traced the affect heuristic across a variety of research paths. These studies reveal that affect guides judgments and decisions.[22] Studies found evidence that affective emotional reactions appear to drive both perceived benefit and perceived risk.[23] Like houses, cars, watches, and other products, stocks exude "affect." They are considered "good" or "bad," beautiful or ugly. They are liked or disliked. Affect plays an overt role in the pricing of houses, cars, and watches, but according to Traditional Finance, affect plays no role in the pricing of financial assets. The BAPM outlines how expected returns are high, not only when objective risk is high, but also when subjective risk is high. High subjective risk comes with negative affect. Investors prefer stocks with positive affect, which inflates the prices of those stocks yet depresses their returns."[24] Hence, if an activity was "liked," people tended to judge its risks as being low and its benefits as being high. However, if an activity was "disliked," the judgments were the converse, with high risk and low benefit.[25]

Availability Heuristic

When a decision maker relies upon knowledge that is readily available in his or her memory, the cognitive heuristic known as "availability" is invoked (**availability heuristic**). Rather

---

22. Lucey and Dowling, "The Role of Feelings in Investor Decision-Making," Journal of Economic Surveys, Vol. 19, No.2 (2005), pp. 211-233.

23. Statman, Fisher, and Anginer, "Affect In A 'Behavioral Asset-Pricing Model", Financial Analyst Journal, Vol. 64, No. 2 (March/April 2008), pp. 20-29.

24. Id. at p. 20.

25. Id. at p. 226.

than examine other alternatives or procedures, pour through research, or investigate further, the decision-makers simply recant knowledge already known to them. Whatever information is available in their memory banks is tapped to reach a decision. This process can lead to decisions based on outdated information, incorrect data, or incomplete information.

In particular, events that bring out emotion, that are vivid in our memory, or that are fairly close in time tend to drive the availability heuristic. One popular example is the fear of flying versus the fear of riding in a car. Many people are fearful of flying based on the belief that it is not as safe as riding in a car. While it is factual that an accident in a plane would likely be more severe than in a car, the incidence of plane accidents reportedly are extremely small in relation to car accidents. The availability heuristic can also explain, in part, why investors tend to give more weight to the recent or short-term activity of a stock instead of a more prolonged or sustained period of time.

Similarity Heuristic

The "**similarity**" **heuristic** is used when a decision or judgment is made when a similar situation occurs. The mind of the individual goes back to a similar decision from a prior situation. This happens even though the situation is not exactly the same. The situation could be a prototype or an analogous situation, but is not the exact same situation. In personal relationships, those influenced by a similarity heuristic tend to select and choose to be around people who are similar to us, whether it is a similar age, gender, culture or interest.

An example of the similarity heuristic in investment decision making is investing in October. Some individuals that may have lost value in the stock market in any of the high profile drops in the stock market in October may be inclined to have an emotional reaction to mild news or price changes in the month of October. The investor, if moved to act by the similarity heuristic, would sell a stock based on the similar situation of time (that is the month of October), whereas the situation is very likely much different than an event that occurred years earlier during the month of October.

The Mindset of Losing Versus Taking Losses

When evaluating cognitive biases, heuristics and other decision-making processes that normal people encounter, one begins to understand that the collection of all decisions made by investors is what makes up a marketplace. This is the very essence of Behavioral Finance, and of all the literature and all the studies available, the common theme about normal investors is that there are mental or psychological mistakes that are made by all investors. Investors all make them, although they do not all make all of these mistakes. Some individuals do not look at their portfolio as a whole as they should. Some people have winning stocks and sell them prematurely. Of course, the investor does not know if it is being sold prematurely because this is occurring in real time and is not being done in hindsight.

On the other end, many people keep losing stocks, also known as losers. They keep the losers because their mindset is that, once they sell the losers, it is as if they admit defeat. However, the rational investor knows that when a stock value goes down, even though a sale is not made, the value is lost. Not only is this a distinction between the rational investor and the normal investor, it also shows how a decision is made to refrain from selling a stock out of the fear of actually having to admit that one lost the value in that stock. Some people sell winners so they can talk about it with their friends or others. Some sell the winners for fear of it going back down in value, when in reality investors all know that one should strive to buy low and sell high.

In short, losing value occurs when the stock price drops. Sometimes, the mind does not allow us to realize the loss until it is official, that being when the stock is sold. This leads us to the next area of study by Behavioralists, which studies and observes cognitive biases or other lines of thinking for individuals when making financial decisions.

Patterns and Types of Cognitive Biases

In the financial advisor-client relationship, the advisor should serve as a fiduciary or act in the client's best interests. Further, the client should follow the advisor's recommendations, as the client is the ultimate decision-maker. The challenge lies in delivering good advice that is *accepted* by the client. These recommendations, hence, must pass through the wealth of emotions, biases and heuristics that the client possesses to deal with the large amount of information that they receive daily, that they receive from friends and colleagues, and that they receive from the advisor.

Despite the well-intentioned client, these emotions, biases and heuristics may come into play. It is therefore beneficial to the advisor (and ultimately beneficial to the client) for the advisor to have a general understanding of the cognitive biases that are prevalent in the realm of financial decision-making.

Of all the information and research, the most commonly reported pattern of cognitive biases contributing to irrational or detrimental financial decision-making is as follows:

Anchoring

Anchoring is defined as attaching or anchoring one's thoughts to a reference point even though there may be no logical relevance or is not pertinent to the issue in question. Anchoring is also known as conservatism or belief perseverance. Anchoring has been reported to be fairly common in situations where decisions are being made in situations that are novel or new to the decision maker.[26]

For example, Kahneman and Tversky (1974) conducted a study where a wheel was spun with the numbers 1 through 100 on it. Study participants were asked if, whether the percentage of U.N. membership accounted for by certain countries was higher or lower than the number on the wheel. Afterwards, the study participants were asked to provide real estimates. It was learned that a seemingly random anchoring value of the number on which the wheel landed had a clear effect on the answer that the participants provided. For example, the average estimate given by participants was twenty-five (25%) percent if the wheel landed on 10, while the average was forty-five (45%) percent if the wheel landed on

---

26. Tversky and Kahneman, "Judgment under Uncertainty: Heuristics and Biases," Science, New Series, Vol. 185, No. 4157. (Sep. 27, 1974), pp. 1124-1131.

60. The random number resulted in an anchoring effect on the participants' responses even though the number had no correlation to the question.

When applying this to the world of investments or finance, investors have been found to base decisions on irrelevant figures, data or other statistics. For example, if the stock of a company has fallen considerably in a short period of time, investors may anchor on a recent or even distant high that the stock achieved, believing that the drop in price provides an opportunity to buy the stock at a discount.

In sum, anchoring is the opposite of representativeness or overreaction. Investors are normally slow to notice changes when things are changing gradually. They feel that they are secure and therefore other things are secure. The investor does not react or does not react timely because of the cognitive bias of conservatism or anchoring. Anchoring can lead to a quick answer to a problem that instead required more diligent search and critical analysis.

Confirmation Bias

A commonly used and popular phrase is that "you do not get a second chance at a first impression." This phrase can be borrowed to explain the **confirmation bias**. People tend to filter information and focus on information supporting their opinions. Other information can either be rationalized or ignored. At times, a first impression may lead to a preconceived opinion about something, and this opinion or belief can be hard to shake in the future. This is referred to as confirmation bias where selective thinking dominates.

For example, an investor may have an idea about a stock or may have heard about a stock from another person. When conducting a brief search from one's iPhone or handheld device, a few articles will appear at the bottom. A quick perusal may have various supporting information about the investment dealing with favorable information, but the investor may also gloss over potential problems with the stock or with the company, such as a lawsuit or other problems with the product. Selective thinking may lead to an incomplete picture for the investor.

Gambler's Fallacy

In the realm of probabilities, misconceptions can lead to faulty predictions as to occurrences of events. The **gambler's fallacy** is one of the incorrect assumptions from the world of probabilities. The oft-used example from calculus class is 100 coin flips.

When watching successive coin flips, if heads is the result successively, the belief is that the odds of that continuing to happen are slimmer, and therefore it is a better probability of betting on tails. While there would be some support for this logic, the likelihood of heads in a coin flip remains at fifty (50%) percent. Because each flip of the coin is a separate action, the probability of the coin flip is no more and no less than fifty (50%) percent. In a more strictly gambling sense, if playing roulette in the casino, if one is betting on an odd number versus an even number, the odds of an even number or an odd number coming up on the spin of the wheel is no larger or smaller on the next spin.

Just like with the roulette wheel, investors may sell stock when it has been successful in consecutive trading sessions because they may not believe the stock is going to continue its upward trend. Decisions based on this alone may be less than optimal due to the gambler's fallacy.

Herding

This cognitive bias is explained simply by looking at the word. People tend to follow the masses or the "herd." Individuals that are herding mimic the actions or decisions of a larger group, even though the individual may not have necessarily made the same choice. It is believed that **herding** is based on a person's desire to conform or be accepted by a certain group, while another reason is that if such a large group of people believe something to be correct, then the chances are that the conclusion or the decision they have made is also sound or correct.

While there certainly are numerous examples of when a herd, if large enough in the investment world, begins investing in a certain stock, it may raise the value of the stock by virtue of the demand for it. However, there are numerous examples of where jumping on the proverbial bandwagon has cost many investors. If the stock price is driven up by demand simply because other herders are buying it, the herd actually creates overvaluation that in the long run may mask issues with the underlying fundamentals of the actual investment. In this case, optimism or herding can misprice the value of the stock.

Hindsight Bias

Another potential bias for an investor is what is called **hindsight bias.** People are all too familiar with the test of foresight versus the test of hindsight. Hindsight is looking back after the fact is known. It is human nature to look back upon an adverse event and want to change it retrospectively. Foresight is what one predicts or projects will occur with current information without knowing the future. Psychologists have repeatedly explained that people have an inborn or innate need to find organization in the world by creating explanations that allow us to believe that events are predictable.[27] That is why too many events that have occurred, in hindsight, seem obvious.

For instance, many people lament the fact that, after a sporting event, the outcome of the game was obvious to them. However, before the contest or game, nobody knew what the outcome would be, nor could they accurately predict consistently outcomes to such sporting events. If hindsight bias is present, then the person who is making the investment decision believes that some past event was obvious or predictable. If it is obvious and predictable, then the decision-maker believes that the next problem will be obvious and predictable, and hence can be avoided. Therefore, the hindsight bias may lull the investor into believing they can perform better or more efficiently when armed with this knowledge or bias.

Overconfidence

The **overconfidence bias** usually concerns an investor that listens mostly to himself or herself. Overconfident investors mostly rely on their skills and capabilities to do their own homework or make their own decisions. Many investment portfolios that are not well diversified are in that condition due to a propensity of investors to believe that they can

---

27. Hawkins and Hastie, "Hindsight: Biased Judgments of Past Events After the Outcomes Are Known," *Psychological Bulletin,* Vol. 107, No. 3 (May 1990), at pp. 311-327.

outperform the market based on their beliefs or skills. It has been widely reported in terms of investing that overconfidence is one of the most common biases that can be detrimental to portfolios and the performance of investors over the long haul.

Overconfidence is believed to be a driver of excess trading. Another study put forth evidence that investors with discount brokerage accounts traded too frequently and, in the process, reduced their returns. It was found that higher trading costs were incurred, but more importantly, the stocks that investors bought did not do as well as the ones that they sold. The author concluded that the excess trading was attributed to overconfidence.[28] Numerous researchers have theorized that some investors trade very frequently because they are overconfident.

Overreaction

The key component between a normal investor and a rational investor is that the normal investor has emotion when making decisions in the stock market. One emotion that is common is an "**overreaction**" towards the receipt of news or information.

An interesting study from 1985[29] involved psychologists' research and investigation into people's tendency to overreact to dramatic news events and whether such behavior affects stock prices. The empirical evidence and data was consistent, as concluded by the authors, with overreaction bias. Interestingly, the results of the study also unearthed information about January returns from prior declared winners and losers, with the portfolios of losers experiencing exceptionally large returns.[30] Yet another study found that overreaction to new information is just as common as under-reaction, leading the author to conclude that overreaction and under-reaction are consistent with market efficiency.[31]

In the world of Traditional Finance, if new information was learned, that information was instantly incorporated into the stock price leading to market efficiency. This theory was partly contradicted in reality because stock market participants overreact to new information. A security's price is then adjusted by an overreaction by a large amount of investors.

People tend to emphasize more on their recent experience rather than on other factors. Representativeness, or overreaction, is the overweighting of sample information. In other words, when the model is unknown - that is, when the way a very large sample of something looks is unknown - people infer too quickly from too small of a sample. Overweighting sample information leads to overreaction. Investors become worried too quickly or are impressed too quickly based on short, incomplete or very small samples. Investors remove their money from mutual funds that have recently performed poorly and place their funds into mutual funds that have recently done well. Overreaction has been linked to short-term

---

28. Odean, "Do Investors Trade Too Much?," American Economic Review, Vol. 89, No. 5 (December 1999), pp. 1279-1298.
29. De Bondt and Thaler, "Does the Stock Market Overreact?," Journal of Finance, Vol. 40, No. 3 (July 1985), pp. 793-808.
30. Id. at 793.
31. Fama, "Market Efficiency, Long Term Returns, and Behavioral Finance," Journal of Finance, Vol. 49, No. 3 (September 1998), pp. 283-306.

market momentum for individual stocks when investors move money to stocks that have performed well and away from those that have performed poorly.

Prospect Theory

Kahneman and Tversky presented the "**Prospect Theory**" in 1979.[32] The Prospect Theory provides that people value gains and losses differently and will base their decisions on perceived gains rather than perceived losses. If someone is provided with two equal choices, one being expressed in terms of possible gains and the other in terms of possible losses, people would chose to express in terms of possible gains, even if it means the same economic result.

Kahneman and Tversky conducted a number of studies where participants answered questions about judgments between two monetary decisions involving perspective losses and perspective gains. The overwhelming majority of the participants chose stating things in terms of gains rather than losses. The result is, under the Prospect Theory, that people would rather a reasonable level of gains even though they have a chance at earning more, and are willing to engage in risk seeking behavior when they can limit their losses. This means that losses are more heavily weighted than an equal amount of gains.

The Disposition Effect

With all the above cognitive biases, heuristics and other mental exercises discussed above, there is another subset of Behavior Finance that should be addressed. Shefrin and Statman (1985)[33] presented the reluctance of an investor to realize a loss in a Behavioral framework where they argued that the reluctance stems from a combination of two cognitive biases and an emotion. The cognitive bias was "faulty framing" where normal investors do not mark their stocks to market prices. Investors create mental accounts when they purchase stocks and continue to mark their value to purchase prices even after market prices have changed. They mark stocks to the market only when they sell their stocks and close their mental accounts. Normal investors therefore do not acknowledge the loss in value, referred to as a paper loss, because an open account means that there is still a chance that the stock price will rise, and the stock is not necessarily a loser, but may still turn into a gain. The normal investor does not consider the stock a loser until the stock is sold, at which time the loss is technically realized in the mind of the normal investor. Interfacing with the faulty framing bias is the cognitive bias of hindsight.

Shefrin and Statman explained that hindsight is linked to the emotion of regret, and realization of losses brings on the pain of regret when investors realize in hindsight that they would have been better off had they avoided buying the stock altogether. Hindsight misleads the investor into believing that they could have foreseen the losing stock and avoided the loss which could also lead to overconfidence for subsequent transactions. A defense against regret is to postpone the realization of the loss until later, yet the fact that the stock price dropped is the real moment when the loss occurred, not upon the actual sale.

---

32. Kahneman and Tversky, "Prospect Theory: An Analysis of Decisions Under Risk," Econometrica, Vol. 47, No. 2 (March 1979), pp. 263-291.
33. Shefrin and Statman, "The Disposition to Sell Winners Too Early and Ride Losers Too Long," Journal of Finance, Vol. 40, No. 3 (July 1985), pp. 777-790.

Another study examined the behavior of individual investors, finding that they realized their profitable stock investments at a much higher rate than their unprofitable ones, except in December. The December sale was obviously explained by motivation for tax purposes.[34]

In summary, the reluctance to realize a loss is a powerful motivator of the normal investor. The "**Disposition Effect**" helps provide some insight into the mind of the normal investor.

Note on Limits to Arbitrage

Behavioral biases among normal investors have an effect on asset prices and returns on investments on a sustained basis only if there are limits to arbitrage that also exist, preventing rational investors from exploiting short-term overvaluation or undervaluation in prices, and in the process, return those prices to their fundamental values. There is some evidence that suggests limits to arbitrage exist in the failure to eliminate obvious and straightforward "mispricing" situations. For instance, in one paper, Mitchell, Pulvino and Stafford (2002) chronicled 82 instances where the market value of a company was less than the market value of the company's stock in its subsidiary.[35] While this implies there are opportunities for arbitrage that lead to swift correction of the mispricing, these authors also warn of barriers to arbitrage.

In short, there are many cases and instances where the market value of spun out subsidiaries exceed that of the parent company that retained a majority stock in the spinout, but in these cases, short-selling of the spinout was difficult, expensive or impossible, reducing or eliminating the arbitrage opportunity. The literature also supports other inherent risks in arbitrage, such as trading by uninformed investors that may cause the mispricings to increase before correction, the inability of the arbitrageur to maintain the position in the face of margin calls, and other high implementation calls for arbitrage trades. Therefore, arbitrage in practice is limited by various areas of risk.

CONCLUSION ABOUT BEHAVIORAL FINANCE

Behavioral Finance involves normal people in various settings, including questions as to why people trade, why they consume more from dividend dollars than from capital funds, why they are eager to invest in hedge funds or why they prefer to invest in socially responsible companies.

This chapter points out how cognitive biases, heuristics and other mental exercises or short-cuts can affect behavior and decisions of investors. As a result, if investors' decisions are subject to their biases, biases also have an effect on stock market pricing. Traditional Finance proponents would explain that bubbles occur when prices are correctly placed and high priced stocks are less risky or have good cash flow prospects. Behavioral Finance proponents would explain bubbles occur because investor sentiment comes in waves and can drive up

---

34. Odean, "Are Investors Reluctant to Realize Their Losses?," Journal of Finance, Vol. 53, No. 5 (October 1998), pp. 1775-1798.

35. Shefrin and Statman, "Explaining Investor Preferences for Cash Dividends", Journal of Financial Economics, Vol. XIII, No. 2 (June 1984), pp. 253-282. See also, H. M. Shefrin and M. Statman, "The Disposition to Sell Winners Too Early and Ride Losers Too Long: Theory and Evidence," Journal of Finance, Vol. XL, No. 3 (July 1985), pp. 777-790. These are cites to some of the other evidence cited above. See also, Shefrin and Statman, "Behavioral Capital Asset Pricing Theory," Journal of Financial and Quantitative Analysis, Vol. 29, No. 3 (Sept. 1994), pp. 323-349.

stock beyond its fundamental value, or if stocks are falling, that fall can lead to a crash because of panic.

Human nature cannot be discounted when trying to understand the market as a whole. Therefore, to have an optimal investment policy and plan for a client, the financial planning practitioner must understand some of the tenets and challenges in Behavioral Finance. While it is hard to make investment decisions without some biases coming into play, understanding and being aware of behavioral biases can aid the investor and financial planning advisor. Everyone makes mistakes including being overconfident, overweighting recent behavior while underrating the long-term view, and refusing to accept a small loss and selling a winning stock prematurely.

If investors and financial planning advisors can understand biases and how they can direct investor behavior, then there is an opportunity for the investor or the financial planning advisor to be mindful of, or to perhaps create an advantage due to, common mistakes made by normal investors. For instance, there may be news that leads numerous investors to overreact. Investors should consider avoiding the over reactive behavior, or perhaps the herding behavior, and consider more long-term goals, or better yet perform more research or investigation into what the actual problem might be.

Quick Quiz 2.5

Highlight the answer to these questions:

1. Understanding behavioral biases can aid the financial advisor.
   a. True
   b. False

2. Biases have no effect on stock prices.
   a. True
   b. False

3. Behavioral Finance is pure and concerned only with risk-reward and risk-return.
   a. True
   b. False

4. Behavioral Finance is more subjective than Traditional Finance and does not have a single cohesive theory.
   a. True
   b. False

True, False, False, True.

While many concepts of psychology and sociology enter into the framework in the world of Behavioral Finance, Behavioral Finance does not abandon many of the concepts and use of scientific method from traditional finance. While not abandoning Traditional Finance, advisors who study or educate themselves in Behavioral Finance may be able to improve their clients' outcomes by providing prudent recommendations tailored to the goals of the client in a way that increases the chances that the clients will use the recommendations. Traditional Finance is pure and concerned with risk-reward and risk-return.

Behavioral Finance, however, is far more subjective, with consideration to a wide range of cognitive biases and areas of psychology and sociology to consider. Behavioral Finance does not have a cohesive single theory. Obviously, much is left to be done for there to be a consensus among Behavioral theorists, and it is not farfetched to believe that the simplicity of the rational investor or the efficient market hypothesis will never be matched. Behavioral Finance is in its infancy. However, Behavioral Finance and its principles can aid investors and financial advisors to improve the investment process, make effective decisions during the advisor-client relationship, and help advisors reach an optimal plan for planning and investing for the client.

Key Terms

Active Listening - Requires the listener's undivided attention. Active listening involves concentration of what the speaker is saying. The listener must put aside irrelevant thoughts.

Affect Heuristic - Deals with judging something, whether it is good or bad.

Anchoring - Attaching or anchoring one's thoughts to a reference point even though there may be no logical relevance or is not pertinent to the issue in question. Anchoring is also known as conservatism or belief perseverance.

Availability Heuristic - When a decision maker relies upon knowledge that is readily available in his or her memory, the cognitive heuristic known as "availability" is invoked.

Behavioral Finance - Contains much of the scientific framework and lessons learned from Traditional Finance, amends some of it with basic assumptions based on normal, more human-like behavior, and supplements other aspects of it with notions from psychology and sociology.

Closed Questions - Seeks a response that is very specific and commonly involves an answer that can be accomplished with a single word or two. Closed questions lead with is, are, do, did, could, would, have, or "is it not true that..."

Cognitive-Behavioral Paradigm (Cognitive-Behavior School of Thought) - Humans are beings are subject to the same learning principles that were established in animal research. The basic principles of classical and operant conditioning are assumed to account for an individuals' behavior and understandings throughout their lives.

Confirmation Bias - A commonly used and popular phrase is that "you do not get a second chance at a first impression." People tend to filter information and focus on information supporting their opinions.

Developmental Paradigm ("Developmental" School of Thought) - Believes that human development occurs in stages over time. Relationships that are formed early in life become a template for establishing relationships in adulthood. As to emotions, the Developmental Paradigm assumes that all humans develop and progress in a predictable sequence.

Disposition Effect - The cognitive bias was "faulty framing" where normal investors do not mark their stocks to market prices. Investors create mental accounts when they purchase stocks and continue to mark their value to purchase prices even after market prices have changed.

Gambler's Fallacy - One of the incorrect assumptions from the world of probabilities; in the realm of probabilities, misconceptions can lead to faulty predictions as to occurrences of events.

Key Terms

Herding - This cognitive bias is explained just by looking at the word. People tend to follow the masses or the "herd."

Hindsight Bias - Another potential bias for an investor. Hindsight is looking back after the fact is known.

Human Communications - Comprised of fundamental elements. Societal groups use a system of signs in their communication process. A sign could be a word, object, gesture, tone, quality, image, substance or other reference according to a code of shared meaning among those who use that sign for communication purposes.

Humanistic Paradigm (The "Humanistic" School of Thought) - Dominated by theorists whose models have their origins from a shared philosophical approach. For a client to grow, the relationship requires a transparent and genuine counselor. The advisor needs a philosophical stance that humankind is basically good and that people have the inherent capability of self-direction and growth under the right set of circumstances.

Nonverbal Behaviors - Nonverbal cues, or body language, can communicate feelings and attitudes from the client to the financial advisor and are mainly provided from the body and the voice. Body position and body movement are important, while voice tone and voice pitch are also telling.

Open Questions - Result in a person answering with a lengthy response that usually begin with words such as how, what, when, where, who and why.

Overconfidence Bias - Usually concerns an investor that listens mostly to himself or herself, overconfident investors mostly rely on their skills and capabilities to do their own homework or make their own decisions.

Overreaction - A common emotion towards the receipt of news or information.

Passive Listening - Described as listening in the normal or usual conversation or conversational setting to which most people are accustomed at seminars, in class, at social gatherings, or at sermons.

Prospect Theory - Provides that people value gains and losses differently and will base their decisions on perceived gains rather than perceived losses.

Similarity Heuristic - Used when a decision or judgment is made when a similar situation occurs.

Traditional Finance (Modern Portfolio Theory) - Also described in the literature as though some of the concepts of the theory are not necessarily modern and have been subject to much debate and change over recent decades. Traditional finance is premised on four basic premises: (1) Investors are Rational; (2) Markets are Efficient; (3) The Mean-Variance Portfolio Theory Governs; and (4) Returns are Determined by Risk (Beta).

DISCUSSION QUESTIONS

1. Identify and discuss the 3 general schools of thought for counseling.

2. What are some examples of open questions versus closed questions?

3. Discuss the benefits and drawbacks to the "why" question of a client?

4. What are your options if you sense a client is saying one thing but believes another?

5. Identify and discuss the 4 basic premises for Traditional Finance.

6. Identify and discuss the 4 basic premises for Behavioral Finance.

7. Identify and describe some differences between a rational investor and a normal one.

8. Discuss what you believe are the reasons how someone can buy lottery tickets and insurance at the same time.

9. Discuss the difference between evaluating a portfolio as a whole versus evaluating a portfolio in mental layers.

10. What should you do as a financial advisor if you believe that a client's heuristic is clouding his or her judgment?

1. Which of the following is considered to be a counseling paradigm or school of thought?

    a. Developmental.

    b. Humanistic.

    c. Cognitive-Behavioral.

    d. All of the above.

2. Which of the following are consistent with the Humanistic Paradigm?

    1. The majority of Humanistic theories view clients as experts on themselves.

    2. The alliance between the counselor and client is extremely important for humanistic counselors and is the basis of the treatment or plan of action.

    3. There needs to be a professional distance between the client and advisor where the advisor should stay close to discussing numbers and data with the client.

    a. 1 only.

    b. 1 and 2.

    c. 1 and 3.

    d. All of the above.

3. Which of the following is NOT a premise in Traditional Finance?

    a. Markets are Efficient.

    b. Investors are Rational.

    c. Markets are Inefficient.

    d. Modern Portfolio Theory Governs.

4. Which of the following are important in nonverbal communication and behavior?

    1. Body positioning.

    2. Body movement.

    3. Voice tone.

    4. Voice pitch.

    a. 1 only.

    b. 1 and 2.

    c. 1 and 3.

    d. All of the above.

5. Which of the following is NOT true in communicating with a client?

    a. Posture means nothing.
    b. Good posture may indicate positive self-esteem.
    c. Slouching may indicate less interest.
    d. None of the above.

6. Which of the following are components of "passive listening?"

    1. Listening in a normal social setting, such as a sermon.
    2. Communication rests on one speaker.
    3. The listener screens out some information.
    4. The listener is thinking about what to say in response which hampers listening.
        a. 1 only.
        b. 1 and 2.
        c. 1 and 3.
        d. All of the above.

7. Which of the following are NOT components of "active listening?"

    a. Requires the listener's undivided attention.
    b. The listener must put aside irrelevant thoughts.
    c. Interruptions or disruptions, such as texting and bathroom breaks, are common.
    d. The listener can nod occasionally to show interest.

8. Which of the following are theories or equations used in traditional finance?

    1. Mean-Variance Theory.
    2. Modern Portfolio Theory.
    3. The Capital Asset Pricing Model.
        a. 1 only.
        b. 1 and 3.
        c. All of the above.
        d. None of the above.

9. Which of the following investors would apply in the realm of Behavioral Finance?

    a. A rational investor who considers his or her portfolio as a whole at all times.
    b. An investor not moved by emotion or biases.
    c. An investor who at times is subject to emotion or cognitive biases.
    d. An investor guided by risk calculations based on Beta alone.

10. Which of the following is are NOT basic premises in Behavioral Finance?

 1. Investors are normal.

 2. Markets are inefficient.

 3. The Behavioral Asset Pricing Model applies.

 a. 2 only.

 b. 1 and 3.

 c. 2 and 3.

 d. All of the above.

11. Which of the following are NOT heuristics or cognitive biases discussed in this chapter that can lead to less than optimal decisions by a normal investor?

 a. The Affect Heuristic.

 b. Overreaction bias.

 c. Overconfidence bias.

 d. Laziness.

12. Which of the following statements are true?

 1. There has been a movement in recent times for the financial industry to be more in touch with psychology and sociology due to their effect and persuasiveness in financial matters.

 2. There has been a movement in recent times for the financial industry to focus on asset prices and ignore psychology and sociology issues.

 3. Behavioral Finance has nothing to do with issues concerning psychology and sociology.

 a. 1 only.

 b. 1 and 3.

 c. None of the above.

 d. All of the above.

13. Which schools of thought for counseling could an advisor combine?

 a. Developmental and Humanistic.

 b. Humanistic and Cognitive-Behavioral.

 c. Developmental and Cognitive-Behavioral.

 d. All 3 schools of thought may be combined.

14. Which of the following choices are false as to open or closed questions?

    a.   Open or closed questions are both effective tools for the financial advisor.

    b.   An open question starts with the phrase "Isn't it true that ..."

    c.   A closed question is narrow and can be answered with a word or two.

    d.   None of the above.

15. Which of the following are true about "why" questions?

    1.   While the "why" questions are tempting and may help understand the client's motives, the "why" question may be ill-advised because it could have limited benefit for the client.

    2.   A "why" question could place the client in a position of having to justify what was done, and that could put the client in a defensive posture.

    3.   "Why" questions are always the best questions to ask.

        a.   1 only.

        b.   2 only.

        c.   1 and 2.

        d.   All of the above.

16. Which of the following is the best choice for Behavioral Finance?

    a.   Behavioral Finance throws out all notions and equations from Traditional Finance.

    b.   Behavioral Finance does not abandon Traditional Finance, though some key assumptions are changed.

    c.   Traditional Finance's introduction of scientific method into financial analysis has no benefit to Behavioral Finance.

    d.   Behavioral Finance is a well-developed, well-matured and settled area of finance.

Quick Quiz Explanations

Quick Quiz 2.1
1. True.
2. True.
3. True.

Quick Quiz 2.2
1. True.
2. True.
3. False. Nonverbal communication, including body language, can play an important role in understanding communications, especially when verbal communication is contrary to body language.

Quick Quiz 2.3
1. False. It is better to pay attention and provide supporting facial and/or body gestures (such as nodding in affirmation) when actively listening to encourage the speaker to continue and to convey that the information is important.
2. True.

Quick Quiz 2.4
1. True.
2. False. Markets are assumed to be efficient in Traditional but not Behavioral Finance.
3. False. Returns are determined by risk (beta) in Traditional but not Behavioral Finance.

Quick Quiz 2.5
1. True.
2. False. Normal investors are susceptible to less than optimal decisions due to cognitive biases. When combining the activity and decision of normal investors in the marketplace, biases can have an effect on stock prices.
3. False. Traditional Finance, not Behavioral Finance, is pure and concerned with risk-reward and risk-return.
4. True.

Financial Planning Approaches: Analysis and Recommendations

LEARNING OBJECTIVES

After reading this chapter, you should be able to:

- List and describe each of the approaches to financial planning analysis and recommendations.
- Describe the lifecycle approach and its benefits.
- Describe the pie chart approach and its benefits.
- Describe the financial statement and ratio analysis approach.
- Understand the relationship between time, savings, and withdrawal rates on retirement planning.
- Understand the exponential nature of the investment assets to gross pay benchmark.
- Describe the two-step, three panel, and metrics approach to financial planning.
- Analyze the various sources of borrowing available to a client and communicate the advantages and disadvantages of each for meeting a client's financial goal.*
- Create a debt management plan for a client that minimizes financing costs and maximizes the potential to reach goals.*
- Explain and compare appropriate financing strategies for purchasing a home.*
- List each benchmark metric for risk management short term savings and investing goals and long-term savings and investing goals.
- Communicate the need for liquid assets and emergency funds and recommend strategies for accumulating the appropriate levels of funds.*
- Calculate savings required to meet financial goals and recommend how to incorporate planned savings into the cash flow plan.*
- Describe the cash flow approach to analysis.
- Identify opportunities and challenges related to a client's cash inflows and outflows and make recommendations to assist the client in meeting their current needs and long-term financial goals.*
- Describe the income tax analysis.
- Describe the strategic approach to financial planning analysis.

- Describe and discuss the present value of all goals approach to financial planning analysis.

* CFP Board Resource Document - Student-Centered Learning Objectives based upon CFP Board Principal Topics.

INTRODUCTION

Prior to developing and presenting financial plan recommendations to a client, the planner and client should mutually define the client's personal and financial goals, needs and priorities. The planner must keep the client's values, attitudes, expectations, and time horizons in mind as they affect the goals, needs, and priorities of the client.

Goals and objectives provide a roadmap for the financial planning process. Goals tend to be broad (such as having sufficient assets to retire), while objectives are more narrow and defined and can effectively be subjected to measurement (e.g., $1,000,000 in investment assets by age 45).

To evaluate the extent to which the client's goals, needs, and priorities can be met by the client's current and future financial resources, the planner must collect and analyze both internal and external data.

REASONABLE ASSUMPTIONS

The planner, in consultation with the client, must establish reasonable assumptions, especially where projections will be used to determine if a goal can be achieved. Some of these assumptions include information about:
- What constitutes an adequate emergency fund (e.g., savings provisions)?
- What is an appropriate emergency fund ratio (the number of months of coverage by cash and cash equivalents of non-discretionary cash flows)?
- What are appropriate debt ratios? What is an appropriate benchmark for this client? When will the client be out of debt?
- What are the personal, property, and liability risks that this client faces and what are the best ways to cover and manage these risks?
- What retirement benchmarks are to be used, including the retirement age, the percentage of pre-retirement income needed to maintain the retirement lifestyle, the retirement life expectancy, any legacy requirements, inflation rates, income tax rates, and expected investment returns consistent with the client's risk tolerance and actual portfolio asset allocation?
- What estimates will be used to provide for any college education goals - ages of children, education inflation rate, current costs of relevant education?
- What estimates will be used to provide for any lump-sum funding goals - today's cost, the inflation rate, the amount needed to provide an adequate down payment?
- What estimates will be used to provide for legacy goals - defined in dollars (today's), the inflation rate, earnings rate, the expected estate and gift tax rates, exclusions, and exemptions (state and federal)?

THE ANALYSIS

Once the financial planner has completed the initial financial planning process steps where the client relationship is established and the required data is collected, the practitioner can begin analyzing and evaluating the client's situation. Agreed upon assumptions can be taken into consideration, and various financial planning approaches can be applied to arrive at plan recommendations. This chapter will focus on the following two steps of the financial planning process: (1) analyzing and evaluating the client's financial status and (2) developing and presenting financial planning recommendations.

FINANCIAL PLANNING PROCESS[1]

EXHIBIT 3.1

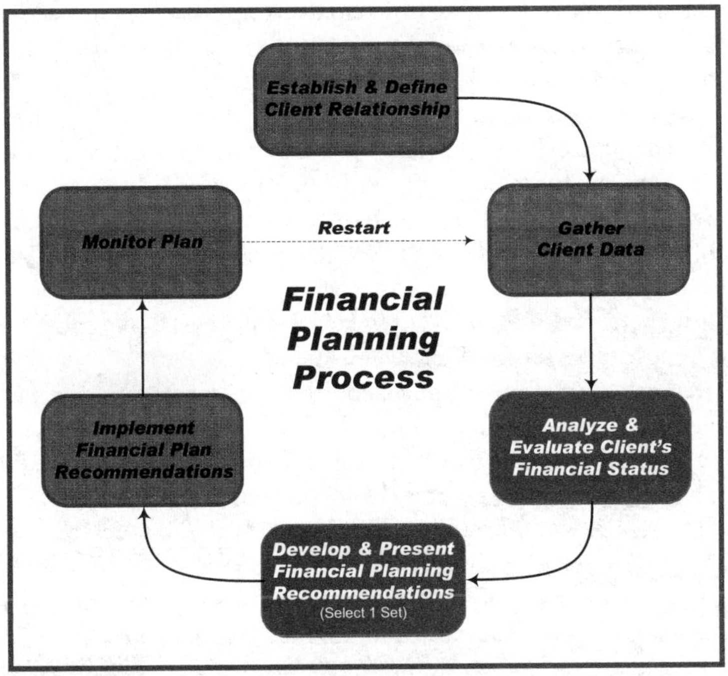

The purpose of the analysis is to identify any weaknesses in the plan and make recommendations that will assist the client in achieving their goals.

THE APPROACHES TO FINANCIAL PLANNING ANALYSIS AND RECOMMENDATIONS

There are a wide array of possible approaches to analyzing, evaluating, and developing recommendations in the financial planning process. Each approach by itself is useful and provides the planner and client with a slightly different perspective of the collected data. These approaches are identified and the benefits of each approach are briefly described below with further explanation later in the chapter.

---

1. Abbreviated from the CFP Board's Financial Planning Practice Standards.

- The **life cycle approach** - Data collection is quick and simple and relatively non-threatening to the client. It provides the planner with a brief overview of the client's financial profile permitting the planner to have a relatively focused conversation with the client. It is generally used very early in the engagement.

- The **pie chart approach** - This approach provides a visual representation of how the client allocates financial resources. It provides a broad perspective on the client's financial status and it is generally used after the collection of internal data and the preparation of financial statements. For example, the balance sheet pie chart illustrates the relative size of liabilities and net worth to total assets, the relative size of cash/cash equivalents, and investment assets to total assets, and personal use assets to total assets. If a benchmark comparison pie chart from the metrics approach (discussed below) is added, it is often revealing for the client.

- The **financial statement and ratio analysis approach** - This approach helps to establish a financial snapshot of the client as of today. The ratio analysis provides an opportunity to assess the client's strengths, weaknesses, and deficiencies by comparing the client's ratios to the benchmark metrics. The ratio approach usually follows the pie chart approach and provides the planner with the actual financial ratios with which to compare the benchmarks in the metrics approach.

- The **two-step/three-panel approach** - A step-by-step approach in which the client's actual financial situation is compared against benchmark criteria. This approach is relatively thorough and presents a manageable approach to the client. It stresses the management of risk, seeks to avoid financial dependence, and promotes savings and investing to achieve financial independence.

- The **present value of goals approach** - This approach considers each short-term, intermediate-term, and long-term goal, determines their respective present value, then sums all of these together and treats the sum as an obligation (liability) that is then reduced by current resources of investment assets and cash and cash equivalents. The resultant is the net future obligation that will need to be retired over the remaining work life expectancy at the expected rate of investment return using an ordinary annuity. This annuity requirement in dollars is then compared to the current annual savings amount in dollars after any implemented risk management and other immediate recommendations and a tax analysis, to determine whether the current savings amount is adequate to fund all goals. As part of determining the ability to save, a pre and post recommendations tax analysis must be preformed to determine whether the client is properly, over, or under-withheld on income taxes.

- The **metrics approach** - This approach uses qualitative benchmarks that provide rules of thumb for a measurement of where a client's financial profile should be. When combined with the two-step/three-panel approach, metrics help establish objectives that are measurable compared to ratio analysis.

- The **cash flow approach** - This approach takes an income statement approach to recommendations. It uses the three-panel approach and uses a pro forma approach (as if) "to purchase" the suggested recommendations. This approach has the effect of driving down the discretionary cash flow. Next, positive cash flows or the sale of assets are identified to finance the recommendations.

- The **strategic approach** - This approach uses a mission, goal, and objective approach considering the internal and external environment and may be used with other approaches.

Using any single approach described above is not likely be adequate to develop a comprehensive financial plan. Employing all of the approaches simultaneously will create some redundancy but considered together will probably produce a comprehensive financial plan that is effective for the client. While a beginner planner may want to use all of the approaches, an experienced financial planner will find it sufficient to use a combination of a select few. For example, it is usually essential in any comprehensive plan to use the cash flow approach because it requires the client to prioritize and monetize each recommendation and determine the overall financial impact of each recommendation on the financial statements. Also, the cash flow approach clarifies the current and future resources to be used and whether or not they are sufficient to implement all of the recommendations or whether some recommendations will have to be deferred until additional resources are available. Experienced financial planners will combine approaches depending on the preferences of the planner and the needs of the client.

Key Concepts

Underline/highlight the answers as you read:

1. List assumptions that the financial planner and client need to consider when developing a comprehensive financial plan.

2. Identify the eight approaches to financial planning analysis and recommendations.

3. Describe the types of information the financial planner gathers and analyzes using the life cycle approach.

4. Identify the three phases of the life cycle approach along with each phase's likely risks and goals.

Exhibit 3.2 portrays common characteristics, by age group, of individuals with typical financial risks and goals. Financial planners should be familiar with these typical characteristics so that their particular client's financial wants, needs, and goals can be anticipated.

Life Cycle Factors							
Age	22-30	25-35	25-35	35-45	45-55	55-65	65-75
Marital Status	Single	Married**	Married	Married	Married	Married	Married
Children***	No	No	Yes	Yes	Yes	Yes	Yes
Grandchildren***	No	No	No	No	No	Yes	Yes
Income	$35-$75k	$35-$75k	$45-$100k	$50-$150k	$75-$200k	$100-$200k	$50-$200k
Net Worth	$10-$20k	$10-$20k	$15-$25k	$20-$40k	$50-$100k	$500-$1,200k	$400-$1,500k
Self Employed	No	No	No	No	Yes	Maybe	No
Typical Risks/Insurance Coverage Needs							
Life Insurance	No	Maybe	Yes	Yes	Yes	Yes	No
Disability	Yes	Yes	Yes	Yes	Yes	Yes	No
Health	Yes	Yes	Yes	Yes	Yes	Yes	Yes
Long-Term Care*	No	No	No	No	No	Maybe Yes	Maybe Yes
Property	Yes	Yes	Yes	Yes	Yes	Yes	Yes
Liability	Yes	Yes	Yes	Yes	Yes	Yes	Yes
Typical Goals							
Retirement Security	Yes	Yes	Yes	Yes	Yes	Yes	In Retirement
Education Funding	No	No	Yes	Yes	Yes	No	No
Gifting	No	No	No	No	No	Yes	Yes
Lump-Sum Expenses	Yes	Yes	Yes	Yes	Yes	Yes	No
Legacy	No	No	No	No	No	Maybe	Maybe

* While younger clients will not typically require long-term care insurance, in some circumstances long-term care may be appropriate.

** Married could be married, divorced, or widow(er).

*** Children and grandchildren are always yes, no, or maybe.

THE LIFE CYCLE APPROACH

Using this approach, the planner gathers and analyzes the following information:

- the ages of the client and spouse;
- the client's marital status;
- the number and ages of children and grandchildren;
- the family income by each contributor;
- the family net worth; and
- whether the client is employed, unemployed, self-employed, or retired.

The life cycle approach is a broad view of the client financial profile and is best employed to provide general information with which to focus a financial discussion with the client when the financial planner only has partial information. For example, a married couple with small children will probably have a goal to save for the college education of their children. Meanwhile they should be concerned about certain other risks such as their untimely death or disability. The life cycle approach gives the planner a 60-75 percent perspective of the risks the client is likely to be concerned about and their likely goals and serves as a foundation for a dialog with the client.

It should be emphasized that there are no absolutes in personal financial planning. Each client is unique. Having said that, many clients fit into similar profiles (see Exhibit 3.2). The ages of the spouses may provide an indication as to what phase of life the client is in, as defined below.

- The **asset accumulation phase** usually occurs in the early 20s to mid 50s when discretionary cash flow for investing is low and the debt to net worth ratio is high.
- The **conservation (risk management) phase** usually occurs from the late 20s to the early 70s, where cash flow, assets, and net worth have increased and debts have decreased somewhat. In addition, risk management of events like unemployment, disability due to illness or accident, and untimely death become a priority.
- The **distribution (gifting) phase** usually occurs from the mid 40s to the end of life and is characterized by the individual having high cash flow, low debt, and high net worth.

The client's life cycle phase helps the planner to understand the client's risks and likely goals. It is entirely possible for a given client to be in two or even all three of these phases at the same time. When special circumstances occur, such as the untimely death of a spouse, the conservation phase may come before the asset accumulation phase for a particular client.

EXHIBIT 3.3

LIFE CYCLES

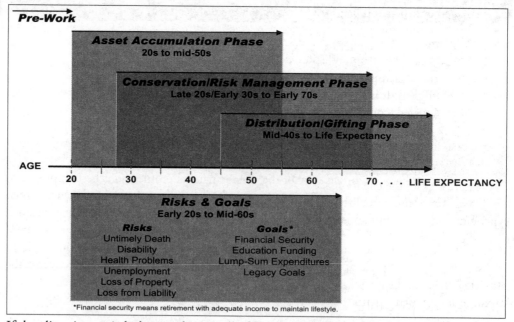

If the client is married, the couple typically files a joint income tax return and relies on both incomes for the payment of family expenses (such as a home mortgage, auto loans, etc.). This situation creates a life insurance and disability insurance need for each spouse. The fact that a client has young children signals a need for life insurance and disability insurance, regardless of the parent's marital status. Young children may also indicate a client's need, or at least desire, for college education funding. If a client has grandchildren, gifts, tuition payment plans, and other transfers during life (gifts) or at death (bequests) to or for grandchildren may be a consideration. Older clients may also be thinking about estate planning needs.

The planner should conduct a comprehensive review of the insurance portfolio for all clients (especially for those in the risk management phase), including the use of life insurance, health insurance, disability insurance, long-term care insurance, and property and liability insurance.

Other client profile characteristics that give insight into the client's needs include:
- Any client that is simultaneously in the accumulation and conservation phase has financial security (retirement) as a long-term goal.
- Generally, the higher a client's net worth and the greater a client's income, the more interest that client has in income tax minimization.
- If a client is self-employed, it creates opportunities to use employer-sponsored retirement plans to assist that client in accomplishing long-term financial security goals.

Analyzing client data to achieve long-term financial goals takes time. Achieving those financial goals takes persistent savings and good investment returns. Unfortunately, risks that are insured against, such as untimely death, disability, health issues, and loss of property or personal liability, are unexpected events that can occur at any time. An uninsured loss can destroy even the best conceived savings and investment plan. Therefore, clients need to make risk management their top priority. A great retirement investment plan with a time horizon of 30 years that relies on persistent savings and investment returns can be abruptly derailed if the client becomes disabled before retirement and has no disability insurance benefits.

The life cycle approach provides financial planners a broad overview of the client's probable risks and likely goals. It is a good place to start, but it lacks the specifics to direct the planner to develop a detailed, comprehensive financial plan.

THE PIE CHART APPROACH

A pie chart focuses the client on the relative size of financial variables. People can only spend what they have and visualizing where the money goes is often a sobering, but helpful experience. The pie chart approach is an effective analytical and illustrative tool for financial planning clients.

The pie chart approach provides the planner and the client with separate pictorial representations of the balance sheet and the statement of income and expenses. These financial statements are discussed in detail in Chapter 4.

The financial statements are prepared first and then depicted in pie charts. One set of pie charts is for the statement of income and expenses (income statement) and the other set is for the balance sheet (statement of financial position). Note that the statement of income and expenses (income statement) is also referred to as the cash flow statement. For purposes of this textbook, it is not referred to as the cash flow statement because not all cash flows are included in the

Key Concepts

Underline/highlight the answers as you read:

1. Identify the financial planning usefulness of the income statement pie chart.

2. Understand the questions that the balance sheet pie chart should answer and illustrate.

3. Identify the reason for creating benchmark pie charts.

statement (such as inheritance of cash). The pie chart approach generally uses percentages of the whole, but can use a dollar approach. The percentage approach is usually more effective for comparison purposes.

INCOME STATEMENT PIE CHART

The questions that the pie chart approach addresses are:
- What percentage of gross pay is the client paying in taxes (income and Social Security)?
- What percentage of the client's gross pay are they saving?
- What percentage of the client's gross pay goes to protection (insurance)?
- What percentage of the client's gross pay is spent on basic housing costs (principal, interest, tax, and insurance or rent plus insurance)?

- What percentage of the client's gross pay is spent on debt repayments both excluding housing costs and including housing costs?
- What percentage of the client's gross pay is left to live on?

For example, the following sample income statement pie chart reflects total living expenses of 54 percent (housing costs 25% plus other living expenses). This is useful information for the planner to analyze considering a client's other characteristics (e.g., age, gross pay, risks, etc.). To build the pie chart, the planner calculates the client's expenses from the income statement as a proportion of the client's gross pay and portrays them in the income statement pie chart.

EXHIBIT 3.4 **INCOME STATEMENT PIE CHART**

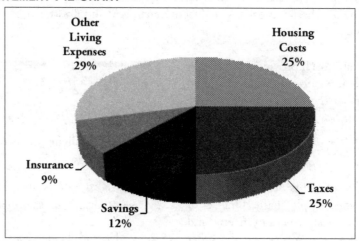

There are many flexible and creative ways to make a pie chart. One useful way is total income arrayed by percentage of:
- savings,
- housing costs,
- other debt payments (ODP),
- insurance other than property insurance,
- all other living costs (OLC),
- taxes other than property taxes, and
- net discretionary cash flows (DCF), presuming that they are positive.

One shortcoming of the pie chart approach, however, is that it is difficult to depict negative cash flows in pie charts.

EXAMPLE 3.1

Assume a client has gross pay of $100,000 and expenses as listed in the table below. The data can be reflected in an income statement pie chart, allowing the client to visualize his financial situation as pertains to income and expenses.

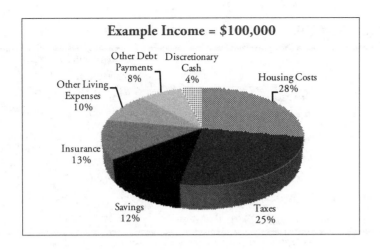

Example Income = $100,000

	Amount	Percentage
Gross Income	$100,000	100%
Taxes	$25,000	25%
Savings	$12,000	12%
Insurance	$13,000	13%
Housing Costs	$28,000	28%
Other Debt Payments (ODP)	$8,000	8%
Other Living Costs (OLC)	$10,000	10%
Discretionary Cash Flow (DCF)	$4,000	4%

It is easy to depict on an income statement pie chart with the percentages that a client is paying for taxes, saving for the future, and paying insurance premiums (25% + 12% + 13% = 50%) to protect the client's assets that have or will be accumulated. That leaves approximately 50 percent of the current income for current living expenses, 10-28 percent of which is typically allocated to housing or shelter costs. Exhibit 3.5 gives targeted example benchmarks for various income statement items.

The pie chart approach assists the planner and client by illustrating if the client is spending too much on debt repayment or too much on housing that may result in either undersaving or being underinsured. The financial planner can then present benchmark pie charts that illustrate where a client should be in order to meet typical goals and objectives.

EXHIBIT 3.5 **INCOME STATEMENT TARGETED EXAMPLE BENCHMARKS**

	Targeted Example Benchmarks*
Taxes (income and payroll)	15 - 30%
Savings (future asset protection)	10 - 18%
Protection (insurance) (past and future asset protection)	5 - 12%
Living - Present	40 - 60%
Housing (Rent or Mortgage Payment)	≤ 28%
Housing and Other Debt Payments	≤ 36%

*These are general and vary widely among individuals.

The pie chart depiction of the income statement provides the planner with an opportunity to discuss with the client where the client is currently from a financial point of view. If the benchmark pie chart is agreed to, a step by step plan to get from the current situation to the benchmark can be established.

BALANCE SHEET PIE CHART

The questions that the pie chart approach addresses include, what percentage of total assets are in the form of:

- cash and cash equivalents?
- investment assets?
- personal use assets?
- current liabilities?
- long-term liabilities?
- net worth?

Quick Quiz 3.1

Highlight the answer to these questions:

1. The life cycle approach utilizes liquidity ratios to analyze the client's financial situation.
   a. True
   b. False

2. The pie chart approach provides a pictorial representation of the balance sheet and the statement of income and expenses.
   a. True
   b. False

False, True.

The balance sheet pie chart is portrayed in two pie charts, one for the asset side of the balance sheet and the other for the liabilities and net worth side of the balance sheet. The asset pie chart is broken down into three categories: cash and cash equivalents, investment assets, and personal use assets.

BALANCE SHEET PIE CHART

EXHIBIT 3.6

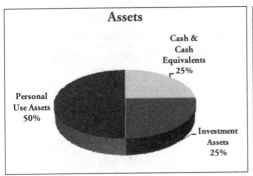

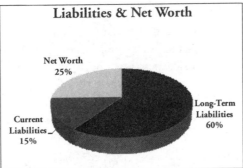

Assume a client has assets (and liabilities and net worth) totalling $300,000. The balance sheet data can be reflected in the following pie charts.

CLIENT SAMPLE BALANCE SHEET PIE CHART

EXHIBIT 3.7

Assets = 100%			Liabilities & Net Worth = 100%		
Cash & Cash Equivalents	$30,000	10%	Current Liabilities	$75,000	25%
Investment Assets	$120,000	40%	Long-Term Liabilities	$150,000	50%
Personal Use Assets	$150,000	50%	Net Worth	$75,000	25%
	$300,000	100%		$300,000	100%

Regardless of the amount of total assets, a portion of assets should be in cash and cash equivalents and a portion should be in investment assets. The percentage needed in cash and cash equivalents is functionally related to the non-discretionary cash outflows on the income statement. The percentage that should be in investment assets is functionally related to the age of the client and the gross pay (See Exhibit 3.8).

The liabilities (both short term and long term) are then integrated into a separate pie chart opposite the assets, along with the client's net worth. If net worth is negative, the client is technically insolvent and the pie charts for the balance sheet may be unreliable.

The planner can compare the age of the client, the gross pay, and non-discretionary cash flows to create additional information from the pie chart. However, even before creating a benchmark pie chart for the example client, we already know that cash and cash equivalents are only 40 percent of current liabilities (10% ÷ 25%) and total debt represents 75 percent of all assets (25% + 50%) with net worth representing only 25 percent of assets (See Exhibit 3.7).

Keeping benchmarks in mind, given a client's characteristics, the financial planner can develop balance sheet benchmark pie charts to use to compare to the client's actual pie charts. This creates the opportunity to have a quick and high level discussion of where the client is currently and where the client should be based on appropriate benchmarks.

The following exhibit provides typical benchmark goals by age range for a client's balance sheet.

| EXHIBIT 3.8 | AN ESTIMATE OF BALANCE SHEET TARGETED BENCHMARKS BY AGES |

		20s - 30s	40s - 50s	60s - 70s
ASSETS*	Cash & Cash Equivalents	5 - 20%	5 - 20%	5 - 20%
	Investment Assets	0 - 30%	30 - 60%	60 - 70%
	Personal Use Assets	55 - 90%	25 - 60%	15 - 30%
LIABILITIES*	Current Liabilities	10 - 20%	10 - 20%	0 - 10%
	Long-Term Liabilities	40 - 72%	16 - 48%	8 - 24%
NET WORTH*	Net Worth	8 - 50%	32 - 74%	66 - 82%

* A more detailed description of each category is provided in Chapter 4. These can vary widely among families.

FINANCIAL PLANNING ASSUMPTIONS USED FOR EXHIBIT 3.8

Assumptions	
Inflation and Raises	3%
Investment Returns	8.5%
Savings Rate	11.5%*
Retirement Accumulation	18 times pre-retirement income**

*Average Savings Rate = 10-13%;   Savings Rate = 11.5% of gross pay.

**Produces an initial wage replacement ratio of 72% of pre-retirement income at retirement at a 4% withdrawal rate (a 4% withdrawal rate is considered a relatively safe withdrawal rate as determined by current research).

Pie charts are very effective tools for helping the client to see pictorially and to understand (especially if the client is a visual learner) where their assets are deployed in cash, in investment assets, or for maintaining their current lifestyle (personal use assets) in retirement.

SUMMARY REGARDING THE LIFE CYCLE AND PIE CHART APPROACHES

The life cycle and pie chart approaches are generally used in the preliminary stages of an engagement to get a general idea of the client and/or to present, in the case of the pie chart approach, a graphical picture of the current and general benchmark situation. These are generally not used for detailed analysis.

THE FINANCIAL STATEMENT AND RATIO ANALYSIS APPROACH

The purpose of calculating and presenting financial ratios is to provide useful planning information to the user. The financial statement and ratio analysis approach uses financial ratios to help clarify and reveal the true financial situation of a client. The approach uses four types of ratios:

- **Liquidity ratios:** measures the client's ability to meet short-term obligations.
- **Debt ratios:** indicates how well the client manages debt.
- **Ratios for financial security goals:** indicates the progress that the client is making toward achieving long-term financial security goals.
- **Performance ratios:** indicates the adequacy of returns on investments, given the risks taken by the client.

Key Concepts

Underline/highlight the answers as you read:

1. Identify the purpose of evaluating liquidity ratios used in the financial statement and ratio analysis approach.

2. Identify the difference between discretionary and non-discretionary cash flows.

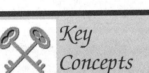

Key Concepts

Underline/highlight the answers as you read:

1. What information is provided by housing ratio 1 and housing ratio 2 and what are the benchmarks for both ratios?

2. How is the savings rate calculated and what are the typical benchmarks for this ratio?

3. Identify the usefulness of the performance ratios.

The information covered in this section is an overview and introduction to financial statement and ratio analysis as one method of analyzing, evaluating, and making financial planning recommendations to a client. **A more detailed explanation of financial statements and financial statement analysis is covered in Chapter 4.** For now, a high level overview of this approach is discussed in this chapter.

LIQUIDITY RATIOS

The emergency fund ratio and the current ratio are the two most common financial ratios used to provide meaningful information for measuring the ability to meet short-term obligations. These are essentially coverage ratios.

Emergency Fund Ratio

$$\text{Emergency Fund Ratio} = \frac{\text{Cash \& Cash Equivalents}}{\text{Monthly Non-Discretionary Cash Flows}} = 3 - 6 \text{ Months}$$

The emergency fund ratio determines the number of months the client can pay non-discretionary cash flows with current liquidity. The risks covered by an emergency fund are those that arise from loss of employment, injury, or some other unexpected occurrence. The benchmark is three-to-six months of non-discretionary cash flow coverage. However, this benchmark is highly dependent on the individual client's situation and the job market at the time of the financial emergency. Therefore, the benchmark should be used cautiously and revised accordingly for a particular client and a particular economic climate. For example, a specialty job may require more than six months for a job seeker to replace, especially for an older worker. On the other hand, a tenured faculty member at a university may be in a low risk situation and would not necessarily need an emergency fund of three months of non-discretionary cash flows. The elimination period of a client's disability policy should also be considered when selecting an emergency fund ratio target.

Definition of Terms

An evaluation of a client's monthly expenses is necessary for the calculation of the emergency fund coverage. Discretionary versus non-discretionary cash flows must be identified to determine the monthly expenses that must be met. Discretionary cash flows are those cash flows that can be avoided in the event of loss of income, whereas non-discretionary cash flows are generally fixed monthly obligations and expenses that are required to be met regardless of the loss of income. Some monthly cash flows may be discretionary or nondiscretionary depending on the client (e.g., church contributions).

| EXHIBIT 3.9 | DISCRETIONARY CASH FLOWS VS. NON-DISCRETIONARY CASH FLOWS |

Common Non-discretionary Cash Flows	Common Cash Flows that may be either Discretionary or Non-discretionary	Common Discretionary Cash Flows
Mortgage Loan Auto Loan Credit Cards Life Insurance Health Insurance Auto Insurance Homeowners (or Renters) Insurance Tuition and Education Expenses Property Taxes Food Auto Maintenance Utilities Clothing	Charitable Contributions Church Donations Lawn Service Child Care	Entertainment Vacations Satellite or Cable TV

While many costs may have both a fixed and variable (controllable) component (e.g., utilities), what the financial planner is looking for is an idea of how many months of coverage exists for those costs that the client considers to be non-discretionary. Ordinarily, income taxes and payroll taxes are not included in the determination of discretionary versus non-discretionary cash flows because the most likely risk triggering the use of the emergency fund is the loss of employment income. However, the financial planner calculating non-discretionary expenditures should consider whether the client is unemployed and if the client is receiving unemployment benefits (unemployment benefits are subject to federal income tax, but not payroll taxes). In addition, some clients who have lost jobs have either outstanding 401(k) plan or other qualified plan loans, which may be treated as a taxable distribution if the loan is not repaid shortly after termination. Still some clients who find themselves unemployed, exhaust their qualified plan balance in such a way as to make the distributions subject to both federal and state income tax. The planner should decide whether any of the above should be considered in the determination of non-discretionary expenses.

Current Ratio

$$\text{Current Ratio} = \frac{\text{Cash \& Cash Equivalents}}{\text{Current Liabilities}} \geq 1.00$$

The current ratio provides insight into the client's ability to meet short-term obligations as they come due. Current liabilities represent those liabilities that will be paid within the next year. A larger current ratio implies more liquidity and thus a greater ability to pay current liabilities as they come due. It may appear that there is a liquidity problem when the current ratio is less than 1. However, most individuals pay their current liabilities and associated interest out of their current income (statement of income) and not out of their cash and cash equivalents (balance sheet). Therefore, to the extent this is true, a current ratio that is less than 1 may be adequate.

It also should be noted that the current ratio can be modified by adding the net positive discretionary cash flow to the numerator, which should provide a better measure of liquidity over a period of time. Of course if net expected discretionary cash flow from the projected income statements is negative, it would have to be subtracted from cash and cash equivalents to provide a clearer picture of liquidity using the current ratio.

DEBT RATIOS

There are four debt ratios used in the financial statement and ratio analysis approach to help the planner determine how well the client manages debt:
- the housing ratio 1 (basic),
- the housing ratio 2 (broad),
- the debt to total assets ratio, and
- the net worth to total assets ratio.

Housing Ratio 1 (Basic)

$$\text{Housing Ratio 1} = \frac{\text{Housing Costs}}{\text{Gross Pay}} \leq 28\%$$

Housing costs include principal payment on the mortgage (or alternately rent), interest, homeowners insurance, property taxes, and association dues, if applicable.

The purpose of housing ratio 1 (HR1) is to calculate the percentage of gross pay that is devoted to basic housing. It does not include utilities, lawn care, maintenance, etc. The benchmark for housing ratio 1 is less than or equal to 28 percent. Generally, a HR1 of 28 percent or less is the initial ratio necessary for a first time home buyer to qualify for a conforming (best) rate mortgage. The conforming rate mortgage generally requires a 20 percent down payment and good credit. Assuming that the mortgage interest rate is fixed and amortized over 15 or 30 years, then as inflation causes salaries and housing values to increase, housing ratio 1 should decline gradually.

The housing ratio 1 benchmark is used traditionally by mortgage lenders to issue conforming (best) rate mortgages. Note that the ratio should decline to roughly five percent (although not in a state with very high property taxes, such as Texas) at retirement, when the mortgage is assumed to be completely paid off and only taxes, association dues, and insurance expenses continue.

Housing Ratio 2 (Broad)

$$\text{Housing Ratio 2} = \frac{\text{Housing Costs} + \text{Other Debt Payments}}{\text{Gross Pay}} \leq 36\%$$

Housing ratio 2 (HR2) combines basic housing costs (HR1) with all other monthly debt payments, including payments for automobile loans, student loans, bank loans, revolving consumer loans, credit card payments, and any other debt payments made on a recurring basis. The housing ratio 2 benchmark is less than or equal to 36 percent of gross pay. The planner should be cautious when considering the client's credit card payments for purposes of this ratio. If the client is only making minimum payments on credit cards, the payback period for such debt could be 17 years or longer, depending on the relationship between the interest rate, the minimum payments, and the original balance. In the situation where a client is only making minimum credit card payments, then the planner should calculate a payment using the interest rate on the card that would retire the credit card debt in 36 to 60 months. The planner can then use that payment for this calculation, rather than the minimum payment the client is actually making, so as to avoid underestimating the relevant ratio. Credit card statements are now required to disclose this type of comparison and may save the planner time and effort.

Debt to Total Assets Ratio

$$\text{Debt to Total Assets Ratio} = \frac{\text{Total Debt}}{\text{Total Assets}} = \text{Benchmark Depends on Client Age}$$

The debt to total assets ratio is essentially a leverage ratio. It reflects what portion of assets owned by a client are financed by creditors. Usually, young people establishing themselves have relatively high debt ratios due to the presence of automobile and student loans. First time home buyers generally have high ratios, even with a 20 percent down payment (implying an 80% mortgage). This ratio, like all other ratios, is best considered over time to monitor the client's progress. This ratio is commonly as high as 80 percent for young people and as low as 10 percent or less for those near retirement age.

Net Worth to Total Assets Ratio

$$\text{Net Worth to Total Assets Ratio} = \frac{\text{Net Worth}}{\text{Total Assets}} = \text{Benchmark Depends on Client Age}$$

The net worth to total assets ratio is the complement of the debt to assets ratio described above. The two add up to one (i.e., as debt declines as a percent of total assets, net worth rises). This ratio provides the planner with the percentage of total assets owned or paid for by the client. It is not surprising that this would be 20 percent for young people and up to 90 to 100 percent for retirement age clients. This ratio once again is best observed over time. Note that the net worth increases as assets increase in value (home and investments) and also increases with additional savings and with the payoff of obligations (liabilities) over time.

RATIOS FOR FINANCIAL SECURITY GOALS

Ratios for financial security goals help the financial planner to assess the progress that the client is making toward achieving long-term goals. The two most common ratios used to assess that progress are the savings rate and the investment assets to gross pay ratio.

Savings Rate

$$\text{Savings Rate} = \frac{\text{Savings} + \text{Employer Match}}{\text{Gross Pay}} = \begin{array}{c}\text{Benchmark Depends on Client Goals}\\ \text{(but at least 10 - 13\%)}\end{array}$$

An appropriate savings rate is critical to achieving long-term goals including retirement, education funding, large lump-sum expenditures (e.g., second home), and legacy plans. The savings rate is calculated by dividing gross savings in dollars, employee elective deferrals into 401(k), 403(b), and 457 plans plus any employer match), and any other savings, by gross pay. The savings rate benchmark depends on the number of long-term goals of the client. If the only goal of the client is financial security (retirement) the benchmark savings rate should be 10 to 13 percent of gross pay. The persistent savings rate needed for a 25-year old with retirement as his only goal should be 10 to 13 percent, excluding Social Security contributions.

If the client has multiple long-term goals, the savings rate must be greater than 10 to 13 percent to meet those goals. For example, a couple, both age 25, earning $75,000 annually with newborn twins who they plan to send to an in-state college for four years, would need a savings rate of 10 to 13 percent for retirement plus an additional two to three percent for education for a combined savings rate of 12 to 16 percent. The education savings rate is dependent on the type of school their children will attend (in-state / lower costs, private / medium costs, or private / higher costs) and the income level of the client because the savings rate for tuition declines as income increases because tuition is a fixed dollar amount. Note: Dividends, interest, capital gains and other types of portfolio income are not counted or included as part of savings since this type of income is already considered as part of the portfolio rate of return. If they were included in both, then they would be double counted. If they were included as part of savings, then the rate of return would have to be reduced to reflect that treatment.

RELATIONSHIP BETWEEN TIME, SAVINGS, AND WITHDRAWAL RATES ON RETIREMENT PLANNING

The following three scenarios will help to illustrate the intricate nature of the savings rate on the retirement capital balance and how the savings rate and capital balance impact the withdrawal rate and the required rate of earnings needed during retirement. The first scenario assumes the client saves for 40 years, while the second scenario assumes 30 years of savings and finally, the third scenario assumes 20 years of savings.

Each of the scenarios assumes a **real rate of return** of 5%, which is reasonable over a long period of time. However, increasing or decreasing this rate will have a significant effect on the final result. These scenarios also assume a retirement life expectancy of 30 years, which is very conservative for most of the population.[1]

The first scenario assumes a wage replacement ratio of 80%. The wage replacement ratio for scenarios 2 and 3 have been reduced from the original 80% to 70% and 60% respectively, to make the models work with a reasonable required **real rate of return** during retirement. Effectively, clients who begin saving later in life are less likely to be able to fund a larger annual withdrawal amount as compared to someone who begins saving at an earlier age. Social Security retirement benefits have purposely been left out of this analysis.

1. Scenarios 1, 2, and 3 assume that savings are made at the end of the year (ordinary annuity) and that withdrawals are made at the beginning of the year (annuity due).

Scenario 1 (40 years of savings, real rate of return 5%, WRR 80%, LE 30 years)

Annual Savings	Annual Savings Rate	Retirement Capital Balance	Annual Needs at Retirement	Required Withdrawal Rate	Required Real Rate of Return
$18,000	18%	$2,174,396	$80,000	3.68%	0.70%
$16,000	16%	$1,932,796	$80,000	4.14%	1.57%
$14,000	14%	$1,691,197	$80,000	4.73%	2.62%
$13,000	**13%**	**$1,570,397**	**$80,000**	**5.09%**	**3.24%**
$12,000	**12%**	**$1,449,597**	**$80,000**	**5.52%**	**3.93%**
$11,000	11%	$1,328,798	$80,000	6.02%	4.73%
$10,000	10%	$1,207,998	$80,000	6.62%	5.65%

Income at retirement assumed to be $100,000.

The highlighted section of Scenario 1 illustrates a person age 25 saving about 12% to 13% of his income for 40 years and accumulating approximately $1.5 million. The result is that he is able to meet an 80% wage replacement ratio with a reasonable required real rate of return (between 3.24 - 3.93%) during retirement. At a 13% savings rate, the $80,000 needs at retirement translate to a 5.09% withdrawal rate. To maintain this withdrawal throughout retirement, a real return of 3.24% would have to be earned. If inflation were 3%, this would equate to an approximate 6.3% nominal return, still quite conservative. The calculation of the required real return assumes he has spent all of his capital at the end of the 30 year period.

Scenario 2 (30 years of savings, real rate of return 5%, WRR 70%, LE 30 years)

Annual Savings	Annual Savings Rate	Retirement Capital Balance	Annual Needs at Retirement	Required Withdrawal Rate	Required Real Rate of Return
$25,000	25%	$1,660,971	$70,000	4.21%	1.71%
$24,000	24%	$1,594,532	$70,000	4.39%	2.02%
$23,000	23%	$1,528,093	$70,000	4.58%	2.36%
$22,000	22%	$1,461,655	$70,000	4.79%	2.72%
$21,000	**21%**	**$1,395,216**	**$70,000**	**5.02%**	**3.11%**
$20,000	**20%**	**$1,328,777**	**$70,000**	**5.27%**	**3.52%**
$19,000	19%	$1,262,338	$70,000	5.55%	3.98%

Income at retirement assumed to be $100,000.

The highlighted section of Scenario 2 illustrates a person 35 years of age required to save close to 20% of his income to drive a retirement plan with a 70% wage replacement ratio. It appears that the 20% savings rate is adequate to drive a reasonable withdrawal rate and a reasonable required rate of return of 3.11 to 3.52%. Note that this person began saving 10 years later than the one in Scenario 1 and can only sustain an annual retirement annuity of $70,000, which is $10,000 less than the wage replacement ratio in Scenario 1.

Scenario 3 (20 years of savings, real rate of return 5%, WRR 60%, LE 30 years)					
Annual Savings	Annual Savings Rate	Retirement Capital Balance	Annual Needs at Retirement	Required Withdrawal Rate	Required Real Rate of Return
$30,000	30%	$991,979	$60,000	6.05%	4.77%
$29,000	29%	$958,913	$60,000	6.26%	5.10%
$28,000	28%	$925,847	$60,000	6.48%	5.44%
$27,000	27%	$892,781	$60,000	6.72%	5.80%
$26,000	26%	$859,715	$60,000	6.98%	6.19%
$25,000	25%	$826,649	$60,000	7.26%	6.60%
$24,000	24%	$793,583	$60,000	7.56%	7.04%

*Income at retirement assumed to be $100,000.

The highlighted section of Scenario 3 illustrates a person 45 years of age with only 20 years to save for retirement. In this scenario, 20 years of savings is driving a 30 year withdrawal period. The result of this scenario is that the required savings rate is very high (29-30%) and the wage replacement ratio is significantly less than the results in Scenario 1 or 2 (60% as opposed to 70% or 80%).

The above three scenarios clearly illustrate the importance of the timing of savings and the duration of savings. These scenarios were based on a constant real rate of return of 5% during the savings period, however investment returns are not constant or linear in financial markets. Rather, there are ups and downs and when returns are down, the account balance at retirement (e.g., if negative returns occur for the three years preceding retirement) can be significantly impacted.

Negative portfolio returns can also seriously damage an investment plan if they occur shortly after retirement when there are no additional savings to be added to the plan. In such a case, there are both withdrawals and negative portfolio returns exacerbating the reduction in the account balance of the retirement fund. This kind of situation increases the probability of running out of money before the end of life (superannuation).

There are a few ways to mitigate the risk of superannuation. Options before retirement include saving more and beginning to save at an earlier age. Saving more means saving based on a model such as the capital preservation model or the purchasing power preservation model or working a few extra years to make certain that the capital balance is sufficient to adequately fund retirement. It is important to generate investment returns that provide a sufficient real rate of return. Equities are an important element of any portfolio that is attempting to generate a positive real rate of return. Once in retirement, the primary way to mitigate the risk of superannuation is to maintain a relatively low withdrawal rate and have a balanced portfolio that can withstand unexpected fluctuations in investment returns.

Social Security and part-time work in retirement has not been included in the above analysis. Social Security, for average income workers, provides as much as 42% of wage replacement and for higher income workers provides as low as 26% of wage replacement (this assumes a same age non-working spouse who is entitled to a 50% benefit of the worker based on the working spouse's earnings history). To adjust these amounts for a single individual, divide the wage replacement percentage for the couple by 150 percent (e.g., 42% ÷ 150% = 28%).

Investment Assets to Gross Pay

Saving 10 to 13 percent of gross pay is sufficient to drive the retirement goal only if the client begins saving at or around age 25. Therefore, it is necessary to calculate a second ratio. The combination of these two ratios provides the planner with a better understanding of the current progress toward achieving the retirement goal. The investment assets to gross pay ratio is the second ratio used to assess a retirement plan that persistently has clients saving 10 to 13 percent of gross pay. As used in this textbook, all investment assets are considered, including cash and cash equivalents and education savings. If the client wants to measure retirement assets separately, the planner can redefine the ratio for retirement assets only by leaving out nonretirement savings (e.g., cash and cash equivalents and education savings).

$$\frac{\text{Investment Assets}}{\text{to Gross Pay}} = \frac{(\text{Investment Assets}) + (\text{Cash} + \text{Cash Equivalents})}{\text{Gross Pay}} = \frac{\text{Benchmark Depends}}{\text{on Client Age}}$$

(see Exhibit 3.10)

For this ratio to be effective, the financial planner needs to make sure that all personal use assets are classified correctly (e.g., most homes and various collectibles are not investment assets for this purpose). In the event that a client has multiple goals such as college education for children, lump sum expenditure goals, retirement goals, and legacy goals, the investment assets used in this calculation should be reduced by those that are devoted to goals other than retirement.

The investment assets to gross pay benchmark is calculated according to age and is generally reliable for a wide range of income levels (e.g., $40,000 to $400,000 annual income).

INVESTMENT ASSETS TO GROSS PAY BENCHMARKS TO ACHIEVE RETIREMENT GOAL **EXHIBIT 3.10**

Benchmark for Investment Assets as a Ratio of Gross Pay by Age	
25	0.2:1
30	0.6 - 0.8:1
35	1.6 - 1.8:1
45	3 - 4:1
55	8 - 10:1
65	16 - 20:1

A continued savings rate of 10 to 13% of gross pay until retirement age 65 will achieve these ratios if invested in a balanced fund that produces reasonable returns. Inflation and pay raises are included in the analysis.

For example, the above information indicates that a client age 35 should have 1.6 to 1.8 times his annual gross pay in investment assets as savings for retirement. A savings rate of 10 to 13 percent of gross pay will facilitate achieving the financial security (retirement) goal. This table of investment asset ratios is consistent with a four to five percent withdrawal rate at retirement that will mitigate against the risk of superannuation.

A frequent question regarding the above benchmark data table is how a defined benefit plan pension or employer-provided pension plan fits into this analysis. A financial planner has two alternatives to address the additional retirement funding provided by a defined benefit plan. The first is to calculate the present value of all benefits and include that amount on the client's balance sheet under investment assets. The second alternative is to reduce the wage replacement needs amount at retirement for the expected pension benefit at that time and then recalculate the client's adjusted needs for the amount of savings necessary to drive the new wage replacement ratios (as adjusted by the portion provided by the pension). In either case, the planner should only include these adjustments when there is reasonable certainty that the client will receive the benefit. The first approach is preferred because it only includes the present value of vested benefits, without making any assumptions about whether the client will remain with his current employer until retirement.

EXAMPLE 3.2	Cindy, age 45, is currently making $78,000 and has been with her employer for 20 years. She is expecting to receive an annual pension of $23,400 at her normal retirement age of 65. The formula is 1.5% per year times final salary of employment.

The present value of the pension today is:

$N = 20$ (life expectancy at 65 to 85)

$i = 4$ (the riskless rate if a strong company)

$PMT_{AD} = \$23,400$ (20 years x 1.5% x $78,000)

$FV = \$0$ (a single life annuity)

$PV_{65} = \$330,734$ (to age 65) (N = 20)

$PV_{45} = \$150,943$ (to age 45) (N = 20)

The $330,734 represents the lump-sum amount needed at age 65 to pay Cindy an annuity of $23,400 per year during her retirement. The $150,943 represents the lump-sum amount that, if set aside today, that will grow to $330,734 at age 65 if invested at 4%. Her salary has intentionally not been adjusted for inflation.

Cindy can add the $150,943 to her balance sheet or reduce her annual needs at retirement by $23,400 at age 65. The balance sheet approach is preferred because many defined benefit pensions are not adjusted for inflation thus making the needs approach more difficult to be precise.

Note, that if Cindy remains with the company until age 65 and her salary continues to grow by 3% per year to $140,877, the present value of her pension benefit at age 65 will be $1,194,685, calculated as follows:

$N = 20$ (life expectancy at 65)

$i = 4$ (the riskless rate if a strong company)

$PMT_{AD} = \$84,526$ (40 years x 1.5% x $140,877)

$FV = \$0$ (a single life annuity)

$PV_{65} = \$1,194,685$ (at age 65)

Another important point to consider when evaluating the investment assets to gross pay ratio is the context of this ratio within the entire set of ratios. For example, if the client is fairly young, owns a principal residence that is debt free, but has an investment assets to gross pay ratio that is low for his age, this may not be a problem. It may be that a similarly situated person with debt on a principal residence has a higher investment assets to gross pay ratio, but a lower savings rate. As long as the client, who is not servicing debt on a residence, has a current and future increasing savings rate, then the investment asset to gross pay ratio should grow quickly. Ultimately, the ratio is intended to help track how the client is progressing towards retiring with the necessary funds to sustain the desired lifestyle.

PERFORMANCE RATIOS

Return on investments, return on assets, and return on net worth are the most common performance ratios used to determine the adequacy of returns on investments for the risks taken.

Return on Investments (ROI)

The Return on Investments (ROI) ratio calculates the rate of return on invested assets. The ratio is calculated by taking the ending balance of investments (I_1) minus the beginning balance of investments (I_0) plus the annual savings (S), divided by the beginning balance of investments.

$$\text{Return on Investments (ROI)} = \frac{I_1 - (I_0 + \text{Savings})}{I_0}$$

This ratio is an appropriate measure of the return on investments made during a year. There is an implicit assumption that savings are made in equal monthly deposits during the year. This calculation produces what is referred to as an arithmetic return (AR), which is appropriate for a one-year period. However, for measuring returns over a long period of time, the arithmetic mean is not as accurate as the geometric average, and will generally overstate the return. The geometric average is equivalent to the internal rate of return, while the arithmetic return is a simple average.

For example, assume that a client had $100 at I_0 and $120 at I_1 and that the client had also saved $10 during the year. The ROI would be $120 - ($100 + $10) ÷ $100 = 10%.

However, if the ROI was calculated exactly using a <u>geometric return</u>, then it would actually be 9.173 percent.

Geometric Return (GR) Calculation

N	=	12 months
PV	=	$100
FV	=	($120)
Payments	=	0.8333 per month ($10 ÷ 12)
i	=	0.76442 per month x 12 = 9.173% (GR)

The ROI of 9.173 percent is the geometric return. The ten percent return as calculated by the initial formula produces the arithmetic return. In order to calculate the ROI we need two balance sheets. Once again, ROI is best calculated over time and geometric returns are more useful to the financial planner than arithmetic returns.

The ROI benchmark comparison should be made using the same asset class returns as the actual investments. For example, it would be inappropriate to compare a balanced fund to the S&P 500 index. Instead, the investment should be compared to a blended index that includes equities and fixed income.

Return on Assets (ROA)

The Return on Assets (ROA) ratio measures total asset returns by calculating the difference between ending assets (A_1) less beginning assets (A_0) plus any savings (S), divided by beginning assets.

$$\text{Return on Assets} = \frac{A_1 - (A_0 + \text{Savings})}{A_0}$$

This ratio must be used cautiously when the client is adding assets that are leveraged with debt. In the event new assets are added to the balance sheet and they are highly leveraged, the financial planner may consider simply adding the net equity to the year-end assets (A_1) for purpose of calculating ROA.

Quick Quiz 3.2

Highlight the answer to these questions:

1. The savings rate is measured to help clients achieve long-term goals including retirement funding, education funding, lump-sum expenditures, and legacy plans.
   a. True
   b. False

2. The savings rate benchmark is client goal oriented, while the investment assets to gross pay benchmark is client age dependent.
   a. True
   b. False

3. Common performance ratios include net worth to total asset ratio, return on investments, and return on assets.
   a. True
   b. False

4. Debt ratios utilized in the financial analysis include housing ratio 1, housing ratio 2, debt to total assets ratio, and net worth to total assets ratio.
   a. True
   b. False

True, True, False, True.

Return on Net Worth (RONW)

The Return on Net Worth (RONW) ratio further refines the performance set of ratios by calculating the rate of return on net worth. The calculation takes ending net worth (NW_1) less the sum of beginning net worth (NW_0) and savings (S), divided by beginning net worth.

$$\text{Return on Net Worth} = \frac{NW_1 - (NW_0 + \text{Savings})}{NW_0}$$

If the client is adding assets with debt, this ratio should help to clarify the ROA ratio.

EXHIBIT 3.11   **SUMMARY OF FINANCIAL STATEMENT RATIOS**

LIQUIDITY RATIOS			
RATIO	**FORMULA**	**MEASURES**	**BENCHMARK**
Emergency Funds	$\dfrac{\text{Cash \& Cash Equivalents}}{\text{Monthly Non-Discretionary Cash Flows}}$	The number of months of non-discretionary expenses in the form of cash and cash equivalents.	3 - 6 months
Current Ratio	$\dfrac{\text{Cash \& Cash Equivalents}}{\text{Current Liabilities}}$	The number of times a client can satisfy their short-term liabilities.	1.0 - 2.0
DEBT RATIOS			
Housing Ratio 1 (Basic)	$\dfrac{\text{Housing Costs}}{\text{Gross Pay}}$	The percentage of income spent on housing debt.	$\leq 28\%$
Housing Ratio 2 (Broad)	$\dfrac{\text{Housing Costs} + \text{Other Debt Payments}}{\text{Gross Pay}}$	The percentage of income spent on housing and all other recurring debt.	$\leq 36\%$
Debt to Total Assets	$\dfrac{\text{Total Debt}}{\text{Total Assets}}$	The percentage of assets being provided by creditors.	As a person ages, this ratio should decline.
Net Worth to Total Assets	$\dfrac{\text{Net Worth}}{\text{Total Assets}}$	The percentage of total assets owned or paid for by client.	Depends on age. 20% for young client and 90-100% for retirement age client.
RATIOS FOR FINANCIAL SECURITY GOALS			
Savings Rate	$\dfrac{\text{Savings} + \text{Employer Match}}{\text{Gross Pay}}$	The percentage of income saved towards a retirement goal.	10 – 13% assuming the client starts early, ages 25-35.
Investment Assets to Gross Pay	$\dfrac{\text{Investment Assets} + \text{Cash \& Cash Equivalents}}{\text{Gross Pay}}$	The progress towards a retirement goal.	Depends on Age 16 to 20 times pre-retirement income at retirement.
PERFORMANCE RATIOS			
Return on Investments	$\dfrac{I_1 - (I_0 + \text{Savings})}{I_0}$	The growth rate of a client's investment assets.	8 – 10%
Return on Assets	$\dfrac{A_1 - (A_0 + \text{Savings})}{A_0}$	A blended growth rate of all assets.	2 – 4%
Return on Net Worth	$\dfrac{NW_1 - (NW_0 + \text{Savings})}{NW_0}$	The growth rate of net worth.	The higher the better. This ratio is likely to become smaller as the client's net worth increases.

GUIDE FOR CALCULATING FINANCIAL RATIOS

Financial ratios can be created and defined using different criteria according to a particular client's situation. For example, one client's non-discretionary spending (e.g., charitable contributions, church donations, etc.) may be defined by different values as compared to another client's non-discretionary spending.

The following exhibit reflects common financial ratios along with an indication of which financial statements contain the data necessary to calculate each ratio. Some ratios may be calculated using both historical and current financial statements. The same ratios can also be calculated using projected financial statements based on a financial planner's recommendations.

This textbook reflects the reality of various client scenarios and calculates ratios based on current information and in some cases based on projected financial statements. Some ratios can be calculated using only one (current) balance sheet and other ratios (performance ratios) require two balance sheets. The calculated ratios in this textbook are reflective of the particular client's scenario and whether one balance sheet or two balance sheets are available. The financial planner should view a ratio as one part of a mosaic; by itself the ratio does not portray the entire financial picture. Ratios should be viewed individually and then as part of the whole financial "mosaic" to obtain a true understanding of a client's entire financial situation.

FINANCIAL STATEMENTS NEEDED TO CALCULATE RATIOS

EXHIBIT 3.12

LIQUIDITY RATIOS			
RATIO	FORMULA	BALANCE SHEET[1]	INCOME STATEMENT
Emergency Funds Ratio[2]	$\dfrac{\text{Cash \& Cash Equivalents}}{\text{Monthly Non-Discretionary Cash Flows}}$	✓	✓
Current Ratio	$\dfrac{\text{Cash \& Cash Equivalents}}{\text{Current Liabilities}}$	✓	

1   Balance sheet ratios may use beginning balance sheet, one year projected, or both.
2   Client must determine non-discretionary payments based on personal values (charitable contributions, church donations, etc.).

EXHIBIT 3.13   FINANCIAL STATEMENTS NEEDED TO CALCULATE RATIOS (CONTINUED)

	DEBT RATIOS		
RATIO	**FORMULA**	**BALANCE SHEET**[3]	**INCOME STATEMENT**
Housing Ratio 1 (Basic)	$\dfrac{\text{Housing Costs}}{\text{Gross Pay}}$		✓
Housing Ratio 2 (Broad)	$\dfrac{\text{Housing Costs} + \text{Other Debt Payments}}{\text{Gross Pay}}$		✓
Debt to Total Assets	$\dfrac{\text{Total Debt}}{\text{Total Assets}}$	✓	
Net Worth to Total Assets	$\dfrac{\text{Net Worth}}{\text{Total Assets}}$	✓	

3   Balance sheet ratios may use beginning balance sheet, one year projected, or both.

	RATIOS FOR FINANCIAL SECURITY GOALS		
RATIO	**FORMULA**	**BALANCE SHEET**	**INCOME STATEMENT**
Savings Rate[4]	$\dfrac{\text{Savings} + \text{Employer Match}}{\text{Gross Pay}}$		✓
Investment Assets to Gross Pay[5/6]	$\dfrac{\text{Investment Assets} + \text{Cash \& Cash Equivalents}}{\text{Gross Pay}}$	✓	✓

4   Include any employer matches for retirement funds.
5   Can be separated by goal. If retirement only, use retirement committed investment assets. Education assets and cash and cash equivalents are not included. If calculating total investment assets to gross pay then: All Investment Assets + Cash and Cash Equivalents ÷ Gross Pay.
6   Use all Investment Assets and Cash and Cash Equivalents also in the ratio calculation.

	PERFORMANCE RATIOS		
RATIO	**FORMULA**	**BALANCE SHEET**	**INCOME STATEMENT**
Return on Investments - Retirement	$\dfrac{I_1 - (I_0 + \text{Savings})}{I_0}$	✓	✓
Return on Investments - Education	$\dfrac{I_1 - (I_0 + \text{Savings})}{I_0}$	✓	✓
Return on Investments - Total	$\dfrac{I_1 - (I_0 + \text{Savings})}{I_0}$	✓	✓
Return on Assets	$\dfrac{A_1 - (A_0 + \text{Savings})}{A_0}$	✓	✓
Return on Net Worth	$\dfrac{NW_1 - (NW_0 + \text{Savings})}{NW_0}$	✓	✓

HESS CASE EXAMPLE OF APPLYING THE PIE CHART, FINANCIAL STATEMENT, AND RATIO ANALYSIS APPROACH

The purpose of this case is to illustrate how the pie chart approach and the ratio analysis approach may be applied to a client scenario. A more detailed application of these approaches will follow in subsequent chapters.

Jack Hess is a 45-year old marketing manager for a national pharmaceutical company. His annual salary is $73,000. He participates in his company's 401(k) retirement plan and his employer matches three percent of his salary. Jack's wife, Marilyn, is a 43-year old make-up artist with an annual salary of $36,000. There are no company retirement plans available for Marilyn. Jack and Marilyn have been married for 18 years and plan to retire in 20 years. They have a 13-year old daughter, Melba, who is in the 8th grade at a private school in their area. Jack and Marilyn anticipate that Melba will attend a private university with tuition of $21,000 annually in today's dollars. Jack and Marilyn have a moderate level of risk tolerance and rank their financial objectives, by priority, as follows:
1. save for retirement,
2. save for private college education for Melba, and
3. have an adequate insurance portfolio.

FINANCIAL STATEMENTS: BALANCE SHEET (12/31/2013)

Statement of Financial Position Jack and Marilyn Hess Balance Sheet as of 12/31/2013					
ASSETS[1]			**LIABILITIES AND NET WORTH**		
Current Assets			**Current Liabilities[2]**		
Checking Account	$18,000		Credit Card Balances	$11,000	
Money Market Account	$12,000		**Total Current Liabilities**		**$11,000**
Total Current Assets		**$30,000**			
Investment Assets			**Long-Term Liabilities[2]**		
401(k) Plan	$86,000		Mortgage Balance (Residence)[3]	$145,000	
IRA	$16,000		Auto Loans	$16,000	
CDs	$15,000		**Total Long-Term Liabilities**		**$161,000**
Growth Mutual Fund	$20,000				
Stock Portfolio[4]	$40,000				
Total Investment Assets		**$177,000**	**Total Liabilities**		**$172,000**
Personal Use Assets					
Personal Residence	$155,000				
Personal Property	$57,000		**Total Net Worth**		**$280,000**
Automobiles	$33,000				
Total Personal Use Assets		**$245,000**			
Total Assets		**$452,000**	**Total Liabilities & Net Worth**		**$452,000**

1. Assets are stated at fair market value.
2. Principal balance only.
3. The mortgage is a 30-year note at 8% with an original balance of $145,000. They just purchased the home.
4. Publicly-traded stock.

FINANCIAL STATEMENTS: STATEMENT OF INCOME AND EXPENSES

Statement of Income and Expenses Mr. and Mrs. Hess Statement of Income and Expenses for 2013 and Expected (Approximate) For 2014		
CASH INFLOWS[1]		**Totals**
Salaries		
Jack's Salary	$73,000	
Marilyn's Salary	$36,000	
Total Cash Inflows		$109,000
CASH OUTFLOWS		
Savings[1]		
Employee - Elective Deferral	$14,600	
Total Savings		$14,600
Ordinary Living Expenses		$26,000
Debt Payments		
Credit Card Payments	$3,300	
Mortgage Loan	$12,768	
Auto Loans	$5,400	
Total Debt Payments		$21,468
Insurance Premiums		
Life Insurance	$1,900	
Health Insurance	$500	
Auto Insurance	$800	
Homeowners Insurance	$1,600	
Total Insurance Premiums		$4,800
Charitable Contributions		$935
Tuition & Education Expenses		$10,000
Entertainment & Vacations		$2,000
Taxes		
Federal Income Taxes	$16,220	
State Income Taxes	$3,175	
Social Security Taxes	$8,033	
Property Tax (Residence)	$2,895	
Total Taxes		$30,323
TOTAL CASH OUTFLOWS		$110,126
NET DISCRETIONARY CASH FLOW		($1,126)

1. Reinvested earnings are not included in gross pay or the savings rate because they are included in the overall expected portfolio rate of return.

FINANCIAL STATEMENTS: PROJECTED BALANCE SHEET (12/31/2014)

Statement of Financial Position
Jack and Marilyn Hess
Projected Balance Sheet as of 12/31/2014

ASSETS[1]			LIABILITIES AND NET WORTH		
Current Assets			**Current Liabilities[2]**		
Checking Account	$16,174		Credit Card Balances	$11,000	
Money Market Account	$12,000		**Total Current Liabilities**		**$11,000**
Total Current Assets		**$28,174**			
Investment Assets			**Long-Term Liabilities[2]**		
401(k) Plan	$89,600		Mortgage Balance (Residence)[3]	$143,789	
IRA	$17,000		Auto Loans	$10,600	
CDs	$15,000		**Total Long-Term Liabilities**		**$154,389**
Growth Mutual Fund	$18,000				
Stock Portfolio[4]	$36,000				
Total Investment Assets		**$175,600**	**Total Liabilities**		**$165,389**
Personal Use Assets					
Personal Residence	$160,000				
Personal Property	$57,000		**Total Net Worth**		**$285,385**
Automobiles	$30,000				
Total Personal Use Assets		**$247,000**			
Total Assets		**$450,774**	**Total Liabilities & Net Worth**		**$450,774**

1. Assets are stated at fair market value.
2. Principal balance only.
3. The mortgage is a 30-year note at 8% with an original balance of $145,000.
4. Publicly-traded stock.

Pie Chart Analysis for Hess Case

From the balance sheet and income statement data, the financial planner can then create pie charts as shown below.

Balance Sheet Data and Pie Charts (12/31/2013)

Assets = 100%		
Cash & Cash Equivalents	$ 30,000	7%
Investment Assets	$177,000	39%
Personal Use Assets	$245,000	54%
	$452,000	100%

Liabilities & Net Worth = 100%		
Current Liabilities	$ 11,000	2%
Long-Term Liabilities	$161,000	36%
Net Worth	$280,000	62%
	$452,000	100%

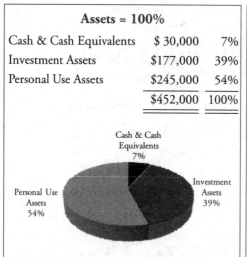

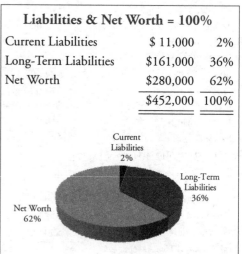

Income Statement Data (For Year 2014)

	Amount	Percentage
Gross Income	$109,000	100%
Taxes	$30,323	27.8%
Savings	$14,600	13.4%
Insurance	$4,800	4.4%
Ordinary Living Expenses	$26,000	23.8%
Other Debt Payments (ODP)	$21,468	19.7%
Charitable, Tuition, Entertainment	$12,935	11.9%
Discretionary Cash Flow (DCF)	($1,126)	(1%)

Income Statement Pie Chart

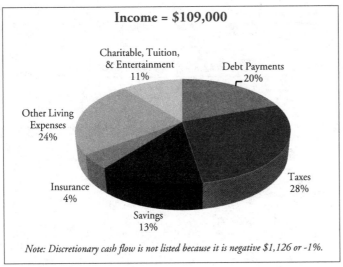

Income = $109,000

Charitable, Tuition, & Entertainment 11%

Debt Payments 20%

Other Living Expenses 24%

Taxes 28%

Insurance 4%

Savings 13%

Note: Discretionary cash flow is not listed because it is negative $1,126 or -1%.

FINANCIAL RATIOS FOR HESS CASE

The ratios below are based on the year beginning balance sheet (2013) except for the performance ratios, that are based on the year-end values (2014).

Liquidity Ratios

$$\text{Emergency Fund Ratio} = \frac{\$30,000}{(\$66,098 \div 12)= \$5,508.17} = 5.44 \text{ Months Coverage (Good)}$$

$26,000	Ordinary Living Expenses
$21,468	Total Debt Payments
$4,800	Total Insurance Payments
$10,000	Tuition & Education Expenses
$2,895	Residence Property Taxes
$935	Charitable Contributions*
$66,098	Total Non-Discretionary Cash Flows

* Charitable contributions are considered non-discretionary by the client.

$$\text{(2013) Current Ratio} = \frac{\$30,000}{\$11,000} = 2.73 \text{ (Good)}$$

$$\text{(2014) Current Ratio} = \frac{\$28,174}{\$11,000} = 2.56 \text{ (Good)}$$

Debt Ratios

$$\text{Housing Ratio 1} = \frac{\$12,768 + \$1,600 + \$2,895}{\$109,000} = 15.8\% \text{ (Very Good)}$$

$$\text{Housing Ratio 2} = \frac{\$12,768 + \$1,600 + \$2,895 + \$3,300 + \$5,400}{\$109,000} = 23.8\% \text{ (Very Good)}$$

$$\text{Debt to Total Assets Ratio} = \frac{\$172,000}{\$452,000} = 38.1\% \text{ (Good) (2013)}$$

$$\text{Debt to Total Assets Ratio} = \frac{\$165,389}{\$450,774} = 36.7\% \text{ (Good) (2014)}$$

$$\text{Net Worth to Total Assets Ratio} = \frac{\$280,000}{\$452,000} = 62\% \text{ (Good) Benchmark Depends on Age (2013)}$$

$$\text{Net Worth to Total Assets Ratio} = \frac{\$285,385}{\$450,774} = 63\% \text{ (Good) Benchmark Depends on Age (2014)}$$

Ratios for Financial Security Goals

$$\text{Savings Rate*} = \frac{\$2,190 + \$14,600}{\$109,000} = 15.4\% \text{ (Good) (\$2,190 = employer match)}$$

(* Excludes reinvestments)

$$\frac{\text{Investment Assets}}{\text{to Gross Pay}} = \frac{\$177,000 + \$30,000}{\$109,000} = 1.90 \text{ times (Weak)}$$

401(k) Plan Savings	
Employee Elective Deferral	$14,600
Employer Match	$2,190
Total	$16,790

Performance Ratios

$$\text{Return on 401(k)} = \frac{\$89,600 - (\$86,000 + \$16,790)}{\$86,000} = -15.5\% \text{ (Very Poor)}$$

$$\frac{\text{Return on}}{\text{Total Investments}} = \frac{\$175,600 - (\$177,000 + \$16,950 + \$2,190)}{\$177,000} = \frac{-11.6\%}{\text{(Very Poor)}}$$

Overall, the ratio approach suggests the Hess' only have two major weaknesses in the amount of savings to gross pay and return on investments. Additional approaches should be applied to reveal a more comprehensive analysis of the Hess financial position. The additional approaches are covered during the remainder of this chapter.

THE TWO-STEP / THREE-PANEL / METRICS APPROACH

TWO-STEP APPROACH

The two-step approach to financial planning recommends covering the risks and saving and investing. The two-step approach considers personal risks as potentially leading to catastrophic losses or dependence on someone else for their financial well being. The two-step approach regards savings and investments as the path to financial security or independence. Dependence on others can be caused by a single catastrophic event that can occur unexpectedly. Financial independence, however, is achieved over a long period of time by saving and investing. In summary, the two-step approach focuses on risk management and appropriate saving and investing.

Key Concepts

Underline/highlight the answers as you read:

1. List the two focuses of the two-step approach and the financial categories analyzed by the three-panel approach.

2. Identify the purpose of the example benchmarks used in the metrics approach.

THREE-PANEL APPROACH

The three-panel approach is a slight refinement of the two-step approach. It divides saving and investing into short and long-term objectives. The three-panel approach provides the planner and the client with a methodology for financial planning in order to achieve the goals of covering the risks, saving, and investing. The exhibit below outlines the three-panel methodology.

THREE-PANEL METHODOLOGY

EXHIBIT 3.14

PANEL 1	PANEL 2	PANEL 3
Risk Management of Personal, Property, and Liability Risks	Short-Term Savings and Investments & Debt Management	Long-Term Savings and Investments
Evaluate the need for and quality of personal insurance:	Evaluate the adequacy of:	Evaluate the adequacy of progress toward:
1. Life Insurance 2. Health Insurance 3. Disability Insurance 4. Long-Term Care Insurance 5. Property Insurance: • Homeowner's Insurance • Auto Insurance • Other Property Insurance 6. Liability Insurance	1. The emergency fund 2. The proportion of income spent on housing 3. The proportion of income spent on debt other than housing debt repayments	1. The retirement goal • the savings rate • investment assets 2. The education funding goal 3. Any large purchase goal 4. Legacy goals • documents • financial

Panel 1 is used to evaluate each of the risks listed and then evaluates the client's actual portfolio of insurance to determine the adequacy of current insurance coverage. The focus is on covering catastrophic risk exposures.

Panel 2 is used to calculate the emergency fund ratio (which is also available from using the financial statement analysis approach). Next, the planner calculates housing ratio 1 and housing ratio 2 and evaluates the quality of client debt. The focus is on meeting short-term obligations and evaluating how well the client is managing debt.

Panel 3 focuses on long-term goals. To meet the financial security goal (ability to maintain the pre-retirement lifestyle throughout retirement) requires persistent savings, adequate investment performance, and investment assets appropriate for the age and gross pay of the client. If the client also expects or wants to provide a college education for children, the savings rate must be increased. If the client also has lump-sum goals (second home, very expensive trip, boat, airplane) the savings rate should increase at least sufficiently to provide a down payment on the lump-sum asset of 20 percent. Finally, all clients need basic estate planning documents (will, durable power of attorney for health care, advance medical directive). If, in addition to the other goals, the client wants to leave a financial legacy, even more savings is required.

As shown in Exhibit 3.15, client A has no children. Client B has two children and plans to send them to an in-state college. Client C plans to send two children to a good private school and plans to buy a second home at the beach in ten years (current cost $250,000). Client D plans to send the children to an exclusive private school and buy a second home for $350,000 in ten years and leave $1,000,000 in purchasing power to the children at death (age 65). Expected earnings is eight percent and inflation is expected to be three percent. The wage replacement ratio is approximately 90 to 100 percent of pre-retirement income.

EXHIBIT 3.15 **SAVINGS RATE NECESSARY FOR VARIOUS CLIENTS / SCENARIOS**

	A Single Age 25 (0 children)	B Married Age 35 (2 children)	C Married Age 40 (2 children)	D Married Age 40 (2 children)
Income	$100,000	$100,000	$150,000	$200,000
Retirement Goal Savings Rate (as a % of gross pay)	10 - 13%	10 - 13%	10 - 13%	10 - 13%
Investment Assets	$2,000	$150,000	$365,000	$500,000
Education Goal	0	3%	5%	7%
Lump-Sum Goal	0	0	3%	3.3%
Legacy Goal	0	0	0	6.30%
Overall Savings Rate Needed (as a % of gross pay)	10 - 13%	13 - 16%	18 - 21%	26.6 - 29.6%

The point is not necessarily how much a person needs, but rather whether the retirement goal is being met by: (1) a savings rate of 10 to 13 percent and (2) investment assets of a certain amount that are an appropriate percentage of gross pay depending on the age of the client. If the client has goals other than retirement (education, lump sum, and/or legacy) the overall savings rate will have to be increased to meet those additional goals.

The three-panel approach is like a recipe or a checklist. An advantage of this approach is that it is easy to follow by both the planner and the client. Keep in mind this methodology does not answer every question in financial planning, nor does it require the analysis of rates of return on investments or evaluate investment risk.

Once the three-panel approach is understood, the financial planner can overlay it with quantitative and qualitative metrics that provide benchmarks to compare to the client's actual financial situation. The result of this analysis will determine deficiencies in the client's risk management portfolio, short-term savings and investing (plus debt management), and long-term savings and investing (to determine if adequate progress is being made towards long-term goals).

METRICS APPROACH

The metrics approach provides quantitative example benchmarks for the financial planner and client to use as guidance for necessary comprehensive financial goals and objectives. Once the practitioner has analyzed and evaluated the client's actual financial situation, the metrics can be applied to establish financial planning recommendations.

Quick Quiz 3.3

Highlight the answer to these questions:

1. The two-step approach considers savings and investments as the financial plan leading to financial security (and independence).
   a. True
   b. False

2. The three-panel approach provides a plan for risk management of personal, property, and liability risks, along with both short-term and long-term savings.
   a. True
   b. False

3. The metrics approach provides finite benchmarks for the financial planner to use as a comparison of client actual to client goal.
   a. True
   b. False

True, True, False.

EXHIBIT 3.16 **EXAMPLE BENCHMARKS (METRICS)**

	Metric	Comment / Recommendation
RISK MANAGEMENT DATA		
Life Insurance	12 - 16 times gross pay, if needed.	The amount certainly depends on needs of dependents.
Health Insurance	Lifetime benefit ≥ $1,000,000.**	Should be guaranteed renewable with reasonable out of pocket limits.
Disability Insurance	60 - 70% of gross pay and at least guaranteed renewable.	Covering both sickness and accident and a hybrid or own occupation definition and appropriate elimination period.
Long-Term Care Insurance	If needed, daily or monthly benefits ≥ average for appropriate facility.	Benefits inflation adjusted and a benefit period ≥ 36 - 60 months.
Homeowners Insurance	≤ full replacement value on both dwelling and content and coverage for open perils.	
Automobile Insurance	≤ full fair market value for comprehensive and collision.	
Liability Insurance	At least a $1,000,000 personal liability policy.	Need sufficient underlying homeowners and auto liability to satisfy PLUP issuer.
SHORT-TERM SAVINGS AND INVESTING GOALS		
Emergency Fund	Equal to 3 - 6 times the monthly non-discretionary cash outflows.	
Housing	Housing ratio1 should be ≤ 28% of gross pay.	Housing ratio 1 should decline to ≤ 5% of gross pay at retirement.
Housing and Debt	The total paid for housing costs and other debt payments ≤ 36% of gross pay.	Other debt payments include, but are not limited to, credit cards, auto loans, and student loans.
LONG-TERM SAVINGS AND INVESTMENT GOALS		
Financial Security (Retirement)	Save 10 - 13% of gross pay (include employer match).	Have an appropriate amount of investment assets relative to gross pay for the client's age.
College Education Funding	Save $3,000/$6,000/or $9,000 per child per year for 18 years in a balanced portfolio (60% stocks/40% fixed income).	Savings is dependent on where the child is expected to attend college (in state/ mid-private/elite-private).
Lump-Sum Goals	Goals like 2nd home, airplane, or boat require savings of at least 20% of the total price as a down payment.	This additional goal will increase the overall savings rate required to achieve all the goals.
Legacy Goals	Every client under age 50 needs basic documents. Those 50 and over may also need trusts and estate planning.	Basic documents include a will, durable power of attorney for healthcare, advanced medical directive (living will), and durable power of attorney for financial matters.

** Historically it was important to make sure that a health care policy has a lifetime limit of at least $1million. However, under Section 2711 of the Patient Protection and Affordable Care Act, lifetime limits are eliminated and no longer a concern.

RISK TOLERANCE AND ASSET ALLOCATION

The three-panel approach and the metrics approach are very helpful in providing a framework and benchmarks for the client and planner. However, clients and planners need tools to develop an investment plan. A proper investment plan is a critical element in the pursuit of most financial planning goals, including retirement and education. The investment plan is a bit like the engine in a car – without it, you cannot reach the destination.

In financial planning, calculating savings for retirement or education is sometimes performed without a significant amount of thought and consideration given to a proper expected investment rate of return. However, this "variable" or "input" is an extremely important factor in determining the amount that needs to be accumulated or saved.

Investing is a challenging component of financial planning as certainty resides only in past and not in future investment performance. However, it is generally accepted that asset allocation is the largest contributor to investment performance over time and the two key components in determining a proper asset allocation are risk tolerance and time horizon.

As part of the investment planning process, the financial planner evaluates the client's goals in terms of both dollar value and time. The client's goals are assessed together with risk tolerance in designing the appropriate investment strategy. The client's risk tolerance is a combination of both the ability and the willingness to accept investment risk. The planner will develop an investment plan considering the client's investment ability (an objective state of being, based on the client's financial profile) and the client's willingness (a subjective state of being) to take on investment risk and to commit dollars over time to reach the investment goals. The ability and willingness of the client to accept risk can be gauged by various factors. For example, the longer the time horizon of a client, the more risk that the client is able to accept in the investment portfolio. The client's ability to accept risk is associated with time horizon, liquidity needs, tax conditions, and unique financial and personal circumstances. The client's willingness to accept risk is associated with the psychological condition of risk tolerance. The risk tolerance questionnaire provides both the planner and the client with a clear understanding of the client's psychological tolerance (willingness) for taking risk.

Financial planners employ tools to assess the client's willingness to accept investment risk, thus helping to determine the client's risk tolerance as part of the investment planning process. Dr. William Droms, CFA, the Powers Professor of Finance in the McDonough School of Business at Georgetown University and a principal at in Droms Strauss Advisors, Inc. has granted us permission to use his Global Portfolio Allocation Scoring System (PASS) in this text.[2] PASS considers both time horizon and risk tolerance in determining an appropriate asset allocation. Step one is to have the client answer the following questions, which have scores ranging from 5 to 1. Once the questions are answered, each of the point values is summed and is used as part of determining the asset allocation.

---

2. More information can be found on Dr. Droms at http://www.droms-strauss.com, as well as the complete article from the Journal of Financial Planning.

Global Portfolio Allocation Scoring System (PASS) for Individual Investors[1]					
Questions	Strongly Agree	Agree	Neutral	Disagree	Strongly Disagree
1 Earning a high long-term total return that will allow my capital to grow faster than the inflation rate is one of my most important investment objectives.	5	4	3	2	1
2 I would like an investment that provides me with an opportunity to defer taxation of capital gains to future years.	5	4	3	2	1
3 I do not require a high level of current income from my investments.	5	4	3	2	1
4 I am willing to tolerate some sharp down swings in the return on my investments in order to seek a potentially higher return than would normally be expected from more stable investments.	5	4	3	2	1
5 I am willing to risk a short-term loss in return for a potentially higher long-run rate of return.	5	4	3	2	1
6 I am financially able to accept a low level of liquidity in my investment portfolio.	5	4	3	2	1

1. More information can be found on Dr. Droms at http://www.droms-strauss.com, as well as the complete article from the Journal of Financial Planning.

The next step is to determine the time horizon of the investment goal and then to use the PASS score to determine the appropriate asset allocation. The higher the score, the more tolerance for risk the client has shown and the more the portfolio can be aggressively allocated.

PASS Score	Short-Term Horizon				Intermediate-Term Horizon				Long-Term Horizon			
	RT1 Target	RT2 Target	RT3 Target	RT4 Target	RT1 Target	RT2 Target	RT3 Target	RT4 Target	RT1 Target	RT2 Target	RT3 Target	RT4 Target
	6 - 12	13 - 18	19 - 24	25 - 30	6 - 12	13 - 18	19 - 24	25 - 30	6 - 12	13 - 18	19 - 24	25 - 30
Cash and Money Market Fund	40%	30%	20%	10%	5%	5%	5%	5%	5%	5%	3%	2%
Treasury Bonds/ Bond Funds	40%	30%	30%	20%	60%	35%	20%	10%	30%	20%	12%	0%
Corporate Bonds/ Bond Funds	20%	30%	30%	40%	15%	15%	15%	10%	15%	10%	10%	4%
Subtotal	100%	90%	80%	70%	80%	55%	40%	25%	50%	35%	25%	6%
International Bond Funds	0%	0%	0%	0%	0%	5%	5%	5%	0%	5%	5%	4%
Subtotal	0%	0%	0%	0%	0%	5%	5%	5%	0%	5%	5%	4%
Index Fund	0%	10%	10%	10%	10%	15%	20%	20%	20%	20%	20%	25%
Large Cap Value Funds/Stocks	0%	0%	5%	5%	5%	5%	10%	10%	10%	10%	5%	5%
Large Cap Growth Funds/Stocks	0%	0%	0%	0%	5%	5%	5%	10%	15%	10%	10%	5%
Mid/Small Growth Funds/Stocks	0%	0%	0%	0%	0%	0%	5%	5%	0%	0%	5%	10%
Mid/Small Value Funds/Stocks	0%	0%	0%	5%	0%	5%	5%	5%	0%	5%	5%	10%
Subtotal	0%	10%	15%	20%	20%	30%	45%	50%	45%	45%	45%	55%
International Stock Funds	0%	0%	0%	5%	0%	5%	5%	10%	0%	5%	10%	15%
Subtotal	0%	0%	0%	5%	0%	5%	5%	10%	0%	5%	10%	15%
Real Estate Funds	0%	0%	5%	5%	0%	5%	5%	10%	5%	10%	15%	20%
Subtotal	0%	0%	5%	5%	0%	5%	5%	10%	5%	10%	15%	20%
Total	100%	100%	100%	100%	100%	100%	100%	100%	100%	100%	100%	100%

PASS defines short-term as three years or less, intermediate-term as three to seven years and long-term as more than seven years. With the PASS score and the time horizon, the asset allocation can be determined. There are other models that can be used to assess risk tolerance and determine an appropriate asset allocation. However, Dr. Drom's PASS is a valid model and his article in the Journal of Financial Planning can be used as an additional reference on the subject.

To simplify and to help determine expected return and to consider risk of asset classes, the asset classes above have been condensed into the following asset classes with corresponding expected returns and expected standard deviations:

	Expected Rates of Return	Standard Deviation of Returns
Cash and Money Market Fund	2.5%	2.0%
Treasury Bonds / Bond Fund	4.0%	4.0%
Corporate Bonds / Bond Fund	6.0%	5.0%
International Bond Funds	7.0%	6.0%
Index Funds	9.0%	14.0%
Large Cap Funds / Stocks	10.0%	16.0%
Mid / Small Funds / Stocks	12.0%	18.0%
International Stock Funds	13.0%	22.0%
Real Estate Funds	8.0%	12.0%

These asset classes are used in Money Education's *Cases in Financial Planning: Analysis and Presentation* textbook. In practice, some of these asset classes might be excluded while other asset classes might be included.

The following chart reflects the condensed asset classes and weightings with the corresponding expected return and estimated standard deviation for each portfolio.[3]

	Short-Term Horizon				Intermediate-Term Horizon				Long-Term Horizon			
	RT1 Target	RT2 Target	RT3 Target	RT4 Target	RT1 Target	RT2 Target	RT3 Target	RT4 Target	RT1 Target	RT2 Target	RT3 Target	RT4 Target
PASS Score	6 - 12	13 - 18	19 - 24	25 - 30	6 - 12	13 - 18	19 - 24	25 - 30	6 - 12	13 - 18	19 - 24	25 - 30
Cash and Money Market Fund	40%	30%	20%	10%	5%	5%	5%	5%	5%	5%	3%	2%
Treasury Bonds/ Bond Funds	40%	30%	30%	20%	60%	35%	20%	10%	30%	20%	12%	0%
Corporate Bonds/ Bond Funds	20%	30%	30%	40%	15%	15%	15%	10%	15%	10%	10%	4%
International Bond Funds	0%	0%	0%	0%	0%	5%	5%	5%	0%	5%	5%	4%
Index Fund	0%	10%	10%	10%	10%	15%	20%	20%	20%	20%	20%	25%
Large Cap Funds/Stocks	0%	0%	5%	5%	10%	10%	15%	20%	25%	20%	15%	10%
Mid/Small Funds/Stocks	0%	0%	0%	5%	0%	5%	10%	10%	0%	5%	10%	20%
International Stock Funds	0%	0%	0%	5%	0%	5%	5%	10%	0%	5%	10%	15%
Real Estate Funds	0%	0%	5%	5%	0%	5%	5%	10%	5%	10%	15%	20%
Total	100%	100%	100%	100%	100%	100%	100%	100%	100%	100%	100%	100%
Expected Return	3.80%	4.65%	5.30%	6.50%	5.33%	6.78%	7.73%	8.58%	6.93%	7.73%	8.51%	9.77%
Expected Standard Deviation (est)	2.79%	3.85%	4.84%	6.40%	5.13%	7.26%	8.73%	10.25%	7.75%	8.94%	10.12%	12.20%

The information in the chart above can be used to support the required returns in a comprehensive case. In practice, this analysis will often be conducted using a software package that incorporates mean variance optimization. However, the above approach is effective for comprehensive cases.

EXAMPLE 3.3

Alice Answers the PASS with the following answers for each of the six questions: strongly agree, agree, agree, neutral, agree, strongly agree. Based on the scoring for each answer, her total score is 25 (5 + 4 + 4 + 3 + 4 + 5). Assuming that she is positioning her portfolio for retirement, a long term goal, then she would be considering the long-term portfolio RT4, with an expected return of approximately 9.77%. She would allocate her portfolio as indicated in the above chart based on the right most column.

THE PRESENT VALUE OF GOALS APPROACH

The present value of goals approach takes each short, intermediate, and long-term goal, determines each individual present value, then sums these present values together and then reduces them by current resources (investment assets and cash and cash equivalents) and then treats the net PV as an obligation to be retired over the remaining work life expectancy at a discount rate equal to the expected portfolio rate of return.

Refer back to Hess Goal (slightly modified for our purposes here). **Note**: New details for example purposes. They now have three goals.

---

3. The standard deviation for each portfolio has been estimated. To calculate it as accurately as possible, a correlation matrix would be required.

Goal 1: Retire

Assume they want to both retire at Jack's age 65 with an 80% wage replacement ratio. Inflation is projected to be 3%, an earnings rate to and through retirement is expected to be 8.0% and life expectancy is expected to be 25 years for both spouses (e.g., to 90 and 88 respectively). Assume Social Security will pay $25,000 in today's dollars at age 67 for Jack and $20,000 for Marilyn.

Wage Replacement Calculation

Income	$109,000	
WRR%	X 0.80	
Total Needs in Today's Dollars	$87,200	
Jack's Social Security (at age 65)	($21,667)	$25,000 (0.8666)
Marilyn's Social Security	($15,000)	$20,000 (0.75)
Needs in Today's Dollars	$50,533	

Note – Social Security benefits are reduced when payments begin prior to full retirement age. In this case, their full retirement age is age 67 and he is beginning his benefits at age 65, while she is beginning her benefits at age 63. The reduction in benefits is equal to 5/9ths of one percent for each of the first 36 months and 5/12ths of one percent for months beyond the first 36 months.

Retirement Calculation

Step 1	Step 2	Step 3
N = 20 (45-65)	PMT_{AD} = $91,268.21902	$FV_{@65}$ = $1,368,681.23
i = 3	N = 25	N = 20
PV = $50,333	i = $((1.08 \div 1.03) - 1) \times 100$	i = 8
PMT = 0	FV = 0	$PV_{@45}$ = $293,648.10
FV = $91,268.21902	$PV_{@65}$ = $1,368,681.23	

Goal 2: Education for Melba, age 13

Facts: Education costs in today's dollars is $21,000 per year for 5 years (added), education inflation is assumed to be 6% per year.

Step 1	Step 2
N = 5 years in college	$FV_{@18}$ = $101,182.46
PMT_{AD} = $21,000 per year	N = 5 (18 - 13) years to college
i = $((1.08 \div 1.06) - 1) \times 100$	i = $((1.08 \div 1.06) - 1) \times 100$
$PV_{@18}$ = $101,182.46	PMT = 0
FV = 0	$PV_{@13}$ = $92,154.34

Goal 3: Created for this example.

Assume that the Hess's want to buy a second home for $300,000 in today's dollars 11 years from now.

Step 1		Step 2	
N	= 11 years to goal	FV	= $415,270.16
i	= 3	N	= 11
PV	= $300,000	i	= 8
PMT	= 0	PV	$178,102.25
FV	= $415,270.16		

Note: This calculation can also be done in one step using an inflation adjusted discount rate.

The summation of the three goals in present value terms is as follows:

Retirement	$293,648.10
Education	$92,154.34
Second Home	$178,102.25
Total PV of all Goals	$563,904.69

The PV of all goals reduced by current resources is:

PV of All Goals	$563,904.69	
Current Resources	$207,000.00	(Investment assets and cash)
Short Fall / PV	$356,904.69	
i	8%	(the earnings rate)
N	20	(to retirement)
FV	0	
PMT_{OA}	$36,351.53	

Once the present value of the goals are summed and then reduced by current resources, the remaining present value of goals can be determined and treated hypothetically as a mortgage to be retired at the expected earnings rate. This will determine how much they need to be saving annually, at year end, to achieve all their goals. That resultant ($36,351.53) can then be compared to their current savings amount to determine its adequacy.

Current Savings Amount	$14,600	Required Annual Savings	$36,351.53
Plus the Employer Match	$2,190	Less Current Savings	$16,790.00
Total Current Savings	**$16,790**	**Necessary Savings Deficit**	**$19,561.53**
The $16,950 on the income statement includes reinvestment which is included in the overall portfolio rate and should not be counted in the savings rate.			

They are $19,561.53 in annual savings short of meeting all of their goals ($36,351.53 - $16,790). They should consider some of their alternatives:

1. Do they have additional discretionary cash flow they can save? No!
2. Are they over withheld on taxes? The answer to this requires a tax analysis (see below).

Tax Analysis (2013)

Itemized Deductions

Mortgage Interest	$11,556
Charitable Contribution	$935
State Income Tax	$3,175
Property Tax	$2,895
Total Itemized Deductions	$18,561

Income	$111,350	
401(k)	($14,600)	
AGI	$96,750	
P&D exempt	($11,400)	3 personal and dependency exemptions
Itemized Deductions	($18,561)	MFJ / itemized deduction - assumed
Taxable Income	$66,789	
Tax from Schedule	$9,148	Tax income / Appendix A - www.money-education.com
Child Credit	($1,000)	
Tax Liability	$8,148	
Tax withheld	($16,220)	
Over withheld	$8,072	Refund due

It is not uncommon that clients are over-withheld. The problem for many people who are over withheld is that they spend rather than save the refund check. If they increase their 401(k) plan contribution or other savings during the year by changing the with-holdings form (W-4), they can increase their savings by $8,072 ÷ 0.85 (the marginal tax rate) and they will be just as well off except they will have no refund.

Below is the revised savings amount resulting from the tax analysis (this amount is calculated without grossing up the over withholding).

401(k) deferral	$14,600	
Employer match	$2,190	(3% of $73,000)
Addition 401(k) deferral	$2,900	(to get to $17,500)
Traditional spouse IRA	$5,172	
New Total Annual Savings	$24,862	

While this amount is still below the $36,351.53 needed, the wage replacement ratio can also be adjusted to reflect the new savings amount. The wage replacement ratio was originally 80% or $87,200 in today's dollars but with the above additional savings, they are currently living on the following:

Gross pay	$109,000	
Less savings	$22,672	(excluding employer match)
Less Social Security taxes	$8,033	
Net	$78,295	(which is a WRR of 71.83%, not 80%)

While they initially wanted and thought they needed an 80% wage replacement ratio, they can actually maintain their lifestyle with a WRR of approximately 72% (71.83%). It is fairly common that a client may have initial desires that exceed what is absolutely necessary to insuring their current standard of living. Through discussions with them, they will likely understand that point.

Consider the following adjustments and alternatives:
1. Delay retirement to normal age retirement of age 67 (2 more years) and reduce the wage replacement ratio to 72% from 80%.
2. Leave all other goals the same as they were.

Impact on calculations:

	$109,000.00	Income
	0.72	WRR
	$78,480.00	Needs in today's dollars
Social Security (Jack)	($25,000.00)	normal age retirement
Social Security (Marilyn)	($17,333.33)	2 years early, not 4 (13.33% reduction)
Needs	$36,146.67	Retirement needs in today's dollars

Step 1	Step 2	Step 3
N = 22 years to retirement	PMT_{AD} = $69,260.76	FV = $993,168.10
i = 3 inflation	i = $((1.08 \div 1.03) - 1) \times 100$	i = 8
PV = $36,146.67	N = 23	N = 22
FV = $69,260.76	$PV_{@67}$ = $993,168.10	PV = $182,683.84

The new calculation of the present value of all goals is as follows along with the change in the necessary savings amount required to achieve all goals.

PV of retirement	$182,683.84	
PV of education	$92,154.34	
PV of second house	$178,102.25	
PV	$452,940.43	
Less resources:	$207,000.00	
Short fall PV	$245,940.43	
N	22	(note 2 more years of working)
i	8%	
PMT_{OA}	$24,110.05	(new savings calculations)
FV_0	0	

It is clear from the revised calculation of the savings and wage replacement ratio that they can meet all their financial goals simply by delaying retirement by two years and revising their wage replacement needs from 80% down to 72%. The amount needed to be saved is $24,110.05 and they are currently saving $24,862 (assuming the Form W-4 changes). But what if they do not like this idea? The client can then consider other choices in various combinations.

1. Only pay for 4 years of college education.
2. Reduce the price of the second home to $200,000 from $300,000 or do not buy a second home.
3. Use a 72% wage replacement ratio.
4. Delay retirement one year instead of two.
5. Perhaps refinance their home.
6. Save more and spend less.

PRESENTATION OF THE PRESENT VALUE OF ALL GOALS APPROACH

When presenting the present value of all goals approach, it is useful to present values at various times and both the overall savings requirements and specific goal savings requirements. As an example, presume the following:

TABLE 1

Goal	Present Value	Annual Savings Required*	Annual Savings Required**
# 1 - Retirement	$300,000.00	$28,926.65	$28,926.65
# 2 - Education	$195,000.00	$18,802.32	$23,652.89****
# 3 - Second Home	$100,840.00	$9,723.21	$9,732.21
Total	$595,840.00	$57,452.18	N/A
Current Resources***	($200,000.00)	($19,284.43)	N/A
Net Needs	$395,840.00	$38,167.75	N/A

* Savings on an annual ordinary annuity basis over the remaining work life expectancy.
** Savings required to the beginning of the draw down.
Other Assumptions:
- Earnings Rate 8% / Inflation 3% / Age 42 / Retire at 65
- Educate 3 children 2, 4, and 6 years old. Education inflation 5%.
- Purchase second home 23 years from now for $300,000.
*** Current resources include investment assets and cash and cash equivalents.
**** Assume the money is needed in 14 years.

By presenting the present value in current real dollar terms, the net needs can be hypothetically treated as an obligation (mortgage) to be repaid at the expected rate of return (in this case, 8%) over the work life expectancy (in this case, 23 years). The resultant ($38,167.75) can then be compared to the current actual savings rate to determine whether current savings are adequate to pay for all goals. Presuming annual savings are not adequate, it is relatively easy to see the cost of each goal in terms of annual required savings and consider priorities. For example, in this case, the client might decide the second home is not important or a less expensive one could suffice. The client could decide that one or two more years of working would be preferable to changing other goals. Keep in mind that an additional year of working: (1) increases Social Security benefits up to age 70, (2) increases savings years by one, (3) increases compounding by one, and (4) decreases consumption by one year. One to two years of delayed retirement can be very significant.

In addition to the Table 1 presentation, it may also be useful to present the values in nominal dollars for each goal at the start of the draw down as in Table 2.

TABLE 2

Goal	Present Values	Future Values	
# 1 - Retirement	$300,000.00	$1,761,439.09	Value at the beginning of retirement
# 2 - Education	$195,000.00	$572,752.76	Value at the start of education*
# 3 - Second Home	$100,840.00	$592,078.39	Value in 23 years
Income**	$170,000	$335,509.71	Value in 23 years

* Assume in 14 years.
** Assume raises are at 3%.

Table 2 data provides a perspective of both the present and future (nominal) dollars required to achieve the financial goals. The current and projected income also provides a relative perspective as between today and the future costs of goals.

In the Table 1 example, it is notable that education (which is sometimes the most important goal) could be fully funded by utilizing all of the current resources. If the goal of the second home were abandoned the required savings rate would decline from approximately 22.5% to 17%. Table 3 depicts various changes and the impact of each change on the required savings rate.

TABLE 3

Alternatives	Current Savings Rate Required	New Savings Rate Required
# 1 - Abandon 2nd home, fully fund education now, retire on time	22.5%	17%
# 2 - Abandon 2nd home, fully fund education now, delay retirement 2 years	22.5%	12.77%
# 3 - Fully fund education now, delay retirement 2 years	22.5%	18.324%

Ultimately, the questions are "What are the priorities of the client" and "How much (savings% or dollars) are they willing to sacrifice to achieve the goals and over what time frame?"

The present value approach assists the planner in understanding the requirements of the goals that the client has specified in present and future dollar terms as well as the corresponding savings required to achieve those goals.

THE CASH FLOW APPROACH

The cash flow approach takes the annual current income statement and adjusts the cash flows by forecasting what they would be after implementing all of the planning recommendations. This approach begins with the discretionary cash flows at the bottom of the income statement and accounts for each of the recommendations in the order of priority. The annual cost of each recommendation is charged against the discretionary cash flows regardless of any negative cash flow impact. The approach separates the recommendations into four impact categories:

Key Concepts

Underline/highlight the answers as you read:

1. Explain the usefulness of the cash flow approach.

2. Identify the three focus areas being managed under the cash flow approach.

3. Define the strategic approach to financial planning.

1. No cash flow impact.
2. Annual recurring positive (very few) or negative cash flow impact.
3. One-time non-recurring positive (sale of an asset) or negative (pay off debt) cash flow impact.
4. Impact that affects the client in a positive or negative way, but does not affect his cash flow on the income statement (an increase in the employer match in the 401(k) plan as a result of increased employee deferrals or the employer no longer matches thus causing a decrease).

RISK MANAGEMENT

The immediate risk management recommendations are usually related to insurance portfolio changes because perils (the cause of a loss) are event driven (e.g., untimely death) or unpredictable, and can occur at any time. It takes a long time for an implemented financial plan to provide financial security for a client, with both savings and investing potentially taking 25 to 40 years to be successful. However, a catastrophic loss caused by a peril associated with personal risks (life, health, disability, or long-term care), property loss, or liability can occur suddenly and completely destroy an otherwise well thought out financial plan. Hence, the importance of implementing insurance portfolio recommendations as the first priority.

Insurance recommendations may have annual recurring positive, negative, or no cash flow impact. Insurance recommendations involve adding, deleting, changing, or replacing some aspect of the insurance portfolio so as to improve the overall catastrophic protection for the client and maximize premium efficiency. The following provides examples of insurance recommendations impact (or lack of) on cash flows.

EXHIBIT 3.17		

1	**No Cash Flow Impact** • Change name of beneficiary • Assign policy to another • Stop driving uninsured vehicle • Clarify the lifetime benefits of an employer provided health plan
2A	**Positive Annual Cash Flow Impact** • Raise deductibles (e.g., auto) • Eliminate duplicate coverage (e.g., disability) • Reduce coverage (e.g., home value declined) • Replace one policy for another (e.g., term life)
2B	**Negative Annual Cash Flow Impact** • Purchase life, health, disability, long-term care, property, or liability insurance • Increasing the amount of current coverage • Lowering deductibles

Insurance recommendations follow the three-panel and metrics approach when a detailed analysis of the insurance portfolio needed for a particular client is conducted. The estimated cash flow impact resulting from changes described in cash flow categories 2A and 2B above can be determined by contacting an insurance agent who sells the product type that is being changed, added, deleted, or replaced (and may also be estimated by a thorough internet search). For purposes of this chapter and the textbook, assume that the planner has previously investigated the costs and/or savings from changing, adding, deleting, or replacing an insurance policy. Therefore, when the planner implements these recommendations into the cash flow statement, it is an accurate estimate of the cost (e.g., the annual per $1,000 cost of term life insurance for a male age 30 is about 70 cents for a 30-year term policy).

Exhibit 3.18 provides an illustration of risk management recommendations for a client along with the cash flow impact and implementation responsibility.

EXHIBIT 3.18

	Recommendation	Annual Recurring Cost <Negative> + Positive*	Non-Recurring Cost	Other	To Be Implemented by Client or Planner
1	Change the beneficiary on life insurance Policy A to wife	None			Client
2	Purchase a $500k 30-year term life insurance policy on husband	<$350.00>			Client
3	Purchase disability insurance for wife 60% of pay, benefits to 65, guaranteed renewable	<$360.00>			Client
4	Change homeowners policy to reflect a decline in value and raise the homeowner's deductible	+$250.00			Client

For the purpose of this textbook, cash flow impacts are estimated.

DEBT MANAGEMENT

The next area of recommendations will either involve debt management or savings and investing depending on the client's priorities. Since debt management has an impact on savings and investments, debt management will be covered first.

Frequently, people have too much debt, have debt with high interest rates, and/or have debt that is not well managed. The analysis of debt includes calculating housing ratios 1 and 2 and comparing those to the well established benchmarks (metrics) of 28% / 36%. In addition, the financial planner should evaluate the quality and the cost of each client's individual debt. Good debt tends to have two components: (1) the interest rate is relatively low in comparison to expected inflation and expected investment returns, and (2) the expected debt repayment period is substantially less than the expected economic life of the asset. An example of good debt is a fixed 15-year mortgage on a home with an economic life of the home in excess of 40 years, a house payment that fits within the housing ratios, and an interest rate of five percent (and the lowest rate available) when the client's raise rate is expected to be four percent, inflation is expected to be three percent, and the client's expected investment return is 8.5 percent. Another example of good debt is a student loan used to provide education tied to a profession (e.g., medicine, law, financial planning, accounting, or engineering) for a person with a reasonable work life expectancy. This type of education is essentially an investment that can provide returns well in excess of the capital cost and over a period much longer than the debt repayment period. It remains important that debt is incurred at a reasonable interest rate.

In addition to good debt, there is also reasonable debt where the debt repayment period is longer or the returns on the debt are positive, but less certain than for good debt. Examples of reasonable debt include 30-year home mortgages at conforming interest rates and student loans that are for general education.

Bad debt is associated with: (1) high interest rates, or (2) when the economic life of the purchase is exceeded by the associated debt repayment period. An example of bad debt is an automobile loan with a small down payment and a 72-month term where the economic life of the automobile is three to five years. Another example of bad debt involves debt with high interest rates, (which includes most credit cards). Consider the following credit card debt and associated pay off schedule ramifications:

Alternative	Balance	Minimum Payment Due	Term to Pay-Off Balance	Implied Interest Rate	Total Estimated Payments
A	$1,912.78	$39.13	16 years	24%	$7,512.79
B	$1,912.78	$75.04	3 years	24%	$2,701.58
C	$1,912.78	$106.26	1.5 years	0%*	$1,912.78

* The rate is 0% interest because it is a promotional program with 18-months free interest but only if the account is completely paid off by the promotional code expiration date.

Note in the above example that if the client only pays the minimum monthly payment (Alternative A), it will take 16 years and cost $7,512.79 to pay for $1,912.78 of debt.

For Alternative C, note that retailers using promotional rates of zero percent, also use low minimum payments that creates a balloon payment at the end of the promotional term. Retailers expect that most consumers will violate the agreement resulting in them having to pay all of the interest from the original date of purchase.

EXHIBIT 3.19	CHARACTERISTICS OF VARIOUS TYPES OF DEBT

Classification of Debt	Interest Rates	Nature of and Economic Life of Asset Purchased	Repayment Period	Examples
Good Debt	Relatively Low	Typically Long Lived	Substantially less than economic life of asset	• Home purchase with 15-year mortgage • Student loan with vocation • Car loan with repayment period of 3 years or less
Reasonable Debt	Competitive	Typically Long Lived	Less than the economic life of asset	• Home purchase with 30-year mortgage • Student loan for general higher education • Car loan with repayment period of 4-5 years
Bad Debt	High	Short or Long Lived or Consumed Expenditure	Longer than economic life of purchase	• Minimum payments on credit card debt • Car loan with repayment period longer than economic life of car

The following table outlines example debt management recommendations for a client, including the cash flow impact and implementation responsibilities.

EXHIBIT 3.20

	Recommendations	Annual Recurring Cost <Negative> + Positive	Non-Recurring Cost (Savings)	Other	To Be Implemented by Client or Planner
A	Refinance a home for 15 years at 5% (current loan at 7.5% on $300,000). 3% closing included in mortgage	+ $4,049.73			Client
B	Pay off balance of credit cards (also eliminates recurring payment)	+ $2,150.00	<$9,000> to pay off		Client
C	Pay off furniture loan	+ $1,802.00	<$3,115> to pay off		Client

SAVINGS AND INVESTING MANAGEMENT

Savings and investing management recommendations require both an increase in savings and an increase in the emergency fund. Once the planner has calculated the savings rate (savings and reinvestment of dividends, interest, and capital gains, plus any employer match/ gross pay), the rate should equal 10 to 13 percent if the client only has one financial goal, that being financial security. As previously stated, if the client and family have multiple financial goals including retirement, college education, and lump-sum goals (e.g., new house or second home) the savings rate must be increased from the 10 to 13 percent to a savings rate necessary to achieve all of the goals. It is possible that the client can be more tax efficient by saving on a pre-tax rather than post-tax basis. Recall that the 10 to 13 percent savings rate is for a client who is between ages 25 and 35 years old.

The rule of thumb for an emergency fund is three to six months of non-discretionary cash flows. The astute planner understands however, that there are no absolutes in financial planning. The more difficult the labor market and the more unique the worker, the longer the worker may be out of work, which is one of the most significant risks addressed by the emergency fund. The following exhibit contains both savings and investing management recommendations. The cash flow impact is listed along with implementation responsibilities.

SAVING AND INVESTING RECOMMENDATIONS

EXHIBIT 3.21

	Recommendation	Annual Recurring Cost <Negative> + Positive	Non-Recurring Cost	Other	To Be Implemented by Client or Planner
A	Increase the 401(k) plan employee deferral by $1,000 from $2,000 to $3,000 (note that there is a tax savings of 15% and an increased employer match)	<$1,000> + $150		+ $500 Employer Match	Client
B	Add to the emergency fund to get to 3 months coverage		<$5,000>		Client

Other approach recommendations may include:

- executing estate planning documents (e.g., will, durable power of attorney for health care, advanced medical directive),
- managing the withholding of taxes (W-4),
- planning for income from part time jobs or changing jobs to earn more,
- annuitizing an annuity to create recurring income,
- planning to take required minimum distributions from IRAs and qualified plans, or
- deciding to begin drawing Social Security retirement benefits.

These additional recommendations require an analysis of the impact on cash flow and should be implemented in order of priority.

Ultimately, the cash flow approach yields a net recurring cash flow number and a net non-recurring cash flow number. If the cash flow impact is positive, all is well, but if the cash flow impact is negative (as it usually is), then the planner will need to look for the money with which to fund the client's recommendations. There are usually three possible sources of funding that may be available:

- savings from refinancing of a home mortgage,
- increased cash flows from adjusting the W-4 exemptions upward, and
- cash flows from the sale of assets on the balance sheet.

These may also be additional cash flows from raising deductibles on insurance policies. While it is often challenging to implement, there can be savings by reducing expenses. However, reducing expenses is generally challenging.

A lack of funding availability will limit the ability to immediately implement recommendations. However, since the recommendations are already prioritized, the planner can simply cut off implementing recommendations at the point where there is no additional funding remaining and later fund the remainder of the recommendations.

The cash flow approach should include:

- a mortgage refinance calculation, both pre and post recommendations;
- a current and projected tax analysis pre and post recommendations;
- a present value analysis of all needs pre recommendations; and
- a consideration of alternatives (e.g., delay retirement, include Social Security).

THE STRATEGIC APPROACH

The strategic approach is characterized by a client mission statement (e.g., to achieve financial security), a set of goals, and a set of objectives. Specifically, the planner can construct a plan driven by the client's mission statement. Then, a needs-driven list of client goals is created. From the list of goals, a detailed list of objectives is created that will all together result in the accomplishment of the mission of the client's financial planning. The planner creates a plan by reviewing relevant internal and external data and produces a plan for the long-run (the mission) with both short and intermediate accomplishment of goals and objectives. The plan incorporates capitalizing on a client's strengths (e.g., good salary or savings rate), overcoming a client's weaknesses (e.g., insufficient insurance), taking advantage of external opportunities, and mitigating external threats.

Note that the strategic approach takes into consideration needs versus wants. Needs are defined as those objectives required by law (e.g., auto liability insurance) or essential to make the financial plan successful (e.g., savings). Wants on the other hand are somewhat discretionary (e.g., purchase a new home). Planning using the strategic approach focuses on the needs-driven versus wants-driven priorities that can be successfully implemented following the design of a financial planning mission, goal and objective oriented arrangement.

The typical structure of the strategic approach to financial planning includes:

MISSION STATEMENT (AN ENDURING LONG-TERM STATEMENT)

- Financial Security – A formal statement of the purpose of the client's financial planning.

GOALS (BROADLY CONCEIVED GOALS)

- Adequate risk management portfolio
- Adequate savings rate for retirement and education
- Adequate emergency fund
- Adequate debt management
- Adequate investment portfolio
- Adequate estate plan

OBJECTIVES (NARROW MEASURABLE OBJECTIVES)

- **Risk Management** – A risk management objective may include the purchase or increase or decrease in coverage of life, disability, liability, or personal property insurance. In addition, the client may need to sell a liability associated asset that is either uninsured or uninsurable.
- **Debt Management** - Objectives associated with debt management may include reducing or eliminating high interest debt, paying off credit card debt, and reducing housing ratios to appropriate levels (HR1 = ≤ 28% and HR2 = ≤ 36%).
- **Tax Management and Emergency Fund** - For tax management purposes, the client may need to adjust income tax over withholding as an objective in order to meet other cash-required objectives. The client's emergency fund balance may need to be increased to meet at least a three to six month balance objective.
- **Savings and Investments** - Savings objectives may include creating, adjusting, or increasing amounts associated with retirement, education, or housing funding.

Quick Quiz 3.4

Highlight the answer to these questions:

1. The cash flow approach adjusts the cash flows on the balance sheet by forecasting what they would be after implementing all client recommendations.
   a. True
   b. False

2. The three areas the cash flow approach focuses on are the risk management, the debt management, and the savings and investment management cash flow areas of the client's financial planning.
   a. True
   b. False

3. The strategic approach is a needs versus wants directed financial plan based on the client's mission statement and goals.
   a. True
   b. False

False, True, True.

Changing the risk of an investment portfolio or either buying or selling existing investments to fit the financial planning mission are possible investment objectives.

- **Estate Plan** - Having estate documents prepared (will, durable power of attorney for financial matters and healthcare, advanced medical directive etc.) is an important objective.

If the planner chooses to start the financial planning process using the strategic approach method, it is likely that this approach will be followed by the use of the cash flow approach and recommendations. This ensures that implementation of the mission, goals, and objectives are feasible.

INVESTMENT ANALYSIS

- Risk tolerance analysis comparison of current implicit rate of return tool with PASS score.
- Investment performance analysis compares current rate of return to the expected rate of return based on the risk tolerance profile applied with the PASS score.

This chapter has discussed several approaches to analyzing a client's financial planning situation. Each of these approaches has advantages and limitations and most advisors will use a combination of approaches to complete a comprehensive financial plan.

Key Terms

Asset Accumulation Phase - This phase is usually from the early 20s to late 50s when additional cash flow for investing is low and debt to net worth is high.

Cash Flow Approach - This approach takes an income statement approach to recommendations. It uses the three-panel approach and uses a pro forma approach (as if) "to purchase" the recommendations thus driving down the discretionary cash flow. Next, positive cash flows or the sale of assets are identified to finance the recommendations which were purchased.

Conservation (Risk Management) Phase - This phase is from late 20s to early 70s, where cash flow assets and net worth have increased and debt has decreased somewhat. In addition, risk management of events like employment, disability due to illness or accident, and untimely death become a priority.

Current Ratio - This ratio provides insight as to the client's ability to meet short-term obligations should this debt all come due immediately.

Debt Management - The analysis of debt because clients can have too much debt, debt that has high interest rates, and debt that is generally not well managed. The analysis of debt includes calculating housing ratios 1 and 2 and comparing those to well established benchmarks (metrics) of 28% / 36%. In addition, the financial planner will evaluate the quality and the cost of each client's individual debt.

Debt Ratios - These ratios indicate how well the client manages debt.

Debt to Total Assets Ratio - This ratio reflects what portion of assets a client has financed or is owned by creditors.

Discretionary Cash Flows - Expenses which can be avoided in the event of loss of income.

Distribution (Gifting) Phase - This phase is from the late 40s to end of life and occurs when the individual has high additional cash flow, low debt, and high net worth.

Emergency Fund Ratio - This ratio determines how many months of non-discretionary cash flows (income statement item) the client can pay for out of current liquidity.

Financial Statement and Ratio Analysis Approach - The ratio analysis provides an opportunity to assess the client's strengths, weaknesses, and deficiencies when the client's ratios are compared to benchmark metrics. The ratio approach usually follows the pie chart approach and provides the planner with the actual ratios with which to compare the benchmarks in the metrics approach.

Key Terms

Housing Ratio 1 (HR1) - This ratio reflects the proportion of gross pay on an annual or monthly basis that is devoted to housing (principal, interest, taxes, and insurance). It does not include utilities, lawn care, maintenance, etc. The benchmark for housing ratio 1 is less than or equal to 28 percent.

Housing Ratio 2 (HR2) - This ratio combines basic housing costs (principal, interest, taxes, and insurance) with all other monthly debt payments, including automobile loans, student loans, bank loans, revolving consumer loans, credit card payments, and any other debt payments made on a recurring basis. The benchmark for housing ratio 2 should be less than or equal to 36 percent of gross pay on a monthly or annual basis.

Investment Assets to Gross Pay Ratio - This ratio assesses a retirement plan that persistently has clients saving 10 - 13 percent of gross pay for retirement.

Life Cycle Approach - This approach provides the planner with a brief overview of the client's financial profile which permits the planner to have a relatively focused conversation with the client. It is used very early in the engagement.

Liquidity Ratios - These ratios measure the ability to meet short-term obligations.

Metrics Approach - This approach uses qualitative benchmarks for a measurement of where a client's financial profile should be. When combined with the two-step/three-panel approach, metrics help establish objectives that are measurable compared to ratio analysis.

Net Worth to Total Assets Ratio - This ratio provides the planner with the percentage of total assets owned or paid for by the client.

Non-discretionary Cash Flows - Mostly fixed expenses which are required to be met monthly or annually regardless of loss of income.

Performance Ratios - These ratios determine the adequacy of returns on investments, given the risks taken.

Pie Chart Approach - This approach is a visual presentation of how the client spends money. It provides a broad perspective on the client's financial status and it is generally used after the collection of internal data and the preparation of financial statements.

Present Value of Goals Approach - This approach considers each short-term, intermediate-term, and long-term goal, determines their respective present value, then sums all of these together and treats the sum as an obligation (liability) that is then reduced by current resources of investment assets and cash and cash equivalents.

Key Terms

Ratios for Financial Security Goals - These ratios assess the progress that the client is making toward achieving long-term financial security goals.

Return on Assets (ROA) Ratio - This ratio measures total asset returns. This ratio must be used cautiously when the client is adding assets that are leveraged with debt.

Return on Investments (ROI) Ratio - This ratio calculates the rate of return on invested assets.

Return on Net Worth (RONW) Ratio - This ratio further refines the performance set of ratios to calculate the rate of return on net worth.

Risk Management - Recommendations usually are related to the insurance portfolio because perils (the cause of a loss) are event driven (e.g., untimely death) or unpredictable, and can occur at any time.

Savings and Investing Management - Management that results in recommendations that require both an increase in savings and an increase in the emergency fund. The savings rate (savings and reinvestment of dividends, interest, and capital gains, plus an employer match/gross pay) should equal 10 - 13 percent if the client only has one goal, that being financial security. If the client and family have multiple goals including retirement, college education, and lump-sum goals (e.g., new house or second home) the savings rate must be increased.

Savings Rate - A rate calculated by taking gross savings in dollars (including reinvestment of interest dividends, distributed (realized) capital gains, employee elective deferrals into 401(k), 403(b), and 457 plans plus any employer match), and any other savings divided by gross pay.

Strategic Approach - This approach uses a mission, goal, and objective approach considering the internal and external environment and may be used with other approaches.

Two-step / Three-panel Approach - A step-by-step approach where the client's actual financial situation is compared against benchmark criteria. It stresses the management of risk, seeks to avoid financial dependence, and promotes savings and investing to achieve financial independence.

1. List and define the eight approaches to financial planning analysis and recommendations.

2. List the three phases of the life cycle approach.

3. What are some of the questions that an income statement pie chart will answer?

4. What are some of the questions that a balance sheet pie chart will answer?

5. What is an advantage to using the pie chart approach with clients?

6. What are the liquidity ratios used in the financial statement and ratio analysis approach?

7. Discuss the difference between discretionary and non-discretionary cash flows.

8. List the four debt ratios used in the financial statement and ratio analysis approach.

9. Discuss the average savings rate for retirement funding and the average retirement withdrawal rate.

10. List the common performance ratios used in the financial statement and ratio analysis approach.

11. Define the two-step approach to financial planning.

12. What do the three panels of the three panel approach cover?

13. Why is the present value approach easy to understand at the completion of the analysis?

14. Discuss the usefulness of the metrics approach.

15. What is the usefulness of the cash flow approach to financial planning?

16. Define the strategic approach to financial planning.

17. Discuss whether capital gains, dividends, interest and other portfolio income should be part of the savings ratio.

MULTIPLE-CHOICE PROBLEMS

1. You have been working with your client, Brenda, for 3 months now. You developed a mission statement, goals, and objectives with the client. You are now constructing a plan that is led by the client's mission statement. Which approach to financial planning are you utilizing?

    a. Life Cycle Approach.
    b. Strategic Approach.
    c. Metrics Approach.
    d. Three Panel Approach.

2. During your work with your new client, Brian, you created several visual representations of how your client spends his money. Which approach to financial planning are you utilizing?

    a. Pie Chart Approach.
    b. Cash Flow Approach.
    c. Financial Statement Approach.
    d. Metrics Approach.

3. Rachel is 30 years old and single. She is healthy, has no children or pets. Rachel works as a human resources coordinator and earns approximately $40,000 per year. Due to her outstanding student loans, she has a fairly low net worth. She rents an apartment but does own her car outright. All of the following are likely insurance coverage needs, except?

    a. Life Insurance.
    b. Health Insurance.
    c. Disability Insurance.
    d. Liability Insurance.

4. David, 33 years of age, and Kristina, 34 years of age, are married with no children. They anticipate having children within the next five years. David and Kristina both have a graduate degree and student loans. They both have good jobs and earn about $110,000 together. They have mortgage debt of $190,000 on their home that is valued at $210,000. They have one car that they share that is not yet paid for and they anticipate buying a second car in the next year. They have no credit card debt. Which of the following is a likely current goal of the couple?

    a. Education Funding.
    b. Gifting.
    c. Charitable Gifting.
    d. Retirement Funding.

5. Paul and Lucy Martin are married and both are 65 years of age. Paul is retired from the military and receives a military pension as well as disability benefits from an injury he sustained during the Vietnam War. Lucy is a retired nurse. Lucy is fairly healthy, although she is borderline diabetic. Paul is diabetic and had a triple bypass several years ago. He also has extensive hearing loss in one ear that he sustained during his military service. Both have a family history of Alzheimer's disease. Their home is paid for and they just purchased a new car with financing. They have three self sufficient adult children and two grandchildren. The Martins have a life insurance policy on each of their adult children they purchased when the children were young with a death benefit of $10,000. All three policies have a cash value of $3,000 each. They also have policies on each other with a death benefit of $100,000. The Martins live comfortably with their pensions but do not have a lavish lifestyle or high net worth. Which of the following is their most important need/goal?

    a. They should immediately begin a gifting plan giving $13,000 to each child each year.
    b. They should investigate long-term care insurance.
    c. They should purchase additional life insurance immediately.
    d. They should purchase a disability policy on Paul.

6. Curtis is 60 years old. He plans to retire in a five years. He has amassed a net worth of $1,500,000 which he expects will sustain him during retirement. He is divorced with two adult independent children. Which phase of the life cycle is Curtis most likely in?

    a. Conservation Phase.
    b. Asset Accumulation Phase.
    c. Distribution Phase.
    d. Income Phase.

7. Your new client, Kerri, age 35, came into your office today. She provided you with the following information for the year:

    - Income - $100,000
    - Taxes - $18,000
    - Rent - $14,000
    - Living Expenses - $40,000
    - Credit Card Debt - $12,000
    - Savings - $5,000
    - Student Loan Payments - $5,000
    - Car Payment - $6,000

After receiving this information you created a pie chart to visually depict where her income was spent. Utilizing targeted benchmarks which of the following statements are you most likely to make during you next meeting?

    a. "You are spending too much on housing."

    b. "Your current living expenses are within the normal range."

    c. "Your mortgage and debt payments are within the normal range."

    d. "Your savings is low but still appropriate for your age."

8. Darrin and Kathi are both 44 years of age. They came to your office today and provided the following financial information:

- Cash and Cash Equivalents – $333,333
- Investment Assets - $333,333
- Personal Use Assets - $333,333
- Current Liabilities - $100,000
- Long-Term Liabilities – $250,000

After meeting with them you created a pie chart to visually depict their current balance sheet. Utilizing targeted benchmarks, which of the following statements are you most likely to make during you next meeting?

    a. "You are within all normal ranges for your age group."

    b. "Your net worth is too low."

    c. "Compared to the other assets, the investment asset holdings are appropriate."

    d. "Your long-term liabilities are excessive."

9. Which of the following is true?

    a. Debt ratios measure the ability to meet short-term obligations.

    b. Liquidity ratios indicate how well a client manages debt.

    c. Ratios for financial security determine the progress that he client is making toward achieving short-term financial security goals.

    d. Performance ratios determine the adequacy of returns on investments given the risks taken.

10. Ronnie visited your office today. He is 55 years of age. He is divorced and has two children. One child recently graduated from college and the other child is just entering into high school. Ronnie earns $350,000 a year as the operator of a very specific type of medical equipment. There are only two of these particular machines in existence. He has provided you the following financial information.

- Cash and Cash Equivalents – $100,000
- Annual Non-Discretionary Expenses - $300,000

Which of the following is true?

    a. Given all the facts and circumstances, Ronnie probably does not have an adequate emergency fund.

    b. Ronnie has an emergency fund ratio of 3 months.

    c. All individuals should have an emergency fund equal to 3 - 6 months.

    d. Disability insurance is irrelevant in determining whether the emergency fund ratio is appropriate.

11. Natalie and Brian visited your office today. They are both in their early 30s and have two children with one on the way. During your meeting they provide you with the following financial information:

- Gross Income per Year - $150,000
- Housing Costs per Year (P & I and T & I) - $24,000
- Other Debt Payments per Year - $50,000
- Total Assets – $300,000
- Total Debt – $200,000

Which of the following is true?

    a. The housing ratio 1 (basic) is within the normal range.

    b. The housing ratio 2 (broad) is within the normal range.

    c. The debt to total assets ratio is 25%.

    d. There are not enough facts to determine the net worth to total assets ratio.

12. Utilizing investment assets to gross pay benchmarks, which of the following individuals is likely on target with their investment assets?

    a. Jimmy age 55 earns $150,000 a year and has invested assets of $900,000.

    b. Sarah age 35 earns $30,000 a year and has invested assets of $15,000.

    c. Terry age 45 earns $60,000 a year and has invested assets of $150,000.

    d. Casey age 25 earns $40,000 a year and has invested assets of $9,000.

13. You currently manage Cody's investment portfolio. He provided you with the following information for the beginning and the end of the year:

- Investment Balance (beginning of the year) - $100,000
- Investment Balance (end of the year) - $115,000
- IRA Balance (beginning of the year) - $75,000
- IRA Balance (end of the year) - $82,000
- Net Worth (beginning of the year) - $1,000,000
- Net Worth (end of the year) - $970,000
- Annual Savings to IRA - $5,000

Which of the following statements is correct?

- a. The return on investments ratio is within the normal range.
- b. The return on the IRA ratio is 10%.
- c. The return on net worth ratio is 3.5%.
- d. The return on investments, return on IRA, and return on net worth ratios are all within the normal range.

14. Utilizing the three panel approach, which of the following would be evaluated in Panel 1 - Risk Management?

- a. Emergency Fund.
- b. Education Fund.
- c. Retirement Fund.
- d. Life Insurance.

15. Robin met with you recently to make some changes to her insurance needs. You have made several recommendations. Which of these recommendations will have a positive cash flow impact from an insurance perspective?

- a. Cancel an insurance policy.
- b. Change the name of the beneficiary on her life insurance policy.
- c. Increase coverage on an existing insurance policy.
- d. Lower the deductible on her auto insurance.

16. CJ bought the following assets this year. Which of these purchases would be considered "bad debt?"

- a. He purchased a slightly used car from a pre-owned dealer. The car has an estimated useful life of 3 years. He put down 5% and financed the balance over 72 months.
- b. He bought a new living room set that cost $5,000. He used his credit card that has a 23% APR. He paid the balance off within one month.
- c. He purchased a home for $500,000. He made a down payment of 20% and financed the remainder over 15 years.
- d. He took a CFP® Certification education program in order to meet the education requirement to take the CFP Certification Examination. He paid $5,000 for the program utilizing a student loan.

17. Adriana is an analyst at High Tech Hedge (HTH) where she earns $150,000 base salary with a bonus of $50,000. HTH sponsors a profit-sharing plan with a 401(k) feature and provides for a dollar for dollar match up to 3% of compensation. Her account had $10,000 of capital gains this year and dividends of $5,000. She defers $15,000 into the 401(k) plan. The employer made no additional contribution to the profit sharing plan. What is her savings rate this year?

    a. 10.5%.
    b. 14%.
    c. 18%.
    d. 31%.

18. Candice earns $85,000 working as an administrative assistant in a public company based in New York. The company provides a matching contribution in the 401(k) plan of 50% up to a maximum contribution of 4% of compensation. Her 401(k) plan account had $20,000 in it at the beginning of the year. She contributed $5,000 to the plan this year and the employer made the matching contribution before year end. The ending balance of the account is $30,000. What is her savings rate this year?

    a. 8.8%.
    b. 9.9%.
    c. 12.5%.
    d. 25%.

19. Janice earns $85,000 working as an administrative assistant in a public company based in New York. The company provides a matching contribution in the 401(k) plan of 50% up to a maximum contribution of 4% of compensation. Her 401(k) plan account had $20,000 in it at the beginning of the year. She contributed $5,000 to the plan this year and the employer made the matching contribution before year end. The ending balance of the account is $30,000. What is her return on her investments this year for the 401(k) account?

    a. 8.8%.
    b. 9.9%.
    c. 12.5%.
    d. 25%.

20. Mark and Caren are 36 years old and plan on retiring at age 62 and expect to live until age 95. They currently earn $250,000 and expect to need $200,000 in retirement. They also expect that Social Security will provide $40,000 of benefits in today's dollars at age 62. They are saving $15,000 each in their 401(k) plans and just had a baby boy they named Albert Rufus or AR for short. They want to save for AR's college education,

which they expect will cost $20,000 in today's dollars and they are willing to fund 4 years of college. They were told that college costs are increasing at 7% per year, while general inflation is 3%. They currently have $150,000 saved in each of their 401(k) plans and they are averaging a 9% rate of return and expect to continue to earn the same return over time. Based on this information, what should they do?

- a. They are currently saving more than they need and can reduce their annual savings.
- b. They are doing just fine and should continue doing what they are doing.
- c. They need to increase their annual savings by about $6,400 now that AR is born and they want to fund his college in addition to retirement.
- d. They should increase their annual savings by about 7.5 percent and they should be fine.

21. Jack and Jill are 41 years old and plan on retiring at age 65 and expect to live until age 95. They currently earn $200,000 and expect to need $100,000 in retirement. They also expect that Social Security will provide $24,000 of benefits in today's dollars at age 65. They are saving $20,000 each in their 401(k) plans and IRAs. Their son, Parker, is expected to go to college in 10 years. They want to save for Parker's college education, which they expect will cost $25,000 in today's dollars and they are willing to fund 4 years of college. They were told that college costs are increasing at 6% per year, while general inflation is 3%. They currently have $500,000 saved in total and they are averaging an 8% rate of return and expect to continue to earn the same return over time. Based on this information, what should they do?

- a. They have saved enough to fund retirement and Parker's education and can stop saving if they wish.
- b. They are doing just fine and should continue doing what they are doing.
- c. They need to increase their annual savings by about $12,000 now if they want to fund college in addition to retirement.
- d. They should increase their annual savings by about 10 percent and they should be fine.

Quick Quiz Explanations

Quick Quiz 3.1
1. False. The life cycle approach is a broad view of the client's financial profile and is useful to focus on further financial discussions when the planner only has partial information. The financial statement and ratio analysis approach utilizes the liquidity ratios to analyze the client's financial situation.
2. True.

Quick Quiz 3.2
1. True.
2. True.
3. False. The net worth to total asset ratio is a debt ratio that measures the total assets owned or paid for by the client. Another common performance ratio is the return on net worth that measures the change in net worth plus savings over a given period of time.
4. True.

Quick Quiz 3.3
1. True.
2. True.
3. False. While some benchmarks may be finite (housing ratios 1 and 2) other benchmarks will vary based on the client's goals (savings rate to include retirement funding, education funding and/or lump-sum funding) and age (risk tolerance for investment choices).

Quick Quiz 3.4
1. False. The cash flow approach adjusts the cash flows from the income statement for forecasting purposes.
2. True.
3. True.

Personal Financial Statements: Preparation and Analysis

LEARNING OBJECTIVES

After reading this chapter, you should be able to:

- Prepare a balance sheet and its components.
- Differentiate cash and cash equivalents, from investment assets, and personal use assets.
- Clarify the difference between short and long-term liabilities.
- Determine the methodology for evaluating various assets.
- Determine net worth.
- List sources of information to properly value assets and liabilities.
- Prepare a statement of income and expenses.
- Define a statement of net worth and a statement of cash flows.
- Construct statements of financial positions and cash-flow statements as applied to clients consistent with sound personal accounting standards.*
- Evaluate client financial statements using ratios and growth rates and by comparing them to relevant norms.*
- Describe the fundamental differences between corporate/business accounting practices and those appropriate for personal financial statements.*
- Describe the value of forecasting and importance of budgeting.
- Describe the purpose of financial statement analysis including vertical and horizontal analysis.
- Prepare a ratio analysis including liquidity ratios, debt ratios, ratios for financial security goals, and performance ratios.
- List appropriate benchmarks for each of the ratios calculated.
- Discuss the limitations of financial statement analysis including, estimating fair market value, inflation, hard to value assets, illiquidity of certain assets, and uncertain returns.
- Discuss sensitivity analysis and Monte Carlo analysis.

* CFP Board Resource Document - Student-Centered Learning Objectives based upon CFP Board Principal Topics.

INTRODUCTION

Personal financial statements are essential for the financial planner to evaluate a client's financial position and to review changes or trends in the client's financial position and financial performance. The planner can use the financial statements to prepare a **financial statement analysis**, which is the process of calculating financial ratios and comparing the actual ratios to industry established benchmarks. Financial statement analysis helps to reveal:

- how well a client is managing debt,
- whether the client is saving enough for retirement or education goals,
- whether the client's risks are adequately covered, and
- how well is the client able to meet short-term financial obligations.

The process of conducting financial statement analysis permits the financial planner to identify weaknesses in the client's financial position and performance. The planner can then develop an appropriate set of actions to respond to and improve upon those weaknesses.

Clients rarely have well prepared personal financial statements. A financial planner should be prepared to assist the client in the preparation of basic financial statements, including a balance sheet and a statement of income and expenses. This chapter explores the preparation and presentation of a client's financial statements. Financial statement

Key Concepts

Underline/highlight the answers as you read:

1. Identify the process and purpose of financial statement analysis.

2. Identify the common principal and supplementary financial statements used as part of the financial planning process.

analysis is also covered in this chapter so that the planner is prepared to evaluate the client's financial position and determine trends in the client's financial position and financial performance.

Preparing financial statements is the process of accounting for asset and liability balances, as well as for income and expenses for a client. For personal financial planning purposes, there are two principal financial statements and two supplementary financial statements.

Principal Financial Statements
- The Balance Sheet (A Statement of Financial Position or A Statement of Assets, Liabilities and Net Worth)
- The Income Statement (A Statement of Income and Expenses)

Supplementary Financial Statements
- The Statement of Net Worth
- The Cash Flow Statement

This chapter primarily focuses on the balance sheet and income statement. Although the statements of net worth and cash flow provide useful information, in practice they are rarely prepared for individuals. This chapter also builds on and expands the approaches and analysis discussed in Chapter 3, including the financial statement and ratio analysis, the pie chart approach, and the two-step / three panel approach.

BALANCE SHEET (STATEMENT OF FINANCIAL POSITION)

A **balance sheet**, or as commonly referred to, a statement of financial position represents the accounting for items the client "owns" (assets) and items that are "owed" (liabilities). The difference between assets and liabilities is the owner's equity (net worth). The balance sheet provides a snapshot of the client's assets, liabilities, and net worth as of a stated date. Typically, a balance sheet is dated "as of 12/31/xx," which represents the value of assets owned, liabilities owed, and resulting net worth at that particular moment in time.

Assets represent anything of economic value that can ultimately be converted into cash. Depending upon the client's intent regarding disposition of an asset, the asset is further classified into one of the following three categories as reflected on the balance sheet:

- Cash and Cash Equivalents (Current Assets)
- Investment Assets
- Personal Use Assets

Key Concepts

Underline/highlight the answers as you read:

1. Identify the main categories listed on a balance sheet.

2. Distinguish between cash and cash equivalents, investment assets, and personal use assets.

3. Distinguish between short-term liabilities and long-term liabilities.

CASH AND CASH EQUIVALENTS

Cash and cash equivalents (current assets) represent assets that are highly liquid, which means they are either cash or can be converted to cash (within the next 12 months) with little to no price concession from their current value. Cash and cash equivalents also represent very safe investments that are unlikely to lose value. An example of a current asset that can be converted to cash within the next 12 months is a certificate of deposit that matures in six months.

Typical assets included in cash and cash equivalents are:
- cash,
- checking accounts,
- money market accounts,
- savings accounts, and
- certificates of deposit (maturity is ≤ 12 months).

Since cash and cash equivalents represent highly liquid "safe" investments, it is important to the client's financial position and financial performance to maintain sufficient levels of cash and cash equivalents to meet liabilities that are due within the next 12 months. Benchmarks and ratios (discussed later in this chapter) assist the planner in determining whether the client is maintaining sufficient levels of cash and cash equivalents.

INVESTMENT ASSETS

Investment assets include appreciating assets or those assets being held to accomplish one or more financial goals. Typical assets included in this category are:

- retirement accounts (401(k) plans, profit sharing plans, IRAs, annuities),
- brokerage accounts,
- education funds,
- cash value in life insurance,
- business ownership interests, and
- the vested portion of any pension plan.

Investment assets are listed on the balance sheet at their current fair market value. As a financial planner, there are important issues to consider when preparing the investment assets section, including:

- ensuring that all investment assets are included (e.g., stock certificates sitting in a safety deposit box), and
- making sure that the current fair market value of the investment is properly determined.

One of the most difficult investment assets to value is ownership in a privately-held business. Unlike a publicly-traded company, there is no established market value for a privately-held company.

- Whether the basis for valuation is a professional opinion versus the owner's opinion,
- If a professional valuation, is it current (completed in the last six to nine months),
- A determination of whether goodwill is associated specifically with the business or with the owner (in the event that the owner leaves the business), and
- Whether the business will be sold to fund retirement and if so, what will be the characteristics of the funding (e.g., short versus long-term funding arrangement).

Important questions to consider with regard to the valuation of a private business include:

- Who prepared the valuation? The valuation may have been prepared by the owner himself, which could result in the value of the business being significantly overstated or understated. Alternatively, a professional valuation expert may have valued the business. However, it is important to understand the purpose of the valuation and to understand important assumptions of the valuation.
- How current is the valuation? The valuation may be accurate or it may be understated or overstated if the underlying assumptions no longer apply.
- Is goodwill associated with the business or with the owner? Some businesses are critically dependent on the owner and founder of the business and can be negatively impacted upon the owner's departure.
- Will the business be sold to fund retirement? It is important to understand how the owner is planning on selling a business and over what time period he expects the proceeds. This information will assist the planning in a conversation about any risks associated with the exit strategy.

For small business owners, a large portion of their net worth is usually invested in the business. Financial planners should be very cautious and conservative when valuing business ownership interests on the balance sheet. If the business is valued too high, the client's financial position will be too optimistic, perhaps resulting in a shortfall at retirement. If the business is valued too low, the client's financial resources may be improperly allocated, jeopardizing other financial goals.

PERSONAL USE ASSETS

Personal use assets are those assets that maintain the client's lifestyle. Examples of assets included in personal use assets are:

- personal residences
- automobiles
- furniture
- clothing
- boats
- jet skis
- vacation homes
- electronics (television, stereo, iPod, etc.)
- collectibles (art, antiques)

The value of personal use assets is usually determined by client estimation as opposed to appraisal. Anytime a financial planner is estimating the value of assets, it is always better to be conservative and not overvalue the assets. Financial statements and financial statement analysis provides insight into the client's financial position, performance, strengths and weaknesses, so accurately valuing assets is an important part of the process.

Although the value of personal use assets will impact net worth, financial planners are more concerned with cash, cash equivalents and investment assets when conducting financial statement analysis. As previously discussed, a properly valued business ownership interest is important, especially if the client is relying on the business to accomplish a retirement goal. However, the **exact** economic or fair market value of personal use assets is less important than the exact fair market value of investment assets. Reasonable and conservative estimates are usually adequate when valuing personal use assets, because the client will likely continue to use their personal use assets to maintain their lifestyle through the retirement years. It is important to periodically determine if there are any major changes in the value of personal use assets, such as the appreciation or depreciation of the primary residence, vacation property, and other high dollar amount items. Also, a question may arise as to whether an item is a personal use asset or an investment asset.

Holly purchases a $50,000 painting and hangs it on her wall. Is it a personal use asset or an investment asset? The determination is dependent on Holly's intent. Does she intend to leave it on her wall to show her family and friends or does she intend to hold it as an appreciating asset to be sold for a profit? If Holly's intent is to leave the painting on the wall to enjoy, then the painting should be classified as a personal use asset on the balance sheet. If Holly's intent is to hold the painting to advance future profit, then the painting should be classified as an investment asset.

EXAMPLE 4.1

LIABILITIES

Liabilities represent financial obligations that the client owes to creditors. To satisfy a liability, either a client-owned asset or some other economic benefit must be transferred to the creditor. A liability may be either a legal obligation or moral obligation that resulted from a past transaction. A legal obligation may be a mortgage or a car payment. If a client borrows money from the bank to purchase a house or a car, then there is a legal obligation to repay the loan (a liability). A moral obligation can result from the pledging of a donation to a charity or a not-for-profit entity. A pledge is not necessarily a legal obligation, but if intended to be honored, it does represent a financial liability.

EXAMPLE 4.2	Ivan is an alumnus of Florida State University and is a football season ticket holder. In April each year, Ivan pledges to contribute $1,000 to the boosters association in return for parking privileges at the football games. Ivan does not have to pay the $1,000 pledge until the end of the year. Ivan has a moral obligation to pay the $1,000, and it should be reflected as a liability on his balance sheet until the $1,000 pledge is paid (assuming he intends to pay the pledge). In some states, pledges to charitable organizations are legally enforceable debts.

Other types of liabilities include unpaid utility bills, credit card bills, insurance premiums that are due and any other debt obligations. Liabilities are valued at their current outstanding balance as of the date of the balance sheet. The current outstanding balance represents the amount owed to the creditor, including amounts for any bills that have been received but not yet paid. Liabilities are categorized according to the timing of when the liability is due or expected to be paid. The categories of liabilities are:

- short-term or current liabilities (expected to be paid within one year), and
- long-term liabilities (expected to be paid beyond one year).

Short-Term (Current) Liabilities

Short-term liabilities represent those obligations that are "current" in nature that are due or expected to be paid within the next 12 months ($\leq$ 12 months).   Examples of liabilities that are included in short-term or current liabilities are:

- Electric, gas, water, garbage, and sewage bills incurred, but not yet paid
- Principal portion of any debt obligations due within the next 12 months (mortgage and auto loan)
- Unpaid credit card bills
- Outstanding medical expenses
- Insurance premiums due
- Unpaid taxes

When reporting debts such as a mortgage or a car loan, only the principal portion of the loan that is due in the next 12 months is reported as a short-term or current liability. This treatment is the correct accounting methodology, but is rarely used by individuals in preparation of personal financial statements. Interest expense for the next 12 months is not reported on the balance sheet. If a loan is paid off today, the payoff amount would include the interest expense incurred since the last payment (plus the outstanding principal) because the interest expense is calculated for having a loan outstanding for the previous month. Liabilities only reflect the amount currently owed by the client. Since interest expense for the next 12 months has yet to be incurred, it is not reflected on the balance sheet.

Long-Term Liabilities

Long-term liabilities are financial obligations owed that are due and expected to be paid beyond the next 12 months. Long-term liabilities are usually the result of major financial purchases and resulting obligations that are amortized over multiple years. Examples of liabilities that are included under long-term liabilities are:

- primary residence loans (mortgage),
- vacation home loans (mortgage),
- automobile loans,
- student loans, and
- any other type of loan or promissory note.

When reporting the outstanding balance of a loan, the current portion of the liability should be reported separately from the long-term portion of the liability. This allows the financial planner to make a comparison between current assets and current liabilities and to evaluate the client's liquidity status and ability to meet short-term financial obligations.

EXAMPLE 4.3

Lisa has a $300,000 mortgage on her house, with a 30-year term at 6% interest. She expects to pay a total of $21,583.81 this upcoming year, including $3,684.04 in principal reduction and $17,899.77 in interest expense. The loan should be properly categorized as a liability on the balance sheet as follows:

Short-Term Liabilities
Mortgage on Primary Residence = $3,684.04

Long-Term Liabilities
Mortgage on Primary Residence = $296,315.96

Total Liabilities = $300,000.00

Note: Even though Lisa knows how much interest expense she will be paying in the next 12 months ($17,899.77), it is not reported as a liability until the interest expense is incurred. If the interest is paid as incurred, it will not be recorded as a liability but rather simply be reflected in the monthly or annual income statement. She is not legally obligated to pay the interest until it accrues each month. Another way to think about this is to consider that she could pay $300,000 today to retire the debt and thus, avoid the interest next year.

VALUING ASSETS AND LIABILITIES

As previously stated, it is important that assets reflect their fair market value and that liabilities are stated at their current outstanding principal balance as of the date of the balance sheet.

NET WORTH

The **net worth** of the client as reflected on the balance sheet represents the amount of total equity (assets - liabilities = net worth) a client has accumulated as of the date of the balance sheet. When evaluating a client's financial position, net worth is an important consideration because it represents an absolute dollar amount reflective of a client's financial position. A positive net worth may imply the client has done a good job of saving, investing, and managing debt. A negative net worth implies that the client is insolvent and potentially facing bankruptcy.

Unfortunately, due to the real estate crisis in years 2008 to 2010 and the high home foreclosure rate, a negative net worth is a reality for many households. In 2009 alone, California experienced a 20 percent decline in real estate values, which was in addition to the 19 percent decline in 2008. For many homeowners this collapse has led to the value of their homes declining significantly below the outstanding debt on the homes. In other words, they are "upside down" on their mortgage (also known as underwater). For some clients who have accumulated savings and investment assets of $200,000 to $300,000, it is possible to have a negative net worth simply due to the decline in real estate values.

Quick Quiz 4.1

Highlight the answer to these questions:

1. The client's balance sheet represents all income earned less expenses incurred for the period being covered.
    a. True
    b. False

2. Cash and cash equivalents are assets that are highly liquid and are either cash or can be converted to cash within the next 12 months.
    a. True
    b. False

3. Investment assets are those assets that help to maintain the client's lifestyle.
    a. True
    b. False

4. Long-term liabilities represent client financial obligations that are owed to creditors beyond the next 12 months.
    a. True
    b. False

False, True, False, True.

Exhibit 4.1 illustrates a balance sheet for Mr. and Mrs. Zacker that reflects the three types of assets, short-term liabilities, long-term liabilities and the resulting net worth.

EXHIBIT 4.1

Statement of Financial Position
Mr. and Mrs. Zacker
Balance Sheet as of 12/31/12

Assets			Liabilities and Net Worth			
Current Assets			**Current Liabilities**			
JT	Cash & Checking	$5,000	W	Credit Cards	$5,000	
JT	CD Maturing in 6 months	$25,000	H	Auto # 1	$5,000	
JT	Money Market	$50,000	W	Auto # 2	$6,000	
			JT	Personal Residence	$10,000	
Total Current Assets		$80,000	**Total Current Liabilities**			$26,000
Investment Assets			**Long-Term Liabilities**			
H	401(k) Plan	$30,000	H	Auto # 1	$14,000	
W	IRA	$50,000	W	Auto # 2	$17,000	
JT	Brokerage Account	$100,000	JT	Personal Residence	$450,000	
W	Value of Business Interests	$500,000				
W	Education Savings	$75,000	**Total Long-Term Liabilities**			$481,000
Total Invested Assets		$755,000				
			Total Liabilities			$507,000
Personal Use Assets						
JT	Personal Residence	$500,000	**Total Net Worth**			$1,008,000
JT	Furniture, Clothing	$125,000				
H	Auto # 1	$25,000				
W	Auto # 2	$30,000				
Total Personal Use Assets		$680,000				
Total Assets		$1,515,000	**Total Liabilities and Net Worth**			$1,515,000

H = Husband Owns
W = Wife Owns
JT = Jointly owned by husband and wife

The balance sheet formula is: Assets = Liabilities + Net Worth.

Alternatively, we can restate the formula, such that: Assets – Liabilities = Net Worth.

These formulas help us understand how financial transactions impact a client's net worth.

EXAMPLE 4.4

Lisa buys a house for $400,000. She makes a $50,000 down payment and finances the balance with a mortgage. How is her net worth impacted from this transaction?

	Assets	- Liabilities	= Net Worth
Cash and Cash Equivalents	($50,000)		($50,000)
Personal Use Assets	+ $400,000		+ $400,000
Mortgage on New House		$350,000	($350,000)
Net Impact	$350,000	- $350,000	= $0

Lisa exchanges one asset ($50,000 cash) for another ($400,000 home) and increases her liabilities ($350,000 mortgage). Therefore, her net worth is not impacted by purchasing the house. However, as time goes by, the increase or decrease in the value of the house will impact her net worth as will the reduction in the principal obligation of the mortgage. The principal reduction is funded most by income that would otherwise have increased another asset category on the balance sheet, such as cash or investments.

EXAMPLE 4.5

One year ago, Elaine purchased a house for $400,000. Today, the house is worth $425,000 and she has reduced her outstanding mortgage principal by $10,000. What is the impact to Elaine's net worth?

	Assets	- Liabilities	= Net Worth
Personal Use Assets	+ $25,000		$25,000
Reduction in Outstanding Mortgage Balance		($10,000)	+ $10,000
Net Impact	$25,000	- ($10,000)	= $35,000

Elaine's net worth increased as a result of the value of her house increasing ($25,000), plus she has paid down her mortgage throughout the year. Since her liabilities have decreased by $10,000, the two actions result in Elaine's net worth increasing by a total of $35,000.

Laureen, her husband and 5 children went on vacation to Disney World for one week. Laureen spent $7,000 on the family vacation and paid for it with money in her savings account. What is the impact to her net worth?

EXAMPLE 4.6

	Assets	- Liabilities	= Net Worth
Cash and Cash Equivalents	($7,000)		($7,000)
Net Impact	($7,000)	-	= ($7,000)

Laureen's net worth has decreased by the $7,000 she spent on the vacation. Although they are certainly priceless, she cannot capture the good times and memories she has from the vacation and report them on her balance sheet.

SOURCES OF INFORMATION

In order to properly and accurately prepare personal financial statements, the financial planner needs source documents from the client to properly value assets and liabilities. Source documents include:

- ✓ bank statements,
- ✓ brokerage statements,
- ✓ loan amortization schedules, and
- ✓ tax returns.

ACCOUNT OWNERSHIP

As part of the balance sheet presentation, it is important to disclose how an asset or liability is titled (owned). The most common forms of ownership are:

- ✓ Fee Simple
- ✓ Tenancy in Common
- ✓ Joint Tenancy with Right of Survivorship (JTWROS)
- ✓ Tenancy by the Entirety
- ✓ Community Property

Key Concepts

Underline/highlight the answers as you read:

1. Distinguish between property owned fee simple and tenancy in common.

2. Distinguish between property owned JTWROS and tenancy by the entirety versus community property.

3. Identify the importance of footnotes to financial statements.

Below is an explanation of the types of ownership. However, Chapter 14 provides a more thorough discussion of this topic.

Fee simple ownership is the complete ownership of property by one individual who possesses all ownership rights associated with the property, including the right to use, sell, gift, alienate, convey, or bequeath the property. Typically, a car is owned fee simple and is titled in the name of one person. When preparing a balance sheet for a husband and wife, (H) is used to designate the asset or liability belongs to the husband only and (W) is used if the asset or liability belongs to the wife only.

Tenancy in common is an interest in property held by two or more related or unrelated persons. Each owner is referred to as a tenant in common. Tenancy in common is the most common type of joint ownership between nonspouses. Each person holds an undivided, but not necessarily equal, interest in the entire property.

Joint Tenancy with Right of Survivorship (JTWROS) is typically how a husband and wife own joint property. Joint tenancy is an interest in property held by two or more related or unrelated persons called joint tenants. Each person holds an undivided, equal interest in the whole property. A right of survivorship is normally implied with this form of ownership, and at the death of the first joint tenant, the decedent's interest transfers to the other joint tenants outside of the probate process according to state titling law. Probate is the process whereby the probate court retitles assets and gives creditors an opportunity to be heard and stake a claim to any assets to satisfy outstanding debts. Because of this right of survivorship, joint tenancy is often called joint tenancy with right of survivorship.

Quick Quiz 4.2

Highlight the answer to these questions:

1. Fee Simple ownership is an interest in property held by two or more related or unrelated persons.
   a. True
   b. False

2. If property is owned tenancy by the entirety or as community property then probate is avoided.
   a. True
   b. False

False, False.

Tenancy by the entirety is similar to property owned as JTWROS between a husband and wife because property ownership is automatically transferred to the surviving spouse upon death. The two tenants own an undivided interest in the whole asset. However, the ownership cannot be severed without the consent of the other spouse.

Community property is a civil law statutory regime under which married individuals own an equal undivided interest in all property accumulated during their marriage. During marriage, the income of each spouse is considered community property. Property acquired before the marriage and property received by gift or inheritance during the marriage retains its status as separate property. However, if any separate property is commingled with community property, it is often assumed to be community property. The states following the community property regime are Arizona, California, Idaho, Louisiana, Nevada, New Mexico, Texas, Washington, and Wisconsin. Community property does not usually have an automatic right of survivorship feature although some states, including Texas and California, have a survivorship option.

As previously indicated, an important distinction between fee simple, tenants in common, and sometimes community property versus JTWROS and tenancy by the entirety is that property owned by the former will pass through probate at the death of the owner. Property owned JTWROS and tenancy by the entirety avoids probate and the decedent's interest transfers automatically. Property owned in a revocable trust would be listed on the balance sheet as trust assets.

FOOTNOTES TO THE FINANCIAL STATEMENTS

Footnotes are an important source of information regarding the financial statements. Footnotes listed on financial statements can provide information such as how the asset or liability is owned. For example, it may state whether the asset is owned individually or jointly. In addition, footnotes can provide information regarding a client's purchase price of an asset, the date the asset or liability was acquired, how the value of an asset was determined and much more. When reviewing financial statements, it is important that the financial planner always read the footnotes.

STATEMENT OF INCOME AND EXPENSES

A **statement of income and expenses** (income statement) represents all income earned or expected to be earned by the client, less all expenses incurred or expected to be incurred during the time period being covered. The heading of the statement of income and expenses identifies the person or persons that the statement applies to, the type of financial statement, and the time period covered by the statement. To indicate the reporting period, the time period is generally listed as "For the Year Ended 12/31/xx" or for "January 1, 2013 – December 31, 2013." Although financial planners typically prepare and work with annual financial statements, the income statement can also be prepared for a monthly or quarterly period of time.

Key Concepts

Underline/highlight the answers as you read:

1. Identify the main categories listed on the statement of income and expenses.

2. Identify examples of recurring income.

3. Identify examples of savings contributions.

4. Distinguish between variable and fixed expenses.

5. Determine how net discretionary cash flow is calculated.

INCOME

Examples of recurring **income** accounts earned by the client are:

- Salary
- Interest
- Dividend
- Pension
- Retirement Account Withdrawal
- Business Income
- Alimony Received

SAVINGS CONTRIBUTIONS

Along with expenses, recurring **savings contributions** must be reported on the statement of income and expenses. Examples include savings contributions to the following types of accounts:

- 401(k) plan
- 403(b) plan
- IRA (Traditional or Roth)
- Education Savings
- Any other type of savings account contributions
- Reinvested dividends, interest, or capital gains

EXPENSES

Recurring **expenses** represent those items that are paid regularly by the client during the time period being presented. Examples of expenses accounts include:

- Mortgage Principal and Interest
- Utilities
- Taxes
- Insurance
- Telephone
- Water
- Cable or Satellite
- Internet
- Cell Phone

Variable and Fixed Expenses

Expenses can be divided into variable and **fixed expenses**. There is less discretion over fixed expenses in the short term. Examples of fixed expense accounts include:

- Mortgage Payment
- Car Payment
- Boat Payment
- Student Loan Payment
- Property Taxes
- Insurance Premiums
- Federal and State Income Taxes Withheld
- Social Security Payments Withheld

Variable expenses are more discretionary than fixed expenses over the short term. A client has more discretion over the amount of variable expenses and this area often presents an opportunity for savings if variable expenses are closely monitored and controlled. Examples of variable expense accounts include:

- Entertainment Expenses
- Vacation Expenses
- Travel Expenses
- Charitable Contributions (may or may not be considered variable or discretionary)

The statement of income and expenses is a compromise in accounting. Note that cash transactions that are non-recurring are not included or reported on the statement of income and expenses. Examples of cash transactions that are non-recurring include:

- the sale of stock,
- an employer's contribution to a retirement plan,
- giving or receiving a gift of cash, or
- an inheritance.

In addition, transactions that are noncash, non-recurring changes in the balance sheet are not reported on the statement of income expenses. Noncash, non-recurring changes in the balance sheet include:

- gifting (or receiving) stock, and
- gifting (or receiving) personal use assets and would only be reported in a statement of changes in net worth.

It is precisely because of the lack of perfection in the income statement that a planner should consider the balance sheet and the income statement together. The two documents provide a significantly more complete picture of the client's financial situation than either document alone.

Quick Quiz 4.3

Highlight the answer to these questions:

1. Main categories listed on the income statement include income, savings contributions, assets, and expenses.
   a. True
   b. False

2. Net discretionary cash flow represents the amount of cash flow still available after all savings, expenses, and taxes have been paid.
   a. True
   b. False

3. The client's income statement can be prepared from the client's W-2 information, credit card statement, and other billing statement information.
   a. True
   b. False

False, True, True.

NET DISCRETIONARY CASH FLOWS

Net discretionary cash flow represents the amount of cash flow available after all savings, expenses, and taxes have been paid. The net discretionary cash flow formula is a result of the statement of income and expenses.

The net discretionary cash flow formula from the income statement is:

Income – Savings – Expenses – Taxes = Net Discretionary Cash Flow

Net discretionary cash flow is a critical item when analyzing the statement of income and expenses. Net discretionary cash flow can be positive, negative, or equal to zero. A positive discretionary cash flow indicates that income is greater than savings, taxes, and expenses. This financial situation creates an opportunity for additional savings to accomplish a financial goal, retire debt, or purchase more comprehensive insurance. A negative net discretionary cash flow is one of the most important weaknesses a financial planner must mitigate against. A negative discretionary cash flow indicates that gross income is less than savings, taxes, and expenses. This financial situation requires steps to reduce expenses, taxes, or savings or to increase income. While a client can likely tolerate a negative net discretionary cash flow for a short period of time, ultimately, a negative net discretionary cash flow can lead to financial disaster, including bankruptcy in the most extreme cases.

The following is a statement of income and expenses for Mr. and Mrs. Zacker as expected for a complete year. This statement provides an efficient method of determining where the Zacker's income is being spent or saved during the year.

EXHIBIT 4.2

Statement of Income and Expenses Mr. and Mrs. Zacker Statement of Income and Expenses Expected (Approximate) for 2013		
CASH INFLOWS		**Totals**
Salary - Husband	$58,000	
Salary - Wife	$100,000	
Total Cash Inflows		**$158,000**
CASH OUTFLOWS		
Savings		
Husband's 401(k) Plan	$5,000	
Wife's 401(k) Plan	$10,000	
IRA Contribution	$5,000	
Education Savings (529 Plan)	$8,000	
Total Savings		**$28,000**
Debt Payments		
Personal Residence (mortgage)	$35,000	
Auto - Husband	$7,000	
Student Loans	$2,500	
Total Debt Payments		**$44,500**
Living Expenses		
Utilities	$3,500	
Gasoline for Autos	$3,000	
Lawn Service	$3,000	
Entertainment	$6,000	
Vacations	$4,000	
Church Donations	$2,000	
Food	$8,000	
Auto Maintenance	$2,500	
Telephone	$3,000	
Clothing	$6,000	
Total Living Expenses		**$41,000**
Insurance Payments		
HO Personal Residence	$4,500	
Auto Premiums	$2,000	
Life Insurance Premiums	$1,000	
Personal Liability Umbrella Premium	$500	
Total Insurance Payments		**$8,000**
Taxes		
Federal Income Taxes Withheld	$15,000	
State Income Taxes Withheld	$7,500	
Social Security Taxes	$9,000	
Property Tax Personal Residence	$4,000	
Total Taxes		**$35,500**
Total Savings, Expenses and Taxes		**$157,000**
NET DISCRETIONARY CASH FLOW		$1,000

SOURCES OF INFORMATION

Preparing a statement of income and expenses during the initial meetings with a client can be difficult because all sources of information may not yet be available. During the initial or subsequent meetings with a client, the planner should obtain the following documents with which to prepare the statement of income and expenses:

- W-2s (reports income and deferred retirement savings),
- credit card statements (provides insight to expenses and spending, with year-end statements being especially informative),
- billing statements (such as utilities, telephone, satellite, internet, water),
- bank statements (especially those with bill payments), and
- Federal and state income statements.

Frequently, a client will not have all of the above documents and may not have complete records of expenses for an entire year. In these situations, financial planners may need to "back into" expenses over the time period being presented. In other words, if the planner knows the increase in cash and cash equivalents over the time period being presented, along with the client's income, the planner can calculate the total amount spent on taxes, savings, and expenses over that time period.

<table>
<tr><td>EXAMPLE 4.7</td><td>Jan's salary last year was $125,000. According to her bank statements dated 12/31 from the previous two years, her cash and cash equivalents increased by $5,000. Her financial planner can assume that $120,000 ($125,000 - $5,000) was spent by Jan on taxes, savings to retirement plans, education, variable, and fixed expenses. The planner's objective now is to fill in the details of the statement of income and expenses to determine how Jan spent the $120,000 last year.</td></tr>
</table>

PROJECTED INCOME STATEMENTS

It is extremely useful to clients that expect a change in life or lifestyle to have the financial planner prepare a projected income statement for the period just following the projected lifestyle change (i.e., children go to college or client retires). Projected financial statements of this sort can help identify shortfalls in cash or excess net-discretionary cash flows.

STATEMENT OF NET WORTH

The purpose of the **statement of net worth** is to explain changes in net worth between two balance sheets by reporting financial transactions that are not reported on the income statement or other financial statements. Example of transactions that would appear on the statement of net worth are:

- Giving or receiving property other than cash
- Inheriting property other than cash
- Employer contributions or matches to retirement savings accounts
- Appreciation or depreciation of assets such as a primary residence, investments, auto, jewelry, etc.

The formula for the statement of net worth is:

> Beginning balance of net worth (from the January 1st balance sheet)
> + additions (appreciation of assets, receiving a gift or inheritance)
> - subtractions (giving gifts other than cash)
> _____
> = Ending balance of net worth (from the December 31st balance sheet)

Few clients will have a statement of net worth and very few financial planners will actually prepare a statement of net worth for a client. The statement of net worth is a supplementary financial statement that captures and reports transactions that affect net worth that are otherwise not reported on the two principal statements (balance sheet and statement of income and expenses).

Key Concepts

Underline/highlight the answers as you read:

1. Recognize the purpose of a statement of net worth.

2. Recognize the purpose of a cash flow statement.

3. Determine what forecasted financial statements should reflect.

4. Identify the importance of budgeting and the steps to the budgeting process.

CASH FLOW STATEMENT

The purpose of the **cash flow statement** is to explain how cash and cash equivalents were used or generated between the period of two balance sheets. The cash flow statement is a supplementary financial statement of non-recurring transactions not reported on the statement of income and expenses. Recall that the income statement only captures monthly or annually recurring income and expenses. The major sections of the cash flow statement includes how nonrecurring cash transactions were used or generated from investment activities and financing activities.

CASH FLOW STATEMENT CATEGORY EXAMPLES

EXHIBIT 4.3

INVESTING ACTIVITIES
• Purchase or sale of a personal use asset, such as a car or house for cash (decrease in cash)
• Purchase or sale of an investment asset, such as a mutual fund or stock (increase or decrease)
• Contributing to a retirement or education savings account (decrease in cash)
• Receiving or making gifts of cash (increase or decrease)
• Cash inheritances (increase in cash)
FINANCING ACTIVITIES
• Principal reduction of any loans (decrease in cash)
• Taking out any new loans (increase in cash)
• Paying off credit card balances (decrease in cash)

The result of all the transactions on the cash flow statement reflects how cash was used or generated between two balance sheets. Few clients will have a cash flow statement and very few financial planners will actually prepare a cash flow statement.

FORECASTING

After preparing the initial financial statements, the planner will work with the client to overcome any weaknesses and accomplish financial goals. Recommendations may include purchasing additional life insurance, contributing more to savings, or retiring debt. The planner should prepare forecasted balance sheets and a statement of income and expenses for next year, three years from now and five years from now. The forecasted financial statements should reflect the following:

- **Implementation of recommendations.** For example, if the planner recommends increasing 401(k) plan savings, the forecasted financial statements should indicate the amount of savings and balance of the 401(k) plan for the next year, the next three years, and the next five years.
- **Inflation adjustment for expenses.** Certain expenses are likely to increase over the next five years, such as insurance premiums, utilities, gasoline for autos, groceries, clothing, etc. The financial planner should prepare forecasted statements of income and expenses based on a historical inflation rate that is likely to continue for the next five years. Fixed interest rate debt payments are not impacted by inflation, so no inflation adjustments should be made to fixed rate loans. However, if the client has any variable interest rate loans that are likely to increase over the next five years, adjustments to the forecasted income statement should include increased debt payment for variable rate loans.
- **Inflation adjustment for income.** If the client expects to receive salary increases each year, those salary adjustments should be reflected in the forecasted statement of income and expenses.
- **Other adjustments.** Other adjustments to the forecasted financial statements may include:
    - Whether the client is retiring and experiencing major changes to their income in the next five year. The financial planner should prepare forecasted financial statements to reflect withdrawing retirement assets to generate income. The possibility of the client living on reduced income during retirement should be evaluated and forecasted in financial statements.
    - Whether the client is expected to retire debt in the next five years. The financial planner should reflect the retiring of debt on the balance sheet to determine the impact on the balance sheet, net worth, and discretionary cash flow on the statement of income and expenses.

- Whether the client expects to begin paying for college education expenses, and how the tuition payments and living expenses for the child impact the financial statements. The planner should reflect the draw down on any college savings and the increased expenses on the income statement associated with a child living away from home while at college.
- Whether the client expects to borrow money for a car, house, boat, college education, etc. The planner should incorporate the debt into the forecasted balance sheet and statement of income and expenses.

Once the financial planner has prepared forecasted financial statements, the planner can conduct financial statement analysis on the forecasted financial statements. Financial statement analysis is discussed later in this chapter.

IMPORTANT OF BUDGETING

The purpose in creating a financial budget is to evaluate the client's spending and savings behavior, and to establish a spending and savings plan to assist the client in achieving their financial goals. Typically, clients are resistant to preparing or using a budget because historically they have been unsuccessful at following budgets. Actual expenses turn out to be higher than they anticipated and they become frustrated by their inability to save or spend as anticipated.

There are three important tips to being successful in preparing and using a budget.
- First, be realistic with spending behavior. It is easy to overlook credit card expenses for shopping or dining out. Credit cards are an easy way to "blow the budget."
- Secondly, budget a line item expense for miscellaneous expenses and unforeseen expenses. Miscellaneous expenses include gifts at the holidays, car repairs, house repairs, traffic tickets, kid's sporting events, etc. As clients get older, the miscellaneous expense item tends to grow.
- Finally, being successful with a budget takes practice. The more often a client prepares a budget and compares their actual spending to a budget, the better they will

Quick
Quiz 4.4

Highlight the answer to these questions:

1. The statement of net worth explains changes to net worth such as employer contributions to retirement savings accounts.
   a. True
   b. False

2. The cash flow statement captures recurring income and expenses for the period being reported.
   a. True
   b. False

3. Forecasted financial statements should reflect recommendations and inflation adjusted income and expenses.
   a. True
   b. False

True, False, True.

become at budgeting. The first few budgets are likely to be unrealistic and not very accurate. Over time, the client will become more comfortable with budgeting and more realistic with their spending, savings, and miscellaneous expenses.

The budgeting process consists of the following steps:
- Establish goals with the client, such as saving for retirement, education, or a lump-sum purchase (a second home, new car, or boat).
- Determine the client's income for a time period, which could be monthly or annually. Income is based on a client's past earnings and expected income for the time period that is being budgeted.
- Determine expenses, both fixed and variable, for the time period of the budget.
- Determine whether the net discretionary cash flow is positive or negative. If net discretionary cash flow is positive, no immediate action is necessary. If net discretionary cash flow is negative, expenses must be reduced or income needs to increase.
- Present expenses as a percentage of income for the time period being presented. At this point, it is necessary to compare expenses as a percentage of income for previous budgets as well. Generally, the expenses as a percentage of income should be level or decreasing over time.

FINANCIAL STATEMENT ANALYSIS

Financial statements are designed to assist users in identifying key relationships and trends within the client's financial situation. Financial statement analysis is a critical part of the "analyze and evaluate" step of the financial planning process, as the financial planner is measuring a client's progress towards attaining financial goals, assessing the client's ability to meet short-term obligations, and overall debt management.

Financial statement analysis is accomplished by conducting vertical analysis, horizontal analysis, and ratio analysis. Trends will help the planner identify if the client is moving in the right direction and is making adequate progress towards attaining the financial goals. It also allows the planner to glean information that the client may not have communicated to the planner that is important to the overall financial plan and to the ability to meet future financial objectives.

Key Concepts

Underline/highlight the answers as you read:

1. Identify the purpose of financial statement analysis and the tools used in the comparative financial statement analysis.

2. Identify the purpose of ratio analysis.

COMPARATIVE FINANCIAL STATEMENT TOOLS

Vertical Analysis

Vertical analysis lists each line item on the income statement as a percentage of total income and presents each line item on the statement of financial position (balance sheet) as a percentage of total assets. The restated percentage is known as a common size income statement or balance sheet. Vertical analysis compares each line item using a common size analysis and strips away the absolute dollar size of the line item. The financial planner is then able to compare trends for each percentage over time. Using the Zacker's statement of financial position from last year (Exhibit 4.1) and the current year (below), the planner is able to prepare a vertical analysis of their balance sheet (Exhibit 4.4).

BALANCE SHEET AS OF 12/31/2013

Statement of Financial Position
Mr. and Mrs. Zacker
Balance Sheet as of 12/31/13

Assets			Liabilities and Net Worth			
Current Assets			**Current Liabilities**			
JT	Cash & Checking	$5,025	W	Credit Cards	$4,985	
JT	CD Maturing in 6 months	$25,125	H	Auto # 1	$4,985	
JT	Money Market	$51,000	W	Auto # 2	$5,700	
			JT	Personal Residence	$9,700	
Total Current Assets		$81,150	**Total Current Liabilities**			$25,370
Investment Assets			**Long-Term Liabilities**			
H	401(k) Plan	$30,090	H	Auto # 1	$12,600	
W	IRA	$49,900	W	Auto # 2	$14,450	
JT	Brokerage Account	$106,000	JT	Personal Residence	$438,750	
W	Value of Business Interests	$475,000				
W	Education Savings	$77,250	**Total Long-Term Liabilities**			$465,800
Total Invested Assets		$738,240				
			Total Liabilities			$491,170
Personal Use Assets						
JT	Personal Residence	$505,000	**Total Net Worth**			$1,007,445
JT	Furniture, Clothing	$125,025				
H	Auto # 1	$22,500				
W	Auto # 2	$26,700				
Total Personal Use Assets		$679,225				
Total Assets		$1,498,615	**Total Liabilities and Net Worth**			$1,498,615

H = Husband Owns
W = Wife Owns
JT = Jointly owned by husband and wife

EXHIBIT 4.4 **BALANCE SHEET VERTICAL ANALYSIS EXAMPLE**

Mr. and Mrs. Zacker			
Current Assets	**12/31/12**	**12/31/13**	**Difference**
JT - Cash & Checking	0.33%	0.34%	+0.01%
JT - CD Maturing in 6 months	1.65%	1.68%	+0.03%
JT - Money Market	3.30%	3.40%	+0.10%
Total Current Assets	**5.28%**	**5.42%**	**+0.13%**
Investment Assets			
H - 401(k) Plan	1.98%	2.01%	+0.03%
W – IRA	3.30%	3.33%	+0.03%
JT - Brokerage Account	6.60%	7.07%	+0.47%
W - Value of Business Interests	33.00%	31.70%	-1.31%
W - Education Savings	4.95%	5.15%	+0.20%
Total Invested Assets	**49.83%**	**49.26%**	**-0.57%**
Personal Use Assets			
JT - Personal Residence	33.0%	33.7%	+0.69%
JT - Furniture, Clothing	8.25%	8.34%	+0.09%
H - Auto #1	1.65%	1.50%	-0.15%
W - Auto #2	1.99%	1.78%	-0.20%
Total Personal Use Assets	**44.89%**	**45.32%**	**-0.44%**
Total Assets	**100.00%**	**100.00%**	
Current Liabilities			
W - Credit Cards	0.33%	0.33%	-0.00%
H - Auto #1	0.33%	0.33%	-0.00%
W - Auto #2	0.40%	0.38%	-0.02%
JT - Personal Residence	0.66%	0.65%	-0.01%
Total Current Liabilities	**1.72%**	**1.69%**	**-0.02%**
Long-Term Liabilities			
H - Auto #1	0.92%	0.84%	-0.08%
W - Auto #2	1.12%	0.96%	-0.16%
JT - Personal Residence	29.70%	29.28%	-0.43%
Total Long-Term Liabilities	**31.74%**	**31.08%**	**-0.67%**
Total Liabilities	**33.46%**	**32.77%**	**-0.69%**
Total Net Worth	**66.54%**	**67.23%**	**+0.69%**

EXHIBIT 4.5

Mr. and Mrs. Zacker		
CASH INFLOWS	For 2013	Totals
Salary-Husband	36.71%	
Salary-Wife	63.29%	
Total Cash Inflows		**100%**
CASH OUTFLOWS		
Savings		
Husband's 401(k) Plan	3.16%	
Wife's 401(k) Plan	6.33%	
IRA Contribution	3.16%	
Education Savings (529 Plan)	5.06%	
Total Savings		**17.71%**
Available for Expenses		**82.29%**
Debt Payments		
Personal Residence (mortgage)	22.15%	
Auto-Husband	4.43%	
Student Loans	1.58%	
Total Debt Payments		**28.16%**
Living Expenses		
Utilities	2.22%	
Gasoline for Autos	1.90%	
Lawn Service	1.90%	
Entertainment	3.80%	
Vacations	2.53%	
Church Donations	1.27%	
Food	5.06%	
Auto Maintenance	1.58%	
Telephone	1.90%	
Clothing	3.80%	
Total Living Expenses		**25.96%**
Insurance Payments		
HO Personal Residence	2.85%	
Auto Premiums	1.27%	
Life Insurance Premiums	0.63%	
Personal Liability Umbrella Premium	0.32%	
Total Insurance Payments		**5.07%**
Taxes		
Federal Income Taxes Withheld	9.49%	
State Income Taxes Withheld	4.75%	
Social Security Taxes	5.70%	
Property Tax Personal Residence	2.53%	
Total Taxes		**22.47%**
Total Savings, Expenses and Taxes		**81.66%**
NET DISCRETIONARY CASH FLOW		**0.63%**

The vertical analysis for the Zackers (Exhibits 4.4 and 4.5) does not reveal any significant issues on the balance sheet or income statement. However, some important observations include a savings rate of 17.7 percent, debt payments of 28 percent and taxes of 22 percent.

Horizontal Analysis

Horizontal analysis lists each item as a percentage of a base year and creates a trend over time. For example, on the income statement, income may be stated over a six-year period from 2009 to 2014, but is reflected as a percentage of 2009 income. Expenses, taxes and savings are all stated as a percentage of a base year amount.

EXAMPLE 4.8

Eric earned $100,000 in 2009 and experienced salary increases each year for the past 6 years, such that his salary in 2013 is now $128,000.

Horizontal analysis of his income is as follows:

Year	2009	2010	2011	2012	2013	2014
Income	100%	105%	115%	125%	127%	128%

The horizontal analysis of income would indicate that Eric's income has increased each year for six years and income in 2014 is 28% more than it was in 2009. Horizontal analysis will be conducted for each line item on the income statement and balance sheet. This analysis provides the financial planner and client with a trend that identifies potential problems or demonstrates improved financial performance.

Consider an abbreviated horizontal analysis for Eric's income and golf expenses over the past five years.

Year	2009	2010	2011	2012	2013	2014
Income	100%	105%	115%	125%	127%	128%
Golf Expenses	100%	110%	120%	130%	140%	150%

Although Eric's income has increased 28% over the past 6 years, his golf expenses have increased 10% each year for the past 6 years (for a total increase of 50%). This past year, his golf expenses were 150% of his golf expenses five years ago. So, if Eric's golf expenses were $10,000 in 2009, he paid $15,000 in golf expenses in 2014. Considering that his income increased by $28,000 on a pre-tax basis, he has spent approximately 18% ($5,000 ÷ $28,000) of his additional income on this one expense item that increased $5,000 since 2009 Horizontal analysis provides us insight to a potentially problematic trend in income or expenses that needs to be addressed.

RATIO ANALYSIS

Ratio analysis is the process of calculating key financial ratios for a client, comparing those metrics to industry benchmarks and then evaluating possible deficiencies. Ratio analysis was introduced in Chapter 3 while discussing the financial statement analysis and the two step / three panel approach to evaluating a client's financial position. This section of Chapter 4 provides a more in-depth discussion of financial statement and ratio analysis. Some overlap exists with topics covered in Chapter 3, for the purpose of providing a thorough discussion of the benefits and application of ratio analysis. Ratio analysis provides a historical perspective of the client's financial position and performance because the ratios are calculated based on historical financial statements. Ratio analysis is both an art and a science. The art portion is being able to interpret the results that will become the basis for recommendations the financial planner makes to the client. The science portion is being able to calculate the financial ratios. When conducting ratio analysis, there is a need for a comparative analysis (benchmarks) to gain perspective about the client's ability to meet short and long-term obligations and goals.

Ratio analysis provides insight to underlying conditions that may not be apparent directly from the financial statements. This type of analysis expresses the relationship between selected items from the income statement and the balance sheet and provides additional information for the financial planner to use in building the client's financial plan.

Limitations

Any single financial ratio has limited use because a single ratio by itself has very little meaning. The ratio begins to take on meaning when it is used for comparison purposes over time to identify trends and when combined with information and insight from other ratios.

Ratios become more meaningful when compared to benchmarks. Benchmarks provide a rule of thumb for analyzing client status as it relates to industry standards. Note that the individual circumstances may cause any benchmark to be inappropriate for a given client. It is important that the financial planner recognize circumstances that may cause a benchmark to be inappropriate and to make adjustments accordingly.

Quick Quiz 4.5

Highlight the answer to these questions:

1. Vertical analysis is a tool for financial statement analysis using a common size comparison of a statement's line items.
   a. True
   b. False

2. Ratio analysis is the process of calculating financial ratios that are compared to example benchmarks for meaningful interpretation of the client's actual financial status.
   a. True
   b. False

3. The emergency fund ratio measure how many times the client can satisfy their short-term liabilities.
   a. True
   b. False

True, True, False.

BRANDON AND JILL BOWDEN

Brandon (age 40) and Jill (age 43) are married with two children, Cole (age 9) and Owen (age 5). Brandon is a vice president with a health care company and Jill manages their family and household. Brandon's salary is $124,000 per year and he contributes three percent of his salary to a 401(k) plan retirement plan while his employer matches $0.50 for every $1 contributed, up to three percent of his salary.

Bowden's Financial Goals
- Save for retirement.
- Save for their children's college education.
- Transfer all assets to their children at Brandon and Jill's death.

Brandon and Jill Bowden's balance sheets for the beginning of this year and the end of the current year are below.

EXHIBIT 4.6   **BALANCE SHEET AS OF 12/31/2012**

Statement of Financial Position
Brandon and Jill Bowden
Balance Sheet as of 12/31/2012

ASSETS			LIABILITIES AND NET WORTH			
Current Assets			**Current Liabilities**			
			(current portion of long-term debt)			
JT Cash & Checking	$3,500		W Credit Cards	$20,000		
JT Money Market	$6,650		W Auto # 2	$4,588		
			JT Personal Residence	$3,812		
Total Current Assets		$10,150	**Total Current Liabilities**			$28,400
Investment Assets			**Long -Term Liabilities**			
H 401(k) Plan	$61,800		W Auto # 2	$16,176		
H Education Savings	$11,500		JT Personal Residence	$342,633		
H High Tech Stock[1]	$7,500					
Total Investment Assets		$80,800	**Total Long-Term Liabilities**			$358,809
Personal Use Assets			**Total Liabilities**			$387,209
JT Personal Residence[2]	$390,000					
H Furniture, Clothing	$95,000		**Total Net Worth**			$222,241
H Auto # 1	$9,000					
W Auto # 2[3]	$24,500					
Total Personal Use Assets		$518,500				
Total Assets		**$609,450**	**Total Liabilities and Net Worth**			**$609,450**

1. Brandon and Jill intend to use this investment for retirement savings.
2. The house was purchased on 1/1/2012 for $375,000 with a loan for $350,000 financed over 30 years at 7%.
3. The car was purchased on 1/1/2012 for $30,000 with $5,000 down, financed over 5 years at 8%.

H = Husband Owns
W = Wife Owns
JT = Jointly owned by husband and wife

LOAN CALCULATION EXPLANATION TO EXHIBIT 4.6

AUTO LOAN CALCULATION		HOME LOAN CALCULATION	
(Present Value) PV =	$25,000	(Present Value) PV =	$350,000
(Term) N =	60	(Term) N =	360
(Interest Rate) i =	$\frac{8\%}{12}$ = 0.667	(Interest Rate) i =	$\frac{7\%}{12}$ = 0.583
(Future Value) FV =	0	(Future Value) FV =	0
(Payment) PMT =	$506.91	(Payment) PMT =	$2,328.56
12/31/11 Principal Balance =	$20,764	12/31/11 Principal Balance =	$346,444
12/31/12 Principal Balance =	$16,176 (Long-Term Liability)	12/31/12 Principal Balance =	$342,632 (Long-Term Liability)
	$4,588 (Current Liability)		$3,812 (Current Liability)

BALANCE SHEET AS OF 12/31/2013

EXHIBIT 4.7

Statement of Financial Position
Brandon and Jill Bowden
Balance Sheet as of 12/31/2013

ASSETS			LIABILITIES AND NET WORTH		
Current Assets			**Current Liabilities**		
JT Cash & Checking	$3,000		W Credit Cards	$25,000	
JT Money Market	$5,000		W Auto # 2	$4,968	
			JT Personal Residence	$4,088	
Total Current Assets		$8,000	**Total Current Liabilities**		$34,056
Investment Assets			**Long-Term Liabilities**		
H 401(k) Plan	$75,000		W Auto # 2	$11,208	
H Education Savings	$15,000		JT Personal Residence	$338,544	
H High Tech Stock[1]	$5,000				
Total Investment Assets		$95,000	**Total Long-Term Liabilities**		$349,752
Personal Use Assets			**Total Liabilities**		$383,808
JT Personal Residence[2]	$400,000				
H Furniture, Clothing	$100,000		**Total Net Worth**		$249,192
H Auto # 1	$8,000				
W Auto # 2	$22,000				
Total Personal Use Assets		$530,000			
Total Assets		**$633,000**	**Total Liabilities and Net Worth**		**$633,000**

1. Brandon and Jill intend to use this investment for retirement savings.
2. The house was purchased on 1/1/2012 for $375,000 with a loan for $350,000 financed over 30 years at 7%.
3. The car was purchased on 1/1/2012 for $30,000 with $5,000 down, financed over 5 years at 8%.

   H = Husband Owns
   W = Wife Owns
   JT = Jointly owned by husband and wife

Loan Calculation Explanation to Exhibit 4.7

Auto Loan Calculation			Home Loan Calculation		
(Present Value) PV =	$25,000		(Present Value) PV =	$350,000	
(Term) N =	60		(Term) N =	360	
(Interest Rate) i =	$\frac{8\%}{12} = 0.667$		(Interest Rate) i =	$\frac{7\%}{12} = 0.583$	
(Future Value) FV =	0		(Future Value) FV =	0	
(Payment) PMT =	$506.91		(Payment) PMT =	$2,328.56	
12/31/13 Principal Balance =	$16,176		12/31/13 Principal Balance =	$342,632	
Principal Balance =	$11,208	(Long-Term Liability)	Principal Balance =	$338,544	(Long-Term Liability)
	$4,968	(Current Liability)		$4,088	(Current Liability)

STATEMENT OF INCOME AND EXPENSES

EXHIBIT 4.8

Statement of Income and Expenses Mr. and Mrs. Bowden Statement of Income and Expenses for Past Year and Expected (Approximate) For This Year		
CASH INFLOWS		**Totals**
Brandon's Salary	$124,000	
Total Cash Inflows		$124,000
CASH OUTFLOWS		
Savings		
Brandon's 401(k) Plan	$3,720	
Education Savings (529 Plan)	$2,000	
Total Savings		$5,720
Debt Payments		
Personal Residence (mortgage)	$27,943	
Jill's Auto	$6,083	
Credit Cards[1]	$7,000	
Total Debt Payments		$41,026
Living Expenses		
Utilities	$5,000	
Gasoline for Autos	$4,000	
Lawn Service	$1,500	
Entertainment	$3,000	
Vacations	$2,500	
Church Donations	$1,000	
Food	$6,000	
Auto Maintenance	$1,000	
Telephone	$2,660	
Clothing	$3,000	
Total Living Expenses		$29,660
Insurance Payments		
HO Personal Residence	$4,500	
Auto Premiums	$2,000	
Life Insurance Premiums	$1,000	
Total Insurance Payments		$7,500
Taxes		
Federal Income Taxes Withheld	$24,800	
State Income Taxes Withheld	$6,200	
Social Security Taxes	$8,420	
Property Tax Personal Residence	$3,500	
Total Taxes		$42,920
Total Savings, Expenses and Taxes		$126,826
NET DISCRETIONARY CASH FLOW		($2,826)

1. The Bowden's make the minimum monthly payments on some of their credit cards.

CATEGORIES OF FINANCIAL RATIOS

Financial statement ratios are classified according to the analysis and insight provided by calculating the ratio. Financial statement ratios are broken down into the following categories:

- **Liquidity Ratios** – Measures the amount of cash and cash equivalents relative to short-term liabilities.
- **Debt Ratios** – Measures how well the client is managing their overall debt structure.
- **Ratios for Financial Security Goals** – Measures the client's progress towards achieving long-term financial security goals.
- **Performance Ratios** – Measure the return a client is generating on assets.

The remaining portion of this chapter discusses the ratios within each category, how the ratio is calculated, associated ratio benchmarks, and how to interpret and apply meaning to each ratio.

Key Concepts

Underline/highlight the answers as you read:

1. Identify the key liquidity ratios used in financial planning ratio analysis.

2. Identify the key debt ratios used in financial planning ratio analysis.

3. Identify the key ratios for financial security goals used in financial planning ratio analysis.

4. Identify the key performance ratios used in financial planning ratio analysis.

5. Determine the various limitations on financial statement analysis.

LIQUIDITY RATIOS

Liquidity ratios provide the financial planner insight into the client's ability to meet short-term obligations with current assets. Liquidity ratios include the emergency fund and current ratio.

EMERGENCY FUND RATIO

The **emergency fund ratio** measures how many months of non-discretionary expenses the client has in the form of cash and cash equivalents or current assets.

The formula for the emergency fund is:

$$\text{Emergency Fund} = \frac{\text{Cash and Cash Equivalents}}{\text{Monthly Non-discretionary Cash Flows}}$$

Current assets are represented by cash and cash equivalents on the balance sheet.

Non-discretionary cash flows are those expenses that exist even if a job or other income source is lost. Non-discretionary cash flows are typically fixed expenses. Examples of non-discretionary expenses include:

- All debt payments (mortgage, car loan, student loan, boat loan, credit cards)
- Utilities
- Insurance premiums
- Property taxes
- Food

Travel, entertainment, and payroll taxes are examples of expenses that would be minimized or eliminated if a job or other income source was lost.

The benchmark for the emergency fund is three to six months and is important to provide for the following risks:

- Job loss
- Elimination period on a disability policy
- Unexpected expenses

Job Loss

The emergency fund can be used to pay monthly non-discretionary expenses in the event of job loss. Often times, it can take months to find a job, especially during periods of a recession like recently experienced during 2008 – 2012 and also during periods of high unemployment.

For clients that have a one wage earner family, the client should be on the high end of the benchmark, such as five to six months. If a financial planner has a client in a two wage earner family, the client can be on the low end of the benchmark, such as three months. With a two wage earner family, if one spouse is still working, a three month emergency fund can pay 50 percent of the monthly non-discretionary expenses, while the working spouse can pay the other 50 percent of the monthly non-discretionary expenses. This assumes, of course, that the spouse that is still employed earns enough to pay 50 percent of the monthly non-discretionary expenses. The planner can help guide the client to an appropriate amount of emergency fund based on individual circumstances.

Elimination Period on a Disability Policy

It is also important for the financial planner to make sure the emergency fund is equal to the elimination period of any disability policy. A disability policy is designed to provide income replacement if the insured is unable to work because of sickness or accident. The elimination period of a disability policy is the amount of time the insured must wait before collecting benefits under the policy. If the elimination period is 180 days, the client must wait six months before collecting benefits under the policy. If the client is unable to work for six months, the emergency fund should be at least six months to satisfy the elimination period of the disability policy.

Unexpected Expenses

A comprehensive financial plan will also account for the unexpected. Often times it is the unanticipated risk that can cause the greatest problems. A financial plan that accounts for the unexpected will better position a client to achieve their financial goals. An emergency fund can help mitigate the impact of unexpected expenses. Examples of unexpected expenses that a planner should anticipate include:

- Large deductibles for a homeowners' insurance policy. Many earthquake and flood policies have the insured paying a percentage of the total loss as a deductible.
- Large deductibles for private health insurance. To help reduce the cost of health insurance, some families purchase high deductible health insurance policies ($5,000 or more deductible per person).
- House repairs or additions for dependent family members that may move into the client's home.
- Large auto repairs, household repairs, etc.

Mitigating Circumstances

Although the emergency fund is important, the planner should keep the emergency fund in perspective when evaluating the client's financial position. Many competing needs may arise, and the client will have limited financial resources to satisfy all of the needs. The financial planner and client must prioritize which competing needs to address first and which needs to postpone until a later time. If the client has access to a home equity line of credit or loan provisions as part of a 401(k) plan or other qualified retirement plan, contributing to the emergency fund may be a lesser priority than purchasing health insurance.

Brandon and Jill Bowden's Emergency Fund

The Bowden's monthly non-discretionary expenses (cash outflows) from the Income Statement are:

Property Tax on Personal Residence	$3,500
Debt Payments (Personal residence, auto, credit cards)	$41,026
Utilities	$5,000
Gasoline for Autos	$4,000
Church Donations	$1,000
Food	$6,000
Auto Maintenance	$1,000
Telephone	$2,660
Insurance Premiums	$7,500
	$71,686

$$\text{Emergency Fund} = \frac{\text{Cash and Cash Equivalents}}{\text{Monthly Non-discretionary Cash Flows}}$$

$$\text{Emergency Fund} = \frac{\$10,150}{(\$71,686 \div 12)} = \frac{\$10,150}{\$5,974} = 1.70 \text{ months (2012)}$$

$$\text{Emergency Fund} = \frac{\$8,000}{(\$71,686 \div 12)} = \frac{\$8,000}{\$5,974} = 1.34 \text{ months (2013)}$$

The Bowden's have an emergency fund of less than two months. This is a weakness that requires planning to overcome in order to have an emergency fund of three to six months. As a one-income family, the Bowden's should have a 6-month emergency fund. However, that would require them to increase their cash and cash equivalents from $8,000 to $35,844 (6 x $5,974 in monthly non-discretionary expenses). Initially a 3-month emergency fund may be the most appropriate recommendation because there may be other sources of emergency funding, such as a home equity line of credit or borrowing provisions from Brandon's 401(k) plan. In addition, it is likely there will be other financial weaknesses the financial planner must help Brandon and Jill overcome, so increasing the emergency fund to three months in the short term will be sufficient. As the financial planner works with Brandon and Jill in the coming years, an evaluation can be made as to when increasing their emergency fund to six months is an appropriate recommendation.

CURRENT RATIO

The **current ratio** measures how many times the client can satisfy their short-term liabilities with cash and cash equivalents. The current ratio is:

$$\text{Current Ratio} = \frac{\text{Cash \& Cash Equivalents}}{\text{Current Liabilities}}$$

Current assets represent cash and cash equivalents on the balance sheet. Current liabilities represent short-term liabilities on the balance sheet.

For the current ratio the industry benchmark is 1.0 – 2.0, with the higher the ratio the better. It is also helpful if the financial planner tracks the current ratio over a period of years to determine the trend. If the ratio becomes too large, it could signify that the client needs to reallocate some current assets to more growth oriented investment assets. If the ratio is decreasing, it will likely lead to a lower emergency fund as well. If the planner addresses the emergency fund first, it will likely lead to an improved current ratio.

Brandon and Jill Bowden's Current Ratio
The current ratio is:

$$\text{Current Ratio} = \frac{\text{Cash \& Cash Equivalents}}{\text{Current Liabilities}} = \frac{\$10,150}{\$28,400} = 0.36 \text{ (2012)}$$

$$\text{Current Ratio} = \frac{\text{Cash \& Cash Equivalents}}{\text{Current Liabilities}} = \frac{\$8,000}{\$34,056} = 0.23 \text{ (2013)}$$

The Bowden's have approximately 20 percent (for 2013) of their current liabilities in the form of current assets. As the Bowden's begin to overcome their emergency fund deficiency, the current ratio will improve at the same time. For example, if the Bowden's increase their emergency fund to three months, they will have $17,922 (3 x $5,974 in monthly non-discretionary expense) in cash and cash equivalents. Assuming their current liabilities do not change, the new current ratio would be 0.53 ($17,922 ÷ $34,056). By increasing the Bowden's emergency fund from 1.34 to 3.0 months, the current ratio would almost double from 0.23 to 0.53.

DEBT RATIOS

The debt management section of ratio analysis provides insight into how well the client is managing debt (too much or the right amount) and the quality of that debt.

Housing Ratio1 (Basic)

Housing ratio 1 was established by the banking industry to determine if the amount of income and housing debt that a client is carrying is appropriate and affordable. If a borrower meets housing ratio 1, he likely will qualify for a conventional mortgage loan at a favorable rate.

The formula for housing ratio 1 is:

$$\text{Housing Ratio 1} = \frac{\text{Housing Costs}}{\text{Gross Pay}} \leq 28\%$$

Housing Costs = PITI
P = Principal
I = Interest
T = Taxes
I = Insurance (home)
Gross Income = Gross pay (before taxes)

Note: The PITI and gross income can be stated on a monthly or annual basis. The PITI and gross income should be stated on the same terms, either both on a monthly basis or both an annual basis.

Brandon and Jill Bowden's Housing Ratio 1

The Bowden's housing costs (PITI and other debt) from the Income Statement are:

Principal and Interest on Personal Residence	$27,943
Property Taxes – Personal Residence	$3,500
Insurance HO Personal Residence	$4,500
	$35,943
Total monthly housing costs ($35,943 ÷ 12)	**$2,995.25**

Their monthly gross pay is:

Total monthly gross pay (Brandon's Salary $124,000 ÷ 12)	**$10,333**

$$\text{Housing Ratio 1} = \frac{\text{Housing Costs}}{\text{Gross Pay}} \leq 28\%$$

$$\text{Housing Ratio 1} = \frac{\$2,995.25}{\$10,333} = 28.9\%$$

The Bowden's housing ratio 1 is 28.9 percent, which is slightly above the industry benchmark of 28 percent. The actual ratio of 28.9 percent is near the benchmark of 28 percent, so the Bowdens may be able to wait one or two years and allow for Brandon's salary increases to bring the ratio down to the benchmark.

For example, if Brandon receives a five percent raise each year for the next two years, the Bowden's housing ratio 1 would be:

$$\text{Next Year} = \frac{\$2,995.25}{\$10,333 \times 1.05} = 27.6\%$$

$$\text{Next 2 Years} = \frac{\$2,995.25}{\$10,333 \times 1.05 \times 1.05} = 26.3\%$$

This is a good example of how forecasted financial statements provide the financial planner with insight as to how financial ratios will be impacted by salary adjustments, inflation, or the implementation of planning recommendations. Care must be exercised, however, when assuming the ratio will "fix itself" based on future salary adjustments. The client may not receive the salary adjustment, the salary adjustment may or may not be as much as forecasted, or increasing expenses may offset the increased salary. In this example, not only would the financial planner be concerned about Brandon actually receiving the salary adjustment, but there is also concern that the property taxes or insurance premiums may increase and offset the increased salary. In this situation, the front end ratio would continue being higher than 28 percent. It is important to monitor the ratio and consider other alternatives such as potentially decreasing the insurance premium or potentially refinancing the mortgage, if possible.

Housing Ratio 2 (Broad)

Housing ratio 2 is also referred to as housing ratio 1 plus all other debt. This ratio was established by the banking industry to determine if the total amount of debt that a client is carrying is appropriate for a given level of income. If housing ratio 2 is met, the borrower will likely qualify for a conventional loan at a favorable rate.

The formula for housing ratio 2 is:

$$\text{Housing Ratio 2} = \frac{\text{Housing Costs + Other Debt Payments}}{\text{Gross Pay}} \leq 36\%$$

Housing Costs = PITI
P = Principal
I = Interest
T = Taxes
I = Insurance (home)
Gross Income = Gross pay before taxes

All other debt payments include:
- Car loan payments
- Boat loan payments
- Student loan payments
- Credit cards payments
- Principal and interest on vacation or second homes
- Any other monthly recurring debt

Recurring debt payments do not include utilities, car insurance, property insurance on a second home or property taxes on a second home.

Note: It is important that PITI, all other debt payments and gross income are stated on the same terms, either all on a monthly basis or all on an annual basis.

Brandon and Jill Bowden's Housing Ratio 2
From their Statement of Income Expenses, this is the Bowden's PITI plus all other recurring debt:

The Bowden's housing costs (PITI) from the Income Statement are:

Principal and Interest on Personal Residence	$27,943
Property Taxes – Personal Residence	$3,500
Insurance HO Personal Residence	$4,500
Jill's Auto	$6,083
Credit Cards	$7,000
	$49,026
Total monthly PITI plus other debt payments ($49,026 ÷ 12)	**$4,086**

Their monthly gross pay is:

Total monthly gross pay (Brandon's Salary $124,000 ÷ 12)	**$10,333**

$$\text{Housing Ratio 2} = \frac{\text{Housing Costs} + \text{Other Debt Payments}}{\text{Gross Pay}} \leq 36\%$$

$$\text{Housing Ratio 2} = \frac{\$4,086}{10,333} = 39.5\%$$

The Bowden's housing ratio 2 of 39.5 percent is slightly above the industry benchmark of 36 percent. Since the housing ratio 1 of 28.9 percent is so close to the industry benchmark of 28 percent, the issue with the housing ratio 2 is related to all other recurring debt. The financial planner should make recommendations to reduce the all other debt payments by either using assets on the balance sheet to retire debt or by increasing monthly debt payments.

Debt to Total Assets Ratio

The **debt to total assets ratio** indicates the percentage of assets that is owned by creditors. The lower this ratio the better, as it indicates that the assets owned have a low amount of debt owed.

To calculate the debt to total assets ratio:

$$\text{Debt to Total Assets Ratio} = \frac{\text{Total Debt}}{\text{Total Assets}} = \text{Benchmark Depends on Client Age}$$

Brandon and Jill Bowden's Debt to Total Assets Ratio

As of 12/31/12

$$\text{Debt to Total Assets Ratio} = \frac{\$387,209}{\$609,450} = 0.6353$$

As of 12/31/13

$$\text{Debt to Total Assets Ratio} = \frac{\$383,808}{\$633,000} = 0.6063$$

The total debt to total assets ratio has improved for the Bowdens over the past year. The financial planner should continue monitoring the debt to total asset ratio trend which should continue decreasing. As housing ratio 2 decreases from retiring all other recurring debt, the debt to total assets ratio will continue to improve.

Quality of Debt

The quality of debt assessment is based on the relationship between the term of the debt and the useful life of the asset. The quality of debt can be classified into three categories: good, reasonable, and bad debt. Any time the useful life of the asset far exceeds the term of the debt, the debt is considered good debt. Examples of good debt include a 3-year car loan, a 15-year home mortgage or any type of debt from student loans. Reasonable debt includes obligations where the useful life of the asset equals the term of the debt. Examples of reasonable debt include a 5-year car loan or a 30-year mortgage. Bad debt implies that the term of the debt far exceeds the useful life of the asset. For example, if a client charges a two-week summer vacation on a credit card, then makes the minimum payments for the next 20 years, the term of the debt when making minimum payments far exceeds the two-week useful life of the vacation. When an assessment as to the quality of the debt has been made, the financial planner can develop recommendations for the client to implement (such as retiring the bad debt).

Quick
Quiz 4.6

Highlight the answer to these questions:

1. The housing ratio 1 industry bench-mark is less than or equal to 28 percent.
   a. True
   b. False

2. The savings rate calculation includes reinvestments and the employer match.
   a. True
   b. False

3. The quality of debt assessment is based on the comparison of the term of the debt on an asset and the useful life of the asset.
   a. True
   b. False

True, True, True.

When working with a client who has bad debt, such as credit card or consumer debt, the planner should develop a plan to help the client retire the debt as soon as possible and within a reasonable amount of time. Consider a client who has $15,000 in credit card debt with an interest rate of 19 percent. The initial minimum payment may be $500, but as each month passes, the minimum payment will continue to decline. By simply making the minimum payment, it can take between 16 to 20+ years to retire this debt. Instead, the client should continue to make a level payment of $500 each month and will be able to retire the debt in less than five years. Another alternative to retiring bad debt includes using assets on the balance sheet to pay down debt. It is the financial planner's responsibility to evaluate the appropriate mix of using assets to pay down debt or retiring the debt within a reasonable amount of time by making monthly payments.

An assessment of the quality of Brandon and Jill's debt reveals that their home is financed over 30 years and the car is financed over five years. The term of the debt on the house and car match the useful life of both assets, so those debt items are reasonable debt. However, according to the Statement of Income and Expenses, the Bowden's are making the minimum monthly payment on their credit cards. It will take almost 15 years to payoff the credit card balances by making the minimum monthly payment, which is clearly bad debt. An important recommendation for the Bowdens is to retire the credit card debt within a reasonable amount of time.

In the event a financial planner discovers that the client is making minimum payments on credit card debt, it would seem reasonable to recalculate housing ratio 2 using a payment more representative of a reasonable term (e.g., 36 months). Credit card minimum payments may require a payback period of 16 to 20+ years. If the credit card debt payment is understated in housing ratio 2, the ratio may indicate everything is below the benchmark when really this is a distortion.

For example, three alternatives for paying off a balance of $2,000 on credit cards charging 20 percent interest are:

Alternative	Balance	Payment	Years	Number of Payments	Total Paid Back
A	$2,000	$34.78	16	192	$6,677.76
B	$2,000	$52.99	5	60	$3,179.26
C	$2,000	$74.32	3	36	$2,675.78

It would seem prudent that if the client were actually paying under alternative A, the planner would recalculate housing ratio 2 using the payment under alternative C.

Net Worth to Total Assets Ratio

$$\text{Net Worth to Total Assets Ratio} = \frac{\text{Net Worth}}{\text{Total Assets}} = \text{Benchmark Depends on Client Age}$$

The **net worth to total assets ratio** is the compliment of the debt to assets ratio described above. These two should add up to one. This ratio provides the planner with the percentage of total assets owned or paid for by the client. It is not surprising that this would be 20 percent for young people and up to 90 to 100 percent for retirement age clients. This ratio once again is best observed over time. Note that the net worth increases as assets increase in value (home and investment), which increases in savings, and with the payoff of obligations (liabilities).

Brandon and Jill Bowden's Net Worth to Total Assets Ratio

$$\text{Net Worth to Total Assets Ratio} = \frac{\text{Net Worth}}{\text{Total Assets}} = \frac{\$249,192}{\$633,000} = 39.37\% \ (2013)$$

The Bowden's net worth to total assets ratio of 39.37 percent is low as compared to the benchmark for their age group. The ratio will improve as the Bowden's assets increase.

RATIOS FOR FINANCIAL SECURITY GOALS

Ratios for financial security goals provide the planner with insight about the progress (adequate or not) that the client is making towards their long-term goals. For example, ratios can answer questions such as: Is the client earning an appropriate rate of return on retirement investments? Is the client saving an appropriate amount? How much has the client accumulated towards a goal based on age?

Savings Rate

The **savings rate** measures the amount a client is saving towards a retirement goal. If a client begins saving for retirement between ages 25 to 35, there is a need to save about 10 to 13 percent of annual gross income. However, if a client does not begin saving at an early age, then a greater percentage of annual income must be saved to overcome the lost years of contributions and compounding interest.

Age Beginning Regular and Recurring Savings*	Savings (as percent of gross pay) Rate Required to Create Appropriate Capital*
25 - 35	10 - 13%
35 - 45	13 - 20%
45 - 55	20 - 40%**

*Assumes appropriate asset allocation for reasonable-risk investor through accumulation years; also assumes normal raises and an 80 percent wage replacement ratio at Social Security normal retirement age and includes Social Security retirement benefits.

**At age 55 the person will have to delay retirement until age 70.

The formula for the savings rate is:

$$\text{Savings Rate} = \frac{\text{Savings + Reinvestments + Employer Match}}{\text{Gross Pay}} = \text{Benchmark Depends on Client Goals}$$

Note: The savings rate includes any employee and employer contributions.

EXAMPLE 4.9

David's salary at United Technologies Industries is $100,000 per year. He contributes 8% of his compensation to his 401(k) plan and his employer matches his contributions dollar for dollar, up to 4% of his compensation. His total savings rate is:

$$\text{Savings Rate} = \frac{\text{Employee Contributions + Employer Contributions}}{\text{Gross Pay}}$$

$$\text{Savings Rate} = \frac{(\$100,000 \times 0.08) + (\$100,000 \times 0.04)}{\$100,000}$$

$$\text{Savings Rate} = \frac{\$8,000 + \$4,000}{\$100,000} = 0.12 \text{ or } 12\%$$

When calculating the savings rate for a husband and a wife, combine both their retirement savings amounts and combine their gross incomes.

EXAMPLE 4.10

Jason and Sally are married. Jason has a salary of $45,000 and Sally has a salary of $75,000. Jason's employer regularly contributes $2,500 to his profit sharing plan. Sally does not participate in her employer's retirement plan, but contributes $5,000 per year to a Roth IRA. Jason and Sally's savings rate is:

$$\text{Savings Rate} = \frac{\text{Employee Contributions} + \text{Employer Contributions}}{\text{Gross Pay}}$$

$$\text{Savings Rate} = \frac{(\$2,500 + \$5,000)}{(\$45,000 + \$75,000)}$$

$$\text{Savings Rate} = \frac{\$7,500}{\$120,000} = 0.0625 \text{ or } 6.25\%$$

Brandon and Jill Bowden's Savings Rate

Recall that Brandon contributes three percent of his compensation to his 401(k) plan and that his employer matches $0.50 for each $1 contributed, up to three percent of his compensation.

Brandon's contribution to his 401(k) plan is 0.03 x $124,000 = $3,720
Brandon's employer match is 0.015 x $124,000 = $1,860

Brandon and Jill are also saving for education expenses in a 529 plan.

$$\text{Savings Rate} = \frac{\text{Employee Contributions} + \text{Employer Contribution} + 529 \text{ Savings}}{\text{Gross Pay}}$$

$$\text{Savings Rate} = \frac{(\$3,720 + \$1,860) + \$2,000 \text{ (education savings)}}{\$124,000}$$

$$\text{Savings Rate} = \frac{\$7,580}{\$124,000} = 0.0611 \text{ or } 6.11\%$$

The Bowden's savings rate of 6.11 percent is well below the industry benchmark of 10 to 13 percent. Recall that the 10 to 13 percent benchmark is to meet a retirement goal only. The retirement only savings rate for the Bowden's is 4.5% [($3,720 + $1,860) ÷ $124,000]. If Brandon increases his 401(k) plan deferral to six percent, his employer will match an additional three percent, bringing Brandon's total savings rate to 10.61 percent (6% + 3% + 1.61 percent (education savings). A 10.61 percent savings rate would be a significant improvement over his current total savings rate of 6.11 percent. The additional savings required by Brandon would only be another three percent of his compensation or $3,720 on a pre-tax basis. On an after tax basis, it would be closer to $3,000. Although the Bowdens have a negative discretionary cash flow of $2,826, this will turn positive once the credit card debt is retired. Once the credit card debt is retired, the Bowdens will have a positive discretionary cash flow of $4,174 ($7,000 - $2,826), which is more than enough to increase Brandon's 401(k) plan deferral by another three percent.

Investment Assets to Gross Pay

Investment assets to gross pay ratio measures progress towards a client's saving goal, based on the client's age and income. The benchmark (as shown in the following table) is a useful metric because it provides insight as to: (1) whether the client has saved enough towards the retirement goal and (2) how much the client needs in retirement assets to generate a certain level of income at retirement.

Age	Investment Assets as a Ratio to Gross Pay Needed at Varying Ages
25	0.20 : 1
30	0.6 - 0.8 : 1
35	1.6 - 1.8 : 1
45	3 - 4 : 1
55	8 - 10 : 1
65	16 - 20 : 1

The benchmark considers income between $50,000 and $250,000 and inflation at approximately two to three percent. It also considers a balanced investment portfolio of 60/40 (equities to bonds) returning five percent over inflation, a savings rate of 10 to 13 percent of gross pay, and a wage replacement ratio of 80 percent of gross pay.

This ratio can answer the question, "For his age, has the client saved enough towards retirement?"

EXAMPLE 4.11	Jan age 45 with an annual salary of $80,000, has saved $250,000 in her retirement accounts. Jan should have at least $80,000 x 3 = $240,000 towards her retirement goal.

How much does the client need in retirement assets to generate a certain level of income?

EXAMPLE 4.12	Peter, age 50, is looking to retire at age 65, with about $100,000 per year in retirement income. Peter will need $100,000 x 16 = $1,600,000 in retirement savings to generate $100,000 per year in retirement income.

Brandon and Jill Bowden's Investment Assets to Gross Pay Ratio

The ratio for Brandon (age 40) and Jill (age 43) is based on their age. They should have three times their gross pay in retirement savings using this calculation:

Savings Amount = Salary x Benchmark
Savings Amount = $124,000 x 3
Benchmark Amount of Investment Assets = $372,000

The most current actual retirement savings for the Bowden's is:

Brandon's 401(k) Plan (2013)	$75,000
High Tech Stock	$5,000
Cash and Cash Equivalents	$8,000
Total	$88,000

$$\text{Actual Ratio} = \frac{\text{Investment Assets + Cash \& Cash Equivalents}}{\text{Gross Pay}} = \frac{\$88,000}{\$124,000} = 0.71:1$$

Their total retirement savings is $88,000, which is well below what is needed based on the benchmark of $372,000. This is a difficult deficiency to overcome in the short term. However, the Bowdens are young enough and have another 20+ years remaining to work and increase their retirement savings. The first step is to increase Brandon's saving ratio from 4.5 percent to nine percent. The financial planner should also recommend looking at additional savings opportunities once some of the Bowden's bad debt is retired. The Bowden's should also evaluate the feasibility of Jill taking on a part time or full time job to help overcome the savings amount shortfall. Note that because in this case the ratio is refined to measure progress towards the retirement goal only, education savings is not included in the calculation.

PERFORMANCE RATIOS

Performance ratios will provide the planner with information regarding the return the client is earning on assets, net worth, and investments. This section of the chapter provides the appropriate ratios and formulas to calculate the ratios. However, using a financial calculator will provide the most accurate, compounded rate of return (see Chapter 7).

Return on Investments (ROI)

Return on investments (ROI) ratio is a critical performance ratio, as it measures the compounded rate of return on a client's investments. If the client's ROI is too low over a number of years, it may result in the client not having sufficient capital to retire or pay for education.

$$\text{Return on Investments} = \frac{I_1 - (I_0 + \text{Savings})}{I_0}$$

I_0	=	Beginning Investments
I_1	=	Ending Investments
S	=	Savings (include employer match)

Beginning investment assets are the investment assets, typically from the preceding year, and ending investment assets are the investment assets on the balance sheet at the end of the current year. Savings includes any amount contributed to a retirement plan by the employee and employer. In addition, savings includes contributions to an education savings account. Average net worth represents an average net worth between two balance sheets. Alternatively, a financial calculator can be used to compute this ratio (see Chapter 7).

An appropriate benchmark for return on investments depends on the time horizon and risk tolerance of the client. Generally, a client with a long-term time horizon, such as 10 years or more, should have a portfolio more heavily weighted towards equities. A client with a long-term time horizon is expected to have a return on equity of eight to ten percent per year. A client with a shorter time horizon would have a portfolio with a higher weighting of bonds and a return on equity of six to eight percent per year. These concepts will be discussed more in the investments chapter (see Chapter 9).

Brandon and Jill Bowden's Return on Investment Ratio

$$\text{ROI} = \frac{\$95,000 - (\$80,800 + \$5,720 + \$1,860)}{\$80,800} = \frac{\$6,620}{\$80,800} = 0.0819 \text{ or } 8.19\%$$

Based on the age of the Bowdens, an ROI on retirement savings of eight to ten percent is expected, so they are within the ROI benchmark. However, the financial planner should review their High Tech Stock, as their portfolio does not appear to be well diversified and the High Tech Stock lost 33 percent of its value last year.

Return on Assets (ROA)

The **return on assets ratio** provides the planner with insight to the general growth rate of a client's assets.

$$\text{Return on Assets} = \frac{A_1 - (A_0 + S)}{A_0}$$

A_0	=	Beginning Assets
A_1	=	Ending Assets
S	=	Savings (include employer match)

Beginning total assets are the total assets, typically from the preceding year, and ending total assets are the total assets on the balance sheet at the end of the current year.

This measure of return is a blended growth rate of all assets a client owns because it considers returns on low yielding assets like savings and checking accounts, personal residence and auto (an asset declining in value), along with higher returning assets like retirement savings, stocks, and bonds. It is reasonable to expect the return on assets to be low, typically between two to four percent annually. The financial planner should monitor this return over time as it will provide insight to the client's mix of assets (cash and cash equivalents versus investment assets versus personal use assets). If the rate of return on assets begins to trend lower, or below three percent, it may indicate too many low returning assets like personal use assets or cash and cash equivalents.

Brandon and Jill Bowden's Return on Assets

$$\text{Return on Assets} = \frac{\$633,000 - (\$609,450 + \$5,720 + \$1,860)}{\$609,450} = \frac{\$15,970}{\$609,450} = 2.62\%$$

A return on assets of 2.62 percent is low in comparison to the typical three to four percent annual return expected on total assets. This return includes cash and cash equivalents that earn less than one percent and personal use assets (which include a house that may or may not increase in value), personal autos (that decline in value) and other personal use assets (such as furniture and clothing which do not increase in value each year). The financial planner should review the client's assets and recommend changes to increase the return.

Return on Net Worth (RONW)

The **return on net worth ratio** provides the planner with insight as to the average growth rate on net worth.

$$\text{Return on Net Worth} = \frac{NW_1 - (NW_0 + S)}{NW_0}$$

NW_0	=	Beginning Net Worth
NW_1	=	Ending Net Worth
S	=	Savings (include employer match)

Beginning net worth is the total net worth, typically from the preceding year, and ending net worth is the total net worth on the balance sheet at the end of the current year.

Brandon and Jill Bowden's Rate of Return on Net Worth

$$\text{Return on Net Worth} = \frac{\$249,192 - (\$222,241 + \$5,720 + \$1,860)}{\$222,241} = \frac{\$19,371}{\$222,241} = 0.0872 \text{ or } 8.72\%$$

A return on net worth of 8.71 percent is reasonable. A financial planner should calculate the return on net worth each year and develop a trend over time. The return on net worth is expected to be higher when a client is working, then begin to decline as the client enters retirement (as assets are drawn down to generate income).

EXHIBIT 4.9 BOWDEN RATIO ANALYSIS

LIQUIDITY RATIOS				
Ratio	**Formula**		**Comment**	**Benchmark**
Emergency Fund Ratio =	$\dfrac{\text{Cash \& Cash Equivalents}}{\text{Monthly Non-Discretionary Cash Flows}}$	$\dfrac{\$8,000}{\$5,974}$ = 1.34 months (2013)	Weak	3 - 6 months
Current Ratio =	$\dfrac{\text{Cash \& Cash Equivalents}}{\text{Current Liabilities}}$	$\dfrac{\$8,000}{\$34,056}$ = 0.23 (2013)	Low	1.0 - 2.0
DEBT RATIOS				
Housing Ratio 1 (HR 1)(Basic) =	$\dfrac{\text{Housing Costs}}{\text{Gross Pay}}$	$\dfrac{\$2,995.25}{\$10,333}$ = 28.9%	Slightly High	≤ 28%
Housing Ratio 2 (HR 2)(Broad) =	$\dfrac{\text{Housing Costs + Other Debt Payments}}{\text{Gross Pay}}$	$\dfrac{\$4,086}{\$10,333}$ = 39.5%	Slightly High	≤ 36%
Debt to Total Assets =	$\dfrac{\text{Total Debt}}{\text{Total Assets}}$	$\dfrac{\$383,808}{\$633,000}$ = 60.63% (2013)	High	As a person ages, this ratio should decline.
Net Worth to Total Assets =	$\dfrac{\text{Net Worth}}{\text{Total Assets}}$	$\dfrac{\$249,192}{\$633,000}$ = 39.37% (2013)	Low	Depends on age. 20% for young client and 90-100% for retirement age client.
RATIOS FOR FINANCIAL SECURITY GOALS				
Savings Rate =	$\dfrac{\text{Savings + Reinvestments + Employer Match}}{\text{Gross Pay}}$	$\dfrac{\$2,000 + \$3,720 + \$1,860}{\$124,000}$ = 6.11%	Low	10 – 13% assuming the client starts early, ages 25-35.
Investment Assets to Gross Pay =	$\dfrac{\text{Investment Assets + Cash \& Cash Equivalents}}{\text{Gross Pay}}$	$\dfrac{\$88,000}{\$124,000}$ = 0.71:1	Low	Depends upon age. At retirement age – 16:1
PERFORMANCE RATIOS				
Return on Investments =	$\dfrac{I_1 - (I_0 + \text{Savings})}{I_0}$	$\dfrac{\$6,620}{\$80,800}$ = 8.19%	Good	8 – 10%
Return on Assets =	$\dfrac{A_1 - (A_0 + \text{Savings})}{A_0}$	$\dfrac{\$15,970}{\$609,450}$ = 2.62%	Low	2 – 4%
Return on Net Worth =	$\dfrac{NW_1 - (NW_0 + \text{Savings})}{NW_0}$	$\dfrac{\$19,371}{\$222,241}$ = 8.72%	Good	The higher the better. This ratio is likely to become smaller as the client's net worth increases.

Exhibit 4.10

LIQUIDITY RATIOS			
RATIO	**FORMULA**	**MEASURES**	**BENCHMARK**
Emergency Funds	$\dfrac{\text{Cash \& Cash Equivalents}}{\text{Monthly Non-Discretionary Cash Flows}}$	The number of months of non-discretionary expenses in the form of cash and cash equivalents.	3 - 6 months
Current Ratio	$\dfrac{\text{Cash \& Cash Equivalents}}{\text{Current Liabilities}}$	The number of times a client can satisfy their short-term liabilities.	1.0 - 2.0
DEBT RATIOS			
Housing Ratio1 (Basic)	$\dfrac{\text{Housing Costs}}{\text{Gross Pay}}$	The percentage of income spent on housing debt.	$\leq 28\%$
Housing Ratio 2 (Broad)	$\dfrac{\text{Housing Costs + Other Debt Payments}}{\text{Gross Pay}}$	The percentage of income spent on housing and all other recurring debt.	$\leq 36\%$
Debt to Total Assets	$\dfrac{\text{Total Debt}}{\text{Total Assets}}$	The percentage of assets being provided by creditors.	As a person ages, this ratio should decline.
Net Worth to Total Assets	$\dfrac{\text{Net Worth}}{\text{Total Assets}}$	The percentage of total assets owned or paid for by client.	Depends on age. 20% for young client and 90-100% for retirement age client.
RATIOS FOR FINANCIAL SECURITY GOALS			
Savings Rate	$\dfrac{\text{Savings + Reinvestment + Employer Match}}{\text{Gross Pay}}$	The percentage of income saved towards a retirement goal.	10 – 13% Assuming the client starts early, ages 25-35.
Investment Assets to Gross Pay	$\dfrac{\text{Investment Assets + Cash \& Cash Equivalents}}{\text{Gross Pay}}$	The progress towards a retirement goal.	Depends upon age. At retirement age – 16:1
PERFORMANCE RATIOS			
Return on Investments	$\dfrac{I_1 - (I_0 + \text{Savings})}{I_0}$	The growth rate of a client's investment assets.	8 – 10%
Return on Assets	$\dfrac{A_1 - (A_0 + \text{Savings})}{A_0}$	A blended growth rate of all assets.	2 – 4%
Return on Net Worth	$\dfrac{NW_1 - (NW_0 + \text{Savings})}{NW_0}$	The growth rate of net worth.	The higher the better. This ratio is likely to become smaller as the client's net worth increases.

LIMITATIONS OF FINANCIAL STATEMENT ANALYSIS

Estimating Fair Market Value

When preparing financial statements, the financial planner must estimate the fair market value of certain assets like the primary residence, second homes, boats, cars, and any collectibles. In addition, if the client owns a small business, it is likely the planner will have to estimate the value of the business as well. This becomes problematic when the client is planning to sell the asset and use the proceeds to fund a goal. The estimate of fair market value must be conservative enough so that the financial goal is not jeopardized because the value was overstated.

Inflation

The impact of inflation makes it very difficult to compare financial statements over multiple years. The financial planner needs to adjust investment returns for inflation to determine a real, after inflation, rate of return. The planner should also adjust income and savings into real, after inflation, dollars. Inflation of even a small rate (e.g., 3%) can have a very serious effect on financial statements over a long period of time (e.g., 10 to 30 years).

Hard to Value Assets

Some assets such as collectibles and private business interests are difficult to value. To the extent the asset is going to fund a financial goal, such as retirement, it is important for the financial planner to use an appraiser to determine an appropriate value of the asset. For example, if a client intends to sell a business ownership interest to fund retirement, the planner wants to make sure the client is going to be able to sell the business interest at the current value of the interest. The planner does not want to report the value of the business interest at $1 million on the balance sheet, only to find out years later that the client can only sell the interest for half of the value reported. If the client was including the business interest in the retirement amount calculation and now has a significant shortfall in retirement assets, it is likely to leave the client unable to retire and looking for a new planner.

Liquidity of Certain Assets

Other assets may be difficult to sell, such as a small business or collectible items. If a client is planning to use illiquid assets to fund a financial goal, the client and financial planner must carefully plan the timing of the sale of the asset, as it may not occur exactly as the client intends. For example, if the client is trying to sell a small business to fund retirement at age 62, the client may have to start looking for a buyer five years before the intended retirement date. It may also result in the client having to retire earlier or later than intended.

Uncertain Returns

Many of the benchmarks covered in this chapter assume a certain level of return. Returns are based on historical returns for asset classes such as stocks and bonds. As the markets continue to evolve over time, future returns may be higher or lower than historical returns, which could positively or negatively impact the financial planner's calculations and benchmarks.

Sensitivity Analysis

Financial statements and retirement and education needs that are projected over long periods of time employ many assumptions such as the rate of increase in income, the tax rate, the savings rate, the inflation rate, and the investment return rate. Retirement age and life expectancy are additional assumptions used for retirement projections. Assumptions made for education funding include the cost of education, when the cost will occur, and how many years the student will be in school. With all of these assumptions and variables, the financial planner needs to subject the plan to some sensitivity analysis. This involves slightly rotating the value of the variable toward the risk. For example, what if the client retires one year earlier than expected or inflation is 3.5 percent instead of the assumption used of three percent? Sensitivity analysis can also be used to illustrate to the client how the plan would be impacted if the client decides to pursue one or two years of additional work and savings (delayed retirement).

Conducting Sensitivity Analysis

Sensitivity analysis is the process of changing key variables in planning assumptions, to determine the overall impact of those changes on the plan. When a planner is calculating the amount needed to save towards an education goal, the financial planner must assume an investment rate of return, an inflation rate of return, and future cost of tuition. Sensitivity analysis involves calculating the amount needed to save for education, if the investment rate of return is two, three or more percentage points lower than the original assumption. The planner would also adjust the tuition inflation rate up and then calculate the amount needed to save for education. The planner would then adjust the tuition inflation rate down and recalculate the amount needed to save for education. Sensitivity analysis provides a range of savings required to meet a goal, based upon differing assumptions and the implications of the assumptions changing.

Conducting Monte Carlo Analysis

Monte Carlo analysis is a mathematical simulation to determine the probability of achieving a given outcome. Monte Carlo analysis is useful for financial planners to help measure the probability of our assumptions being true or false. Suppose a client, age 62, has $1 million in a retirement savings account and wants to know how much can be withdrawn each year for income. If a planner assumes a historical rate of return of eight percent on the investment assets, the planner may suggest $90,000 a year in withdrawals which should last for 30 years. However, if the client experiences negative returns during the first three to four years of retiring, then retirement savings will be depleted in less than ten years. By conducting Monte Carlo analysis, the planner may determine that there is a 20 percent probability of running out of money within ten years of retiring. Then appropriate steps can be taken to adjust the annual withdrawal amount to decrease the probability of running out of money to a more tolerable level.

Key Terms

Assets - A balance sheet category that represents anything of economic value that can ultimately be converted to cash.

Balance Sheet - A statement of financial position that represents the accounting for items the client "owns" (assets) and items that are "owed" (liabilities). The balance sheet provides a snapshot of the client's assets, liabilities, and net worth as of a stated date.

Cash and Cash Equivalents - A balance sheet category that represents assets that are highly liquid, which means they are either cash or can be converted to cash (within the next 12 months) with little to no price concession from their current value.

Cash Flow Statement - Explains how cash and cash equivalents were used or generated between two balance sheets.

Community Property - A civil law originating statutory regime under which married individuals own an equal undivided interest in all property accumulated during their marriage. Property acquired before the marriage and property received by gift or inheritance during the marriage retains its status as separate property.

Current Ratio - Measures how many times the client can satisfy their short-term liabilities.

Debt Ratios – Measures how well the client is managing their overall debt structure.

Debt to Total Assets Ratio - Indicates what percentage of assets is being provided by creditors. The lower this ratio the better, as it indicates that the assets owned have a low amount of debt owed.

Emergency Fund Ratio - Measures how many months of non-discretionary expenses the client has in the form of cash and cash equivalents or current assets.

Expenses - An income statement category. Expenses represent those items that are paid regularly by the client during the time period being presented. Examples of expenses include mortgage principal and interest, utilities, taxes, insurance, telephone, water, cable or satellite, internet, and cell phone.

Fee Simple Ownership - The complete ownership of property by one individual who possesses all ownership rights associated with the property, including the right to use, sell, gift, alienate, convey, or bequeath the property.

Financial Statement Analysis - The process of calculating financial ratios and comparing the actual ratios to industry established benchmarks.

Key Terms

Fixed Expenses - Those expenses that are due and payable regardless of whether income is available to cover the cost. There is less discretion over fixed expenses in the short term. Examples of fixed expenses include mortgage payment, car payment, boat payment, student loan payment, property taxes, and insurance premiums.

Horizontal Analysis - Lists each financial statement item as a percentage of a base year and creates a trend over time.

Housing Ratio 1 - Established by the banking industry to determine if the amount of income and housing debt (PITI) are appropriate and affordable.

Housing Ratio 2 - Also referred to as housing ratio 1 plus all other debt. This ratio was established by the banking industry to determine if the total amount of debt is appropriate for a given level of income. If housing ratio 2 is met, the borrower will likely qualify for a conventional loan.

Income - An income statement category. Examples of recurring income earned by the client includes salary, interest, dividend, pension, retirement account withdrawal, and business income.

Investment Assets - A balance sheet category that includes appreciating assets or those assets being held to accomplish one or more financial goals.

Investment Assets to Gross Pay Ratio - Measures progress towards a client's retirement goal, based on the client's age and income.

Joint Tenancy with Right of Survivorship (JTWROS) - Typically how a husband and wife own joint property. Joint tenancy is an interest in property held by two or more related or unrelated persons called joint tenants. Each person holds an undivided, equal interest in the whole property. A right of survivorship is normally implied with this form of ownership, and at the death of the first joint tenant, the decedent's interest transfers to the other joint tenants outside of the probate process according to state titling law.

Liabilities - A balance sheet category that represents client financial obligations that are owed to creditors.

Liquidity Ratios – Measures the amount of cash and cash equivalents relative to short-term liabilities.

Long-Term Liabilities - Financial obligations owed that are due beyond the next 12 months. Long-term liabilities are usually the result of major financial purchases and resulting obligations that are being paid off over multiple years (house, vacation, boat, student loan).

Key Terms

Monte Carlo Analysis - A mathematical simulation to determine the probability of success of a given plan. Monte Carlo analysis is useful for financial planners to help measure the probability of assumptions being true or false.

Net Discretionary Cash Flow - Represents the amount of cash flow available after all savings, expenses, and taxes have been paid.

Net Worth - A balance sheet category that represents the amount of total equity (assets - liabilities = net worth) a client has accumulated.

Net Worth to Total Assets Ratio - The compliment of the debt to assets ratio. These two should add up to one. This provides the planner with the percentage of total assets owned or paid for by the client.

Performance Ratios – Measures the return a client is generating on assets.

Personal Use Assets - A balance sheet category that includes those assets that help to maintain the client's lifestyle.

Ratio Analysis - The process of calculating key financial ratios for a client, comparing those metrics to industry benchmarks and then making an evaluation regarding any deficiencies.

Ratios for Financial Security Goals – Measures the client's progress towards achieving their long-term financial security goals.

Return on Assets Ratio - Formula provides the planner with insight to the general growth rate of a client's assets.

Return on Investments (ROI) Ratio - A critical performance ratio, as it measures the compounded rate of return on a client's investments.

Return on Net Worth Ratio - Provides the planner with insight as to the average growth rate on net worth.

Savings Contributions - An income statement category. Examples of savings contributions include 401(k) plan, 403(b) plan, IRA (traditional or Roth), education savings, any other type of savings account, and reinvested dividends, interest, or capital gains.

Savings Rate - Measures the amount a client is saving towards a retirement goal.

Sensitivity Analysis - The process of changing key variables in planning assumptions, to determine the overall impact of those changes.

Key Terms

Short-Term Liabilities - Represent those obligations that are "current" in nature or due within the next 12 months (≤ 12 months).

Statement of Income and Expenses - A financial statement that represents all income earned or expected to be earned by the client, less all expenses incurred or expected to be incurred during the time period being covered.

Statement of Net Worth - Explains changes in net worth between two balance sheets by reporting financial transactions that are not reported on the income statement or other financial statements.

Tenancy by the Entirety - Similar to property owned JTWROS between a husband and wife because property ownership is automatically transferred to the surviving spouse upon death.

Tenancy in Common - An interest in property held by two or more related or unrelated persons. Each owner is referred to as a tenant in common. Tenancy in common is the most common type of joint ownership between nonspouses.

Variable Expenses - Those expenses that can be dispensed with and are more discretionary over the short term. Examples of variable expenses include entertainment expenses, vacation expenses, travel expenses, and charitable contributions.

Vertical Analysis - Lists each line item on the income statement as a percentage of total income and presents each line item on the balance sheet as a percentage of total assets. The restated percentage is known as a common size income statement or balance sheet.

1. List and define the major categories on the assets side of the balance sheet.

2. List and define the liabilities categories on the balance sheet.

3. Discuss how assets and liability values are reflected on the balance sheet.

4. Define and discuss the net worth category listed on the balance sheet.

5. List documents that a client can provide to the financial planner as sources of information to properly prepare financial statements.

6. List and define the common forms of property ownership.

7. Discuss the difference between income and savings contribution categories listed on the income statement.

8. Define the expense category of the income statement and give examples of variable and fixed expenses.

9. Define net discretionary cash flow.

10. What is the purpose of the statement of net worth?

11. What is the purpose of the cash flow statement?

12. List what should be reflected on forecasted financial statements.

13. What is a financial planner's purpose in creating a client's budget?

14. Define and explain the purpose of financial statement analysis.

15. Define vertical and horizontal analysis as comparative financial statement tools.

16. Define ratio analysis.

17. Define the emergency fund ratio.

18. Define housing ratios 1 and 2.

19. Define the savings rate.

20. Define performance ratios.

MULTIPLE-CHOICE PROBLEMS

1. Your client, Tom, asked you to prepare his financial statements. He believes that his wife is the root of all of their financial problems because of her spending habits. His wife, on the other hand, believes that most of their money goes to pay routine expenses like, house, auto, etc. Which financial statement will help them resolve this disagreement?

   a. Balance Sheet.
   b. Income Statement.
   c. Statement of Net Worth.
   d. Statement of Financial Position.

2. Your client, Meg, asked you several questions about her balance sheet. She doesn't understand how the assets, liabilities and net worth are related. Which of the following statements is true?

   a. Net Worth = Assets + Liabilities.
   b. Assets = Net Worth − Liabilities.
   c. Liabilities = Assets − Net Worth.
   d. A balance sheet reflects how the assets, liabilities, and net worth changed over the year.

3. Craig's financial planner is preparing his balance sheet. Which of the following would not generally be considered "cash and cash equivalents?"

   a. Cash value in life insurance.
   b. Money market account.
   c. Certificate of deposit with a 6 month maturity.
   d. Checking account.

4. Craig's financial planner is preparing his balance sheet. Which of the following would be considered an "investment asset?"

   a. A certificate of deposit with a maturity of exactly 1 year.
   b. The unvested portion of a pension plan.
   c. A vacation home.
   d. An education fund.

5. Which of the following statements concerning the valuation of assets on the balance sheet is correct?

    a. Since a financial planner has access to all of the client financials, a privately-held small business is easier to value than a publicly traded company.

    b. Assets should be valued on the balance sheet using replacement cost.

    c. An actuary should be retained to value all personal use assets.

    d. Money market accounts are unlikely to lose value over time.

6. Which of the following would not generally be considered a short-term liability?

    a. An automobile loan.

    b. Credit card bills.

    c. Medical expenses.

    d. Unpaid taxes.

7. Jay purchased a new home for $100,000. He put $20,000 down and financed the $80,000 balance. What is the impact of this transaction on his net worth?

    a. His net worth increases.

    b. His net worth decreases.

    c. His net worth remains the same.

    d. The net worth will decrease with each mortgage payment made.

8. Nathan and Evan (two brothers) are joint property owners. Nathan owns 60% and Evan owns 40%. How is this property owned?

    a. Sole Ownership / Fee Simple.

    b. Tenants in Common.

    c. Joint Tenancy.

    d. Tenancy by the Entirety.

9. Which of the following property ownership regimes has a right of survivorship feature?

    a. Sole Ownership / Fee Simple.

    b. Tenancy in Common.

    c. Tenancy by the Entirety.

    d. Community Property.

10. Which of the following statements concerning income and expenses listed on the Income Statement is correct?

    a. Charitable contributions are always a discretionary expense.

    b. Reinvested dividends is an example of income.

    c. Entertainment expenses is an examples of a fixed expense.

    d. Social Security taxes withheld is an example of a fixed expense.

11. A financial planner is currently preparing a client's cash flow statement. Which of the following would the planner classify as a financing activity?

    a. The purchase of a new residence.

    b. A contribution to a retirement account.

    c. A cash inheritance.

    d. Paying a credit card debt.

12. A client, Marie, age 35, came into a financial planner's office today. She provides the planner with the following information for the upcoming year:

- Income - $100,000
- Principal and Interest payments on home mortgage - $14,000
- Homeowners insurance - $1,000
- Property taxes - $5,000
- Living Expenses - $40,000
- Credit Card Debt Payments - $12,000
- Savings - $5,000
- Student Loan Payments - $5,000
- Car Payment - $6,000

When considering the targeted benchmarks, which of the following statements is the planner most likely to make during the next meeting?

    a. Both the basic and broad housing ratio are within the normal range.

    b. Both the basic and broad housing ratio are outside the normal range.

    c. The basic housing ratio is within the normal range, but the broad housing ratio is not.

    d. The broad housing ratio is within the normal range, but the basic housing ratio is not.

13. Roger and Julie are married. Roger is a police officer and earns $50,000 per year. He contributes 10% of his salary to his retirement plan. His employer also makes a 5% match contribution. Julie stays at home with their children and contributes $5,000 to an IRA. What is their total saving rate?

    a. 10.0%.

    b. 20.0%.

    c. 20.5%.

    d. 25.0%.

14. While meeting with your new client about his retirement needs you have made several assumptions regarding income growth, savings rate, inflation rates, and investment returns. You engage in the process of changing some of the key assumptions to determine the overall impact of those changes on the financial plan. What is this process called?

    a. Sensitivity Analysis.

    b. Objectivity Analysis.

    c. Monte Carlo Analysis.

    d. Las Vegas Analysis.

Quick Quiz Explanations

Quick Quiz 4.1
1. False. This is the definition of the statement of income and expenses (income statement). The balance sheet represents the items the client owns (assets), the items that are owed by the client (liabilities), and the difference between the two (net worth).
2. True.
3. False. This is the definition of personal use assets. Investment assets are appreciating assets that are being held to accomplish financial goal(s). Investment assets include retirement accounts, brokerage accounts, education funds, etc.
4. True.

Quick Quiz 4.2
1. False. This is the definition of tenancy in common property ownership. Fee simple ownership is the complete ownership of property by one individual.
2. False. Community property does not usually avoid probate, but tenancy by the entirety and Joint Tenancy with Right of survivorship both do avoid probate.

Quick Quiz 4.3
1. False. Assets are listed on the balance sheet.
2. True.
3. True.

Quick Quiz 4.4
1. True.
2. False. This is the definition of an income statement not a cash flow statement. The cash flow statement explains how cash and cash equivalents were used or generated between two balance sheets.
3. True.

Quick Quiz 4.5
1. True.
2. True.
3. False. This is the definition of the current ratio. The emergency fund ratio measures how many months of non-discretionary expenses the client has in cash and cash equivalents.

Quick Quiz 4.6
1. True.
2. True.
3. True.

Risk Management for the Individual Client

LEARNING OBJECTIVES

After reading this chapter, you should be able to:

- Describe and explain the personal risk management process and its seven steps.
- Determine and select the best risk management alternatives using the risk management decision chart for individuals.
- Explain the causes and contributors to losses including perils and hazards.
- Identify the requisites for an insurable risk.
- Describe insurance as a legal contract including the elements of a valid contract and the unique characteristics of an insurance contract.
- Describe insurance on the person including life insurance.
- Identify the three methods used to determine the amount of life insurance needed and be able to calculate each.
- Describe the types of life insurance including term and permanent.
- Describe a health insurance plan and differentiate between an indemnity plans and managed care options.
- Describe the risk associated with long-term disability and the coverages that long-term disability plans provide.
- Describe long-term care insurance, activities of daily living, and important features associated with long-term care insurance policies.
- Describe homeowners and renters insurance policies.
- Describe automobile insurance policies and which factors affect premium rates.
- Describe personal liability umbrella insurance policies and the risks that they mitigate against.
- Describe how insurers use risk pooling to pay for losses incurred by policyholders.*
- Explain the factors that affect policyholder premiums and recommend strategies for reducing household insurance costs.*
- Identify and measure liability, automobile, homeowner's, flood, earthquake, health, disability, long-term care, and life risks.*

* CFP Board Resource Document - Student-Centered Learning Objectives based upon CFP Board Principal Topics.

INTRODUCTION

This chapter introduces the reader to the basics of risk management for an individual and identifies the risks that a typical client faces. A financial plan can then be developed for managing those risks with the ultimate objective being that the client will avoid the consequences of such risks were they to happen and avoid becoming financially dependent on loved ones or the state. This chapter is a primer and is not designed to take the place of a full semester course in insurance.

The chapter will provide sufficient risk management information for a financial planner to apply this knowledge to relatively simple client risk management scenarios. If the client's risk management situation is complex, the planner needs to have completed at least a full course in insurance and perhaps also needs to consult with an insurance expert.

THE PERSONAL RISK MANAGEMENT PROCESS

Personal risk management is a systematic process of identifying, evaluating, and managing pure risk exposures faced by an individual. Pure risk is the chance of a loss or no loss occurring, but with pure risk there is no chance of experiencing a gain.

There are seven steps in the personal risk management process:
- Determining the objectives of the risk management program.
- Identifying the risks to which the individual is exposed.
- Evaluating the identified risks for the probability of occurrence and severity of the loss.
- Determining the alternatives for managing the risks.
- Selecting the most appropriate alternative for each risk.
- Implementing the risk management plan selected.
- Periodically evaluating and reviewing the risk management program.

Determining the Objectives of the Risk Management Program

The first step in the risk management process is to determine the objectives of the risk management program. Vaguely defined risk management objectives can conflict with each other and thus be disjointed. Risk management objectives can range from obtaining the most cost-effective protection against risk to continuing income after loss. A client's stated objective may be to insure only those risks that have the potential of catastrophic financial loss and to do so at the minimum premium using as many premium management techniques as are available (e.g., deductibles, co-pays, annual cost comparisons).

Key Concepts

Underline/highlight the answers as you read:

1. Identify the six steps to the personal risk management process.

2. Identify the difference between personal risks, property risks, and liability risks.

3. Distinguish between loss frequency and loss severity.

Identifying Risk Exposures

The next step is to identify all possible **pure risk** exposures of the client. Pure risk represents the possibility of loss, but no possibility of gain. The risk exposures for an individual may be subdivided into **personal risks** that may cause the loss of income (untimely death, disability, health issues), or alternatively cause an increase in the cost of living (disability, health issues), **property risks** that may cause the loss of property (automobile, home, or other asset), and **liability risks** that may cause financial loss (injury to another for which the client is determined to be financially responsible).

Evaluating the Identified Risks

Evaluating the potential frequency and severity of losses is the next step in the risk management process. **Loss frequency** is the expected number of losses that will occur within a given period of time. **Loss severity** refers to the potential size or financial damage of a loss. By identifying loss frequency and severity, the planner can prioritize the urgency of dealing with each specific risk.

Recall that probability is useful when applied to large numbers. However, depending on probability-based predictions for any single individual is not recommended. To the individual, the potential financial severity of the losses, even coupled with a low probability of occurrence, is critical to the risk analysis.

Clients should insure against those **perils** (the proximate or actual cause of a loss, such as fire, liability, or accidental death) that upon occurrence could lead to severe financial hardship. We refer to these as catastrophic financial risks. However, catastrophic risks are relative. The loss of a car to a person who depends on it to get to work and has no other money to replace it may be catastrophic, while the loss of a car to a wealthy person may be incidental. Generally, even those persons owning houses without mortgages cannot risk leaving such an asset uninsured.

Key Concepts

Underline/highlight the answers as you read:

1. Identify the four responses to managing risk.

2. Identify the risk management decisions associated with particular risk exposures.

A general approach to insuring individual risks is as follows:

- For untimely death (earlier in life) - if there are dependents who depend on the income of the person, that person needs income replacement insurance (life insurance).
- For disability (pre-retirement) - most workers need disability insurance as income replacement insurance at least until they have sufficient assets to no longer need employment. Those unemployed will find it difficult to get disability insurance as it is like life insurance (income replacement).
- For healthcare - it is rare that a person can self insure for health care. So, in general, everyone needs health care coverage.

- For property losses - property owners should insure only up to the fair market value of the property. High deductibles should be used as self insurance or loss sharing to manage premiums. Both coverages and costs should be reevaluated annually.
- For liability - most people need a personal liability umbrella policy (PLUP). The minimum coverage is usually $1,000,000 and may be as high as $5,000,000 depending on the risks and the financial resources of the person.

Determining and Selecting the Best Risk Management Alternatives

Insurance is not necessary, or even available, for every risk of financial loss that an individual faces. Choosing the appropriate risk management response depends largely on the potential frequency and severity of loss exposures faced. Where more than one tool is deemed appropriate, the costs and benefits of each should be examined to determine which is the most economical and beneficial.

There are four responses to managing risks:
- **Risk avoidance** - Avoiding an activity so that a financial loss cannot be incurred.
- **Risk reduction** - Implementing activities that will result in the reduction of the frequency and/or severity of losses.
- **Risk retention** - The state of being exposed to a risk and personally retaining the potential for loss.
- **Risk transfer** - Transferring or shifting the risk of loss through means such as insurance or a warranty.

It is important to choose the best risk management response for any particular risk. Exhibit 5.1 is a decision chart for selecting appropriate risk management tools.

EXHIBIT 5.1   **RISK MANAGEMENT DECISION CHART FOR INDIVIDUALS**

	Low Frequency of Occurrence	High Frequency of Occurrence
High Severity (catastrophic financial loss) (e.g., long-term disability)	Transfer and/or share risk using insurance	Avoid Risk
Low Severity (non-catastrophic financial loss) (e.g., car gets dented in parking lot)	Retain Risk	Retain / Reduce Risk (park away from heavy parking area)

Exposures that are a combination of high frequency and high severity should be avoided. Exposures that are low in frequency but high in potential severity are best handled by insurance coverage. The high-severity losses can leave a client in a dire financial position, yet the low frequency makes sharing the cost of losses with others economically feasible. Examples of high-severity / low-frequency loss exposures include fire damage to a house or a loss due to an automobile collision.

The remaining types of losses are both low severity in nature. Transferring low-severity losses to an insurer is generally not economically feasible because the insurer has substantial expenses associated with processing numerous small claims. The risk of low-severity losses is generally retained by the asset owner. When low-severity losses occur with high frequency, their aggregate impact can have financially devastating effects. So, it is recommended that high-frequency, low-severity losses not just be retained but also managed in an effort to reduce frequency.

Quick Quiz 5.1

Highlight the answer to these questions:

1. Personal risk management is a systematic process for identifying, evaluating, and managing pure risk exposures.
   a. True
   b. False

2. Perils are the proximate or actual cause of a loss that upon occurrence can lead to a severe financial hardship.
   a. True
   b. False

3. Risk avoidance is the implementation of activities that will result in the reduction of the frequency and/or severity of losses.
   a. True
   b. False

4. Risk transfer is the shifting of the risk of loss through means such as insurance or a warranty.
   a. True
   b. False

True, True, False, True.

Implementing a Risk Management Plan Based on the Selected Alternatives

A risk management plan should reflect the chosen response to each risk scenario. If risk reduction is the appropriate response to a given risk, the proper risk reduction program must be designed and implemented. If a decision is made to retain a risk, the individual should determine whether an emergency fund will be used (pet needs medical care). If the response to a given risk is to transfer the risk through insurance, an assessment and selection of the appropriate insurer will follow.

Periodically Evaluating and Reviewing the Individual Risk Management Program

The purpose of periodic evaluation and review is twofold. First, the risk management process does not take place independently from external influences. Things change over time, and risk exposures can change as well. The risk management response that was most suitable last year may not be the most prudent this year, and adjustments may need to be made. Second, errors in judgment regarding the selected alternatives may occur, and periodic review allows the planner and client to discover such errors and revise the risk management plan as necessary.

CAUSES OF AND CONTRIBUTORS TO LOSSES

PERILS

Too often the concept of risk, or the chance of loss, is confused with the terms peril and hazard. A peril is the proximate or actual cause of a loss. Common perils include accidental death, disability caused by sickness or accident, and property losses caused by fire, windstorm, tornado, earthquake, burglary, and collision.

Insurance policy coverage may be written in either an open-perils or named-perils format. **Open-perils policies** are called "all-risks" policies, because they cover all risks of loss (perils) that are not specifically excluded from the contract. All-risks proved to be somewhat misleading to the consumer, implying that "all" risks were covered. So, the industry has moved toward the use of the term open-perils to describe this type of coverage. More specifically, an open-perils policy is one in which all perils or causes of loss are covered, unless they are specifically listed under the exclusions section of the policy. A **named-perils policy** provides protection against losses caused by the perils that are specifically listed as covered in the policy. Because there is always a chance of loss being caused by an unknown peril, an open-perils policy is preferable to a named-perils policy. Consequently, the open-perils policy premium is somewhat higher than a named perils policy because it provides broader coverage.

HAZARDS

A **hazard** is a condition that creates or increases the likelihood of a loss occurring. The three main types of hazards are:

- Physical hazard
- Moral hazard
- Morale hazard

Physical Hazard

A **physical hazard** is a tangible condition or circumstance that increases the probability of a peril occurring and/or the severity of damages that result from a peril. Examples of physical hazards include high blood pressure, winding roads, and bad eyesight.

Key Concepts

Underline/highlight the answers as you read:

1. Distinguish between an open-perils policy and a named-perils policy.

2. Identify the three main types of hazards.

3. Identify the four conditions necessary for a risk to be insurable.

Moral Hazard

A **moral hazard** is a character flaw or level of dishonesty an individual possesses that causes or increases the chance for a loss. In property insurance claims, a good example of a moral hazard is arson. Fraud in auto and health claims is a moral hazard situation that also occurs frequently. Dishonest insureds often justify their claims because the loss is insured. These types of losses result in premium increases for all insureds.

Morale Hazard

A **morale hazard** is indifference to losses based on the existence of insurance. Many people think that because they have insurance there is no need to be concerned about protecting their property. As a direct result of the indifference, the chance of loss is increased. Persons may contend that because they are insured, there is no reason to lock their homes or cars. This should not be confused with a moral hazard, which, for example, would be burning their house down or purposely rear-ending another motor vehicle to collect insurance.

INSURABLE LOSSES

REQUISITES FOR AN INSURABLE RISK

Several conditions must exist before a risk is considered insurable:

- A large number of homogeneous (similar) exposure units must exist to help develop statistics for forecasting losses (frequency and severity).
- Insured losses must be accidental from the insured's standpoint. Intentional acts of the insured resulting in a loss are generally not insurable.
- Insured losses must be measurable and determinable.
- The loss must not pose a catastrophic risk for the insurer who has limited reserves.

Insurance is likely unavailable or priced extremely high for risks that are generally not insurable. Risks that are too large cannot be insured due to high premium cost that makes purchasing the insurance impractical. Also, risks that are challenging to measure will be difficult for the insurer to quantify and predict. The insurer in such a circumstance would almost certainly price the premium high in the event a loss occurred that was higher than the insurer was able to anticipate and quantify. A financial planner needs to assist the client in identifying insurable and uninsurable risks as part of the personal risk management process. Then direction can be given for the appropriate alternatives to risk management.

INSURANCE AS A LEGAL CONTRACT

A contract is valid only if the legal system enforces the terms and conditions of the contract. Our legal system has established certain principles upon which insurance contracts are based and interpreted when claims or disputes arise. What constitutes a legally binding contract? The elements of a valid contract are listed below.

ELEMENTS OF A VALID CONTRACT

- Offer and acceptance (one party makes the offer, the other party accepts, rejects, or counters).
- Legal competency of all parties (generally at least age 18).
- Consideration (usually money or the promise to pay).
- Lawful purpose (the purpose of the contract is not for an unlawful activity).

Key Concepts

Underline/highlight the answers as you read:

1. Identify the elements of a valid contract.

2. Identify some of the unique characteristics of an insurance contract.

3. Determine the purpose of life insurance.

4. Identify the methods of determining the amount of life insurance needed.

5. Distinguish the difference between term life insurance and permanent life insurance.

Insurance as a contract has some unique characteristic, including:

- It is unilateral - Only the insurer is making a promise, therefore it is a unilateral contract.
- It is aleatory - What is paid in by the insured and paid out by the insurer may not be equal amounts.
- It is adhesive - The insured had no opportunity to negotiate terms; thus ambiguities are charged to the insurer.
- It implies utmost good faith - The insurance applicant is truthful in disclosure of pertinent material facts and the insurer discloses critical contract information.
- It is a contract based on the principle of indemnity (insured cannot make a profit from a claim on insurance).
- The insured must have an insurable interest.
- The coverage is conditioned upon the payment of premiums.

As a result of the characteristic of adhesiveness, when interpreting insurance contracts courts resolve any ambiguity in favor of the insured. This result is equitable since insurance contract language is customarily selected by the insurer and the insured has no opportunity to clarify the language. Therefore, court decisions concerning contract ambiguity will weigh in favor of coverage rather than noncoverage.

Insurance companies are regulated by individual states. Local regulation is effective because states know their local and regional markets and the needs of consumers within those markets. States have a direct interest in protecting consumers by making sure insurers remain solvent so that they can meet their contractual obligations of paying claims. In addition, states oversee sales, marketing, policy terms and conditions of insurance products to ensure consumers are protected when making purchases and filing claims. All insurance products sold in a state must be pre-approved by that state's insurance commissioner.

INSURANCE ON THE PERSON

Insurance on the person includes life insurance, health insurance, disability insurance, and long-term care insurance. In this section we will provide a discussion of whether or not a particular client needs (as opposed to wants) any of these four types of insurance. If the client needs the insurance, the planner should consider: (1) how much do they need, (2) what type do they need, and (3) what are some of the key provisions for inclusion that should be considered.

LIFE INSURANCE

Life insurance at its core is income replacement insurance. If a person dies suddenly, what kind of financial hardship results? Would the spouse and/or dependents be left without the income the person has expected to and wanted to provide them? If a person has no dependents, that person typically does not need life insurance to cover this risk. Conversely, if there are people who could not afford to lose the income of the person were that person to die, that person should have life insurance. Dependency is the critical issue to life insurance needs and assists in differentiating between a need versus a want. Married couples who are dependent on the income of both spouses to pay a mortgage need life insurance, as do spouses with dependent children.

Assuming a person needs life insurance, how much should they have? There are three methods used to determine the amount of life insurance needed. They are:

- The Human Life Value Method
- The Financial Needs Method
- The Capitalization of Earnings Method

The Human Life Value Method

The **human life value (HLV) method** uses projected future earnings as the basis for measuring life insurance needs. The HLV method projects the individual's income throughout his remaining work life expectancy. Then, using a discount rate (usually the risk-free rate of return or the inflation rate), the present value of the individual's future earnings is determined. Note that cash flows are adjusted downward by amounts that would have otherwise been used for personal consumption and for the payments of taxes on income. The net amount is known as the FSE (family's share of earnings).

Quick Quiz 5.2

Highlight the answer to these questions:

1. A hazard is a condition that creates or increases the likelihood of a loss occurring.
   a. True
   b. False

2. Moral hazard is the indifference to losses based on the existence of insurance.
   a. True
   b. False

3. The elements of a valid contract include offer and acceptance, legal competency of the parties, legal consideration, and lawful purpose.
   a. True
   b. False

True, False, True.

EXAMPLE 5.1

Fred, who is married and the father of one, is 35 years old and expects to continue to work until age 64. He earns $65,000 per year and expects annual salary increases of 3%. Fred expects inflation to be 3% over his working life, and the appropriate risk-free discount rate is 6%. His personal consumption is equal to 20% of his after-tax earnings, and his combined federal and state marginal tax bracket is 25%.

STEP 1: CALCULATE THE FAMILY'S SHARE OF EARNINGS (FSE)	
Annual Earnings $65,000	= Annual Taxes = $65,000 x 0.25 = $16,250
Personal Consumption	= (After-tax income x consumption %)
	= [(($65,000 - $16,250) x 0.20)]
	= $9,750
FSE (Family's Share of Earnings)	= Annual Earnings - (annual income taxes + annual personal consumption)
	= $65,000 - ($16,250 + $9,750)
	= $39,000

STEP 2: CALCULATE WORK LIFE EXPECTANCY (WLE)	
WLE	= The expected age at retirement less the current age
	= 64 - 35
WLE	= 29 years

STEP 3: DETERMINE HUMAN LIFE VALUE (HLV)*	
Future Value (FV)	= 0
Annual PMT_{OA}	= $39,000
Interest Rate (i)	= 2.91262 [[(1.06 ÷ 1.03 inflation rate) - 1] x 100]
Term of Years (n)	= 29
Human Life Value (PV)	= $756,642 (Present Value of an ordinary income)

* See Chapter 7 for assistance with time value of money calculations.

The $756,642 HLV represents the present value of Fred's life contributions to his family excluding taxes and his consumption. This is the amount of life insurance that is needed using the human life value approach. It would be reduced by any current life insurance.

The Financial Needs Method

The **financial needs method** evaluates the income replacement and lump-sum needs of survivors in the event of an income producer's untimely death. The impact of inflation over time is taken into consideration when using this approach by identifying the timing of the cash flow needs and calculating the present value of each.

A family that loses an income producer is likely to have some or all of the following common financial needs:

- Lump-sum (cash) needs
- Final expenses and debt repayment needs
- Mortgage liquidation or payment fund needs
- Education expense needs

- Emergency expense needs
- Income (cash flow) needs
- Readjustment period needs
- Dependency period needs
- Spousal life income (pre-and post retirement) needs

Lump-Sum (Cash) Needs

The deceased's survivors are expected to maintain a certain lifestyle. Most clients want to make sure that their dependents will not suffer a decrease in standard of living.

Final Expenses and Debt Repayment Needs

A fund for final expenses and debts is needed immediately by the survivors to pay for a deceased's out-of-pocket medical expenses prior to death, funeral costs, and other unplanned expenditures. Estate administration expenses, federal estate taxes, state death taxes, inheritance taxes, and income taxes must also be funded from a source outside the estate if insufficient liquid assets are in the estate to cover these costs.

Mortgage Liquidation or Payment Fund Needs

The family may wish to pay off an existing mortgage at the time of the breadwinner's death. This can be an effective way to reduce the cash flow needs of the surviving family.

Education Expense Needs

If an educational funding plan is not already in place, funds may be set aside for college and postcollege education. If the survivors choose not to set aside funds, and educational expenses will occur in the future, the expenses should be factored into the life income needed by the family.

Emergency Expense Needs

The purpose of this funding is to provide survivors with a cash reserve for unforeseen expenses that may arise as the family makes a transition to life without the deceased.

Readjustment Period Income Needs

The readjustment period typically lasts for one to two years following the death of the breadwinner. During this period, the family should receive approximately the same amount of income it received while the deceased was alive. Families will usually have certain non-recurring expenses as they adjust to a new lifestyle. For a family that will experience a decline in its standard of living, this period income allows the family to achieve the necessary readjustment.

Dependency Period Income Needs

The dependency period is one in which others (the deceased's spouse, children, and, in some cases, parents) would have been dependent on the deceased had she survived. In most cases, income needs are largest during this period. The length of the dependency period is determined by the number of dependents, their ages, and the deceased's contribution to the family's total income.

Spousal Life Income Needs

At some point the children will no longer be dependent upon the surviving spouse. However, the surviving spouse may still need to replace a part of the wage earner's income (especially if the surviving spouse was not an income earner). Surviving spouses who re-enter the workforce often find it difficult to find employment that enables them to maintain their prior standard of living. Therefore, it may be advisable to arrange lifetime income for the surviving spouse.

Two income periods should be considered: (1) the blackout period, and (2) the period during which the surviving spouse receives Social Security benefits. The blackout period refers to the period of time beginning when survivor Social Security benefits to the surviving spouse are discontinued (usually when the last child reaches age 16) and ending when the spouse begins to receive Social Security retirement benefits at age 60 or later. During the blackout period, income must be provided by employment, insurance, investments, or some other source. Once Social Security benefits resume, the amount of supplemental income may be reduced.

If both spouses earned income prior to the first death, a smaller percentage of total family income must be replaced upon one of the spouses's death. If, however, the sole breadwinner of the family has died, the ability (or desire) of the surviving spouse to secure employment must be considered.

In most cases, the children of the deceased will be entitled to Social Security benefits. The benefits received by the spouse, as caretaker of the children and on behalf of the children, will decrease the income needs of the family during the dependency period. In addition, if parents were dependents of the deceased, any Social Security benefits received by them as a result of the death of their adult child may also decrease the income needs during the period.

Assume Fred, age 35, earns $65,000 annually. His spouse, Frederica, age 34, is a homemaker, and they have one child, who just turned age 6. The couple assumes an average annual inflation rate of 3%. Fred and Frederica have set the following goals and assumptions:

EXAMPLE 5.2

Income needed - readjustment period (1 yr.)	$55,250
Income needed - dependency period	$55,250
Income needed - "empty nest" period	$40,000
Income needed - retirement	$36,000
Estate expenses and debts	$15,000
Education fund needed (in today's dollars)	$72,000
Emergency fund needed	$15,000
Investment assets (cash/cash equivalents) current	$200,000
Expected Social Security income while child is under 16	$20,000
Expected Social Security income while child is 17 and 18	$10,000
Expected Social Security income in retirement	$18,000
Frederica's life expectancy	85 years
Frederica expects Social Security benefits to begin	Age 60
Discount rate	6%

Given the previous information, how much life insurance does Fred need?

Step 1: Calculate the family's income (cash flow) needs for each period.

	Readjustment (1 year)	Child's Age (7 - 16)	Child's Age (17 - 18)	Empty Nest/ Blackout Period of Surviving Spouse (Age 46 - 60)	Retirement Period for Surviving Spouse (25 years)
Frederica's Age	34-35	35-45	45-46	46-60	66-80
Fred's (Would Be) Age	36	36-46	46-47	47-61	
Annual Income Needed	$55,250	$55,250	$55,250	$40,000	$36,000
Less: Assumed OASDI (Social Security)	$20,000	$20,000	$10,000	$0	$18,000
Net Annual Income Needed (PMT)	$35,250	$35,250	$45,250	$40,000	$18,000
$i = (\frac{1.06}{1.03}) - 1 \times 100$	2.9126	2.9126	2.9126	2.9126	2.9126
N = Years Needed	1	10	2	15	25
PV of net annual income needed (use begin mode)	$34,252	$310,832	$89,219	$494,547	$325,730
Discount Period	0	1	11 years	12 years	26 years
Present Value Today	**$34,252**	**$302,035**	**$65,058**	**$350,417**	**$154,410**

PV of total annual income needed: $906,172 ($34,252 + $302,035 + $65,058 + $350,417 + $154,410)

Step 2: Calculate the family's lump-sum funding needs.

Final expenses and debts	$15,000
Education funding needed (in today's dollars)	$72,000
Emergency fund	$15,000
Total lump-sum funding needs	**$102,000**

Step 3: Calculate the life insurance death benefit needed.

Total life insurance needed	$1,008,172	($906,172 + $102,000)
Less current life insurance	$0	
Less current liquid assets	($200,000)	
Net death benefit of life insurance needed	**$808,172**	

The Capitalization of Earnings Method

The **capitalization of earnings method** uses a fraction to determine life insurance needs. The initial numerator is the client's gross income and the initial denominator is the riskless rate of return (typically the yield on U.S. Treasury Bonds).

Recall the Fred examples (Example 5.1 and 5.2):

$$\frac{\text{Income}}{\text{Treasury Bond}} \quad \frac{\$65,000}{0.06} = \$1,083,333 \text{ Life Insurance Needed}$$

This calculation does not initially take into consideration taxes, consumption, or inflation. However, adjustments can be made to the numerator for taxes (\$16,250) and for personal consumption (\$9,750) and to the denominator for inflation (3%).

$$\frac{\$65,000 - \$16,250 - \$9,750}{[(1.06 \div 1.03) - 1]} = \frac{\$39,000}{0.029126} = \$1,339,000 \text{ Life Insurance Needed}$$

Summary	Life Insurance Needed
Human Life Value Method	$756,642
Financial Needs Method	$808,172
Capitalization Income Method	$1,339,000

Using all three of these methods, we conclude that if life insurance is needed, it should be sufficient if it is approximately 12 - 16 x the client's gross pay (\$65,000 x 12 = \$780,000 to \$65,000 x 16 = \$1,040,000). (Note that the average of the three methods is \$967,938.)

TYPES OF LIFE INSURANCE

There are two general types of life insurance, term and permanent. Permanent is frequently broken down into whole (ordinary life) and universal life. Ordinary life offers a death benefit along with a savings component. Universal life offers more flexibility than ordinary life including the availability of altering the death benefit, savings component, and premium payments. The basic difference between term life insurance and permanent life insurance is that where permanent insurance has a savings and investment component, term does not.

Term life insurance is "pure insurance" and is for a stated temporary period of time (10, 20, 25, 30 years). Term insurance is attractive to consumers because the premiums are significantly lower than the premiums for permanent policies. (See Exhibit 5.2 - life insurance premium cost comparisons per \$1,000 of coverage.)

Term life insurance can be annually renewed usually with an increasing premium or it can be level premium for the entire term. A policy that is annually renewed will have increasing premiums to correspond with the increasing risk of mortality as individuals age. Fixed premium term insurance (e.g., 20, 30 years) is attractive because over time it becomes easier to pay the premium assuming the client is receiving pay increases. Initially the premium is higher than an annual renewable term policy because you are paying for not only this year's mortality risk, but also for part of the future mortality risk. Annual renewable term with an increasing premium is attractive initially because of the low initial premium in comparison to level premium term.

Most people with incomes less than $250,000 to $400,000 buy term insurance because they can get a death benefit that is sufficiently large and for a relatively small premium. The following exhibit compares the costs of varying term policies and permanent life insurance (universal life).

Quick Quiz 5.3

Highlight the answer to these questions:

1. The human life value method of measuring life insurance needs evaluates the income replacement and lump-sum needs of survivors in the event of the insured's death.
   a. True
   b. False

2. The capitalization of earnings method uses the client's gross income divided by the riskless rate of return to arrive at the initial amount of life insurance need.
   a. True
   b. False

3. Term life insurance has both a savings and an investment component.
   a. True
   b. False

False, True, False.

EXHIBIT 5.2	LIFE INSURANCE PREMIUM COSTS COMPARISON FOR TERM AND UNIVERSAL (PER $1,000 OF COVERAGE)

Age	Term* (10 year)	Term* (25 year)	Term* (30 year)	Universal Life
25	$0.25	$0.52	$0.60	$2.31
30	$0.25	$0.56	$0.64	$2.92
35	$0.26	$0.65	$0.72	$3.77
40	$0.31	$0.96	$1.04	$4.74
45	$0.51	$1.52	$1.68	$5.99
50	$0.83	N/A	N/A	$7.45
55	$1.40	N/A	N/A	$9.05
60	$2.39	N/A	N/A	$11.74
65	$4.08	N/A	N/A	$15.40

Price is per $1,000 of coverage ($ per 000).
For very healthy non-tobacco using male insured.
* Usually available to terminate at or before age 75.

HEALTH INSURANCE

A health insurance plan is an arrangement that provides benefits to the insured in the event of sickness or personal injury. Health insurance coverage can include hospitalization coverage, major medical, and indemnity or managed care plan coverage (health maintenance organizations, preferred provider organizations, and point of service plans). In general, health insurance plans should provide lifetime benefits of at least $1 million for each person. Otherwise, they are probably inadequate.

Indemnity Coverage

Indemnity coverage allows the insured to choose health care providers. The insured can go to any doctor, hospital, or other medical provider. Reimbursement is based on services provided and a deductible or portion of services billed may be required of the insured. The policy may have an annual limit to the insured's out-of-pocket expenses where additional covered services beyond the limit are paid in full. Covered services may be restricted and prior authorization may be required for high cost medical services.

A High Deductible Health Plan (HDHP) is an inexpensive health insurance plan that provides benefits after a high deductible is met. The following exhibit reflects minimum and maximum deductibles for HDHPs.

DEDUCTIBLE LIMITS FOR HDHPs, 2012 AND 2013

EXHIBIT 5.3

	Minimum Deductible		Maximum Deductible and Out of Pocket Expenses	
	2012	2013	2012	2013
Individual	$1,200	$1,250	$6,050	$6,250
Family	$2,400	$2,500	$12,100	$12,500

This type of health plan may be a good option for the client interested in financial planning services that are focused on budgeting expenses.

Managed Care Options

A Health Maintenance Organization (HMO) plan provides access to a network of participating medical providers including physicians, hospitals, and other medical professionals and facilities. The insured selects a network primary care physician who provides medical services and coordinates the insurance care. A HMO plan generally requires less out of pocket expenses by the insured and a co-payment for services such as office visits and pharmacy prescriptions is typically required.

A Preferred Provider Organization (PPO) charges on fee-for-service basis. The medical providers are paid by the insurer on an agreed upon discounted fee schedule. The insured is encouraged to use in-network healthcare providers to maintain lower costs. If the insured chooses an out-of-network medical provider, additional expenses may be incurred.

A Point-of-Service (POS) plan coordinates care through a primary care doctor that makes referrals to other providers who participate in the plan. Referrals by the primary care physician to an out of plan provider, is typically covered in full. If the insured self-refers to an out of network provider, then additional expenses (co-insurance payment) will be incurred.

Patient Protection and Affordable Care Act

The Patient Protection and Affordable Care Act was passed by Congress and then signed into law by the President on March 23, 2010. On June 28, 2012 the Supreme Court rendered a final decision to uphold the health care law. The law, which is thousands of pages long, is phased in over several years and expected to extend heath care coverage to 30 million Americans, who would otherwise be uninsured. The law attempts to make transform the US health care system, including providing better access, eliminating medical limits, eliminating the issue of pre-existing conditions, expanding Medicaid access, and imposing penalties on individuals and some businesses for not having health care insurance. It is far too soon to fully understand the full impact of this law. However, what is certain is that this law will dramatically change health care in the United States.

LONG-TERM DISABILITY

The likelihood of long-term disability is far greater than that of untimely death. Actuaries estimate that one in three individuals will suffer a disability that lasts 90 days or more. One of ten persons will be permanently disabled before age 65.

Disability insurance provides replacement income to the insured while the insured is unable to work because of sickness (illness) or injury (accident).

The coverage should include accidental bodily injury and illness. The illness coverage may exclude preexisting conditions (such as colitis).

Key Concepts

Underline/highlight the answers as you read:

1. Determine the purpose of disability insurance.

2. Identify the various definitions of disability and the associated insurance coverage.

The critical issues and provisions related to disability insurance include:
- the definition of disability,
- coverage for both sickness and accidents,
- the amount of benefits per month / year,
- the term of benefits,
- the elimination period (waiting period of self insurance), and
- whether or not the policy is noncancelable (the insurer cannot cancel and cannot raise premiums - expensive) or guaranteed renewable (the insurer cannot cancel but can raise premiums if the increase is on everyone in the class or pool).

The range of disability definitions include:

Own Occupation: This disability coverage is determined by whether or not the insured can carry out each and every one of the duties of his employment. If the insured cannot perform each and every one of his usual duties, then he will qualify for disability benefits. This coverage may be either to retirement or may be for a set term of one, two, or five years.

Any Occupation: If disability coverage is defined as any occupation, the insured is considered disabled if he cannot work in any occupation for which he is qualified for by education, training, or experience. If the insured can perform the duties of employment that is comparable to the job held prior to the illness or injury, benefits may be discontinued.

Hybrid (sometimes called split definition): Some disability policies, especially group disability policies, offer a definition of disability that contains characteristics from both own occupation and any occupation classifications. For example, a hybrid disability policy may offer own occupation for five years and any occupation after that time period.

Partial Disability: A disability policy may offer coverage for partial disability where the insured can perform either a part of his own occupation or a portion of the previous time in his own occupation. If the insured meets the definition of partial disability, then the insured would receive a proportion of the disability benefit.

Elimination Period: The time during which an insured must be disabled and before disability income benefits will begin. A common elimination period is 90 days with shorter elimination periods resulting in higher premiums and longer elimination periods resulting in lower premiums.

Noncancelable Insurance: A disability policy's noncancelable provision ensures that the insurance will not be cancelled and that the premiums will remain fixed for the term of the policy.

Guaranteed Renewable Insurance: A guaranteed renewable feature of a policy obligates the insurer to continue coverage as long as premiums are paid on the policy. While renewal is guaranteed, premiums can increase if they are increased on the entire group.

Quick Quiz 5.4

Highlight the answer to these questions:

1. Critical provisions related to disability insurance include the definition of disability, coverage for both sickness and accidents, and whether the policy is noncancelable or guaranteed renewable.
   a. True
   b. False

2. The noncancelable provision of a disability policy ensures that the insurance will not be cancelled and that the premiums will remain fixed for the term of the policy.
   a. True
   b. False

3. The guaranteed renewable feature of a disability insurance policy obligates the insurer to continue coverage as long as appropriate premiums are paid on the policy.
   a. True
   b. False

True, True, True.

EXHIBIT 5.4 **DISABILITY POLICY CHARACTERISTICS**

Policy Characteristics	Low Coverage	Medium Coverage	High Coverage
Monthly Benefit	$6,000	$6,000	$6,000
Elimination Period	90 days	90 days	90 days
Benefit Period	5 years	to age 67	to age 67*
Noncancelable	No	No (guaranteed renewable)	Yes
Occupation Specific	No	No	Yes
Partial Benefits (if go back to work part time)	Yes	Yes	Yes
Cost of Living Increases	No	No	Yes

Example policy for 40 year old with annual income of $100,000.
*Or for life if disability occurs before age 50.

Exhibit 5.5 provides sample premiums (by age) for disability policies with low, medium, and high coverage.

EXHIBIT 5.5 **DISABILITY POLICY MONTHLY PREMIUMS (FOR EXHIBIT 5.4 POLICIES)**

Age	Low Coverage	Medium Coverage	High Coverage
30	$68	$102	$168
35	$75	$120	$213
40	$100	$137	$263
45	$119	$155	$322
50	$148	$183	$380
55	$195	$218	$411
60	$267	$258	$453

Example individual policy for annual income of $100,000.

EXHIBIT 5.6 **LONG-TERM DISABILITY SUMMARY OF ISSUES AND METRICS**

Issue	Adequate Coverage
Coverage	Both sickness and accidental
Term of Benefits	To retirement or for life
Amount of Benefit	60 - 70% of gross pay
Elimination Period	Depends on emergency fund but generally 90 - 180 days
Definition of Disability	Own occupation or hybrid of own (up to 5 years under this definition of coverage), and any occupation for which insured is educated, experienced, or trained for balance
Cancelable	Noncancelable or guaranteed renewable

LONG-TERM CARE INSURANCE

Long-term care insurance pays benefits when the insured is unable to perform at least two of the activities of daily living (ADL). Those activities typically include: eating, bathing, dressing, toileting, transferring (walking), and continence. If the insured cannot perform two or more of these activities of daily living or has cognitive impairment, the policy normally pays benefits. Assisting an insured with ADLs is referred to as custodial care (not skilled medical care). Services can be provided in an adult day care center, an assisted living center, or at home.

A client who anticipates qualifying for Medicaid services for long-term care might consider not purchasing long-term care insurance. In addition, the client with financial resources to cover long-term care may not want to purchase long-term care insurance. The client who falls in between (cannot afford to self insure long-term care and does not anticipate qualifying for Medicaid) may want to seriously consider purchasing long-term care insurance.

It is less expensive to purchase long-term care insurance at a younger age (pre-50) and purchasing the insurance at a younger age also reduces the likelihood of being rejected for coverage. Most policies have a waiting (elimination) period from when the long-term care is first needed until when the policy begins to pay benefits. The longer the waiting period, the lower the policy premium.

The benefit period can vary from two years to a lifetime. Premiums can be reduced by selecting coverage for three to four years instead of a lifetime. Most policies pay on an expense-incurred basis (reimbursement versus indemnity) up to the policy limits. When purchasing a long-term care policy, an inflation protection provision should be considered to protect the client from the loss of purchasing power of long-term care services. Additional important policy features include:

- Guaranteed renewable - The policy must be renewed by the insurer although the premiums can increase if they are increased for the entire class of policyholders.
- Waiver of premium - No further premiums are due once the insured begins receiving benefits.

HOMEOWNERS AND RENTERS INSURANCE

Key Concepts

Underline/highlight the answers as you read:

1. Identify the insurance coverages in a package homeowners insurance policy.

2. Identify the six parts of a personal automobile policy (PAP).

3. Determine the purpose of a personal liability umbrella policy.

A home represents a major asset to the client. The frequency of a loss of a home is small, but the severity if it happens is potentially financially catastrophic. The key to homeowners insurance coverage, like any other property insurance, is having the correct risks (perils) covered and having them covered for the proper value (replacement value). **Homeowners insurance coverage** is a package policy covering dwelling, dwelling extensions (garage), personal property, loss of use, medical payments for others, and liability. Standard homeowner policies do not cover flood or earth movement (earthquake, mud slide). In addition, those properties located in an area prone to hurricanes may require a separate policy for wind and hail damage.

Homeowner policies range from covering 18 perils (broad) to open perils (open or "all") and from actual cash value (ACV = replacement cost - depreciation) to replacement value. There may be mixed coverages with open perils and replacement value on the dwelling and broad and actual cash value on personal property. Most homeowners and renters are not knowledgeable about insurance and should generally purchase open perils and replacement value for all property in a homeowners policy. This may require an endorsement for personal property since many homeowners and renters policies only have broad perils covered for personal property and then only for actual cash value.

Homeowners policies do not cover everything that can happen. Generally homeowners policies cover damage from fires, tornadoes (wind), trees falling, theft, and loss of use. However, homeowners policies frequently do not cover damage from earth movement (quake, mudslide, sink hole), mold, rising water (flood), sewer backup (without rider), war, nuclear accidents, neglect, dogs, and intentional acts by the insured or family, and some do not cover acts of terrorism.

In addition, valuable collections or items (guns, wine, coins, stamps, cash, jewelry) while perhaps covered may be limited in value to the amount for which they are covered (e.g., up to $1,000 or some other limit). If the client has such collections, they probably need a policy rider.

SUMMARY OF DISASTERS COVERED BY HOMEOWNERS POLICIES[1]

EXHIBIT 5.7

Perils	Dwelling & Personal Property — Broad HO-2*	Dwelling — Special HO-3*	Personal Property — Special HO-3	Personal Property — Renters HO-4	Personal Property — Condo/Co-op HO-6	Dwelling & Personal Property — Modified Coverage HO-8
1. Fire or lightning	x	x	x	x	x	x
2. Windstorm or hail	x	x	x	x	x	x
3. Explosion	x	x	x	x	x	x
4. Riot or civil commotion	x	x	x	x	x	x
5. Damage caused by aircraft	x	x	x	x	x	x
6. Damage caused by vehicles	x	x	x	x	x	x
7. Smoke	x	x	x	x	x	x
8. Vandalism or malicious mischief	x	x	x	x	x	x
9. Theft	x	x	x	x	x	x
10. Volcanic eruption	x	x	x	x	x	x
11. Falling object	x	x	x	x	x	
12. Weight of ice, snow or sleet	x	x	x	x	x	
13. Accidental discharge or overflow of water or steam from within a plumbing, heating, air conditioning, or automatic fire-protective sprinkler system, or from a household appliance.	x	x	x	x	x	
14. Sudden and accidental tearing apart, cracking, burning, or bulging of a steam or hot water heating system, an air conditioning or automatic fire-protective system.	x	x	x	x	x	
15. Freezing of a plumbing, heating, air conditioning or automatic, fire-protective sprinkler system, or of a household appliance.	x	x	x	x	x	
16. Sudden and accidental damage from artificially generated electrical current (does not include loss to a tube, transistor or similar electronic component).	x	x	x	x	x	
17. All perils except flood, earthquake, war, nuclear accident, landslide, mudslide, sinkhole and others specified in your policy. Check your policy for a complete list of perils excluded.		x				

* HO-1, HO-2 and HO-3 refer to standard Homeowners Policies.

Note: HO-1 has been discontinued in most states. The 18th peril is not listed and is glass breakage, which is covered by HO-2 (broad form).

---

1. Excerpt from Insurance Information Institute, "What Types of Disasters are Covered?"

AUTOMOBILE INSURANCE

Automobile liability insurance is required in every state. Many people also buy automobile property insurance (comprehensive - theft, and collision - damage from a wreck). The owner of an automobile is concerned about risks associated with the financial loss due to damage to the owned automobile, damage to the property of others, and bodily injury to the insured, family members, and to others.

The **personal automobile policy (PAP)** is a package policy that protects against loss for the three risks mentioned above. The PAP contract is organized into six parts.
- **Part A** - Liability coverage for bodily injury and property damage to others.
- **Part B** - Medical payments coverage (used to mitigate damage and not necessarily related to fault); may benefit anyone in the accident.
- **Part C** - Uninsured motorist coverage - covers uninsured and underinsured motorist who cause damage to the insured passengers or the insured's property.
- **Part D** - Coverage for damage to the insured automobile, comprehensive (e.g., theft, tree falling etc.) and collision (striking any inanimate object while moving).
- **Part E** - Duties of the insured (notify insurer, file proof of claim, and cooperate with any investigation).
- **Part F** - General Provisions - Various provisions including that coverage is only valid in the U.S., its territories, and Canada (not Mexico or other foreign countries).

EXCLUSIONS

The PAP has exclusions for liability for public livery (the transporting of people or goods for hire), intentional acts, business use of auto, use without permission, for the insured's property, and bodily injury to an employee (except domestic employee).

Exclusions for medical payments include public livery, use without permission, business use, racing, and intentional acts.

Exclusions for uninsured motorist coverage include public livery, regular use of non-owned or nondeclared auto, use without permission, and business use.

Exclusions for damage to the insured's automobile includes public livery, use without permission, racing, intentional acts, business use and, in addition, some items found in the car may not be covered (e.g., radar detectors and electronic equipment not permanently installed).

RATES

Automobile rates vary by zip code, marital status, age, sex, and driving record. In order to manage premiums effectively, the insured should solicit regular quotes (every one to two years) and should raise deductibles. The following exhibit lists the average annual automobile insurance premium by state from highest to lowest.

Rank	State	Average Premium	Rank	State	Average Premium
1	Louisiana	$2,536	26	Maryland	$1,372
2	Oklahoma	$2,047	27	Alabama	$1,345
3	Michigan	$2,013	28	Arkansas	$1,334
4	West Virginia	$2,002	29	Colorado	$1,322
5	Washington, D.C.	$1,866	30	Utah	$1,315
6	Montana	$1,856	31	Washington	$1,305
7	Rhode Island	$1,830	32	South Dakota	$1,303
8	Wyoming	$1,732	33	Indiana	$1,301
9	California	$1,709	34	Virginia	$1,297
10	Georgia	$1,694	35	New Mexico	$1,274
11	Connecticut	$1,665	36	Minnesota	$1,264
12	Texas	$1,661	37	Nebraska	$1,244
13	Florida	$1,654	38	Oregon	$1,241
14	Delaware	$1,652	39	Tennessee	$1,228
15	New Jersey	$1,608	40	Nevada	$1,223
16	Pennsylvania	$1,598	41	Illinois	$1,192
17	Hawaii	$1,594	42	Arizona	$1,176
18	Kentucky	$1,572	43	New Hampshire	$1,133
19	Mississippi	$1,502	44	South Carolina	$1,108
20	Missouri	$1,455	45	Ohio	$1,099
National Average		$1,438	46	Vermont	$1,063
21	Alaska	$1,431	47	North Carolina	$1,022
22	North Dakota	$1,426	48	Idaho	$1,011
23	New York	$1,413	49	Wisconsin	$987
24	Kansas	$1,410	50	Vermont	$985
25	Massachusetts	$1,378	51	Maine	$889

Source: Insure.com; http://www.insure.com/car-insurance/car-insurance-rates.html

It should be noted that personal automobile policies do not cover other types of vehicles (e.g., boats, motorcycles, etc.). In addition, the PAP does not cover business automobiles.

PERSONAL LIABILITY INSURANCE

Today, lawsuits are common. Juries and judges are awarding larger amounts of money than ever before. Claims arise from incidents at home, while driving an automobile, boat, recreational vehicle, motorcycle and other activities (snow skiing). The question is, are the underlying liability coverages for homeowners policies and automobile insurance packages sufficient to meet the award if a person is judged to be at fault?

Generally, liability policies provide for a legal defense as well as for paying a claim up to the limit of the policy. However, if the insurer is willing to pay the limit of the policy, then legal defense is not required and the client is on their own. <u>Almost all homeowner policies have inadequate liability coverages.</u> Automobile policies that have limits for bodily injury to others of $100,000 or even $300,000 per person may prove to be inadequate.

Quick Quiz 5.5

Highlight the answer to these questions:

1. The personal automobile policy (PAP) is a package policy that protects against loss for liability, comprehensive, and collision risks.
   a. True
   b. False

2. The PAP includes coverage for use with permission, business use, and unintentional acts.
   a. True
   b. False

3. The lack of catastrophic liability coverage in homeowners and auto insurance creates the need for an excess liability policy (PLUP).
   a. True
   b. False

True, False, True.

This lack of catastrophic liability coverage creates the need for an excess liability policy known as a **personal liability umbrella policy (PLUP)**. PLUP is usually sold in millions of dollars coverage (e.g. $1M, $3M, $5M) and provides excess liability coverage and legal defense for claims that may arise and that exceed the limits of the underlying homeowners and automobile policies. The PLUP also covers the entire family and fills in the liability gap that exists between the homeowners and automobile policy. The PLUP is relatively inexpensive ($1,000,000 in Louisiana is $300 per year, $4,000,000 in Maryland is $450 per year) and is based on the risk analysis by the underwriter of the insured.

The PLUP is usually sold by the automobile or home insurer and the amount needed is not balance sheet dependent, but rather risk dependent (e.g., what has been the amount of recent awards in a particular state for common, although infrequent, accidental perils).

CONCLUSION

The chapter presents an introduction to the most common types of client risk. Risk management issues are a priority as part of the personal financial plan because catastrophic loss can lead to financial planning failure. A full course in insurance and/or consultation with an insurance expert is recommended for all planners aspiring to competently assist clients with important risk management issues.

Key Terms

Capitalization of Earnings Method - A method that initially uses a numerator of gross income and denominator of riskless rate of return to determine life insurance needs. It can be further adjusted to account for taxes, personal consumption, and inflation.

Disability Insurance - Insurance that provides replacement income to the insured while the insured is unable to work because of sickness (illness) or injury (accident).

Financial Needs Method - A method that evaluates the income replacement and lump-sum needs of survivors in the event of an income producer's untimely death.

Hazard - A condition that creates or increases the likelihood of a loss occurring.

Homeowners Insurance Coverage - A package policy covering dwelling, dwelling extensions (garage), personal property, loss of use, medical payments for others, and liability.

Human Life Value (HLV) Method - A method that uses projected future earnings after taxes and individual consumption to determine the family's share of earnings (FSE) as the basis for measuring life insurance needs.

Liability Risk - A risk that may cause financial loss (injury to another for which the client is determined to be financially responsible).

Life Insurance - At its most basic is income replacement insurance.

Loss Frequency - The expected number of losses that will occur within a given period of time.

Loss Severity - The potential size or financial damage of a loss.

Moral Hazard - A character flaw or level of dishonesty an individual possesses that causes or increases the chance for a loss.

Morale Hazard - Indifference to losses based on the existence of insurance.

Named-Perils Policy - A policy that provides protection against losses caused by the perils that are specifically listed as covered in the policy.

Open-Perils Policies - Policies that are called "all-risks" policies, because they cover all risks of loss (perils) that are not specifically excluded from the contract.

Perils - The proximate or actual cause of a loss, such as fire, liability, or accidental death.

Key Terms

Personal Automobile Policy (PAP) - A package policy that protects against loss due to damage to the owned automobile, damage to the property of others, and bodily injury to the insured, family members, and others.

Personal Liability Umbrella Policy (PLUP) - A policy usually sold in millions of dollars coverage (e.g. $1M, $3M, $5M) and provides excess liability coverage and legal defense for claims that may arise and that exceed the limits of the underlying homeowners and automobile policies.

Personal Risk - A risk that may cause the loss of income (untimely death, disability, health issues), or alternatively cause an increase in the cost of living (disability, health issues).

Personal Risk Management - A systematic process for identifying, evaluating, and managing pure risk exposures faced by an individual.

Physical Hazard - A tangible condition or circumstance that increases the probability of a peril occurring and/or the severity of damages that result from a peril.

Property Risk - A risk that may cause the loss of property (automobile, home, or other asset).

Pure Risk - A risk for which there is a possibility of loss, but no possibility of gain. The possibility of a home being damaged or destroyed by a fire is an example of a pure risk. Most pure risks are insurable.

Risk Avoidance - Avoiding an activity so that a financial loss cannot be incurred.

Risk Reduction - Implementing activities that will result in the reduction of the frequency and severity of losses.

Risk Retention - The state of being exposed to a risk and personally retaining the potential for loss.

Risk Transfer - Transferring or shifting the risk of loss through means such as insurance or a warranty.

DISCUSSION QUESTIONS

1. Describe the personal risk management process.

2. List four responses to managing risk.

3. Define a peril.

4. Define the three main types of hazard.

5. List some of the unique characteristics of an insurance contract.

6. What are three methods used to determine the amount of life insurance needed?

7. Discuss the characteristics of term life insurance.

8. Define the difference between own occupation and any occupation disability definitions and the associated coverage.

9. Discuss the coverage available under a homeowners insurance policy.

10. Define a personal automobile policy (PAP).

11. Discuss why there is a need for personal liability insurance.

12. Differentiate between noncancellable and guaranteed renewable.

1. During your recent meeting with Ron, a new client, you discussed the concept of risk. You defined several terms for Ron. Which of the following terms is defined as: the possibility of loss, but no possibility of gain?

    a. Pure Risk.
    b. Perils.
    c. Risk Transfer.
    d. Open-perils.

2. Which of the following would <u>not</u> be considered a personal risk?

    a. Becoming disabled due to a car accident.
    b. Injuring a passenger in your vehicle during an auto accident that was your fault.
    c. Dying at age 42 given a normal life expectancy of age 80.
    d. Being diagnosed with a curable form of cancer.

3. Nathan, age 35, came into your office today. He has been a client of yours for a long time. He has neglected his insurance portfolio up until this point and wants to complete the personal risk management process. Together you determine that his insurance objective is to "insure, in the most economical way, only those risks that have the potential of causing catastrophic financial loss." You also identified all of the possible risk exposures. In evaluating these risks, which of the following is true?

    a. Loss severity is the expected number of losses that will occur within a given period of time.
    b. Death is always catastrophic.
    c. Most, if not all clients, need health insurance.
    d. Perils are the proximate or actual cause of a loss that upon occurrence always leads to financial hardship.

4. You recently met with your client, Don, age 40. Don is widowed and has one dependent child. During your meeting with him you discussed the concept of risk management. Which of the following statements regarding the ways to manage risk is incorrect?

    a. The selling of Don's Jet Ski is an example of risk reduction.
    b. Not purchasing life insurance is an example of risk retention.
    c. Purchasing a warranty is an example of risk transfer.
    d. Insurance is not necessary for every risk of financial loss.

5. If a risk has a high frequency of occurrence and a high severity, you should:

    a. Transfer the risk.

    b. Retain the risk.

    c. Reduce the risk.

    d. Avoid the risk.

6. Ginny and Max own a rental home on the Gulf Coast. They insured their property with their local insurance company. The policy provides protection against losses caused by perils that are specifically listed as covered in the policy. What type of policy do they have?

    a. All-risk policy.

    b. Open-perils policy.

    c. Named-perils policy.

    d. Identified-perils policy.

7. Jennifer had a very bad year. She wrecked her car in January when she ran a red light (because she could not see properly having left her contacts at home) and crashed into another car completely destroying both cars. The insurance company was very nice to her and she purchased a new car with the insurance proceeds. Jennifer decided that since she had insurance, it really did not matter if she took proper care of her new car because she could always get a new one. Jennifer got in the habit of leaving her new car unlocked and it was stolen. After Jennifer bought another car she decided that she really liked the insurance adjuster and wanted to see him again, so one day she purposefully set her car on fire. In her carelessness, she also caught her hand on fire. Jennifer was depressed over her circumstances and decided she didn't want to go back to work. She filed a falsified disability claim for the loss of use of her hand (even though she could still use her hand). Which of the following statements is true?

    a. Driving with poor eyesight is not a hazard.

    b. Leaving the car unlocked is a morale hazard.

    c. Burning the car on purpose is a morale hazard.

    d. Filing a false disability claim is a morale hazard.

8. Which of the following is most likely to be an insurable risk?

    a. Intentionally burning down your house.

    b. War.

    c. Gambling losses.

    d. An automobile accident due to negligence.

9. You recently met with your client, Tripp, to discuss his insurance policies. Tripp was reading a book on contracts and wanted to know how his insurance contract related to the material he was reading and to his circumstances. During your conversation, Tripp made several statements to clarify that he understood insurance. Which of the following statements would you have told him was incorrect?

   a. An insurance contract is unilateral, where both parties agree to a legally enforceable promise.

   b. The insurance contract is aleatory, where unequal monetary values are exchanged.

   c. An insurance contract is based on the principal of indemnity, where the insured cannot make a profit from a claim on insurance.

   d. An insurance contract is a contract of adhesion, where the insured accepts the contract as written and is unable to negotiate the terms of the contract.

10. Erin purchased a life insurance policy on her own life. Her husband Mike is the beneficiary of the policy. Which of the following is not a necessary legal element of the contract?

    a. Offer and acceptance.

    b. Legal competency of all parties.

    c. Consideration.

    d. Listed beneficiary.

11. Joe wants to purchase a life insurance policy on his own life. He is interested in learning about the various approaches to determine the amount needed. Which of the following is not true regarding the three most common approaches?

    a. The human life value method estimates the present value of income generated over a person's work life expectancy and is then adjusted for the expected consumption of the survivors.

    b. The financial needs method evaluates the income replacement and lump-sum needs of the survivors after the insured dies.

    c. The capitalization of earnings method determines need by dividing the client's gross income by the riskless rate of return.

    d. In practice a financial planner would utilize all three methods and then determine the client's needs based on a combination of factors including affordability.

12. Which of the following is true regarding the financial needs method used to determine life insurance needs?

    a.   Most clients are fine with their dependents suffering a decrease in their standard of living.

    b.   The readjustment period typically lasts for one to two years following the death of the breadwinner.

    c.   Final expenses and debts are not a key feature of this method because they are generally limited in amount and often not due for a long time after death.

    d.   The so-called blackout period is the period of time between the insured's death and when the insurance death benefit is actually paid out.

13. Josh, age 30, is a single father of one daughter, Nicole, age 11. Josh works for an advertising agency with an annual income of $40,000. Due to his messy divorce and several student loans that drain his financial resources, Josh lives paycheck to paycheck. His doctor recently discovered that he has high cholesterol and Josh is worried that his health may fail. He wants to purchase a life insurance policy to protect Nicole in the event of his untimely death (his employer does not yet offer a group plan). Assuming he wants to buy as much coverage as possible for the cheapest price, which of the following policies should he buy?

    a.   A whole life insurance policy.

    b.   A universal policy.

    c.   A single premium whole life policy.

    d.   A 20-year term insurance policy.

14. Julie is a doctor that specializes in performing heart surgery on babies. She has a long-term disability policy that covers her in the event that she can no longer perform this type of surgery due to disability. What type of long-term disability insurance policy does she have?

    a.   Hybrid occupation.

    b.   Own occupation.

    c.   Any occupation.

    d.   Specific occupation.

15. Zach and Laura recently purchased a new home. They came to your office to ask several questions about their homeowner's policy. Which of the following is true regarding homeowners insurance?

    a.   Most policies cover all possible losses.

    b.   Most policies cover all possessions within the home.

    c.   Zach and Laura should probably have an open perils and replacement value for all property covered under the homeowners policy.

    d.   Broad peril coverage means the insurance company covers "all" perils.

16. Jim's car was totaled in a wreck. He failed to yield to oncoming traffic and Jim was found to be at fault. The driver of the car he hit did not have insurance. Jim's own car insurance policy reimbursed him for the property damage to his own vehicle. What type of coverage would pay for this?

    a. Liability coverage.

    b. Uninsured motorist coverage.

    c. Comprehensive coverage.

    d. Collision coverage.

17. Tom is interested in purchasing a personal liability umbrella policy (PLUP). He has asked you to educate him on this type of policy. Which of the following is true?

    a. PLUPs are very expensive.

    b. Most people do not need a PLUP.

    c. PLUPs are usually sold in million dollars of coverage.

    d. Since Tom owns a home and a car with no other assets other than clothing, dishes, etc., he does not need a PLUP.

Quick Quiz Explanations

Quick Quiz 5.1
1. True.
2. True.
3. False. This is the definition for risk reduction. Risk avoidance is avoiding an activity so that a financial loss cannot be incurred.
4. True.

Quick Quiz 5.2
1. True.
2. False. This is the definition of a morale hazard. A moral hazard is a character flaw or level of dishonesty an individual possesses that causes or increases the chance for a loss.
3. True.

Quick Quiz 5.3
1. False. This is the definition of the financial needs method of measuring life insurance need. The human life value method uses projected future earnings as the basis for measuring life insurance needs.
2. True.
3. False. Permanent insurance has both a savings and investment component. Term life insurance has no savings or investment component.

Quick Quiz 5.4
1. True.
2. True.
3. True.

Quick Quiz 5.5
1. True.
2. False. Business use is not an included coverage under a PAP. Exclusions from coverage under a PAP includes liability for public livery, intentional acts, business use of auto, use without permission, for insured's property, and bodily injury to an employee (except domestic employee).
3. True.

John & Mary Burke Case and Case Analysis

LEARNING OBJECTIVES

After reading this chapter, you should be able to:

- Describe an initial meeting and summarize data and draw conclusions for the life cycle approach.
- Prepare a comprehensive engagement letter.
- Gather internal and external data and prepare financial statements.
- Create the pie chart approach.
- Prepare financial statement analysis using a ratio analysis approach.
- Prepare each of the ratios and compare them to the benchmark.
- Prepare the two-step, three panel, metrics approach with schedules.
- Prepare the cash flow approach.
- Prepare the tax analysis approach.
- Prepare the strategic approach.
- Prepare the present value of all goals approach.
- Make a presentation to the client using current and projected financial statements and ratios.
- Prepare a closing engagement letter that includes the responsibility for implementation and monitoring.

JOHN AND MARY BURKE CASE

This chapter presents a financial planning case incorporating the introductory information in Chapter 1, the financial planning approaches in Chapter 3, the financial statement analysis in Chapter 4, and the risk management information in Chapter 5 of this textbook. The Burke case analysis is presented in a basic fashion to assist the developing financial planner in understanding the importance of professionally providing the fundamental tasks as well as complicated tasks throughout the comprehensive financial planning process.

	Dialog of Phone Conversation **December 15, 2012, 1:00 p.m.**
Mike Mitchell:	Hello Mr. Burke (formal, show respect). This is Mike Mitchell returning your call from this morning. I understand you are interested in developing a financial plan for your family. Is that correct (questioning)?
John Burke:	Yes, thank you for returning my call. You come highly recommended from my good friend and mentor, Sally Robbins, who I believe is one of your financial planning clients.
Mike Mitchell:	Well thank you. Yes, Sally has been a client for some time now. I appreciate you letting me know that Sally recommended our services.
John Burke:	You're welcome.
Mike Mitchell:	I expect you want to set up an appointment? How about you and your wife meeting with me at 9:00 a.m. on January 4th at my office? Would that work for you? The meeting would last about two hours, giving us time to get to know each other. There is no charge for the initial meeting.
John Burke:	January 4th is fine and I know where your office is located. Do I need to bring anything?
Mike Mitchell:	Well, I would like to send you an email with a list of items to bring. I'll mention them now (internal data collection): your recent bank statements, investment account statements, all insurance policies, 5 years of tax returns (if you have them), employer benefits brochures, and a set of financial statements (if you have them). No need to write all of this down, I will email you a detailed list. What is your email address?
John Burke:	jburke@hotmail.com
Mike Mitchell:	Ok, great. Please do not worry if you do not have all these things; just bring what you can. The whole process takes time. By the way, would you mind if I asked you a few brief questions to help me form a picture of you and your family (life cycle information)?
John Burke:	No, go ahead.
Mike Mitchell:	Your wife's name is Mary, correct?
John Burke:	Yes.
Mike Mitchell:	How old are each of you?
John Burke:	We are both 30 years old and have been married for 3 years. I was previously married and have a 4 year old son, Patrick, but we are estranged. He lives out of state.
Mike Mitchell:	Fine. Do you plan on having additional children in the near future?

John Burke:	Yes, we would like to adopt 2 newborns in the next few years and are already approved by the adoption agency.
Mike Mitchell:	What is your approximate income and does Mary work?
John Burke:	Mary works as an administrative assistant at an accounting firm making $26,000 per year. I am an assistant marketing manager with Atlanta Gas. My annual income is $36,000 or $3,000 per month. I pay $350 a month to my ex wife for child support.
Mike Mitchell:	Good, I have a good picture now. Do you happen to know what your net worth is? And, do you own your home?
John Burke:	I am guessing our net worth is about $10,000 or so. We are just getting started and we currently rent and are saving to buy a home. We hope you can help us get on the right track.
Mike Mitchell:	That's great. It has been very nice talking with you. Do you have any questions for me at this time?
John Burke:	No, thank you.
Mike Mitchell:	I will send the email to you by tomorrow and I will see you and Mary at my office January 4th at 9:00 a.m. Please do not hesitate to call me if anything comes up during the interim.
John Burke:	Thanks, I am looking forward to meeting you in person. Goodbye.
Mike Mitchell:	Thank you. Goodbye.

Dialog of Phone Conversation to 850-555-9876 December 15, 2012, 10:00 a.m.	
Robin:	Good morning, Mitchell and Mitchell Financial Planners.
Caller:	Is Mr. Michael Mitchell available?
Robin:	He is currently in a meeting. May I have him return your call?
Caller:	Yes, please. This is John Burke. I am calling about financial planning for myself and my wife, Mary. My phone number is 850-555-4321.
Robin:	I can have Mr. Mitchell call you back between 1:00 and 1:30pm. Is that a good time for you?
Mr. Burke:	Yes, thank you. By the way, please tell him I was referred to him by Sally Robbins.
Robin:	I will. Thank you. Goodbye.

Based on the initial telephone communication, here is the relevant information collected:

Summary of Data Collected - Life Cycle Approach	
Ages	John 30, Mary 30
Marital Status	Married Filing Jointly filing status
Children	John has one child, age 4 (living out of state, estranged), they would like two to three within the next five years.
Grandchildren	None
Net Worth	Approximately $10,000
Income	$36,000 John, $26,000 Mary
Self-Employed	No
Other	John pays $350 per month in child support. One of their goals is to save for a home.

MIKE MITCHELL'S PRELIMINARY CONCLUSIONS REGARDING THE BURKES:
(USING THE LIFE CYCLE APPROACH)

The life cycle data suggests the Burkes are in the accumulation and risk management phases. Therefore, they need a thorough risk management analysis: life needs, health, disability, property and liability. They also need to save at least 10 - 13 percent of their income for the basic goal of retirement security and probably need a savings rate greater than 10 - 13 percent to accommodate the college education of two to three children.

- Their personal risks are:
  - untimely death,
  - health problems, and
  - disability risks.
- They are probably underinsured for catastrophic risks.
- They likely have cars that need the proper liability and property insurance coverage.
- They likely need but do not have a personal liability umbrella policy.
- Their potential goals are:
  - buying a house,
  - savings for children's education, and
  - beginning to save for retirement.
- They probably do not have personal financial statements.
- They probably have a wide assortment of debt.

Dear Mr. Burke:

Thank you for calling me. It was a pleasure to talk with you yesterday and I look forward to our meeting on January 4th.

Please bring with you as many of the following items as you can but do not worry if you do not have everything. (You can bring originals and we can copy them or you can bring copies for us to keep.)

Insurance:
- All life insurance policies - the type - the death benefit, the annual premium(s), who pays the premium(s), who owns the policy, the insured, the beneficiary;
- Any Disability policies - who is insured, amount of premium, who pays the premium(s);
- Health insurance policies - who is covered, deductibles, co-pays, etc.
- Automobile insurance policies - who is covered, amount of premium(s);
- Homeowner's policies - what is covered, deductibles, etc.;
- Any liability policies - amount of premium(s); and
- Any long-term care policies.

Banking and Investments:
- All recent statements for checking and savings accounts;
- All recent statements and year-end statements if available for all brokerage and investment accounts; and
- All 401(k) Plan, 403(b) Plan statements.

Tax Returns:
- Five years of Federal income tax returns if you have them.

Wills, Trust:
- All copies of wills, durable powers of attorney for health care, advance medical directives; and
- Any trust documents for which you are either grantor or beneficiary if you have them.

Employee Benefits:
- Any employer brochures describing employee fringe benefits that you receive or can receive for both you and Mary.
- Summary plan description for employer-sponsored plans.

Financial Statements:
- Any prepared personal financial statements, balance sheet, and income statement.
- If you do not have financial statements, we can create them for you. Bring a list of assets and debts with interest rates, balances, and terms.
- If you can, prepare an annual or monthly statement of your income and expenses.

Call me if you have any questions. I look forward to seeing you and Mary at 9:00 a.m. on the 4th at my office.

Regards,

Mike Mitchell, CFP®
Partner
Mitchell and Mitchell
850-555-9876

At the first meeting - January 4, 9:00 a.m. - Mike Mitchell Notes

I met with John and Mary Burke and we had a good initial meeting. I described that our services involve comprehensive financial planning. They identified several financial goals. I inquired about additional savings opportunities at their place of employment. I discovered that at this time they have no plans for college education of Patrick (age 4). They did a great job of bringing in their information that I had requested in my email and I will be putting that together in a case file. While they did not have financial statements prepared, they were able to list for me their assets and liabilities. I told them that in the case file I would send them, there would be financial statements that we prepared, a prepared pie chart graphic, and some ratios for their review. I mentioned that if we were missing any data we would contact John by email.

I informed them that for this engagement we would bill $3,000 for the initial plan. Any additional services are billed per diem at the rate of $200 per hour for myself and $125 per hour for any assistant time. John informed me that his father would be paying for the comprehensive financial plan. I also explained that it would take us about twelve weeks to complete the process if we met once a week for about an hour. We discussed implementation and they indicated that where they could, they would handle the implementation.

We set the next meeting for January 18th to allow time for us to build the case file and prepare the financial statements.

ENGAGEMENT LETTER

Financial Planning Offices of Mitchell and Mitchell

January 4, 2013

John and Mary Burke
1420 Elm Street
Pensacola, FL 32501

RE: Financial Planning Engagement Letter

Dear Mr. and Mrs. Burke:

This letter will confirm the terms of our recent conversation regarding the financial planning services we will provide for you. The primary objective of our engagement is to prepare a review of your personal financial situation. This review will identify your personal financial goals and objectives, and will include possible strategies to achieve them. Our analysis and recommendations are based on information provided by you that will be relied upon.

The initial phase involves accumulating and organizing facts about your current financial status, identifying specific goals and objectives, and agreeing upon planning assumptions. After your financial information has been received, the data will be analyzed and projections will be made. Subsequent meetings will be held to verify the accuracy of the data and will allow you to validate the assumptions used. Alternative courses of action to meet goals and alleviate any issues will be comprehensively discussed. We will meet over a period of approximately twelve weeks (based on weekly meetings).

The methods that you choose to follow for the implementation of the financial planning recommendations are at your discretion. As you have indicated, you will be responsible for all decisions regarding implementation of the recommendations.

The fee for your comprehensive financial plan has been determined by our mutual agreement and is $3,000 which is due and payable upon return of this Engagement Letter and will be paid by John Burke's father. Please note that this fee is for the written financial plan alone and the plan shall contain all of our recommendations to you through the date of its delivery. In addition, please be advised that this fee does not include preparation of any legal documents or tax returns.

We anticipate beginning the engagement immediately. If this letter meets with your approval, please sign the enclosed copy in the space provided and return it to us. You are free to terminate this agreement at any time and we will bill you for the portion of work that is complete.

We thank you for the opportunity to be of service, and we welcome you as a valued client.

Sincerely,
Michael A. Mitchell, CFP®

I/We agree to the above terms & conditions:

Client Signature: _____ Date: _____
          John Burke

Client Signature: _____ Date: _____
          Mary Burke

| Mike Mitchell's Email to John Burke |
| January 11, 2013 |

Dear John and Mary:

I am sending you our complete case file of internal and external data collected along with:
- an Income Statement for the year 2013,
- a Statement of Financial Position as of 1/01/2013,
- a pie chart of your current Income Statement along with a benchmark pie chart, and
- a pie chart of your current Statement of Financial Position along with a benchmark pie chart.

Please review these for accuracy and we can discuss them at our next meeting on the 18th.

Regards,

Mike Mitchell, CFP®
Partner
Mitchell and Mitchell
850-555-9876

PERSONAL BACKGROUND AND INFORMATION COLLECTED

THE FAMILY

John Burke, age 30, is an assistant manager in the marketing department of Florida Gas. His annual salary is $36,000. His wife, Mary, is an administrative assistant with an accounting firm. Mary is also 30 years old and has an annual salary of $26,000.

John and Mary have been married for three years and have no children from their marriage. They hope to have two to three children in the next five years. However, John has one child, Patrick (age 4), from a former marriage. Patrick lives with his mother, Kathy, out of state and as a result, John has not seen Patrick for three years.

John pays $350 per month in child support to Kathy for Patrick until he reaches age 18. John also pays for a term life insurance policy on himself for Kathy (beneficiary) as a result of the divorce. The contingent beneficiary on the policy is Patrick. Patrick's education is fully funded by a 529 Plan established by Kathy's father.

EXTERNAL INFORMATION

ECONOMIC INFORMATION
- Inflation is expected to be 3.0% annually.
- The Burke's salaries should increase 4.0% for the next five to ten years.
- There is no state income tax.
- It is expected that there will be a slow growth economy; stocks are expected to return an average of 9.0% annually.

BANK LENDING RATES

- 15-year mortgage rate is 5.0%.
- 30-year mortgage rate is 5.5%.
- Secured personal loan rate is 8.0%.
- Credit card rates are 18%.
- Prime rate is 3.0%.

EXPECTED INVESTMENT RETURNS

- Their expected rate of return is 8.5%.

	Return	Standard Deviation
Cash and Money Market Fund	2.5%	2.5%
Guaranteed Income Fund	2.5%	2.5%
Treasury Bonds/ Bond Funds	4.0%	4.0%
Corporate Bonds/ Bond Funds	6.0%	5.0%
Municipal Bonds/ Bond Funds	5.0%	4.0%
International Bond Funds	7.0%	6.0%
Index Fund	9.0%	14.0%
Large Cap Funds/Stocks	10.0%	16.0%
Mid/Small Funds/Stocks	12.0%	18.0%
International Stock Funds	13.0%	22.0%
Real Estate Funds	8.0%	12.0%

INTERNAL INFORMATION

INSURANCE INFORMATION

Life Insurance

	Policy A*	Policy B	Policy C
Insured	John	John	Mary
Face Amount	$500,000	$50,000	$26,000
Type	Term	Group Term	Group Term
Cash Value	$0	$0	$0
Annual Premium	$600	$178	$50
Who pays premium	John	Employer	Employer
Beneficiary	Kathy then Patrick	Kathy	John
Policy Owner	Kathy	John	Mary
Settlement options clause selected	None	None	None

John is required, as a result of the divorce, to maintain a term life insurance policy (Policy A) of $500,000. The premiums are $50 per month.

Health Insurance

John and Mary are both covered under John's employer health plan. The policy is an indemnity plan with a $300 deductible per person per year and an 80/20 major medical coinsurance clause with a family annual stop loss of $2,000 for each person. Patrick's health insurance is provided by his mother.

Long-Term Disability Insurance

- John is covered by an "own occupation" policy with premiums paid by his employer. The benefits equal 60 percent of his gross pay after an elimination period of 90 days. The policy covers both sickness and accidents and is guaranteed renewable. The term of benefits is to age 66.
- Mary is not covered by disability insurance.

Long-Term Care Insurance

- Neither John nor Mary have long-term care insurance.

Renters Insurance

- The Burkes have an HO4 renters policy (a Contents Broad Form policy that covers contents and liability) without endorsements. The annual premium is $600.
- Content coverage is $25,000 and liability coverage is $100,000.

Automobile Insurance

- Both their car and truck are covered.
- They do not have any separate insurance on John's motor scooter.

Type	PAP
Bodily Injury	$50,000/$100,000
Property Damage	$10,000
Medical Payments	$5,000 per person
Physical Damage	Actual Cash Value
Uninsured Motorist	$25,000/$50,000
Comprehensive Deductible	$200
Collision Deductible	$500
Premium (annual)	$3,600

Personal Liability Insurance

- Neither John nor Mary have PLUP coverage.

INVESTMENT INFORMATION

John owns 1,000 shares of Crossroads Inc. stock that was inherited by him. Its current value is $8,000 and it pays a dividend of 34 cents per share for a total of $340 per year which is included in investment income.

John also owns 100 shares of Gladwell, Inc. stock that was received by him as a gift. The adjusted taxable basis is $4,000 and the fair market value is $4,000. Both the Gladwell and Crossroads stocks are large cap stocks.

Five years ago, John invested in a balanced mutual fund that was initially started with $8,000 he received as a gift. He has reinvested all dividends and capital gains each year. The gains and dividends together reported on their tax returns from the balanced mutual fund were as follows:

	Dividends & Interest	Capital Gains	Total
5 Years Ago	$160	$140	$300
4 Years Ago	$170	$580	$750
3 Years Ago	$180	$1,020	$1,200
2 Years Ago	$190	$600	$790
Last Year	$200	$760	$960

The 401(k) plan portfolio is invested in a balanced mutual fund expected to earn 8.5%. Their overall expected investment rate of return is 8.5%.

Risk Tolerance Questionnaire

Global Portfolio Allocation Scoring System (PASS) for Individual Investors[1]

Questions	Strongly Agree	Agree	Neutral	Disagree	Strongly Disagree
1. Earning a high long-term total return that will allow my capital to grow faster than the inflation rate is one of my most important investment objectives.	J	M			
2. I would like an investment that provides me with an opportunity to defer taxation of capital gains to future years.		M	J		
3. I do not require a high level of current income from my investments.		J, M			
4. I am willing to tolerate some sharp down swings in the return on my investments in order to seek a potentially higher return than would normally be expected from more stable investments.	J	M			
5. I am willing to risk a short-term loss in return for a potentially higher long-run rate of return.		J	M		
6. I am financially able to accept a low level of liquidity in my investment portfolio.		J	M		

J = John, M = Mary

---

1. Global Portfolio Allocation Scoring System (PASS) for Individual Investors - developed by Dr. William Droms (Georgetown University) and Steven N. Strauss, (DromsStrauss Advisors Inc.) - model used with permission.

FINANCIAL STATEMENTS: STATEMENT OF FINANCIAL POSITION 1/1/2013

Statement of Financial Position
John and Mary Burke
Balance Sheet as of 1/1/2013

ASSETS[1]			LIABILITIES AND NET WORTH		
Current Assets			**Current Liabilities[2]**		
JT Checking Account	$3,000		H Credit Card Balance Visa	$9,000	
JT Savings Account	$0		W Credit Card Balance MC	$5,000	
Total Current Assets		$3,000	**Total Current Liabilities**		$14,000
Investment Assets			**Long-Term Liabilities[2]**		
H Crossroads Inc. (1,000 Shares)[3]	$8,000		H Student Loan - John[4]	$54,298	
H Gladwell Inc. (100 Shares)	$4,000		W Auto Loan - Mary	$10,047	
H Balanced Mutual Fund	$12,000				
H 401(k) Plan Account Balance	$4,320		**Total Long-Term Liabilities**		$64,345
Total Investment Assets		$28,320			
Personal Use Assets			**Total Liabilities**		$78,345
W Auto - Mary	$18,500				
H Truck - John	$12,000		**Total Net Worth**		$10,475
H Motor scooter - John	$2,000				
JT Personal Property & Furniture	$25,000				
Total Personal Use Assets		$57,500			
Total Assets		**$88,820**	**Total Liabilities & Net Worth**		**$88,820**

1. Assets are stated at fair market value.
2. Liabilities are stated at principal only as of January 1, 2013 (prior to January payments). The current portion of long-term liabilities of the student loan and the auto loan were unknown at the time this financial statement was prepared. The current portion of these two loans should be classified as a current liability.
3. Crossroads Inc.'s current dividend is $0.34 per year per share.
4. The interest rate on the student loan is 6.9% for a 10-year term on a consolidation loan John just made.

JT = Joint Tenancy
H = Husband
W = Wife

FINANCIAL STATEMENTS: INCOME STATEMENT

Statement of Income and Expenses Mr. and Mrs. Burke Statement of Income and Expenses for Past Year and Expected (Approximate) For 2013		
CASH INFLOWS		**Totals**
Salaries		
John's Salary	$36,000	
Mary's Salary	$26,000	
Investment Income*	$1,300	
Total Cash Inflows		$63,300
CASH OUTFLOWS		
Savings		
Savings - House down payment	$2,500	
401(k) Plan Contribution	$1,080	
Total Savings		$3,580
Fixed Outflows		
Child Support	$4,200 ND	
Life Insurance Payment (Term)	$600 ND	
Rent	$8,400 ND	
HO 4 Renters Insurance	$600 ND	
Utilities	$720 ND	
Telephone	$360 ND	
Auto payment P&I	$3,600 ND	
Auto Insurance	$3,600 ND	
Gas, Oil, Maintenance for Auto	$2,400 ND	
Student Loan Payments	$7,695 ND	
Credit Card Payments	$3,000 ND	
Total Fixed Outflows		$35,175
Variable Outflows		
Taxes - John FICA	$2,754	
Taxes - Mary FICA	$1,989	
Taxes - Federal Tax Withheld	$12,660	
Food	$3,600 ND	
Clothing	$1,000 ND	
Vacations	$1,500	
Total Variable Outflows		$23,503
Total Cash Outflows		$62,258
NET DISCRETIONARY CASH FLOWS		$1,042

ND = Non-Discretionary

INCOME TAX INFORMATION

The filing status of the Burkes for federal income tax is married filing jointly. Patrick is claimed as a dependent on Kathy's tax return as part of John and Kathy's divorce agreement. There is no state income tax. Their average income tax rate is 17 percent and their marginal income tax rate is 25 percent.

RETIREMENT INFORMATION

John currently contributes three percent of his salary to his 401(k) plan. The employer matches each $1 contributed with $0.50 up to a total employer contribution of three percent. Mary has a 401(k) plan that provides a match of 25 percent of her contributions up to six percent. Mary has never contributed to her 401(k) plan.

GIFTS, ESTATES, TRUSTS, AND WILL INFORMATION

- John has a will leaving all of his probate estate to Patrick. He did not change the will after his marriage to Mary.
- Mary does not have a will.
- The Burkes live in a common law property state.

INFORMATION REGARDING ASSETS AND LIABILITIES

AUTOMOBILE

The automobile was purchased January 1, 2011 for $19,993 with 20 percent down and 80 percent financed over 60 months with payments of $300 per month.

FINANCIAL GOALS

The Burke's financial goals include:
- Increase savings rate and amount.
- Debt reduction and an adequate emergency fund.
- Have an appropriate risk management portfolio.
- Save enough for a down payment on a home of 20 percent of $180,000 in today's dollars for purchase in three years. Property taxes are expected to be one percent of the value of home. Homeowners insurance (HO3 endorsed - a Special Form Homeowner's policy that covers a wide variety of perils) will be one percent of the value of the home.
- For education, they plan to spend $20,000 per year for four years each for each of the two children at the child's age 18. The expected education inflation rate is five percent. Assume they have twins two years from now for the calculation of education funding.
- For retirement, they want to plan for 100% ($62,000) wage replacement at age 65, without any consideration of Social Security, which would be $20,000 for him at age 67 and $15,000 for her at age 67. If they cannot achieve that they will consider a compromise between delaying retirement and lowering the wage replacement ratio

as long as the wage replacement is no less than 75% and the delayed retirement is no later than age 67. They expect to live to age 95.

- Assume a portfolio rate of return of 8.5%.
- Develop a comprehensive financial plan, including estate planning documents.

CASE ANALYSIS

Based on the initial telephone communication, here is the relevant information collected.

Summary of Data Collected - Life Cycle Approach	
Ages	John 30, Mary 30
Marital Status	Married Filing Jointly filing status
Children	John has one child, age 4 (living out of state, estranged), they would like two to three within the next five years.
Grandchildren	None
Net Worth	Approximately $10,000
Income	$36,000 John, $26,000 Mary
Self-Employed	No
Other	John pays $350 per month in child support. One of their goals is to save for a home.

MIKE MITCHELL'S PRELIMINARY CONCLUSIONS REGARDING THE BURKES:
(USING THE LIFE CYCLE APPROACH)

The life cycle data suggests the Burkes are in the accumulation and risk management phases. Therefore, they need a thorough risk management analysis: life needs, health, disability, property and liability. They also need to save at least 10 - 13 percent of their income for the basic goal of retirement security and probably need a savings rate greater than 10 - 13 percent to accommodate the college education of two to three children.

- Their personal risks are:
    - untimely death,
    - health problems, and
    - disability risks.
- They are probably underinsured for catastrophic risks.
- They likely have cars that need the proper liability and property insurance coverage.
- They likely need but do not have a personal liability umbrella policy.
- Their goals are:
    - buying a house,
    - savings for children's education, and
    - saving for retirement.
- They probably do not have personal financial statements.
- They probably have a wide assortment of debt.

APPLYING FINANCIAL PLANNING APPROACHES

The Burke client relationship has now been established and the internal and external data has been collected. Next, the financial planner is ready to analyze and evaluate the client's financial status. The following approaches will be applied in order to form client recommendations.

- Pie Chart Approach
- Financial Statement Analysis-Ratio Analysis Approach
- The Two-Step / Three-Panel / Metrics Approach
- The Present Value of All Goals Approach
- The Cash Flow Approach
- Strategic Approach

Each approach is applied to the Burke case for practical application purposes so that the financial planner can learn how to identify weaknesses in the financial situation. In addition, the practitioner can also learn how to use the varied approaches together to analyze and evaluate the client's financial circumstances to arrive at the best recommendations for the client.

PIE CHART APPROACH

INTRODUCTION

The pie chart approach to analysis provides the financial planner and the client with a visual representation of the balance sheet and the income statement. The financial statements are prepared first and then they are depicted in pie charts. The pie charts provide a fairly high level view, rather than a detailed analysis, and are only used as a starting point for discussions with the client. They do, however, provide the planner with sufficient insight to the client's financial profile to have that high level conversation. Below each pie chart are the planner's observations, which affords the opportunity for a more in-depth discussion with the clients on each observation point.

DATA FOR PIE CHART APPROACH - BALANCE SHEET 1/1/2013

Burke Balance Sheet

Assets = 100%			Liabilities & Net Worth = 100%		
Cash or Cash Equivalents	$3,000	3.38%	Current Liabilities	$14,000	15.76%
Investment Assets	$28,320	31.88%	Long-Term Liabilities	$64,345	72.44%
Personal Use Assets	$57,500	64.74%	Net Worth	$10,475	11.79%
	$88,820	100.00%		$88,820	100.00%

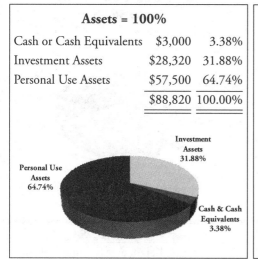 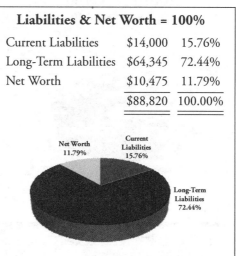

Benchmark Balance Sheet (From Fundamentals of Financial Planning)

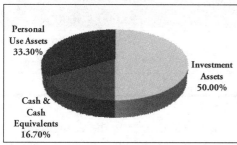 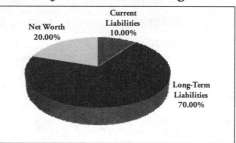

Note: The balance sheet benchmarks are never exactly precise, but it is clear that the Burkes should have a greater amount of money in an emergency fund and more investment assets for their current age. It is also clear that relative to the benchmarks, debt is high.

Observations

The balance sheet pie chart indicates the following:
- cash and cash equivalents are low (3.4%), therefore the emergency fund and current ratios are also probably low,
- the net worth is low relative to the client's age, and
- investment assets are low relative to gross pay.

These deficiencies can be overcome in a relatively short period of time by increasing the savings rate, reducing debt, and managing interest rates on debt.

DATA FOR PIE CHART APPROACH - INCOME STATEMENT 1/1/2013

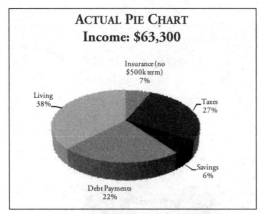

ACTUAL PIE CHART
Income: $63,300

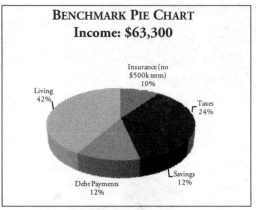

BENCHMARK PIE CHART
Income: $63,300

Income	100%	$63,300
Other Living Expenses	21.77%	The balance of living expenses*
Debt Payments	22.58%	($3,600 + $7,695 + $3,000)
Savings Rate	5.66%	$3,580 ÷ $63,300
Insurance	6.64%	($3,600 + $600)
Housing Costs	14.22%	($8,400 + $600)
Taxes	27.49%	($2,754 + $1,989 + $12,660)
Discretionary Cash Flows	1.64%	$1,042

* $4,200 + $720 + $360 + $2,400 + $3,600 + $1,000 + $1,500

Note: The initial savings rate is 5.66%, but with the employer match, the savings rate is 6.5 percent. If you consider the child support of $350 per month and life insurance payment as required by the court of $50 per month as debt, the financial picture is weaker. Keep in mind that benchmarks are averages for a group and may not apply exactly to a client's personal financial situation.

Observations

The first observation is that the expenditures for debt repayments is high (22.58%) and the savings rate (5.66%) is low. In addition, the expenditure percentage for insurance looks to be low relative to the benchmark. Each of these issues will require investigation and resolution. While it is not uncommon to have percentages like these, the Burkes are more likely to meet their goals by reducing debt, increasing savings, and making sure they are adequately protected by insurance.

The overall savings rate with the employer 401(k) plan match is 6.5 percent and can easily be increased by John increasing his elective deferral to receive the maximum match from his employer. An additional $1,080 elective deferral would generate an additional match of $540 and would change the savings rate to 9.1%.

FINANCIAL STATEMENT ANALYSIS - RATIO ANALYSIS APPROACH

Introduction

The liquidity ratios provide insight into the client's ability to pay short-term obligations and fund an emergency. The housing ratios and total debt to asset ratios help the financial planner to assess the client's ability to manage debt. The savings rate provides the planner with a good perspective of whether the client is committed financially to all of his goals, which includes saving for retirement and other goals. In addition, the investment assets to gross pay ratios help the planner to determine the progress of the client in achieving the goal of financial security based on the client's age and income. Lastly, the performance ratios indicate how well the investment assets have performed to benchmarks. The ratios should be compared to appropriate benchmarks to be meaningful.

BURKE'S RATIO ANALYSIS

LIQUIDITY RATIOS				
Ratio	**Formula**		**Comment**	**Benchmark**
Emergency Fund Ratio =	$\dfrac{\text{Cash \& Cash Equivalents}}{\text{Monthly Non-Discretionary Cash Flows}}$	$\dfrac{\$3,000}{\$3,315} = 0.91 < 1$ month	Very Weak	3 - 6:1
Current Ratio =	$\dfrac{\text{Cash \& Cash Equivalents}}{\text{Current Liabilities}}$	$\dfrac{\$3,000}{\$14,000} = 0.21\%$	Very Weak	1 - 2
DEBT RATIOS				
Housing Ratio 1 (HR 1) =	$\dfrac{\text{Housing Costs}}{\text{Gross Pay}}$	$\dfrac{\$9,000}{\$63,300} = 14.22\%$	Strong	$\leq 28\%$
Housing Ratio 2 (HR 2) =	$\dfrac{\text{Housing Costs + Other Debt Payments}}{\text{Gross Pay}}$	$\dfrac{\$23,295}{\$63,300} = 36.80\%$	Weak	$\leq 36\%$
Debt to Total Assets =	$\dfrac{\text{Total Debt}}{\text{Total Assets}}$	$\dfrac{\$78,345}{\$88,820} = 88.21\%$	Weak	Age Dependent
Net Worth to Total Assets =	$\dfrac{\text{Net Worth}}{\text{Total Assets}}$	$\dfrac{\$10,475}{\$88,820} = 11.79\%$	Weak	Age Dependent
RATIOS FOR FINANCIAL SECURITY GOALS				
Savings Rate =	$\dfrac{\text{Savings + Employer Match}}{\text{Gross Pay}}$	$\dfrac{\$3,580 + \$540}{\$63,300} = 6.5\%$	Weak	Goal Driven At Least 10-13%
Investment Assets to Gross Pay =	$\dfrac{\text{Investment Assets + Cash \& Cash Equivalents}}{\text{Gross Pay}}$	$\dfrac{\$28,320 + \$3,000}{\$63,300} = 0.49:1$	Very Weak	1:1 Age Dependent
PERFORMANCE RATIOS				
Return on Investments =	$\dfrac{I_1 - (I_0 + \text{Savings})}{I_0}$	Unavailable (Need beginning and ending balance sheet)		N/A
Return on Assets =	$\dfrac{A_1 - (A_0 + \text{Savings})}{A_0}$	Unavailable (Need beginning and ending balance sheet)		N/A
Return on Net Worth =	$\dfrac{NW_1 - (NW_0 + \text{Savings})}{NW_0}$	Unavailable (Need beginning and ending balance sheet)		N/A

Comments on Calculated Ratios

Many of the Burke's ratios are currently low, but can be substantially improved over the next few years.

The Burkes are just getting started in their married life and while many of their ratios are weak today, they have a long work life expectancy. They will want to build an emergency fund, increase savings, and pay off their credit card debt. They may even want to delay the purchase of a home if the rent they are paying will be substantially less than the net after tax amount of the mortgage they will be paying. This decision will depend on market rates of rent, cost of houses, interest rates for mortgages, and marginal tax rates presuming mortgage interest remains an itemized deduction for income tax purposes. This analysis should be made in the three to five year period ahead.

THE TWO-STEP / THREE-PANEL / METRICS APPROACH

INTRODUCTION

The two-step approach (cover the risks, save and invest), looks at personal risks as potentially leading to catastrophic financial results and dependence on someone else for well being. Savings and investments are the road to financial security or independence in the long run. Generally, dependence can be caused by an event that can occur at any moment, whereas financial independence is earned over a long period of time.

A modification to the two-step approach is the three-panel approach, which provides the planner and the client with a methodology for planning. Step 1 is to evaluate each of the insurance risks and then evaluate the client's actual portfolio of insurance to determine the adequacy of the current coverage. Step 2 is to calculate the emergency fund ratio and housing ratios (or take them from the financial statement analysis approach). Step 3 focuses on the long-term savings and investments in order to meet the financial security goal (retirement with adequate income to maintain the pre-retirement lifestyle) and requires persistent savings, adequate investment performance, and a benchmark of investment assets appropriate for the age and gross pay of the client. Step 3 also considers education goals, lump-sum goals, and legacy goals. The goal of the three-panel / metrics approach is to identify specific recommendations for the client to improve the overall financial plan.

Risk Management Data

	Actual	Metric	Comment / Recommendation
Personal Insurance:			
Life Insurance[1,2]	$50,000 + $26,000	$360k - $576k $260k - $416k	They are significantly underinsured for life insurance.
Health Insurance	Indemnity 80 /20 Stop Loss $2,000 Life-Term Benefit	Same	Okay
Disability Insurance	John - 60% of Gross Pay/ Guaranteed Renewable / 90-day Elimination/ Own Occupation Mary - None	John is fine. Mary needs disability insurance.	Mary needs disability insurance
Long-Term Care Insurance	None	None at this time	Okay
Property and Liability Insurance:			
Homeowners Insurance	HO4 without endorsements	HO4 with endorsements	Add endorsements for all risk and replacement value.
Automobile Insurance[3]	$50,000/$100,000/$10,000	$100k/$300k/$50k	Upgrade the liability per the requirements of PLUP carrier and re-quote the premium. Should be in $2,000 - $2,500 range.
Motor Scooter Insurance	None	$\leq$ FMV + Liability	Stop driving, add insurance, or sell motor scooter.
Liability Insurance	None	Need $1M PLUP coverage.	Add PLUP coverage of $1M.

[1] Note that the owner of the $500,000 term policy is John's ex-wife, Kathy, and that is why it is not included here.

[2] They need to change Policy B beneficiary to Mary from Kathy at no cost.

[3] Note that they requested auto quotes, but due to their driving records, the premium was not lowered.

Short-Term Savings and Investments

	Actual	Metric	Comment / Recommendation
Emergency Fund	0.91 month	3 - 6 months	Deficient
Housing Ratio 1 (HR1)*	14.22%	$\leq$ 28%	Excellent
Housing Ratio 2 (HR2)	36.8%	$\leq$ 36%	Fair - need to improve metric for home purchase.

*Although the Burkes do not own a home, the financial planner should calculate their housing ratios using their rent and renter's insurance in the calculation.

Debt Management Data

	Balance	Interest Rate	Payment	Balance of Term	Comment / Recommendation
Credit Cards	$14,000	18% /yr.	$250 / month	124 months	Pay off if possible.
Auto	$10,047	4.75% /yr.	$300 / month	36 months	Pay as agreed.
Student Loans	$54,298	6.9%/ yr.	$7,695 / year	10 years	Pay as agreed.

Long-Term Goals

	Actual	Metric	Comment / Recommendation
Overall Savings Rate	6.5%	At least 10 - 13%	Too Low to Meet Goals / Increase
Investment Assets / Gross Pay	0.49:1	1:1	Too Low for Age / Increase Over Time

HOME PURCHASE ANALYSIS - SCHEDULE A

Home Down Payment Calculation

The purpose of this calculation is to determine the funds required to meet a 20 percent down-payment for the Burke's home purchase goal.

PV	=	$180,000 (current price of home)
N	=	3 (periods until expected purchase)
i	=	3% inflation
PMT	=	0
FV	=	$196,690.86 (future value of house) x 20% = $39,338 down payment required
PV$_{Today}$	=	$30,798 based on 8.5% earnings rate

Mortgage on Home

The purpose of the following computations is to determine the projected debt ratios should the Burkes purchase a home.

PV ($196,690.86 x 0.80)	=	$157,352.69 (loan amount)
N (term in months)	=	360 months
i (interest rate)	=	5.5 ÷ 12
FV (balance in 30 yrs)	=	0
PMT$_{OA}$ (monthly payment)	=	$893.43 (principal and interest)

	Monthly	Annually
Principal and Interest	$893.43	$10,721
Property Taxes	$163.92	$1,967
HO Insurance	$163.92	$1,967
Total House Payment	**$1,221.27**	**$14,655**

Projections for the Home Purchase (in three years)

- Projected income = $62,000 x $(1.04)^3$ = $69,742 in three years.
- Therefore, HR1 = 21.01% [Excellent ($14,655 ÷ $69,742)].
- As adjusted HR2 = 32% [Okay, qualifies ($14,655 + $7,695 ÷ $69,742)].
- Assume the car and credit cards are paid off and the student loan is the only debt remaining.

SAVINGS SCHEDULE - SCHEDULE B

The following schedule projects the savings requirement and debt retirement needed to meet the Burke's 3-year goals.

Objective	Cash Needed	Comment / Recommendation
Save	$39,338	Will need to save $12,117 at 8.5% per year for three years.
Pay off auto	$10,047	Will be paid off in three years with current payments of $3,600 per year.
Pay off credit cards	$14,000	Will be paid off immediately by using the proceeds from the sale of assets.
Total Cash Needed	**$63,385**	**Cash required in the next three years.**

PAYMENT SCHEDULE - SCHEDULE C

Knowing the debt retirement issues illustrated in Schedule B, the practitioner can plan for debt reduction on a monthly basis. Note that for comparison purposes, if the Burkes pay $250 per month on their credit card balance, they would remain with a $5,000 balance (plus interest) in three years.

Scheduled Payments	Annual Payment	Current Balance	Balance 3 Years Future	Payments
Auto Loan	$3,600	$10,047	$0	$300 / month
Credit Cards*	$3,000	$14,000	$5,000 + interest	$250 / month

* Note that the credit cards, however, will be paid off now with the sale of some of the assets.

AUTO INTEREST - SCHEDULE D

Determine the interest rate on the auto loan.

Automobile Interest Rate Calculation		Calculation	
Purchase Price	$19,993.00		
20% Down	- 3,998.60	FV	= 0
Balance	$15,994.40	PV	= $15,994.00
Payment	$300	PMT	= ($300)
Term	60	N	= 60 months
Therefore i = annual rate	4.75%	i	= 0.3957 x 12 = 4.75%

COMMENTS ON THREE-PANEL / METRICS APPROACH ANALYSIS

The Burkes need life insurance because they are dependent on each other's income to support their current lifestyle and they have told the financial planner that they want to have two to three children fairly soon.

Their health insurance is adequate although they are dependent on their employer for coverage. They would be covered under COBRA for 18 to 36 months if John was terminated.

The Burkes need disability insurance on Mary because it provides for income replacement.

The homeowners (renters) policy can be improved by endorsing the personal property coverage for all risks and for replacement value. The standard HO4 policy has coverage for 18 perils (not all) and actual cash value (not replacement value).

The Burkes should also purchase a personal liability insurance policy. The PLUP issuer will likely require that they increase their liability coverages to $100k/$300k/$50k. They need to annually shop the automobile insurance premium because it is high due to their recent driving records.

The emergency fund needs to be increased. The Burke's currently cover about one month (0.91) of non-discretionary cash flow with their cash and cash equivalents. They would be in financial difficulty if one or both of them lost their jobs.

The Burkes housing ratio 1 is excellent at 14.22 percent, but the back ratio of 36.8 percent already indicates they have too much debt. They will need to improve this ratio significantly before buying a home.

The Burkes need to pay off the credit cards and pay off the automobile loan within the 36 months remaining. Schedule D above reflects the calculation of the rate of interest on the auto loan (4.75%).

The Burkes overall savings rate, including the employer match, is only 6.5 percent of gross pay. It needs to be 10 to 13 percent of gross pay just to drive the financial security (retirement) goal. If the Burke's are going to have a home purchase goal and college education goal for two to three children, and a build the emergency fund goal, they are going to need to increase the savings rate to 10 to 13 percent for retirement, save an average of 18 percent for the home purchase down payment (see Schedule A), and four to five percent for college education (total 32 to 36% (See Schedule B). This is an important task and they might consider delaying the home purchase until such time as they have saved the 20 percent down payment. They need to increase the 401(k) plan deferrals to maximize employer matches.

Schedule C illustrates that the client will have the auto paid off in three years and can at that time add the $3,600 per year to their savings rate.

The three-panel / metrics approach dictates that the recommendations are prioritized (see the cash flow approach) and that there is an estimate of the impact of each on the income statement and balance sheet (see projected financial statements later in this chapter). In the case of the Burkes, the financial planner is able to improve the insurance portfolio, increase savings and increase the employer match to the maximum in the 401(k) plan, and pay off the credit cards. The credit card debt reduction is accomplished by selling the individual stocks and the motor scooter. The individual stocks were not diversified and the scooter was not insured. The complete rearrangement provides the Burkes with a much better financial plan.

The financial planner should note that the client will need to address the large student loans balance and it will take time to save for the home they expect to purchase especially if they have two to three children relatively soon. The Burkes have been advised that they need to get their wills and other estate planning documents in order and they expect to do that in Year 2.

It is important for the financial planner to take note of where they can usually find the resources to pay for the recommendations. The places we find resources are:
- refinancing a home mortgage at a lower rate,
- reducing our withholding of income tax,
- the sale of assets from the balance sheet (usually from an inappropriate or no longer desired investment or personal use asset), and
- changing lifestyle (this is the last place we look because it requires behavioral change like cutting vacations).

Sometimes there simply are not sufficient financial resources to solve all the problems immediately. That is why in the cash flow approach recommendations are listed in order of priority. In the event there are insufficient financial resources, the financial planner and client simply solve the problems that they can today and use future resources as they become available. Whatever financial weaknesses the client has generally took some time to develop, and may also take some time to resolve.

RISK TOLERANCE AND ASSET ALLOCATION

The chart below depicts the scoring system for the PASS risk tolerance questionnaire. Based on the Burke's answers, their PASS[1] score is 23.5, which corresponds to the RT3 target.

Global Portfolio Allocation Scoring System (PASS) for Individual Investors						
Questions	Strongly Agree	Agree	Neutral	Disagree	Strongly Disagree	John & Mary
1. Earning a high long-term total return that will allow my capital to grow faster than the inflation rate is one of my most important investment objectives.	5	4	3	2	1	4.5
2. I would like an investment that provides me with an opportunity to defer taxation of capital gains to future years.	5	4	3	2	1	3.5
3. I do not require a high level of current income from my investments.	5	4	3	2	1	4
4. I am willing to tolerate some sharp down swings in the return on my investments in order to seek a potentially higher return than would normally be expected from more stable investments.	5	4	3	2	1	4.5
5. I am willing to risk a short-term loss in return for a potentially higher long-run rate of return.	5	4	3	2	1	3.5
6. I am financially able to accept a low level of liquidity in my investment portfolio.	5	4	3	2	1	3.5
						23.5

Below are the recommended portfolios based on the time horizon and answers to the risk tolerance questionnaire.

	Short-Term Horizon				Intermediate-Term Horizon				Long-Term Horizon			
	RT1 Target	RT2 Target	RT3 Target	RT4 Target	RT1 Target	RT2 Target	RT3 Target	RT4 Target	RT1 Target	RT2 Target	RT3 Target	RT4 Target
PASS Score	6 - 12	13 - 18	19 - 24	25 - 30	6 - 12	13 - 18	19 - 24	25 - 30	6 - 12	13 - 18	19 - 24	25 - 30
Cash and Money Market Fund	40%	30%	20%	10%	5%	5%	5%	5%	5%	5%	3%	2%
Treasury Bonds/ Bond Funds	40%	30%	30%	20%	60%	35%	20%	10%	30%	20%	12%	0%
Corporate Bonds/ Bond Funds	20%	30%	30%	40%	15%	15%	15%	10%	15%	10%	10%	4%
Subtotal	100%	90%	80%	70%	80%	55%	40%	25%	50%	35%	25%	6%
International Bond Funds	0%	0%	0%	0%	0%	5%	5%	5%	0%	5%	5%	4%
Subtotal	0%	0%	0%	0%	0%	5%	5%	5%	0%	5%	5%	4%
Index Fund	0%	10%	10%	10%	10%	15%	20%	20%	20%	20%	20%	25%
Large Cap Value Funds/Stocks	0%	0%	5%	5%	5%	5%	10%	10%	10%	10%	5%	5%
Large Cap Growth Funds/Stocks	0%	0%	0%	0%	5%	5%	5%	10%	15%	10%	10%	5%
Mid/Small Growth Funds/Stocks	0%	0%	0%	0%	0%	0%	5%	5%	0%	0%	5%	10%
Mid/Small Value Funds/Stocks	0%	0%	0%	5%	0%	5%	5%	5%	0%	5%	5%	10%
Subtotal	0%	10%	15%	20%	20%	30%	45%	50%	45%	45%	45%	55%
International Stock Funds	0%	0%	0%	5%	0%	5%	5%	10%	0%	5%	10%	15%
Subtotal	0%	0%	0%	5%	0%	5%	5%	10%	0%	5%	10%	15%
Real Estate Funds	0%	0%	5%	5%	0%	5%	5%	10%	5%	10%	15%	20%
Subtotal	0%	0%	5%	5%	0%	5%	5%	10%	5%	10%	15%	20%
Total	100%	100%	100%	100%	100%	100%	100%	100%	100%	100%	100%	100%

---

1. Global Portfolio Allocation Scoring System (PASS) for Individual Investors - developed by Dr. William Droms (Georgetown University) and Steven N. Strauss, (DromsStrauss Advisors Inc.) - model used with permission.

This information and the risk and return information are used to determine and estimate the expected return for the current portfolio versus the recommended PASS[1] portfolio.

	Current Porfolio (Dollars)	Current Portfolio Percentage	PASS Recommended Portfolio	Difference	Expected Rates of Return	Current Expected Return	PASS Expected Return
Cash and Money Market Fund	$3,000	9.6%	3%	6.6%	2.5%	$75	$23
Treasury Bonds/ Bond Funds	$0	0.0%	12%	-12.0%	4.0%	$0	$150
Corporate Bonds/ Bond Funds	$8,160	26.1%	10%	16.1%	6.0%	$490	$188
International Bond Funds	$0	0.0%	5%	-5.0%	7.0%	$0	$110
Index Fund	$8,160	26.1%	20%	6.1%	9.0%	$734	$564
Large Cap Funds/Stocks	$12,000	38.3%	15%	23.3%	10.0%	$1,200	$470
Mid/Small Funds/Stocks	$0	0.0%	10%	-10.0%	12.0%	$0	$376
International Stock Funds	$0	0.0%	10%	-10.0%	13.0%	$0	$407
Real Estate Funds	$0	0.0%	15%	-15.0%	8.0%	$0	$376
	$31,320	100.0%				$2,499	$2,664
					Expected Return	7.98%	8.51%

As indicated above, the expected return slightly increases over the current portfolio and the return is consistent with the required return in the case. In addition, the portfolio should be better positioned to reflect the risk tolerance of the Burkes.

THE PRESENT VALUE OF ALL GOALS APPROACH

Recall from Chapter 3 that the present value of all goals approach is a relatively quick way to determine if the client's annual savings amount is sufficient to satisfy all goals. The method requires the calculation of the present value of each separate goal. The current investment assets and cash are then deducted from that total. The resultant is treated as an obligation (mortgage) and is retired over a period no longer than the remaining work life expectancy as an ordinary annuity, using the expected investment rate of return as the interest rate. The calculated annuity in dollars is then compared to the current savings amount as adjusted to determine whether the client is saving enough. This is one of our favorite approaches.

Goals:

1. Retirement - $62,000 in today's dollars, 3% inflation, at 65 to 95 without consideration of Social Security.
2. Education of 2 children - $20,000 per year in today's dollars, starting in 20 years. Inflation is expected to be 5%. The children will attend college for 4 years each. They do not plan to pay for Patrick.
3. Home down payment - $36,000 down payment in three years from now.

---

1. Global Portfolio Allocation Scoring System (PASS) for Individual Investors - developed by Dr. William Droms (Georgetown University) and Steven N. Strauss, (DromsStrauss Advisors Inc.) - model used with permission.

Calculation of Retirement Needs in PV Terms

N = 35	PMT_{AD} = $174,459.47	FV = $2,718,862.76
i = 3	N = 30	N = 35
PV = $62,000	i = (1.085 ÷ 1.03 - 1) x 100	i = 8.5
FV = $174,459.47	$PV_{@65}$ $2,718,862.76	PV_{Today} = $156,439.51

Calculation of Education Needs in PV Terms

PMT_{AD} = $20,000	FV = $152,423.22 (for 2 children)
i = (1.085 ÷ 1.05 - 1) x 100	N = 20 (children born 2 years from now)
N = 4	i = (1.085 ÷ 1.05 - 1) x 100
$PV_{@18}$ = $76,211.60757	PV_{Today} = $79,112.00

Calculation of Home Down Payment in PV Terms

N = 3	FV = $39,338.17
i = 3	i = 8.5
PV = $36,000	N = 3
FV = $39,338.17	PV = $30,798.17

SUMMARY OF THE PRESENT VALUE OF ALL GOALS

Retirement	$156,439.51	
Education	$79,112.00	
Home Down Payment	$30,798.11	
Total PV of All Goals	$266,349.62	
Less Current Resources	<$31,320.00>	(this is before using $14,000 to pay off credit cards)
Net PV of All Goals	$235,029.62	
N	35	(years to retirement)
i	8.5%	(portfolio expected rate of return)
PMT_{OA}	$21,197.17	(annual savings needed as an ordinary annuity)
Current Savings Amount	- $4,120.00	
Tax Analysis Savings	- $7,618.00	(See Schedule D)
Shortfall of Savings	$9,459.17	

The Burke's are still $9,459.17 short on annual savings. However, by adding the additional savings of $1,080 + $1,560 + $660 (see cash flow approach), they will reduce the shortfall to $6,159.17. Their current wage replacement ratio is 100% but if they save as above, the real needed WRR is $62,000 less savings of $15,038 and less Social Security of $4,743 or $42,219 which is only 68.095%, not 100%. So, you could use a wage replacement ratio of 70-75%, which would reduce the PV of retirement needs by at least $39,109.88 and thus the annual savings needed by $3,527.30, making then only approximately $2,600 annual savings short which they could make up with increased savings from raises over the 35 years.

THE CASH FLOW APPROACH

The cash flow approach essentially adjusts the cash flows on the income statement to what they would be after implementing all of the immediate short-term recommendations that the planner has suggested. It starts with the discretionary cash flows at the bottom of the income statement and accounts for each recommendation in the order of priority by charging the cost of the expense (recommendation) against the discretionary cash flows, regardless of any negative cash flow impact. The analysis is prepared carefully to differentiate between recurring and non-recurring cash flows.

BURKE CASH FLOW APPROACH WITH RECOMMENDATIONS

	Impact on Income Statement Recurring Cash Flows	Impact on Statement of Financial Position Non-Recurring Cash Flows	Comments/Explanations
Beginning Cash Flow (Income Statement)	**$1,042**		From the original income statement
Recommendations:			
Risk management:			
Term life insurance for John	($375)		Buy $500,000 term
Term life insurance for Mary	($250)		Buy $500,000 term
Disability insurance for Mary	($600)		Buy disability
Homeowners insurance	($100)		Endorse
Automobile insurance	($400)		Upgrade
Motor scooter	$0	$2,000	Sell motor scooter
Personal liability umbrella	($200)		$1,000,000 PLUP
Prepare proper estate documents		($1,000)	
Debt management:			
Pay off credit cards		($14,000)	Reduces expenditures by $3,000 per year
Savings from credit card payoffs	$3,000		Pay off credit cards with proceeds from asset sale
Increase John's 401(k) plan deferrals*	($1,080)		3% additional
Begin Mary's 401(k) plan deferrals*	($1,560)		6% of salary
Tax Savings from 401(k) plan deposits	$660		From income tax reductions (25% of 401(k) plan deferrals)
Savings from Change in W=4**	$7,618		This will initially go to the emergency fund
Ending cash flow after implementation	$7,755		This is the positive recurring cash flow to add to savings
Sell assets to pay credit card (Crossroads and Gladwell stock)		$12,000	Sold stocks, etc. to pay off credit cards
TOTAL of Changes in Cash Flows	$7,755	($1,000)	

Note that the numbers in parenthesis are expenditures.

* The Burkes had to choose between increasing savings to the 401(k) plan and paying down on the student loans. They expect John will get a substantial raise in 4-5 years and choose to save rather than pay the student loans even though they were at 6.9% interest. There also is a possibility that their parents will help with the student loans.

** See Tax Analysis.

ASSETS SOLD TO PAY OFF CREDIT CARDS - SCHEDULE A

Assets Sold to Pay Off Credit Cards	
Motor scooter	$2,000
Crossroads Inc.	$8,000
Gladwell Inc.	$4,000
TOTAL	**$14,000**

STRATEGIC APPROACH

INTRODUCTION

The strategic approach encompasses establishing a mission, a mission statement, a set of goals, and a set of objectives. The planner analyzes the mission, goals, and objectives given both internal client data and relevant external data and creates a plan for the long-run accomplishment of the mission with the short and intermediate accomplishment of objectives and goals.

MISSION STATEMENT (AN ENDURING LONG-TERM STATEMENT)

- Financial security (maintaining lifestyle without the need for current employment).

GOALS (BROADLY CONCEIVED GOALS)

- Adequate risk management portfolio.
- Adequate savings rate for retirement and education.
- Adequate emergency fund.
- Adequate debt management.
- Adequate investment portfolio.
- Adequate estate plan.

OBJECTIVES (NARROW MEASURABLE OBJECTIVES)

Risk Management
- Immediately buy term life insurance on both John and Mary at $500,000 each.
- Purchase disability insurance on Mary at 60% to 70% of gross pay with a 90 day elimination period.
- Add endorsement for HO4 to all risk / replacement value.
- Upgrade liability on automobile insurance to meet PLUP carrier requirements.
- Sell motor scooter.
- Add PLUP of $1,000,000.

Debt Management
- Pay off credit cards ($14,000).
- Keep credit card purchases to $1,000 per year.

Tax Management and Emergency Fund

- Use the extra $7,618 in income tax overwithholding to build an emergency fund. (See Schedule D - Tax Analysis on the following pages).

Savings and Investments

- Increase John's 401(k) plan deferral to $2,160 (increasing the employer match to $1,080).
- Have Mary defer $1,560 to her 401(k) plan (employer match is $1,560 x 0.25 = $390).
- Move all 401(k) plan investments to a balanced portfolio.

Estate Plan

Have estate planning documents prepared (will, durable power of attorney for healthcare, advance medical directive) within the second year (expected cost = $1,000).

COMMENTS ON STRATEGIC APPROACH

The strategic approach takes into consideration needs versus wants. Needs are defined as necessary by law (e.g., auto liability insurance) or required to make the plan work (e.g., savings). Wants on the other hand are somewhat discretionary (e.g., home purchase, vacation).

Even if the planner started with the strategic approach, the financial planning method would probably follow with the cash flow approach and recommendations to be assured that the implementation is feasible.

PRESENTATION TO JOHN AND MARY BURKE
PROJECTED FINANCIAL STATEMENTS AND RATIOS

The next step for the financial planner is to project financial statements at least one year out to be able to present to the client where they will be in a year if they follow and implement the recommendations. This is one way to help clients get and stay motivated while implementing the plan. In order to project both the balance sheet and the income statement and to prepare pro forma (projected) ratios, the planner will need to prepare schedules of savings and earnings. For the Burkes, the planner has prepared schedules A - E and the projected financial statements.

SCHEDULE A - ANALYSIS OF JOHN'S 401(k) PLAN

	Beginning Balance January 1	Employee Deferrals	Employer Match	Earning Rate 8.5%*	Ending Balance December 31
2013	$4,320	$2,160	$1,080	$505	$8,065
2014	$8,065	$2,246	$1,123	$830	$12,264
2015	$12,264	$2,336	$1,168	$1,191	$16,959
2016	$16,959	$2,429	$1,215	$1,596	$22,199

* Earnings are for 1/2 year on new deposits. Rounded.

SCHEDULE B - ANALYSIS OF MARY'S 401(k) PLAN

	Beginning Balance January 1	Employee Deferrals	Employer Match	Earning Rate 8.5%	Ending Balance December 31
2013	$0	$1,560	$390	$83	$2,033
2014	$2,033	$1,622	$406	$259	$4,320
2015	$4,320	$1,687	$422	$456	$6,885
2016	$6,885	$1,755	$439	$678	$9,757

* Earnings on the balanced mutual fund is 8.5% for 1/2 year on new deposits. Rounded to nearest $1.

SCHEDULE C - COMBINED SAVINGS RATE AFTER RECOMMENDATIONS (NOT INCLUDING TAX OVERWITHHELD)

	Savings
House Savings	$1,200
John's 401(k) Plan Deferral	$2,160
Employer 401(k) Plan Match	$1,080
Mary's 401(k) Plan Deferral	$1,560
Employer 401(k) Plan Match	$390
Tax Analysis	$7,618
	*$14,008 ÷ $62,000 = 22.59% current savings rate

* $6,390 + $7,618 (tax)

SCHEDULE D - INCOME TAX ANALYSIS

The Burkes average income tax rate is approximately 8 percent (8% x $63,300 = $5,042) and their marginal income tax rate is 15 percent. The Burkes are overwithheld by approximately $7,618 annually ($12,660 - $5,042). The Burkes should invest the $7,618 annually in the emergency fund by changing the income tax withholding form (W-4) to 1 (for self) and 1 (for spouse) and saving approximately $635 per month to the emergency fund.

Abbreviated Tax Analysis

	2012	2013**	2013 After Recommendations
Gross Income	$63,300	$63,300	$63,300
401(k) - John	($1,080)	($1,080)	($2,160)
401(k) - Mary			($1,560)
AGI	$62,220	$62,220	$59,580
Personal & Dependency Exemptions	$7,600	$7,800	$7,800
Standard or Itemized Deduction	$11,900	$12,200	$12,200
Taxable Income	$42,720	$42,720	$39,580
Tax Liability (estimated)	$5,538	$5,438	$5,042
Withholding	$12,660	$12,660	$12,660
Over Withheld Refund Expected*	$7,122	$7,212	$7,618

* This could be added to savings on an annual basis.

**Assume 3% inflation causing adjustment to exemptions, standard deduction, and brackets.

FINANCIAL STATEMENT: PROJECTED STATEMENT OF FINANCIAL POSITION

<table>
<tr><td colspan="4" align="center">Statement of Financial Position
Mr. and Mrs. Burke
Projected Balance Sheet 12/31/2013</td></tr>
<tr><td colspan="2" align="center">ASSETS[1]</td><td colspan="2" align="center">LIABILITIES AND NET WORTH</td></tr>
<tr><td>Current Assets</td><td></td><td>Current Liabilities[2]</td><td></td></tr>
<tr><td>Cash and Cash Equivalents[4]</td><td>$12,418</td><td>Credit Card Balance</td><td>$0</td></tr>
<tr><td>Total Current Assets</td><td>$12,418</td><td>Total Current Liabilities</td><td>$0</td></tr>
<tr><td colspan="4"></td></tr>
<tr><td>Investment Assets</td><td></td><td>Long-Term Liabilities[2]</td><td></td></tr>
<tr><td>Crossroads Inc. (1,000 Shares)</td><td>$0</td><td>Student Loan[3] - John</td><td>$50,350</td></tr>
<tr><td>Gladwell Inc. (100 Shares)</td><td>$0</td><td>Auto Loan - Mary</td><td>$6,856</td></tr>
<tr><td>House Down Payment</td><td>$1,200</td><td></td><td></td></tr>
<tr><td>Balance Mutual Fund</td><td>$13,020</td><td>Total Long-Term Liabilities</td><td>$57,206</td></tr>
<tr><td>John's 401(k) Plan</td><td>$8,065</td><td></td><td></td></tr>
<tr><td>Mary's 401(k) Plan</td><td>$2,033</td><td></td><td></td></tr>
<tr><td>Total Investment Assets</td><td>$24,318</td><td></td><td></td></tr>
<tr><td colspan="4"></td></tr>
<tr><td>Personal Use Assets</td><td></td><td>Total Liabilities</td><td>$57,206</td></tr>
<tr><td>Auto - Mary</td><td>$18,500</td><td></td><td></td></tr>
<tr><td>Truck - John</td><td>$12,000</td><td>Total Net Worth</td><td>$35,030</td></tr>
<tr><td>Motor scooter - John</td><td>$0</td><td></td><td></td></tr>
<tr><td>Personal Property & Furniture</td><td>$25,000</td><td></td><td></td></tr>
<tr><td>Total Personal Use Assets</td><td>$55,500</td><td></td><td></td></tr>
<tr><td>Total Assets</td><td>$92,236</td><td>Total Liabilities & Net Worth</td><td>$92,236</td></tr>
</table>

1. Assets are stated at fair market value.
2. Liabilities are stated at principal only as of December 31, 2013 before January payments.
3. The interest rate on the student loan is 6.9% for 10 years on a consolidation loan.
4. The $7,618 from tax analysis was added to cash.

Schedule E - Reconciliation of Year-End Net Worth

Change in Projected Net Worth January 1, 2013 - December 31, 2013	
Beginning Net Worth	**$10,475**
Home Savings	$1,200
Emergency Fund Growth	$1,800
Debt Reduction (student loan)	$3,948
Debt Reduction (automobile loan)	$3,191
Growth of John's Mutual Fund	$1,020
Growth of John's 401(k) Plan	$3,745
Growth of Mary's 401(k) Plan	$2,033
Cash from Tax Analysis	$7,618
Total Ending Net Worth	**$35,030**

REVIEW OF PRESENT VALUE APPROACH WITH REVISED WRR

RECALCULATE WAGE REPLACEMENT RATIO

	$	%
Income	$62,000	100%
Revised Savings	$14,008 ($6,390* + $7,618**)	<22.59%>
Social Security Taxes	$4,743	<7.65%>
New Wage Replacement Ratio	**$43,249**	**69.76%**

Does not count the investment income. That is, in portfolio rate of return.

**Savings plus tax savings*

REVISED RETIREMENT CALCULATION AT 70% WRR WITHOUT SOCIAL SECURITY

Age 62		Age 65	
PV	= $43,249	PV	= $43,249
N	32	N	35
i	= 3%	i	= 3%
FV	$111,369.75	FV	$121,666.737
PMT_{AD}	$111,369.75	PMT_{AD}	$121,666.737
N	33	N	30
i	(1.085/1.03 - 1) x 100	i	(1.085/1.03 - 1) x 100
$PV_{@62}$	$1,802,308.58	$PV_{@62}$	$1,896,582.19
$PV_{@30}$	= $132,475.43	$PV_{@30}$	= $109,126.65

PV OF ALL GOALS WITH RETIREMENT AT AGE 62 AND WRR OF 70%

Retirement @ 62/70%	$132,475.43	
Education	$79,112.00	
Home Down Payment	$30,798.11	
Emergency Fund Amount	$7,618.00	(From 1st Year Tax Analysis)
	$249,985.54	
Less Resources	$18,320.00	$31,320 - $13,000 (e.g., credit cards, estate documents, scooter)
	$231,665.54	

PV	$231,66.54	
i	8.5	
N	32	
PMT_{OA}	$21,253.57	Compared to actual revised savings of $14,008
	$231,665.54	

This plan will not work.

PV OF ALL GOALS WITH RETIREMENT AT AGE 65 AND WRR OF 70%

		Allocated	% of Salary
Retirement	$109,126.65	$9,842.06	15.9%
Education	$79,112.00	$7,135.06	11.5%
Home	$30,798.11	$2,777.66	4.5%
Emergency Fund	$7,618.00	$687.06	1.1%
	$226,654.76	$20,441.85	33.0%
Less Resources	$18,320.00	$1,652.27	2.7%
	$208,334.76	**$18,789.58**	**30.3%**

PV	$208,334.76
i	8.5
N	35
PMT$_{OA}$	$18,789.58 vs. $14,008 ($4,781.58 short)

DISCUSSION WITH CLIENT

The savings amount as fixed is too low to drive their quite ambitious goals of retirement, education, a home down payment, and providing an emergency fund. They are around $4,800 short, even with delaying their retirement to age 65.

What are their options?
1. Delay retirement further.
2. Include Social Security.
3. Plan for an increasing savings amount as a percentage of this income rather than a fixed amount of $14,008.
4. Save even more.

What are the major reasons the plan does not work?
If you consider the savings rate necessary for each goal over the work life expectancy at age 65, the breakdown is as follows:

Retirement	15.9%
Education	11.5%
House	4.5%
Emergency Fund	1.1%

Even with their resources they have to save 30.3% of income to reach their goals. They are currently saving 22.6%. Alternatively, Option 4 above seems infeasible. They need to seriously consider some combination of Options 1, 2, and 3 above. A plan is clearly in the making that is achievable.

Statement of Income and Expenses
Mr. and Mrs. Burke
Statement of Income and Expenses for Past Year and
Expected (Approximate) For 2014

CASH INFLOWS			
Salaries			
John's Salary	$37,440		
Mary's Salary	$27,040		
Investment Income***	$2,067		
Total Cash Inflows			$66,547
CASH OUTFLOWS			
Savings			
Savings - House down payment	$1,200		
Reinvestment of Investment Income***	$2,067		
401(k) Plan Contribution - John	$2,246		
401(k) Plan Contribution - Mary	$1,622		
Total Savings			$7,135
Fixed Outflows			
Child Support/Court Rqd. Insurance	$4,800	ND	
Rent	$8,400	ND	
HO 4 Renters Insurance*	$718	ND	
Utilities*	$742	ND	
Telephone	$360	ND	
Auto payment P&I	$3,600	ND	
Auto Insurance	$4,000	ND	
Gas, Oil, Maintenance for Auto*	$2,472	ND	
Student Loan Payments	$7,695	ND	
Insurance (Life, Disability, PLUP)	$1,425	ND	
Fee for Estates Documents	$1,000		
Credit Card Payments**	$1,000	ND	
Total Fixed Outflows			$36,212
Variable Outflows			
Taxes - John and Mary FICA	$4,933		
Taxes - Federal Tax Withheld	$5,042		
Food*	$3,708	ND	
Clothing	$1,000	ND	
Vacations	$1,500		
Total Variable Outflows			$16,183
Total Cash Outflows			$59,530
NET DISCRETIONARY CASH FLOWS			**$7,017**

*Subject to 3% inflation
**They continue to incur $1,000 yearly in credit card debt for incidentals.
*** Not included in savings rate. It is included in portfolio rate of return.

SCHEDULE F - PROJECTED SELECTED RATIOS

End of Year 1 Projected Ratios December 31, 2013		
	Beginning of Year 1	**End of Year 1**
Current Ratio	0.21	N/A no C.L.
Emergency Fund Ratio	0.91 x	3.7x*
HR 1	14.22%	14.14%
HR 2	36.8%	33.21%
Net Worth / Total Assets	11.79%	32.39%
Savings Rate	6.5%	22.59%
Investment Assets / Gross Pay	0.4947 x	0.4516 x**

* Denominator is based on beginning of year totals.

** The reason the end of year 1 investment assets to gross pay ratio is down from 0.4947 x to 0.4516 x is because the client sold the two stocks to pay off the credit card debt. This was a strategic choice of the client. If the $12,000 that decision represented were added to the year-end investment assets to gross pay ratio it would be 0.6376 x, so the Burkes are making good progress.

SUMMARY

Assuming the Burkes follow and implement all of the recommendations, they will have significantly increased their emergency fund ratio, reduced both housing ratios 1 and 2, almost tripled their net worth, and increased their savings rate from 6.5 percent to 22.59 percent at the end of the first year. These are remarkable results to accomplish in one year. If the Burkes continue on the plan, they will meet their financial goals as they come due.

Financial Planning Offices of Mitchell and Mitchell

April 18, 2014

John and Mary Burke
1420 Elm Street
Pensacola, FL 32501

RE: Financial Plan

Dear Mr. and Mrs. Burke:

This letter will confirm the completion of our services related to your current financial plan. At this time we have delivered your financial plan based on your goals and objectives. The financial plan was reviewed in detail with you at our April 11, 2013 meeting. As previously indicated our analysis and recommendations are based on information provided by you that were relied upon.

In addition, the methods that you choose to follow for the implementation of the financial planning recommendations are at your discretion. As you have indicated, you will be totally responsible for all decisions regarding implementation of the recommendations. The financial plan presented provides the following recommendations for your implementation:

Financial Planning Category	Specific Planning Area	Recommendation
Risk Management		
	Life Insurance	Both John and Mary need additional life insurance ($500,000 each) to protect each other and to protect any future child.
	Disability Insurance	Mary needs disability insurance in the event of loss of income due to disability.
	Homeowner's/Renters Insurance	There is a need to increase coverage on the renter's policy by endorsing the personal property coverage for all risks and for replacement value.
	Personal Liability Insurance	There is a need to purchase personal liability insurance. This may require the need to increase automobile liability coverage.
*Debt Management		
	Credit Cards, Auto and Student Loans	The credit cards need to be paid off immediately and the auto and student loans need to be paid as agreed. Note that the parents may assist with student loan debt.

Financial Planning Offices of Mitchell and Mitchell

**Savings Management		
	Emergency Fund	The emergency fund will be increased to reach a 3-6 month balance, rather than the current .91 month balance from savings from tax analysis.
	Retirement Savings	Currently the overall savings rate is 6.5% of gross pay (including employer match). For the retirement savings goal, the savings rate needs to be increased to 10-13%. John needs to increase his 401(k) plan deferral for maximum employer match and Mary needs to begin contributing to her 401(k) plan.
	Home Purchase Savings	The savings rate needs to reach 18% of gross pay for the home purchase 20% down payment ($39,338 needed in three years). Note that the parents may contribute towards down payment.
	College Savings for Children	The savings rate for college education for children should be 4-5% of gross pay per child.
Investment Management		
	Retirement Plans	All 401(k) plan investments need to be placed in a balanced portfolio.
Estate Planning Management		
	Estate Planning Documents	Have estate documents (will, durable power of attorney for healthcare, advance medical directive, etc.) prepared within two years.

*Note that the credit card debt can be paid off by funds acquired from the sale of the motor scooter and the sale of Crossroads and Gladwell stock.
**The savings rate can be increased after the automobile is paid off.

We thank you for the opportunity to be of service. Please contact us with any questions you may have regarding your current financial plan. We look forward to continuing a long term relationship with you as your financial situation requires additional planning services.

Sincerely,

Michael A. Mitchell, CFP®

Time Value of Money

LEARNING OBJECTIVES

After reading this chapter, you should be able to:

- Describe and prepare a timeline of the cash flows associated with time value money.
- List the time value of money variables.
- Calculate the present value of the dollar type problem.
- Understand what an annuity is and the difference between an ordinary annuity and an annuity due.
- Calculate the present by you of an ordinary annuity.
- Calculate present by you of an annuity due.
- Calculate the future value of an ordinary annuity.
- Calculate the future value of an annuity due.
- Differentiate the future value of an ordinary annuity versus an annuity due.
- Solve a time value of money problem for i, PV, N, PMT, or FV.
- Solve time value of money problems using uneven cash flows.
- Calculate NPV.
- Calculate IRR.
- Calculate the inflation adjusted rate of return.
- Calculate serial payments.
- Prepare and amortization schedule.
- Apply time value of money concepts to financing and mortgages.
- Calculate present value and future value of single amounts, annuities, annuities due, uneven cash flows and serial payments.*
- Calculate amortization payments and annual savings required to meet a goal.*
- Calculate NPV and IRR and be able to apply the techniques to financial planning problems.*

* CFP Board Resource Document - Student-Centered Learning Objectives based upon CFP Board Principal Topics.

INTRODUCTION

Time Value of Money (TVM) is a mathematical concept that determines the value of money, at a point or over a period of time, at a given rate of interest. There is an expression that "a dollar received today is worth more than a dollar received tomorrow." Most people would choose money today if offered the option between receiving it today or one year later. For example, if a person has $100 today, it could be invested and earn a rate of return that would increase the $100 to something more than that in one year. Money received in the future forgoes the potential earnings from today to the time the funds are received.

Time value of money concepts begin with two key values, the present value and the future value. The **present value** is the value today of one or more future cash flows discounted to today at an appropriate interest rate. The **future value** is the value at some point in the future of a present amount or amounts after earning a rate of return, for a period of time.

Time value of money concepts allow questions to be answered, such as how much $100 earning three percent is worth in one year. TVM also allows a financial planner and the client to answer other quantitative questions, such as:

- If I invest a certain sum of money into my IRA each year beginning now, and assuming a fixed interest rate and identified time period, how much will I have at the end of the period?
- If my goal is to pay for my children's college education, how much do I need to save each year beginning today or at some time in the future?
- If I borrow money to buy a house or car, how much is my monthly payment?
- If I want to retire debt early, how much in additional principal payments would be required?
- Should I purchase a piece of equipment for my business or rent it?
- What is my annual rate of return on an investment?

Throughout this chapter, the tools and skills necessary to answer these questions and more are provided. The chapter begins with an approach to solve time value of money calculations using a financial calculator. The appendix to this chapter, located online at money-education.com, provides other methods of solving time value of money calculations, such as mathematical formulae, factor tables and accumulation schedules. Today, most financial planners use a financial calculator, but these other methods are helpful to illustrate the actual mathematical calculations and concepts behind the time value of money calculations. Note that additional TVM calculations for education funding and retirement funding are found in Chapters 8 and 11, respectively.

For all time value of money calculations in this chapter, keystrokes are provided for the HP 10BII and HP 12C financial calculators. This chapter assumes a basic working knowledge of a financial calculator such as how to add, subtract, multiply, divide, powers, roots and string calculations. Refer to the calculator manual for operation instructions, especially for the HP 12C, that uses reverse polish notation where every operator ([+], [-], [x], [÷]) follows all of its operands.

APPROACH FOR SOLVING TIME VALUE OF MONEY CALCULATIONS

Solving time value of money calculations requires both an understanding of time value of money concepts and the knowledge and skill to properly operate a financial calculator. To avoid common keystroke and data entry errors, it is important to establish a disciplined approach to working TVM calculations. One such approach is the following four-step method:

1. Start with a timeline of cash flows.
2. Write down the TVM variables.
3. Clear all registers in the financial calculator.
4. Populate the TVM variables in the calculator.

As you work through the examples in this chapter, be sure to practice the four-step approach. For those that are experienced and confident with a financial calculator, you may decide to only use steps 3 and 4. For those less experienced with a financial calculator and time value of money concepts, steps 1 through 4 should be used with all the problems.

Key Concepts

Underline/highlight the answers as you read:

1. Identify some of the questions that financial planners are able to answer using time value of money concepts.

2. Identify the four steps approach to solving a time value of money calculation.

3. Define positive inflows and negative outflows used on a timeline and in TVM calculations.

STEP ONE: START WITH A TIMELINE

A timeline is a useful tool that illustrates the amount, timing, and direction (inflows versus outflows) of cash flows for a TVM calculation. A timeline graphically depicts all TVM variables, which helps easily identify present value, future value, an interest rate, and the number of periods. The example below demonstrates the setup of a timeline.

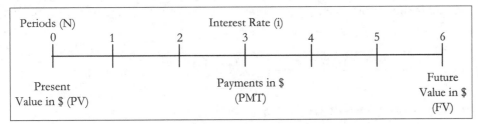

Present Value (PV): Represents the value of the cash flow today in dollars.

Payments (PMT): Represents any recurring payments, such as an income stream or debt repayment.

Future Value (FV): Represents the dollar value at some point in the future, of a current deposit(s), earning a rate of return over a period of time.

Periods (N): Represents the number of periods of compounding, which may be annual, semi-annual, quarterly, monthly or daily. In the above timeline there are six periods.

Interest Rate (i): Represents the rate being earned on an investment or interest paid on a loan.

When drawing a timeline, it is important to identify the direction of the cash flow such as whether the cash flow is an inflow or outflow. To determine the direction of a cash flow, consider whether the cash flow is being received or is being paid. When an amount is being received, the direction of the cash flow is positive. When an amount is being paid or invested, the direction of the cash flow is negative. A cash inflow is a positive amount on the timeline. A cash outflow is a negative amount on the timeline. This textbook uses < > to represent outflows on the timeline.

Examples of cash inflows, which are positive amounts:
- A client is receiving annuity payments each month during retirement.
- A client takes out a loan to purchase a house.
- The lump-sum amount that is accumulated after a period of savings.
- Any type of income received during retirement, inheritance, or distribution of savings.

Examples of cash outflows, which are negative amounts:
- A client makes tuition payments.
- Any type of periodic savings or a lump-sum amount contributed / deposited to a savings account.
- Periodic repayment of any type of debt.
- The purchase of a piece of equipment or investment.

Values are entered as positive amounts in the financial calculator when they are cash inflows (see examples above). Values that represent cash outflows (examples above) are entered as negative numbers (note that answers will calculate as a negative amount when the facts indicate the calculation is being solved for a cash outflow). To change the sign between a positive and negative value being entered into a financial calculator, use one of the following keys:

10BII Keystrokes	12C Keystrokes
[+/-]	[CHS]

STEP TWO: WRITE DOWN THE TVM VARIABLES

Write down the time value of money input variables before entering them into a financial calculator. When writing down the variables, always write them down in the same order as they appear on the financial calculator, from left to right (N, i, PV, PMT, and FV).

The variables on the financial calculator correlate to the timeline drawn in step #1. Listed below are the letters on the financial calculator and an explanation of how they relate to the timeline.

N: Represents the **N**umber of "Periods" or the term. Periods or term can be stated as the number of years, quarters, months or days.

I/YR (HP 10BII) or i (HP 12C): Represents the **i**nterest rate or discount rate. The interest rate is typically stated on an annual, semi-annual, quarterly or monthly basis.

PV: Represents the "**P**resent **V**alue" on the timeline. The present value is the value of an amount, as of today or at time period zero on the timeline.

PMT: Represents "**P**ayments" on the timeline, which can be debt payments, savings contributions, income payments received or any other type of periodic cash flow. The PMT register is only used for even cash flows or cash flows of an equal amount.

FV: Represents "**F**uture **V**alue" on the timeline. The future value is the value of an amount at some point in the future, at some interest rate, for some period of time.

STEP THREE: CLEAR ALL REGISTERS IN THE FINANCIAL CALCULATOR

Before starting any calculation of a time value of money problem, it is critical to completely clear the financial calculator. If the calculator is not cleared, it is possible to calculate a wrong answer based on a previously inputted value that remains in the memory or financial registers of the calculator.

10BII Keystrokes	*12C Keystrokes*
[ORANGE] [C ALL]	[f] [CL*X*]

Quick
Quiz 7.1

Highlight the answer to these questions:

1. Examples of inflows on a timeline include payments of education tuition and repayments of debt.
    a. True
    b. False

2. The four steps of solving time value of money problems include creating a timeline, writing down TVM values, clearing calculator registers, and populating the appropriate variables.
    a. True
    b. False

False, True.

STEP FOUR: POPULATE THE TVM VARIABLES IN THE CALCULATOR

Always populate the input values in the financial calculator in the same order as they are written down in step #2 (N, i, PV, PMT, and FV). By entering the values in the same order as written down, you are less likely to skip or forget to enter a value. To enter a value, simply press the number and then the TVM register on the financial calculator. To solve for a TVM register once all the values are populated, press the TVM register (e.g., i, N, PV, etc.) that is being solved (see [FV] in Example 7.1).

How much is $100 deposited today, worth in one year, if it earns 5% interest?

EXAMPLE 7.1

10BII Keystrokes	12C Keystrokes
1 [N]	1 [n]
5 [I/YR]	5 [i]
100 [+/-] [PV]	100 [CHS] [PV]
0 [PMT]	0 [PMT]
[FV]	[FV]
Answer: 105.00	**Answer: 105.00**

TIME VALUE OF MONEY CONCEPTS

PRESENT VALUE OF $1

The **present value of a future amount** of $1 is the current value today of that $1. The future amount is discounted over time using a discount rate (an interest rate that reflects the individual's risk or opportunity cost that could be earned on a similar project or investment) to arrive at the present value. The present value of $1 is used when calculating how much should be deposited today to meet a financial goal in the future.

Key Concepts

Underline/highlight the answers as you read:

1. Distinguish between present value and future value of a lump-sum deposit and that of an annuity.

2. Distinguish between an ordinary annuity and an annuity due.

EXAMPLE 7.2

John requires $25,000 in 5 years as a down payment for a house. Assume John can earn a 6 percent rate of return, compounded annually. How much must John deposit today to have the $25,000 in 5 years?

10BII Keystrokes	12C Keystrokes
5 [N]	5 [n]
6 [I/YR]	6 [i]
0 [PMT]	0 [PMT]
25,000 [FV]	25,000 [FV]
[PV]	[PV]
Answer: <18,681.45>	**Answer: <18,681.45>**

FUTURE VALUE OF $1

The future value of $1 is the value of a present lump-sum deposit after earning interest over a period of time. The future value of $1 is used when determining a future amount based on today's lump-sum deposit that will be earning interest (e.g., a certificate of deposit).

The interest that an investment earns can be simple or compound interest. When using simple interest, the interest rate is only applied to the original investment. Compound interest involves earning interest on the original balance, plus interest on any previously accumulated interest. Throughout this chapter, and in most time value of money calculations made by a financial planner, compound interest is used.

EXAMPLE 7.3

Holly deposits $30,000 into an account earning 4% interest, compounded annually. How much will her account balance be in 3 years?

10BII Keystrokes	12C Keystrokes
3 [N]	3 [n]
4 [I/YR]	4 [i]
30,000[+/-] [PV]	30,000[CHS] [PV]
0 [PMT]	0 [PMT]
[FV]	[FV]
Answer: 33,745.92	**Answer: 33,745.92**

PERIODS OF COMPOUNDING OTHER THAN ANNUAL

Annual compounding assumes that the interest earned is calculated and applied to the beginning of the year balance, only once each year, at the end of the year. If interest is compounded semi-annually, quarterly, monthly or daily, there are more than one period of compounding per year as the following chart illustrates.

Compounding	Periods of Compounding Per Year
Annual	1 time
Semi-Annual	2 times
Quarterly	4 times
Monthly	12 times

In Example 7.3, Holly earned four percent interest per year, compounded annually for three years. What would her account balance be if the interest were compounded semi-annually, quarterly, or monthly? For this type of calculation, the period and interest rate must all be stated in the same terms. The following chart summarizes the impact to the period and interest rate, based upon the periods of compounding per year. Note that the more periods of compounding, the larger the final balance, as summarized in Exhibit 7.2.

PERIODS OF COMPOUNDING IMPACT TO TERM AND INTEREST RATE

EXHIBIT 7.1

Compounding	Periods of Compounding Per Year	Impact to Period (N)	Impact to Interest Rate (i)
Annual	1x	None	None
Semi-Annual	2x	Years x 2	Rate ÷ 2
Quarterly	4x	Years x 4	Rate ÷ 4
Monthly	12x	Years x 12	Rate ÷ 12

EXAMPLE 7.4

Holly deposits $30,000 in an account earning 4% interest, compounded *semi-annually*. How much will her account balance be in 3 years?

10BII Keystrokes	12C Keystrokes
3 x 2 = [N]	3 [ENTER] 2 [x] [n]
4 ÷ 2 = [I/YR]	4 [ENTER] 2 [÷] [i]
30,000[+/-] [PV]	30,000[CHS] [PV]
0 [PMT]	0 [PMT]
[FV]	[FV]
Answer: 33,784.87	**Answer: 33,784.87**

Notice that for a semi-annual problem, there are two periods of compounding each year. The number of years is multiplied by two and the interest rate is divided by two. Also, notice that the greater the frequency of compounding the higher the future value.

EXAMPLE 7.5

Holly deposits $30,000 in an account earning 4% interest, compounded *quarterly*. How much will her account balance be in 3 years?

10BII Keystrokes	12C Keystrokes
3 x 4 = [N]	3 [ENTER] 4 [x] [n]
4 ÷ 4 = [I/YR]	4 [ENTER] 4 [÷] [i]
30,000[+/-] [PV]	30,000[CHS] [PV]
0 [PMT]	0 [PMT]
[FV]	[FV]
Answer: 33,804.75	**Answer: 33,804.75**

Notice that for a quarterly compounding problem, there are four periods of compounding each year. The number of years is multiplied by four and the interest rate is divided by four.

EXAMPLE 7.6

Holly deposits $30,000 in an account earning 4% interest, compounded *monthly*. How much will her account balance be in 3 years?

10BII Keystrokes	12C Keystrokes
3 x 12 = [N]	3 [ENTER] 12 [x] [n]
4 ÷ 12 = [I/YR]	4 [ENTER] 12 [÷] [i]
30,000[+/-] [PV]	30,000[CHS] [PV]
0 [PMT]	0 [PMT]
[FV]	[FV]
Answer: 33,818.16	**Answer: 33,818.16**

Notice that for a monthly compounding problem, since there are 12 periods of compounding each year, the number of years is multiplied by 12 and the interest rate is divided by 12.

COMPOUNDING SUMMARY

EXHIBIT 7.2

Account balance after investing $30,000 for 3 years at 4% interest			
Annual Compounding	Semi-Annual Compounding	Quarterly Compounding	Monthly Compounding
$33,745.92	$33,784.87	$33,804.75	$33,818.16

The more often the periods of compounding, the larger the future account balance because the interest rate is being compounded (or calculated on previous interest earnings) more frequently. This results in interest on previous interest earnings. Financial calculators are able to accommodate periods of compounding other than one year. For example, the HP 10BII can be set to semi-annual periods of compounding by pressing 2 [ORANGE] [P/YR], which would avoid having to manually adjust the number of periods and interest rate. However, the problem with this approach is that it is easy to forget that a financial calculator is set to something other than annual periods of compounding. Throughout this chapter, assume that the calculator is always set to one period of compounding per year. Any adjustments to the periods of compounding will be made manually by making the appropriate adjustment to the number of periods, interest rate and/or payments.

For any HP 10BII calculators, be sure to set default compounding periods to one for the remainder of this chapter. The HP 10BII is set by default to 12 periods of compounding. To change the calculator to 1 period of compounding per year:

10BII Keystrokes	12C Keystrokes
1[ORANGE][P/YR]	Not applicable as the HP 12C is set to one period of compounding per year.

ANNUITIES

Ordinary Annuity vs. Annuity Due

An **annuity** is a recurring cash flow, of an equal amount that occurs at periodic (but regular) intervals. Annuities are reflected on a financial calculator as a PMT (payment). An **ordinary annuity** occurs when the timing of the first payment is at the end of a period. The period may be the end of a week, month, quarter, or the end of a year. An **annuity due** occurs when the timing of the first payment is at the beginning of the period. The period may be the beginning of a week, month, quarter, or year.

Examples of an ordinary annuity:
- Most debtor payments (car loans, student loans, or mortgages).
- Many savings contributions to an IRA or 401(k) if regular and recurring and made at month, quarter, or year end.

Examples of an annuity due:
- Rents (usually paid in advance).
- Tuition payments (usually paid at the beginning of the term in advance).
- Retirement income (usually paid at the beginning of the month or year in advance).

The mathematical difference between an ordinary annuity and an annuity due is captured on a timeline by reflecting whether the first payment occurs at time period zero or at time period one. For an annuity due, the first payment occurs at time period zero. For an ordinary annuity, the first payment occurs at time period one.

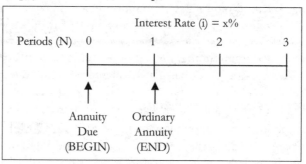

EXAMPLE 7.7

Kenny deposits $100 into a savings account, at the end of each year, for three years, earning 5% annually. What is the account value in three years?

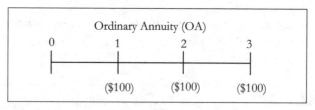

EXAMPLE 7.8

Kenny deposits $100 into a savings account, at the beginning of each year, for three years, earning 5% annually. What is the account value in three years?

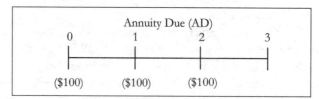

Once the timing of the cash flows has been illustrated on a timeline, the financial planner needs to identify the timing of the annuity as part of the keystrokes for the financial calculator. For an annuity due, the financial calculator should be in "BEGIN" mode, to signify the timing of the first payment is at the beginning of the period. Both the 10BII and 12C will display "BEGIN" when the calculator is in BEGIN mode. For an ordinary annuity, the calculator should be in "END" mode. When the 10BII and 12C are in END mode, the

BEGIN is no longer displayed. The calculators do not display END when in end mode. If the financial calculator is in END mode, the following keystrokes will set the calculator to BEGIN mode:

10BII Keystrokes	12C Keystrokes
[ORANGE] [BEG/END]	[g] [BEG]

If the financial calculator is in BEGIN mode, the following keystrokes will set the calculator to END mode:

10BII Keystrokes	12C Keystrokes
[ORANGE] [BEG/END]	[g] [END]

Calculation for Example 7.7 (Ordinary Annuity)

10BII Keystrokes	12C Keystrokes
3 [N]	3 [n]
5 [I/YR]	5 [i]
0 [PV]	0 [PV]
100 [+/-] [PMT]	100 [CHS] [PMT]
[FV]	[FV]
Answer: 315.25	**Answer: 315.25**

Calculation for Example 7.8 (Annuity Due)

10BII Keystrokes	12C Keystrokes
[ORANGE] [BEG/END]	[g] [BEG]
3 [N]	3 [n]
5 [I/YR]	5 [i]
0 [PV]	0 [PV]
100 [+/-] [PMT]	100 [CHS] [PMT]
[FV]	[FV]
Answer: 331.01	**Answer: 331.01**

Notice that the difference in the future values between the annuity due ($331.01) and the ordinary annuity ($315.25) is simply the difference between the first (period 0) payment for the annuity due and the last (period 3) payment for the ordinary annuity compounded by five percent (e.g., $15.76). Also, the future value of an annuity due will always be greater than the future value of an ordinary annuity by exactly the interest earned on the first payment of the annuity due over the total term. Another way to look at the problem is to see that the annuity due has one more period of compounding. Therefore, $315.25 x (1.05) = $331.01.

PRESENT VALUE OF AN ORDINARY ANNUITY OF $1 (EVEN CASH FLOWS)

The **present value of an ordinary annuity of $1** is today's value of an even cash flow stream received or paid over time. The present value of an ordinary annuity assumes that the first annuity payment is made at the end of a period. Examples of questions that may be answered using the present value of an ordinary annuity may include:

- If a client needs x dollars each year while in retirement, how much should be deposited today?
- Given the amount of debt repayment, how much was originally borrowed?
- How much would a client be willing to pay today for an annuity or income stream that begins at the end of the year?

Quick Quiz 7.2

Highlight the answer to these questions:

1. The present value of a future amount is the value of a present lump-sum deposit after earning interest over a period of time.
   a. True
   b. False

2. An annuity due occurs when the timing of the payment is at the end of a period (e.g., end of month, end of quarter, end of year).
   a. True
   b. False

False, False.

EXAMPLE 7.9

William wants to withdraw $12,000 at the end of each year (ordinary annuity) from a savings account for the next 5 years. How much must he deposit today, if the account earns 6%, compounded annually? (Note: The calculator is set to end mode for this question.)

10BII Keystrokes	12C Keystrokes
5 [N]	5 [n]
6 [I/YR]	6 [i]
12,000 [PMT]	12,000 [PMT]
0 [FV]	0 [FV]
[PV]	[PV]
Answer: <50,548.37>	**Answer: <50,548.37>**

PRESENT VALUE OF AN ANNUITY DUE OF $1 (EVEN CASH FLOWS)

The difference between the present value of an ordinary annuity and **present value of an annuity due of $1**, is the timing of the first payment. For the ordinary annuity, the timing of the first payment is at the end of the period, whereas for an annuity due the timing of the first payment is at the beginning of a time period (today) representing today's value of that even cash flow stream. On a timeline, the first payment occurs at time period zero (now).

William wants to withdraw $12,000 at the beginning of each year from a savings account for the next 5 years, to pay for his college tuition. How much must he deposit today, if the account earns 6%, compounded annually?

EXAMPLE 7.10

10BII Keystrokes	12C Keystrokes
[ORANGE] [BEG/END]	[g][BEG]
5 [N]	5 [n]
6 [I/YR]	6 [i]
12,000 [PMT]	12,000 [PMT]
0 [FV]	0 [FV]
[PV]	[PV]
Answer: <53,581.27>	**Answer: <53,581.27>**

Notice that if William waits until the end of the year to make his first withdrawal, he would deposit $3,032.90 ($53,581.27 - $50,548.37) less than if he makes the first withdrawal at the beginning of the year. By waiting until the end of the year to make his first withdrawal, he is able to take advantage of compounding interest on his entire deposit of $50,548.37. Whereas, if William takes a withdrawal immediately, he is only earning interest on his deposit, less the initial withdrawal or $41,581.27 ($53,581.27 - $12,000).

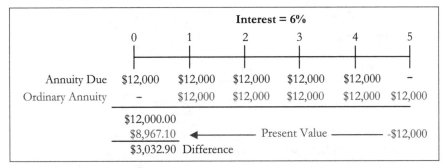

As previously stated, the present value of an annuity due will always be greater than the present value of an ordinary annuity. The difference is the last payment made under the ordinary annuity discounted to time period zero at the given interest rate as compared to the first payment made under the annuity due. In Example 7.10, the $12,000 at time period five is worth $8,967.10 at time period zero. ($12,000 - $8,967.10 = $3,032.90).

FUTURE VALUE OF AN ORDINARY ANNUITY OF $1 (EVEN CASH FLOWS)

The **future value of an ordinary annuity of $1** is the value of equal periodic payments or deposits, at some point in the future. The future value of an ordinary annuity assumes that deposits are made at the end of a period or end of a year. This calculation is useful to determine the value of saving contributions over time, earning a constant compounded rate of return.

<table>
<tr><td>**EXAMPLE 7.11**</td><td>Lisa deposits $2,500 into an account at the end of each year. If she earns 6% compounded annually, how much will the account be worth in 7 years? (Note that the calculator should be set to END mode).</td></tr>
</table>

10BII Keystrokes	12C Keystrokes
7 [N]	7 [n]
6 [I/YR]	6 [i]
0 [PV]	0 [PV]
2,500 [+/-] [PMT]	2,500 [CHS] [PMT]
[FV]	[FV]
Answer: 20,984.59	**Answer: 20,984.59**

FUTURE VALUE OF AN ANNUITY DUE OF $1 (EVEN CASH FLOWS)

The **future value of an annuity due of $1** is the future value of equal periodic deposits, made at the beginning of the period. This calculation is useful to determine the value of savings contributions at some point in the future for payments made at the beginning of each period, assuming a compounded rate of return.

<table>
<tr><td>**EXAMPLE 7.12**</td><td>Lisa deposits $2,500 into an account at the beginning of each year. If she earns 6% compounded annually, how much will the account be worth in 7 years? (Note that the calculator should be set to BEGIN mode)</td></tr>
</table>

10BII Keystrokes	12C Keystrokes
[ORANGE] [BEG/END]	[g][BEG]
7 [N]	7 [n]
6 [I/YR]	6 [i]
0 [PV]	0 [PV]
2,500 [+/-] [PMT]	2,500 [CHS] [PMT]
[FV]	[FV]
Answer: 22,243.67	**Answer: 22,243.67**

Remember that the present value of an annuity due will always be greater than the present value of an ordinary annuity because of the timing of the first withdrawal and compounded interest. Likewise, the future value of an annuity due will also always be greater than the future value of an ordinary annuity because of the additional periods of compounding. To equate the two examples above, multiply the ordinary annuity by (1 + i) or (1.06) to get the value of the annuity due. Thus, $20,984.59 x 1.06 = $22,243.67.

FUTURE VALUE OF AN ORDINARY ANNUITY VS ANNUITY DUE COMPARISON

The future value of an annuity can be separated into individual future value calculations for each cash flow. For example, the future value of a series of deposits made over a number of years can be determined by calculating the future value of each individual deposit.

Future Value of an Ordinary Annuity of $1

In Example 7.11, Lisa deposits $2,500 at the end of each year for seven years, earning six percent compounded annually. The future value of her account can be determined by calculating the future value of each $2,500 deposit. Her first deposit, for example, has six periods of compounding with a future value of $3,546.30. Whereas, her last deposit of $2,500 at the end of the seventh year has zero periods of compounding, resulting in a future value is $2,500.

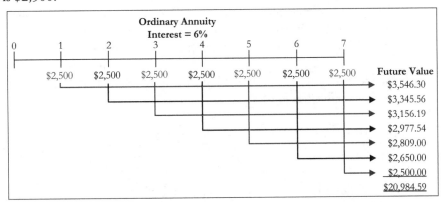

Future Value of an Annuity Due of $1

The difference in the future value between an ordinary annuity (OA) of $1 and an annuity due (AD) of $1 is attributed to additional periods of compounding for the first annuity due deposit. For example, consider Example 7.12 where Lisa deposits $2,500 at the beginning of each year for seven years, earning six percent compounded annually. Again, the future value of her account can be determined by calculating the future value of each $2,500 deposit. Lisa's first deposit has seven periods of compounding, therefore the future value of the first deposit is $3,759.08. Whereas, her last deposit of $2,500 at the beginning of the sixth year only has one period of compounding and a future value of $2,650.

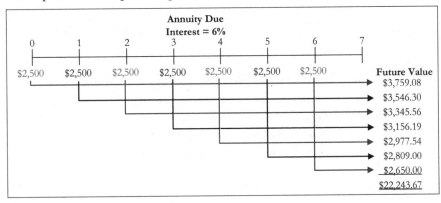

Note that the additional earnings of $1,259.08 ($22,243.67 - $20,984.59) under the annuity due calculation are attributable to the additional compounding of the first deposit under the annuity due $3,759.08 in comparison to the last (7th) deposit under the ordinary annuity $2,500 ($3,759.08 - $2,500.00 = $1,259.08).

ORDINARY ANNUITY PAYMENTS FROM A LUMP-SUM DEPOSIT

The **ordinary annuity payments from a lump-sum deposit** are the payments that can be generated at the end of each period, based on a lump-sum amount deposited today. This calculation is useful in determining an:

- Amount of payment required to repay a loan.
- Amount of income payments that can be generated from a lump-sum amount.

EXAMPLE 7.13

Jan has an investment account with a balance of $200,000. She intends to make withdrawals each year for the next 10 years from this account. If the investment account earns 7%, compounded annually, how much can Jan receive at the end of each year? (Note that the calculator should be set to END mode).

10BII Keystrokes	12C Keystrokes
10 [N]	10 [n]
7 [I/YR]	7 [i]
200,000 [+/-] [PV]	200,000 [CHS] [PV]
0 [FV]	0 [FV]
[PMT]	[PMT]
Answer: 28,475.50	**Answer: 28,475.50**

ANNUITY DUE PAYMENTS FROM A LUMP-SUM DEPOSIT

The **annuity due payments from a lump-sum deposit** are the payments that can be generated at the beginning of each period, based on a lump-sum amount deposited today. This calculation is useful in determining:

- Amount of retirement income payments that can be generated from a lump-sum amount.
- Amount of periodic income payments that can be generated from a lump-sum amount.

EXAMPLE 7.14

Peter won $3,000,000 in the Florida lottery. He intends to receive income payments at the beginning of each year, for the next 12 years. Assuming the proceeds are invested with a 3% annual return, how much can Peter receive at the beginning of each year? (Note that the calculator should be set to BEGIN mode).

10BII Keystrokes	12C Keystrokes
[ORANGE] [BEG/END]	[g] [BEG]
12 [N]	12 [n]
3 [I/YR]	3 [i]
3,000,000 [+/-] [PV]	3,000,000 [CHS] [PV]
0 [FV]	0 [FV]
[PMT]	[PMT]
Answer: 292,608.02	**Answer: 292,608.02**

SOLVING FOR TERM (N)

Term calculations provide the amount of time required to accomplish a financial goal. This calculation is useful in determining an:

- Amount of time required to attain an account balance given a certain rate of return.
- Amount of time to retire a debt.

Ivan has $25,000 invested in a mutual fund that earns 9% per year. Ivan wants to know how long it will take for his investment to double?

EXAMPLE 7.15

10BII Keystrokes	12C Keystrokes
9 [I/YR]	9 [i]
25,000 [+/-] [PV]	25,000 [CHS] [PV]
50,000 [FV]	50,000 [FV]
0 [PMT]	0 [PMT]
[N]	[n]
Answer: 8.0432	**Answer: 9.0**

Notice that the HP 10BII calculates the time for Ivan to double his investment as 8.04 years, whereas the HP 12C calculates 9 years. A limitation of the 12C is that it rounds to integers (whole numbers) when calculating periods or term. To verify which answer is correct, we can use both 8.04 and 9.0 to determine which term results in the closest amount to $50,000.

Using 9 as the number of years to double Ivan's investment. If the registers have not been cleared, simply press FV.

10BII Keystrokes	12C Keystrokes
9 [N]	9 [n]
9 [I/YR]	9 [i]
25,000 [+/-] [PV]	25,000 [CHS] [PV]
0 [PMT]	0 [PMT]
[FV]	[FV]
Answer: 54,297.33	Answer: 54,297.33

Using 8.0432 as the number to double Ivan's investment:

10BII Keystrokes	12C Keystrokes
8.0432 [N]	8.0432 [n]
9 [I/YR]	9 [i]
25,000 [+/-] [PV]	25,000 [CHS] [PV]
0 [PMT]	0 [PMT]
[FV]	[FV]
Answer: 49,999.86	Answer: 50,007.74

Using 8.0432 results in the closest future value of Ivan doubling his money from $25,000 to $50,000 (earning 9% per year, compounded annually). If using the HP 12C, be mindful of the integer rounding when calculating term.

SOLVING FOR INTEREST RATE (i)

Interest rate calculations provide the financial planner and client with the interest rate that is required to attain a certain goal and also may be used to calculate the interest rate being charged on a debt obligation.

EXAMPLE 7.16

Joe borrowed $25,000 to buy a new car. His payment is $600 per month, at month end, and he is making equal monthly payments for the next four years. What is the implicit interest rate on this loan?

10BII Keystrokes	12C Keystrokes
4 x 12 = [N]	4 [ENTER] 12 [x] [n]
25,000 [PV]	25,000 [PV]
600 [+/-] [PMT]	600 [CHS] [PMT]
0 [FV]	0 [FV]
[i]	[i]
Answer: 0.5930 per month, so multiply by 12 to state the interest rate on an annual basis 7.1158 (0.5930 x 12).	**Answer: 0.5930** per month, so multiply by 12 to state the interest rate on an annual basis 7.1158 (0.5930 x 12).

UNEVEN CASH FLOWS

So far, the discussions regarding annuity payments have focused on even dollar amounts, recurring at periodic equal intervals. When an investment or project has periodic cash flows that are not even dollar amounts or not at even intervals, the calculation is referred to as an **uneven cash flow** calculation.

During the discussion of the next two topics (Net Present Value and Internal Rate of Return) it will be necessary to use the uneven cash flow keys on a financial calculator.

For the HP 10BII, the following keys are used for uneven cash flow problems:

- **CFj:** Represents the periodic cash flows. The "j" represents each period of cash flows.
- **Nj:** Represents the number of consecutive times the periodic cash flow is an even amount. This key allows you to reduce the number of keystrokes in the calculation by entering the number of consecutive times a periodic cash flow occurs.

For the HP 12C, the following keys are used for uneven cash flow problems:
- **CF0:** Represents the cash flow amount at time period zero.
- **CFj:** Represents the periodic cash flows after time period zero. The "j" represents each period of cash flows beyond zero.
- **Nj:** Represents the number of consecutive times the periodic cash flow is an even amount.

Key Concepts

Underline/highlight the answers as you read:

1. Identify the methods for solving uneven cash flows, net present value, and IRR.

2. Define an inflation adjusted rate of return and determine its use.

3. Distinguish between serial payments and annuity payments.

4. What is an amortization schedule?

The following example demonstrates how to use the CFj and Nj buttons.

EXAMPLE 7.17

Sheryl makes the following investments into her savings account:

Year 0 – 4: $200 (a total of 5 deposits)

Year 5 – 10: $300 (a total of 6 deposits)

Year 11 – 15: $400 (a total of 5 deposits)

Note that there is no answer to this cash flow scenario. It is only meant to illustrate how to use the [Nj] key to populate multiple periods of even cash flows.

The keystrokes using CFj, the Nj shortcut is:

10BII Keystrokes	*12C Keystrokes*
200 [+/-] [CFj]	200 [CHS] [g] [CF0]
200 [+/-] [CFj] *	200 [CHS] [g] [CFj] **
4 [ORANGE] [Nj]	4 [g] [NJ]
300 [+/-] [CFj]	300 [CHS] [g] [CFj]
6 [ORANGE] [Nj]	6 [g] [NJ]
400 [+/-] [CFj]	400 [CHS] [g] [CFj]
5 [ORANGE] [Nj]	5 [g] [NJ]

* The HP10 BII does not permit the use of the Nj shortcut at this point. You must enter the cash flow at time period zero and time period one separately. However, the is not the case for the 10BII+ calculator.

** The HP12C permits the use of the Nj shortcut at this point. You do not have to enter the cash flow at time period zero and time period one, separately.

NET PRESENT VALUE

Net Present Value (NPV) is used in capital budgeting by managers and investors to evaluate investment alternatives. NPV measures the excess or shortfall of cash flows based on the discounted present value of the future cash flows, less the initial cost of the investment. NPV uses the investor's required rate of return as the discount rate. NPV assumes that the cash flows generated from the project are reinvested at the required rate of return or discount rate. The formula for NPV is:

NPV = Present Value of the Future Cash Flows – Cost of the Investment

OR

NPV = PV of CF – Cost (initial outlay)

A positive NPV indicates that the project or investment is generating cash flows in excess of what is required based on the required rate of return. A negative NPV means that the project or investment is not generating cash flows sufficient enough to meet the required rate of return. An NPV equal to zero indicates that the investment is generating a stream of cash flows with a rate of return equal to the required rate of return.

EXAMPLE 7.18

David purchased a new printer for his book publishing company. The printer was purchased for $10,000 and is expected to generate the following cash flows for the next four years at the end of each year:

Year 1: $3,000

Year 2: $4,000

Year 3: $2,500

Year 4: $1,000

Assume the printer can be sold for $2,000 at the end of year 4 and David's required rate of return is 8%. What is the net present value and should he purchase the printer?

10BII Keystrokes	12C Keystrokes
10,000 [+/-] [CFj]	10,000 [CHS] [g] [CF0]
3,000 [CFj]	3,000 [g] [CFj]
4,000 [CFj]	4,000 [g] [CFj]
2,500 [CFj]	2,500 [g] [CFj]
1,000 + 2,000 =[CFj]	1,000 [Enter] 2,000 [+]
8 [I/YR]	[g] [CFj]
[ORANGE] [NPV]	8 [i]
	[f][NPV]
Answer: 396.80	Answer: 396.80

Since the NPV is greater than zero, David should consider purchasing the printer. The value of $396.80 represents the difference between the present value of the future cash flows discounted at the required rate of return less the initial investment.

Recall the NPV formula, which is:

NPV = Present Value of the Future Cash Flows – Cost of the Investment

EXAMPLE 7.19

What is the present value of the future cash flows from this new printer David is considering?

NPV = PV of CF – Cost of Investment

$396.80 = PV of CF – $10,000

$10,000 + $396.80 = PV of CF

$10,396.80 = PV of CF

The calculation can be proved as follows:

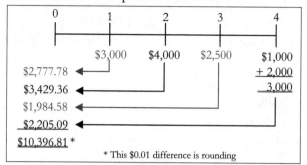

Year	Cash Flow	Discounted Present Value
Year 1	$3,000	$2,777.78
Year 2	$4,000	$3,429.36
Year 3	$2,500	$1,984.58
Year 4	$1,000 + $2,000 = $3,000	$2,205.09
Total Discounted Present Value of Cash Flow Stream		**$10,396.81**

EXAMPLE 7.20

Lisa anticipates making the following tuition payments for her son, Carson, who is starting his first year of college today.

Year	Tuition Payment
Year 1	$10,000
Year 2	$10,000
Year 3	$15,000
Year 4	$15,000

How much must Lisa have in a college savings account to make the tuition payments above, if she can earn 5%, each year, on her investments?

10BII Keystrokes	12C Keystrokes
10,000 [+/-] [CFj]	10,000 [CHS] [g] [CF0]
10,000 [+/-] [CFj] *	10,000 [CHS] [g] [CFj] **
15,000 [+/-] [CFj]	15,000 [CHS] [g] [CFj]
2 [ORANGE] [NJ]	2 [g] [Nj]
5 [I/YR]	5 [i]
[ORANGE] [NPV]	[f] [NPV]
Answer: <46,086.82>	**Answer: <46,086.82>**

The HP10 BII does not permit the use of the Nj shortcut at this point. You must enter the cash flow at time period zero and time period one separately. However, the is not the case for the 10BII+ calculator.

** *The HP12C permits the use of the Nj shortcut at this point. You do not have to enter the cash flow at time period zero and time period one, separately.*

Quick Quiz 7.3

Highlight the answer to these questions:

1. Uneven cash flows are periodic cash flows that are not the same dollar amount.
   a. True
   b. False

2. NPV measures the excess or shortfall of cash flows based on the discounted present value of future cash flows (less the initial cost/investment).
   a. True
   b. False

3. IRR is the calculation of the simple interest annual rate of return.
   a. True
   b. False

True, True, False.

INTERNAL RATE OF RETURN (IRR)

The **Internal Rate of Return (IRR)** is the compound rate of return that equates the cash inflows to the cash outflows. IRR allows for the comparison of projects or investments with differing costs and cash flows. An investment is considered acceptable when the IRR equals or exceeds the client's required rate of return. Alternatively, an investment should be rejected if the IRR is less than the client's required rate of return.

IRR is that discount rate that will cause the sum of the discounted present value of all the future cash flows to equal the cost of the investment. An important assumption about the internal rate of return is that it assumes that cash flows are reinvested at the internal rate of return.

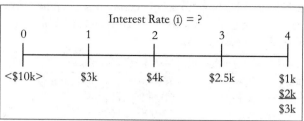

EXAMPLE 7.21

David purchased a new printer for his book publishing company. The printer was purchased for $10,000 and is expected to generate the following cash flows for the next four years:

Year 1: $3,000

Year 2: $4,000

Year 3: $2,500

Year 4: $1,000

Assume the printer can be sold for $2,000 at the end of year 4 and David's required rate of return is 8 percent. What is David's internal rate of return if he purchases the printer?

10BII Keystrokes	12C Keystrokes
10,000 [+/-] [CFj]	10,000 [CHS] [g] [CF0]
3,000 [CFj]	3,000 [g] [CFj]
4,000 [CFj]	4,000 [g] [CFj]
2,500 [CFj]	2,500 [g] [CFj]
1,000 + 2,000 = [CFj]	1,000 [ENTER] 2,000
[ORANGE] [IRR/YR]	[+] [g] [CFj]
	[f] [IRR]
Answer: 9.81%	**Answer: 9.81%**

The NPV for this problem is positive, meaning David is earning a return greater than his required rate of return. His required rate of return was 8%, but the actual internal rate of return on this investment would be 9.81%.

As previously mentioned, the internal rate of return calculation can be used to measure the compounded rate of return, when considering uneven cash flows.

EXAMPLE 7.22

Three years ago, Sydney purchased a stock for $75. Over the past three years, the stock has paid the following dividends.

Year 1: $2.25

Year 2: $2.50

Year 3: $2.75

At the end of the third year, the stock was selling for $85. What was Sydney's compounded rate of return (IRR)?

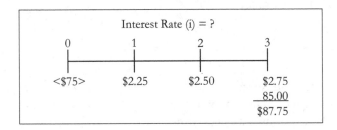

10BII Keystrokes	12C Keystrokes
75 [+/-] [CFj]	75 [CHS] [g] [CF0]
2.25 [CFj]	2.25 [g] [CFj]
2.50 [CFj]	2.50 [g] [CFj]
2.75 + 85 = [CFj]	2.75[ENTER]85 [+][g][CFj]
[ORANGE] [IRR/YR]	[f][IRR]
Answer: 7.45%	**Answer: 7.45%**

INFLATION ADJUSTED RATE OF RETURN

An **inflation adjusted rate of return** adjusts the nominal rate of return into a real (after inflation) rate of return. **Nominal interest rates** are the actual rate of return earned on an investment. Real rates of return are adjusted for inflation's impact. The formula for the real rate of return is:

$$\text{Real Rate of Return} = \frac{(1 + Rn)}{(1 + i)} - 1 \times 100$$

Where:

   Rn = nominal rate of return or investment rate of return

   i = inflation rate

Assume $5 is invested for one year earning 6% and the inflation rate during that one year is 3%. What is the inflation adjusted rate of return?

EXAMPLE 7.23

Return: $5 x 1.06 = $5.30

Inflation: $5 x 1.03 = $5.15

Difference: $5.30 - $5.15 = $0.15

The return above and beyond the impact of inflation is:

$0.15 ÷ $5.15 = 0.029126214 or 2.91% (rounded)

Using the real rate of return formula:

Real Rate of Return = [(1 + Rn) ÷ (1 + i) – 1] x 100

Real Rate of Return = [(1.06) ÷ (1.03) – 1] x 100

Real Rate of Return = [1.0291 – 1] x 100

Real Rate of Return = 0.0291 x 100

Real Rate of Return = 2.91%*

(caution: rounding 2.9126214 to 2.91 will cause a slight error)

The inflation adjusted rate of return should be used when there is an account balance growing at one rate of return and simultaneously an expense is growing at a different rate of return (or when there are investment returns at one rate and inflation (loss of purchasing power) at another rate). An inflation adjusted rate of return should be used in an education funding situation where there is a lump-sum amount growing at an investment rate of return and tuition expense is growing at a tuition inflation rate.

| EXAMPLE 7.24 | Frank and Stephanie are planning for their son's education. Tuition currently costs $15,000 per year and is paid in advance (annuity due) and they expect their son to attend college for 4 years, beginning today. They expect their investments to earn 7.5% per year and for tuition inflation to be 5% each year. How much must Frank and Stephanie invest today, to meet their goal? |

10BII Keystrokes	*12C Keystrokes*
[ORANGE] [BEG/END] 4 [N] 1.075 ÷ 1.05 - 1 x 100 = [I/YR]* 15,000 [PMT] 0 [FV] [PV]	[g] [BEG] 4 [n] 1.075 [ENTER] 1.05 [÷] 1 [-] 100 [x] [i]* 15,000 [PMT] 0 [FV] [PV]
Answer: 57,939.24	**Answer: 57,939.24**

The inflation adjusted [i] = 2.3809524 unrounded.

An inflation adjusted rate of return can be also used for retirement funding where there is a lump-sum amount earning an investment return and the income being generated by the lump sum is adjusted for inflation each year. If a client wants income throughout retirement equivalent to "today's dollars," an inflation adjusted rate of return must be used.

| EXAMPLE 7.25 | Karen and Dave are planning to retire today. They would like to receive $25,000 per year in today's dollars, at the beginning of each year, for the next 25 years. |

Karen and Dave expect their investments to earn 8% per year and inflation to be 2% each year. How much must Karen and Dave have today, to meet their goal?

10BII Keystrokes	12C Keystrokes
[ORANGE] [BEG/END]	[g] [BEG]
25 [N]	25 [n]
1.08 ÷ 1.02 - 1 x 100 = [I/YR]*	1.08 [ENTER] 1.02 [÷] 1 [-] 100 [x] [i]*
25,000 [PMT]	25,000 [PMT]
0 [FV]	0 [FV]
[PV]	[PV]
Answer: 342,198.97	**Answer: 342,198.97**

* The inflation adjusted [i] = 5.8823529 unrounded.

SERIAL PAYMENTS

Serial payments are different from annuity payments in that annuity payments are an equal dollar amount throughout the payment period. **Serial payments** are adjusted upward periodically throughout the payment period at a constant rate, usually in order to adjust for inflation's impact. Each serial payment will increase, to maintain the real dollar purchasing power of the investment.

Joe wants to purchase a boat in 4 years, which costs $50,000 in today's dollars. He can earn 8% on his investments and expects inflation to be 2.5% per year. What serial payment should Joe make at the end of the first, second, third, and fourth year to be able to purchase the boat in four years?

EXAMPLE 7.26

10BII Keystrokes	12C Keystrokes
4 [N]	4 [n]
1.08 ÷ 1.025 - 1 x 100 = [I/YR]	1.08 [ENTER] 1.025 [÷] 1 [-] 100 [x] [i]
0 [PV]	0 [PV]
50,000 [FV]	50,000 [FV]
[PMT] = 11,537.69	[PMT] = 11,537.69
x 1.025 = 11,826.13*	1.025 [x] = 11,826.13*
Answers	**Answers**
End of First Year: <11,826.13>	End of First Year: <11,826.13>
x 1.025 = End of Second Year: <12,121.79>	1.025 [x] = End of Second Year: <12,121.79>
x 1.025 = End of Third Year: <12,424.83>	1.025 [x] = End of Third Year: <12,424.83>
x 1.025 = End of Fourth Year: <12,735.45>	1.025 [x] = End of Fourth Year: <12,735.45>

* Note: The calculated first payment for a serial payment is determined using the same keystrokes as an ordinary annuity, but the calculated payment is then increased by the inflation rate to determine the first serial payment at the end of year one.

EXAMPLE 7.27

Serial Payment Proof:

Joe needs $50,000 in today's dollars. In 4 years he will need:

10BII Keystrokes	12C Keystrokes
4 [N] 2.5 [I/YR] 50,000 [PV] 0 [PMT] [FV] **Answer: 55,190.64**	4 [n] 2.5 [i] 50,000 [PV] 0 [PMT] [FV] **Answer: 55,190.64**

Accumulation Schedule (Proof):

Year	Year-End Deposits (Payments)	8% Interest on Ending Balance	Ending Balance
1	$11,826.13	0	$11,826.13
2	$12,121.79	$946.09	$24,894.01
3	$12,424.83	$1,991.52	$39,310.36
4	$12,735.45	$3,144.83	$55,190.64

DEBT REPAYMENTS

Time value of money concepts can be used to calculate the monthly, quarterly, or annual payment necessary to retire a debt obligation. Debt repayment calculations can be used for any type of debt including student loans, credit cards, mortgages or car loans. In addition to the payment required to retire the debt, the financial planner can determine the amount of interest and principal paid over a period of time.

Remember, most debt repayments are ordinary annuities (they are made in arrears), so repayment calculations are in END mode. Even though most mortgage payments are made at the beginning of the month, the repayment is still an ordinary annuity (because each payment includes a portion of principal repayment and interest expense incurred from the loan being outstanding for the previous month).

EXAMPLE 7.28

Ken and Amy bought a house for $400,000 on August 1. They made a down payment of 20% and financed the balance over 15 years at 5% annual interest. What is their monthly mortgage payment and when do they make it? (Note that they make the first payment one month in arrears.)

10BII Keystrokes	12C Keystrokes
15 x 12 = [N]	15 [ENTER] 12 [x] [n]
5 ÷ 12 = [I/YR]	5 [ENTER] 12 [÷] [i]
400,000 x 0.80 = [PV]	400,000 [ENTER]
0 [FV]	0.80 [x] [PV]
[PMT]	0 [FV]
	[PMT]
Answer: <2,530.54>	**Answer: <2,530.54>**

Their first payment is due on September 1. How much interest will they pay in the first calendar year (4 payments)?

10BII Keystrokes	12C Keystrokes
1 [INPUT] 4	4 [f] [AMORT]
[ORANGE] [AMORT] [=] 4,818.84-principal	
[=]	
Answer: <5,303.32>	**Answer: <5,303.32>**

Note: They will make four payments during the current calendar year (September, October, November, and December). Therefore, the loan must be amortized for four months.

Their first payment is due on September 1. How much principal will they repay in the first calendar year?

10BII Keystrokes	12C Keystrokes
See above	[x ≷ y]
([=] 4,818.84-principal)	
Answer: <4,818.84>	**Answer: <4,818.84>**

Their first payment is due on September 1. What is the outstanding principal balance on their loan at calendar year end?

10BII Keystrokes	12C Keystrokes
[=]	320,000 [ENTER]
	4,818.83 [-]
Answer: 315,181.16	**Answer: 315,181.16**

AMORTIZATION SCHEDULE

An **amortization schedule** illustrates the repayment of debt over time. Each debt payment consists of both interest expense and principal repayment. The further into the repayment of a debt, the bigger the portion of the payment that is applied to the outstanding principal. The following yearly amortization schedule illustrates the repayment of Ken and Amy's 15 year mortgage, from the previous example but assumes the loan was taken out January 1 and the first payment was made January 31.

Inputs:	
Amount Borrowed	$320,000
Interest Rate	5%
Term	15

Year	Beginning Balance	Payment	Principal Amount	Interest Amount	Ending Balance
1	$320,000	($30,366.48)	($14,700.32)	($15,666.15)	$305,299.68
2	$305,300	($30,366.48)	($15,452.42)	($14,914.06)	$289,847.26
3	$289,847	($30,366.48)	($16,243.00)	($14,123.48)	$273,604.27
4	$273,604	($30,366.48)	($17,074.02)	($13,292.46)	$256,530.25
5	$256,530	($30,366.48)	($17,947.56)	($12,418.92)	$238,582.70
6	$238,583	($30,366.48)	($18,865.79)	($11,500.69)	$219,716.91
7	$219,717	($30,366.48)	($19,831.00)	($10,535.48)	$199,885.92
8	$199,886	($30,366.48)	($20,845.59)	($9,520.89)	$179,040.33
9	$179,040	($30,366.48)	($21,912.09)	($8,454.39)	$157,128.24
10	$157,128	($30,366.48)	($23,033.16)	($7,333.32)	$134,095.09
11	$134,095	($30,366.48)	($24,211.58)	($6,154.90)	$109,883.51
12	$109,884	($30,366.48)	($25,450.29)	($4,916.19)	$84,433.23
13	$84,433	($30,366.48)	($26,752.37)	($3,614.11)	$57,680.86
14	$57,681	($30,366.48)	($28,121.07)	($2,245.41)	$29,559.80
15	$29,560	($30,366.48)	($29,559.80)	($806.68)	$0.00

Note: The amortization table could have easily been prepared on a monthly rather than yearly basis.

Note: According to the amortization schedule, the ending balance of the mortgage after the first year is $305,299.68 which is different than the $315,181.16 originally calculated (Example 7.28) due to the original loan only being amortized for four months. In the amortization schedule above, the loan was amortized for a full 12 months for each year.

OTHER PRACTICAL APPLICATIONS

The time value of money principles covered in this chapter can also be applied to every day decisions that clients face. Some other questions that can be answered using time value of money include:

- Should a client take the cash rebate or zero percent financing on a new car?
- Should a client pay points to reduce their mortgage payment when purchasing a new home?
- Should a lottery winner receive a lump-sum payment or annuity over 20 years?

CASH REBATE OR ZERO PERCENT FINANCING

When a client is considering a car purchase or other expensive item that requires financing, special terms may be offered. The seller may offer a cash rebate or zero percent financing and the client must determine which offer is the most financially beneficial. Time value of money skills can be applied to answer this question.

Jan is considering purchasing a new car for $40,000. The dealer is offering two options on the purchase:

- Option 1: Receive a $5,000 rebate on the price of the car and finance the balance over 5 years at 4% interest, or
- Option 2: Finance the vehicle for 6 years at 0% interest, but no rebate.

EXAMPLE 7.29

If Jan elects option #1, her payment would be:

10BII Keystrokes	12C Keystrokes
5 x 12 = [N]	5 [ENTER] 12 [x] [n]
4 ÷ 12 = [I/YR]	4 [ENTER] 12 [÷] [i]
40,000 – 5,000 = [PV]	40,000[ENTER]
0 [FV]	5,000 [-] [PV]
[PMT]	0 [FV]
	[PMT]
Answer: <644.58>	**Answer: <644.58>**

The HP 12C can automatically accommodate monthly compounding by pressing the number of years [g] [N], which will multiply the number of years by 12 and populate the number of months into the [n] register. The 12C will also account for monthly interest by pressing the annual interest [g] [i], which will divide the annual interest rate by 12 and populate the [i] register.

Her total cost under option #1 is $38,675 ($644 x 60 months).

If Jan elects option #2, her payment would be:

10BII Keystrokes	12C Keystrokes
6 x 12 = [N] 0 [I/YR] 40,000 [PV] 0 [FV] [PMT] **Answer: <555.56>**	6 [g] [n] 0 [i] 40,000 [PV] 0 [FV] [PMT] **Answer: <555.56>**

Her total cost under option #2 would be $40,000 ($555.56 x 72 months).

Based on the total cost (purchase price – rebate + interest expense), Jan would be better off by electing option #1 and selecting the rebate, as she would save $1,325 ($40,000 - $38,675) over the repayment period.

PAYMENT OF POINTS ON A MORTGAGE

Another type of financing decision a client may consider is whether or not to pay points on a mortgage to reduce the interest rate. Points are a percentage of the amount being borrowed that is paid by the borrower to the lender. The higher the points paid, the lower the interest rate on the loan. The decision to pay (or not pay) points is primarily a function of the time of ownership of the property, so the borrower can recoup the points paid through savings on a lower interest rate (interest expense). Time value of money concepts can be applied to determine the appropriate amount of points to pay or not pay when borrowing to purchase a house.

EXAMPLE 7.30

Sylvia is considering purchasing a new home for $500,000. She intends to put 20% down and finance $400,000, but is unsure which financing option to select. Sylvia is considering the following financing options:

- Option 1: Fixed rate mortgage over 30 years at 5.5% interest, zero points.
- Option 2: Fixed rate mortgage over 30 years at 5% interest, plus two discount points.

How long would her financial planner recommend that she live in the house to justify option #2?

First, determine how much paying the points will cost Sylvia. Paying two discount points will cost her $8,000 ($400,000 x 0.02).

Second, determine the monthly mortgage payment under each financing option.

Option #1

10BII Keystrokes	12C Keystrokes
30 x 12 = [N]	30 [g] [n]
5.5 ÷ 12 = [I/YR]	5.5 [g] [i]
400,000 [PV]	400,000 [PV]
0 [FV]	0 [FV]
[PMT]	[PMT]
Answer: <2,271.16>	**Answer: <2,271.16>**

Option #2

10BII Keystrokes	12C Keystrokes
30 x 12 = [N]	30 [g] [n]
5 ÷ 12 = [I/YR]	5 [g] [i]
400,000 [PV]	400,000 [PV]
0 [FV]	0 [FV]
[PMT]	[PMT]
Answer: <2,147.29>	**Answer: <2,147.29>**

Third, determine the cost savings and amount of time required to payback the $8,000 paid in discount points.

Option #1 Payment: $2,271.16

Option #2 Payment: $2,147.29

Savings Per Monthly Payment: $123.87 ($2,271.16 - $2,147.29).

$8,000 ÷ $123.87 = 64.6 months or 5.4 years (64.6 ÷12).

Therefore, if Sylvia intends to live in the new house for more than 5.4 years, she would be better off with option #2 and paying the discount points now.

Note: If the $8,000 is included on the mortgage, the payment would be comparable at $2,190.23 (savings of $80.93 per month). The ownership period to recoup the $8,000 would then be: $8,000 ÷ $80.93 = 98.9 months or 8.2 years.

LOTTERY WINNINGS - LUMP SUM OR ANNUITY

Should a client (or financial planner) be so fortunate as to win a lump-sum amount from a lottery, a decision must be made whether to take a lump-sum distribution or an annual annuity. Along with many other considerations, the lottery winner should decide whether an almost risk-free rate of return can be earned that is greater than what is implied in an annuity payout. If a risk-free rate of return can be earned that is greater than what is being implied in an annuity payout, the lottery winner should take the lump-sum amount. If the lottery winner is unable to earn a risk-free return greater than what is implied in the annuity, then the annuity should be considered. Ultimately, the decision will be based on many factors including the winner's expected earnings rate.

EXAMPLE 7.31

Big Money Bob won $50 million in the New York lottery. He can elect to receive a single lump-sum payout of $22 million after taxes or receive an annuity of $1,500,000 after tax, at the end of each year for the next 20 years. What rate of return would he need to earn to make the lump-sum payout, equivalent to the annuity payment? Should Bob take the lump-sum payment or the annuity?

What rate of return would he need to earn to make the lump-sum payout equivalent to the annuity payment?

10BII Keystrokes	12C Keystrokes
20 [N]	20 [n]
22,000,000 [+/-] [PV]	22,000,000 [CHS] [PV]
1,500,000 [PMT]	1,500,000 [PMT]
0 [FV]	0 [FV]
[I/YR]	[i]
Answer: 3.15%	**Answer: 3.15%**

Should Bob take the lump-sum payment or the annuity?

If Bob can invest the lump-sum payout and earn a return greater than 3.15% tax-free (without risk) he should take the lump-sum payout. If Bob is uncertain if he can earn a riskless 3.15%, he should consider electing the annuity payment. There may be other considerations that impact Bob's decision, such as immediate lump-sum needs or other considerations. This example is only intended to illustrate how time value of money may be used in the decision making process. There are other considerations such as current financial needs and the ability to manage assets that must be considered.

CONCLUSION

The important time value of money concepts, including ordinary annuity and annuity due, are necessary subjects for the financial planner to master in order to properly understand and assist clients with goal-oriented recommendations. Common financial planning needs such as retiring debt, financing decisions, and goal attainment (i.e., retirement and education funding) require time value of money knowledge to properly serve clients. Financial planners must immerse themselves in this subject matter to effectively and successfully practice in their chosen profession.

Key Terms

Amortization Schedule - Illustrates the repayment of debt, over time. Each debt payment consists of both interest expense and principal repayment.

Annuity - A recurring cash flow, of an equal amount that occurs at periodic (but regular) intervals.

Annuity Due - Occurs when the timing of the first payment is at the beginning of the first period. The period may be the beginning of a month, quarter, or year.

Annuity Due Payment from a Lump-Sum Deposit - The payment that can be generated at the beginning of each period, based on a lump-sum amount deposited today.

Future Value - The value at some point in the future of a present amount or amounts after earning a rate of return, for a period of time.

Future Value of an Annuity Due -The future value of equal periodic deposits, made at the beginning of the period.

Future Value of an Ordinary Annuity - The value of equal periodic payments or deposits, at some point in the future. The future value of an ordinary annuity assumes that deposits are made at the end of a period or end of a year.

Inflation Adjusted Rate of Return - The nominal rate of return adjusted for inflation. The real (after inflation) rate of return equals $[(1+Rn) \div (1 + i) - 1] \times 100$, where Rn is the nominal return and i is the inflation rate.

Internal Rate of Return (IRR) - A compounded annual rate of return. IRR allows for the comparison of projects or investments with differing costs and cash flows. The rate that equates the PV of a series of cash flows to an initial investment.

Net Present Value (NPV) - Measures the excess or shortfall of cash flows based on the discounted present value of the future cash flows, less the initial cost or investment. NPV uses the investor's required rate of return for similar projects as the discount rate.

Nominal Interest Rates - The actual rate of return earned on an investment.

Ordinary Annuity - Occurs when the timing of the first payment is at the end of a period. The period may be, for example, the end of a month or the end of a year.

Ordinary Annuity Payment from a Lump-Sum Deposit - The payment that can be generated at the end of each period, based on a lump-sum amount deposited today.

Key Terms

Present Value - The value today of one or more future cash payments discounted at an interest rate.

Present Value of a Future Amount - The current value today of a future amount. The future amount is discounted over time using a discount rate (an interest rate that reflects the individual's risk or opportunity cost that could be earned on a similar project or investment) to arrive at the present value.

Present Value of an Annuity Due - The timing of the first payment is at the beginning of a time period (today) representing today's value of that even cash flow stream. On a timeline, the first payment occurs at time period zero (now).

Present Value of an Ordinary Annuity - Today's value of an even cash flow stream received or paid over time. The present value of an ordinary annuity assumes that the first annuity payment is made at the end of a period.

Serial Payments - Payments that are adjusted upward periodically throughout the payment period at a constant rate, in order to adjust for inflation's impact.

Time Value of Money (TVM) - A mathematical concept that determines the value of money, over a period of time, at a given rate of interest.

Uneven Cash Flow - An investment or project that has periodic cash flows that are not the same dollar amount.

DISCUSSION QUESTIONS

1. Define time value of money.

2. Discuss the difference between the present value and the future value of money.

3. List and define the four steps to solving time value of money calculations.

4. Define the present value of a future amount.

5. Define the future value of a lump-sum amount.

6. Discuss the difference between ordinary annuity and annuity due.

7. Define present value of an ordinary annuity.

8. Define the present value of an annuity due.

9. Define the future value of an ordinary annuity.

10. Define the future value of an annuity due.

11. Distinguish between an ordinary annuity payment with a lump-sum deposit versus an annuity due payment with a lump-sum deposit.

12. Define Net present Value (NPV).

13. Define Internal Rate of Return (IRR).

14. Define an inflation adjusted rate of return.

15. Define a serial payment.

16. Define what an amortization schedule illustrates.

17. List and define the three methods used for the retirement funding calculation.

18. List applications other than education, retirement funding, mortgages, and loans for TVM.

MULTIPLE-CHOICE PROBLEMS

1. Steve and his wife Christine recently opened an investment account with the intention of saving enough to purchase a house. Their goal is to have $45,000 for a down payment in 5 years. Their account will guarantee them a return of 8% compounded annually. How much do they need to put into the account right now to reach their goal?

   a. $30,626.24.
   b. $39,546.09.
   c. $46,778.96.
   d. $51,214.75.

2. Jordan invested $12,500 to help her friend Dylan start his own cooking school five years ago. The business proved to be successful far beyond Dylan's expectations. Today he is returning a check to Jordan and has told her that as best as he could figure, she was receiving the equivalent of about 38% per year for her initial investment. What is the amount of the check Dylan has for Jordan today?

   a. $44,632.49.
   b. $56,733.57.
   c. $62,561.25.
   d. $66,980.35.

3. Colleen's grandfather set up a savings account for her with a $25,000 gift when she was first born. The account accumulated interest annually at a rate of 6% per year and no other deposits were made to the account. Colleen is 21 years old today. To date, how much has accumulated in Colleen's account?

   a. $79,231.88.
   b. $84,989.09.
   c. $98,656.75.
   d. $101,378.92.

4. DRI Enterprises needs to have a lump-sum deposit of $200,000 for the purchase of a surety bond in 6 months. They wish to immediately deposit a sum of cash into a short-term account paying 4% per year, compounded on a monthly basis. How much will they need to deposit into this account to have enough to purchase the bond?

   a. $175,890.46.
   b. $188,907.43.
   c. $196,046.25.
   d. $211,013.89.

5. Claire just won the lottery and has been told that she can either accept annual payments at the beginning of each year of $173,695 per year for the next 20 years or she can receive a lump-sum settlement. Claire figures she could invest the money at 6.34% (the same rate as the annuity). What would the amount of the lump-sum settlement be?

     a. $1,989,309.23.

     b. $2,061,320.61.

     c. $2,152,659.03.

     d. $2,589,645.97.

6. Mark and Sonya would like to have the opportunity to buy a home in the next five years. They currently have $15,000 saved toward this goal in an investment account paying 7% annual interest, compounded on a monthly basis. In addition to this, Mark and Sonya add an additional $250 every month at the end of the month. Given this information, what amount can you tell Sonya and Mark that they will have for a down payment when they are ready to purchase their home?

     a. $21,398.45.

     b. $37,465,87.

     c. $39,162.60.

     d. $45,733.58.

7. Alberto saved enough tip money from working at the casino to place $125,500 in an investment account generating 9.25% compounded monthly. He wants to collect a monthly income of $1,350, at the beginning of each month, for as long as the money lasts. Approximately, how many months will Alberto have this income coming to him?

     a. 139.

     b. 145.

     c. 152.

     d. 162.

8. David purchased stock 15 years ago for $325.75. He sold the stock today for $2,500. Given this information, what is the average annual compound rate of return that David realized on this stock?

     a. 10.09%.

     b. 12.39%.

     c. 13.12%.

     d. 14.55%.

9. Kelly has asked her accountant, Darla, to determine whether her company, Gaggin Industries, a leader in chain manufacturing, should purchase a new machine for $155,000 that can be sold at the end of 5 years for $125,000 and during that time will generate cash flows as follows: Year 1) + 4,000; Year 2) +7,000 and Years 3 - 5) + $15,000. She told Darla to determine her NPV with her cost of capital at 11.5%. With her NPV calculated, what will Darla tell her?

    a. Do not purchase the machine because NPV is negative.

    b. Purchase the machine because NPV is negative.

    c. Do not purchase the machine because NPV is positive.

    d. Purchase the machine because NPV is positive.

10. Donna plans to save for a vacation to Costa Rica in 18 months. She will be putting the money into a short-term investment account earning 4% annually. How much will Donna have to put away at the beginning of each month if the total package cost for the trip is $3,500?

    a. $170.34.

    b. $188.37.

    c. $212.69.

    d. $246.73.

11. Liam bought a piece of equipment for $10,000. He paid $3,000 for upgrades during year 1 and the equipment generates $2,000 in cash flow for year 1. In year 2 the equipment generated $3,000 and in year 3 it generated $4,000, but Liam sells it for $6,000 and pays a $500 commission. What is his IRR?

    a. 3.4%.

    b. 3.9%.

    c. 4.4%.

    d. 4.9%.

12. With interest rates at 4.875% for a 30-year fixed mortgage, Dan, age 48, plans to buy a house for $825,000. He wants to put half of the purchase price down. What will his monthly mortgage payment be for principal and interest?

    a. $2,182.98.

    b. $2,768.55.

    c. $3,176.43.

    d. $3,493.67.

13. Bobby bought a house for $275,000, by putting 15% down and borrowing the balance. His note is for 30 years at 7.5% interest. If his first payment is due August 1st of the current year, how much interest will he pay this year?

    a. $5,498.11.
    b. $6,989.46.
    c. $7,293.78.
    d. $7,667.13.

14. Bobby bought a house for $275,000, by putting 15% down and borrowing the rest. His note is for 30 years at 7.5% interest. If his first payment is due August 1st of the current year, how much principal did he pay in the current year?

    a. $878.29.
    b. $925.14.
    c. $985.43.
    d. $1,612.28.

15. Cindy won the California lottery. She can take a single lump-sum payout of $12.5 million dollars or receive $825,000 per year for the next 25 years. What rate of return would Cindy need to break even if she took the lump-sum amount instead of the annuity?

    a.   3.75%.
    b.   4.29%.
    c.   4.98%.
    d.   5.31%.

16. Danny buys a house for $500,000, putting 20% down. His loan is for 30 years at 6% and he includes closing costs of 3% into his mortgage. How much is his monthly payment (rounded to whole dollars)?

    a. $2,457.
    b. $2,470.
    c. $2,754.
    d. $2,785.

17. Frank and Stephanie have an 18 year old son who is going to college this year, for four years. The tuition is $15,000 per year and is expected to increase at 4% per year. They believe they can earn 6% per year on their investment, what lump-sum amount must they deposit today, to pay for their son's education?

      a. $55,095.18.

      b. $56,626.37.

      c. $57,222.71.

      d. $58,323.15.

18. In five years, Joe wants to buy a boat that costs $75,000 in today's dollars. He can earn 8% return on his investments and he expects the boat to increase in price by 3% each year. What will Joe's serial payment at the end of the second year be, if he wants to buy the boat in 5 years?

      a. $11,097.12.

      b. $13,612.65.

      c. $14,021.03.

      d. $14,441.67.

1. Calculate the present value of $3 million to be received in 30 years assuming an annual interest rate of 10%.

2. Calculate the present value of $75,000 to be received in 20 years assuming an annual interest rate of 8%.

3. Calculate the present value of $10,000 to be received in 10 years assuming an annual interest rate of 6%.

4. Calculate the present value of $50,000 to be received in 5 years assuming an annual interest rate of 8%, compounded monthly.

5. Calculate the present value of $200,000 to be received in 7 years assuming an annual interest rate of 12%, compounded monthly.

6. Calculate the present value of $300,000 to be received in 10 years assuming an annual interest rate of 6%, compounded monthly.

7. Calculate the future value of $10,000 invested for 30 years assuming an annual interest rate of 8%.

8. Calculate the future value of $15,000 invested for 10 years assuming an annual interest rate of 8%.

9. Calculate the future value of $5,000 invested for 10 years assuming an annual interest rate of 15%.

10. Calculate the future value of $24,000 invested for 12 years assuming an annual interest rate of 18%, compounded monthly.

11. Calculate the future value of $3,000 invested for 50 years assuming an annual interest rate of 12%, compounded monthly.

12. Calculate the future value of $8,000 invested for 360 months assuming an annual interest rate of 11%, compounded monthly.

13. Calculate the present value of an ordinary annuity of $5,000 received annually for 7 years assuming a discount rate of 8%.

14. Calculate the present value of an ordinary annuity of $10,000 received quarterly for 20 years assuming a discount rate of 9%.

15. Calculate the present value of an ordinary annuity of $3,000 received monthly for 12 years assuming a discount rate of 10%.

16. Calculate the present value of an annuity of $300,000 received annually that begins today and continues for 10 years, assuming a discount rate of 9%.

17. Calculate the present value of an annuity of $5,000 received quarterly that begins today and continues for 20 years, assuming a discount rate of 8%.

18. Calculate the present value of an annuity of $12,000 received monthly that begins today and continues for 25 years, assuming a discount rate of 6%.

19. Calculate the future value of an ordinary annuity of $6,500 paid annually for 23 years, assuming an annual earnings rate of 6%.

20. Calculate the future value of an ordinary annuity of $5,000 paid every quarter for 20 years, assuming an annual earnings rate of 8%.

21. Calculate the future value of an ordinary annuity of $3,000 paid every month for 25 years, assuming an annual earnings rate of 10%.

22. Calculate the future value of an annual annuity of $1,500 beginning today and continuing for 10 years, assuming an earnings rate of 6%.

23. Calculate the future value of a quarterly annuity of $3,000 beginning today and continuing for 15 years, assuming an annual earnings rate of 8%.

24. Calculate the future value of a monthly annuity of $150 beginning today and continuing for 100 years, assuming an annual earnings rate of 12%.

25. Calculate the annual payment that can be received over 30 years from a single investment of $1,000,000 earning 7%, compounded annually.

26. Calculate the quarterly payment to be received over 10 years from a single investment of $50,000 earning 12%, compounded quarterly.

27. Calculate the monthly payment to be received over 15 years from a single investment of $250,000 earning 9.2%, compounded monthly.

28. Calculate the payment to be received at the beginning of each year for 5 years from an investment of $250,000 earning 6%, compounded annually.

29. Calculate the monthly payment for a home loan of $400,000 financed at 4% over 30 years.

30. Calculate the NPV of a machine which is bought for $5,000, sold at the end of year 5 for $2,500.00, and produces the following cash flows: year 1) +$700; year 2) +$600; year 3) +$500; year 4) +$400; year 5) +$300, assume the cost of capital is 8%.

31. Calculate the IRR of a project that requires an initial cash outflow of $9,000.00 and will be sold at the end of year 5 for $4,500.00. The project produces the following cash flows:

Year 1: +$300
Year 2: +$600
Year 3: +$1,200
Year 4: +$2,400
Year 5: +$4,800

32. Calculate the number of years it will take $5,000 to grow to $25,000 assuming an annual rate of return of 12%.

33. Today Brian purchased an antique car for $15,000. He expects it to increase in value at a rate of 7% compounded annually for the next 10 years. How much does he expect the car to be worth at the end of the 10th year?

Quick Quiz Explanations

Quick Quiz 7.1

1. False. These are examples of cash outflows. Cash inflows include receiving an annuity and receipt of income during retirement.
2. True.

Quick Quiz 7.2

1. False. This is the definition of future value of a lump sum. Present value of a future amount is the current value today of a future amount that is discounted over time to arrive at a present value.
2. False. This is the definition of an ordinary annuity. An annuity due occurs when the timing of the payment is at the beginning of the period (e.g., beginning of month etc.).

Quick Quiz 7.3

1. True.
2. True.
3. False. IRR is a compounded annual rate of return that allows a comparison of projects or investments with differing costs and cash flows.

Education and Education Funding

LEARNING OBJECTIVES

After reading this chapter, you should be able to:

- Describe current higher education costs and know the cost besides tuition.
- Describe historical tuition inflation rate and determine its impact on education cost.
- Describe financial aid and the expected family contribution amount.
- Identify the various types of financial aid including grants and loans.
- Describe qualified tuition plans including prepaid tuition plans and college savings plans.
- Articulate the role of U.S. government savings bonds in higher education funding.
- Describe the tax implications for education expenses and student loan interest deduction.
- Describe the American opportunity tax credit and the lifetime learning credit.
- Calculate education funding needs using the uneven cash flow method, the traditional method, the account balance method, and the hybrid approach.
- Calculate the funds needed to meet the education goals for members of the client's family.*
- Recommend the appropriate use of funding sources including loans, scholarships, grants, and fellowships in funding education.*
- Compare, contrast and recommend appropriate education savings vehicles given tax implications, risk tolerance, investment alternatives, and funds needed.*

* CFP Board Resource Document - Student-Centered Learning Objectives based upon CFP Board Principal Topics.

INTRODUCTION

Besides wanting a healthy happy baby, one of parent's most common desires is for their child to grow up and go to college. While not always the case, paying for children's college education is now one of the top goals for many families. Therefore, education planning and funding represents an important area of expertise most financial planners should develop. Planners should be able to answer client questions regarding:

- How much is current tuition?
- How much is tuition expected to increase in the future?
- Other than tuition, what other costs are associated with a college education?
- What types of financial aid are available and where is information regarding financial aid found?
- What are the tax advantaged plans, income tax deductions, and tax credits available for education funding?

CURRENT EDUCATION COSTS

According to the U.S. Department of Education's National Center for Education Statistics, undergraduate enrollment in postsecondary institutions increased from 7.4 million in 1970 to 18.6 million undergraduates in Fall 2011. It is forecasted that undergraduate enrollments will increase to 17.5 million in 2018.

The reason more families are sending their children to college is because of the disparity in wages between workers with a high school diploma compared to workers with an undergraduate or master's degree.[1]

- High School Diploma - $33,176
- Bachelor's Degree - $54,756
- Masters Degree - $65,676
- Doctorate Degree - $80,652
- Professional Degree - $86,580

Over the course of a lifetime, the average annual earnings difference between high school graduates and those workers with a postsecondary degree, for workers age 25 and older (2012) was:

- High School Diploma – 1.0
- Bachelor's Degree – 1.65
- Masters Degree – 1.98
- Doctorate Degree – 2.43
- Professional Degree – 2.61

Over the course of a lifetime, workers with a bachelor's degree will earn 66 percent more than a worker with a high school diploma. Workers with a professional degree will earn 274 percent more than a worker with a high school diploma.

As more and more families send their children to college, it places a larger financial burden on families to plan for and fund this expense. According to College Board's *Trends in College Pricing 2012*, the average annual tuition and fees for 2012 was as follows:

---

1. Bureau of Labor Statistics, Current Population Survey, Annual Social and Economic Supplement, March 23, 2012.

- Public University In State Tuition - $8,655
- Public University Out of State Tuition - $21,706
- Private University Tuition - $29,506

OTHER COSTS BESIDES TUITION

The above tuition and fees exclude living expenses associated with attending college, such as room and board, transportation, insurance, internet access, etc. The total cost of attending college is significantly greater than just tuition and fees. According to the College Board's *Trend in College Pricing 2012*, tuition and fees account for 67 percent of the total cost of attending a private four-year college, 39 percent of the total cost for in-state public universities. Although the other costs besides tuition are similar to what one would experience as part of every day life without going to college, the issue is that if a student is attending college full-time, instead of working, how does the student pay for the other costs? There's an opportunity cost associated with going to college, rather than working to provide income to pay for ordinary living expenses. It is not uncommon for the total cost of education to be twice tuition and fees.

Key Concepts

Underline/highlight the answers as you read:

1. Identify all costs associated with funding a college education and the impact of tuition inflation on education funding.

2. Identify the financial aid process and describe the three formulas used to determine the EFC.

FUTURE TUITION COSTS

A financial planner should be able to forecast the future cost of tuition and other costs. Such forecasting will require an understanding of the historical tuition inflation rate and inflation rate for other costs besides tuition.

The following exhibit compares the tuition inflation rate[2] to the consumer price index from 1970 - 2010.

---

2. College tuition inflation rates are based on the average rate of tuition increases at public universities (both in-state and out-of-state tuition), private and not-for-profit universities. Source: trends.collegeboard.org.

EXHIBIT 8.1 **TUITION INFLATION (PER YEAR)**

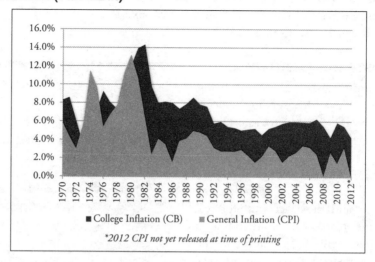

The exhibit below reflects the cumulative impact of college inflation and general inflation over time. Beginning with $100 in 1970 and subjecting it to the impact of general inflation over the 40 year period results in an equivalent purchasing power of $606 in 2011. In other words, the general cost of items in 2011 cost 6.06 times the 1970 cost. The impact of college tuition is even more staggering. The 2011 equivalent of $100 of tuition in 1970 is $1,754, meaning that it cost 17.54 times as much in 2010 as it did in 1970. The compound increase for general inflation and college tuition is 4.5 percent and 7.24 percent, respectively.

EXHIBIT 8.2 **TUITION INFLATION (CUMULATIVE)**

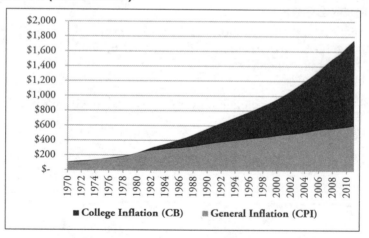

Over the last 10 years, tuition inflation has averaged 5.7 percent higher than regular inflation, as measured by CPI. During this time, tuition inflation has been approximately twice the rate of the CPI. A tuition inflation rate of six percent would indicate that a family with a child born today, can expect the current cost of tuition to increase 150 percent over the next 18 years. If tuition is currently $15,000 per year, the client can expect to pay over $40,000 per year when the child starts college at age 18. A financial planner must first forecast future tuition and related costs, then create a plan that will allow the client to fund their education goal.

Notice that during periods of recession, like the early 80s and 90s, tuition rates increase the most dramatically. During a recession, the unemployment rate is increasing, causing state tax revenues to decrease. State governments will react by reducing their budget, potentially impacting the state funding of higher education. In this situation, state universities are likely forced to increase tuition. Periods of tuition inflation of eight percent or higher occur during the worst of economic times with high unemployment, so it can significantly impact families that have not saved enough for college education funding. Those families are likely to turn to financial aid to bridge the gap between funds available for education and the higher cost of attending college. For families that have children ten plus years away from college, there are alternatives to relying on financial aid. Alternatives include tax-deferred savings, tax deductions, and tax credits, which will all be discussed later in the chapter.

FINANCIAL AID AND THE EXPECTED FAMILY CONTRIBUTION AMOUNT

Financial aid represents an important tool for families that are inadequately prepared to pay for their children's college education. Most financial aid is administered by the U.S. Department of Education, (states and universities offer aid as well), and consists of grants, loans for students and parents, and work study programs. According to the U.S. Department of Education, 85 percent of all full-time undergraduate students received some type of financial aid, either federal or state provided financial aid, in 2009 – 2010.[3]

WHERE TO FIND INFORMATION ABOUT FINANCIAL AID

Information about financial aid is available online, at high schools and college campuses. The U.S. Department of Education[4] offers information about financial aid offered by the federal government. The U.S. Department of Education provides a list of all state higher education agency websites. The state higher education agency[5] websites provide information about financial aid available by state.

In addition to online resources, many high schools and all college campuses have a financial aid office and financial aid counselors. Students and parents should contact their high school and prospective universities to schedule a time to meet with a financial aid counselor. The counselors can provide details on financial aid that is available, as well as qualification requirements and deadlines for applying.

3. chronicle.com/article/share-of-students-receiving/13201b.
4. studentaid.ed.gov/PORTALSWebApp/students/english/index.jsp.
5. wdcrobcolp01.ed.gov/Programs/EROD/org_list.cfm?category_ID=SHE.

FINANCIAL AID PROCESS

The financial aid process is initiated by completing the **Free Application for Federal Student Aid (FAFSA)**. This form is used to determine a student's eligibility for all types of financial aid, including grants, work study, and loans. The FAFSA[6] is used to determine the Expected Family Contribution amount (EFC). The EFC is calculated based on the information provided in the FAFSA, as a family's income and assets are applied to a Federal Methodology, which determines the family's financial strength and how much it can contribute towards education costs. The Federal Methodology determines the EFC using one of three methods:

- Regular Formula: Income and Assets
- Simplified Method
- Automatically Assessed Formulas

REGULAR FORMULA: INCOME AND ASSETS

The regular formula considers a family's income and assets. This is the formula that is used for most families. The federal methodology considers the following:

- Income
- Assets
- Dependency status
- Household size
- Number of children in college
- Cost of supporting the family

The regular formula considers 12 percent of the parent's discretionary net worth available for education. Adjustments are made to net worth to determine the discretionary net worth such as protecting certain assets, like a family business or farm. For students, 50 percent of their income is deemed available for education and 35 percent of their net worth is available. The EFC is a combination of the parent's expected contribution, plus the student's contribution from income and the student's net worth.

SIMPLIFIED METHOD

The simplified method does not consider the family's assets. In order to qualify for the simplified formula:

- The parents must file 1040A, 1040EZ or is not required to file a federal income tax return, and
- The total adjusted gross income of the parents is less than $50,000.

---

6. fafsa.ed.gov.

In order to qualify for the simplified formula, when the student is not claimed as a dependent:

- Student (and spouse, if married) must file a Form 1040A, Form 1040EZ or is not required to file a federal income tax return, and
- Student's (and spouse, if married) adjusted gross income is less than $50,000.

AUTOMATICALLY ASSESSED FORMULAS

The automatically assessed formulas, simply calculates the EFC at zero. In order to qualify for this method:

- Student or parents file a Form 1040A, Form 1040EZ or the student and parents are not required to file a federal income tax return, and
- Student or parents' adjusted gross income is $20,000 or less.

Quick
Quiz 8.1

Highlight the answer to these questions:

1. The Expected Family Contribution (EFC) for financial aid can be calculated using the simplified method, which does not consider the family's assets.
   a. True
   b. False

2. The financial aid process is initiated by completing the Student Aid Report.
   a. True
   b. False

True, False.

Once the EFC is determined by using one of the three Federal Methodologies, the EFC is subtracted from the cost of attendance at a university, which can include living expenses. The formula is:

$$\begin{array}{l} \text{Cost of Attendance} \\ \underline{- \text{ Expected Family Contribution (EFC)}} \\ = \text{Financial Need} \end{array}$$

Once the FAFSA is completed, student's can then request that the information contained in the FAFSA be provided to universities. Families can request a copy of a Student Aid Report from the Department of Education, which will contain information provided on the FASFA, including the EFC.

Universities will prepare a financial aid package, which helps students satisfy their financial need. Financial aid may consist of grants (money that doesn't have to be repaid), loans and work study programs (where the student can work on or off campus to help pay for education expenses). After determining a student's financial need, a university may not be able to offer an aid package that provides 100 percent of education expenses.

EXAMPLE 8.1

Jeff and Betty have a daughter, Olivia, who is applying to Northwest State University. The total cost of attendance is $20,000 per year and their EFC is $5,000 per year. The financial aid office has put together an aid package covering $12,000 per year. The gap of $3,000 ($20,000 - $5,000 - $12,000) must be covered by other possible resources such as student or parent education loan(s).

TYPES OF FINANCIAL AID

GRANTS

Grants are money provided to students for postsecondary education that does not require repayment. Grants are typically awarded based on financial need. The federal government only awards grants for undergraduate studies. The following grants are discussed in this chapter:

Key Concepts

Underline/highlight the answers as you read:

1. Define a college grant?

2. Identify different types of education grants and the qualifications required for each grant.

- Federal Pell Grant
- Teacher Education Assistance for College and Higher Education (TEACH) Grant
- Academic Competitiveness Grant (ACG)
- National Science and Mathematics Access to Retain Talent (SMART) Grant
- Federal Supplemental Educational Opportunity (FSEOG) Grant

Federal Pell Grant

A **Federal Pell Grant** is need based financial aid for students that have not earned an undergraduate degree or a professional degree. A Pell Grant does not have to be repaid and is awarded based on financial need.

Pell Grants are based on an academic year, from July 1st to June 30th. The amount of a Pell Grant awarded to a student is dependent upon the family's EFC, cost of attendance, and whether the student is attending full-time or part-time. The maximum Pell Grant award for the 2012-13 award year (July 1, 2012 to June 30, 2013) is $5,550 and is paid directly to the school or paid directly to the student. As a benefit to military families, the maximum Pell Grant amount is awarded to students whose parent or guardian died as a result of military duty in Iraq or Afghanistan after September 11, 2001 (if the student was under 24 years old at the time of the parent or guardian's death).

Teacher Education Assistance for College and Higher Education (TEACH) Grant

The **Teacher Education Assistance for College and Higher Education (TEACH) Grant** provides up to $4,000 per year for students that intend to teach in a public or private elementary, middle, or high school that serves a community of low-income families. If a student fails to meet the teaching requirements, the grant is converted to a Federal Direct Unsubsidized Stafford Loan, which must be repaid by the student. Recipients of the TEACH grant have a six-month grace period after the grant is converted to a Stafford Loan before repayment must begin. If a TEACH grant is converted to a Stafford Loan, interest accrues from the first date the funds were disbursed.

In order to be eligible for the TEACH grant, applicants must meet the following criteria:
- Complete a FAFSA;
- Be a U.S. citizen or eligible noncitizen;
- Be enrolled in an undergraduate, post-baccalaureate or graduate program at a university that participates in the TEACH Grant program;
- Be enrolled or plan to complete courses that prepare a student for a career in teaching;
- Score above the 75th percentile on college admission testing or maintain a Grade Point Average (GPA) greater than or equal to 3.25; and
- Sign a TEACH Grant Agreement to Serve each year the grant is received.

For each TEACH Grant eligible program for which TEACH Grant funds are received, the student must serve as a full-time teacher for a total of at least four academic years within eight calendar years after completing or withdrawing from the academic program for which the TEACH Grant was received.

Academic Competitiveness Grant (ACG)

The **Academic Competitiveness Grant (ACG)** is for students graduating from a rigorous secondary school program of study. Rigorous secondary school programs are designated by stated education agencies and recognized by the Secretary of Education. The ACG is awarded to first year postsecondary students in the amount of $750 and second year postsecondary students in the amount of $1,300. A program can be deemed a rigorous secondary school program whether it is a public school, private school, or home school as long as it meets minimum education requirements in english, math, science, and social studies. A list of each state's requirements to be deemed a rigorous secondary school program of study is available at the U.S. Department of Education's website.

To be eligible for an ACG the recipient must:
- Be a U.S. citizen or eligible noncitizen;
- Be a Federal Pell Grant recipient;
- Be enrolled at least half-time in a degree program;
- Be a first or second-year undergraduate student or a student in a certificate program of at least one year in a degree program at a two-year or four-year degree-granting institution;
- Have completed a rigorous secondary school program of study; and
- If a first-year student — not have been previously enrolled in an ACG-eligible program while at or below age of compulsory school attendance; or
- If a second-year student — have at least a cumulative 3.0 GPA on a 4.0 scale as of the end of the first year of undergraduate study.

National Science and Mathematics Access to Retain Talent (SMART) Grant

The **National Science and Mathematics Access to Retain Talent (SMART) Grant** is available during the third and fourth years of undergraduate studies. To be eligible, students must be eligible for the Pell Grant and are majoring in:

- Physical science
- Life science
- Computer science
- Mathematics
- Technology
- Engineering
- Critical foreign language
- Non-major single liberal arts program

In addition, the recipient must maintain a GPA of 3.0 in the field of study. The National SMART Grant pays up to $4,000 per year and is paid in addition to the Pell Grant. The combined National SMART Grant and Pell Grant cannot exceed the cost of attendance. If the amount of eligible students for the National SMART Grant exceeds funding, eligible students will receive a pro rata reduction in their National SMART Grant amount.

Federal Supplemental Educational Opportunity Grant (FSEOG Grant)

The **Federal Supplemental Educational Opportunity Grant (FSEOG)** is awarded to students with exceptional financial need. Pell Grant recipients with the lowest EFC are considered first for a FSEOG. Students awarded the FSEOG can receive between $100 to $4,000 per year.

Campus Based Aid

Campus based aid is administered directly by the financial aid office of the university. The three types of campus based aid are Federal Supplementary Educational Opportunity Grant, Federal Work Study and Federal Perkins Loan Program. Schools may offer some or all three campus based aid programs. Unlike the Federal Pell Grant, which provides funding to all students that qualify, campus based aid may or may not be available if a student qualifies. Once the school has allocated their campus based aid, no further aid can be allocated from that program for the year. Students should apply early for financial aid, as the campus based aid may not always be available.

Quick Quiz 8.2

Highlight the answer to these questions:

1. Pell Grants are based on an academic year, the family's EFC, cost of attendance, and whether the student is attending full-time or part-time.
   a. True
   b. False

2. The TEACH grant provides up to $4,000 per year and is converted to a Federal Direct Unsubsidized Stafford Loan if teaching requirements are not met.
   a. True
   b. False

3. The FSEOG is awarded to students graduating from a rigorous secondary school program of study.
   a. True
   b. False

True, True, False.

FINANCIAL AID - LOANS

The U.S. Department of Education and many colleges and universities offer low interest rate loans for students and parents. Unlike grants, most loans are not based on financial need but are part of an overall financial aid package offered to students. Some loans are based on financial need, such as the Federal Perkins Loan and Subsidized Stafford Loans, which are discussed below.

Stafford Loans

Stafford Loans are student loans administered by the U.S. Department of Education. Prior to July 1, 2010, there were two types of Stafford Loans: the Federal Family Education Loan (FFEL) and Direct

Key Concepts

Underline/highlight the answers as you read:

1. Identify the types of student and parent loans available for college funding.

2. Define the repayment terms available for government funded loans.

3. Identify the consequences of defaulting on student loans.

Stafford Loan. However, as part of The Student Aid and Fiscal Responsibility Act, passed on March 30, 2010, the federal government is eliminating the FFEL program. Education loans will now only be issued by the U.S Department of Education as part of the Direct Loan program. With the Direct Loan program, the funds are provided by the federal government, whereas under the FFEL, the funds were provided by a bank or other lender. As part of The Student Aid and Fiscal Responsibility Act, students with low incomes and large loan balances are only required to repay up to 10 percent of their income each year. Previously, the law permitted up to 15 percent of a borrower's income to repay student loans. In addition, The Student Aid and Fiscal Responsibility Act forgives loans after 20 years of repayment, whereas prior to the Act, borrowers were eligible for loan forgiveness after 25 years of repayment.

A student may qualify for subsidized or unsubsidized Direct Loans. Qualification for a subsidized or unsubsidized loan is based on a student's financial need. For a subsidized loan, the federal government pays interest on the loan while the borrower is attending school and during the six-month grace period after graduation before repayment begins. With an unsubsidized loan, the borrower is responsible for interest from the time the funds are dispersed. Students may pay the interest expense as it is incurred or allow the interest to be added to the loan's outstanding principal.

The following are maximum limits on the amount that can be borrowed under the Stafford Loan program for a full academic year:
- First year students: $5,500 but no more than $3,500 of this amount can be in subsidized loans.
- Second year students: $6,500 but no more than $4,500 of this amount can be in subsidized loans.
- Beyond the second year: $7,500 but no more than $5,500 of this amount can be in subsidized loans.

For undergraduate students that are independents (not claimed as a dependent on parent's tax return) and for dependent students whose parents did not qualify for a Parent Loan for Undergraduate Students (PLUS) Loan, the following are maximum limits on the amount that can be borrowed under the Stafford Loan program in a full academic year:

- First year students: $9,500 but no more than $3,500 of this amount can be in subsidized loans.
- Second year students: $10,500 but no more than $4,500 of this amount can be in subsidized loans.
- Beyond the second year: $12,500 but no more than $5,500 of this amount can be in subsidized loans.

For graduate or professional degree students, the following are maximum limits on the amount that can be borrowed under the Stafford Loan program in a full academic year:

- Each Year: $20,500 but no more than $8,500 of this amount can be in subsidized loans.

The maximum amount of Stafford Loan debt a student can graduate with from graduate school is $138,500, which also includes amounts borrowed for undergraduate studies. Some health profession programs will allow students to borrow up to $224,000. No more than $65,500 out of the $138,500 can be in subsidized loans.

Stafford Loan funds are paid directly to the school, which applies the loan proceeds to tuition, fees, room, and board. Any remaining amounts will be paid directly to the student. Funds are paid through the school in at least two installments.

Students pay two fees associated with Stafford Loans. The first fee is an origination fee of 1.5 percent of the loan amount, which is used to offset the cost of administering the loan. The second fee is an annual interest rate. The interest rate for unsubsidized Stafford Loans is 6.8 percent. Prior to July 1, 2006 interest rates on Stafford Loans were variable, but limited to a cap of 8.25 percent. Interest rates for Stafford Loans can be found at the U.S. Department of Education's website.[7]

The interest rate on new subsidized Stafford Loans is being reduced over a four-year period. The interest rate reduction only applies to loans dispersed during the time periods shown below. It does not apply to any previously dispersed loans and it does not apply to unsubsidized Stafford Loans.

---

7. http://ifap.ed.gov/ifap

The following is a summary of the interest rate reduction schedule for Direct Subsidized Stafford Loan:

Funds Dispersed	Interest Rate
July 1, 2009 – June 30, 2010	5.6%
July 1, 2010 – June 30, 2011	4.5%
July 1, 2011 – June 30, 2012	3.4%
July 1, 2012 – June 30, 2013	3.4%

For borrowers on active military duty, the interest rate on Direct Stafford Loans is capped at six percent.

Borrowers must begin repaying a Stafford Loan after a six-month grace period that begins after graduation, leaving school, or dropping below half-time status. For subsidized Stafford Loans, the borrower is not responsible for interest payments during the grace period. However, for unsubsidized Stafford Loans, the borrower still incurs interest charges, during the grace period, that will need to be repaid.

Students generally have 10 to 25 years to repay a Stafford Loan. There are four repayment methods for a Stafford Loan, which include:
- Standard Repayment
- Extended Repayment
- Graduated Repayment
- Income Based Repayment

Standard Repayment
A standard repayment schedule will amortize the loan for up to a 10-year time period, with minimum monthly payments of at least $50. The standard repayment schedule has the borrower repaying the loan in the shortest amount of time. The shorter repayment schedule allows the borrower to pay the least amount of interest on the loan, as compared to the other repayment schedules.

Extended Repayment
The extended repayment schedule allows borrowers with more than $30,000 outstanding in either FFEL Stafford Loans or Direct Stafford Loans, to repay the loans over a period of time not to exceed 25 years. Since the repayment period under an Extended Repayment schedule is up to 15 years longer than the Standard Repayment schedule, borrowers can expect to pay significantly more in interest using the Extended Repayment plan.

Dominic has $40,000 in Direct Stafford Loans and is considering the Standard Repayment over 10 years or Extended Repayment over 25 years. The summary below compares the difference in payments and interest between the two repayment plans.

EXAMPLE 8.2

	Standard	Extended
Term	10 years	25 years
Amount of Loan	$40,000	$40,000
Interest Rate	6.8%	6.8%
Monthly Payment	$460.32	$277.63
Total Interest Paid Over Life of Loan	$15,238	$43,289

Although the Extended Repayment schedule will result in a lower monthly payment, the borrower will pay three times the amount of interest, in comparison to the Standard Repayment schedule. Borrowers should consider their cash flow and ability to make monthly payments. During a borrower's initial working years after graduating, they may not be able to afford the higher payments. However, as the borrower's earnings increase, the payment amount should be increased, in order to retire the debt in a reasonable amount of time.

Graduated Repayment

The graduated repayment schedule allows borrowers to repay a Stafford Loan for up to 10 years. Borrowers are able to initially make low payments, but the payments will increase every two years. This allows borrowers to increase their loan payments, as their income increases. Under the graduated repayment schedule, no monthly loan payment will be more than three times the lowest monthly loan payment.

Income Based Repayment

The Income Based Repayment (IBR) schedule is a new repayment schedule that went into effect on July 1, 2009. The IBR schedule will cap the monthly payment based on the borrower's income and family size. To qualify for the IBR schedule, the amount of payment calculated using the IBR method must be less than the monthly payment under the standard repayment schedule over a 10-year term.

The following loans are available to use the IBR schedule:
- Stafford loans (FFEL or direct)
- PLUS loans made to graduate or professional students (PLUS loans made to parents are not eligible)
- Consolidation student loans

Other benefits of the IBR schedule include:
- The monthly payment will be 15 percent of discretionary income and cannot be more than required under the standard 10-year repayment plan.
- If the repayment amount calculated under the IBR schedule is less than the monthly interest that is due, the federal government will pay the interest for up to three consecutive years. Beyond the third year, any interest deficiencies will be added to the outstanding balance of the loan.
- If a borrower has been paying under the IBR schedule for 25 years, still has a balance due and meets certain other requirements, the balance due will be cancelled.

- If a borrower is making payments under the IBR schedule for 10 years, has Direct Stafford Loans and has been working in public service for 10 years, the remaining balance due can be cancelled. If a borrower has FFEL Stafford Loans, it is possible to convert the loans to a Direct Stafford Loan to take advantage of the 10 Year Public Service Loan Forgiveness Program. The borrower will still have to meet the 10-year payment requirement on a Direct Stafford Loan.

Income Contingent Repayment

The income contingent repayment (ICR) schedule is for Direct Stafford Loans and Direct Graduate PLUS Loans only. Parent Direct PLUS Loan borrowers are not eligible for the ICR repayment schedule (PLUS Loans are discussed later in this chapter). The amount of payment under the ICR schedule is the lesser of:

- The amount required under a 12-year repayment schedule times an income percentage factor that varies based on annual income or,
- 20 percent of the borrower's monthly discretionary income.

If the payments calculated under the ICR schedule are insufficient to pay the monthly interest expenses, the unpaid portion is capitalized, or added to the outstanding principal, once per year. If after 25 years, the loan has not been repaid, the outstanding balance will be cancelled.

Income Sensitive Repayment

The income sensitive repayment schedule is for FFEL Stafford Loans only. This repayment schedule will vary, based on the borrower's income. As the borrower's income increases (or decreases), the repayment amount will increase (or decrease). The repayment period for an Income Sensitive Repayment Schedule is up to 10 years.

If a borrower becomes unable to repay a student loan, it is possible to request a deferment or forbearance. During this time, payments are suspended but may or may not incur interest expense. For a subsidized Stafford Loan, the borrower will not be responsible for interest payments during the forbearance period. However, for unsubsidized Stafford Loans, the borrower is still responsible for interest charges during the forbearance period.

Federal Perkins Loan Program

The **Federal Perkins Loan** program is for undergraduate and graduate students with exceptional financial need. The Perkins Loan is a low interest rate loan (5%), which is offered through a university's financial aid office. The university serves as the lender and the federal government provides the funds. Students can borrow up to $5,500 each year of undergraduate studies (up to $27,500). Graduate students can borrow up to $8,000 per year (up to $60,000, including the amount borrowed as an undergraduate).

Repayment on the Federal Perkins Loan begins after a nine-month grace period. The grace period begins once the student graduates, leaves school or drops below half-time status.

Parent PLUS Loans

PLUS Loans are for parents to borrow to help pay for a dependent's undergraduate education expenses. The dependent student must be attending at least half-time, in an eligible school, and in an eligible program. PLUS Loans are not based on financial need, but are instead based on the parent's credit history. PLUS Loans are appropriate for parents that have not saved enough for the child's education, their child is close in age to attending college, and the parents have sufficient cash flow to repay the loans.

PLUS Loans are available as a Direct PLUS Loan from the U.S. Department of Education or a FFEL PLUS Loans from a lender affiliated with a university. Although no new FFEL PLUS Loans will be issued after July 1, 2010, many parents will still be repaying previously issued FFEL PLUS Loans. The amount of a PLUS Loan a parent may borrow is the cost of attendance less any other financial aid awards. The school determines the amount of PLUS Loan the borrower is eligible to receive. Loan funds are dispersed in at least two equal payments. The funds are sent to the school and are used to pay tuition, fees, room and board. Any remaining funds are paid directly to the parents or can be held by the school for future education expenses.

The interest rate on PLUS Loans depends on whether it is a Direct or FFEL PLUS Loan. The interest rate for a Direct PLUS Loan is fixed at 7.9 percent. The interest rate for a FFEL PLUS Loan is fixed at 8.5 percent. Prior to July 1, 2006, the interest rate was variable. Interest on PLUS Loans begins as soon as the first disbursement is paid. There are no subsidized PLUS Loans and repayment begins either 60 days after the loan is fully disbursed or may be postponed until six months after the dependent student ceases to be enrolled on at least a half-time basis. The parents can elect either repayment method.

In addition to the interest expense, PLUS Loans also charge a fee of up to four percent of the amount borrowed.

Similar to a Stafford Loan, PLUS Loans are eligible for deferment or forbearance. While the loan is in forbearance, it continues to accrue interest that can be paid immediately or added to the outstanding principal of the loan.

PLUS Loans for Graduate and Professional Degree Students
PLUS Loans for Graduate and Professional Degree Students (or **Graduate PLUS Loans**) are for student's seeking graduate and professional degrees. A Graduate PLUS Loan is based on the parent's credit history and is not based on financial need. In order to receive a Graduate PLUS Loan, students must have applied for the maximum Stafford Loan amount available for graduate students. The amount of Graduate PLUS Loans available is based on the cost of attendance, less other financial aid.

The interest rate for Graduate PLUS Loans is fixed at 7.9 percent for Direct Graduate PLUS Loans and 8.5 percent for previously issued FFEL Graduate PLUS Loans.

Repayment of Student Loans

After graduating, leaving school, or falling below half-time status, borrowers have a grace period before repayment begins. The grace period depends on the type of loan, as described below.

Loan	Grace Period
PLUS Loans	60 Days after Final Disbursement*
Stafford Loans (Direct and FFEL)	Six Months
Federal Perkins Loans	Nine Months

* For a Parent PLUS Loan borrower, where the funds are disbursed on or after July 1, 2008, the borrower can elect to defer payment for six months after the student is no longer enrolled at least half-time. For a Graduate PLUS Loan or PLUS Loan where the parent is the student, repayment can be deferred for six months after the borrower is no longer enrolled at least a half-time.

Consolidation Loans

Consolidation loans take all of a student's outstanding loans and consolidate them into one payment. The interest rate for a consolidation loan is based on a weighted average of the interest rates of the loans being consolidated.

The following loans are eligible for consolidation:

- Subsidized and unsubsidized Direct and FFEL Stafford Loans
- Federal Perkins Loans
- Parent PLUS Loans
- Graduate PLUS Loans

Prior to the Higher Education Reconciliation Act of 2005, a borrower enrolled in school at least half-time could request to begin repaying a Stafford Loan early. By entering repayment early, the borrower could apply for a Direct or FFEL Consolidation Loan. However, as a result of the Higher Education Reconciliation Act of 2005, borrowers may not begin repaying a Stafford Loan or apply for a consolidation loan until after the six month grace period that begins once the borrower falls below half-time status. PLUS Loans are eligible for consolidation once the funds are fully dispersed.

Quick Quiz 8.3

Highlight the answer to these questions:

1. Students must pay the interest expense as incurred for an unsubsidized Stafford Loan.
   a. True
   b. False

2. The four repayment plans for a Stafford Loan include the standard repayment, extended repayment, graduated repayment, and income based repayment.
   a. True
   b. False

3. Parent PLUS Loans are for parents to borrow to help pay for a dependent's undergraduate education expenses and are based on financial need.
   a. True
   b. False

4. The interest rate on consolidated loans is based on a weighted average of the interest rates of the loans being consolidated.
   a. True
   b. False

False, True, False, True.

Repayment of a consolidation loan begins within 60 days of the funds being dispersed and the repayment period is from 10 to 30 years. Borrowers should keep in mind that although the consolidation loan payment may be less than the original payments, if the repayment period is being extended to 30 years, the total cost of repayment can be significantly more under a consolidation loan because of the total interest expense. As with all debt, every effort should be made to retire the debt within a reasonable amount of time.

CONSEQUENCES OF DEFAULTING ON STUDENT LOANS

For many families, student loans represent the only way to pay for a college education. Approximately 60%, or 12 million students, borrow each year to fund college expenses.[8] Today, there are about 37 million students that have outstanding student loan balances.[9]

Total student loan debt in the U.S. has risen steadily from $363 billion in 2005, to nearly $1 trillion dollars in 2012. The average amount of student loan debt, per borrower, was $15,561 in 2005 and has risen to $24,301 in 2012.[10]

Year	Student Loan Debt
2005	363
2006	434
2007	507
2008	579
2009	664
2010	758
2011	841
2012	902

Consumer debt peaked just prior to the financial crisis in 2008. Student loan debt is the only form of debt that has increased since 2008. Balances of student loan debt is greater than both auto loans and credit cards debt. Student loan debt is now the largest form of consumer debt outside of mortgages.

The sheer magnitude of student loan debt presents a major threat to the financial security of student borrowers. Approximately one-third of all student debt is owed by individuals age 30 and under. This same age group is currently experiencing one of the highest unemployment rates in the country at 11.8% (as of October 2012).[11] From 2004 – 2009, only 37% of federal student loan borrowers made their loan payments on time, without postponing their payments or becoming delinquent. Two out of every 5 student loan borrowers, or about 40%, are delinquent at some point during the first five years after entering repayment.[12] When considering the high unemployment rate and amount of student loan debt in the

---

8. Chronicle of Higher Education.
9. Federal Reserve Board of New York.
10. Newyorkfed.org/studentloandebt
11. washingtontimes.com/blog/inside-politics/2012/oct/5/under-30-unemployment-rate-118-percent
12. Institute for Higher Education Policy

under 30 age group, it's understandable why many of these young people are forced to move back in with their parents after graduating, are unable to purchase their own homes, and are forced to delay starting their own families.

Students who do not complete their degrees struggle the most when it comes to repaying their student loans. From 2004 - 2009, 33% of undergraduate federal student loan borrowers that left school before completing their degree became delinquent and 26 percent defaulted, compared to 21% who earned a degree but became delinquent without defaulting and 16% who defaulted.[13] Almost half (48%) of borrowers age 25-35 indicate they are unemployed or underemployed, which is the primary reason they are delinquent or have defaulted on their student loan.[14]

Student loan debt is one of the exceptions in bankruptcy and is not a dischargeable debt. Borrowers that file for Chapter 7 bankruptcy must make payments to the bankruptcy trustee for five years to repay a portion of the debts owed to unsecured creditors. During this time, borrowers must continue to make the full payment due under their student loan obligations. It's quite possible, after 5 years of payments to unsecured creditors under Chapter 7 bankruptcy, to still face years of student loan payments.

Cosigners

Neither Perkins nor Stafford loans require a cosigner. Private student loans often require a parent to co-sign for the loan. From the lender's perspective, a loan to a student is a high risk because students likely have no assets, no credit history and a very uncertain future income stream. When parents or grandparents co-sign a loan, they become responsible for repaying the loan, if the student falls behind on their payments. If a child becomes delinquent on a student loan, the lender may initiate collection efforts against the cosigner. If the loan is past due, late fees, additional interest, penalties and collection costs will be added to the outstanding balance, which will ultimately negatively impact both the child and cosigner's credit report. To collect the outstanding student loan, the cosigner's wages may be garnished and/or state or federal income tax refunds may be withheld. In addition, a cosigner's Social Security benefit may be reduced to repay an outstanding student loan if such loan is owed to the federal government.

In 2007, about 60,000 retirees had their Social Security benefit reduced, due to outstanding student loans. In the first half of 2012, approximately 115,000 retirees had their Social Security benefit reduced, almost double since 2007. This represents a major risk to a retiree's income during retirement because up to 15% of a Social Security benefit may be withheld, although benefits of $750 or less are generally not reduced.[15] Considering that 45% of people age 48 to 64 do not save enough for basic needs during retirement, a reduction to in Social Security benefits for student loan repayment can significantly delay retirement or even impact the ability to pay for necessary medication and medical care.[16]

---

13. IHEP
14. Demos and Young Invincibles
15. smartmoney.com/borrow/student-loans/grandmas-new-financial-problem-college-debt-1344292084111
16. Employee Benefit Research Institute

Defaulting on student loans can have severe and long-term financial consequences for the borrower and co-signer. Families should try all possible alternatives to reduce the amount borrowed for education such as savings, grants, work-study, living at home after graduating for a period of time and taking advantage of an Income Based Repayment schedule which permits payments over 25 years and limits the amount of repayment to 15% of discretionary income.

FINANCIAL AID - FEDERAL WORK STUDY

Federal Work Study (FWS) are jobs on campus or off campus for undergraduate or graduate students to help students pay for their education expenses. To be eligible, students must complete the FAFSA and have financial need. Universities will pay students in the FWS an hourly rate, not less than the minimum wage. The amount of earnings in an FWS program cannot exceed the amount of a total FWS award, as described in the student's financial aid package.

TAX DEFERRED SAVINGS, DEDUCTIONS, CREDITS OR OTHER EDUCATION PLANNING BENEFITS

This chapter's discussion so far has focused on paying for a college education with loans, grants, and work-study provided by financial aid. For families that are planning for a college education goal that is 10 or more years away, there are other opportunities besides financial aid. Congress has passed laws establishing savings accounts that allow families to save towards an education goal and permit the account to grow on a tax-deferred basis. If the funds are used for qualified education expenses, then any distributions from the savings accounts are tax-free.

The types of tax-deferred savings vehicles permitted by Congress are:
- Qualified Tuition Plans (Includes Prepaid Tuition and College Savings Plans)
- Coverdell Education Savings Accounts
- U.S. Government Savings Bonds

Although each of the savings vehicles have different characteristics, features and rules, they all share the same basic principal of excluding any appreciation and earnings from taxable income, as long as the funds are used for qualified education expenses. The Internal Revenue Service's Publication 970 provides information on education funding.

QUALIFIED TUITION PLANS

Qualified tuition plans or Savings Plans, allow families to save for education expenses on a tax-deferred basis. Section 529 of the Internal Revenue Code authorized states to adopt qualified tuition plans, either as a prepaid tuition plan or a college savings plan.

Prepaid Tuition

States will sponsor a **prepaid tuition plan** that will allow a parent to purchase college credits today and use those credits when the child attends college. States typically require parents to reside in the state where they are purchasing prepaid tuition credits and then use those credits to attend a college that is part of the state university system. Prepaid tuition plans are designed to only pay the cost of tuition, not room and board. When the credits in a prepaid tuition plan are used to attend college, there are no income tax consequences to the parents for the difference between the amount paid for the college credits and the current cost of the college credits.

A popular misconception about prepaid tuition is that credits are purchased at "today's cost." In fact, many states will charge a premium over the current cost per credit hour when parents purchase prepaid tuition credits. Currently, only 11 states still offer prepaid tuition plans. Those states are: Florida, Illinois, Maryland, Massachusetts, Michigan, Mississippi, Nevada, Pennsylvania, Texas, Virginia, and Washington. Many states have been forced to close their prepaid tuition plans due to education costs increasing faster than anticipated and poor investment returns.

Another type of prepaid tuition plan is the Independent 529 Plan (I-529), which allows parents to purchase prepaid tuition credits to over 270 private universities across the country. Parents purchase prepaid tuition credits that can be used to attend universities such as Stanford, Notre Dame, Emory and MIT. Parents can use the credits purchased to attend any of the 270 plus private universities that participate in the program. Students must still meet entrance requirements, which are separate and independent of the prepaid tuition plan. There is no preferential acceptance to private universities because the parents participate in an Independent 529 Plan.

Key Concepts

Underline/highlight the answers as you read:

1. Distinguish between a prepaid tuition plan and a college savings plan.

2. Identify the levels and types of education expenses that can be funded using distributions from a Coverdell education savings account.

3. Identify the criteria required for an individual to receive the income exclusion benefit associated with U.S Government Series EE and I bonds.

The disadvantages to prepaid tuition is that universities in the home state may not offer a curriculum that appeals to the student or the student may be offered a scholarship to attend a university out of their home state. If parents decide to cancel the prepaid tuition plan or not use the tuition credits, the rules vary by state, but generally parents will receive what they paid for the tuition credit, less some administrative expenses. Some states will return any earnings on the investments.

Planners should advise clients to carefully research their states' prepaid tuition plans before investing. Many plans are facing difficulty as the investment returns have not outpaced or maintained tuition inflation rates. Some states are facing significant shortfalls in the amount of assets in the prepaid tuition plans, which are not keeping up with the cost of tuition at the universities in the state and the tuition credit hours promised are exceeding the assets of the plan. As a result, many states have closed their prepaid tuition plans or have frozen the plans to prevent future purchases. However, most states offer a guarantee that the state will make up any shortfall between plan assets and the cost of tuition.

Prepaid tuition credits are considered assets of the parent for financial aid purposes. As previously discussed, a smaller percentage of a parent's income and assets are deemed available for education than the child's. Anytime an asset is treated as an asset of the parent, it results in more favorable treatment when determining the amount of financial aid the family qualifies to receive.

College Savings Plan

College Savings Plans (or 529 Savings Plans) allow for college saving on a tax-deferred basis with attendance at any eligible education institution. According to the IRS, "An eligible education institution is any college, university, vocational school, or other postsecondary educational institution eligible to participate in a student aid program administered by the U.S. Department of Education." Distributions from a College Savings Plan are federal and state income tax-free, as long as they are used to pay for qualified education expenses. Qualified education expenses include: tuition and fees, books, supplies and equipment. Qualified education expenses also include room and board for students enrolled at least half-time and cannot exceed the greater of:

- Allowance for room and board as part of the cost of attendance provided by the school as part of the financial aid process or,
- The actual amount charged if the student resides in housing owned or operated by the university.

The American Recovery and Reinvestment Act of 2009 expanded qualified education expenses to include computer technology or equipment. Computer technology and equipment includes any computer and related peripheral equipment, such as a printer, internet access and software used for educational purposes.

A federal income tax deduction is not permitted for contributions to a College Savings Plan. However, states that have a state income tax will generally offer a state income tax deduction for those residents that contribute to their state's College Savings Plan.

There are no phase-outs (income limitations) on who can contribute to a College Savings Plan and a Savings Plan can be opened benefiting anyone (e.g., family member, friend, neighbor or the owner of the plan). The owner of the Savings Plan can change the beneficiary at any time without gift tax consequences as long as the new beneficiary is a family member assigned to the same generation as the original beneficiary. A family member includes the following beneficiaries:

- Son, daughter, stepchild, foster child, adopted child
- Brother, sister, stepbrother or stepsister
- Stepfather or stepmother
- Son or daughter of a brother or sister
- Brother or sister of father or mother
- Son-in-law, daughter-in-law, and first cousin

A transfer which occurs by reason of a change in the designated beneficiary, or a rollover of credits or account balances from the account of one beneficiary to the account of another beneficiary, will be treated as a taxable gift by the old beneficiary to the new beneficiary if the new beneficiary is assigned to a lower generation than the old beneficiary, as defined in IRC

Section 2651, regardless of whether the new beneficiary is a member of the family of the old beneficiary. The transfer will be subject to the generation-skipping transfer tax if the new beneficiary is assigned to a generation that is two or more levels lower than the generation assignment of the old beneficiary.[17]

EXAMPLE 8.3

In Year 1, Bob makes a contribution to a College Savings Plan on behalf of Bob's child, Beth. In Year 4, Bob directs that a distribution from the account for the benefit of Beth be made to an account for the benefit of Bob's grandchild, Dylan. The rollover distribution is treated as a taxable gift by Beth to Dylan, because, under section 2651, Dylan is assigned to a generation below the generation assignment of Beth.

Contributors to a Savings Plan are permitted to open a Savings Plan in any state. The funds in that Savings Plan can be used to pay for qualified education expenses at any eligible institution regardless of whether the institution is in the same state as the Savings Plan or not.

EXAMPLE 8.4

Holly lives in Georgia and contributes to New York's Savings Plan, for the benefit of her daughter Sydney. Sydney decides to attend the University of Southern California (USC). Holly is permitted to use the funds in her New York Savings Plan to pay qualified tuition expenses for Sydney to attend USC.

EXAMPLE 8.5

Debbie lives in California and contributes to California's Savings Plan for the benefit of her son, Bryan. Bryan decides to attend Massachusetts Institute of Technology (MIT). Debbie is permitted to use the funds in her California Savings Plan to pay qualified education expenses for Bryan to attend MIT.

Contributions to a Savings Plan are limited to the amount necessary to provide for the qualified education expenses of the beneficiary. Individual states will impose contribution limits per beneficiary, based on the most expensive university in a state. A student may be the beneficiary of multiple Savings Plans.

A contributor can contribute up to the annual gift tax exclusion amount ($14,000 in 2013) and not incur any gift tax liability. A husband and wife can elect gift splitting and give two times the annual gift tax exclusion amount or $28,000 ($14,000 x 2 for 2013) in one year, per beneficiary and not incur gift tax liability. In addition to the annual exclusion, each person has a $5,120,000 (as of 2012) lifetime applicable gift tax exclusion.

---

17. Treas. Reg. 1.529-5(3).

College Savings Plans permit a contributor to contribute up to five times the annual gift tax exclusion amount or $70,000 (5 x $14,000) as a lump sum, in one year. The $70,000 gift tax exclusion is for one beneficiary and the contributor will not incur gift tax liability if the contributor elects to treat the gift as an annual exclusion gift, for that year of the gift, and for each of the next four years. A married couple can elect gift splitting and contribute a lump-sum amount of $140,000 (5 x $14,000 x 2) in one year, per beneficiary and not incur gift tax liability. The IRS will recognize 1/5 of the contribution as being contributed each year, even though the lump-sum amount was contributed in one year.

EXAMPLE 8.6	Dave opens a Savings Plan for his favorite nephew, Matthew. In 2013, Dave can contribute a maximum amount of $70,000 (5 x $14,000 for 2013) into a Savings Plan for Matthew and not incur gift tax consequences since the IRS will only count 1/5 of the total contribution as being contributed each year.
EXAMPLE 8.7	Jerry and Mary decide to open a Savings Plan for their favorite grandson, Marcus. In 2013, Jerry and Mary can contribute a maximum amount of $140,000 in one year to Marcus' Savings Plan and not incur gift tax consequences.

Distributions from a Savings Plan used for purposes other than for qualified education expenses are subject to taxation as ordinary income to the extent of earnings within the account and the distribution may be subject to a 10 percent penalty. Exceptions to the 10 percent penalty rule are listed below.

If the distribution is due to: • Death of the beneficiary.   • Disability of the beneficiary.
If the distribution is included in income because the beneficiary received: • Tax-free scholarship.   • Veterans' educational assistance.   • Employer-provided educational assistance.   • Any other nontaxable (tax-free) payments (other than gifts or inheritances) received as educational assistance.
If the beneficiary is attending a U.S. military academy, and the distribution is not in excess of the cost of attendance.
If the distribution is included in income only because the qualified education expenses were taken into account in determining the American Opportunity or Lifetime Learning Credits (discussed later in this chapter).

EXAMPLE 8.8

Sydney, an accomplished high school gymnast, received an athletic scholarship worth $35,000 per year from Stanford University to compete on the gymnastics team. Sydney's parents may take a distribution from her Savings Plan for $35,000. They will include the earnings on the $35,000 distribution in ordinary income, but there is no 10% penalty on the earnings because the distribution is taken as a result of the beneficiary's athletic scholarship.

EXAMPLE 8.9

Sydney forgoes her scholarship to Stanford and instead uses her gymnastic skills to join the circus as part of the flying trapeze show. Sydney's parents are less than thrilled with her decision and decide to withdraw all of the funds in her Savings Plan and purchase a boat to sail around the world. The earnings associated with the withdrawal will be included as ordinary income for Sydney's parents and subject to a 10% penalty.

Investment options for Savings Plans typically include mutual funds and annuities and most Savings Plans offer age banded investments that become more conservative as the beneficiary becomes closer to age 18.

Savings Plans offer a unique advantage for grandparents looking for ways to provide for the grandchildren's college education. Funds in a Savings Plan are not included in the grandparent's gross estate when calculating any estate tax due. The grandparent's contribution is recognized over a five year period. If during that five year period the grandparents die, any remaining years (excluding the year of death) are brought back into the gross estate.

Grandparents still retain control over the asset and have the flexibility to change the beneficiary or remove the funds from the Savings Plan. Another benefit for a grandparent owned Savings Plan is that the value of the Savings Plan is generally not included in the financial aid calculation.

Assets in a College Savings Plan owned by the parent are considered assets of the parent

Quick Quiz 8.4

Highlight the answer to these questions:

1. Prepaid tuition plans allow a parent to purchase college credits today for availability when the child attends college.
   a. True
   b. False

2. Distributions for qualified education expenses from a College Savings Plan are federal and state income tax-free when the student is attending any eligible educational institution.
   a. True
   b. False

3. The American Recovery and Reinvestment Act of 2009 expanded qualified education expenses to include books, supplies, and equipment.
   a. True
   b. False

True, True, False.

for financial aid purposes. Remember, a smaller percentage of a parent's income and assets are deemed available for education than the child's. Anytime an asset is treated as an asset of the parent, it results in more favorable treatment when determining the amount of financial aid the family qualifies to receive.

COVERDELL EDUCATION SAVINGS ACCOUNT

A **Coverdell Education Savings Account (ESA)** is a tax deferred trust or custodial account established to pay for qualified higher education or qualified elementary / secondary school expenses. A unique benefit of Coverdell ESA is the ability to use the proceeds of a Coverdell to pay for private elementary, middle or high school expenses. A College Savings Plan is only eligible to pay for postsecondary education expenses.

For a Coverdell ESA, qualified higher education expenses include tuition, fees, books, room, board, and computer related expenses. Qualified elementary and secondary expenses include tuition, fees, books, supplies, equipment, tutoring, computer related expenses, and special needs services for special needs beneficiaries. Qualified elementary and secondary expenses also include room and board, uniforms and transportation if required or provided by the institution.

Distributions from a Coverdell ESA used for qualified education expenses are tax-free, as long as the distribution does not exceed the qualified education expenses, reduced by any financial assistance.

EXAMPLE 8.10	Cole receives a $15,000 per year scholarship to attend Notre Dame. The cost of attending Notre Dame is $35,000 per year. Cole may take a tax-free distribution from his Coverdell ESA, up to $20,000 ($35,000 - $15,000).

Any distributions in excess of qualified education expenses or distributions not used for qualified education expenses will cause the earnings to be taxable as ordinary income and to be subject to a 10 percent penalty.

Although a distribution is included in income, it may not subject to a 10 percent penalty. Following is a list of the exceptions to the 10 percent penalty rule.

If the distribution is due to:
•   Death of the beneficiary.
•   Disability of the beneficiary.
If the distribution is included in income because the beneficiary received:
•   Tax-free scholarship.
•   Veterans' educational assistance.
•   Employer-provided educational assistance.
•   Any other nontaxable (tax-free) payments (other than gifts or inheritances) received as educational assistance.
If the beneficiary is attending a U.S. military academy, and the distribution is not in excess of the cost of attendance.
If the distribution is included in income only because the qualified education expenses were taken into account in determining the American Opportunity or Lifetime Learning Credits (discussed later in this chapter).

When the Coverdell ESA is established the beneficiary must be under age 18 or qualify as a special needs beneficiary. Contributions to a Coverdell ESA are limited to $2,000 per beneficiary and are not deductible for federal or state income taxes. Although a beneficiary can have multiple Coverdell ESAs, the total annual contribution to all Coverdell accounts cannot exceed $2,000 per beneficiary. Contributions to Coverdell accounts must be in cash and contributions are not permitted once the beneficiary attains age 18. Note: Unless Congress changes the law, contribution limits are scheduled to decrease from $2,000 to $500 in 2013. In addition, distributions will be tax free only if they are not Hope or Lifetime Learning credits claimed. Finally, withdrawals for elementary and secondary education expenses will not be permitted.

The phase-out for contributing to a Coverdell ESA is based on the taxpayer's Modified Adjusted Gross Income (MAGI). For most taxpayers, MAGI is the same as adjusted gross income (AGI). The phase-out limits for a Coverdell ESA are:
- Single: $95,000 - $110,000
- Married Filing Jointly: $190,000 - $220,000

Assets from one Coverdell can be rolled over to another Coverdell, however, only one rollover within a 12-month period is permitted. The beneficiary designation for a Coverdell can also be changed and not subject to income tax as long as the new beneficiary is a member of the family and is under the age of 30. Funds in a Coverdell ESA must be distributed within 30 days of the beneficiary attaining age 30.

A Coverdell ESA is treated as an asset of the parent for financial aid purposes.

U.S. GOVERNMENT SAVINGS BONDS

U.S. Government Series EE (issued after 1989) and Series I bonds can be redeemed to pay for qualified education expenses with the interest earned on the bonds excluded from taxable income. For purposes of excluding interest income using U.S. Government savings bonds, qualified education expenses only include tuition and fees. Expenses for only room and board are not permitted.

In order to receive the income exclusion benefit, the bond must be purchased in the name of the parent (or parents), the bonds must be issued when the owner is at least 24 years old, and the bonds must be redeemed in the year that qualified education expenses are incurred. The qualified education expenses must be for the taxpayer, the taxpayer's spouse, or dependents of the taxpayer.

There are also MAGI based income limitations determining who can benefit from the interest income exclusion for Series EE and I bonds.

The income limitations (as of 2012) are:
- Single: $72,850 - $87,850
- Married Filing Jointly: $109,250 - $139,250

If a taxpayer's MAGI is less than the threshold, then the taxpayer is eligible to exclude the interest income. If a taxpayer's MAGI is greater than the threshold limit then interest income is not excludable for a series EE or I bond. If the taxpayer's MAGI is between the lower and upper phaseout limit, the taxpayer will be permitted to exclude a portion of the interest from taxable income.

In addition to the ability to exclude the interest earned on a Series EE or I bonds in the year qualified education expenses are incurred, owners of these bonds may convert the bonds into a College Savings Plan (529 Plan) or Coverdell Education Savings Account. Since only cash may be contributed to a Savings Plan or Coverdell account, the bonds must first be redeemed, and then invested in the Savings Plan or Coverdell ESA.

Series EE and I bonds are deemed assets of the owner of the bond for financial aid purposes. So, if the parents own the bonds, then the bonds are deemed owned by the parents for financial aid purposes.

Quick Quiz 8.5

Highlight the answer to these questions:

1. Coverdell account contributions must be in cash, no future contributions are allowed once the beneficiary turns 18, and final distributions must be made within 30 days of the beneficiary attaining age 30.
   a. True
   b. False

2. Qualified education expenses, including tuition, fees, and room and board can be paid with Series EE and I bonds allowing the interest earned to be excludable from taxable income.
   a. True
   b. False

True, False.

TAX DEDUCTIONS FOR EDUCATION EXPENSES

Congress permits taxpayers to deduct education related expenses for income tax purposes. While not as valuable as tax credits, deductions reduce taxable income, whereas tax credits are a dollar for dollar reduction in tax owed.

Deductions that are taken before calculating adjusted gross income are valuable because the taxpayer does not have to itemize deductions on their tax return to take advantage of some specific deductions. Examples of deductions before adjusted gross income related to education expenses include:
- Student Loan Interest Deduction
- Tuition and Fees Deduction

STUDENT LOAN INTEREST DEDUCTION

Generally, the interest expense on most personal loans is not tax deductible, with few exceptions, including mortgage interest on a primary residence. The tax law does allow taxpayers that pay interest related to a student loan to deduct up to $2,500 of interest expense per year. Taxpayers do not have to itemize their deductions to receive the student loan interest deduction because the deduction is taken before adjusted gross income (also known as an adjustment for AGI).

Taxpayers with income in excess of the phase-out thresholds are not eligible to deduct student loan interest expense. The phase-outs (as of 2012) are based on MAGI:
- Single: $60,000 - $75,000
- Married Filing Jointly: $125,000 - $155,000

Key Concepts

Underline/highlight the answers as you read:

1. Identify the criteria required to receive the student loan interest deduction and the deduction for tuition and fees.

2. Distinguish between the American Opportunity Tax Credit and the Life-time Learning Credit.

3. Distinguish between scholarships and fellowships.

4. Identify the income tax consequences associated with education funding from IRA distributions.

To qualify for the student loan interest deduction, the student loan proceeds must have been used to pay for qualified education expenses. Qualified education expenses include tuition and fees, books, supplies, equipment, and other necessary expenses such as transportation, room and board. The qualified education expenses must have been paid by the taxpayer, the taxpayer's spouse, or a dependent of the taxpayer.

As part of the student loan interest deduction, not only is the interest expense on a student loan deductible, but so are loan origination fees, credit card interest expenses, and any capitalized interest expenses. Loan origination fees are financial institution charges associated with issuing a loan. The origination fee is included on a pro-rata basis over the repayment period as a student loan interest expense deduction.

<table>
<tr><td>**EXAMPLE 8.11**</td><td>Ivan receives a $4,000 student loan used for qualified education expenses. His lender charges an origination fee of 3% or $120. Ivan repays the loan over a 10-year period, therefore he is entitled to deduct $12 ($120 ÷ 10) per year for the origination fee. In addition to the origination fee deduction, Ivan can deduct the interest expense paid on the loan as part of the student loan interest deduction.</td></tr>
</table>

Credit card interest is deductible as part of the student loan interest deduction if the credit card charges incurred were for qualified education expenses. If the taxpayer is carrying a large credit card balance, it may be difficult to determine the portion of the outstanding balance that is only associated with qualified education expenses. In addition, because of high interest rates on credit cards, the $2,500 student loan interest expense limit will be attained with only $10,000 - $15,000 in credit card debt.

Capitalized interest is the interest expense that is added to the outstanding balance of a loan, while the taxpayer is enrolled at least half-time. Remember, with unsubsidized Stafford Loans, the borrower can either pay the interest expenses as incurred or capitalize the interest expense.

LOAN FORGIVENESS

Usually, any discharge of indebtedness or forgiveness of debt is considered income for federal and state income tax purposes unless a specific exception applies under Internal Revenue Code Section 108. Therefore, if someone borrowed $1,000 and the loan is subsequently forgiven, it would generally be treated as taxable income. There is an exception under IRC 108 for specific student loans.

Generally, student loan forgiveness is excluded from income if the forgiveness is contingent upon the student working for a specific number of years in certain professions.[18] Public service loan forgiveness, teacher loan forgiveness, law school loan repayment assistance programs, and the National Health Service Corps Loan Repayment Program are not taxable. Loan discharges for closed schools, false certification, unpaid refunds, and death and disability are considered taxable income. The forgiveness of the remaining balance under income-contingent repayment and income-based repayment after 25 years in repayment is considered taxable income.

TAX CREDITS FOR EDUCATION RELATED EXPENSES

The federal tax law permits two types of tax credits for education related expenses. The two types of tax credits are:
- The American Opportunity Tax Credit (formerly the Hope Scholarship Credit)
- Lifetime Learning Credit

---

18. IRC Section 108(f).

Credits are more valuable to taxpayers than income tax deductions, as credits are a dollar for dollar reduction in any federal income taxes owed.

THE AMERICAN OPPORTUNITY TAX CREDIT (FORMERLY THE HOPE SCHOLARSHIP CREDIT)

The **American Opportunity Tax Credit (AOTC)** was created by the American Recovery and Reinvestment Act of 2009 and amended by the Tax Relief, Unemployment Insurance Reauthorization, and Job Creation Act of 2010. The new legislation increased the amount of the tax credit and provided other benefits beyond that of the Hope Credit. The AOTC is currently available through 2012.

The AOTC provides a tax credit of up to $2,500 per student per year for the first four years of qualified education expenses for postsecondary education. The tax credit is calculated as follows:
- 100% x the first $2,000 of qualified education expenses, plus
- 25% x the second $2,000 of qualified education expenses

Since the AOTC is "per student," a family that has multiple children in the first four years of college may qualify for multiple American Opportunity Tax Credits in one year.

> John has two children, Bob and Sara, who are attending the University of Oregon. John pays qualified education expenses of $6,000 for Bob and $3,000 for Sarah. John is entitled to an AOTC of $2,500 for Bob [(100% x $2,000) + (25% x $2,000)] and $2,250 for Sara [(100% x $2,000) + (25% x $1,000)] for a total tax credit of $4,750.

EXAMPLE 8.12

Qualified education expenses include tuition and fees (including student activity fees) as long as those fees are paid directly to the university. Qualified education expenses also include books, supplies and equipment, but they do not have to be purchased directly from the university.

To qualify for the AOTC the taxpayer must pay qualified education expenses for the taxpayer, the taxpayer's spouse or dependent of the taxpayer. In addition, taxpayers with income in excess of the phase-out thresholds are not eligible for the AOTC. The phase-outs are based on MAGI:
- Single: $80,000 - $90,000
- Married Filing Jointly: $160,000 - $180,000

LIFETIME LEARNING CREDIT

The **Lifetime Learning Credit** provides a tax credit of up to $2,000 (2012) per family for an unlimited number of years of qualified education expenses. The qualified education expenses must be related to a postsecondary degree program or to acquire or improve job skills. The tax credit is calculated as follows:
- 20% x qualified education expenses (up to $10,000).

EXAMPLE 8.13	Patrick and Jill are married and both have an undergraduate degree. Patrick goes back to school for a certificate in financial planning while Jill goes back to school to earn her master's degree in nursing. Patrick incurs $5,000 of qualified education expenses and Jill incurs $15,000 of qualified education expenses. Patrick and Jill can take a total Lifetime Learning Credit of $2,000 (($5,000 + $15,000) x 20% limited to $2,000 maximum credit) in the current year. Next year, if Patrick and Jill incur the same amount of qualified education expenses, they can take another $2,000 Lifetime Learning Credit.

Qualified education expenses include tuition and fees, student activity fees, books, supplies and equipment as long as those fees are paid directly to an eligible education institution. An eligible education institution is any accredited public, nonprofit and private profit-making postsecondary institution eligible to participate in a student aid program administered by the U.S. Department of Education.

To qualify for the Lifetime Learning Credit the taxpayer must pay qualified education expenses for the taxpayer, the taxpayer's spouse, or dependent of the taxpayer. In addition, taxpayers with income in excess of the phase-out thresholds are not eligible for the Lifetime Learning Credit. The phase-outs are based on MAGI:
- Single: $52,000 - $62,000
- Married Filing Jointly: $104,000 - $124,000

An important difference between the AOTC and the Lifetime Learning Tax Credit is that AOTC qualified education expenses include related expenses of books, supplies and equipment, regardless of whether the expenses are paid directly to the university. The Lifetime Learning Credit requires related educational expenses such as activity fees, course books, supplies, and equipment be paid directly to the university in order for these expenses to be included in the credit.

There are many similarities between the AOTC and Lifetime Learning Credits such as the timing of when qualified expenses count toward an education tax credit calculation, adjustments to qualified education expenses, no double dipping on benefits and nonqualified education expenses.

Timing of When Qualified Expenses Count Toward the Tax Credit Calculation
When calculating qualified education expenses for the AOTC and Lifetime Learning Credits, the taxpayer may include expenses paid in December, related to attending the university during the first three months of the following year. This includes whether the taxpayer uses cash from their checking account or funds from a loan.

EXAMPLE 8.14	Robin paid $15,000 winter tuition for her daughter Reese on December 15th, for classes that begin January

24th. Robin paid $2,000 from her checking account and used $13,000 from a PLUS Loan to pay the remaining $13,000. Robin is permitted to use the $2,000 paid from her checking account and $2,000 of the $13,000 from the PLUS Loan when calculating the AOTC or Lifetime Learning Credit.

Adjustments to Qualified Education Expenses

If the student receives any tax-free education assistance, the amount of qualified education expenses is reduced by that amount before calculating the AOTC or Lifetime Learning Credit. Examples of tax-free education support include:

- Pell Grants
- Tax-Free Scholarships
- Employer Provided Education Assistance
- Tax-Free Distribution from a Savings Plan or Coverdell ESA

A gift or inheritance used for qualified education expenses does not reduce the amount of expenses considered when calculating the AOTC or Lifetime Learning Credit.

Sally's daughter Jessica is attending Arizona State University and receives a Pell Grant in the amount of $4,000. Qualified tuition expenses for Jessica to attend Arizona State are $7,000 per year. Sally may only use $3,000 ($7,000 - $4,000) of the qualified education expenses to calculate the AOTC or Lifetime Learning Credit.

EXAMPLE 8.15

Laureen's son Dominic is attending Duke University and incurs $35,000 of qualified tuition expenses. Laureen takes a distribution from Dominic's 529 Savings Plan in the amount of $33,000. Laureen may only use $2,000 ($35,000 - $33,000) of the qualified education expenses to calculate the AOTC or Lifetime Learning Credit.

EXAMPLE 8.16

No Double Dipping on Benefits

There are coordination of benefit rules when using multiple tax-deferred savings, tax deductions and tax credits to pay for higher education expenses. The general rule is that a taxpayer is not allowed to receive a double benefit for the same expenses. The following specific rules apply:

- The taxpayer cannot claim both the AOTC and the Lifetime Learning Credits for the same child in the same year.
- The taxpayer cannot claim both the AOTC and the Lifetime Learning Credits for the same qualified education expenses.
- The taxpayer cannot use the same expenses used for a tax-free distribution from a Qualified Tuition Plan (529 Savings Plan) or Coverdell ESA and use those expenses to calculate an AOTC/Hope or Lifetime Learning Credit.

- The taxpayer cannot claim an AOTC or Lifetime Learning Credit if the taxpayer received tax-free education assistance, such as a scholarship, grant or employer provided education assistance.

Nonqualified Education Expenses

The AOTC and the Lifetime Learning Credits do not allow certain education related expenses to be counted as qualified education expenses. Examples of expenses that are not qualified education expenses for the AOTC and Lifetime Learning Credits are:

- Room and Board
- Insurance
- Student Health Fees
- Transportation Expenses

The above expenses are not qualified expenses for the AOTC and Lifetime Learning Credit, even if the fees are a condition of enrollment and are paid directly to the education institution.

EXHIBIT 8.3	**SUMMARY OF EDUCATION RELATED TAX CREDITS**	

	American Opportunity	Lifetime Learning
Calculation	100% x 1st $2,000 + 25% of 2nd $2,000	20% x up to $10,000
Maximum Amount	$2,500	$2,000
Phase-Out (2011)	Single: $80 - $90k MFJ: $160 - $180k	Single: $52 - $62k MFJ: $104 - $124k
Qualified Education Expenses include Textbook and Equipment	Yes - Does not have to be paid directly to the university	Yes - Only if paid directly to the university
Qualified Education Expenses include Room and Board	No	No

OTHER EDUCATION SOURCES OF FUNDING

This section discusses some of the tax advantages and disadvantages of using scholarships, fellowships, IRA distributions, and custodial accounts to pay for post-secondary education expenses. A planner should understand all of the tax consequences of each of these education related benefits.

SCHOLARSHIPS AND FELLOWSHIPS

Scholarships are a grant of financial assistance made available to students to assist with the payment of education related expenses. Scholarships are available for academic or athletic achievement. Many private organizations will also fund scholarships based on various fields of study, religious affiliations, or military service. Scholarships can be provided to undergraduate or graduate students.

Information on various scholarships and organizations awarding scholarships can be found on the Federal Student Aid website,[19] which is an office of the U.S. Department of Education. There is also a research tool for scholarships available on the website.[20]

Fellowships are typically paid to students for work, such as teaching while studying for a Master's degree or conducting research while working towards a Doctorate of Philosophy degree (Ph.D.). Fellowships can also be provided to an M.D. working on a specialty field of medicine. Fellowships can last from a few weeks to a few years, depending on the depth and level of work involved.

A scholarship or fellowship is tax-free to the recipient if the recipient is:
- A candidate for a degree at an eligible education institution, and
- The recipient uses the proceeds to pay for qualified education expenses.

The recipient is considered a candidate for a degree if:
- The recipient is attending a primary or secondary school or is pursuing a degree at a college or university, or
- The recipient is attending an accredited education institution (that is authorized to provide full credit towards a bachelor's degree or higher, or provides training for students for gainful employment in a recognized occupation).

An eligible education institution is one that maintains a regular faculty and curriculum, and normally has an enrolled student body at a place where education activities are conducted.

Qualified education expenses for the purpose of tax-free scholarships and fellowships include tuition and fees, course related expenses such as books, supplies, and equipment that are required by the eligible education institution.

A scholarship or fellowship may be taxable if the scholarship or fellowship is used for:
- Expenses that do not qualify
- Payments for services
- Scholarship prizes

EXPENSES THAT DO NOT QUALIFY

Expenses that do not qualify as qualified education expenses for the purpose of tax-free scholarships include:
- Room and Board
- Transportation Expenses
- Equipment and Other Fees not Required for Attendance

The above expenses are not qualified expenses for the tax-free scholarships and fellowships, even if the fees are a condition of enrollment and are paid directly to the education institution. Scholarships and fellowships used to pay the above expenses will lose their tax-

19. https://studentaid.ed.gov
20. https://studentaid2.ed.gov/getmoney/scholarship/v3browse.asp

free status and the recipient must include that portion of the scholarship or fellowship in taxable income.

PAYMENT FOR SERVICES

If a scholarship or fellowship is intended to compensate the recipient for past, present or future services, such as teaching or research, then the scholarship or fellowship is included in taxable income.

| EXAMPLE 8.17 |

Brian receives a fellowship to attend Duke University's medical school in the amount of $80,000 per year. As a condition of the fellowship, Brian must serve one year on staff at Duke University's Hospital upon his graduation from medical school. Since the fellowship requires one year of work in the future, the fellowship represents a payment for services and must be included in Brian's income in the year he receives the fellowship.

SCHOLARSHIP PRIZES

Generally, scholarships won as a result of a competition and awarded as a prize are included in taxable income unless the scholarship meets the following requirements:

Quick Quiz 8.6

Highlight the answer to these questions:

1. Up to $2,500 of student loan interest is income tax deductible (before adjusted gross income) for loans used for qualified education expenses.
   a. True
   b. False

2. The American Opportunity Tax Credit provides a tax credit of up to $2,000 (2012) per family for an unlimited number of years of qualified education expenses.
   a. True
   b. False

3. Scholarships are nontaxable and typically paid to students for work, such as teaching while studying for a Master's degree or conducting research while working towards a Doctorate of Philosophy degree.
   a. True
   b. False

True, False, False.

The recipient is:
- A candidate for a degree at an eligible education institution, and
- The recipient uses the proceeds to pay for qualified education expenses

AND

The recipient is considered a candidate for a degree if:
- The recipient is attending a primary or secondary school or is pursuing a degree at a college or university, or
- The recipient is attending an accredited education institution.

IRA DISTRIBUTIONS

Distributions from an IRA are another source of funds to pay for college education. However, these distributions have tax implications that need to be considered. In addition, the planner should work with the client to determine if taking distributions from an IRA will adversely impact retirement goals.

With distributions from IRAs, taxpayers need to be concerned with whether the distribution is subject to income tax and whether it is subject to a penalty. Distributions from a traditional IRA are generally included in taxable income and may be subject to an early withdrawal penalty if the distribution is made prior to the attainment of age 59½. However, there is an exception to the penalty if the distribution from the IRA is used to pay for higher education expenses.[21] Therefore, distributions from an IRA can be used for college funding, but will generally be treated as taxable income.

There are also tax implications to using distributions from Roth IRAs as a source of funds for college funding. Roth IRAs are generally funded with after tax contributions or conversions from traditional IRAs.

The tax characteristics of funds held in a Roth IRA take one of three forms:
- Contributions
- Conversions
- Earnings

Contributions to a Roth IRA consist of after tax dollars for which no tax deduction is taken at the time of the contribution. Contributions to a Roth IRA represent the owner's basis in the IRA and can be withdrawn, without tax consequences at any time.

Conversions represent pre-tax dollars, typically in a Traditional IRA, that were converted to a Roth IRA. The account owner recognized income on the amount converted and the conversion became after tax dollars since income was recognized and income taxes were paid on the converted amount. Conversions represent the owner's basis in the IRA and can be withdrawn, without tax consequences at any time. However, conversions withdrawn within five years of the date of conversion may be subject to a 10 percent penalty.

Earnings represent the growth from investing contributions and conversions. Distributions of earnings may be tax-free, if the distribution is a qualified distribution.

A qualified distribution from a Roth IRA must meet the following two requirements:

1. The distribution must occur at least five years after the Roth IRA owner established and funded the Roth IRA

AND

2. At least one of the following requirements must be met:
   - The Roth IRA holder must be at least age 59½ when the distribution occurs
   - The Roth IRA owner becomes disabled
   - Death of the Roth IRA owner
   - Distributed assets limited to $10,000 are used towards the purchase or rebuilding of a first home for the Roth IRA holder or a qualified family member

---

21. This exception does not apply to distributions from qualified plans.

If the distribution is a qualified distribution, there is no tax or penalty associated with the distribution. If the distribution is not a qualified distribution, then any amount distributed in excess of the contributions and conversions will be treated as taxable income, but will not be subject to the 10 percent penalty if the funds are used for higher education expenses.

As mentioned above, it is important to keep in mind that using assets in an IRA to fund education expenses may impact the attainment of a client's retirement goal. It may be more appropriate to borrow for education expenses, as you cannot borrow to finance a retirement goal.

UNIFORM GIFT TO MINORS ACT (UGMA) & UNIFORM TRANSFER TO MINORS ACT (UTMA) CUSTODIAL ACCOUNTS

The **Uniform Gift to Minors Act (UGMA)** allows minors to own cash or securities. The **Uniform Transfer to Minors Act (UTMA)** allows minors to own cash, securities, and real estate. The UGMA / UTMA accounts are governed by state law that requires the custodian of the account, usually a parent or grandparent, to manage the account for the benefit of the minor child. When the child reaches age of majority (18 or 21 depending on the state), the child can access the account without permission of the custodian.

Quick Quiz 8.7

Highlight the answer to these questions:

1. Traditional IRA distributions by an individual prior to age 59½ made for qualified education expenses are subject to a 10% tax penalty.
   a. True
   b. False

2. An UGMA account allows a minor to own cash or securities and an UTMA account allows minors to own cash, securities, and real estate.
   a. True
   b. False

3. An employer provided education assistance program only reimburses employees for education expenses directly related to the employee's current job duties.
   a. True
   b. False

False, True, False.

UGMA and UTMA accounts were popular education savings accounts, prior to the passage of Section 529 (Prepaid Tuition and Savings Plans). However, there are two primary disadvantages to using UGMA / UTMA accounts to fund a college education.

The first disadvantage is that once a child reaches the age of majority, he can use the assets in an UGMA / UTMA for something other than a college education. The account custodian, or parent, will be unable to control the asset to ensure the funds are used for a college education.

The second disadvantage is that the earnings in the UGMA / UTMA may cause a "kiddie tax" issue. The kiddie tax rules state that if unearned income is above a certain threshold ($2,000 in 2013), then the additional unearned income is taxed at the parent's tax rate. Unearned income is any income that is not derived from working, which includes interest, dividends, and realized capital gains.

To be subject to the kiddie tax rules, one of the following conditions must be present:
- Children under the age of 19
- Full time students under the age of 24[22]

William, age 8, has an UGMA account that earned $2,500 in interest in 2013. Since William is under age 19 and has unearned income in excess of $2,000, he is subject to the kiddie tax rules. The first $2,000 will be taxed at William's tax rate, $500 will be taxed at his parent's tax rate.	**EXAMPLE 8.18**
Frankie, age 19, has unearned income of $3,000 in his UGMA account in 2013. Frankie signed a contract to play professional hockey out of high school and is not attending college. Since Frankie is older than 18 years old and is not a full time student, he is not subject to the kiddie tax. The entire $3,000 will be taxed at Frankie's tax rate.	**EXAMPLE 8.19**
Owen, age 21, is attending college full time. He has unearned income of $1,500 in his UGMA account in 2013. Although Owen is a full time student under the age of 24, his unearned income is below $2,000 (2013) therefore he is not subject to the kiddie tax. The entire $1,500 of unearned income will be taxed at Owen's tax rate.	**EXAMPLE 8.20**

EMPLOYER PROVIDED EDUCATION ASSISTANCE

An **employer provided education assistance program** is a program established by an employer to reimburse employees for education expenses. The education expenses may or may not be directly related to the employee's current job duties; it depends on the employer's policy. Reimbursement of education expenses by an employer, up to $5,250 (2013) per year, is not taxable to the employee. Any education expenses reimbursed above $5,250 are included in income for the employee.

To qualify for the tax-free reimbursement of education expenses, the employer's education assistance program must be in writing, and the reimbursement must be for tuition, fees, books, supplies, and equipment.

---

22. IRC Section 152(C)(3).

EDUCATION FUNDING

By using our time value of money skills, we are able to determine the lump sum required to fund a college education or annual savings required to attain a lump sum to pay for college. **Education funding** represents a coalescing of many of the concepts covered in the chapter and are some of the more challenging time value of money calculations. There are four primary methods for solving an education funding calculation, which are:

- Uneven Cash Flow Method
- Traditional Method
- Account Balance Method
- Hybrid Approach

Key Concepts

Underline/highlight the answers as you read:

1. Identify the steps of the uneven cash flow method used for education funding.

2. Identify the four methods used to calculate education funding.

College education funding calculations can be made by various methods. The planner can use real, rather than nominal dollars or vice versa. The financial planner can use an annuity due concept coupled with either a real or nominal dollar calculation or an ordinary annuity concept. Some additional college education funding alternatives include:

- Fully fund the plan today, as a grandparent might by using a 529 Plan.
- Fund the plan from date of birth to the start date of college.
- Fund the plan from date of birth through the expected college years (or some other fixed period).
- Fund the savings in an ordinary annuity funding plan on a monthly or yearly basis.
- Fund the savings in an annuity due funding plan on a monthly, yearly, or serial payment basis.

All of these possible variations make education funding calculations seem quite different whereas they are relatively similar. The traditional method uses real dollars and an annuity due funding plan to determine the present value of the education today. The account balance method uses nominal dollars initially and then an annuity due concept. The hybrid approach uses an ordinary annuity concept and will not be covered in this chapter. Refer to Chapter 6 for information and examples related to the hybrid approach and establishing timelines for time value of money calculations.

UNEVEN CASH FLOW METHOD

The uneven cash flow method is a good approach for education funding calculations because it consists of only two steps and it works for any type of education funding situation. Other methods may not work if a client continues saving while the child is attending college and will only work if the client stops saving when the child starts going to college.

The uneven cash flow method has two steps:

1. Determine the net present value of the cash flow stream in today's dollars. This step will determine the lump-sum amount needed today, to fund the college education goal. During this step, be sure to use an inflation adjusted rate of return.
2. Determine the annual savings required to fund the education goal. During this step, be sure to determine how long the client intends to save and whether the savings payments are at the beginning or end of the year.

Saving Until the Child Reaches College Age

In this example, we will determine the amount required to save each year, assuming the client saves until the child reaches college age.

EXAMPLE 8.21

Jan wants to plan for her daughter's education. Her daughter, Rachel was born today and will go to college at age 18 for five years. Tuition is currently $15,000 per year, in today's dollars. Jan anticipates tuition inflation of 7% and believes she can earn an 11% return on her investments. How much must Jan save at the end of each year, if she wants to make her last payment at the beginning of her daughter's first year of college?

Step #1: Determine the NPV at time period zero of the cash flows. Recall that this step determines the amount that could be deposited today, to satisfy the education funding need.

10BII Keystrokes	12C Keystrokes
0 [CFj]	0 [g] [CF0]
0 [CFj]	0 [g] [CFj]
17 [ORANGE] [NJ]	17 [g] [Nj]
15,000 [+/-] [CFj]	15,000 [CHS] [g] [CFj]
5 [ORANGE] [NJ]	5 [g] [Nj]
1.11 ÷ 1.07 - 1 x 100 = [I/YR]	1.11 [ENTER] 1.07 [÷] 1[–] 100 x [i]
[ORANGE] [NPV]	[f] [NPV]
Answer: 36,046.41	**Answer: 36,046.41**

Step #2: Determine the annual savings required to meet the education goal. Note: During this step it is important to determine two items: (1) How long does the client intend to save and (2) When will the savings payments be made? In this problem, Jan's daughter was born today and Jan intends to save until the beginning of her daughter's first year of college or 18 years of savings. Jan also intends to "save at the end of each year" which indicates that this is an ordinary annuity problem (END mode).

10BII Keystrokes	12C Keystrokes
18 [N]	18 [n]
11 [I/YR]	11 [i]
36,046.41 [PV]	36,046.41 [PV]
0 [FV]	0 [FV]
[PMT]	[PMT]
Answer: <4,680.37>	**Answer: <4,680.37>**

Therefore, Jan must save $4,680.37 each year, at the end of each year, for the next 18 years to satisfy her education goal.

Saving Until the Child's Last Year of College
In this section, we will assume that the client is going to save until the child's last year of college and how this funding approach impacts the annual savings required.

EXAMPLE 8.22

Assume that Jan decides to save until the beginning of her daughter's last year of college, how much would Jan have to save at the end of each year to meet her goal? Recall the other facts are: tuition is currently $15,000 per year, tuition inflation is 7%, Jan's investment return is expected to be 7%, and her daughter will go to college at age 18 for five years.

Step #1: Determine the NPV at time period zero of the cash flows. This step in the problem does not change from the previous example.

10BII Keystrokes	12C Keystrokes
0 [CFj]	0 [g] [CF0]
0 [CFj]	0 [g] [CFj]
17 [ORANGE] [NJ]	17 [g] [Nj]
15,000 [+/-] [CFj]	15,000 [CHS] [g] [CFj]
5 [ORANGE] [NJ]	5 [g] [Nj]
1.11 ÷ 1.07 - 1 x 100 = [I/YR]	1.11 [ENTER] 1.07 [÷] 1[–] 100 x [i]
[ORANGE] [NPV]	[f] [NPV]
Answer: 36,046.41	**Answer: 36,046.41**

Step #2: Determine the annual savings required to meet the education goal. Recall we must determine two items: (1) How long does the client intend to save and (2) When will the savings payments be made? In this problem, Jan's daughter was born today and Jan intends to save until the beginning of her daughter's **last** year of college or 22 years of savings. Jan also intends to "save at the end of each year" which indicates that this is an ordinary annuity problem (END mode).

10BII Keystrokes	12C Keystrokes
22 [N]	22 [n]
11 [I/YR]	11 [i]
36,046.41 [PV]	36,046.41 [PV]
0 [FV]	0 [FV]
[PMT]	[PMT]
Answer: <4,408.95>	**Answer: <4,408.95>**

EXAMPLE 8.23

Instead of Jan making her savings payments at the end of each year, lets assume she makes her savings payments at the beginning of each year. So, if Jan decides to save until the beginning of her daughter's last year of college, how much would Jan have to save at the beginning of each year to meet her goal? Recall the other facts are: Tuition is currently $15,000 per year, tuition inflation is 7%, Jan's investment return is expected to be 7%, and her daughter will go to college at age 18 for five years.

Step #1: Determine the NPV at time period zero of the cash flows. There are no changes to this step of the calculation.

10BII Keystrokes	12C Keystrokes
0 [CFj]	0 [g] [CF0]
0 [CFj]	0 [g] [CFj]
17 [ORANGE] [NJ]	17 [g] [Nj]
15,000 [+/-] [CFj]	15,000 [CHS] [g] [CFj]
5 [ORANGE] [NJ]	5 [g] [Nj]
1.11 ÷ 1.07 - 1 x 100 = [I/YR]	1.11 [ENTER] 1.07 [÷] 1[−] 100 x [i]
[ORANGE] [NPV]	[f] [NPV]
Answer: 36,046.41	**Answer: 36,046.41**

Step #2: Determine the annual savings required to meet the education goal. We must determine: (1) How long does the client intend to save and (2) When will the savings payments be made? In this problem, Jan's daughter was born today and Jan intends to save at the beginning of the year and until the beginning of her daughter's **last** year of college. Since Jan is going to start saving today, that represents the first savings payment, such that when her daughter is 22, Jan will be making her 23rd savings payment.

10BII Keystrokes	12C Keystrokes
[ORANGE] [BEG/END] 23 [N] 11 [I/YR] 36,046.41 [PV] 0 [FV] [PMT] **Answer: 3,928.45**	[g] [BEG] 23 [n] 11 [i] 36,046.41 [PV] 0 [FV] [PMT] **Answer: 3,928.45**

Multiple Children

The best approach to use in calculating education funding for multiple children is using the uneven cash flow method. This method allows the planner to combine multiple cash flows during the same time periods.

EXAMPLE 8.24

Joe has two children, Sydney age 5 and William age 2, that he wants to provide for their education funding. Currently, tuition is $10,000 per year and tuition inflation is 6%. Joe expects to earn 10% on his investments and he expects the children to start college at age 18 and go to college for 4 years. Joe wants his last savings payment to be made when the oldest child starts college. How much must Joe save at the end of each year?

Step #1: Determine the NPV at time period zero of the cash flows. Recall that this step determines the amount that could be deposited today, to satisfy the education funding need.

10BII Keystrokes	12C Keystrokes
0 [CFj] 0 [CFj] 12 [ORANGE] [NJ] 10,000 [+/-] [CFj] 3 [ORANGE] [NJ] 20,000 [+/-] [CFj] 10,000 [+/-] [CFj] 3 [ORANGE] [NJ] 1.10 ÷ 1.06 - 1 x 100 = [I/YR] [ORANGE] [NPV] **Answer: <44,334.65>**	0 [g] [CF0] 0 [g] [CFj] 12 [g] [Nj] 10,000 [CHS] [g] [CFj] 3 [g] [Nj] 20,000 [CHS] [g] [CFj] 10,000 [CHS] [g] [CFj] 3 [g] [Nj] 1.10 [ENTER] 1.06 [÷] 1 [–] 100 x [i] [f] [NPV] **Answer: <44,334.65>**

Step #2: Determine the annual savings required to meet the education goal. Note: During this step it is important to determine two criteria: (1) How long does the client intend to save and (2) When will the savings payments be made? In this problem, Joe's oldest child is 5 and he intends to save until she starts college, which is in 13 years. He also indicates that he wants to "save at the end of each year" which indicates that this is an ordinary annuity problem (END mode).

10BII Keystrokes	12C Keystrokes
13 [N]	13 [n]
10 [I/YR]	10 [i]
44,334.65 [PV]	44,334.65 [PV]
0 [FV]	0 [FV]
[PMT]	[PMT]
Answer: <6,241.37>	**Answer: <6,241.37>**

TRADITIONAL METHOD

The traditional method of education funding uses real dollars and the annuity due funding plan to calculate the present value of the cost of education.

Continuing with Example 8.21 where Jan is interested in funding the college education of her daughter, Rachel, the traditional method is applied.

EXAMPLE 8.25

Step 1: Determine the present value at age 18 using real dollars.

10BII Keystrokes	12C Keystrokes
[ORANGE] [BEG/END]	[g] [BEG]
5 [N]	5 [n]
1.11 [÷] 1.07 – 1 x 100 = [I/YR]	1.11 [ENTER] 1.07 [÷] 1 [-] 100 [x] [i]
15,000 [PMT]$_{AD}$	15,000 [PMT]$_{AD}$
0 [FV]	0 [FV]
[PV]	[PV]
Answer: <69,785.90>	**Answer: <69,785.90>**

Step 2: Determine the present value at age zero using real dollars.

10BII Keystrokes	12C Keystrokes
[**ORANGE**] [BEG/END] 18 [N] 1.11 [÷] 1.07 – 1 x 100 = [I/YR] 0 [PMT] 69,785.90 [FV] [PV] **Answer: <36,046.41>**	[g] [BEG] 18 [n] 1.11 [ENTER] 1.07 [÷] 1 [-] 100 [x] [i] 0 [PMT] 69,785.90 [FV] [PV] **Answer: <36,046.41>**

Step 3: Treat the present value calculated above as an opportunity for grandparent(s) to fully fund a 529 Plan (at a cost of $36,046.41). Alternatively, determine the amount the parents will have to save by treating the present value as a mortgage to be paid off by Rachel's age 18 as an ordinary annuity or annuity due at the earnings rate (in this example, 11%).

10BII Keystrokes	12C Keystrokes
18[N] 11 [I/YR] 0 [FV] 36,046.41 [PV] [PMT]OA **Answer: <4,680.37>***	18 [n] 11 [i] 0 [FV] 36,046.41 [PV] [PMT]$_{OA}$ **Answer: <4,680.37>***

* Annual payment amount.

SUMMARY OF SAVINGS OPTIONS

A financial planner should be able to present a client with alternative strategies to save for a college education, such that the best strategy that is highly likely to be maintained by the client is implemented. Options to lower the amount of annual savings required include continuing to save while the child is in college and making savings payments at the beginning of each year. The primary consideration for the client when determining which funding strategy to use is the amount of current income available for education savings.

	Saving Until Age 18	Saving Through College (Age 22)	Saving Through College (Age 22) and Saving at the Beginning of each Year
Annual Savings	$4,680.37	$4,408.95	$3,928.45
Total Savings Contributions	$84,246.66	$96,996.90	$90,354.35

Traditional Method and Serial Payments

As indicated, the traditional method of education fund uses real dollars and the annuity due funding plan to calculate the present value of the cost of education.

EXAMPLE 8.26

John and Betty Shelton would like to save for their son, Bob's, college education. They expect Bob, who was born today, to attend a private college for 4 years starting at age 18. Current tuition at the college of their choice is $20,000 per year. Tuition inflation rate is expected to be 7 percent, while CPI is expected to be 3 percent. The Shelton's expect to earn twelve percent after-tax return on their investments. How much should they deposit in a lump-sum amount into a college fund today to fully fund the education?

10BII Keystrokes	12C Keystrokes
[**ORANGE**] [BEG/END]	[g] [BEG]
4 [N]	4 [n]
1.12 ÷ 1.07 - 1 x 100 = [I/YR]	1.12 [ENTER] 1.07 [÷] 1[–] 100 x [i]
20,000 [PMT]	20,000 [PMT]
0 [FV]	0 [FV]
[PV]	[PV]
Answer: <74,800.51>	**Answer: <74,800.51>**
18 [N]	18 [n]
4.6729 [I/YR]	4.6729 [i]
0 [PMT]	0 [PMT]
74,800.51 [FV]	74,800.51 [FV]
Answer: 32,876.69	**Answer: 32,876.69**

EXAMPLE 8.27

Assume the same Shelton education funding situation except instead of a lump sum invested today, the Sheltons would like to invest annually in equal payments at the <u>end</u> of each year (ordinary annuity). What should their annual investment be assuming the last investment is made when Bob is 18 years old?

10BII Keystrokes	12C Keystrokes
18 [N]	18 [n]
12 [I/YR]	12 [i]
0 [FV]	0 [FV]
32,876.69 [PV]	32,876.69 [PV]
[PMT]$_{OA}$	[PMT]$_{OA}$
Answer: 4,534.92	**Answer: 4,534.92**

EXAMPLE 8.28

Assume the same Shelton education funding situation except they would like to invest annually in equal payments at the <u>beginning</u> of each year (annuity due). What should their annual investment be assuming the last investment is made when Bob is 18 years old?

10BII Keystrokes	12C Keystrokes
[**ORANGE**] [BEG/END]	[g] [BEG]
18 [N]	18 [n]
12 [I/YR]	12 [i]
0 [FV]	0 [FV]
32,876.69 [PV]	32,876.69 [PV]
[PMT]$_{AD}$	[PMT]$_{AD}$
Answer: <4,049.03>	**Answer: <4,049.03>**

Serial Payments

EXAMPLE 8.29

Assume the same Shelton education funding situation except that instead of a lump sum invested today, the Sheltons would like to make serial saving payments until Bob is 18 years old. What would be their first and second payments (with a tuition inflation rate of 7 percent)?

10BII Keystrokes	12C Keystrokes
18 [N]	18 [n]
4.6729 [I/YR]	4.6729 [i]
74,800.51 [FV]	74,800.51 [FV]
0 [PV]	0 [PV]
[PMT]$_{OA}$	[PMT]$_{OA}$
Answer: 2,741.05	**Answer: 2,741.05**

$$PMT_0 = 2,741.05$$

$$PMT_1 = 2,741.05 \times 1.07 = 2,932.93$$

$$PMT_2 = 2,932.93 \times 1.07 = 3,138.23$$

The first payment is equal to payment at time zero ($2,741.05) increased by inflation for one year. All subsequent payments are increased by the rate of inflation over the prior period's payment.

ACCOUNT BALANCE METHOD

The account balance method is a three-step approach that determines the lump-sum amount needed when the child starts college and how much must be saved to attain that lump-sum amount. Note that the method assumes parents will stop saving when the child starts college and begins withdrawals.

Seth was born today. Harold and Maude Clark anticipate that Seth will begin college at age 18. College education expenses are $25,000 per year in today's dollars
and are expected to increase at an annual rate of six percent. The Clarks can earn an after-tax annual return of
11 percent. How much should the Clarks deposit at the
end of each year to pay for Seth's education. The last
deposit will be made when Seth reaches his 18th birth-
day.

EXAMPLE 8.30

Step #1: Calculate the future value cost of one year of
Seth's education in 18 years (based on today's cost of
$25,000-in nominal dollars).

10BII Keystrokes	12C Keystrokes
18 [N]	18 [n]
6 [I/YR]	6 [i]
25,000 [PV]	25,000 [PV]
0 [PMT]	0 [PMT]
[FV]	[FV]
Answer: 71,358.48	**Answer: 71,358.48**

Step #2: Calculate the amount of education funding
needed at Seth's age 18.

10BII Keystrokes	12C Keystrokes
[ORANGE] [BEG/END]	[g] [BEG]
4 [N]	4 [n]
1.11 ÷ 1.06 - 1 x 100 = [I/YR]	1.11 [ENTER] 1.06 [÷] 1[−] 100 x [i]
0 [FV]	0 [FV]
71,358.48[PMT]$_{AD}$	71,358.48 [PMT]$_{AD}$
[PV]	[PV]
Answer: 266,720.48	**Answer: 266,720.48**

Step #3: Calculate how much in annual savings is necessary to reach the age 18 savings goal.

10BII Keystrokes	12C Keystrokes
18 [N]	18 [n]
11 [I/YR]	11 [i]
266,720.48 [FV]	266,720.48 [FV]
0 [PV]	0 [PV]
[PMT]$_{OA}$	[PMT]$_{OA}$
Answer: 5,292.50	**Answer: 5,292.50**

COMPARISON OF THE ACCOUNT BALANCE METHOD TO THE TRADITIONAL METHOD

Step #1: Calculate the present value of the cost of Seth's education in real dollars at his age 18.

10BII Keystrokes	12C Keystrokes
[ORANGE] [BEG/END]	[g] [BEG]
4 [N]	4 [n]
1.11 ÷ 1.06 - 1 x 100 = [I/YR]	1.11 [ENTER] 1.06 [÷] 1 [–] 100 x [i]
0 [FV]	0 [FV]
25,000[PMT]$_{AD}$	25,000 [PMT]$_{AD}$
[PV]	[PV]
Answer: 93,443.86 (in real dollars)	**Answer: 93,443.86 (in real dollars)**

Step #2: Calculate the present value today of the cost of funding Seth's education at 18.

10BII Keystrokes	12C Keystrokes
18 [N]	18 [n]
1.11 ÷ 1.06 - 1 x 100 = [I/YR]	1.11 [ENTER] 1.06 [÷] 1
93,443.86 [FV]	[–] 100 x [i]
0 [PMT]$_{OA}$	93,443.86 [FV]
[PV]	0 [PMT]$_{OA}$
	[PV]
Answer: 40,760.80	**Answer: 40,760.80**

Step #3: Calculate how much in annual savings is necessary to reach the age 18 savings goal.

10BII Keystrokes	12C Keystrokes
18 [N]	18 [n]
11 [I/YR]	11 [i]
0 [FV]	0 [FV]
40,760.80 [PV]	40,760.80 [PV]
[PMT]$_{OA}$	[PMT]$_{OA}$
Answer: 5,292.50	**Answer: 5,292.50**

HYBRID APPROACH

The hybrid approach combines the concepts of the uneven cash flow and account balance methods.

EXAMPLE 8.31

Kathy and Dave are planning to save for their daughter Aubrey's college education. Aubrey was born today and will attend college for 4 years, starting at age 18. Tuition currently costs $20,000 per year and tuition inflation is expected to be 6%. They believe they can earn 9% on their investments. How much must Kathy and Dave save at the end of each year using the hybrid approach?

Step #1: Determine the present market value of the tuition payments at age 17.

10BII Keystrokes	12C Keystrokes
4 [N] 1.09 ÷ 1.06 - 1 x 100 = [I/YR] 20,000 [PMT] 0 [FV] [PV] **Answer: <74,644.84>**	4 [n] 1.09 [ENTER] 1.06 [÷] 1[–] 100 x [i] 20,000 [PMT] 0 [FV] [PV] **Answer: <74,644.84>**

Step #2: Determine the present value of the lump sum calculated from Step #1, at time period zero.

10BII Keystrokes	12C Keystrokes
17 [N] 1.09 ÷ 1.06 - 1 x 100 = [I/YR] 0 [PMT] 74,644.84 [FV] [PV] **Answer: <46,446.08>**	17 [n] 1.09 [ENTER] 1.06 [÷] 1[–] 100 x [i] 0 [PMT] 74,644.84 [FV] [PV] **Answer: <46,446.08>**

Step #3: Determine the annual savings required to fund the college tuition.

10BII Keystrokes	12C Keystrokes
18 [N] 9 [I/YR] 46,446.08 [PV] 0 [FV] [PMT] **Answer: <5,304.71>**	18 [n] 9 [i] 46,446.08 [PV] 0 [FV] [PMT] **Answer: <5,304.71>**

The hybrid approach is used the least of the methods because the ordinary annuity concept can be confusing to the first-time learner. Note that with the same facts, all methods lead to the same answer.

EXHIBIT 8.4   SUMMARY OF EDUCATION FUNDING METHODS

Method	Real or Nominal Dollars	Number of Steps to Present Value	Total Steps to Annual Funding	Annuity Method of Calculation*
Uneven Cash Flow	Real	1	2	Annuity Due
Traditional	Real	2	3	Annuity Due
Account Balance	Nominal/Real	2 steps to Future Value (at college age 18)	3 Total	Annuity Due
Hybrid	Real	2 steps to Present Value	3	Ordinary Annuity

*The use of the annuity due calculation generally means that present value is calculated using 18 periods. The use of ordinary annuity calculation (hybrid approach) uses 17 periods.

CONCLUSION

For many families, paying for their children's college education is one of their top two or three largest financial goals, next to retiring and paying off debt. It is the responsibility of the financial planner to help the client prioritize how to allocate their cash flow and savings. Paying off a mortgage, fully funding a retirement, and saving an adequate amount for education may not be possible for some families. The planner should advise the client as to all of the education funding options, including financial aid (grants, loans, and work study) and scholarships. The planner should also advise the family regarding tax-deferred savings, tax deductions, and tax credits.

With the average cost of tuition ranging from $7,000 for a public state university and up to $30,000+ for a private university, it is important for the financial planner to also consider other cost factors besides tuition when determining the total cost of attendance, (such as room and board, insurance, travel, entertainment etc.). The total cost of attending college is likely to be an additional 50 to 75 percent of the cost of tuition. Tax deferred savings is an ideal way to save for education funding for clients with the means to save for a college education and a time horizon greater than 10 years. The longer the time horizon until the child enters college, the more beneficial tax deferred savings becomes. As the education funding section of this chapter demonstrated, the longer the time horizon (savings period), the less the family must save each year. The planner should present alternative saving strategies to the client to determine which strategy is most likely to be implemented (based on the amount of income available for education funding).

For clients that do not have the means to save for college education or do not have a sufficient time horizon to take advantage of tax deferred savings, the financial planner must advise the family as to the various types of financial aid, such as grants and loans. It is also important that the planner advise the client as to the tax consequences of grants, loans, scholarships and possible tax deductions and credits related to education. With changing tax laws, education planning can be a challenging area for planners that is also very rewarding when helping a family achieve education funding goals for their children.

Quick Quiz 8.8

Highlight the answer to these questions:

1. The traditional method for education funding calculation is the best approach to use for education funding when the client continues to save while the child is attending college.
   a. True
   b. False

2. The account balance method used for education funding calculation is a three-step approach that determines the lump-sum amount needed when the child starts college and how much is saved to attain that amount.
   a. True
   b. False

3. They hybrid approach used for education funding calculation combines the concepts of the uneven cash flow and traditional methods.
   a. True
   b. False

False, True, False.

Key Terms

Academic Competitiveness Grant (ACG) - A grant for students graduating from a rigorous secondary school program of study. Rigorous secondary school programs are designated by stated education agencies and recognized by the secretary of education.

American Opportunity Tax Credit (AOTC) - Created by the American Recovery and Reinvestment Act of 2009. The new legislation increased the amount of the tax credit and provided other benefits. The AOTC provides a tax credit of up to $2,500 (2012) per student for the first four years of qualified education expenses for postsecondary education.

College Savings Plans (529 Savings Plans) - A plan that allows for college saving on a tax-deferred basis with attendance at any eligible education institution. Distributions from a College Savings Plan are federal and state income tax-free, as long as they are used to pay for qualified education expenses.

Coverdell Education Savings Account (ESA) - A tax deferred trust or custodial account established to pay for qualified higher education or qualified elementary / secondary school expenses.

Education Funding - Determination of the lump sum or annual savings required to pay for college.

Employer Provided Education Assistance Program - A program established by an employer to reimburse employees for education expenses. The education expenses may or may not be directly related to the employee's current job duties; it depends on the employer's policy.

Federal Pell Grant - Need based financial aid for students that have not earned an undergraduate degree or a professional degree. A Pell Grant does not have to be repaid. Pell Grants are awarded based on financial need.

Federal Perkins Loan - A program for undergraduate and graduate students with exceptional financial need. The Perkins Loan is a low interest rate loan (5%), which is offered through a university's financial aid office. The university serves as the lender and the federal government provides the funds.

Federal Supplemental Educational Opportunity Grant (FSEOG) - A grant awarded to students with exceptional financial need. Pell Grant recipients with the lowest EFC are considered first for a FSEOG.

Federal Work Study (FWS) - Jobs on campus or off campus for undergraduate or graduate students to help students pay for their education expenses. To be eligible students must have financial need.

Fellowships - Paid to students for work, such as teaching while studying for a Master's degree or conducting research while working towards a Doctorate of Philosophy degree (Ph.D.). Fellowships can last anywhere from a few weeks to a few years, depending on the depth and level of work involved.

Free Application for Federal Student Aid (FAFSA) - A form used to determine a student's eligibility for all types of financial aid, including grants, work study, and loans. The FAFSA is used to determine the Expected Family Contribution amount (EFC).

Key Terms

Graduate PLUS Loans - Loans for student's seeking graduate and professional degrees. A Graduate PLUS Loan is based on the parent's credit history and is not based on financial need.

Grants - Money provided to students for postsecondary education that does not require repayment.

Lifetime Learning Credit - Provides a tax credit of up to $2,000 (2012) per family for an unlimited number of years of qualified education expenses. The qualified education expenses must be related to a postsecondary degree program or to acquire or improve job skills.

National Science and Mathematics Access to Retain Talent (SMART) Grant - A grant available during the third and fourth years of undergraduate studies. The National SMART Grant pays up to $4,000 per year and is paid in addition to the Pell Grant.

PLUS Loans - Loans for parents to borrow to help pay for a dependent's undergraduate education expenses. PLUS Loans are not based on financial need, but are instead based on the parent's credit history.

Prepaid Tuition Plan - A plan that will allow a parent to purchase college credits today and use those credits when the child attends college.

Qualified Tuition Plans (Savings Plans) - A plan that allows families to save for education expenses on a tax-deferred basis. Section 529 of the Internal Revenue Code authorized states to adopt qualified tuition plans. The two types of qualified tuition plans are prepaid tuition and college savings plans.

Scholarships - A grant of financial assistance made available to students to assist with the payment of education related expenses. Scholarships are available for academic or athletic achievement. Scholarships can be provided to undergraduate or graduate students.

Stafford Loans - Student loans administered by the U.S. Department of Education.

Teacher Education Assistance for College and Higher Education (TEACH) Grant - A grant that provides up to $4,000 per year for students that intend to teach in a public or private elementary, middle, or high school that serves a community of low-income families.

Uniform Gift to Minors Act (UGMA) - Allows minors to own cash or securities. The UGMA/UTMA accounts are governed by state law that requires the custodian of the account, usually a parent or grandparent, to manage the account for the benefit of the minor child.

Uniform Transfer to Minors Act (UTMA) - Allows minors to own cash, securities, and real estate. The UGMA/UTMA accounts are governed by state law that requires the custodian of the account, usually a parent or grandparent, to manage the account for the benefit of the minor child.

U.S. Government Series EE (issued after 1989) and Series I Bonds - Bonds that can be redeemed to pay for qualified education expenses and the interest earned on the bonds is excluded from taxable income. For purposes of excluding interest income using U.S. Government savings bonds, qualified education expenses include tuition and fees, but do not include room and board.

DISCUSSION QUESTIONS

1. List and define the three methods used to determine the Expected Family Contribution (EFC) for financial aid.

2. Distinguish the difference between an educational grant and an educational loan.

3. List the repayment options for a Stafford Loan.

4. What are the two types of PLUS Loans?

5. What are the consequences for defaulting on student loans?

6. Define the two types of qualified tuition plans.

7. Define a Coverdell Education Savings Account (ESA).

8. Discuss a tax advantage to the student loan interest deduction.

9. Distinguish between the American Opportunity Tax Credit and the Lifetime Learning Credit.

10. Discuss tax deductions / tax credits restrictions as pertains to education expenses.

11. Discuss the differences between scholarships and fellowships.

12. Explain the disadvantages to using UGMA / UTMA accounts to fund a college education.

13. Discuss the features of a nontaxable employer provided education assistance program.

14. List and briefly describe the four primary methods for calculating the amount needed for education funding.

1. Which of the following statements concerning educational tax credits and savings opportunities is correct?

    a. The Lifetime Learning Credit is equal to 10% of qualified educational expenses up to a certain limit.

    b. The American Opportunity Tax Credit (AOTC) is only available for the first 3 years of postsecondary education.

    c. A parent who claims a child as a dependent is entitled to take the AOTC credit for the educational expenses of the child.

    d. The contribution limit for Coverdell Education Savings Accounts is applied per year per donor.

2. Mitch and Jennifer have AGI of $125,000 and have not planned for their children's education. Their children are ages 17 and 18 and the parents anticipate paying $20,000 per year, per child for education expenses. Which of the following is the most appropriate recommendation to pay for the children's education?

    a. 529 Savings Plan.

    b. PLUS Loan.

    c. Pell Grant.

    d. Coverdell ESA.

3. Tan and Chia are contemplating making a contribution to their grandchildren's education fund. They are both retired, have a significant amount of discretionary income and are concerned about estate transfer taxes. Which of the following education planning techniques would you recommend?

    a. Prepaid Tuition.

    b. Coverdell ESA.

    c. UGMA or UTMA.

    d. 529 Savings Plan.

4. All of the following statements are true, except:

    a. The American Opportunity Tax Credit is only available for the first four years of post-secondary education.

    b. The Lifetime Learning Credit is only available for the first two years of post-secondary education.

    c. The American Opportunity Tax Credit is awarded on a per student basis.

    d. The Lifetime Learning Credit is awarded on a per family basis.

5. Which of the following types of aid are not need based?

    a. Pell Grant.
    b. Plus Loan.
    c. Perkins Loan.
    d. Subsidized Stafford Loan.

6. The following type of financial aid is awarded to students with a low EFC, and funds are guaranteed to be available if a student qualifies:

    a. Pell Grant.
    b. Plus Loan.
    c. Work Study.
    d. Stafford Loan.

7. Roshan is a freshman at Florida State University where his tuition is $4,000. Shante, his older sister, is a graduate student at Expensive University, where tuition is $25,000. What is the maximum tax credit Roshan and Shante's parents can take?

    a. $2,000.
    b. $3,650.
    c. $3,800.
    d. $4,500.

8. What is one of the primary differences between a Coverdell ESA and a 529 Savings Plan?

    a. A Coverdell can be used for private elementary, middle, or high school.
    b. A Coverdell does not have a phase-out limit for participation.
    c. A 529 Savings Plan has a phaseout limit for participation.
    d. A Coverdell allows 5-year proration of contributions.

9. Reba has a son, Chad (age 18), a freshman at Tulane University with tuition of $30,000 per year. Reba's AGI is $45,000. She takes a withdrawal of $20,000 from her 529 Savings Plan and pays the remaining $10,000 in tuition out of her checking account. Which of the following would you recommend?

    a. Take a Lifetime Learning Credit of $2,000.
    b. Take a American Opportunity Tax Credit (AOTC) of $2,500.
    c. Cannot take AOTC or Lifetime Learning Credit because she took a 529 distribution.
    d. Take AOTC and Lifetime Learning Credit totaling $4,500 ($2,000 + $2,500).

10. Peter wants to save some money for his daughter Gwen's education. Tuition costs $12,500 per year in today's dollars. His daughter was born today and will go to school starting at age 18. She will go to school for 4 years. Peter can earn 11% on his investments and tuition inflation is 7%. How much must Peter save at the end of each year, if he wants to make his last savings payment at the beginning of his daughter's first year of college?

   a. $2,694.56.
   b. $2,789.04.
   c. $3,167.33.
   d. $3,176.43.

11. Kim and Nick are planning to save for their daughter Chloe's college education. Chloe was born today and will attend college for 4 years, starting at age 18. Tuition currently costs $15,000 per year and tuition inflation is expected to be 6%. They believe they can earn 9% on their investments. How much must Kim and Nick save at the end of each year, if they want to make their last savings payment at the beginning of Chloe's first year of college?

   a. $3,869.03.
   b. $3,892.07.
   c. $3,965.04.
   d. $3,978.53.

12. What is the present value of all college education for 5 children ages 0, 1, 1, 3, and 5 if the cost of education is today's dollars is $17,000 per year, education inflation is 5%, and the parents expected portfolio rate of return is 8.5%? The children are expected to be in college 4 years and they will each start at age 18.

   a. $88,775.02.
   b. $148,958.22.
   c. $192,007.89.
   d. $203,085.22.

13. What is the present value of the cost of college education for 4 children ages 1, 3, 5, and 7. The current cost of college is $25,000. The children will begin college at age 18 and be in college for 4 years. Education inflation is expected to be 6% and the parents portfolio rate of return is 8%.

   a. $294,000.
   b. $295,000.
   c. $300,000.
   d. $305,000.

14. Using previous information, how much do the parents have to save annually at year end through the education of the youngest child at pay all college costs?

    a. $17,418.31.

    b. $29,381.57.

    c. $29,921.11.

    d. $30,526.52.

15. Lanie is a single mom who has 3 children, ages 1, 5 and 9. While she is struggling a bit, she would like to pay for half of their education at a public college. The annual cost of education is currently $20,000 and has been increasing at 6% and is expected to continue. Her portfolio that was established for education has $25,000 in it and earns an average rate of return of 8%. If she would like to fund half of four years of college for each of the children, how much must she save each year at the end of the year, for the next nine years (round to the nearest $100)?

    a. $9,400.

    b. $10,700.

    c. $12,300.

    d. $15,800.

16. George has been in academia his entire career and wholeheartedly believes that education is the key to success. He has two daughters, Cindy and Susie. Cindy is a lingerie and swimsuit model who also believes in education, as well as fashion. Cindy has two children, Red and Mauve, who are ages 4 and 2 today. She is also headed to the hospital at this very moment to deliver her third child, who will be named Olive. Susie is an engineer, who used to play rugby in college and also believes in education. Her children, Copper and Mercury, are ages 3 and 5 today, respectively. George believes that with $100,000, a student should be able to obtain a great education, even if it is not the exact amount necessary to fund all of a student's time in college. George would to provide each of his grandchildren with the ability to have $100,000 of purchasing power when they turn 18. Education costs are approximately $30,000 per year at private schools and about $15,000 at public schools. Education costs have been increasing at a consistent rate of 7% per year and are expected to continue, while inflation has been at a steady 3% per year. How much should he set aside today to fund his goal for his grandchildren if he can earn a rate of return of 9%?

    a. $136,383.

    b. $179,983.

    c. $212,444.

    d. $377,520.

17. CJ is 40 and wants to retire in 25 years. He expects to live until age 95. He currently has a salary of $100,000 and expects that he will need about 75% of that if he were retired. He thinks he needs to accumulate $1 million (future dollars) and he will be fine. He currently has $150,000 saved for his retirement that is earning 9%. He is able to save $20,000 towards his retirement. However, he is willing to use some or all of this to fund education for his grandchild, Bob, if and when his retirement objective appears to be set in terms of funding. Edward, Bob's dad and CJ's son, wants Bob to go to school for six years and expect that it will cost $50,000 per year in today's dollars. Inflation has been modest at 3%, while education has been increasing at 6% per year. Edward would like to know how much he should save every year to fund Bob's college expenses assuming that he can max out his dad's (CJ) contribution, which would begin in one year and stop when Bob goes to school. Edward would also begin contributing in one year and stop when Bob goes to school and wants to assume he can earn 9% per year. How much does Edward need to save each year? (round answer to nearest $1,000)

    a. $0 - Dad has it covered.

    b. $4,000.

    c. $9,000.

    d. $15,000.

Quick Quiz Explanations

Quick Quiz 8.1
1. True.
2. False. The financial aid process is initiated by completing the Free Application for Federal Student Aid (FAFSA). The Student Aid Report is available after the completion of the FAFSA and contains the EFC.

Quick Quiz 8.2
1. True.
2. True.
3. False. The grant for students graduating from a rigorous secondary school program of study is the ACG. The FSEOG is awarded to students with exceptional financial need (those with the lowest EFC).

Quick Quiz 8.3
1. False. For an unsubsidized Stafford Loan, the borrower is responsible for interest from the time the funds are disbursed. However, the student may pay the interest expense as incurred or may choose to allow the interest to be added to the loan's outstanding principal. Interest is paid by the federal government on subsidized loans while the borrower is in school and during the six-month grace period before repayment begins.
2. True.
3. False. PLUS Loans are not based on financial need.
4. True.

Quick Quiz 8.4
1. True.
2. True.
3. False. The Act expanded education expenses to include computer technology or equipment (computer and related peripheral equipment) used for educational purposes.

Quick Quiz 8.5
1. True.
2. False. Qualified education expenses do not include room and board when using redeemed Series EE and I bonds funds.

Quick Quiz Explanations

Quick Quiz 8.6
1. True.
2. False. This is the definition for the Lifetime Learning Credit. The American Opportunity Tax Credit provides a tax credit of up to $2,500 (2011) per student for the first four years of qualified education expenses.
3. False. This is the definition for a Fellowship. Scholarships are made available to students to assist with the payment of education related expenses and are for academic or athletic achievement.

Quick Quiz 8.7
1. False. IRA distributions made prior to age 59½ are typically made subject to a 10% tax penalty, which is waived when used for qualified education expenses.
2. True.
3. False. The education expenses may or may not be directly related to the employee's current job duties depending on the employer's policy.

Quick Quiz 8.8
1. False. The uneven cash flow method is the best approach to use when saving continues through the years of college attendance.
2. True.
3. False. The hybrid approach used for education funding calculation combines the concepts of the uneven cash flow and account balance methods.

Investments

LEARNING OBJECTIVES

After reading this chapter, you should be able to:

- Understand risk tolerance and how it is measured.
- Understand historical returns and the relationship between equities, bonds, and treasuries.
- Describe the investment planning process.
- Describe the components of an investment policy statement.
- Describe and calculate the various measurements of investment returns.
- Identify the various types of investment risk and how they are measured.
- Be able to calculate standard deviation and semi-variance and describe beta.
- Be able to identify the risk-adjusted performance measures including Sharpe, Traynor, and Jensen.
- Describe modern portfolio theory, the efficient frontier, and the capital asset pricing model.
- Define portfolio statistics including correlation coefficient, the coefficient of determination, and portfolio risk for a two asset portfolio.
- Describe alternative investments such as equity, debt, real estate, and derivatives.
- Identify the methods of valuing an equity security.
- Identify the risks to investing in bonds, real estate and derivatives.
- Describe investment companies, unit investment trusts exchange traded funds, open-ended investment companies, closed-ended investment companies, and various types of mutual funds.
- Understand asset allocation and investment analysis for an individual client.
- Identify the regulatory authorities that impact elements of the financial planning process. (Examples include regulation of accountancy, legal practice, real estate law, insurance regulation, etc.)*
- Differentiate between investment knowledge that is proper to use in the evaluation of securities and insider information.*

- Demonstrate a comprehensive understanding of investment advisor regulation and financial planning aspects of the ERISA.*
- Explain the relevant licensing, reporting and compliance issues that may affect the business model used by a financial planning firm.*

* CFP Board Resource Document - Student-Centered Learning Objectives based upon CFP Board Principal Topics.

INTRODUCTION

Investing is the process whereby capital resources are allocated and committed by investors with the expectation of earning future positive economic returns. The overall investment return expected is primarily a function of, and usually dependent upon, the riskiness of the investment. Investment returns can be in the form of current income (interest or dividends) and/or capital appreciation. This chapter discusses the relationship between risk and return and provides the financial planner with the means to measure both risk and return for the individual client/investor. Investment alternatives are then reviewed, as well as the importance of asset allocation and investment performance analysis.

Financial planners employ tools to assess the client's ability and willingness to accept investment risk, thus determining the client's risk tolerance as part of the investment planning process. An **investment policy statement** is a written document, agreed upon by the client and the advisor, which specifically identifies the investment goals of the clients and the strategies and parameters, such as risk tolerance, time horizon, asset allocation, and acceptable investment vehicles, that will be employed to reach such goals. The investment goals are stated in dollar terms and also in terms of time. To achieve the investment goals, the client should be expected to invest at a risk level consistent with an assessment of his risk tolerance. The risk tolerance assessment can be used to build an investment portfolio that has the desired expected returns that will help to achieve the client's goals. All of these factors are included in the investment planning process and are expressed in an investment policy statement (discussed later in this chapter).

INVESTMENT PLANNING

As part of the investment planning process, the financial planner evaluates the client's goals in terms of both dollar value and time. The client's goals are assessed together with risk tolerance in designing the appropriate investment strategy. The client's risk tolerance is a combination of an ability and willingness to accept investment risk. The planner will develop an investment plan considering the client's investment ability (an objective state of being, based on the client's financial profile) and willingness (a subjective state of being) to take on investment risk and to commit dollars over time to reach the investment goals. The risk tolerance questionnaire provides both the planner and the client with a clear understanding of the client's tolerance for taking risk.

RISK TOLERANCE (ABILITY TO HANDLE RISK)

Ability to take on investment risk is a function of objective measures (the client's financial profile) such as the investment goals, the time horizon for each goal, the need for liquidity, the client's tax situation, and the unique circumstances facing the investor, such as a high ability to save, high salary, or low living expenses relative to income. Basically, the more a person can save, the longer the time horizon for the investment goals, and the less current the need for liquidity, the greater the investor's ability to take on risk. However, ability does not mean willingness, which is psychological in nature.

RISK TOLERANCE QUESTIONNAIRE (WILLINGNESS TO TAKE ON RISK)

A **risk tolerance questionnaire** evaluates an investor's willingness to take on risk by inquiring about risk issues, usually by asking questions or evaluating statements such as:

- In a volatile stock market that is expected to be down 20 percent, what percentage of your portfolio are you willing to lose?
- Rank your understanding of the stock market.
- Rank your comfort level with investing in the stock market.
- By what percentage do you want your stock portfolio to increase during an up market?

These questions and statements can help the planner determine whether the client is physiologically risk averse or risk tolerant. A risk averse investor is more conservative and requires significantly more return in order to consider investing in a higher risk investment. A risk tolerant investor is more willing to accept risk for a small increase in return than a risk averse investor.

Key Concepts

Underline/highlight the answers as you read:

1. Identify the purpose of a risk tolerance questionnaire.

2. Determine how the ability and willingness of the client to accept risk is gauged.

3. Identify the four steps of the investment planning process.

4. Identify the components of an investment policy statement.

Other questions the financial planner should ask to further evaluate risk tolerance include the investment time horizon of the investor, as follows:

- At what point in time does the investor expect to require the use of the invested capital?
- How much does the investor have in an emergency fund and how long will the funds last?
- What are the investor's short-term, intermediate term, and long-term goals?

EXHIBIT 9.1 SAMPLE RISK TOLERANCE QUESTIONNAIRE (ABBREVIATED)

RISK TOLERANCE QUESTIONNAIRE

How much do you have in cash reserves to cover non-discretionary cash flows?
1. Less than two months.
2. Two to three months.
3. Three to five months.
4. Six months or more.

How long is it until you need the money from your investment for your goal?
1. Five years or less.
2. Six to ten years.
3. Ten to fifteen years.
4. Greater than fifteen years.

If the stock market is down 20% or more for the year, how much of your investment are you willing to lose?
1. None.
2. 5% or less.
3. 10% or less.
4. It does not matter as long as the investments are appropriate for my objective.

Which statement best describes your investment experience?
1. None.
2. I have little background in purchasing stocks, some mutual funds.
3. I am comfortable with purchasing mutual funds, bonds, and stocks.
4. I have extensive investment experience with mutual funds, bonds, stocks, and derivates.

If the stock market is up 20% for the year, how much do you expect your investments to return?
1. Less than ½ of the market, however preserving capital is my primary goal.
2. Half of the market but protecting against potential losses by a riskier portfolio is not preferred.
3. 15-20% by accepting a sufficient amount of risk.
4. More than 20% by investing in an investment portfolio more risky than the market.

Total Score:_____ (Add the point value next to each response)

Point Ranges:	Recommended Portfolios:
16 - 20: Aggressive	Aggressive: 80% Equities / 20% Bonds
11 - 15: Moderately Aggressive	Moderately Aggressive: 65% Equities / 35% Bonds
6 - 10: Moderate	Moderate: 50% Equities / 50% Bonds
1 - 5: Conservative	Conservative: 20% Equities / 80% Bonds

Note: See the Approaches chapter for a discussion of the Global Portfolio Allocation Scoring System (PASS) for Individual Investors - developed by Dr. William Droms (Georgetown University) and Steven N. Strauss, (DromsStrauss Advisors Inc.). PASS will be used in the Rudolph Part 1 case.

The ability and willingness of the client to accept risk can be gauged by various factors. For example, the longer the time horizon of a client, the more risk that the client is able to accept in the investment portfolio. The client's ability to accept risk is associated with time horizon, liquidity needs, tax conditions, and unique circumstances. The client's willingness to accept risk is associated with the psychological condition of risk tolerance.

The charts below identify various potential risk tolerance levels. For example, if the client's ability to take on investment risk is higher than the client's willingness, then the financial planner needs to educate the client accordingly.

	Ability	Willingness
Low		✓
Medium	✓	
High	✓	

If the client's ability to take on investment risk is lower then the client's willingness, then the financial planner needs to educate until the client has a clearer understanding of his objective financial ability.

	Ability	Willingness
Low	✓	
Medium		✓
High		✓

Typically, only when the client's willingness and ability to take risk are equal does the financial planner proceed to develop an investment strategy. However, if willingness remains less than ability after the client is fully informed, then the planner will have to use the willingness measure to develop an investment strategy. The reverse is not true.

Once the client's risk tolerance is understood, it can be translated into a risk measurement (conservative, moderate, or aggressive) that is then used to guide investment choices.

The more risk the client is able and willing to accept, the greater the allocation of the investment portfolio to equities, which have greater volatility than bonds. Volatility is measured by standard deviation, which also measures the total riskiness of an investment portfolio. If the client's portfolio is appropriately diversified, the financial planner can use beta for risk measurement, otherwise standard deviation should be used. Semivariance is an additional measure of risk that only takes into consideration downside volatility. The chart below illustrates the historical risk (as measured by standard deviation) and return relationship between equities, bonds, and Treasury bills.

EXHIBIT 9.2 **HISTORICAL RISK AND RETURN RELATIONSHIP BETWEEN EQUITIES, BONDS, AND TREASURY BILLS 1900 - 2008)**

	Return	Risk* (Standard Deviation)	Range of Expected Annual Returns
Equities	11.2%	20.2%	-29.2 to 51.6
Government Bonds	5.5%	8.3%	-11.1 to 22.1
Government Bills	4.0%	2.8%	-1.6 to 9.6
Inflation	3.1%	4.9%	-6.7 to 12.9

*Expected returns in a normal market in a year range by 2 standard deviations +/-.

Source: Elroy, Dimson, Paul Marsh, and Mike Staunton. Triumph of the Optimists: 101 Years of Global Investment Returns

Expected Return

Expected return is generally the compound annual rate of return expected for an investment or investment portfolio. The return an investor expects from an investment is primarily a function of the riskiness of the investment(s). If an investor is investing in a risk-free asset, like a short-term U.S. Treasury bill, then both the expected rate of return and the required rate of return are likely to be relatively low. If an investor takes on substantially more risk by investing in a small startup company, the investor will require a higher expected rate of return. There are various methods of calculating actual return, which are discussed later in this chapter.

THE INVESTMENT PLANNING PROCESS

The **investment planning process** is a series of steps the financial planner and client follow to build an investment portfolio, which is designed to achieve the client's investment goals. The investment planning process consists of the following four steps:

1. The client and planner create a written investment policy statement (with risk tolerance having been derived from the risk tolerance questionnaire and financial profile), which serves as a guide to the client's investment strategy. The written investment policy statement assists the client by helping to ensure realistic return expectations consistent with acceptable risk and enforces discipline in the investment process.

2. The planner examines the external environment focusing on the expected short-term and intermediate term economic, political, social, legal, and tax conditions.

3. The planner and client select an investment portfolio consistent with the investment policy statement.

4. Periodic monitoring, updating, and evaluating of investment performance by the planner is required, as well as revisiting those conditions described in step 2 above.

INVESTMENT POLICY STATEMENT

An investment policy statement is a written document, agreed upon by the client and the advisor, which specifically identifies the investment goals of the clients and the strategies and parameters, such as risk tolerance, time horizon, asset allocation, and acceptable investment vehicles, that will be employed to reach such goals. The statement guides the financial planner and client regarding appropriate investment choices and serves as a benchmark to measure performance.

The investment policy statement should begin with a broad set of goal(s) such as:

- Capital appreciation for retirement
- Capital appreciation for the education goal
- Generate income to fund retirement
- Capital appreciation and preservation for a down payment on a house

The client's objectives expressed in terms of both risk and expected return should also be included in the investment policy statement. A client's return objective can be expressed either as a broad measure (capital appreciation, capital preservation, or current income) or as an absolute or relative percentage return (i.e., 8% or a spread of 4% over inflation). The returns on various asset classes for various years are presented later in this chapter.

The investment policy statement should also include a section that establishes the conditions under which the investment portfolio will be rebalanced. Rebalancing will generally be necessary when the overall riskiness of the portfolio attains a level that is inappropriate for the investor or the amount allocated to a particular asset class is inappropriate because of gains or losses in that particular asset class. By establishing a predetermined rebalancing threshold and policy, the advisor and client have a plan with which to manage the investment portfolio.

An additional section of the investment policy statement covering constraints to the investment policy should be included. The financial planner should be aware of the types of constraints that may impact the selection of investments. Constraints generally include:

- Liquidity needs (i.e., for a retiree)
- Investment time horizon
- Tax issues (taxable versus tax-deferred account)
- Social
- Legal
- Regulatory issues
- Unique circumstances to the client (i.e., dependant parent(s), high net worth client, special needs children, etc.)

Quick Quiz 9.1

Highlight the answer to these questions:

1. A risk tolerance questionnaire identifies an investor's investment goals and guides the investor regarding appropriate investment choices.
   a. True
   b. False

2. The expected return is a function of the riskiness of an investment and is the rate of return expected for an asset or investment portfolio.
   a. True
   b. False

3. The investment planning process includes creating an investment policy statement, examines the external environment, involves selecting a portfolio consistent with the investment policy statement, and includes the periodic monitoring, updating and evaluating of investment performance.
   a. True
   b. False

False, True, True.

The following is a sample investment policy statement that covers the criteria necessary to manage a client's investment portfolio selection.

EXHIBIT 9.3 **SAMPLE INVESTMENT POLICY STATEMENT**

Investment Policy Statement
Client: Michael
Age: 42 (divorced)

Goals:
- Save for retirement
- Retirement Goal: 80% of pre-retirement income at age 67
- Provide college education funding for four children (Jordan age 6, Colin age 4, Cate age 2 & Caroline age 1)
- Education Goal: Provide each child with $30,000 in today's dollars for college at their age 18

Returns and Inflation
- Expected Return: 8.5% annually or 5.5% real returns
- Expected Inflation: 3% annually
- Expected Education Inflation: 5% annually

Risks and Inflation
- Risk Tolerance: Moderately aggressive
- Risk Measure: Standard deviation for overall portfolio of 12%

Rebalance
- When the overall portfolio standard deviation is outside the range of 12% +/-2%

Constraints
- Time Horizon Retirement: 25 years
- Time Horizon Education: 12-18 years
- Liquidity Needs: none for 12 years.
- Tax Rate: 35% marginal federal and no state income tax
- Regulatory Issues: none
- Unique: Income of $250,000 annually, lives modestly, saves 18-20% of current income, pays modest child support.

The next section of this chapter focuses on several methods of measuring investment returns, which allows a financial planner to assist clients in comparing investment performance among and between various investments.

MEASURING INVESTMENT RETURNS

The following methods of calculating actual return are discussed in this section of the chapter:
- The Holding Period Return (HPR)
- The Arithmetic (Average) Return (AR)
- The Geometric Return (GR)
- The Weighted Average (Expected) Return (WAR)

- The Internal Rate of Return (IRR)
- Dollar Weighted and Time Weighted Returns

THE HOLDING PERIOD RETURN (HPR)

The **holding period return** represents the total return for an investment or portfolio over the period of time the investment or portfolio was held. The holding period return is not a compound rate of return because there is no consideration for the time period over which the investment was made. While the calculation is straightforward, it is primarily useful when the holding period is one year. If comparing the holding period return between investments, it is important that the holding periods are the same for the two investments, so as to make a fair comparison of performance. Note that holding period return is not an annual return.

Key Concepts

Underline/highlight the answers as you read:

1. Identify the six ways to measure actual investment returns.

2. Identify which measurements of actual investment returns take compounding into consideration and which ones do not.

3. Determine the difference between systematic risk and unsystematic risk.

4. Determine the different measurements of investment risks.

$$\text{HPR} = \frac{\text{Selling Price - Purchase Price +/- Cash Flows}}{\text{Purchase Price}}$$

Carson purchases a stock at $100 per share, receives $5 of dividends per share, and later sells the stock at $125. His holding period return is:

EXAMPLE 9.1

$$\text{HPR} = \frac{\text{Selling Price - Purchase Price +/- Cash Flows}}{\text{Purchase Price}}$$

$$\text{HPR} = \frac{\$125 - \$100 + \$5}{100}$$

HPR = 30%

While a 30% return sounds great, it does not speak to the time period over which it was earned. If the investment was held for 10 years, the return would only average 3% annually.

THE ARITHMETIC (AVERAGE) RETURN (AR)

The **arithmetic or average return** is also known as the simple average return. The arithmetic return does not take compounding into consideration, because it is a simple average return. It is the sum of all returns, divided by the number of periods:

$$AR = \frac{\sum_{i=1}^{n} r_i}{n}$$

EXAMPLE 9.2

Rachael has owned a stock for three years, with the following returns:

Year 1: 12%

Year 2: 5%

Year 3: <2%>

The arithmetic return is:

$$\frac{12 + 5 + (2)}{3} = 5\%$$

While the arithmetic return is useful, it also has limitations. Since it does not take compounding into consideration, the AR can provide misleading results, especially with volatile returns.

EXAMPLE 9.3

Aiden purchases a stock for $100 per share. At the end of the first year, the stock is worth $200 per share, representing a 100% return. At the end of the second year, the stock has declined to $100, representing a 50% loss.

The average return is calculated as:

$$\frac{100\% + (50\%)}{2} = 25\%$$

The average return is calculated as 25%. However, the actual return cannot possibly be 25% when the value of the stock at the end of the second year is the same as the value when it was purchased. Clearly, the actual return is 0%. Since the arithmetic return does not take compounding into consideration, the result is misleading. To overcome this limitation, the geometric return is preferred.

THE GEOMETRIC RETURN (GR)

The **geometric return** is a time-weighted compounded rate of return. In other words, the geometric return takes compounding into consideration. The formula for the geometric return is:

$$GR = \sqrt[n]{(1 + r_1)(1 + r_2)\ldots (1 + r_n)} - 1 \times 100$$

Bennett purchases a stock for $100 per share. At the end of the first year, the stock is worth $200 per share, representing a 100% return. At the end of the second year, the stock has declined to $100, representing a 50% loss.

EXAMPLE 9.4

The geometric return is calculated as follows:

$$\sqrt[2]{(1 + 100\%)(1 - 50\%)} - 1 \times 100$$

Answer: 0%

Notice that the geometric return calculates the actual return of 0% because it takes into consideration compounding. It is a more precise calculation than the arithmetic return discussed above.

Caitlynn has owned a stock for three years, with the following returns:

EXAMPLE 9.5

Year 1: 12%

Year 2: 5%

Year 3: <2%>

$$\sqrt[3]{(1.12)(1.05)(0.98)} - 1 \times 100$$

Answer: 4.8442%

Note: this answer is equivalent to the internal rate of return (IRR). You should also quickly be able to calculate the arithmetic return, which is equal to 5%. The geometric mean will generally be less than or equal to the arithmetic mean.

THE WEIGHTED AVERAGE (EXPECTED) RETURN (WAR)

The **weighted average return** is based on the dollar amount or percentage of a portfolio invested in each asset or security. Investments with a larger allocation or weighting will contribute more to the overall return of the portfolio whereas investments with a smaller allocation or weighting will contribute less to the overall return of the portfolio.

Karen owns the following securities in her portfolio. What is the weighted average expected return of the portfolio?

Security	Fair Market Value	Expected Return
A	$10,000	10%
B	$15,000	8%
C	$25,000	6%

Security	Fair Market Value	Total Portfolio Value	Expected Return	% of Portfolio	Weighted Return
A	$10,000	$50,000	x 10%	20%	0.020
B	$15,000	$50,000	x 8%	30%	0.024
C	$25,000	$50,000	x 6%	50%	0.030
				Weighted Average Expected Return	0.074 or 7.4%

THE INTERNAL RATE OF RETURN (IRR)

The **Internal Rate of Return (IRR)** is the compounded annual rate of return for investments of differing cash inflows and cash outflows. The internal rate of return assumes that any periodic payments are reinvested at the internal rate of return. If an investor reinvests the income at a lower rate that the IRR, then the investor's actual IRR will be lower than originally calculated.

EXAMPLE 9.6

Three years ago, William purchased a stock for $20. Over the past three years, the stock has paid the following dividends, which William has reinvested.

Year 1: $1.00

Year 2: $1.25

Year 3: $1.50

At the end of the third year, the stock price is $24. What is William's compounded rate of return (IRR) if he sells the stock for $24?

10BII Keystrokes	12C Keystrokes
20 [+/-] [CFj]	20 [CHS] [g] [CF0]
1.00 [CFj]	1.00 [g] [CFj]
1.25 [CFj]	1.25 [g] [CFj]
1.50 [+] 24 [=] [CFj]	1.50 [ENTER] 24 [+] [g] [CFj]
[ORANGE]	[f]
[IRR/YR]	[IRR]
Answer: 12.08%	**Answer: 12.08%**

DOLLAR-WEIGHTED AND TIME-WEIGHTED RETURNS

The dollar and time-weighted returns are internal rates of return or compounded rate of return measures. A dollar-weighted return is the IRR based on the investor's actual cash flows. The time-weighted return is the IRR based on the security's cash flow.

Frank purchases 1 share of XO stock for $75. One year later the stock pays a dividend of $5, and Frank purchases an additional share for $90. Frank sells both shares of the stock one year later for $100 per share. What is Frank's dollar-weighted and time-weighted return?

EXAMPLE 9.7

Dollar-Weighted Return

Period	Cash Flow	
0	($75)	
1	($85)	$5 dividend - $90 share purchase
2	$200	2 shares sold at $100 each

10BII Keystrokes	12C Keystrokes
75 [+/-] [ORANGE] [CFj]	75 [CHS] [g] [CF0]
85 [+/-] [ORANGE] [CFj]	85 [CHS] [g] [CFj]
200 [ORANGE] [CFj]	200 [g] [CFj]
[ORANGE] [IRR]	[f] [IRR]
Answer: 16.19%	**Answer: 16.19%**

Time-Weighted Return

Period	Cash Flow	
0	($75)	
1	$5	$5 dividend
2	$100	Ending share price

10BII Keystrokes	12C Keystrokes
75 [+/-] [ORANGE] [CFj]	75 [CHS] [g] [CF0]
5 [ORANGE] [CFj]	5 [g] [CFj]
100 [ORANGE] [CFj]	100 [g] [CFj]
[ORANGE] [IRR]	[f] [IRR]
Answer: 18.85%	**Answer: 18.85%**

An investor is always concerned with dollar-weighted returns because dollar-weighted returns take into consideration exactly when the shares were purchased (at what price), any subsequent cash flows (such as dividends) and when (and at what price) the shares were sold. Mutual funds always report time-weighted returns because they are concerned about the price of the fund at the beginning of a period, the end of a period and any distributions made during the period. Depending on the cash flows of the investor, he may experience similar or vastly different rates of return compared to the investment time weighted return.

TYPES OF INVESTMENT RISKS AND MEASURING INVESTMENT RISKS

Risk is the uncertainty associated with investment returns. More specifically, risk is the possibility that actual returns will be different from what is expected. There is a direct relationship between risk and an investor's expected return. As risk increases, so does the investor's expected rate of return. The risk premium is the amount of return above the risk-free rate of return that an investor will require to invest in a risky asset. The risk-free rate is generally considered to be the U.S. Treasury rate. The risk premium is determined by the amount of risk associated with an investment. This next section of the chapter discusses the components of risk, the measurement of risk and how to maximize an investor's return for any given level of risk.

TYPES OF INVESTMENT RISKS

Systematic Risk
Systematic risk represents the risk that is inherent in the "system" and cannot be eliminated through diversification. The system represents U.S. market risk. Regardless of how many stocks and industries are combined into a portfolio, the portfolio will still be subject to at least one systematic risk. Examples of systematic risk are:
- Purchasing Power Risk
- Reinvestment Rate Risk
- Interest Rate Risk
- Market Risk
- Exchange Rate Risk

Purchasing Power Risk
Purchasing power risk is the risk that inflation will cause prices to increase and a dollar today will not be able to purchase the same amount of goods and services tomorrow. Investments that provide a fixed return, such as a bond paying a fixed interest rate, will be subject to more purchasing power risk than those investments that tend to change in value as prices change, such as commodities.

Reinvestment Rate Risk
Reinvestment rate risk is the risk that an investor will not be able to reinvest income received from current investments at the same rate of return as the current investment return. Investments that pay current income, such as a bond paying interest or a stock paying a dividend, are subject to reinvestment rate risk. Investments that do not pay current income, such as a non-dividend paying stock or a zero coupon bond are not immediately subject to reinvestment rate risk. Once an investment is sold, the investor is subject to reinvestment rate risk.

Interest Rate Risk

Interest rate risk is the risk that changes in interest rates will inversely impact both equities (stocks) and bonds. Generally, as interest rates increase (decrease), the price of equities and bonds decreases (increases). Changes in interest rates impact the cost of borrowing for companies, the discount rate or required rate of return for investors when valuing securities and the overall attractiveness of alternative investments.

Market Risk

Market risk is the risk that in the short term, the daily fluctuations of the market tend to bring all securities in the same direction. Many securities are highly correlated with the market. The old expression, "during high tide all boats rise, during low tide all boats fall" holds true for the market and security prices. When the market increases, most equities will also increases in price. When the market declines, most equities will decrease in price.

Exchange Rate Risk

Exchange rate risk is the risk that international investments and domestic companies that import or export goods are subject to changes in the relationship between the price of a dollar and foreign currencies. Changes in foreign currency rates can adversely effect the value of foreign investments or of domestic investments with substantial foreign operations.

Unsystematic Risk

Unsystematic risk represents the risk that can be diversified away by combining multiple stocks from multiple industries into one portfolio. Unsystematic risks are unique to one firm, industry or country and can be reduced and perhaps eliminated by building a diversified portfolio. Examples of unsystematic risk are:
- Business Risk
- Country Risk
- Default Risk
- Executive Risk
- Financial Risk
- Government / Regulation Risk

Business Risk

Business risk is the inherent risk of conducting business within a particular industry. Different industries have different risks that make their industry unique. Microsoft is primarily in the software development industry and it faces the risk of copyright infringement and illegal copying and distribution of it's software. Those risks are significantly different than Exxon Mobile, which is subject to commodity pricing risk and regulatory risk. Business risk is associated with the asset side of the balance sheet.

Country Risk

Country risk is the risk of political and economic stability or instability for a country that a company faces when doing business in that particular country. Starting and operating a business in the U.S. has significantly different country risk than starting and operating a business in Iraq or Venezuela.

Default Risk

Default risk is the risk that a company may not be able to repay its debt obligations. If a company has any type of debt, it is subject to default risk. Debt may include bonds issued by a company or municipality. Default or credit risk is on the liability side of the balance sheet.

Executive Risk

Executive risk is the risk of moral character of the executives running the company. The extent to which executives break laws, regulations, or ethical standards that may negatively impact a company and investment returns. Executives may also manage a business to generate short-term returns at the expense of long-term gains. The short-term gains may mask the risks to the long-term success of the company.

Financial Risk

Financial risk is the amount of leverage the company is using in its capital structure. Leverage is a measure of the amount of debt a company uses to capitalize the business. Capital structure may consist of a combination of both debt and equity. The more debt a company takes on, the more leverage it is using and the more financial risk that is present. Companies like Microsoft and Apple have zero debt in their capital structure, so there is no financial risk. However, the airline and cable industries use high degrees of leverage because of the large initial and continuing capital investment required. Historically, both the airline and cable industries are subject to significant financial risk. Financial risk is on the liability side of the balance sheet.

Government/Regulation Risk

Government or regulation risk is the potential risk that a country may pass a law or regulation that negatively impacts a particular industry. In 2003, Japan stopped importing beef from the U.S. due to a mad cow disease breakout in the U.S. At the time, Japan was the top international importer of beef from the U.S. The impact of Japan's decision on the U.S. beef industry is an example of government or regulation risk.

One of the goals in building a portfolio is to combine stocks from a broad range of industries, which will eliminate diversifiable risk and reduce the overall variability of returns within the portfolio. As carefully selected securities are added to a portfolio, the total riskiness of the portfolio, as measured by standard deviation, is reduced. On average, a portfolio with approximately 20 carefully selected securities will result in a diversified portfolio.

TOTAL RISK

EXHIBIT 9.4

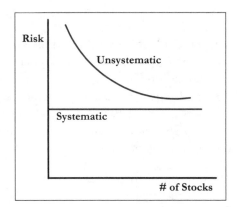

Exhibit 9.4 illustrates how unsystematic risk is reduced and may be eliminated in a well diversified portfolio, such that the only relevant risk is systematic risk. As more securities from multiple industries are combined within a portfolio, both unsystematic risk and total risk in the portfolio will be reduced.

MEASURING INVESTMENT RISKS

Investment risk is broadly defined as the uncertainty surrounding returns. Risk can be measured using both Beta (β) and Standard Deviation (σ). Beta is used to measure the risk for a well diversified investment portfolio, while standard deviation is used to measure the total risk of any investment portfolio regardless of whether the portfolio is well diversified.

Beta

Beta is a common measure of risk that is derived from regression analysis when comparing the returns for a particular security or portfolio to market benchmark returns. Beta is a measure of systematic risk and provides a comparison of the volatility of a security or portfolio to the market benchmark. The market is predefined as having a beta of 1.0. Portfolios that have a beta greater than 1.0 are more volatile than the market, whereas portfolios with a beta less than 1.0 are less volatile than the market. A portfolio with a beta of 1.50 is 50 percent more volatile than the market. A beta that is negative means that the security or portfolio generally moves the opposite direction of the market. The discussion of the capital asset

Quick Quiz 9.2

Highlight the answer to these questions:

1. The holding period return represents the time period and investment return is measured.
   a. True
   b. False

2. The geometric return is known as the simple average return.
   a. True
   b. False

3. Purchasing power risk is a type of unsystematic risk and is the risk that inflation will cause prices to increase.
   a. True
   b. False

True, False, False.

pricing model later in the chapter illustrates how beta can be used to determine the expected return for an investment or portfolio.

Since beta only measures systematic risk, it is a good measure of risk only when the portfolio is well diversified. Diversified portfolios have little or no unsystematic risk and, therefore, the majority of diversified portfolio returns are a result of systematic risk or market risk. However, if a portfolio is not well diversified (much of the return is due to unsystematic risk) then beta does not capture all of the relevant risk. If beta does not capture all of the relevant risk, then beta is not an appropriate measure of total risk and the planner should use standard deviation as the appropriate risk measure.

The beta of a stock can be found on Yahoo finance (finance.yahoo.com) under the key statistics for a company. The beta of a mutual fund can be found on Morningstar (morningstar.com) under fund research.

Standard Deviation

Standard deviation measures the total risk of an investment. The larger the standard deviation, the more risky the asset. Standard deviation also measures the amount of variation around a historical average or mean return. A small standard deviation indicates that the annual returns are close to the average return, while a large standard deviation indicates a large variation around the average return and therefore, more uncertainty. Standard deviation is calculated using the following formula:

$$\sigma_r = \sqrt{\frac{\sum_{t=1}^{n} (r_t - \bar{r})^2}{n}}$$

If all the data points are known, the standard deviation of a population formula (σ_r) will calculate the standard deviation. If, however, only a set of data or sample from a population is used, the standard deviation of a sample size (S_r) can be used.

$$S_r = \sqrt{\frac{\sum_{t=1}^{n} (r_t - \bar{r})^2}{n-1}}$$

EXAMPLE 9.8

For example, the returns for a portfolio over the last three years are as follows:

Year 1   8%

Year 2   10%

Year 3   12%

The average return is ten percent [(0.08 + 0.10 + 0.12) ÷ 3] and the standard deviation is two percent.

$$S_r = \sqrt{\frac{(8\% - 10\%)^2 + (10\% - 10\%)^2 + (12\% - 10\%)^2}{3 - 1}}$$

$$S_r = \sqrt{\frac{4\% + 0\% + 4\%}{2}}$$

$$S_r = 2$$

Alternatively, a financial calculator can be used to calculate the standard deviation.

Given the annual returns below, which investment is more risky (using standard deviation as the risk measure)?

EXAMPLE 9.9

	Investment A	Investment B
Year 1	10%	21%
Year 2	13%	19%
Year 3	7%	23%

Keystrokes for Investment A:

10BII Keystrokes	12C Keystrokes
10 [Σ+]	10 [Σ+]
13 [Σ+]	13[Σ+]
7 [Σ+]	7 [Σ+]
[ORANGE] [Sx] [Sy]	[g] [.]
Answer: 3 or 3%	**Answer: 3 or 3%**

Keystrokes for Investment B:

10BII Keystrokes	12C Keystrokes
21[Σ+]	21 [Σ+]
19 [Σ+]	19[Σ+]
23 [Σ+]	23 [Σ+]
[ORANGE] [Sx] [Sy]	[g] [.]
Answer: 2 or 2%	**Answer: 2 or 2%**

Therefore, investment A is more risky than investment B because the standard deviation for A is greater than the standard deviation of B. It is important to note that the key strokes above are calculating the standard deviation based on a sample of returns as opposed to the population of returns.

Normal distributions are frequently used in science and other fields to describe the distribution of occurrences or outcomes from a specific event. It turns out that investment returns are often distributed in the shape of a normal distribution, allowing us to make estimates about potential investment outcomes.

A **normal distribution** describes how investment returns are dispersed around the average return. A normal distribution results in a bell shaped curve, as depicted in the following graph.

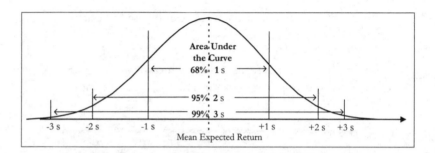

A normal distribution will have the following distribution expectations.

Standard Deviation	Probability of Returns
+/- 1	68%
+/- 2	95%
+/- 3	99%

The two charts above illustrate that for a normal distribution, 68% of outcomes will fall within one standard deviation from the mean return, 95% of outcomes will fall within two standard deviations from the mean and that 99% of all outcomes will fall within three standard deviations from the mean. The mean return is calculated as a simple average and the standard deviation is calculated as described above.

Consider the example from above with returns of 8%, 10%, and 12%. The mean of this distribution is 10% and it has a standard deviation of 2%. Therefore, the range from the mean minus one standard deviation to the mean plus one standard deviation should contain 68% of all outcomes. This range is from 8% (10% - 2%) to 12% (10% + 2%). It follows that 95% of outcomes will fall between 6% and 14% by moving out two standard deviations from the mean and 99% of outcomes will fall between 4% and 16% by moving out three standard deviations from the mean.

The normal distribution relationship allows the advisor to predict probabilities of returns (outcomes), which can assist in determining the likelihood of reaching specific goals of a client and understanding the likelihood of receiving negative returns.

EXAMPLE 9.10

Mutual fund SCG has an average return of 12% and a standard deviation of 12%. What is the probability that the fund will return less than 0% in a given year?

At +/- 1 standard deviation from the average, 68% of the area under the curve is covered. By taking the 68% and dividing by 2, the area between 0 to 12% is 34%. Add 34% to the probability that the returns are greater than 12% (note that this is 50% of the area under the curve) equals 84% of the area under the curve. By subtracting 84% from 100% = 16% (the probability that the fund returns less than 0%).

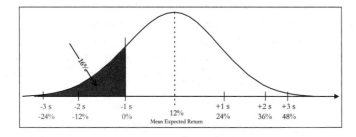

EXAMPLE 9.11

Mutual fund HLG has an average return of 10% and a standard deviation of 5%. What is the probability that the fund will return less than 0%?

At +/- 2 standard deviations from the average, 95% of the time the fund will have a return between 0 - 10%, therefore 5% (100% - 95%) of the time the return will be greater than 10% or less than 0%. The probability of a return less than 0% is one half of that or 2.5% (5% ÷ 2).

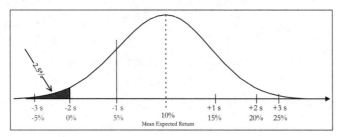

EXAMPLE 9.12

Mutual fund WJG has an average return of 9% and a standard deviation of 3%. What is the probability that the fund will return less than 0%?

At +/- 3 standard deviations from the average, 99% of the time the fund will have a return between 0 - 9%, therefore 1% (100% - 99%) of the time the return will be greater than 9% and less than 0%. The probability of a return less than 0% is 0.5% (1% ÷ 2).

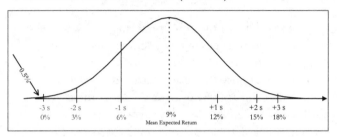

Semivariance

Investors certainly complain about volatility below their average return, but usually not above their average return. While standard deviation measures volatility or variation around the average return, both above and below the average, **semivariance** measures the possibility of returns below the average. Therefore, semivariance is a measure of downside risk. For investors seeking to minimize their downside risk, managing semivariance will reduce the probability of a large loss in their portfolio. The formula for semivariance is as follows:

$$ SV = \frac{1}{n-1} \times \sum_{r_t < \bar{r}}^{n} (r_t - \bar{r})^2 $$

Where:

n = number of returns below the mean

$\bar{r}$ = mean return

EXAMPLE 9.13

Holly has the following stocks and actual returns in her investment portfolio:

Average Return		Less Than Average Return	
Stock A	12%	Stock A	N/A
Stock B	5%	Stock B	(2%)*
Stock C	8%	Stock C	N/A
Stock D	<6%>	Stock D	(13%)*
Stock E	16%	Stock E	N/A
Average Return	**7%**	* 5% - 7% = (2%) and (6%) - 7% = (13%)	

Holly's average return is 7% or $\dfrac{12\% + 5\% + 8\% + <6\%> + 16\%}{5}$.

Semivariance is calculated as follows:

1. Determine the securities that performed below the portfolio average of 7%, which are stocks B (5%) and D (-6%).

2. Subtract the actual return from the average return for each stock below the portfolio and square the difference.

Stock B: $(5\% - 7\%)^2 = 4$

Stock D: $(-6\% - 7\%)^2 = 169$

Sum the squares and divide by one less than the number of observations (n-1), which is the same as using the standard deviation formula for a sample of a population.

$$(4 + 169) \div (2 - 1) = 173$$

Therefore, the mean semivariance for Holly's portfolio is 173. The larger the semivariance the more downside volatility in the portfolio. Note that the semi-standard deviation is simply the square root of the simi-variance.

RISK ADJUSTED RETURN MEASURES

When evaluating the return performance for any security or portfolio, calculating the actual total return is insufficient for a proper analysis. The actual return does not take into consideration the riskiness of the investment. It is important for the financial advisor and client to ask, "did I receive an appropriate amount of return, given the riskiness of the investment?" The **risk adjusted performance measures** are Sharpe, Treynor and Jensen's Alpha, which can be used to measure the performance of any type of investment including stocks, bonds and mutual funds and portfolios. These risk adjusted performance measures are used when evaluating mutual funds and other securities and are discussed later in this chapter.

Quick Quiz 9.3

Highlight the answer to these questions:

1. Beta measures the total risk of an investment.
   a. True
   b. False

2. A normal distribution describes how returns are dispersed around the average return.
   a. True
   b. False

False, True.

MODERN PORTFOLIO THEORY

Modern Portfolio Theory was developed by Harry Markowitz, who concluded that investors will seek to maximize their expected returns, for any given level of risk. Effectively, it is a methodology for developing and constructing portfolios. Harry Markowitz found that different combinations of securities produced portfolios with varying returns and volatilities. He realized that he could create portfolios with specific expected returns at varying levels of risk or portfolios with varying returns at a specific level of risk. By identifying the portfolios with the highest return per unit of risk, he created the **efficient frontier**.

EXHIBIT 9.5 EFFICIENT FRONTIER

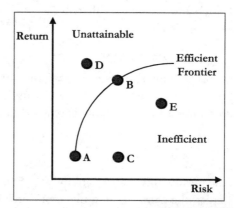

Compare various portfolios from above based on their risk-return relationship:

- Portfolio A vs. Portfolio C: Investors prefer Portfolio A because it provides the same amount of returns as Portfolio C, but with less risk.
- Portfolio B vs. Portfolio C: Investors prefer Portfolio B because it provides a higher return than Portfolio C, for the same amount of risk.
- Portfolio B vs. Portfolio E: Investors prefer Portfolio B because it provides a higher return and less risk than Portfolio E.

RESULTS OF THE EFFICIENT FRONTIER

Portfolios A and B lie on the efficient frontier, therefore portfolios A, B and all portfolios that lie on the efficient frontier represent the highest return achievable for any given level of risk. Any portfolio that lies below the efficient frontier (such as Portfolios C and E) is **inefficient** because there is another portfolio that provides a higher level of return, for that same level of risk. Since the efficient frontier represents the most efficient portfolios in terms of the risk-return relationship, no portfolios can lie above the efficient frontier. The efficient frontier represents portfolios of 100 percent of risky assets.

The **Capital Asset Pricing Model (CAPM)** calculates the relationship of risk and return for an individual security using Beta (ß) as its measure of risk. CAPM is derived by combining a risk-free asset, with risky assets from the original efficient frontier. The result is a new efficient frontier.

 *Key Concepts*

Underline/highlight the answers as you read:

1. Determine what the Efficient Frontier represents.

2. Identify what the Capital Asset Pricing Model calculates.

3. Determine the difference between the Security Market Line and the Capital Market Line.

4. Determine the methods used to measure correlation of securities and portfolios relative to other securities or the market.

EFFICIENT FRONTIER

EXHIBIT 9.6

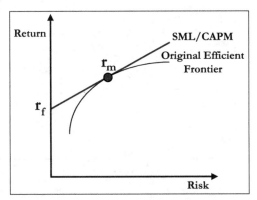

The tangent point of the old efficient frontier and the new efficient frontier is a market portfolio and represents 100 percent risky assets. The basic theory that links return and risk for all assets is the capital asset pricing model (CAPM). The CAPM formula is often referred to as the Security Market Line (SML) equation because its inputs and results are used to construct the SML. The difference between the return of the market (r_m) and the risk-free rate of return (r_f) is considered the risk premium (r_m - r_f). The risk premium is the increase in return an investor should be compensated to take on the risk of a market portfolio versus investing in a risk-free asset. The CAPM formula is:

$$r = r_f + \beta(r_m - r_f)$$

Where:

- r = Required or expected rate of return.
- r_f = Risk-free rate of return.
- β = Beta, which is a measure of the systematic risk associated with a particular portfolio.
- r_m = Return of the market.
- r_m - r_f = Risk premium.

> If mutual fund XYZ has a beta of 1.5, the total return of the market is 10% and the risk-free rate of return is 3%, what is the expected return for mutual fund XYZ?
>
> $r = r_f + \beta(r_m - r_f)$
>
> $r = 0.03 + 1.5(0.10 - 0.03)$
>
> $r = 0.03 + 1.5(0.07)$
>
> $r = 0.135$ or 13.5%

EXAMPLE 9.14

The relationship between risk and return as defined by the CAPM (when graphically plotted) results in the **Security Market Line (SML)**. Both the CAPM and SML assume an investor will earn a rate of return at least equal to the risk-free rate of return. The SML may be used to determine an expected return for individual securities.

EXHIBIT 9.7 **SECURITY MARKET LINE**

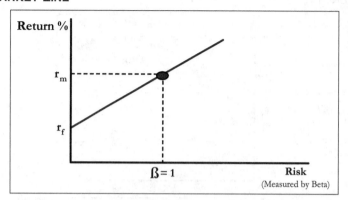

The SML suggests a linear relationship between risk and return. For each unit of nondiversifiable risk, as measured by Beta, the SML results in an expected return. The SML represents the risk-return relationship for an individual security.

CAPITAL MARKET LINE

The **Capital Market Line (CML)** is the macro aspect of the Capital Asset Pricing Model (CAPM). It specifies the relationship between risk and return in all possible portfolios. The CML is not used to evaluate the performance of a single security. The formula for the CML is:

$$r_p = r_f + \sigma_p \left(\frac{r_m - r_f}{\sigma_m} \right)$$

Where:

r_p = Required portfolio rate of return.
r_f = Risk-free rate of return.
r_m = Return on the market.
σ_m = Standard deviation of the market.
σ_p = Standard deviation of the portfolio.

EXHIBIT 9.8 **CAPITAL MARKET LINE**

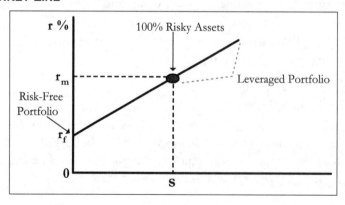

The CML graph suggests that in order to receive higher level of returns, an investor must take on additional risk. Clients are often enticed into the latest and greatest mutual fund that had the best returns for the previous year. It is important for the advisor to caution the investor to consider the amount of return, relative to the amount of risk. Risk adjusted returns are discussed later in this chapter.

Quick Quiz 9.4

Highlight the answer to these questions:

1. The efficient frontier compares various securities based on their risk-return relationship.
   a. True
   b. False

2. The Capital Market Line specifies the relationship between risk and return in all possible portfolios.
   a. True
   b. False

3. Coefficient of Determination is a measure of how much return is a result of the correlation to the market or what percentage of a security's return is a result of the market.
   a. True
   b. False

4. The risk of a portfolio can be measured through determination of the interactivity of beta and the covariance of securities in the portfolio.
   a. True
   b. False

False, True, True, False.

PORTFOLIO STATISTICS

As previously discussed, diversification is achieved by combining stocks from multiple industries and various types of securities, such as stocks and bonds. In this section, portfolio statistics that determine the amount of diversification achieved is discussed. To develop a diversified portfolio, the financial planner must understand the relationship between asset classes and how the returns for securities change relative to each other.

Correlation Coefficient

Correlation coefficient measures the movement of one security relative to that of another security. Correlation ranges from +1 to -1 and provides the investor with insight as to the strength and direction two assets move relative to each other. A correlation of +1 suggests that two assets are perfectly positively correlated. A correlation of 0 suggests that assets are completely uncorrelated or there is no relationship between the price change of the two securities. A correlation of -1 suggests a perfectly negative correlation. For example, if the correlation between Stock A and Stock B is -1, then it is expected that Stock B will decrease by 10% when Stock A increases by 10%.

EXAMPLE 9.15

Jim uses electricity to cool his house in the summer. As the temperature outside increases, so does his consumption of electricity. Jim's consumption of electricity is positively correlated to the temperature outside. As one goes up, so does the other.

Jim uses gas to heat his house in the winter. As the temperature outside decreases, his consumption of gas increases. His consumption of gas is negatively correlated to the temperature outsides. As the temperature outside goes down, his consumption of gas increases.

Jim is attempting to determine the correlation between his consumption of electricity, relative to the distance he commutes to work. Since there is no correlation between his consumption of electricity and the distance he commutes to work, they are uncorrelated.

Correlation is measured using the greek symbol rho or r and plays an important role in determining the overall volatility of a portfolio. The benefit of diversification occurs when securities with correlations of less than one are added to a portfolio. Correlation is a key concept in the Efficient Frontier and in building efficient portfolios. Anytime correlation is less than 1, the overall volatility of the portfolio is reduced. This concept will be discussed in more detail at the end of the *Portfolio Risk* section of this chapter.

Covariance

Covariance is the measure of how two securities change or move together when combined. In other words, how the price movements between two securities are related to each other. Covariance is a measure of relative risk. If the correlation coefficient is known, covariance can be calculated as follows:

$$COV_{AB} = (\sigma_A)(\sigma_B)(\rho_{AB})$$

EXAMPLE 9.16

If the standard deviation for asset A and asset B are 30% and 12%, respectively, and the correlation coefficient between assets A and B is 0.18, what is the covariance?

$$COV_{AB} = (0.30)(0.12)(0.18)$$
$$COV_{AB} = 0.0065$$

Since COV_{AB} is positive, when asset A has a positive return, asset B will also have a positive return.

Coefficient of Determination (r-squared OR r^2)

The **coefficient of determination** (r-squared or r^2) is a measure of how much return for a security or a portfolio is attributable to changes in the market. R-squared ranges from 0 to 100 and the closer to 100 that the r-squared is for a security, the more that the return for that security is a result of the market. If r-squared is 100 for a mutual fund, then 100 percent of return for that fund is a result of the market. For example, for an S&P 500 index fund, the r-squared should be 100. If the r-squared for some other fund is 50, then only 50 percent of the return is attributable to changes in the market. To calculate r-squared, simply square the correlation coefficient.

If mutual fund JMG has a correlation coefficient of 0.90, then its r-squared is 0.81 (0.90 x 0.90), which means 81% of fund JMG's return is a result of market changes.

EXAMPLE 9.17

R-squared also provides the investor with insight into the diversification of a portfolio, because the higher the r-squared, the higher percentage of return that is the result of the market (systematic risk) and the less from unsystematic risk. R-squared also tells the investor whether Beta is an appropriate measure of risk or not. If r-squared is greater than 0.70, then the portfolio is well diversified and Beta is an appropriate measure of risk. If r-squared is less than 0.70, then the portfolio is not well diversified and Beta is not an appropriate measure of risk and standard deviation should be used to measure total risk.

EXAMPLE 9.18

Mutual fund JMG has a 10-year geometric return of 15%, with a standard deviation of 20%. Fund JMG has a Beta of 1.5 with a correlation of 0.80 to the S&P 500 (which is the market). What percent of the JMG return is a result of market returns to the S&P 500?

The correlation coefficient is 0.80, therefore r-squared is 0.64 (0.80 x 0.80), which means that 64% of the return for mutual fund JMG is a result of the S&P 500 (the market).

R-squared can also be used to determine the appropriate benchmark with which to measure performance. The higher the r-squared, the more of the security's return is explained by that market. Therefore, the better the market serves as a benchmark for performance comparisons.

EXAMPLE 9.19

William is considering which of the two indexes below to compare the performance of mutual fund SCG against.

	Index 1	Index 2
Beta	0.60	0.95
Standard Deviation	8%	12%
R-Squared	0.60	0.89

Using r-squared, Index 2 explains 89% of the returns for mutual fund SCG, therefore William should measure the performance of mutual fund SCG using Index 2.

Portfolio Risk (Two Asset Portfolio)

The risk of a portfolio can be measured through determination of the interactivity of the standard deviation and covariance of securities in the portfolio. This process also utilizes the weight of both securities involved, the standard deviations of the respective securities and the correlation coefficient of the two securities. To determine the standard deviation of a two asset portfolio, the following formula is used:

$$\sigma p = \sqrt{(w_A)^2(\sigma_A)^2 + (w_B)^2(\sigma_B)^2 + (2)(w_A)(w_B)(COV_{AB})}$$

Where:

w_A	=	Weight of Asset A.
σ_A	=	The standard deviation of Asset A.
w_B	=	Weight of Asset B.
σ_B	=	The standard deviation of Asset B.

COV_{AB} = Covariance formula [$COV_{AB} = (\sigma_A)(\sigma_B)(\rho_{AB})$].

EXAMPLE 9.20

Sydney has a portfolio with the following two investments:

	Amount	Standard Deviation	Weighting
Stock # 1	$60,000	15%	60%
Stock # 2	$40,000	8%	40%

What is the standard deviation of the portfolio if the correlation is 1, 0 and -1, respectively?

If correlation is 1:

$$\sigma p = \sqrt{(0.60)^2(0.15)^2 + (0.40)^2(0.08)^2 + (2)(0.60)(0.40)(0.15)(0.08)1}$$

$$\sigma p = \sqrt{0.00810 + 0.00102 + 0.00576}$$

$$\sigma p = 12.198\%$$

If correlation is 0:

$$\sigma p = \sqrt{(0.60)^2(0.15)^2 + (0.40)^2(0.08)^2 + (2)(0.60)(0.40)(0.15)(0.08)0}$$

$$\sigma p = \sqrt{0.00810 + 0.00102}$$

$$\sigma p = 9.55\%$$

If correlation is -1:

$$\sigma p = \sqrt{(0.60)^2(0.15)^2 + (0.40)^2(0.08)^2 + (2)(0.60)(0.40)(0.15)(0.08)-1}$$

$$\sigma p = \sqrt{0.00810 + 0.00102 - 0.00576}$$

$$\sigma p = 5.797\%$$

Summary Chart	
r	σp
r = 1	12.198%
r = 0	9.55%
r = -1	5.797%

Notice that as the correlation coefficient decreases, the portfolio becomes less volatile (and less risky), as measured by standard deviation. Diversification benefits begin when correlation is something less than 1. As soon as assets do not move in the same exact direction and strength (correlation is less than 1), the standard deviation of the portfolio is reduced. The greatest diversification benefits occur when the correlation is equal to negative 1.

From a practical application perspective, not many portfolios only have two assets. Portfolios have many securities and even though the above formula could be extended to accommodate a multi-asset portfolio, it would be mathematically cumbersome without the aid of computer software. Instead, tools are available to professionals, such as Morningstar Principia, that will calculate the standard deviation, beta, and other characteristics of a multi-asset portfolio.

INVESTMENT ALTERNATIVES

The primary goal when building an investment portfolio is to construct a well diversified portfolio that provides the greatest return, for the level of risk that the investor is willing to accept. Each investment security has its own unique risk and return characteristics. The next section of this chapter discusses investment alternatives, advantages, disadvantages, and risk and return relationships. The following are some investment alternatives:

- Equity
- Debt
- Real Estate and Tangible Investments
- Derivatives

EQUITY

Equity represents ownership in a business or property. The most common form of equity is common stock. Shareholders of common stock are entitled to a pro rata share of the profits generated and distributed by a company. Common shareholder's claim on company assets and earnings are subordinate to the company's creditors. Return on equity is due to capital appreciation and from return of profits in the form of dividend income.

The advantages of equity investments are:

- The historical and expected returns are higher with equity than with debt.
- Equities are easy to invest in, either directly by purchasing shares through a broker or investing indirectly through a mutual fund.

- Stocks listed on major exchanges are marketable and current prices are easily obtained.

The disadvantages of equity investments are:
- The volatility and risk associated with equities
- It is difficult to consistently select equities that earn their expected return and out perform the market.
- Most equities do not pay significant dividends, which may result in little or no current income.

Stock Valuation

Part of the investment process is to determine the intrinsic value of an equity security. **Intrinsic value** is the underlying value of a security, considering both the future cash flows and the riskiness of the security. Stock valuation is unique to each investor, as each investor's required rate of return will differ from others, based on the riskiness of a security. Although there are multiple valuation models, theories and methods, the purpose of this section is to introduce two basic stock valuation tools and how to apply these tools. The stock valuation methods include the dividend valuation models (zero growth dividend model and constant growth dividend model) and the earnings based valuation model (P/E approach).

The dividend valuation models consider the future cash flows that will be generated by the security. The dividend valuation models discount the future cash flows, based on the investors required rate of return, to obtain a present value.

The P/E approach is an earnings based valuation model that determines the intrinsic value of the security based on the company's future earnings and how much investors are willing to pay for each dollar of earnings.

Zero Growth Dividend Model

The **zero growth dividend model** assumes that a security pays annual income or a dividend, each and every year, and the amount of the dividend does not change. This model values a security based on the stock's capitalized amount of the annual dividends. The zero growth dividend model formula is:

$$V = \frac{D}{r}$$

Where:
- V = Intrinsic value of a stock.
- D = Annual dividends.
- r = Required rate of return.

Robin is considering purchasing a stock that pays an annual dividend of $2.52. The stock is expected to continue paying $2.52 and is currently trading at $20 per share. Robin has a required rate of return of 12%, should she purchase the stock?

EXAMPLE 9.21

$$V = \frac{D}{r}$$

$$V = \frac{\$2.52}{0.12}$$

$$V = \$21.00$$

Since Robin believes the stock is worth $21, and the stock is currently trading at $20, she should consider purchasing the stock.

If Robin's required rate of return is 15%, how much would she be willing to pay for the stock?

EXAMPLE 9.22

$$V = \frac{D}{r}$$

$$V = \frac{\$2.52}{0.15}$$

$$V = \$16.80$$

If Robin's required rate of return is 9%, how much would she be willing to pay for the stock?

EXAMPLE 9.23

$$V = \frac{D}{r}$$

$$V = \frac{\$2.52}{0.09}$$

$$V = \$28.00$$

Required Rate of Return	Implicit Intrinsic Value	Relationship	If Stock Price is $20, Robin Should...
9%	$28.00	As the required rate of return decreases, the intrinsic value increases.	Buy Now
12%	$21.00	Robin's original required rate of return.	Buy Now
15%	$16.80	As the required rate of return increases, the intrinsic value decreases.	Sell

Constant Growth Dividend Discount Model

The **constant growth dividend discount model** values a company's stock by discounting the future stream of cash flows or dividends. This model assumes that dividends will grow indefinitely at a constant growth rate. The constant growth dividend model is most appropriate to value mature companies, with steady and predictable growth rates in earnings and dividends. The constant growth dividend formula is:

$$V = \frac{D_1}{(r - g)}$$

Where:
- V = Intrinsic value of a stock.
- D_1 = Next period's dividends.
- r = Required rate of return.
- g = Dividend growth rate.

The constant growth dividend model uses the "next period's dividend" when determining the intrinsic value. Next period's dividend is a function of this periods dividend x (1 + dividend growth rate).

EXAMPLE 9.24

A stock recently paid a dividend of $3.00. The market price of the stock is $50 and the dividend growth rate is 3%. If an investor's required rate of return is 9%, what is the intrinsic value of this stock?

$$V = \frac{D_1}{(r - g)}$$

$$V = \frac{(\$3.00 \times 1.03)}{(0.09 - 0.03)}$$

$$V = \frac{\$3.09}{0.06}$$

$$V = \$51.50$$

This model also captures the relationship between dividends and required return. As the dividend increases or the required rate of return decreases, the intrinsic value of the security will increase. Alternatively, as the dividend decreases, or the required rate of return increases, the intrinsic value of the security will decrease.

EXAMPLE 9.25

Continuing with the above example where the stock recently paid a dividend of $3.00, the dividend growth rate is 3% and the investor's required rate of return is 9%. The chart below demonstrates the relationship between the dividend and the intrinsic value of the stock. As the dividend decreases, the intrinsic value also decreases. As the dividend increases, the intrinsic value also increases for a given required rate of return.

Assumed Dividend	Required Rate of Return	Dividend Growth Rate	Intrinsic Value
$2.00	9%	3%	$34.33
$3.00	9%	3%	$51.50
$4.00	9%	3%	$68.67

The chart below demonstrates the relationship between the required rate of return and the intrinsic value of the stock. As the required rate of return decreases, the intrinsic value of the stock increases. As the required rate of return increases, the intrinsic value decreases.

Assumed Dividend	Required Rate of Return	Dividend Growth Rate	Intrinsic Value
$3.00	8%	3%	$61.80
$3.00	9%	3%	$51.50
$3.00	10%	3%	$44.14

P/E Approach

The **price earnings (P/E) approach** to valuing equity securities is an earnings based valuation model that places a premium on the amount investors are willing to pay for each dollar of earnings. The P/E ratio is a measure of the relationship between a stock's price and its earnings. P/E ratios are useful to value the stock of a company that pays no dividends. The relationship of price to earnings is known as the P/E multiplier, and is used to determine the price of a stock. The formula for the PE approach is:

$$P/E = \frac{\text{Price per Share}}{\text{Earnings per Share}}$$

OR

$$\text{Price per Share} = P/E \times \text{Earnings per Share}$$

Phyllis' Home Furnishings recently reported earnings per share of $3.50. The stock has a fair market value of $59.50 per share. The P/E ratio is 17 ($59.50 ÷ $3.50). If earnings next year are expected to be $4.00 per share and the stock trades at its current P/E ratio of 17, the stock should be worth $68 (17 x $4.00) per share.

EXAMPLE 9.26

DEBT

Debt represents the lending of funds in return for periodic interest payments and the repayment of the principal debt obligation. **Bonds** are a debt issuance where the bond issuer makes a promise to make periodic coupon payments (interest) and repayment of the par value (principal) at maturity.

Bonds can assist an investor in accomplishing a variety of investment goals. If an investor is income oriented, bonds are appropriate since they provide periodic income. If the investor's goal is capital appreciation, bonds may provide capital gains depending on changes in interest rates and credit spreads. Bond values and prices are inversely related to changes in interest rates. As interest rates increase, bond prices will decrease. As interest rates decrease, bond prices will increase.

Bonds provide diversification benefits to a stock portfolio by reducing the overall volatility in such a portfolio because the correlation between bonds and equities is relatively low. Bonds are only about 24 percent correlated to stocks. However, the correlation will fluctuate based on the time period for which it is being calculated.

Bonds are generally less risky than equities because of interest payments and collateral (many bonds have specific assets as collateral) and they have priority as to claims before equity holders in bankruptcy.

The disadvantages of bonds are:
- Bonds generally provide lower rates of return than equities.
- Bond prices are inversely related to changes in interest rates. As interest rates increase, bond prices decrease.

Types of Bonds

There are three primary issuers of bonds, the U.S. government, municipalities (state and local governments) and corporations. The U.S. government issues bonds to finance the national debt and to fund deficit spending. The three primary types of bonds issued by the U.S. government are:
- Treasury Bills - have maturities less than 12 months.
- Treasury Notes - have maturities between 2 - 10 years.
- Treasury Bonds - have maturities greater than 10 years.

Interest earned on **U.S. government bonds** is excluded from state and local income taxes, but is included for federal income taxes. Bonds issued by the U.S. government are considered default risk free because they are backed by the full faith and credit of the U.S government.

Municipal Bonds

Municipal bonds are issued to fund projects and spending for state or local governments. The three primary types of municipal bonds are general obligation bonds, revenue bonds, and private activity bonds.

General obligation municipal bonds are backed by the taxing authority that issued the bonds. The bonds are repaid through taxes that are collected by the municipality. General obligation bonds are considered the least risky of the various types of municipal bonds.

Revenue bonds are issued to raise capital to fund a particular revenue generating project. The revenue generated by the project will be used to repay the bond issuance. For example, revenue bonds can be used to fund construction of a highway and the revenue from tolls can be used to retire the debt.

A **private activity bond** is issued to finance a joint project between the private sector and a municipality. Private activity bonds are often issued to fund the building of professional sports stadiums.

Interest income earned on a municipal bond is tax-free at the federal level and may be exempt from income tax at the state level. States do not generally tax interest from municipal bonds issued by that state but may tax interest income from municipal bonds issued by other states. Therefore, purchasing a bond from your state of residence will likely result in tax-free income.

Corporate Bonds

Corporate bonds are issued by firms to raise capital to fund ongoing operations, retire debt, fund capital projects or acquisitions. Corporate bonds have default risk because the company is backing the bonds with a promise to repay the bondholder. Corporate bonds can be backed by an asset of the company, such as equipment, financial securities, or a pool of loans. Income received from corporate bonds is taxable both at the federal and state level.

Zero Coupon Bonds

Zero coupon bonds are bonds that are sold at a deep discount to par value and do not make periodic interest payments. Instead, the bonds increase in value each year, so that at maturity the bonds are worth their par value. Zero coupon bonds create a "phantom income" issue where the increase in value of the bond each year is recognized as taxable income, but no actual cash is received. Zero coupon bonds may be either Treasury, municipal, or corporate bonds.

Risks to Investing in Bonds

Like any financial security there are risks to investing in bonds. Some of the most important risks to consider when investing in bonds are:
- Interest rate risk.
- Reinvestment rate risk.
- Purchasing power risk.
- Default risk.
- Call risk.

Interest Rate Risk

Interest rate risk is the risk that changes in interest rates will cause changes in the price of a bond. Interest rate changes are inversely related to bond price changes. As interest rates increase, bond prices will decrease. As interest rates decrease, bond prices increase. Some bonds are more sensitive to changes in interest rates than others. This means that some bonds will experience larger percentage price changes than other bonds, given the same change in interest rates. The longer the term to maturity and the lower the coupon rate, the more sensitive the bond is to changes in interest rates. The following graph depicts the relationship between bond prices, term, and interest rates presuming a six percent coupon paying $30 semi annually.

| EXHIBIT 9.9 | BOND PRICING RELATIONSHIPS |

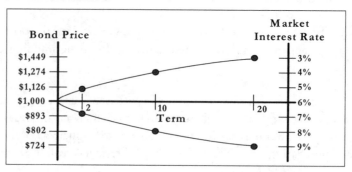

| EXHIBIT 9.10 | BOND PRICING AT VARIOUS INTEREST RATES (20-YEAR TERM) |

3%	6%	9%
N = 40 (20 x 2)	N = 40 (20 x 2)	N = 40 (20 x 2)
i = 1.5 (3 ÷ 2)	i = 3 (6 ÷ 2)	i = 4.5 (9 ÷ 2)
PMT = 30	PMT = 30	PMT = 30
FV = 1,000	FV = 1,000	FV = 1,000
PV = $1,449	PV = $1,000	PV = $724

Assume that a bond is paying a six percent coupon and market interest rates decrease or increase. What happens to the price of the bond? Notice, the longer the term of the bond, the bigger the price change of the bond when interest rates change.

The concept regarding bond sensitivity to changes in interest rates is explained by a concept called duration, which is beyond the scope of this textbook. However, duration is an effective measure of a bond's sensitivity to changes in interest rates with the higher the number indicating a higher sensitivity.

Reinvestment Rate Risk

Reinvestment rate risk is the risk that an investor may not be able to reinvest the proceeds (interest and principal) from a bond at the same rate of return as was invested previously. As interest rates decrease, an investor will have a more difficult time reinvesting at the same rate of return as before, without taking on additional risk. The effect of reinvestment rate risk is that the actual IRR (or yield to maturity) for the bond investment will be less than initially expected.

Purchasing Power Risk

Purchasing power risk is the risk that inflation will erode the investor's purchasing power. For example, one dollar today will likely not be able to purchase the same amount of goods and services tomorrow, one month from now, or one year from now. Also, an investor that purchases a ten year term bond will receive a coupon payment every six months for ten years and the par value of the bond at maturity. As inflation causes prices to increase, the coupon payments have less purchasing power and the par value of the bond will not purchase the same amount of goods and services ten years from now that it would today. Fixed income investments that are used to mitigate the risk of purchasing power loss are bonds that make adjustments for inflation. Two examples include U.S. Treasury issued I bonds, which adjust the interest rate for inflation and TIPS (Treasury Inflation Protected Securities), which adjust the par value for inflation.

Default Risk

Default risk is the risk that the bond issuer will be unable to timely repay the interest or principal of the bonds. Rating agencies such as Moody's and Standard & Poor's rate company's bond issuance on the likelihood of the company being able to repay both principal and interest. Companies that receive the highest credit ratings have the least amount of default risk, therefore they tend to pay the lowest yields. Bonds that receive the lowest credit ratings have the highest amount of default risk, therefore they are required to pay the highest yields to compensate investors for the higher default risk.

Call Risk

Call risk is the risk that a bond will be retired early by the issuing company. Bonds that have a call feature entitle the issuer to retire the bond before maturity by paying a call price, an amount generally above the par value to compensate investors for the bond being called. Many bond investors have the objective of generating income, so having the bond called early forces the bondholder to find another bond, of similar risk, paying the same rate of return (an example of retirement risk). Often, companies will retire bonds because the interest rate on the bond is higher than the current prevailing interest rates or the company wants to simply retire the debt or refinance the debt at a lower rate of interest.

Application of Bonds in a Portfolio

When structuring an investment portfolio, the primary objective of the client will determine the total percentage of the portfolio allocated to bonds. If the primary objective is growth and diversification, (assuming a long-term time horizon and appropriate risk tolerance), only 20 - 40 percent of the portfolio would likely be invested in bonds. However, if the investor's primary goal is income and diversification, then a larger weighting towards bonds, perhaps in excess of 40 percent is expected.

An important consideration when investing in bonds is the type of bond and the type of taxability of the account that will hold the bonds. For example, a municipal bond that is "double tax-free" is ideally held in a taxable account. There is no additional tax benefit to holding a municipal bond in an account that is tax-deferred such as an IRA or 401(k) plan. Bonds that create taxable events, such as corporate bonds or zero coupon bonds are ideally held in a tax-deferred account. Remember, corporate bonds pay taxable interest income each year and zero coupon bonds create "phantom income," so tax deferred accounts, such as IRAs and 401(k) plans are ideal for holding those types of bonds.

REAL ESTATE

Real estate represents an asset class that is often overlooked in an investment portfolio. Real estate may be an important component in an investment portfolio because of the low correlation between real estate and equities/bonds. Generally, real estate performs well during periods of high inflation whereas equities and bonds generally decrease in value as interest rates rise to mitigate the impact of inflation. Investors not only invest in real estate for the diversification benefits but also to generate income. Purchasing commercial or residential real estate that is expected to generate rental income may assist an income oriented investor to attain their investment goals.

Real estate investment trusts (REITs) are a type of mutual fund that pools investor contributions to purchase real estate or make construction or mortgage loans. There are three general types of REITs:

- Equity trusts that buy, operate, and sell real estate in the hopes of earning a return in the form of capital appreciation for the property they own.
- Mortgage trusts issue construction and mortgage loans. Mortgage trusts' investment return is in the form of interest on the loans.
- Hybrid trusts invest in a combination of the ownership of real estate and issuing loans. Hybrid trusts' return is a combination of capital appreciation and income.

Quick Quiz 9.5

Highlight the answer to these questions:

1. The zero growth dividend model assumes that a security pays annual income or a dividend, each and every year, and the amount of the dividend does not change.
   a. True
   b. False

2. Risks associated with bond investment include interest rate, reinvestment rate, purchasing power, default, and call risks.
   a. True
   b. False

3. Mortgage trusts are a type of REIT that issues construction and mortgage loans with return being in the form of interest on the loans.
   a. True
   b. False

4. Calls give the holder the right to sell the underlying security at a certain price by a certain date.
   a. True
   b. False

True, True, True, False.

DERIVATIVES

Derivatives are financial securities that derive their value from some underlying asset. Examples of derivatives include options, warrants, and futures. **Options** include both calls and puts. **Calls** give the holder the right to buy the underlying security at a certain price by a certain date. **Puts** give the holder the right to sell the underlying security at a certain price by a certain date. A **warrant** is a long-term option that gives the holder the right to buy a certain number of shares of stocks in a particular company by a certain date. A **futures contract** is a commitment to make or take the delivery of an amount of a certain item at a specified date at an agreed upon price. The underlying asset for options may be a stock, currency, treasury security, or index. The underlying asset for warrants are stocks. The underlying asset for futures contracts are commodities and financial securities. A commodity may be corn, wheat, cotton, gold, or oil. A financial security may be a currency, Treasury security, or stock index.

Derivatives are a contracts between buyers and sellers. The seller of a derivative security receives a premium and the buyer pays the premium. Under the terms of the derivatives contract the buyer and seller agree to trade the underlying asset, at a pre-determined price known as the strike price, and the contract is good until a certain date (the expiration date). Derivatives are a contract for a finite period of time, making them "expiring assets," which means each day that passes the derivative loses a little value related to the shorter expiration period.

Derivatives can be complex and risky, depending on the trading strategy. The actual trading mechanics, strategies, and valuation of options is beyond the scope of this textbook.

INVESTMENT COMPANIES

Investment companies are financial services companies that sell shares of stock to the public and use the proceeds to buy portfolios of securities. Mutual funds are one type of investment company in which investors buy shares in a fund and own a pro rata portion of the investment portfolio, entitling them to a share of capital gains, interest and dividend income. Other types of investment companies include unit investment trusts and exchange-traded funds. Investment companies are generally nontaxable entities. In order to maintain nontaxable status, an investment company must meet the following criteria:[1]

- It must earn at least 90 percent of its income from interest, dividends and capital gains, which are generated by investing in stocks, bonds and other financial securities.
- At least 90 percent of its income must be distributed to the share-holders annually.

Key Concepts

Underline/highlight the answers as you read:

1. Identify the different types and characteristics of investment companies.

2. Determine the difference between open-end investment companies and closed-end investment companies.

3. Identify the four different types of risk adjusted performance measures.

4. Determine the difference between an absolute risk adjusted performance measurement and a relative risk adjusted performance indicator.

5. Determine how an investor's asset allocation can be determined.

- Investment in any one company is limited to five percent of the funds assets and ten percent of the voting stock of the issuing company.
- No more than 25 percent of the funds assets can be invested in the securities of the issuing company.

Investment companies are regulated by the Securities and Exchange Commission and directly by the Investment Company Act of 1940.[2] This act requires investment companies to disclose to shareholders the investment companies objective, financial condition, structure, and operations. The Investment Company Act of 1940 does not provide the SEC with the authority to make judgments regarding investment decisions or merits of investments held by the investment company.

The types of investment companies are:
- Unit Investment Trusts
- Exchange Traded Funds
- Open-End Investment Companies
- Closed-End Investment Companies

UNIT INVESTMENT TRUSTS

A **unit investment trust (UIT)** is an investment company that passively manages a portfolio of either stocks or bonds, known as a bond or equity UIT. Typically, municipal bonds are the most popular form of a unit investment trust where investors purchase shares in the UIT, income is generated from the bonds and distributed to shareholders. An equity UIT could be considered an exchange traded fund (ETF), discussed below. For an equity UIT, the investor's motivation is typically profit from capital appreciation of the stocks held by the trust.

When a UIT is established, the trust establishes a termination date. Once the termination date is reached, all assets are liquidated and the proceeds are returned to the shareholders. In the case of a bond UIT, the termination date is the maturity date of the bonds. Once the bonds mature, the principal proceeds are repaid to the shareholders. Since UIT's are passively managed, no additional securities are purchased or sold once the trust is established. Essentially, investors in a UIT know exactly what securities will be held throughout the life of the UIT. A list of those securities is provided in the prospectus of the UIT.

Shares of a UIT are traded at Net Asset Value (NAV). Typically, a sponsor of a UIT will offer shares during a one time offering. Any subsequent trading of the UIT is between the investor and sponsor. If an investor decides to redeem shares in a UIT, the UIT will redeem those shares at net asset value. The primary advantages to a UIT are the diversification offered by holding many bonds in the trust and the periodic income payments. The primary disadvantage is the loss in purchasing power for UIT's that are held for a long period of time. As income payments from the UIT remain constant, inflation will erode the investors purchasing power.

---

1. IRC Section 851.
2. http://www.sec.gov/about/laws.shtml

$$\text{Net Asset Value } = \frac{\text{Market Value of Investments Held } - \text{ Liabilities}}{\text{Shares Outstanding}}$$

EXCHANGE TRADED FUNDS

Exchange traded funds (ETF's) are another form of an investment company. An ETF invests in securities that are included in a particular index. The ETF attempts to mimic the performance of an index, by simply buying shares of the stocks in that index, in the same proportion that the stocks are included in the index. For example, QQQ represents the NASDAQ 100, SPIDERS or SPDR represents the S&P 500, Diamonds or DIA represents the Dow Jones Industrial Average. In 1993, the American Stock Exchange developed and launched the first ETF, which was the Standard and Poor's Depositor Receipts (SPDR), which tracked the performance of the S&P 500. There are now hundreds of ETFs with assets reaching $1 Trillion during 2011.

An ETF is passively managed, similar to a UIT, such that active security analysis and selection is not needed or conducted. ETF's trade on exchanges and are bought and sold through a broker. Occasionally an ETF is required to rebalance its portfolio when new stocks are added or removed from an index.

Advantages of an ETF

ETFs offer individual investors several advantages over traditional mutual funds including: intraday trading, the opportunity to purchase on margin, tax efficiency, instant diversification sales, and low cost investment.

Intraday Trading

ETFs are similar to mutual funds in that a share represents a pro rata ownership percentage of a basket of underlying securities. However, ETFs can be bought and sold throughout the day, without any timing restrictions. ETFs can also be purchased on margin and can be sold short, but such short sales are not subject to the uptick rule. In addition, investors can use limit orders and can, unlike mutual funds, buy and sell at predetermined prices.

Tax Efficient Holdings

Another advantage to ETFs is that they are tax efficient because they have very low turnover of the assets within the portfolio. Since ETFs own the stocks that comprise an index and the assets within an index change infrequently, this results in low turnover. The only time an ETF liquidates a position is when the index changes. Anytime an actively managed mutual fund sells an investment at a gain, either capital gains or ordinary income is passed along to the shareholders. Since ETFs are passively managed, which does not involve active buying and selling of securities, any underlying assets that appreciate in value are simply reflected in the ETF's per share price. Once an investor decides to sell the ETF, tax consequences will follow, but the timing is up to the investor.

Diversification

Immediate diversification is another benefit of an ETF because the investor is really purchasing a basket of securities that represent the market. Owning a basket of stocks mitigates the risk of one particular stock performing poorly, which may be offset by other stocks performing well. Building a diversified portfolio (reducing risk as measured by standard deviation), is a key component to meeting long-term goals through proper asset allocation.

Low Cost Investment

ETFs have very low expenses associated with managing the fund because they are passively managed. For example, the Vanguard S&P 500 index fund has an expense ratio of 0.18 percent, whereas SPDRs have an expense ratio of 0.12 percent. Keep in mind that since ETFs are purchased through a broker, there are commissions associated with a purchase.

OPEN-END INVESTMENT COMPANIES

An **open-end investment company**, also referred to as a mutual fund, is an investment company that buys and sells shares to investors directly. This type of investment company has increased dramatically in popularity over the last 30 years. In 1940 there were only 40 mutual funds, and by 1980, that number had grown to slightly over 500. Today, there are well over 8,000 mutual funds, managing over $8 trillion dollars in assets. As more individuals take personal responsibility for their retirement and education goals, the role of mutual funds and percent of individuals participating in funds has increased dramatically. Currently, 45 percent of all U.S. households own a mutual fund, compared to less than six percent in 1980.[3]

One of the primary reasons for the increase in the number of mutual funds has been less reliance on defined benefit plans or pension plans offered by corporations and more reliance on self funded retirement plans such as 401(k) plans or IRAs. Mutual funds offer investors the opportunity to take advantage of the tax deferred nature of these plans, while investing in well diversified portfolios, managed by professional money managers.

In addition to more individuals relying on their own personal savings and investments for retirement, there has been a cultural shift in the attitude towards who is paying for their children's college education. In the 1950 - 70 time period, parents (and children) did not have an expectation that parents would pay for their children's college education. Many students relied on loans, grants, personal savings and worked through college. Over the last 20 to 30 years, there has been a shift in attitude among parents (and children) towards parents assuming the responsibility of paying for their children's education. With long-term planning and using mutual funds as the primary savings vehicle over a child's first 18 years, parents are able to plan for one of the largest expenditures in their lifetime. Mutual funds have been the investment vehicle of choice for many parents, combined with plans that offer a tax deferred or even tax-free benefit if funds are used for qualified education expenses.

Advantages of Mutual Funds

Mutual funds offer individual investors many advantages including diversification, professional management, better than the average returns, low cost method of investing, and many convenient services.

---

3. http://www.icifactbook.org/fb_sec6.html

Diversification

Mutual funds offer investors an easy and economical method of diversifying a portfolio. Many mutual funds have 100 or more securities in their portfolio, offering an investor instant diversification with a relatively low initial investment. For example, consider an investor with $5,000 to invest who wants to build a diversified portfolio. The investor would have difficulty purchasing shares of all the companies that comprise the S&P 500. With such a small initial investment, it is virtually impossible to build a portfolio of stocks to match the performance of the S&P 500. However, with as little as $1,000 an investor can purchase a mutual fund that owns 100 or more stocks in its portfolio and the investor is immediately diversified. Alternatively, the investor can purchase shares in an index mutual fund, which matches the performance of select indexes.

Professional Management

With the busy lifestyles many working individuals and families maintain, it is often difficult to find the time or interest to research investment opportunities, analyze current positions and make well-timed investment decisions. Professional mutual fund managers have teams of analysts researching hundreds and thousands of companies on a daily basis to determine the most attractive investments given the fund's objectives. In addition, mutual fund managers and their teams of analysts have investment selection experience, which is helpful when making asset selections, given current and anticipated economic conditions.

Higher than Average Investor Returns

Historically, individual investors underperform the broader market indices. For example, individual equity investors earned just 3.83 percent versus the S&P 500 gain of 9.14 percent for the twenty year period ending December 31, 2010.[4] The actual returns of individual investors were slightly higher than the rate of inflation during the same period of time, which was 2.57 percent. Reasons for the individual investor's poor performance include selling during market declines, not continuing periodic investments during market declines, and poor asset allocation.

Fund managers are better able to maintain a disciplined approach to investing, whereas the average investor tends to make emotion-based decisions rather than relying on well-researched facts. Individual investors also have a tendency to buy when the market is high and sell when it is low leading to significantly lower than average returns.

Low Cost Method of Investing

Many mutual funds have minimum initial investments anywhere between $1,000 to $2,500 or more to open an account. Many mutual funds will waive the initial investment requirement if an investor enrolls in a periodic monthly investment plan. Consider that most bonds are priced in denominations of $1,000 and many stocks are priced at $20 to $100 or more, therefore, it can be difficult for an individual investor to build a diversified portfolio with a modest initial investment. Mutual funds allow for all investors to have access to professionally managed, well diversified portfolios, regardless of their initial investment. This low cost method of investing in equity and bond securities opens these markets up to many investors who otherwise would not have the means to invest in these securities.

---

4. 2011 Quantitative Analysis of Investor Behavior, Dalbar Inc., March 2011.

Other Services

Many fund families provide convenient services for investors. Services such as conversions from one fund to another, within the same family, but with a different objective. Other services include systematic withdrawal plans for retirees or investors with income needs, that allow the investor to receive periodic payments from the mutual fund on a monthly or quarterly basis. In addition, fund families also provide wire transfer services, periodic investment plans, record keeping, and automatic reinvestment of interest and dividends.

Disadvantages to Mutual Funds

While mutual funds offer many advantages to investors, mutual funds have unique disadvantages as well. Disadvantages include poor performance relative to a benchmark, liquidity constraints, expenses, and built in capital gains.

Performance

In the short run (three to four years) many, if not most mutual funds do not outperform their appropriate investment benchmarks. Only a small percentage of mutual funds outperform the appropriate index even over time. One explanation for this underperformance is that mutual funds have expenses that must be incurred for the operation of the fund. In addition, funds must maintain cash reserves to meet redemptions, which undermines the fund's ability to be fully invested and only generate money market type returns for cash reserves.

Consider that from 1990 - 1999, the average equity mutual fund gained almost 24 percent, compared to the S&P 500, which grew at 28 percent over the same time period. The lower return from mutual funds can be at least partially attributed to fees and expenses from managing the portfolio.

Liquidity

While liquidity is a primary advantage of mutual funds, it can also be a disadvantage. To accommodate cash flowing in and out of a fund on a regular basis, funds must maintain significant cash reserves that are uninvested. This results in a fund not being fully invested and having lower rates of return than what could be achieved if the fund was fully invested. Maintaining cash reserves to meet redemptions is one of the obstacles that prevents mutual funds from consistently beating their benchmark. One of the ways funds attempt to overcome the need for maintaining cash reserves is through leverage using futures contracts. Futures contracts essentially allow the fund to control a large amount of the underlying index with a small investment. If the index increases in value, so will the value of the futures contract. Alternatively, if the index decreases in value, the futures contract will also lose value.

Fees, Loads, and Expenses

Investors should be conscious of fees, loads, and expenses of mutual funds. While all funds will have operating and management expenses, some funds have fairly high sales charges. The higher the fund costs, the more difficult it will be to outperform the appropriate benchmark and the lower the overall return to the investor.

Built in Capital Gains

Mutual funds have securities in their portfolio that may have significantly appreciated in value. The appreciation is essentially a built in capital gains that need to be distributed to the shareholders. Once the security is sold, the capital gains will be allocated to each shareholder, typically at year end. If an investor is unfortunate enough to purchase a mutual fund late in the year and did not participate in the appreciation the fund experienced over the previous year, the investor may be paying capital gains taxes on capital gains that were never realized. Investors should be careful about purchasing mutual funds with significant amounts of unrealized capital gain. This is one of the reasons mutual fund investors will postpone making a large fund purchase in November or December, instead opting to make the purchase the following year in January or February. Investors do not want to be hit with large capital gains at year end, when they did not participate in the funds appreciation. However, if the investor does receive an interest and capital gains distribution and the funds are reinvested, the cost of the new shares will increase the investor's tax basis in the mutual fund.

CLOSED-END INVESTMENT COMPANIES

Closed-end investment companies are another type of investment company that trade on stock market exchanges. Closed-end funds do not generally issue additional shares after their initial offering. Shares of a closed-end fund will trade on an organized exchange, such as the New York Stock Exchange or Nasdaq Stock Exchange, which means shares are generally not redeemable by a fund family. Instead, shares are traded between investors, with the assistance of a broker.

Shares of a closed-end fund generally trade at a discount or premium to net asset value, depending upon the demand for the fund shares. Since a closed-end fund does not issue additional shares after the initial public offering, a closed-end fund generally has a fixed capitalization. An open-end fund has unlimited capitalization because the fund family will issue additional shares as investors buy more shares. Since closed-end funds have a fixed capitalization and shares are not redeemed by the fund family, the fund manager has greater flexibility regarding investments and does not have to maintain significant amounts of cash to meet redemptions. This allows the manager to be fully invested resulting in the opportunity to earn higher returns than those returns generated when holding cash.

TYPES OF MUTUAL FUNDS

Equity Funds

Equity mutual funds typically invest in equity securities, but may have different overall objectives. Typical objectives include large, mid, or small cap growth, large, mid, or small cap value stocks, balanced funds and growth and income. Investor's objectives when investing in equity mutual funds may be capital appreciation or income through ownership of preferred or common stock with high dividend payments. Equity mutual funds have consistently provided investors with higher rates of return than fixed-income funds, however equity funds are more volatile. Equity funds are appropriate for investors with a long-term time horizon and who prefer to minimize tax consequences. Tax consequences associated with equity funds are typically capital gains (assuming a turnover of 12 months or greater), whereas fixed income funds typically generate ordinary income, which is taxed at a higher tax rate than capital gains.

Fixed Income Funds

Fixed income or bond funds typically invest in bonds of various maturities. A fixed income fund's primary objective is to create income for its shareholders and protect principal, which is appropriate for many retirees and investors looking to diversify their portfolio.

Fixed income mutual funds are well diversified, but there are still inherent risks associated with these funds. The two primary risks are interest rate risk and reinvestment rate risk. Since fixed income mutual funds invest primarily in bonds, their value is sensitive to changes in interest rates. During the early 2000's when the market experienced declining interest rates, fixed income mutual funds performed well because as interest rates decreased, the bonds held by these funds increased in value.

Growth Funds

Growth mutual funds typically invest in large and mid cap stocks, where price appreciation is the primary objective. Growth funds invest in growth stocks that can be characterized as stocks that are more risky, have high PE ratios and have little to no dividends. Growth funds are considered more aggressive than most other funds and are appropriate for investors that have a high risk tolerance.

Aggressive Growth Funds

Aggressive growth funds typically invest in small cap stocks, where price appreciation is the primary objective. Aggressive growth funds are more risky than growth funds because of the volatility associated with small cap, growth stocks. Typically, small cap, growth stocks have little to no earnings, rapid sales growth, high PE ratios and no dividends. Aggressive growth funds are appropriate for investors with a very high risk tolerance.

Value Funds

Value funds typically invest in securities that are deemed to be out of favor or extremely under-valued. Value funds, invest in value stocks that are characterized by very low PE ratios and have a high dividend yield. Value funds are less volatile than growth funds and are preferred by more conservative investors because of the low volatility. During the early 2000's, when many growth stocks performed poorly because of concern over valuation and earnings, value funds significantly outperformed growth funds.

Balanced Funds

Balanced funds typically invest in both fixed income securities and equity securities. The objective of a balanced fund is to provide both income from fixed income securities and growth potential from equity securities. Anywhere between 25 to 50 percent of a balanced fund can be invested in fixed income securities. Balanced funds are less volatile than growth or value funds.

Income Funds

Income funds typically invest in corporate and government bonds. The primary objective is generating income, rather than capital appreciation. Income funds offer investors a low cost method of investing in bonds. Considering that most bonds are in denominations of $1,000, income funds provide investors even with small initial investments, the opportunity to participate in an income fund. In addition, income funds offer investors diversification because of the low correlation between equity and bond funds. Finally, income funds are more conservative and less risky than an equity fund.

Growth and Income Funds

Similar to a balanced fund, **growth and income funds** invest in both equities and fixed income securities. However, a much larger percentage of the fund is allocated to equities in a growth and income fund. In fact, a growth and income fund can have up to 90 percent of its capital invested in equities. Growth and income funds are more risky than a balanced fund, but less risky than a growth or aggressive growth fund. A growth and income fund is appropriate for investors with a moderate to high risk tolerance.

Sector Funds

A **sector fund** restricts investments to a particular segment of the market. For example, there are technology, healthcare, telecommunications, financial, and pharmaceutical sector funds, just to name a few. Sector funds concentrate their holdings to firms that operate within a particular industry. Sector funds are more risky than most mutual funds because they are not diversified across industries. Sector funds do not eliminate the industry or business risk associated with a particular segment of the market. Sector funds are appropriate for investors who are speculating that a segment of the market may outperform other segments of the market.

Specialty Funds

Specialty funds that restrict their investments to firms that are good corporate citizens and do not operate in industries such as alcohol, gambling, or tobacco and are considered socially responsible funds. In addition, Green Funds are mutual funds that only invest in companies that are environmentally friendly. Historically, returns for socially responsible funds have under-performed the market.

In contrast to socially responsible funds, there are funds that invest only in "sin stocks." Sin stocks include the alcohol, tobacco, and gambling stocks. These funds tend to outperform socially responsible funds and can be considered defensive stocks during periods of a recession.

Quick Quiz 9.6

Highlight the answer to these questions:

1. A closed-end investment company is an investment company where investors purchase their shares from and sell them back to the mutual fund itself.
   a. True
   b. False

2. Balance funds typically invest in a total mix of both fixed income securities and bonds.
   a. True
   b. False

False, False.

Money Market Mutual Funds

Money market mutual funds provide investors with access to short-term, high quality, large denomination investments. Money market mutual funds invest in short-term government securities, certificates of deposit, commercial paper and bankers acceptance. Commercial paper are in denominations of $100,000, which are beyond the access of many individual investors. Money market mutual funds typically have a net asset value of $1.00 and provide investors with a slightly higher rate of return than a typical checking or savings account.

Index Funds

An **index fund** purchases a basket of stocks to match or replicate the performance of a particular industry. Index funds include Vanguard or ETrades S&P 500 Index fund, which matches the performance of the S&P 500. There are index funds for the S&P Midcap 400 and the Russell 2000, just to name a few.

Index funds take the approach, "if you can't beat 'em, join 'em." Over the long term it is difficult to outperform the market. Even professional money managers have a difficult time beating the market, especially after considering expenses. Actively managed funds have three distinct disadvantages over index funds. Those disadvantages include maintaining cash reserves, higher expense ratios, and turnover costs. Actively managed funds maintain cash reserves to meet redemptions and to take advantage of investment opportunities. Index funds simply use cash to meet redemptions, all excess cash is used to purchase an appropriate weighting of each stock within an index. Derivatives are used to leverage the remaining cash, so that the index does not materially underperform the market due to cash on hand. Actively managed funds also have a higher expense ratio to compensate the fund managers and staff for market research and security selection. Within an index fund, expenses are significantly lower, since there is no active asset selection process. Index funds typically have expense ratios between 20 and 40 basis points (0.20% - 0.40%), whereas actively managed funds can have expense ratios from 100 to 200 basis points (1.0% - 2.0%). Finally, actively managed funds turnover their holdings as often as once or more per year. The buying and selling of securities creates transaction costs that diminish returns. When considering the disadvantages of actively traded mutual funds, it is easy to understand why index funds tend to outperform actively managed funds.

Small, Mid, and Large Cap Funds

Small, mid, and large cap funds may have an objective regarding the size of a firm's market capitalization before making an investment. Capitalization of a firm is determined by multiplying the stock price by the number of shares outstanding. Below is a breakdown of the categories of companies for market size:
- Small Cap - Less than or equal to $1 billion
- Mid Cap - Between $1 and $5 billion
- Large Cap - Greater than $5 billion

Capitalization is an important consideration, especially when matching an investor's risk tolerance to an appropriate mutual fund. Small cap stocks and mutual funds that focus on small cap stocks are more volatile that large cap stocks or funds that invest in large caps. Small cap stocks are more volatile because they are more likely to experience large percentage increases or decreases in revenue or earnings. Comparatively, it is easier for the regional coffee house chain to double revenues and earnings relative to a company like Starbucks.

International Funds

International funds invest in securities and firms that are outside of the U.S. domestic market. International funds provide investors with the opportunity to diversify some U.S. market risk. International funds provide diversification benefits because of the low correlation between the U.S. and foreign markets. With improved technology and reliance on imports and exports, U.S. markets are more highly correlated with foreign markets than they were 15 to 20 years ago. As a result, this correlation translates into less diversification benefits than seen in the past.

International funds present unique risks to investors. Foreign firms may not have the same financial reporting requirements as in the U.S., therefore it can be difficult to properly value foreign firms. In addition, investors in international mutual funds are subject to exchange rate risk. Even though the mutual fund trades in U.S. dollars, the investments held by the mutual fund, may be denominated in foreign currencies.

Global Funds

The major difference between international and **global funds** is that global funds not only invest in foreign securities and markets, but also in U.S. domestic securities. As with international investing, there are unique risks such as laws regarding financial reporting and tariffs, which may be significantly different than laws in the U.S.

PERFORMANCE MEASURES

With over 8,000 mutual funds to choose from, how does an individual investor or investment advisor select an appropriate fund? The most important starting point is determining the investor's goals and objectives. Other considerations that should be included are the investor's risk tolerance and time horizon and their impact on an appropriate asset allocation. The next step is to evaluate securities and / or mutual funds to determine whether or not the security and / or mutual fund fits into the investor's established goals and objectives on the investment policy statement.

When evaluating a mutual fund, many individual investors consider the five-year average return of the fund and overall expenses. Some investors may think the higher the five-year return, the better. While this may be a good starting point, professional financial advisors understand that evaluating a fund based on its five-year historical return does not complete the story. Fund managers may have taken on additional risk, which resulted in a higher five-year average return than other funds, but may not have adequately compensated investors for all the risk taken. Mutual funds should be evaluated on a risk adjusted return basis. Those funds with the highest risk adjusted return are providing investors with the highest amount of return, given the riskiness of their investments.

In addition to evaluating a fund's risk adjusted return, professional advisors use databases of mutual fund information, such as Morningstar, to evaluate a fund's performance and narrow the 8,000 mutual funds down to a few that meet the client's goals and objectives. These databases contain a substantial amount of data regarding mutual funds and allow the user to build criteria regarding the riskiness of the fund, the expenses, manager tenure, historical performance, asset turnover, minimum initial investments, investment objective and more criteria. By inputting the investment criteria, the software will generate of list of appropriate funds to be considered. For individual investors who do not have access to Morningstar, much of the same information can be found in a funds prospectus or by visiting a website such as Morningstar.com.

The primary determining factor when evaluating the performance of a mutual fund or of any investment is the investment return calculated on a risk adjusted basis. There are four risk adjusted performance measures to consider, Jensen's Alpha, Sharpe, Treynor and the Information Ratio.

JENSEN'S ALPHA

Jensen's Alpha is an absolute risk adjusted performance measure. The term absolute indicates that Jensen's Alpha is an independent (versus relative) measure of the fund manager's performance compared to the expected returns based on the risk of the portfolio. A positive Alpha indicates the fund manager exceeded expectations, while a negative alpha indicates the fund manager did not produce enough return, given the level of risk undertaken. The formula for Jensen's alpha is:

$$\alpha_p = r_p - [r_f + \beta_p(r_m - r_f)]$$

Where:

r_p = Actual return of the portfolio

r_f = Risk-free rate of return

r_m = Expected return of the market

α_p = Alpha, the difference between the actual return generated by the fund and the expected return

β_p = Beta of the portfolio

Alternatively, alpha can be expressed as follows:

Alpha = Actual Return - Expected Return

Expected Return = CAPM formula $[r_f + \beta_p(r_m - r_f)]$

Alpha is the difference between the actual return generated by the fund and the expected return, given the level of riskiness of the fund, as measured by beta. Expected return is calculated using the Capital Asset Pricing Model formula. The higher the alpha the better, meaning the more return generated for a given level or risk. However, Jensen uses beta as its risk measure so if the portfolio is not well diversified, the calculated alpha may be misleading. The determination of a well diversified portfolio is an r-squared greater than or equal to 0.70.

EXAMPLE 9.27	Holly's mutual fund has a beta of 1.20 and generated an 11% return, while the S&P 500 generated a 10% return. R-squared is 0.85. The risk-free rate of return is

3%. What is Jensen's alpha and did the fund manager exceed expectations?

Alpha = Actual Return - Expected Return

Alpha = 0.11 - [0.03 + 1.2(0.10 - 0.03)]

Alpha = 0.11 - 0.114

Alpha = - 0.004

Holly's mutual fund has a negative alpha. Her fund slightly underperformed the market on a risk adjusted basis. Notice if the investor only compared the actual return of 11% relative to the S&P 500 return of 10%, the investor may incorrectly infer that the fund outperformed the market. It is critical for a mutual fund investor to evaluate a fund's performance on a risk adjusted basis.

SHARPE RATIO

The **Sharpe ratio** is a relative risk adjusted performance indicator, meaning the ratio by itself does not provide any insight. A Sharpe ratio for one fund needs to be compared to the Sharpe ratio for another fund to take on meaning. The fund with the highest Sharpe ratio provides the investor with the highest return for the risk taken. The formula for Sharpe is:

$$S_p = \frac{r_p - r_f}{\sigma_p}$$

Where:

r_p = Actual return of the portfolio

r_f = Risk-free rate of return

σ_p = Standard deviation of the portfolio

This formula provides the investor with the incremental return above the risk-free rate of return. Sharpe ratio is also a measure of the amount of incremental return, for each unit of risk. After calculating the Sharpe ratio for a set of funds or portfolios, the investor ranks the Sharpe ratios from highest to lowest. The fund with the highest Sharpe ratio will provide the investor with the best risk adjusted performance and the most return, per unit of risk. Notice that Sharpe uses standard deviation as its risk measure, thus not needing to assume a diversified portfolio.

EXAMPLE 9.28

Jill wants to know which of the following mutual funds provided her with the best risk adjusted return. Using the Sharpe ratio, which fund provided the highest return, per unit of risk, if the risk-free rate of return was 3% and the S&P 500 returned 12%?

	Total Return	Beta	Standard Deviation	R-Squared	Sharpe
Fund A	10%	0.75	4%	0.50	1.75
Fund B	15%	1.00	8%	0.68	1.50

Fund A

$$S_p = \frac{r_p - r_f}{\sigma_p} = \frac{0.10 - 0.03}{0.04} = 1.75$$

Fund B

$$S_p = \frac{r_p - r_f}{\sigma_p} = \frac{0.15 - 0.03}{0.08} = 1.50$$

Sharpe Ranking:
Fund A = 1.75
Fund B = 1.50

Fund A has the highest Sharpe ratio, therefore it provided the higher return, per unit of risk. In other words, Fund A provided Jill with 1.75% incremental return above the risk-free rate of return, for each unit of risk, as measured by standard deviation. Notice that the 1.75 is a relative measure and has no absolute meaning.

TREYNOR RATIO

The **Treynor ratio**, like Sharpe, is also a relative risk adjusted performance indicator. A Treynor ratio for one fund requires comparison to the Treynor ratio for another fund. The fund with the highest Treynor ratio provides the investor with the highest return for risk undertaken. The formula for Treynor is:

$$T_p = \frac{r_p - r_f}{\beta_p}$$

Where:
r_p = Actual return of the portfolio
r_f = Risk-free rate of return
β_p = Beta of the portfolio

Laureen is evaluating two mutual funds. She is interested in determining which fund offers the highest risk adjusted return, based on its Treynor measure. Which of the two below would you recommend?

EXAMPLE 9.29

	Total Return	Beta	Standard Deviation	R-Squared	Treynor
Fund C	10%	0.75	4%	0.80	0.093
Fund D	20%	1.25	12%	0.89	0.136

Fund C

$$T_p = \frac{r_p - r_f}{\beta_p} = \frac{0.10 - 0.03}{0.75} = 0.093$$

Fund D

$$T_p = \frac{r_p - r_f}{\beta_p} = \frac{0.20 - 0.03}{1.25} = 0.136$$

Treynor Ranking:

Fund D = 0.136

Fund C = 0.093

Therefore Fund D provided the greater risk adjusted return. Fund D provided 0.136% return for each unit of risk. Keep in mind that Treynor is a relative measure as is Sharpe, but Jensen is an absolute measure.

When to Use Alpha, Sharpe and Treynor

R-squared helps to determine which risk adjusted performance measure should be used. R-squared measures how well diversified a portfolio is and how much return is due to the market. The higher the r-squared, the more well diversified the portfolio, the more reliable beta is as a measure of total risk. If $r^2 \geq 0.70$, then the portfolio is considered well diversified and beta is an appropriate measure of total risk. Once r-squared falls below 0.70, the portfolio is considered undiversified, meaning beta is not a reliable measure of total risk.

If beta is an appropriate measure of total risk ($r^2 \geq 0.70$), then Treynor and Alpha can be used since both use beta in their calculations. If beta is not an appropriate measure of total risk (r-squared < 0.70) then standard deviation is the appropriate measure of total risk and Sharpe should be used as the risk adjusted performance measure.

INFORMATION RATIO (IR)

The **information ratio** measures the excess return above a benchmark, such as the S&P 500, per unit of risk. This formula is similar to the Sharpe ratio, however the Sharpe ratio measures the excess return above the risk-free rate of return and the information ratio measures the excess return above a benchmark. The formula for the information ratio is:

$$IR = \frac{(R_p - R_b)}{\sigma_A}$$

Where:

r_p = Actual return of the portfolio
r_b = Return of the benchmark
σ_A = Standard deviation of the active return (tracking error)

The information ratio provides investors with insight regarding the fund managers excess returns above the benchmark. A high information ratio can be the result of high actual returns, a low return for the benchmark or a low standard deviation.

Quick Quiz 9.7

Highlight the answer to these questions:

1. Jensen's Alpha is an absolute risk adjusted performance measurement that indicates whether the fund manager exceeded expectations or underperformed.
   a. True
   b. False

2. Treynor ratio is a relative risk adjusted performance indicator that compares a Treynor ratio for one fund to the Treynor ratio for another fund.
   a. True
   b. False

True, True.

EXAMPLE 9.30

Consider the following:

- Mutual Fund ABC had a return of 15% and a standard deviation of 12%.
- Mutual Fund XYZ had a return of 10% and a standard deviation 5%.
- The benchmark index has returns of 5%.

Mutual Fund ABC's IR

$$IR = \frac{(R_p - R_b)}{\sigma_A} = \frac{0.15 - 0.05}{0.12} = 0.83$$

Mutual Fund XYZ's IR

$$IR = \frac{(R_p - R_b)}{\sigma_A} = \frac{0.10 - 0.05}{0.05} = 1.00$$

Mutual Fund XYZ experienced lower returns than Mutual Fund ABC, but Mutual Fund XYZ has a higher information ratio than Mutual Fund ABC. A higher information ratio indicates that Mutual Fund XYZ manager provided higher returns more efficiently by taking on less risk.

ASSET ALLOCATION

Asset allocation is the process of dividing a portfolio into various asset classes. The chart below illustrates the appropriate riskiness or volatility of a portfolio (for a retirement goal) as measured by standard deviation. The investor's risk tolerance (ability and willingness) determines whether the client is a conservative, moderate, or aggressive investor.

STANDARD DEVIATION EXPRESSED IN %

EXHIBIT 9.11

Age:	25-30	31-35	36-40	41-45	46-50	51-55	56-60	61-65	66-70	71+
Conservative	10%	9.6%	9.1%	8.7%	8.2%	7.8%	7.3%	6.9%	6.4%	6%
Moderate	12%	11.4%	10.9%	10.3%	9.8%	9.2%	8.7%	8.1%	7.6%	7%
Aggressive	14%	13.3%	12.7%	12%	11.3%	10.7%	10%	9.3%	8.7%	8%

Based on the investor's time horizon and risk tolerance (as measured above by standard deviation), an allocation between equities and bonds can be recommended, as follows (% allocated to equities / % allocated to bonds):

EQUITIES % / BOND %

EXHIBIT 9.12

Age:	25-30	31-35	36-40	41-45	46-50	51-55	56-60	61-65	66-70	71+
Conservative	50/50	47/53	43/57	40/60	37/63	33/67	30/70	27/73	23/77	20/80
Moderate	65/35	61/39	57/43	53/47	48/52	44/66	40/60	36/64	32/68	28/73
Aggressive	80/20	75/25	70/30	65/35	60/40	55/45	50/50	45/55	40/60	35/65

When considering the riskiness of a portfolio, as measured by standard deviation, and the allocation between equities and bonds based on the time horizon, we can then determine an expected rate of return. The expected rate of return based on historical equity returns of 10.4 percent and corporate bond returns of 5.6 percent. Keep in mind that these are long-range historical returns and future returns may or may not be close to historical returns.

Age:	25-30	31-35	36-40	41-45	46-50	51-55	56-60	61-65	66-70	71+
Conservative	8.0%	7.8%	7.7%	7.5%	7.4%	7.2%	7.0%	6.9%	6.7%	6.6%
Moderate	8.7%	8.5%	8.3%	8.1%	7.9%	7.7%	7.5%	7.3%	7.1%	6.9%
Aggressive	9.4%	9.2%	9.0%	8.7%	8.5%	8.2%	8.0%	7.8%	7.5%	7.3%

The expected returns should be consistent with the required rate of return to attain the goals identified in the investment policy statement. If the expected returns are lower than the required return, the investor may have to take additional risk or change assumptions such as the amount of savings toward a goal, delaying the time horizon to take advantage of additional savings, and compounding of earnings

INVESTMENT ANALYSIS FOR AN INDIVIDUAL CLIENT

During the data gathering phase of the financial planning process, the client is likely to provide a number of investment statements including brokerage accounts, savings accounts, mutual funds, education savings accounts, and retirement savings plans (IRAs, 401(k) plans, etc). The financial planner must analyze and evaluate the investments of a client to determine if the asset allocation is appropriate, if the riskiness of the portfolio is appropriate and what changes need to be made to the portfolio. The process of analyzing investments includes:

1. Develop an investment policy statement.
2. Calculate characteristics of the portfolio including historical annual return, beta, standard deviation, and expected return.
3. Evaluate whether the portfolio is consistent with the investment policy statement. The evaluation should consider each category of the investment policy statement, such as:
   - Is the current portfolio appropriate given the goals of the client?
   - Are the investments appropriate give the time horizon for the client?
   - Based on the expected return in the investment policy statement, is the allocation of the portfolio such that the expected return is attainable?
   - Based on standard deviation and beta, is the riskiness of the client appropriate based on a risk tolerance questionnaire?
   - Based on constraints in the investment policy statement, are any of the current investments violating or contradictory to the constraints?
   - Are the types of securities held in taxable versus nontaxable accounts appropriate?
4. Make recommendations to rebalance and realign the investment portfolio such that it is consistent with the investment policy statement.

The investment analysis for an individual client is one of the most important components to developing a comprehensive financial plan. Investment analysis can occur simultaneously when applying any of the approaches described earlier in the textbook, such as financial statement analysis, the cash flow approach, metrics approach, or pie chart approach.

Key Terms

Aggressive Growth Funds - Typically invest in small cap stocks, where price appreciation is the primary objective.

Alpha - The difference between the actual return generated by the fund relative to the expected return give the level of riskiness of the fund, as measured by beta.

Arithmetic or Average Return - The sum of all returns divided by the number of periods.

Asset Allocation - The dividing of a portfolio into various asset classes.

Balanced Funds - Typically invest in both fixed income securities and equity securities.

Beta - A measure of systematic risk and provides the correlation of the volatility of a portfolio as compared to the market benchmark.

Bonds - A debt issuance where the bond issuer makes a promise to make periodic coupon payments (interest) and repayment of the par value (principal) at maturity.

Business Risk - The inherent risk of doing business in a particular industry.

Call Risk - The risk that a bond will be retired early by the issuing company.

Calls - Gives the holder the right to buy the underlying security at a certain price by a certain date.

Capital Asset Pricing Model (CAPM) - Calculates the relationship of risk and return for an individual security using Beta (ß) as its measure of risk.

Capital Market Line (CML) - The macro aspect of the Capital Asset Pricing Model (CAPM). It specifies the relationship between risk and return in all possible portfolios.

Closed-end Investment Companies - Another type of investment company that trade on stock market exchanges. Closed-end funds do not generally issue additional shares after their initial offering.

Coefficient of Determination - A measure of how much return is a result of the correlation to the market or what percentage of a security's return is a result of the market.

Constant Growth Dividend Discount Model - Values a company's stock by discounting the future stream of cash flows or dividends.

Corporate Bonds - Bonds issued by firms to raise capital to fund ongoing operations, retire debt, fund capital projects or acquisitions.

Key Terms

Correlation Coefficient - Measures the movement of one security relative to that of another security.

Country Risk - The risk of political and economic stability of a country that a company faces when doing business in a particular country.

Covariance - The measure of two securities when combined and their interactive risk (relative risk).

Debt - The lending of funds in return for periodic interest payments and the repayment of the principal debt obligation.

Default Risk - The risk that a company may not be able to repay its debt obligations.

Derivatives - Financial securities that derive their value from some underlying asset.

Efficient Frontier - Compares various portfolios based on their risk-return relationship.

Equity - Represents ownership in a business or property.

Equity Mutual Funds - Typically invest in equity securities.

Exchange Rate Risk - The risk that international investments and domestic companies that import or export goods are subject to changes in relationship to the price of a dollar, relative to foreign currencies.

Exchange Traded Funds (ETF's) - Another form of an investment company. An ETF invests in securities that are included in a particular index.

Executive Risk - The risk of moral character of the executives running the company. The extent to which executives break laws, regulations, or ethical standards that may negatively impact a company.

Expected Return - The rate of return expected for an asset or investment portfolio.

Financial Risk - The amount of leverage the company is using in its capital structure. Leverage is a measure of the amount of debt a company uses to capitalize the business.

Fixed Income or Bond Funds - Typically invest in bonds of various maturities.

Future Contract - A commitment to deliver an amount of a certain item at a specified date at an agreed upon price.

General Obligation Bonds - Bonds backed by the taxing authority that issued the bonds. The bonds are repaid through taxes that are collected by the municipality.

Key Terms

Geometric Return - A time-weighted compounded rate of return.

Global Funds - Not only invest in foreign securities and markets, but also in U.S. domestic securities.

Government or Regulation Risk - The potential risk that a country may pass a law or regulation that negatively impacts a particular industry.

Growth and Income Funds - Invest in both equities and fixed income securities. However, a much larger percentage of the fund is allocated to equities.

Growth Mutual Funds -Typically invest in large and mid cap stocks, where price appreciation is the primary objective.

Holding Period Return - Represents the time period an investment return is measured by an investor.

Income Funds - Typically invest in corporate and government bonds.

Index Fund - Purchases a basket of stocks to match or replicate the performance of a particular industry.

Information Ratio - Measures the excess return above a benchmark, such as the S&P 500, per unit of risk.

Interest Rate Risk - The risk that changes in interest rates will inversely impact both equities (stocks) and bonds.

Internal Rate of Return (IRR) - The compounded annual rate of return for investments of differing cash costs and cash flows.

International Funds - Invest in securities and firms that are outside of the U.S. domestic market.

Intrinsic Value - The underlying value of a security, when considering future cash flows and the riskiness of the security.

Investing - The process where capital resources are allocated and committed by investors with the expectation of earning a future positive economic return.

Investment Companies - Financial services companies that sell shares of stock to the public and use the proceeds to buy portfolios of securities. Mutual funds are one type of investment company where investors buy shares in a fund and own a pro rata portion of the investment portfolio, entitling them to a share of capital gains, interest and dividend income.

Investment Planning Process - Comprised of steps the financial planner and client follow to build an investment portfolio designed to accomplish the client's investment goals.

Key Terms

Investment Policy Statement - A written document that specifically identifies an investor's investment goals.

Jensen's Alpha - Absolute risk adjusted performance measurement.

Market Risk - The risk that in the short term, the daily fluctuations of the market tend to bring all securities in the same direction.

Modern Portfolio Theory - An approach to plan and construct a portfolio.

Money Market Mutual Funds - Invests in short-term government securities, certificates of deposit, commercial paper and bankers acceptance.

Municipal Bonds - Bonds issued to fund projects and spending for state or local governments. The three primary types of municipal bonds are general obligation bonds, revenue bonds, and private activity bonds.

Normal Distribution - Describes how returns are dispersed around the average return.

Open-end Investment Company - Also referred to as a mutual fund, is an investment company where investors purchase their shares from and sell them back to the mutual fund itself.

Options - Includes both calls and puts.

Price Earnings (P/E) Approach - Valuing equity securities is an earnings based valuation model that places a premium on the amount investors are willing to pay for each dollar of earnings.

Privacy Activity Bonds - Bonds issued to finance a joint project between the private sector and a municipality. Private activity bonds are often issued to fund the building of professional sports stadiums.

Purchasing Power Risk - The risk that inflation will cause prices to increase and a dollar today will not be able to purchase the same amount of goods and services tomorrow.

Puts - Gives the holder the right to sell the underlying security at a certain price by a certain date.

Real Estate Investment Trusts (REITs) - A type of mutual fund that pools investor contributions to purchase real estate or make construction or mortgage loans.

Reinvestment Rate Risk - The risk that an investor will not be able to reinvest income received from current investments at the same rate of return as the current investment return.

Key Terms

Revenue Bonds - Bonds issued to raise capital to fund a particular revenue generating project. The revenue generated by the project will be used to repay the bond issuance.

Risk - The uncertainty associated with investment returns. It is the possibility that actual returns will be different from what is expected.

Risk Adjusted Performance Measures - Sharpe, Treynor and Jensen's Alpha, which can be used to measure the performance of any type of investment including stocks, bonds and mutual funds.

Risk Tolerance Questionnaire - Evaluates a client's willingness to take risk by addressing risk issues.

Sector Fund - Restricts investments to a particular segment of the market. For example, there are technology, healthcare, telecommunications, financial, and pharmaceutical.

Security Market Line (SML) - The relationship between risk and return as defined by the CAPM (when graphically plotted).

Semivariance - Measures the possibility of returns below the average. Therefore, semivariance is a measure of downside risk.

Sharpe Ratio - A relative risk adjusted performance indicator, meaning the ratio by itself does not provide any insight. A Sharpe ratio for one fund needs to be compared to the Sharpe ratio for another fund to take on meaning.

Small, Mid, and Large Cap Funds - May have an objective regarding the size of a firm's market capitalization.

Specialty Funds - Restrict their investments to firms that are good corporate citizens and do not operate in industries such as alcohol, gambling, or tobacco and are considered socially responsible funds.

Standard Deviation - Measures the total risk of an investment.

Systematic Risk - Represents the risk that is inherent in the "system" and cannot be eliminated through diversification. The system represents U.S. market risk.

Treynor Ratio - A relative risk adjusted performance indicator. A Treynor ratio for one fund requires comparison to the Treynor ratio for another fund.

Unit Investment Trust (UIT) - An investment company that passively manages a portfolio of either stocks or bonds, known as a bond or equity UIT.

Key Terms

Unsystematic Risk - Represents the risk that can be diversified away, by combining multiple stocks, from multiple industries, into one portfolio.

U.S. Government Bonds - Bonds issued by the U.S. government to finance the national debt and to fund deficit spending. The three primary types of bonds issued by the U.S. government are Treasury Bills, Treasury Notes, and Treasury Bonds.

Value Funds - Typically invest in securities that are deemed to be out of favor or extremely under-valued.

Warrant - A long-term option that gives the holder the right to buy a certain number of shares of stocks in a particular company by a certain date.

Weighted Average Return - Based on the dollar amount or percentage of a portfolio invested in each asset. Investments with a larger allocation or weighting will contribute more to the overall return of the portfolio.

Zero Coupon Bonds - Bonds sold at a deep discount to par value and do not pay periodic interest payments. Instead, the bonds increase in value each year, so that at maturity the bonds are worth their par value.

Zero Growth Dividend Model - Values a security based on the stock's capitalized amount of the annual dividends.

1. Discuss important issues covered by a risk tolerance questionnaire.

2. Discuss a client's ability and willingness to accept risk associated with personal investment.

3. Define the steps involved in the investment planning process.

4. Discuss the purpose of an investment policy statement.

5. List the different ways to measure actual investment returns.

6. Define risk that is associated with investment choices.

7. What is the difference between systematic and unsystematic risk and how are they measured?

8. What is used to measure investment risk?

9. What is the modern portfolio theory and the efficient frontier?

10. Define the difference between the Capital Market Line and the Security Market Line.

11. Differentiate between correlation coefficient, covariance, and coefficient of determination.

12. Discuss the three types of measuring models used in this textbook to value equity.

13. Discuss how bonds can assist an investor to accomplish a variety of investment goals.

14. List the types of risks inherent to investing in bonds.

15. Discuss why an investor may choose to invest in real estate.

16. What are the different types of derivatives?

17. Define an investment company and list types of investment companies.

18. List the different types of closed-end funds.

19. What are the risk adjusted performance measures?

20. Define asset allocation.

1. Sylvia has a two assets in her portfolio, asset A and asset B. Asset A has a standard deviation of 40% and asset B has a standard deviation of 20%. 50% of her portfolio is invested in asset A and 50% is invested in asset B. The correlation for asset A and asset B is 0.90. What is the standard deviation of her portfolio?

   a. Greater than 30%.

   b. Less than 30%.

   c. Equal to 30%.

   d. Not enough information to determine.

2. Using the constant growth dividend valuation model, calculate the intrinsic value of a stock that pays a dividend this year of $2.00 and is expected to grow at 6%. The beta for this stock is 1.5, the risk-free rate of return is 3% and the market return is12%.

   a. $20.19.

   b. $28.75.

   c. $35.33.

   d. $48.27.

3. Michael has an investment with the following annual returns for four years:

   Year 1: 12%
   Year 2: -5%
   Year 3: 8%
   Year 4: 18%

   What is the arithmetic mean (AM) and what is the geometric mean (GM)?

   a. AM = 8.25%, GM = 7.91%.

   b. AM = 8.25%, GM = 10.64%.

   c. AM = 10.75%, GM = 7.91%.

   d. AM = 10.75%, GM = 10.64%.

4. The type of risk which measures the extent to which a firm uses debt securities and other forms of debt in its capital structure to finance is known as:

   a. Business risk.

   b. Systematic risk.

   c. Default risk.

   d. Financial risk.

5. The type of risk which CANNOT be eliminated through diversification is:

    a. Unsystematic Risk.

    b. Company Specific Risk.

    c. Systematic Risk.

    d. Business Risk.

6. Municipal bonds that are backed by the income from specific projects are known as:

    a. Income bonds.

    b. Revenue bonds.

    c. General obligation bonds.

    d. Debenture bonds.

7. Tom Taylor wants to accumulate wealth, but he has told his financial planner that he is risk-averse. What should the financial planner advise Tom to do regarding his current asset investment choices, considering his risk tolerance and his goal of accumulating wealth?

    a. Invest in products which bring the highest return regardless of risk.

    b. Invest in products producing high income because fixed income products are generally safe.

    c. Put Tom's assets in 100% cash equivalents because he is risk-averse.

    d. Determine Tom's true risk tolerance.

8. A bond fund had the following yearly returns:

    Year 1 at 14%
    Year 2 at 7%
    Year 3 at -3%
    Year 4 at 18%
    Year 5 at 9%

    What is the standard deviation of the returns?

    a. 6.04.

    b. 7.13.

    c. 7.97.

    d. 8.43.

9. If the risk/return performance of a stock lies above the Security Market Line, the stock is said to have a:

    a. Positive correlation coefficient.

    b. Positive alpha.

    c. Positive expected return.

    d. Positive covariance.

10. Bob Conrad's investment portfolio consists of several types of stocks, bonds, and money market instruments. The portfolio has an overall standard deviation of 12%, a beta of 1.06, and a total return for the year of 11%. Bob is considering adding one of two alternative investments to his portfolio. Stock A has a standard deviation of 13%, a beta of 0.87, and a correlation coefficient with the portfolio of 0.6. Stock B has a standard deviation of 11%, a beta of 0.97, and a correlation coefficient of 0.95. Which stock should Bob consider adding to his portfolio, and why?

    a. Stock A because it has a lower correlation coefficient.

    b. Stock A because it has a lower beta than that of the portfolio.

    c. Stock B because it has a lower standard deviation than that of the portfolio.

    d. Stock B because it has a higher correlation coefficient.

11. The Performance Fund had returns of 19% over the evaluation period and the benchmark portfolio yielded a return of 17% over the same period. Over the evaluation period, the standard deviation of returns from the Fund was 23% and the standard deviation of returns from the benchmark portfolio was 21%. Assuming a risk-free rate of return of 8%, which one of the following is the calculation of the Sharpe index of performance for the Performance Fund over the evaluation period?

    a. 0.3913.

    b. 0.4286.

    c. 0.4783.

    d. 0.5238.

12. Which of the following statements regarding investment risk is correct?

    1. Beta is a measure of systematic, non-diversifiable risk.

    2. Rational investors will form portfolios and eliminate systematic risk.

    3. Rational investors will form portfolios and eliminate unsystematic risk.

    4. Systematic risk is the relevant risk for a well-diversified portfolio.

    5. Beta captures all the risk inherent in an individual security.

        a. 1 and 5.

        b. 2 and 5.

        c. 1, 3 and 4.

        d. 2, 3 and 4.

13. Mutual fund XYZ has a beta of 1.5, a standard deviation of 12%, and a correlation to the S&P 500 of 0.80. How much return of fund XYZ is due to the S&P 500?

    a. 20%.

    b. 64%.

    c. 80%.

    d. 100%.

14. As a measure for risk, the Capital Market Line (CML) uses the:

   a. Risk-free rate of return.
   b. Beta of the market.
   c. Standard deviation of the market.
   d. Portfolio weighted beta.

15. Given a mean of 13% and a deviation of 9%, what is the range for 99% of all possible results?

   a. 1 standard deviation (68%) -4% to 22%.
   b. 2 standard deviation (95%) -5% to 31%.
   c. 3 standard deviation (99%) -14% to 40%.
   d. None of the above.

16. Which index should Jan use as a benchmark when evaluating the performance of her XYZ mutual fund?

	Index 1	Index 2	Index 3	Index 4
Beta	0.75	1.1	1.25	1.5
r-squared	0.80	0.90	0.95	0.50

   a. Index 1.
   b. Index 2.
   c. Index 3.
   d. Index 4.

17. What is the return that a client should expect from a security that last year returned 11.7% with a standard deviation of 0.146, a beta of 1.2, when the overall market return is expected to be 10.93%, and U.S. Treasury is expected to earn 3.56%?

   a. 11.7%.
   b. 12.4%.
   c. 13.3%.
   d. 14.6%.

18. An investor with a required rate of return of 12.5% is looking at a stock that currently pays a $3.75 dividend per share, has a dividend growth rate of 6%, and is selling in the market for $60.00 per share. What would you recommend?

   a. Buy; it meets the buyer's return requirements and is underpriced.
   b. Buy; it does not meet the buyer's return requirements, but it is underpriced.
   c. Do not buy; it does not meet the buyer's return requirements and is overpriced.
   d. Do not buy; it meets the buyer's return requirements, but is overpriced.

19. The primary difference between open-end and closed-end investment companies is:

    a. Closed end funds always sell at par value.

    b. Open-end funds do not charge sales fees.

    c. Closed-end funds guarantee the Net Asset Value (NAV) at the time of sale or purchase.

    d. Closed-end funds sell only a limited number of shares.

20. Which of the following returns do mutual funds use when reporting a five-year historical return?

    a. Time-Weighted Return.

    b. Dollar-Weighted Return.

    c. Arithmetic Mean.

    d. Holding Period Return.

21. Walt Drizzly stock is currently trading at $45 and pays a dividend of $3.50. Analysts project a dividend growth rate of 5%. Your client, Toby Benjamin, requires a rate of 12% to meet his stated goal. Toby wants to know if he should purchase stock in Walt Drizzly.

    a. Yes, the stock is undervalued.

    b. No, the stock is overvalued.

    c. No, the required rate of return is higher than the projected growth rate.

    d. Yes, the required rate is higher than the expected rate.

22. Match the investment characteristic(s) listed below which describe(s) a unit investment trust.

    a. Passive management of the portfolios.

    b. Self-liquidating investments usually holding bonds.

    c. Both a and b.

    d. Neither a nor b.

23. Given the following diversified mutual fund performance data, which fund had the best risk-adjusted performance if the risk-free rate of return is 5.7%?

- Fund A: Average rate of return = 7.82%, Standard deviation of annual return = 7.60% and Beta = 0.950
- Fund B: Average annual return = 12.87%, Standard deviation of annual return = 15.75% and Beta = 1.250
- Fund C: Average annual return = 10.34%, Standard deviation of annual return = 18.74% and Beta = 0.857
- Fund D: Average annual return = 7.50%, Standard deviation of annual return = 8.10% and Beta = 0.300

    a. Fund B, because the annual return is highest.

    b. Fund C, because the Sharpe ratio is lowest.

    c. Fund D, because the Treynor ratio is highest.

    d. Fund A, because the Treynor ratio is lowest.

24. Match the investment characteristic(s) listed below which describe(s) closed-end investment companies.

    a. Passive management of the portfolios.

    b. Shares of the fund are normally traded in major secondary markets.

    c. Both a and b.

    d. Neither a nor b.

25. In computing portfolio performance, the Sharpe index uses _____, while the Treynor index uses _____ for the risk measure.

    a. standard deviation; correlation coefficient.

    b. beta; standard deviation.

    c. standard deviation; beta.

    d. standard deviation; coefficient of variation.

26. The following investment return will result in what dollar weighted return? An initial outlay of $50,000, with three years of additional outflows of $10,000 each, and inflows as follows: $0 the first year, $20,000 in years 2 and 3, and sale of the property at the end of year 3 for $75,000.

    a. 27.64%.

    b. 14.04%.

    c. 18.32%.

    d. 20.67%.

27. Using the CAPM formula, what return should a client expect from a security that returned 10% with a standard deviation of 6%, a beta of 1.5, when the overall market return has been 8%, and the risk-free rare is around 2%?

    a. 8%.

    b. 9%.

    c. 10%.

    d. 11%.

28. Match the investment characteristic(s) listed below which describe(s) an open-end investment company.

    a. Only passive management of the portfolios.

    b. Shares of the fund are normally traded in major secondary markets.

    c. Both a and b.

    d. Neither a nor b.

29. Which of the following is/are characteristics of a municipal bond unit investment trust?

    1. Additional securities are not added to the trust.

    2. Shares may be sold at a premium or discount to net asset value.

    3. Shares are normally traded on the open market (exchanges.)

    4. The portfolio is self-liquidating.

    a. 1 only.

    b. 1 and 4.

    c. 2 and 3.

    d. 2 and 4.

30. A fixed income security whose price has fallen as a result of an increase in interest rates in the market place is said to be subject to:

    a. Interest rate risk.

    b. Reinvestment rate risk.

    c. Purchasing power risk.

    d. Exchange rate risk.

31. The type of risk which may be eliminated through diversification is:

    a. Market Risk.

    b. Purchasing Power Risk.

    c. Interest Rate.

    d. Business Risk.

32. The risk which a firm may not be able to meets its debt obligations is known as:

    a. Business risk.
    b. Interest rate.
    c. Default risk.
    d. Financial risk.

33. William has an investment with the following annual returns for four years:

    - Year 1: -2%
    - Year 2: 9%
    - Year 3: 15%
    - Year 4: 5%

    What is the Arithmetic Mean (AM) and what is the Geometric Mean (GM)?

    a. AM = 6.12%, GM = 6.57%.
    b. AM = 6.12%, GM = 6.02%.
    c. AM = 6.75%, GM = 6.02%.
    d. AM = 6.75%, GM = 6.57%.

34. An investor purchased a bond for $980, received $75 in interest, and then sold the bond for $950 after holding it for seven months. What is the holding period return?

    a. 4.6%.
    b. 4.7%.
    c. 4.8%.
    d. 4.9%.

35. Which method of portfolio evaluation allows the comparison of a portfolio manager's performance to the expected return, using Beta as the measure of risk?

    a. The Treynor Model.
    b. The Jensen Model.
    c. Information Ratio.
    d. The Sharpe Model.

36. What is the weighted average beta of the following portfolio?

- Stock L has a beta of 1.45 and constitutes 10% of the portfolio;
- Stock M has a value of $125,000,with a beta of 0.93;
- While Stock N makes up 40% of the portfolio with a beta of 0.65, and
- Stock O, with a 2.2 beta has a dollar value of $175,000.

    a. 1.24.

    b. 1.31.

    c. 1.54.

    d. 1.76.

37. Which of the following statements regarding investment risk is correct?

1. Beta is a measure of systematic, non-diversifiable risk.
2. Rational investors will form portfolios and eliminate systematic risk.
3. Rational investors will form portfolios and eliminate unsystematic risk.
4. Systematic risk is the relevant risk for a well-diversified portfolio.
5. Beta captures all the risk inherent in an individual security.

    a. 1, 2 and 5.

    b. 1, 3 and 4.

    c. 2 and 5.

    d. 2, 3 and 4.

38. Which of the following reveals the relationship of a given security's movement relative to that of the market?

    a. Beta.

    b. Correlation coefficient.

    c. R-Squared.

    d. Standard deviation.

39. The ideal correlation for portfolio construction is:

    a. +1.0.

    b. -1.0.

    c. 0.0.

    d. +0.70.

40. Which of the following would be considered a systematic risk?

    a. Business Risk.

    b. Financial Risk.

    c. Company-specific Risk.

    d. Market Risk.

Quick Quiz Explanations

Quick Quiz 9.1
1. False. A risk tolerance questionnaire evaluates a client's willingness to take risk by addressing risk issues (e.g., understanding of stock market, comfort level with investing in stock market etc.). An investment policy statement identifies an investor's investment goals and guides the investor regarding appropriate investment choices.
2. True.
3. True.

Quick Quiz 9.2
1. True.
2. False. The simple average return is the arithmetic or average return. The geometric return is a time-weighted compounded rate of return.
3. False. Purchasing power risk is a type of systematic risk.

Quick Quiz 9.3
1. False. Standard deviation measures the total risk of an investment. Beta is a measure of systematic risk.
2. True.

Quick Quiz 9.4
1. False. The Efficient Frontier compares various portfolios based on their risk-return relationship.
2. True.
3. True.
4. False. The risk of a portfolio can be measured through determination of the interactivity of standard deviation and the covariance of securities in the portfolio.

Quick Quiz 9.5
1. True.
2. True.
3. True.
4. False. Puts give the holder the right to sell the underlying security at a certain price by a certain date. Calls give the holder the right to buy the underlying security at a certain price by a certain date.

Quick Quiz 9.6
1. False. An open-end investment company is an investment company where investors purchase their shares from and sell them back to the mutual fund itself. A closed-end investment company trades on stock market exchanges.
2. False. Balance funds typically invest in both fixed income securities and equity securities.

Quick Quiz 9.7
1. True.
2. True.

David and Amy Rudolph Case & Case Analysis Part 1

LEARNING OBJECTIVES

After reading this chapter, you should be able to:
- Describe an initial meeting and summarize data and draw conclusions for the life-cycle approach.
- Prepare a comprehensive engagement letter.
- Gather internal and external data and prepare financial statements.
- Create the pie chart approach.
- Prepare financial statement analysis using a ratio analysis approach.
- Prepare each of the ratios and compare them to the benchmark.
- Prepare the two-step, three panel, metrics approach with schedules.
- Prepare the cash flow approach.
- Prepare the strategic approach.
- Make a presentation to the client using current and projected financial statements and ratios.
- Prepare a closing engagement letter that includes the responsibility for implementation and monitoring.

DAVID & AMY RUDOLPH CASE - INTERNAL DATA

THE FAMILY

David Rudolph (age 51, born on December 4th) is the owner of an office furniture company, DR Office Furniture Inc., (DRI) and is married to Amy Rudolph (age 35, born on February 14th) who is a self-employed real estate broker. David's salary is $275,000. The client's net worth is $4.3 million; of which $3.325 million is the value of his business, DRI.

This is both David and Amy's second marriage. David has a 30-year-old son, Trevor, from his first marriage. Trevor is married and has one child, Trevor Jr. (age 2). Amy has a child from her former marriage, Madelyn (age 14, born on March 31st), who lives with Amy's former husband, George (age 35, born on October 23rd), who is her legal guardian. David and Amy have a child on their own, Danny (age 1). Amy was divorced from George two years ago and they have a very contentious relationship.

Amy is self-employed and has Schedule C net income of $150,000 per year before self-employment tax or any deduction for any qualified or tax advantaged retirement plan.

PERSONAL AND FINANCIAL OBJECTIVES

1. They want to provide for Danny and Madelyn's education.
2. They want to retire debt free when David reaches age 62 (when they both plan to retire).
3. They need adequate retirement income.
4. They want to have adequate risk management coverage.
5. David is primarily concerned with providing income to Amy for the duration of her life and secondarily, leaving the remainder of his estate to their child, Danny.

SUMMARY OF INITIAL DATA COLLECTED - LIFE CYCLE APPROACH

Using the approaches learned earlier in the textbook, the financial planner will initially prepare the life cycle characteristics approach. This approach seeks to efficiently establish which phase or phases of the life cycle the client is in and to then deduce from that assessment the likely client goals and risks of the client. The life cycle approach, while easy and efficient, lacks sufficient detail to permit the financial planner to prepare a complete financial plan.

Based on the initial client communication, the information collected is as follows:

Summary of Data Collected - Life Cycle Approach	
Ages	• David (age 51) • Amy (age 35)
Marital Status	• Married (likely MFJ income tax filing status)
Children & Grandchildren	• Trevor (age 30) - From David's previous marriage with one child Trevor Jr. (age 2) • Madelyn (age 14) - From Amy's previous marriage, lives with George (former husband) • Danny - Child of David and Amy (age 1)
Net Worth	• Approximately $4.3 million (DRI dependent)
Income	• Amy $150,000 self employed (Schedule C) - proprietorship • David owner of DRI / employer $275,000
Self-Employed	• Amy is self employed with no employees • David is owner / employer of a C corporation (DRI) with 31 employees

Preliminary Conclusions Regarding the Rudolphs (Life Cycle Approach)

Using the information from the life cycle approach, the financial planner can get an indication of the Rudolph family's risks and probable goals. Notice that David (age 51) and Amy (age 35) are in their middle years, suggesting that they are in both the asset accumulation and conservation (risk management) phases. They have children and a grandchild, suggesting a need for education funding for their child and a possible interest in setting up a 529 Savings Plan for the grandchild. Having a young child clearly establishes the need for both life and disability insurance for income replacement (both parents). David and Amy probably file joint federal and state income tax returns. Amy's Schedule C income creates the opportunity to establish a Keogh (self employed) retirement plan (could be a SEP, SIMPLE, or qualified plan such as a 401(k) plan or profit sharing plan). The net worth of $4.3 million suggests the need for estate planning.

What a financial planner does not know about the Rudolph's using the life cycle approach is the quality of the relationship between the parties (which could seriously affect the planning), what specific insurance coverages they have, what their ratios are (e.g., savings rate), or what their detailed financial statements look like. We can, however, deduce that they are probably interested in retirement planning, a comprehensive review of their risk management, investments, estate planning portfolios, and education funding. DRI is their largest asset so there are valuation, disposition, and lack of diversification issues. The Rudolphs may or may not have conflicting goals relating to retirement and the management and interaction with children and grandchildren.

RUDOLPH CASE FILE - ADDITIONAL DATA

External Information

Economic Information
- General inflation is expected to average 2.5% annually for the foreseeable future.
- Education inflation is expected to be 6% annually.
- Real GDP has been 2.75% and is expected to continue to be 2.75% for the next several years.
- It is expected that the S&P 500 will return approximately 9% this year and for the foreseeable future.
- T-bills are considered the appropriate proxy for the risk-free rate of return and are currently earning 3.5%.

Bank Lending Rates
- 15-year conforming mortgage is 4.75%.
- 30-year conforming mortgage is 5.0%.
- Any closing costs associated with mortgage refinance are an additional 3% of the amount mortgaged.
- The secured personal loan rate is 8.0%.
- Credit card rates are 18%.

ECONOMIC OUTLOOK - INVESTMENTS

	Return	Standard Deviation
Small Company Stocks	12%	18%
Large Company Stocks (Actively Managed)	10%	16%
S&P 500	9%	14%
Corporate Bonds	7%	5%
Long-term Treasury Bonds	6%	4%
T-bills	3.5%	2%

ADDITIONAL INTERNAL INFORMATION

INSURANCE INFORMATION

Life Insurance

Policy 1	
Insured	David Rudolph
Face Amount	$2,000,000
Type	Whole Life Policy
Cash Value	$120,000
Annual Premium	$10,000
Beneficiary	David Rudolph
Owner	David Rudolph

Policy 2	
Insured	David Rudolph
Face Amount	2x Salary=$550,000
Type	Group Term - Employer Provided
Cash Value	$0
Annual Premium	$700
Beneficiary	David Rudolph
Owner	David Rudolph

Policy 3	
Insured	Amy Rudolph
Face Amount	$250,000
Type	Term Policy Ten Year Level Term
Cash Value	$0
Annual Premium	$500
Beneficiary	Madelyn
Owner	Amy Rudolph

Health Insurance

David currently has an indemnity group health and major medical hospitalization plan through his company. Amy, David, and Danny are currently covered by his health insurance plan. DRI pays the entire premium for the health insurance policy. Madelyn is covered under both David and George's health insurance plans. David's plan has the following characteristics:

- $500 per individual deductible
- $1,000 total family deductible
- 80% co-insurance clause for major medical
- $3,000 annual family stop loss limit

Long-Term Disability Insurance

Long-Term Disability Policy - David	
Type	Own Occupation
Insured	David
Guaranteed Renewable	Yes
Benefit	60% of Gross Pay
Premium Paid By	Employer
Residual Benefits Clause	Yes
Elimination Period	90 Days
Annual Premium	$2,000

Amy is not covered by a long-term disability insurance policy.

Long-Term Care Insurance

Neither David nor Amy have long-term care insurance.

Property and Liability Insurance
Homeowners Insurance

Personal Residence	
Type	HO3 without endorsements
Dwelling	$1,500,000
Other Structures	$150,000
Personal Property	$500,000
Personal Liability	$100,000
Medical Payments	$10,000
Deductible	$1,000
Co-Insurance %	80 / 20
Annual Premium	$4,200

Lake House	
Type	HO3 without endorsements
Dwelling	$200,000
Other Structures	$20,000
Personal Property	$100,000
Personal Liability	$100,000
Medical Payments	$10,000
Deductible	$1,000
Co-Insurance %	80 / 20
Annual Premium	$3,500

There is no flood insurance on the personal residence or the lake house.

Auto Insurance

	Auto #1 David's Car	Auto # 2 Amy's Car
Type	Personal Automobile Policy (PAP)	Personal Automobile Policy (PAP)
Liability (Bodily Injury)	$100,000/$300,000/$50,000	$100,000/$300,000/$50,000
Medical Payments	$10,000	$10,000
Uninsured Motorist	$100,000/$300,000	$100,000/$300,000
Collision Deductible	$1,000	$500
Comprehensive Deductible	$500	$250
Annual Premium	$900	$1,200

Boat Insurance
There is no boat insurance (property or liability).

Liability Insurance

There is no personal liability umbrella policy (PLUP).

FINANCIAL STATEMENTS: STATEMENT OF FINANCIAL POSITION (BEGINNING OF YEAR)

EXHIBIT 10.1

Statement of Financial Position
David and Amy Rudolph
Balance Sheet as of 1/1/2013

ASSETS[1]			LIABILITIES AND NET WORTH		
Current Assets			**Current Liabilities[2]**		
JT Cash & Checking	$20,000		W Credit Cards	$15,000	
JT Money Market	$250,000		**Total Current Liabilities**		$15,000
Total Current Assets		$270,000			
Investment Assets			**Long-Term Liabilities[2]**		
H DR Office Furniture, Inc[3]	$3,325,000		JT Principal Residence	$1,185,264	
H Brokerage Account	$410,000		H Lake House	$153,434	
H Education Account[4](529)	$46,000		H Boat	$78,734	
H 401(k) Plan w/ Roth	$32,000		**Total Long-Term Liabilities**		$1,417,432
W Traditional IRA	$11,000				
W Roth IRA	$16,000				
Total Investment Assets		$3,840,000	**Total Liabilities**		$1,432,432
Personal Use Assets					
JT Principal Residence	$1,300,000				
H Lake House	$450,000				
JT Furniture, Clothing	$100,000		**Total Net Worth**		$4,642,568
H Car # 1	$25,000				
W Car # 2	$35,000				
H Boat	$55,000				
Total Personal Use Assets		$1,965,000			
Total Assets		$6,075,000	**Total Liabilities & Net Worth**		$6,075,000

1. Assets are stated at fair market value.
2. Liabilities are stated at principal only as of January 1, 2013 before January payments.
3. This is David's 75% interest and the value is based on his estimate.
4. This is for Madelyn and Danny. David currently saves $6,000 per year into this account (see portfolio).

Title Designations:
H = Husband (Sole Owner)
W = Wife (Sole Owner)
JT = Joint Tenancy with Survivorship Rights

Statement of Financial Position
David and Amy Rudolph
Balance Sheet as of 12/31/13 (and 1/1/2014)

ASSETS[1]			LIABILITIES AND NET WORTH			
Current Assets			**Current Liabilities[2]**			
JT Cash & Checking	$25,000		W Credit Cards	$15,000		
JT Money Market	$270,000		**Total Current Liabilities**		$15,000	
Total Current Assets		$295,000				
Investment Assets			**Long-Term Liabilities[2]**			
H DR Office Furniture, Inc[3]	$3,325,000		JT Principal Residence	$1,169,619		
H Brokerage Account	$500,000		H Lake House	$148,038		
H Education Account[4] (529)	$46,000		H Boat	$70,276		
H 401(k) Plan w/ Roth	$50,000		**Total Long-Term Liabilities**		$1,387,933	
W Traditional IRA	$15,000					
W Roth IRA	$20,000					
Total Investment Assets		$3,956,000	**Total Liabilities**		$1,402,933	
Personal Use Assets						
JT Principal Residence	$800,000					
H Lake House	$450,000					
JT Furniture, Clothing	$100,000		**Total Net Worth**		$4,313,067	
H Car # 1	$25,000					
W Car # 2	$35,000					
H Boat	$55,000					
Total Personal Use Assets		$1,465,000				
Total Assets		$5,716,000	**Total Liabilities & Net Worth**		$5,716,000	

1. Assets are stated at fair market value.
2. Liabilities are stated at principal only as of December 31, 2013 before January payments.
3. This is David's 75% interest and the value is based on his estimate.
4. This is for Madelyn and Danny. David currently saves $6,000 per year into this account (see portfolio).

Title Designations:
H = Husband (Sole Owner)
W = Wife (Sole Owner)
JT = Joint Tenancy with Survivorship Rights

EXHIBIT 10.3

Statement of Income and Expenses
David and Amy Rudolph
Statement of Income and Expenses for Past Year (2013) and
Expected (Approximate) For This Year (2014)

Cash Inflows			Totals
David's Salary	$275,000		
Amy's Salary	$150,000		
Total Cash Inflows			$425,000
Cash Outflows			
Savings			
Money Market	$1,000		
401(k) Plan	$22,000		
Education (529 Plan)	$6,000		
Total Savings			$29,000
Taxes			
Federal Income Taxes Withheld & Estimated Payments	$64,800		
State Income Taxes Withheld	$22,000		
David's Social Security Taxes	$10,609		
Amy's Social Security Taxes & Estimated Payments	$17,593		
Property Tax Principal Residence	$8,000	ND	
Property Tax Vacation Home	$4,000	ND	
Total Taxes			$127,002
Debt Payments (Principal & Interest)			
Principal Residence	$86,335	ND	
Lake House	$15,967	ND	
Boat	$15,201	ND	
Credit Cards	$15,000	ND	
Total Debt Payments			$132,503
Living Expenses			
Utilities Principal Residence	$5,000	ND	
Lake House Expenses (net of rental income of $5,000)	$15,000	ND	
Gasoline for Autos	$5,000	ND	
Lawn Service	$2,000	ND	
Entertainment	$15,000		
Vacations	$25,000		
Church Donations	$10,000	ND	
Clothing	$18,000	ND	
Auto Maintenance	$2,000	ND	
Satellite TV	$1,800	ND	
Food	$8,000	ND	
Miscellaneous	$10,000	ND	
Total Living Expenses			$116,800
Insurance Payments			
HO Insurance Principal Residence	$4,200	ND	
HO Insurance Lake House	$3,500	ND	
Auto Premiums	$2,100	ND	
Life Insurance #1	$10,000	ND	
Life Insurance #3	$500	ND	
Total Insurance Payments			$20,300
Total Cash Outflows			$425,605
Net Discretionary Cash Flows			($605)

ND = Non-Discretionary cash flow per mutual understanding between financial planner and client.

INVESTMENT INFORMATION

As part of a financial planning engagement, David and Amy fill out a risk tolerance questionnaire. Their answers to the questions in the Global Portfolio Allocation Scoring System (PASS) are as follows:

Global Portfolio Allocation Scoring System (PASS) for Individual Investors						
Questions	Strongly Agree	Agree	Neutral	Disagree	Strongly Disagree	David & Amy
1. Earning a high long-term total return that will allow my capital to grow faster than the inflation rate is one of my most important investment objectives.		D	A			3.5
2. I would like an investment that provides me with an opportunity to defer taxation of capital gains to future years.		D	A			3.5
3. I do not require a high level of current income from my investments.		D, A				4
4. I am willing to tolerate some sharp down swings in the return on my investments in order to seek a potentially higher return than would normally be expected from more stable investments.		D	A			3.5
5. I am willing to risk a short-term loss in return for a potentially higher long-run rate of return.			D, A			3
6. I am financially able to accept a low level of liquidity in my investment portfolio.		D, A				4

Global Portfolio Allocation Scoring System (PASS) for Individual Investors – developed by Dr. William Droms (Georgetown University) and Steven N. Strauss, (DromsStrauss Advisors Inc.) – model used with permission.

21.5

Based on the scoring of 5 for "Strongly Agree" and decreasing by 1 for each column to the right with 1 point for "Strongly Disagree," the Rudolphs score is 21.5. This score equates to the RT3 Target portfolio.

EXHIBIT 10.4 **PASS FOR INDIVIDUAL INVESTORS**

	Short-Term Horizon				Intermediate-Term Horizon				Long-Term Horizon			
	RT1 Target	RT2 Target	RT3 Target	RT4 Target	RT1 Target	RT2 Target	RT3 Target	RT4 Target	RT1 Target	RT2 Target	RT3 Target	RT4 Target
PASS Score	6 - 12	13 - 18	19 - 24	25 - 30	6 - 12	13 - 18	19 - 24	25 - 30	6 - 12	13 - 18	19 - 24	25 - 30
Cash and Money Market Fund	40%	30%	20%	10%	5%	5%	5%	5%	5%	5%	3%	2%
Treasury Bonds/ Bond Funds	40%	30%	30%	20%	60%	35%	20%	10%	30%	20%	12%	0%
Corporate Bonds/ Bond Funds	20%	30%	30%	40%	15%	15%	15%	10%	15%	10%	10%	4%
Subtotal	**100%**	**90%**	**80%**	**70%**	**80%**	**55%**	**40%**	**25%**	**50%**	**35%**	**25%**	**6%**
International Bond Funds	0%	0%	0%	0%	0%	5%	5%	5%	0%	5%	5%	4%
Subtotal	**0%**	**0%**	**0%**	**0%**	**0%**	**5%**	**5%**	**5%**	**0%**	**5%**	**5%**	**4%**
Index Fund	0%	10%	10%	10%	10%	15%	20%	20%	20%	20%	20%	25%
Large Cap Value Funds/Stocks	0%	0%	5%	5%	5%	5%	10%	10%	10%	10%	5%	5%
Large Cap Growth Funds/Stocks	0%	0%	0%	0%	5%	5%	5%	10%	15%	10%	10%	5%
Mid/Small Growth Funds/Stocks	0%	0%	0%	0%	0%	0%	5%	5%	0%	0%	5%	10%
Mid/Small Value Funds/Stocks	0%	0%	0%	5%	0%	5%	5%	5%	0%	5%	5%	10%
Subtotal	**0%**	**10%**	**15%**	**20%**	**20%**	**30%**	**45%**	**50%**	**45%**	**45%**	**45%**	**55%**
International Stock Funds	0%		0%	5%	0%	5%	5%	10%	0%	5%	10%	15%
Subtotal	**0%**	**0%**	**0%**	**5%**	**0%**	**5%**	**5%**	**10%**	**0%**	**5%**	**10%**	**15%**
Real Estate Funds	0%		5%	5%	0%	5%	5%	10%	5%	10%	15%	20%
Subtotal	**0%**	**0%**	**5%**	**5%**	**0%**	**5%**	**5%**	**10%**	**5%**	**10%**	**15%**	**20%**
Total	**100%**	**100%**	**100%**	**100%**	**100%**	**100%**	**100%**	**100%**	**100%**	**100%**	**100%**	**100%**

Global Portfolio Allocation Scoring System (PASS) for Individual Investors – developed by Dr. William Droms (Georgetown University) and Steven N. Strauss, (DromsStrauss Advisors Inc.) – model used with permission.

The above asset allocation and the following expected returns (see the approaches chapter) can be used to determine an expected return.

ASSET CLASS EXPECTED RETURN AND STANDARD DEVIATION

EXHIBIT 10.5

	Expected Rates of Return	Standard Deviation of Returns
Cash and Money Market Fund	2.5%	2.0%
Treasury Bonds / Bond Fund	4.0%	4.0%
Corporate Bonds / Bond Fund	6.0%	5.0%
International Bond Funds	7.0%	6.0%
Index Funds	9.0%	14.0%
Large Cap Funds / Stocks	10.0%	16.0%
Mid / Small Funds / Stocks	12.0%	18.0%
International Stock Funds	13.0%	22.0%
Real Estate Funds	8.0%	12.0%

The following exhibit depicts the PASS allocation multiplied by the expected rates of return for each asset class, which results in an overall expected return of 8.51% However, to be on the conservative side and since they scored on the lower side of the RT3 Target, the Rudolphs have requested that an eight percent (8%) required rate of return be used as part of the analysis.

CALCULATION OF EXPECTED PORTFOLIO RETURN

EXHIBIT 10.6

	PASS Recommended Portfolio	Expected Rates of Return	PASS Expected Return
Cash and Money Market Fund	3%	2.5%	0.075%
Treasury Bonds/ Bond Funds	12%	4.0%	0.480%
Corporate Bonds/ Bond Funds	10%	6.0%	0.600%
International Bond Funds	5%	7.0%	0.350%
Index Fund	20%	9.0%	1.800%
Large Cap Funds/Stocks	15%	10.0%	1.500%
Mid/Small Funds/Stocks	10%	12.0%	1.200%
International Stock Funds	10%	13.0%	1.300%
Real Estate Funds	15%	8.0%	1.200%
		Expected Return	8.51%

Other Investment Information
- David expects to be able to sell his interest at retirement in DRI to fund his retirement.
- Their emergency fund is primarily invested in a taxable money market account earning 0.75 percent.

Description of Investment Assets

DR Office Furniture, Inc.

When valuing his business, David's accountant advised him to use a multiple of revenue approach. David's accountant suggested using a multiple of 2.5 x revenue. David estimated the value of the business on revenues for 2012.

Brokerage Account

The brokerage account consists of the mutual funds described below. Any interest and dividends earned on the investments is reflected in the account balance and is not counted or separately stated on the income statement.

INVESTMENT PORTFOLIO - MUTUAL FUNDS AS OF 12/31/2013

Mutual Funds									
Name	Shares	Cost per Share	NAV	Beta	R^2 to S&P 500	Yield	One Year Return	Standard Deviation	Total FMV
A	2,526	$50	$75	1.1	0.76	0.9%	6%	0.16	$189,450
B	1,468	$25	$20	0.98	0.95	1.2%*	12%	0.15	$29,360
C	2,570	$22	$87	1.24	0.88	0.5%	14%	0.14	$223,590
D	1,200	$45	$48	0.78	0.5	1.4%	4%	0.13	$57,600
								Totals	$500,000

* The dividend for mutual fund B is expected to grow at 3% per year.

David is considering replacing Mutual Fund A with Mutual Fund Z. Both mutual funds have a similar investment objective.

Mutual Fund									
Name	Shares	Cost per Share	NAV	Beta	R^2 to S&P 500	Yield	One Year Return	Standard Deviation	Total FMV
Z	-	-	$89	1.35	0.89	0.75%	7.5%	0.17	-

Education and Education Account (529)

The contributions to this account are invested in a diversified portfolio of mutual funds based on the age of the youngest beneficiary. David selected an overall investment strategy that resulted in "moderate risk" investments. The current annual cost of education in today's dollars is $20,000 with an expected inflation rate of six percent. The Rudolphs currently plan to pay for four years each for Madelyn and Danny.

DRI 401(k) Plan with Roth Account

David is uncertain about which retirement plan mutual funds to allocate his contributions to, so he decided to keep 100 percent of the account balance in cash. David made his first contribution to this account in 2013.

Traditional IRA

The Traditional IRA is invested in a series of zero coupon bonds. The investment returns in this account over the past five years have been:

Year	Returns
1	6.50%
2	4.75%
3	- 3.25%
4	- 2.5%
5	5.25%

David is uncertain what his compounded investment rate of return has been and whether the investments are appropriate for his goals.

Roth IRA

The Roth IRA is currently invested in a tax-free municipal bond mutual fund, earning 1.75 percent per year. The income is reinvested and not reflected on the income statement.

INCOME TAX INFORMATION

The Rudolphs are in the 35 percent marginal income tax bracket for federal income tax purposes and their state income tax rate is five percent. Capital gains are taxed at 15 percent at the federal level and five percent at the state level.

RETIREMENT INFORMATION

David has a safe harbor 401(k) plan through his company (DRI). He contributes the maximum of his salary each year, plus any permissible catch-up contribution (currently $16,500 + $5,500 = $22,000). His company matches dollar for dollar on the first three percent of salary and then $0.50 on the dollar on the next two percent of salary to a maximum contribution of four percent of his covered compensation. David also has an integrated profit sharing plan through his company (DRI). The company adds the amount necessary to the profit sharing plan to maximize the overall defined contribution limit of $49,000 (currently). This limit does not include the $5,500 catchup provision to the 401(k) plan. Amy is self-employed and does not currently have any retirement plan. David's total savings, including the employer match, is $54,500 per year.

The Rudolphs define adequate retirement income as 80 percent of pre-retirement income. They both plan to live until age 95 after retiring at age 62 but only want to consider his age in retirement capital needs projections. He is expecting to receive $20,000 at normal age retirement (age 67) in Social Security benefits but will only receive $14,000 in today's dollars at age 62.

ESTATE INFORMATION

David has not arranged for any estate planning. Amy has a will leaving all of her assets outright to her daughter, Madelyn. Other than Amy's will, she has not arranged for any other estate planning.

OTHER INFORMATION REGARDING ASSETS AND LIABILITIES

Personal Residence

The Rudolphs purchased their personal residence for $1,500,000 two years ago on January 1, 2012. Their mortgage payment is $7,195 per month. They borrowed $1,200,000 over 30 years at six percent. They were considering refinancing the house but decided not to when the appraised value came in at only $800,000 due to market conditions. They pay their homeowner's insurance premiums and property taxes separately from their mortgage. Their property taxes are $8,000 yearly.

Lake House

The lake house was formerly David's personal residence for the last 15 years (1999). He purchased the lake house for $250,000, by putting down 20 percent and borrowing the rest at seven percent for 30 years. His current payment is $15,967 per year. The lake house is rented for 14 days a year to one of David's key customers for $5,000. The $5,000 is used against expenses and is included in the income statement. The property taxes are $4,000 a year and homeowners insurance is $3,500 per year. Both taxes and insurance are paid separately.

Boat

The Rudolph's purchased their boat for $125,000 four years ago in January 2009. It is a 54' Hatterus with twin inboard motors. Their boat payment is $1,267 per month. They borrowed $100,000 over 10 years at nine percent on a signature loan to finance the purchase of the boat. The Rudolph's do not have a separate property or liability insurance policy on the boat.

DR Office Furniture, Inc. (DRI)

David started DR Office Furniture, Inc. over 20 years ago. Today, it is one of the largest office furniture companies in the southeast. Over the years, David has sold 25 percent of the equity in his company to his top employees. The value of the business is expected to grow at three percent each year. Paul Carter, Brian Conner, and Sally Walker (the top employees) have agreed to buy the business in 11 years. David insists that this sale will provide an adequate capital balance upon which to retire. DR Office Furniture, Inc. has traditionally offered employees health insurance, group term life insurance, a 401(k) plan with a Roth component and an integrated profit sharing plan. The profit sharing plan requires age 21 and one year of service for participation. David usually receives the maximum allowed for the combination of the profit sharing plan and 401(k) plan deferrals, including matching and catch-ups.

PIE CHART APPROACH

INTRODUCTION

The pie chart approach to financial planning (as discussed in Chapter 3) gives a visual representation of both the client's balance sheet and the income statement. The Rudolph's pie chart analysis of the income statement is shown below.

DATA FOR PIE CHART APPROACH - INCOME STATEMENT
DAVID AND AMY RUDOLPH 1/1/2014

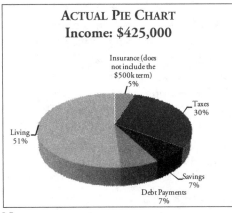

ACTUAL PIE CHART
Income: $425,000

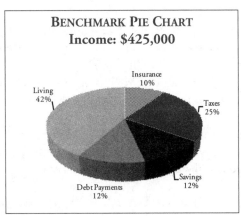

BENCHMARK PIE CHART
Income: $425,000

Notes:
- Debt payments excludes both mortgages. The mortgages are included in living expenses.
- The savings percentage does not include the employer contributions to the 401(k) plan and the integrated profit sharing plan.
- Living expenses = $116,800 + $86,335 + $15,967

Income	100%	$425,000
Other Living Expenses	27.48%	The balance of living expenses - $116,800
Other Debt Payments*	7.11%	($15,201 + $15,000)
Savings Rate	6.82%	($1,000 + $22,000 + $6,000)
Insurance**	2.97%	($2,100 + $10,000 + $500)
Housing Costs** (Personal Residence Only)	23.18%	($86,335 + $8,000 + $4,200)
Housing Costs** (Lake House)	5.52%	($15,967 + $3,500 + $4,000)
Taxes**	27.06%	($64,800 + $22,000 + $10,609 + $17,593)
Discretionary Cash Flows	(0.14%)	- $605

* Other debt payments excludes both mortgages.
** Property taxes and insurance on residences is included with housing costs.

Observations

Although the overall savings rate of 6.82 percent appears to be low, it increases to 14.4 percent (which is excellent) when calculated (later in the case) including the employer contributions.

The Rudolphs are spending 28.7 percent of their overall income on the principal residence and lake house, not including utilities and other expenses. Vacations are listed at $25,000. These two expenses (housing and vacations) combined suggest that perhaps the Rudolphs should consider vacationing at the lake house and paying off or refinancing the seven percent mortgage.

Unfortunately, the Rudolphs are underwater (negative equity) in the principal residence, but mortgage rates are one percent less than when they first bought the house. If they paid down the mortgage to $640,000 (80% loan to value) and then refinanced, they would have a monthly payment of approximately $3,538.73 instead of $7,195.00. To refinance the house, it would require $529,619 of cash, which does not look promising.

Because of the decline in the value of the principal residence, the Rudolphs should definitely challenge the property tax assessment, which could reduce their property taxes to as little as $4,000 and increase their discretionary cash flows by the $4,000 savings.

DATA FOR PIE CHART APPROACH - BALANCE SHEET
DAVID AND AMY RUDOLPH 12/31/2013

RUDOLPH BALANCE SHEET

Assets = 100%		Liabilities & Net Worth = 100%	
Cash or Cash Equivalents	$295,000	Current Liabilities	$15,000
Investment Assets	$3,956,000	Long-Term Liabilities	$1,387,933
Personal Use Assets	$1,465,000	Net Worth	$4,313,067
	$5,716,000		$5,716,000

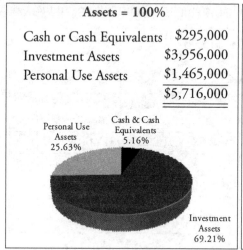

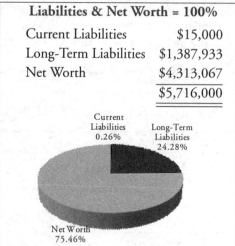

BENCHMARK BALANCE SHEET

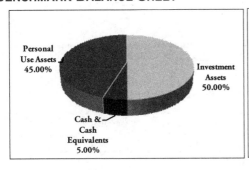
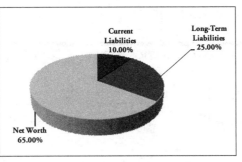

Observations

The Rudolphs balance sheet looks excellent with five percent cash and cash equivalents. The most significant issue is the valuation of DRI. The footnote to the Balance Sheet dated 1/1/2014 indicates that the DRI value is based on David's estimate. The company value represents 77 percent of their net worth and 84 percent of their investment assets. To justify a valuation of this magnitude, the net after-tax cash flows need to be approximately $500,000 per year, discounted for 25 years at 15 percent. It is probably wise to have the buyer employees begin to buy sooner rather than later. It is also a good idea to get an expert to value the business. David continues to own 75 percent of the business and could continue to control the business with 50.1 percent ownership and perhaps even less. The objective is to reduce the risk of a large investment in a single asset.

FINANCIAL STATEMENT ANALYSIS - RATIO ANALYSIS APPROACH

INTRODUCTION

The financial statement analysis - ratio analysis approach utilizes ratios to gain insight into the client's financial situation. The approach assesses: (1) the client's ability to pay short-term obligations and fund an emergency, (2) the client's ability to manage debt, (3) whether the client is committed financially to all of his goals, (4) to determine the progress of the client in achieving the goal of financial security based on the client's age and income, and (5) to indicate how well the investment assets have performed to benchmarks. The ratios should be compared to appropriate benchmarks to provide a more meaningful analysis.

EXHIBIT 10.7   RATIO ANALYSIS

LIQUIDITY RATIOS BASED ON 2014 FINANCIAL STATEMENTS

Ratio	Formula		Comment	Benchmark
Emergency Fund Ratio*	$\dfrac{\text{Cash \& Cash Equivalents}}{\text{Monthly Non-Discretionary Cash Flows}}$	$\dfrac{\$295,000}{\$20,134} = 14.65$	Very Strong	3 - 6:1
Current Ratio	$\dfrac{\text{Cash \& Cash Equivalents}}{\text{Current Liabilities}}$	$\dfrac{\$295,000}{\$15,000} = 19.7:1$	Very Strong	0.5:1

Monthly non-discretionary cash flows = $18,867 as indicated on Statement of Income and Expenses by ND ($241,603 / 12).

DEBT RATIOS BASED ON 2014 FINANCIAL STATEMENTS

Ratio	Formula		Comment	Benchmark
Housing Ratio 1 (HR 1) (Includes both homes.)	$\dfrac{\text{Housing Costs}}{\text{Gross Pay}}$	$\dfrac{\$122,002}{\$425,000} = 28.7\%$	High	$\leq 28\%$
Housing Ratio 2 (HR 2) (Includes both homes.)	$\dfrac{\text{Housing Costs} + \text{Other Debt Payments}}{\text{Gross Pay}}$	$\dfrac{\$152,203}{\$425,000} = 35.8\%$	High	$\leq 36\%$
Debt to Total Assets	$\dfrac{\text{Total Debt}}{\text{Total Assets}}$	$\dfrac{\$1,402,933}{\$5,716,000} = 24.54\%$	Very Strong	Age Dependent
Net Worth to Total Assets	$\dfrac{\text{Net Worth}}{\text{Total Assets}}$	$\dfrac{\$4,313,067}{\$5,716,000} = 75.46\%$	Very Strong	Age Dependent

RATIOS FOR FINANCIAL SECURITY GOALS BASED ON 2013 FINANCIAL STATEMENTS

Ratio	Formula		Comment	Benchmark
Savings Rate (Overall)	$\dfrac{\text{Savings} + \text{Reinvestments} + \text{Employer Match}}{\text{Gross Pay}}$	$\dfrac{\$61,500}{\$425,000} = 14.47\%$	Very Strong	Goal Driven At Least 10-13%
Savings Rate (Retirement)	$\dfrac{\text{Employee Contributions} + \text{Employer Contributions}}{\text{Gross Pay}}$	$\dfrac{\$54,500}{\$425,000} = 12.82\%$	Very Strong	10 - 13%
Investment Assets to Gross Pay (Does not include education savings.)	$\dfrac{\text{Investment Assets} + \text{Cash \& Cash Equivalents}}{\text{Gross Pay}}$	$\dfrac{\$3,910,000 + \$295,000}{\$425,000} = 9.9:1$	Very Strong	Approx. 4:1 at Age 50

PERFORMANCE RATIOS BASED ON 2013 AND 2014 FINANCIAL STATEMENTS

Ratio	Formula		Comment	Benchmark
Return on Investments =	$\dfrac{I_1 - (I_0 + \text{Savings})}{I_0}$	$= 1.42\%$ (See calculation below)	Poor	8-10%
Return on Assets =	$\dfrac{A_1 - (A_0 + \text{Savings})}{A_0}$	$= -6.92\%$ (See calculation below)	Very Poor**	2-4%

Return on Net Worth =	$\dfrac{NW_1 - (NW_0 + \text{Savings})}{NW_0}$	= -8.42% (See calculation below)	Very Poor**	The higher the better. This ratio is likely to become smaller as the client's net worth increases.

** The substantial decrease in the value of the Rudolph's principal residence has resulted in a negative return on total assets and a negative return on net worth.

PERFORMANCE RATIOS CALCULATIONS***

Return on Investments = (Excludes cash and cash equivalents)	$\dfrac{\$3,956,000 - (\$3,840,000 + \$29,000 + \$32,500)}{\$3,840,000} = 1.42\%$
Return on Assets =	$\dfrac{\$5,716,000 - (\$6,075,000 + \$29,000 + \$32,500)}{\$6,075,000} = -6.92\%$
Return on Net Worth =	$\dfrac{\$4,313,067 - (\$4,642,568 + \$29,000 + \$32,500)}{\$4,642,568} = -8.42\%$

*** $32,500 of savings is derived from the employer match of 4% of $245,000 (covered compensation for qualified plans) which equals $9,800 plus $22,700 from the profit sharing plan. (See Schedule C Part 2.)

Observations

The short-term liquidity and ability to pay ratios are excellent. The two housing ratios are high. However, both ratios consider the Rudolph's owning two homes. The other debt ratios are appropriate. The Rudolph's overall savings rate is excellent at 14.47 percent as is their retirement savings rate of 12.8 percent and the investment assets to gross pay ratio at 9.9:1 for his age.

Once again, the issue is the reliability and certainty of the valuation of DRI. David says it grows in value at an annual rate of three percent This should be demonstrated by net after-tax cash flows growing year over year by at least three percent.

The investment performance ratios are poor, but are somewhat skewed because of no change in the balance sheet value of DRI and the decline in the value of the principal residence. The performance ratios need to be compared to market returns for the year. However, investment returns are best measured over a longer time period (five years) and then compared to market benchmarks.

The performance ratios suggest the financial planner should take a much closer look at the investment portfolios and the valuation of DRI. The decline in the value of the principal residence has less consequences if the Rudolphs intend to remain living in the house for the long term.

THE TWO-STEP/THREE-PANEL/METRICS APPROACH

INTRODUCTION

The next approach used is the two-step approach (manage the risks and save and invest) modified to be applied as the three-panel approach, with metrics added. First the Rudolph's risk management portfolio is evaluated, followed by their short-term emergency fund, housing ratios, and debt management. Finally, the Rudolph's long-term goals are analyzed.

RISK MANAGEMENT DATA - SCHEDULE A

	Actual	Metric	Comments / Recommendations
Life Insurance:			
Policy 1 - David	$2,000,000	$2,750,000	Adequate coverage Ownership issue for estate tax Change beneficiary
Policy 2 - David	$550,000		Group Term - okay Change beneficiary
Policy 3 - Amy	$250,000	$1,500,000	Depends on risk tolerance and priorities Change owner Consider trust for Madelyn
Health Insurance	Yes	Adequate	Adequate coverage DRI provided
Disability Insurance			
David	60% Gross Pay / Guaranteed Renewable	60 - 70%	Adequate coverage DRI provided - Taxable
Amy	None		Consider adding disability insurance
Long-Term Care Insurance	None	36-60 months of savings	Examine merits of adding - This is a low priority
Property & Liability Insurance			
Personal Residence	$1,500,000	≤ FMV	Reduce coverage to FMV Endorse HO3
Lake House	$200,000	≤ FMV	Consider raising coverage to FMV Endorse HO3
Automobile # 1 and # 2	100 / 300	100 / 300	Adequate coverage Consider raising deductibles
Boat	None	≤ FMV	At minimum, need liability insurance
Liability Insurance	None	$1 - 4 million	Need PLUP = $1 - $4 million

Observations

There is a question whether Amy's life insurance is adequate, but determining that will require additional conversations with the client to arrive at a conclusion. The fact that David is the owner of his life insurance policies will cause inclusion in his gross estate at his death. During the estate planning phase of the engagement, the financial planner should explore other (trust) ownership options. In any event, he should change the beneficiary to Amy.

Amy needs disability insurance to protect her stream of income.

The Rudolphs need to reduce the homeowners insurance coverage on the residence, increase it on the lake house, and endorse the personal property for all risk and replacement value. A separate property and liability policy on the boat is needed.

The Rudolphs also need to add a personal liability umbrella policy of coverage ranging from $1,000,000 - $4,000,000 to protect against personal law suits. They need to be sure to notify the PLUP provider about the boat and both homes.

SHORT-TERM SAVINGS AND INVESTMENTS - SCHEDULE B

	Actual	Metric	Comments
Emergency Fund	14.65 x	3 - 6 month	More than adequate.
Housing Ratio:			
1 - Principal Residence	23.2%	≤ 28%	
2 - Principal Residence	30.3%	≤ 36%	
1 - Lake House	5.52%	≤ 28%	
1 - Combined	28.7%	≤ 28%	These are high for their ages but do not exceed the metric.
2 - Combined	35.8%	≤ 36%	
Evaluation of Debt			The personal residence is underwater and this will have to be resolved to be able to refinance. Mortgage rates are low enough to refinance and thus improve housing ratios 1 & 2. However on personal residence there is a loan to value issue.

Observations

The Rudolphs emergency fund is substantial at 14.65 times monthly non-discretionary cash flows. They are right up against the maximum metric for both HR1 and HR2 when the two properties are combined. The client may want to pay off all credit and debt. In order to refinance the principal residence, the Rudolphs would have to pay the mortgage down to $640,000 to meet the 80 percent loan to value requirements of most lenders. This option seems unlikely.

Informational Inputs		
Non-Discretionary Cash Flows	$20,134 per month $241,603 annually	Income Statement
Cash and Cash Equivalents	$295,000	Balance Sheet
Principal Residence (PR)	P&I & T&I = $98,535	Income Statement
Lake House (LH)	P&I & T&I = $23,467	Income Statement
Other Debt Payments (Boat)	$15,201	Income Statement
Credit Card Payments	$15,000	Income Statement
Gross Pay	$425,000	Income Statement

LONG-TERM SAVINGS AND INVESTMENTS - SCHEDULE C

To achieve financial security (retirement) requires persistent savings of 10 to 13 percent of gross pay and investment assets that are appropriate for the age of the client and the gross pay. Many clients have multiple goals such as retirement, education funding, lump-sum expenditures, and legacy aspirations. The more goals a client has the greater the need for an increased savings rate.

SCHEDULE C - PART 1

	Actual	Metric	Comments
Retirement Security Goal			
Overall Savings Rate	14.47%	At least 10% - 13% of gross pay	Excellent
Retirement Savings Rate	12.82%	10% - 13% of gross pay	The total savings rate is consistent with the retirement goal.
Investment Assets as % of Gross Pay	9.9 x	8 x	They currently exceed the necessary investment assets for retirement (for their age). Education assets are excluded. Valuation of DRI is critical.
Educational Funding	$6,000 per year	$6,000 per year	Adequate
Lump-Sum Goals	None	None	Okay
Estate Planning	None	Documents	Critical estate planning documents and planning needed.

Informational Inputs * **	
Savings:	
• 401(k) Plan Deferred	$16,500
• 401(k) Plan Match	$9,800
• 401(k) Plan Catch-Up	$5,500
• Profit Sharing Plan	$22,700
TOTAL RETIREMENT	**$54,500**
Education Savings	$6,000
Money Market	$1,000
TOTAL SAVINGS	**$61,500**
Salary (gross pay)	$425,000
Investment Assets less Education Assets =	$3,910,000

* Income Statement plus 401(k) plan match plus profit sharing plan.
** Essentially no estate planning completed.

Observations

The Rudolphs have an excellent savings rate of 14.47 percent ($54,500 + $6,000 + $1,000 ÷ $425,000) overall and have investment assets equal to 9.9 x their gross pay which, using David's age (51), the benchmark or metric is 8x. The most significant issue is the value of the business. DRI makes up 84 percent of the investment assets. There is a serious issue regarding valuation and concern over whether the employees will be willing and able to buy the business in eleven years, at David's retirement. This issue is central to the overall plan and alternatives will have to be developed.

THE CASH FLOW APPROACH

The cash flow approach adjusts the cash flows on the income statement as projected after implementing all of the financial planner's recommendations. The approach starts with the discretionary cash flows at the bottom of the income statement and accounts for the recommendations in the order of priority by charging the cost of the expense against the discretionary cash flows regardless of any negative cash flow impact. The analysis is prepared carefully to differentiate between recurring cash flows and non-recurring cash flows.

Rudolph Cash Flow Approach with Recommendations			
	Income Statement Recurring Impact	Balance Statement Non-Recurring Impact	Comments/Explanations
Beginning Cash Flow (Income Statement)	($605)		
Recommendations:			
Risk Management:			
• Term Life Insurance for Amy	($750)		$1,000,000 for 20 years
• Disability Insurance for Amy	($3,000)		60% Gross Pay / Guaranteed Renewable 90 day to 65
• Long-Term Care			Do nothing now
• Homeowners - principal residence and lake house	($400)		Endorse personal property to all risk / replacement value. Lower dwelling value on principal residence. Raise dwelling value on lake house.
• Boat Property and Liability Insurance	($800)		Cover both property and liability.
• Personal Liability Insurance $2M	($400)		Advise PLUP carrier of boat.
Debt Management:			
• Pay off credit cards	+ $10,000	($15,000)	Recurring $5,000 expenditure
• Pay off boat loan	+ $15,201	($70,276)	
• Refinance Lake House Mortgage	+ $1,735		New loan balance $152,479
Retirement Savings:			
• Amy's 401(k) Plan Roth	($16,500)		401(k) plan individual
• Tax savings on 401(k) plan	0		Average 20% tax rate (Roth = 0)*
Estate Planning:			
• Documents for David and Amy		($1,000)	Will,** Durable Power of Attorney, Advance Medical Directive; need to begin estate planning process.
TOTALS	+ $4,481	($86,276)	Creates positive annual cash flow (reflected in income statement), reduces cash and cash equivalents by $86,276 thus negatively impacting the emergency fund ratio.

( ) indicates a negative impact on cash flow and + indicates a positive impact on cash flow.

* Amy will use the Roth account and therefore will make after-tax contributions.

** David's will naming Amy and Danny as heirs.

Debt Management			
	Old Information (Loan)	New Loan	Comments
Refinance Lake House			
• Loan	$200,000	$152,479.14	($148,038 + 3%)
• Term	360 months	180 months	
• Interest Rate	7%	4.75%	
• Payment per month	($1,330.60)	($1,186.03)	Saves $144.57 per month Saves $1734.84 annually
Alternative:			
• Pay Off Lake House	($148,038)		Saves $15,967 annually
• Pay Off the Boat: Expenditures	($70,276)		Saves $15,201 annually
• Pay Off Credit Cards	($15,000)		Saves $15,000 annually
• Total Debt Pay Off	($233,314)		Saves $46,168 annually

Observations

The Rudolphs have debt that is expensive, such as the boat (10%) and the lake house (7%). The financial planning recommendations are to pay off the boat and credit cards, and to refinance the lake house over 15 years at 4.75 percent to coincide with the retirement objective. These actions would increase the discretionary cash flows by $4,481 per year (Schedule D). They could alternatively payoff the boat, lake house, and credit cards increasing their cash flows annually by another $15,967, giving them net discretionary cash flows (even after Amy's 401(k) plan contribution) of $15,967 + $4,481 = $20,448. The problem is that it would take $233,314 from cash and cash equivalents to pay off the debt.

STRATEGIC APPROACH

MISSION STATEMENT

- Financial Security (the ability to maintain one's lifestyle without employment income).

GOALS

- Adequate risk management portfolio.
- Adequate savings rate for retirement and education.
- Adequate emergency fund.
- Adequate debt management.
- Adequate investment portfolio.
- Adequate estate plan.

PERSONAL AND FINANCIAL OBJECTIVES OF THE RUDOLPHS

1. They want to provide for Danny and Madelyn's education.
2. They want to retire debt free when David reaches age 62 (when they plan to retire).
3. They need adequate retirement income.
4. They want to have adequate risk management coverage.
5. David is concerned about providing income for Amy and leaving the remainder of his estate to their child, Danny.
6. The Rudolph's want to have an appropriate investment portfolio.

PERSONAL AND FINANCIAL OBJECTIVES RECOMMENDED BY THE FINANCIAL PLANNER

Risk Management

- Consider changing the ownership and beneficiary for David's life insurance policy #1 to Amy with contingent beneficiary as Danny.
- Purchase individual disability policy on Amy.
- Endorse the principal residence and lake house homeowners policies for all risk and replacement value.
- Purchase a personal liability umbrella policy (PLUP) $1 - $4 million.

Budgeting

- Refinance the lake house or pay it off.
- Protest the property taxes on their principal residence because of the decline in value.

Retirement

- Amy should establish a retirement plan: SEP, SIMPLE, 401(k) plan, or profit sharing plan.
- DRI makes up 84 percent of investment assets and the sale to employees at David's retirement is questionable. David should sell off at least a portion of this asset as soon as possible.
- David insists that retirement income is covered with DRI. The financial planner recommends, and David agrees, to a valuation and then a capital needs analysis within the next year.

Tax

- An appropriate retirement plan for Amy would shelter income tax and reduce payroll taxes.

Entity

- Amy should change her business entity status from sole proprietorship to an S Corporation or LLC.

Estate Plan

- Have estate documents prepared (will, durable power of attorney for health care, advance medical directive).

Debt Management

- David and Amy are not yet able to meet their goal of being debt free at David's age 62 because of the 30-year mortgage on the principal residence and the 15-year mortgage on the lake house.

Investments

- David is very disappointed in his current investment performance except for his business.

PRESENTATION TO DAVID AND AMY RUDOLPH - FINANCIAL STATEMENTS AND RATIOS POST RECOMMENDATIONS

NEW EMERGENCY FUND RATIO

$20,134.00	Old emergency fund monthly non-discretionary expenses
$445.83	Increases in risk management costs $\dfrac{\$5,350}{12}$
($2,244.67)	Decreases in debt management $\dfrac{\$26,936}{12}$
0	401(k) plan contribution does not affect non-discretionary cash flows
$18,335.16	New non-discretionary cash flows
$208,724.00	New cash & cash equivalent $295,000 - $86,276 non-recurring expenditures
11.38%	New emergency fund ratio $\dfrac{\$208,724.00}{\$18,335.16}$ (excellent)

NEW SAVINGS RATE (EE = EMPLOYEE, ER = EMPLOYER)

David	401(k) Plan (EE) Deferral	$16,500	
	Over 50 Catch-Up	$5,500	
	ER Match	$9,800	
	Profit Sharing (ER)	$22,700	
	David Total	**$54,500**	(See Retirement Information)
	Education	$6,000	
	Money Market	$1,000	
Amy	401(k) Plan (EE) Deferral	$16,500	
	Combined Total	**$78,000**	
	New Savings Rate:	$\dfrac{\$78,000}{\$425,000}$ = 18.35% Excellent	

HOUSING RATIOS

New Housing Ratio - Combined HR 1 (after refinance of lake house)

Principal - P & I	$86,335.00
Principal - HO	$4,200.00
Lake House - P & I	$14,232.36 ($1,186.03 x 12)
Lake House - HO	$3,500.00
Endorsements	$400.00
Principal - Property Tax	$8,000.00 *This is to be protested.
Lake House - Property Tax	$4,000.00
	$120,667.36

$$\frac{\$120,667.36}{\$425,000} = 28.39\% \text{ (slightly exceeds 28\%)}$$

New Housing Ratio - Combined HR 2

$$\$120,667.36 + \$5,000^* = \frac{\$125,667.36}{\$425,000} = 29.57\% \text{ (good)}$$

* credit card recurring payment

INVESTMENT ANALYSIS

Following the investment analysis process, the financial planner should develop an investment policy statement and then analyzes the portfolio performance against the investment policy statement.

The Rudolph's investment policy statement is as follows:

Rudolph's Investment Policy Statement January 1, 2014	
Retirement Goals	• Generate adequate retirement income. • Retire debt free.
Education Goals	• Provide for Danny and Madelyn's education.
Return Requirements	• They require an 8% return on their overall portfolio.
Risk Tolerance	• They have a moderate risk tolerance.
Time Horizon	• Retirement for David is 10 years away. • Retirement for Amy is 10 years away. • Education for Danny is 16 years away. • Education for Madelyn is 3 years away.
Constraints	• They have liquidity issues with a majority of their net worth being in a small business that they are planning to sell and then use the proceeds for retirement. • They have a very short time horizon to fund Madelyn's education, which is only four years away.

INVESTMENT PORTFOLIO ANALYSIS

The analysis of an investment portfolio is accomplished by comparing the objectives in the investment policy statement to the actual performance of the investment portfolio. The Rudolph's investments are compared to their investment policy statement for an analysis of their progress towards accomplishing their goals.

Overall Investment Growth

The Rudolph's investment assets grew from $3,840,000 (2012) to $3,956,000 (2013). The Rudolphs made investment contributions of $61,500 ($29,000 plus $32,500 from the employer, as indicated on Schedule C - Part 2), which means they only earned an annual return of 1.42 percent. This overall rate of return is too low given their time horizon and risk tolerance. One likely issue is the valuation of DRI which has not increased. There are other issues that are contributing, to a lesser extent, to the low annual return such as the Roth IRA return of 1.75 percent and 401(k) plan with Roth entirely invested in cash.

Recommendations:
- Obtain an updated valuation on DRI.
- Reallocate the investments in the Roth IRA and 401(k) plan with Roth to be more consistent with the investment goals.

Education Goal Investment Growth

The 529 Savings Plan balance was $46,000 at the beginning of 2013 and ended the year (12/31/2013) at $46,000. However, the Rudolphs contributed $6,000 to the fund during 2013. Therefore the account declined 13 percent for the year.

With a 529 Savings Plan, the investment options may be limited based on the age of the children and their time horizon until they enter college. Some 529 Savings Plans have the option of an aggressive allocation or moderate allocation based on the child's age. In the Rudolph's case, there is not enough information to determine the riskiness of the investments held. However, since some 529 Savings Plans become more conservative as the beneficiary approaches age 18, it is likely that the Rudolph's education investments are appropriate. The client and planner agree to investigate.

Recommendations:
- The financial planner should review the investment options for the 529 Savings Plan to determine if the funds are appropriately allocated between aggressive and moderate risk investments.

Risk Tolerance
- They have a moderate risk tolerance.

Time Horizons
- Retirement for David is 10 years away.
- Retirement for Amy is 10 years away.
- Education for Danny is 16 years away.
- Education for Madelyn is 3 years away.

Although the financial planner was not provided with the riskiness of each investment, certain conclusions can be drawn based on the investments held.

DRI
The Rudolphs have significant single asset risk because 77 percent of their net worth is based on the value of DRI. Although David's top three employees have agreed to purchase the business, there is some risk that the employees will be unable or unwilling to buy the remainder of DRI at the time projected. There are still other risks that must be discussed with the client, such as:
- *Business Risk* - what are the inherent risks of doing business in the office furniture industry?
- *Executive Risk* - what if something happens to any of the key employees, will the others still be able to purchase the business?
- *Financial Risk* - how do the key employees intend to finance the purchase of the business and will David receive a lump sum or annuity payout?
- *Valuation Risk* - does the revenue multiple of 2.5x represent an appropriate value for the business? The business valuation may be dated, so we should consider an updated valuation based on net after-tax cash flows.

These are all important questions regarding the financial security of the Rudolph's. Their goal is to reduce the risk and diversify their investment portfolio. Throughout the monitoring phase of the financial planning process, the financial planner should continue to work with the Rudolphs to eliminate the single asset risk.

Investment Portfolio of Mutual Funds (Brokerage Account)

The brokerage account consisting of mutual funds has a standard deviation of 15 percent, which appears to be reasonable for their time horizon and risk tolerance. However, when considering the client's investment in DRI and the brokerage account together, the brokerage account may create a diversification issue with too heavy a weighting on equities. The Rudolphs only have the Traditional IRA of $15,000 and Roth IRA of $20,000 invested in fixed income investments. The Rudolphs need 30 to 40 percent of their investment assets allocated to fixed income investments because of the correlation between equities and fixed income investments and the diversification benefits from proper asset allocation.

401(k) Plan with Roth Account

The allocation to cash in this portfolio is too conservative. The financial planner needs to work with David to select an appropriate allocation between equities and fixed income investments in this account. His current allocation is 100 percent cash, which is not appropriate given his time horizon and risk tolerance. Additional information is required from David's plan administrator regarding available investment options.

Traditional IRA

The traditional IRA holds a series of zero coupon bonds. Zero coupon bonds generate "phantom income" or income that is taxed, but not actually received until the bond is sold. Holding zero coupon bonds in a tax deferred account is appropriate to avoid the phantom income issue. However, the financial planner needs to gather more information regarding the types of bonds, the term of the bonds and credit rating of the bonds to make an evaluation regarding the riskiness of these bonds. The planner also needs to review the expected returns.

Roth IRA

Investments that are expected to experience significant capital appreciation are most appropriate for a Roth IRA. Since municipal bonds generate income that is free from federal income taxes, and possibly state income taxes as well, municipal bonds are best held in a taxable account not in a Roth.

Overall Recommendations Regarding Retirement Assets:
- The asset allocation is too heavily weighted towards equities and not enough to fixed income investments because of DRI. It is likely that the standard deviation of the portfolio is significantly higher than 15 percent when considering the riskiness of DRI. Adding bonds to the portfolio will held reduce the overall riskiness of the investment portfolio.
- Since the Rudolph's are 11 years away from selling DRI, they should consider annual valuations and develop a plan to begin selling part of the business to the key

employees so they can build a more diversified portfolio and reduce some of their risk.

Other Investment Observations

- A small percentage of the Rudolph's investment assets are in tax-deferred retirement savings accounts. David and Amy are only 11 years away from retirement, but we should consider taking advantage of tax-deferred savings for both of them during this period.

- David is considering replacing Mutual Fund A in his portfolio with Mutual Fund Z. Mutual Fund Z is showing a higher one-year return than Mutual Fund A. However, the funds should be evaluated on a risk adjusted basis. Since the r-squared for both mutual funds is greater than 0.70, we can rely on Beta as a reasonable measure of total risk and we can use the Treynor ratio to determine which fund returned the higher risk adjusted rate of return. The calculation is as follows:

Treynor Ratio	$\dfrac{\text{Actual Return} - \text{Risk Free Rate}}{\text{Beta}}$
Mutual Fund A	$\dfrac{6\% - 3.5\%}{1.1} = 2.27\%$
Mutual Fund Z	$\dfrac{7.5\% - 3.5\%}{1.35} = 2.96\%$

Mutual Fund Z provides a higher risk adjusted rate of return than Mutual Fund A. Replacing Mutual Fund A with Mutual Fund Z may be an appropriate recommendation.

- David is uncertain regarding their compounded rate of return on the retirement bonds, so the financial planner should use the geometric mean to determine the compounded rate of return. The calculation is as follows:

Geometric Mean $\quad \sqrt[5]{(1.065)(1.0475)(0.9675)(0.9750)(1.0525)} - 1 \times 100 = {}^{*}2.06\%$

*This is a fairly low compounded rate of return for bond investments, which would be expected to be in the five to six percent range. The financial planner needs to evaluate the type of bonds, the credit quality and possibly replace the current zero coupon bonds.

POST RECOMMENDATION BALANCE SHEET - ABBREVIATED - SCHEDULE F

Assets		Liabilities and Net Worth	
Current Assets		**Current Liabilities**	
Cash & Cash Equivalents	$208,724	Credit Cards	$0
Invested Assets	$3,956,000	**Long-Term Liabilities**[1]	$1,322,098
Personal Use Assets	$1,465,000	Net Worth	$4,307,626
Total Assets	$5,629,724	**Total Liabilities & Net Worth**	$5,629,724

CHANGE IN NET WORTH - RECONCILIATION

$4,313,067	Before Recommendations
$4,307,626	After Recommendations
$5,441	Net Reduction
$4,441	Lake House closing costs 3% ($148,038 x 0.03)
$1,000	Paid for basic estate planning documents ($1,000)

RETIREMENT GOAL

The retirement goal was 80 percent of income in today's dollars ar age 62 (11 years from now) and using his life expectancy to age 95 (33 years). The inflation rate is assumed to be 2.5 percent and the portfolio earnings rate is assumed to be eight percent.

Calculation of Retirement Needs at Year 1 of Retirement:

N = 11

i = 2.5

PV = $326,000 ($340,000 less Social Security of $14,000)

PMT = 0

FV = $427,740.25

---

1. Long-term liabilities include the principal residence and the lake house.

Calculation of Capital Needs at Retirement (Annuity Approach):

N	=	33
i	=	[(1.08 / 1.055) -1) x 100]
FV	=	0
PMT_{AD}	=	$427,740.25
$PV_{@62}$	=	$6,902,528.41

Calculation of Capital Needs in Present Value Terms:

N	=	11
i	=	8
FV	=	$6,902,528.41
PMT	=	0
$PV_{@51}$	=	$2,960,376.12

It is clear that even without additional savings, the Rudolph's have sufficient assets to retire but the valuation of assets is heavily dependent on the valuation of DRI.

EDUCATION GOAL

The education goal for Madelyn and Danny, as stated, is four years of college beginning at age 18. The current cost is $20,000, the expected education inflation is six percent, and the expected earnings rate is eight percent.

Calculation of 4 Years of College in Today's Dollars:

N	=	4
i	=	[(1.08 / 1.06) -1) x 100]
PMT_{AD}	=	$20,000
$PV_{@18}$	=	$77,805.09
FV	=	0

Calculation for Madelyn Age 14:

N	=	4
i	=	[(1.08 / 1.06) -1) x 100]
FV	=	$77,805.09
PV	=	$72,199.87

Calculation for Danny Age 1:

N	=	17
i	=	[(1.08 / 1.06) -1) x 100]
FV	=	$77,805.09
PV	=	$56,624.43

Summary of Education Costs in Present Value Terms:

Madelyn	$72,199.87
Danny	$56,624.43
Total	$128,824.30

Again, the Rudolph's have sufficient assets to pay for the education goal.

SUMMARY

When the Rudolphs came to the financial planner they had the following strengths and weaknesses:

STRENGTHS

1. Income $425,000 annually.
2. Savings rate of 14.47%.
3. Net Worth of $4.3 million.
4. Investment assets of $3.956 million.
5. Adequate life insurance on David.
6. Adequate health insurance.
7. Adequate disability insurance on David.
8. Excess homeowners insurance on residence.
9. Adequate automobile insurance, although deductibles were too low.
10. Excellent ratios, except investment performance ratios.

WEAKNESSES

1. Low net discretionary cash flows (negative $605).
2. Questionable life insurance on Amy.
3. Inadequate disability insurance on Amy.
4. No long-term care insurance on David or Amy.
5. Inadequate property insurance on lake house.
6. No property and liability insurance on the boat.
7. No personal liability umbrella policy.
8. Poor investment returns.
9. No estate planning documents.
10. Negative equity on the client's principal residence.
11. The interest rates for the debt on the boat and the lake house are too high.
12. Property taxes on the personal residence are too high.

RECOMMENDATIONS - IMPLEMENTED

The financial planner solved the client's weaknesses as follows:

- The financial planner is continuing to work on the investment returns and is encouraging the clients to consider life insurance on Amy and long-term care for both David and Amy.
- The valuation of DRI is critical to the retirement plan and David should have a complete valuation prepared by an independent and qualified appraiser within a couple of months.
- The boat loan is paid off and the lake house is refinanced over 15 years.
- The revised annual net discretionary cash flows are $4,481 (from negative $605).

UNMET GOALS

The retirement income goal of 80 percent of pre-retirement income is questionable at David's age 62 until the appraisal of DRI is complete.

The goal to be debt free at David's age 62 (retirement) is questionable given the mortgage on the principal residence.

Investment returns remain an issue that will require periodic monitoring and reevaluation.

Retirement Planning Accumulations and Distributions

LEARNING OBJECTIVES

After reading this chapter, you should be able to:
- Identify the factors affecting retirement planning.
- Draw the exponential graph representing the required investment assets as a percent of gross pay at various ages to age 65.
- Explain why saving early is usually better than saving later.
- Explain the impact of inflation on purchasing power.
- Compare two of the common approaches to managing withdrawals.
- Identify the costs that may decrease and those that may increase from pre-retirement to retirement.
- Distinguish between the top down and the bottom up approaches to determining the wage replacement ratio.
- Identify the various sources of retirement income.
- Calculate the capital needs analysis using an annuity approach.
- Calculate the capital needs analysis using a capital preservation approach.
- Calculate the capital needs analysis using a purchasing power approach.
- Discuss the various methods for sensitivity analysis as it is applied to capital needs analysis.

FACTORS AFFECTING RETIREMENT PLANNING

Individuals face many decisions regarding retirement planning. In particular, they must decide what retirement means to them. Does retirement mean withdrawing from the workforce when financially able, or does it mean changes in lifestyle and family situations? For most, it is a major lifestyle change resulting from a significant shift in how they spend their time, money, and energy.

Adequate retirement planning requires an understanding of the factors that affect retirement planning and the proper interrelationship of these factors. While this chapter discusses the major factors affecting retirement planning, it does not examine every factor that affects retirement planning. The major factors are:

- the remaining work life expectancy (RWLE),
- the retirement life expectancy (RLE),
- the savings amount and rate,
- the annual income needed (needs) during retirement,
- the wage replacement ratio (WRR),
- the sources of retirement income,
- inflation expectations,
- investment returns, and
- other qualitative factors.

A retirement plan based on these factors must produce sufficient income at retirement to ensure that a comfortable pre-retirement lifestyle is maintained throughout the retirement period. A discussion of each factor, its associated risks, and the calculations essential to retirement planning (capital needs analysis) is presented below.

REMAINING WORK LIFE EXPECTANCY (RWLE)

Work life expectancy (WLE) is the period of time a person is expected to be in the work force. This time period may be as long as 30 to 40 years and is essential to retirement planning because it is the period during which one saves and accumulates funds to use during retirement. Increasing or decreasing the work life expectancy impacts the time period over which individuals can save for retirement. The United States has seen a substantial decline in the overall WLE in the last several years primarily due to individuals pursuing advanced education (undergraduate and graduate degrees), delaying their entry into the workforce, and those taking early retirement, which hastens their exit from the workforce.

Normal retirement has historically been age 65 primarily because Social Security designated it as such and other employer provided retirement plans followed suit. The age at which recipients of Social Security can begin receiving benefits is age 62, but they must wait until Full Retirement Age to receive their full benefits under the system. The average retirement age in the United States has decreased since the 1970s due to a variety of factors including early retirement options from employer plans, early retirement under Social Security (age 62) and to some extent positive investment performance during the 1980s and 1990s increasing retirees' wealth.

However, Census Bureau data show that the trend of earlier retirement is reversing and the age at which people are retiring has risen over the last several years. For example, in March 2009, 52 percent of men aged 62 to 64 were employed, compared with 42 percent in 1990 and 47 percent in 2000. Among women 62 to 64 years old, 41 percent were working in March 2009, compared with 28 percent in 1990 and 35 percent in 2000.[1]

---

1. Congressional Research Service, "Older Workers: Employment and Retirement Trends" by Patrick Purcell, September 16, 2009.

This trend of delaying retirement is due to a variety of factors, but heavily impacted by economic issues. The stock market crash of 2008 and the lingering recession and lack of an economic recovery from 2008 through 2012 severely impacted the wealth of those that are contemplating retirement.[2] There also appears to be a trend of partial retirement, where an employee will continue working on a reduced schedule as a transition into retirement. This allows employers to reduce cost but maintain experienced employees. The Pension Protection Act of 2006 provided an opportunity for employees to begin receiving pension benefits while employed after the attainment of age 62.

The trends discussed above are illustrated in the chart below.

LABOR FORCE PARTICIPATION FOR WORKERS 65 AND OLDER

EXHIBIT 11.1

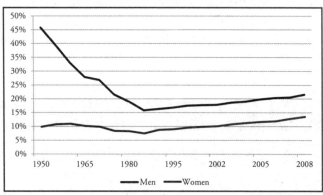

U.S. Bureau of Labor Statistics

Exhibit 11.1 illustrates that the retirement age has steadily declined over the last four decades, but has been reversing direction in the most recent years, with some individuals now retiring before age 62. Exhibit 11.2 focuses on the percentage of individuals in the U.S. that actually retire between the ages of 62 and 65 inclusively, identified as area A on the graph. The chart shows that 93 percent of U.S. residents retire between ages 62 and 65. It is important for financial planners to understand this because it provides a benchmark to use when calculating retirement needs. The planner must also realize that seven percent of these individuals do not retire between 62 and 65. Thus, the planner needs to speak with the client to determine the age at which the client is planning to retire.

Key Concepts

Underline/highlight the answers as you read:

1. What are the major factors affecting retirement planning?

2. Define work life expectancy and retirement life expectancy.

3. When will most clients retire?

4. Explain the work life expectancy/retirement life expectancy dilemma.

---

2. It should be noted that retirement assets were $17.9 trillion in 2007 and dropped to $13.9 trillion in 2008, but have increased to $17.5 trillion at the end of 2010. (http://www.ici.org/pdf/2011_factbook.pdf)

EXHIBIT 11.2

AVERAGE RETIREMENT AGE (U.S.)

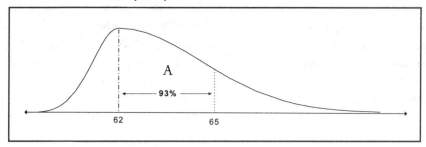

A is the area between ages 62 and 65 and represents 93% of the area under the curve.

The **remaining work life expectancy (RWLE)** is the work period that remains at a given point in time before retirement. For example, a 30-year-old client who expects to retire at age 65 has a RWLE of 35 years. Determining the RWLE is important for the financial planner because it tells the planner the remaining number of years the client has to save for retirement.

RETIREMENT LIFE EXPECTANCY (RLE)

Quick Quiz 11.1

Highlight the answer to these questions:

1. Approximately 93% of individuals retire between ages 60 and 70.
   a. True
   b. False

2. The RLE is the time period beginning at retirement and extending until death.
   a. True
   b. False

3. As the RLE increases because of early retirement, there is generally an increased need of funds to finance the RLE and a shortened WLE in which to save and accumulate assets.
   a. True
   b. False

False, True, True.

Retirement life expectancy (RLE) is the time period beginning at retirement and extending until death. Currently, many retirees live as long as 20 to 40 years in retirement. However, this longevity has not always been the case. In 1900, the average life expectancy for a newborn child was 47 years[3], and many individuals worked as long as they were able. The concept of retirement, as we know it today, did not exist. Exhibit 11.3 presents data depicting the increase in life expectancy at birth from 1949 to 2007 and Exhibit 11.4 depicts the increase in life expectancy at age 65.

Population trends provide the financial planner with a good understanding of how long a person may live in their retirement. Women born in 2007 are expected to live on average 80.7 years, while men born in 2007 are expected to live on average 75.8 years. The average woman retiring in 2007 at age 65 would be expected to be in retirement for 19.8 years. Similarly, a man retiring in 2007 at age 65 would be in retirement for 17.1 years. The

---

3. This life expectancy is biased due to a high infant death rate at the time.

problem with this information is that the average life expectancy is just that - an average. 50 percent of women who were age 65 in 2007 are expected to live longer than 19.8 years and 50 percent of men who were age 65 in 2007 are expected to live longer than 17.1 years. In addition, the older an individual gets, the more likely they are to live beyond their average life expectancy at birth. Proper planning is needed because if the retired individual lives longer than planned for, there is a risk of running out of money. This risk is referred to as **superannuation**.

LIFE EXPECTANCY AT BIRTH (U.S. 1949 - 2007)

EXHIBIT 11.3

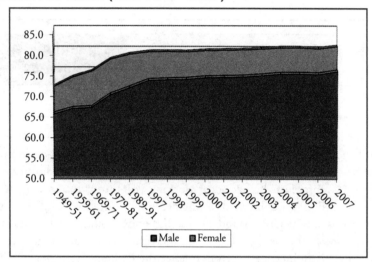

Source: Centers for Disease Control, Trend Tables, United States 2010 (www.cdc.gov)

LIFE EXPECTANCY AT AGE 65 (U.S. 1949 - 2007)

EXHIBIT 11.4

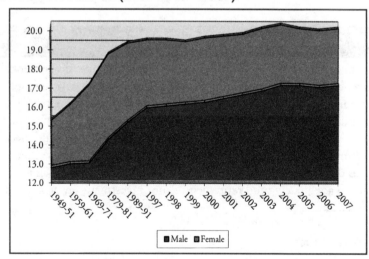

Source: Centers for Disease Control, Trend Tables, United States 2010 (www.cdc.gov)

THE WLE AND THE RLE RELATIONSHIP

It is important for the financial planner to understand the WLE and the RLE relationship. Since there is a fixed time between life and death, each period of time changes inversely with the other. If the WLE increases or decreases, the individual must shorten or lengthen the pre-work life expectancy (PWLE) or RLE. Thus, the planner must estimate each period to determine the ability to save and the financial needs while in retirement. When clients are unable to save adequately, the planner and client can adjust the periods in order to meet the client's needs. For example, if a client is unable to meet the needed retirement goal at 62, the planner can discuss lengthening the WLE by continuing to work and, thus, shortening the RLE in order to meet the retirement need. Exhibit 11.5 visually depicts this relationship.

| EXHIBIT 11.5 | THE WLE/RLE DILEMMA |

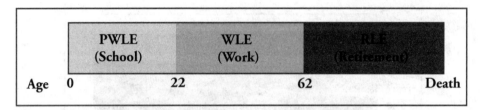

The area to the left of WLE represents the prework life expectancy (PWLE), which continues until the person enters the work force on a full time basis. Generally, the PWLE ends between the ages of 18 to 26, with the average age at 22. The middle area, the work life expectancy (WLE), represents the period of working years prior to retirement. This period begins at the end of the PWLE and ends at the beginning of retirement. The retirement life expectancy (RLE) usually begins around age 62 and ends around age 85 but may continue beyond age 100. Notice that as the RLE period increases due to early retirement and longer life expectancy, there is an increased need to finance the RLE and a shortened WLE in which to save and accumulate assets. Careful planning is needed long before the attainment of the desired retirement age to meet the funding requirements for a financially secure retirement.

SAVINGS AND INVESTMENT ISSUES

The savings amount, the savings rate, the timing of savings, and investment decisions are important concepts in retirement planning. If people were adequately saving for retirement beginning at an early age (25 to 35), they would need to save approximately 10 to 13 percent of their gross annual income and invest in a broad portfolio of growth investments over their entire work life to adequately fund their retirement goal. They would need to be ever mindful of investment returns and inflation to ensure sufficient savings and accumulations. Unfortunately, as demonstrated below, most of our society saves at a much lower savings rate than is necessary to adequately fund retirement, is not investment savvy, and is insensitive to the impact of inflation.

THE SAVINGS AMOUNT

If individuals do not begin saving at an early age, then they must save a greater amount of their gross earnings to compensate for the missed years of contributions and compounding of investment returns. Exhibit 11.6 illustrates the amount individuals must save if they begin saving at different times.

REQUIRED SAVINGS RATE FOR RETIREMENT
(ASSUME $0 OF ACCUMULATED SAVINGS AT THE BEGINNING AGE)

EXHIBIT 11.6

Age Beginning Regular and Recurring Savings*	Savings (as percent of gross pay) Rate Required to Create Appropriate Capital*
25 - 35	10 - 13%
35 - 45	13 - 20%
45 - 55	20 - 40%**

*Assumes appropriate asset allocation for reasonable-risk investor through accumulation year; also assumes normal raises and an 80 percent wage replacement ratio at Social Security normal retirement age and includes Social Security retirement benefits.

** At age 55, the person will realistically have to delay retirement until age 70.

Exhibit 11.6 illustrates a significant problem with delaying saving for retirement, namely, the need to save large amounts because there is less savings time to accumulate a sufficient amount of capital to retire. Saving requires foregoing current consumption and most individuals find it difficult to decrease consumption by 20 to 30 percent, especially when they have been accustomed to maintaining a certain standard of living.

As an alternative to Exhibit 11.6, consider Exhibit 11.7, which assumes that each person is saving 10 to 13 percent of gross pay, including any employer retirement plan contributions. Assuming that the person saves 10 to 13 percent and also has an investment account balance equal to what they need at each age, they are making adequate progress toward the goal of financial security. If the person does not have the appropriate investment assets or is saving less, the problem will eventually surface. Therefore, both investment assets and savings rate issues are relevant.

 *Key Concepts*

Underline/highlight the answers as you read:

1. What are the savings and investment concepts that are important to retirement planning?

2. Why is it important to begin to save early for retirement planning?

3. Why is it important to understand investment decisions and their consequences in retirement planning?

4. How is inflation relevant to retirement planning?

511

EXHIBIT 11.7 **BENCHMARK FOR INVESTMENT ASSETS AS A PERCENTAGE OF GROSS PAY**

Age	Investment Assets as a Ratio to Gross Pay Needed at Varying Ages
25	0.20 : 1
30	0.6 - 0.8 : 1
35	1.6 - 1.8 : 1
45	3 - 4 : 1
55	8 - 10 : 1
65	16 - 20 : 1

The benchmarks as calculated consider incomes between $50,000 and $350,000, inflation at approximately two to three percent, a balanced investment portfolio of 60 / 40 equities to bonds returning five percent over inflation, a savings rate of 10 to 13 percent of gross pay and a wage replacement ratio of 80 percent of gross pay. To the extent that any of these assumptions are incorrect for a particular person, the results may be misleading and require a specific personal calculation. These benchmarks are only a beginning.

Note that Exhibit 11.7 illustrates that a person planning to retire at age 65 will need investment assets approximately 16 to 20 times the pre-retirement gross pay. A person at age 55 who plans to retire at 65 will need investment assets equal to eight times their current gross pay and will need to continue to save 10 to 13 percent of gross pay, including any employer contributions to achieve adequate retirement funding. More precise calculations are addressed throughout this chapter. While this is only a benchmark, it works well for incomes between $50,000 and $350,000, inflation at two to three percent, and a balanced portfolio earning about five percent over inflation.

EXAMPLE 11.1

Assume Carrie, age 45, comes to you and is currently earning $100,000 per year. She has $350,000 (3.5 times her annual earnings) of investment assets (cash, mutual funds, retirement funds, etc.), not including personal use assets (equity in personal residence) and is saving $10,000 of her gross pay (10%). Carrie is concerned about making adequate progress towards her retirement goals. Assuming that Carrie is invested in an appropriate investment portfolio, she appears to be making adequate progress towards retirement if that is her only goal. Note that she will have to save more if she wants to spend longer in retirement. Assume she can earn 8% with inflation of 3%. She will run out of money at age 89.

Step 1: Determine Future Income at Age 65	
Current Earnings - PV	$100,000
Inflation - I	3%
WLE - N	20 years
Future Earnings - FV	$180,611

Step 2: Determine Needs at Retirement	
WRR	80%
Retirement Payment	$144,489 ($180,611 x 80%)

Step 3: Project Savings at Retirement	
Current Assets - PV	$350,000
Annual Savings - PMT	$10,000
Earnings Rate - I	8%
Work Life Expectancy - N	20 years
Assets at Retirement - FV	$2,088,955

Step 4: Determine Period of Time Funds will Last	
Asset at Retirement - PV	($2,088,955)
Annual Inflation Adjusted Annuity Payment - PMT_{AD}	$144,489
Inflation Adjusted Earnings Rate - I	4.85437 ((1.08/1.03)-1) x 100
Funds at End - FV	$0
Years in Retirement that Funds will Last (Approximate)	24 Years

*Note that savings amount will increase each year with raises.

SAVINGS RATE

The **savings rate** identifies the average savings amount in the U.S. based on consumption. The savings rate is interpreted as personal saving as a percentage of disposable personal income. According to the Bureau of Economic Analysis, the personal savings rate has declined significantly since the 1980s. In fact, the personal savings rate fell to 1.4 percent in 2005, but has increased slightly since that time. Exhibit 11.8 illustrates the sharp decline. The growth in personal expenditures may be the cause of the drop in savings over the past few years and suggests that individuals are not saving enough for retirement. This low savings rate identifies a major concern for all planners. Recall that in order to meet just the retirement goal, a savings rate of 10 to 13 percent of gross pay over a long period is necessary.

U.S. PERSONAL SAVINGS RATE (1980-2010)

EXHIBIT 11.8

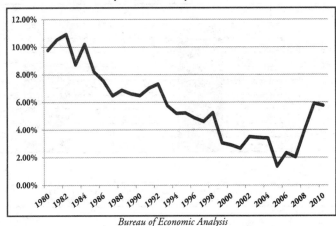

Bureau of Economic Analysis

TIMING OF SAVINGS

The earlier a person saves, the greater the number of future compounding periods available prior to retirement. A greater number of compounding periods leads to a lower required savings rate and a larger accumulation of capital at retirement. When saving is delayed, the power of compounding is lost and individuals must compensate by saving a greater percentage of their disposable income.

EXAMPLE 11.2

Lori saves $2,500 a year from age 25 until age 34 (inclusive) and invests the money in an account earning eight percent annually. Lori stops investing at age 34, but does not withdraw the accumulation until age 65. Lori's accumulation at age 65 is $393,588 even though she only deposited $25,000. In contrast, Peter saves $2,500 a year from age 35 until age 65 inclusively and invests in a similar account to Lori, earning eight percent annually. Even though Peter saved $52,500 more than Lori, he will have accumulated $85,223 less than Lori at age 65. The deposits and balance at age 65 for Lori and Peter are presented in Exhibit 11.9.

EXHIBIT 11.9 | **TIME/SAVINGS EXAMPLE (ACCUMULATION AT AGE 65, ORDINARY ANNUITY)**

	Lori	Peter
Total Invested (10 Years)	$25,000	$77,500 (30 Years)
Balance at age 65	$393,588	$308,365
Earnings Rate	8%	8%

While Peter invested more than three times as much as Lori, Lori has 22 percent more than Peter at age 65. This result demonstrates the power of compound earnings over the longer period of 41 years versus 31 years. Exhibit 11.10 illustrates this phenomenon graphically.

EXHIBIT 11.10 | **ACCUMULATION OF UNEQUAL DEPOSITS OVER VARYING TIME PERIODS**

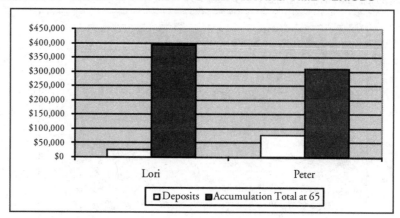

INVESTMENT CONSIDERATIONS

A successful retirement plan is dependent on a successful investment plan. A retirement plan is dependent on savings over time, but is also dependent on the earnings and growth of those funds during the asset accumulation phase and throughout retirement. An investment plan must take into consideration the risk tolerance of the investor as well as the time horizon of the goal. In addition, consideration must be given to historical and expected returns from the various asset classes, diversification, and the types assets included in tax-deferred accounts versus taxable accounts. All of these factors go into constructing a portfolio to achieve specific goals, such as retirement planning.

The risk tolerance of an investor is essentially the willingness and ability to accept risk for potential returns. As indicated below, assets with larger returns typically have larger risks or larger variations in returns. Risk tolerance is typically assessed through questionnaires, an understanding of the investor's experience with risky assets and with the time horizon of the investment goal. If both the willingness and the ability to accept risk are high, the risk tolerance is high. If both the willingness and the ability are low, then the risk tolerance is low. If, however, there is a mismatch between ability and willingness (one high and the other low), then it suggests that the investor may need additional education.

The **suitability** of an investment or portfolio is greatly impacted by the time horizon of an investment goal. Longer-term goals can generally tolerate higher amounts of risk than shorter-term goals. Investments for the accomplishment of short-term goals should generally consist of relatively safe or stable assets. Investments for the accomplishment of long-term goals can consist of assets that generate higher returns, but have a tendency to fluctuate more sharply when markets or the economy changes.

When investors are young, their investment portfolio should typically be dominated by common stocks because, due to long time horizons, young investors can generally afford the additional risk of common stocks. As investors near retirement, their asset allocation generally begins to shift so that it becomes less risky while still maintaining some growth component to mitigate against the risk of inflation. It is important to keep in mind that more than 50 percent of individuals who reach the age of 65 will live for more than 20 years. Therefore, equities are a critical ingredient in an investor's (retiree's) portfolio because they provide for growth over longer-term time horizons.

A fundamental understanding of investment choices and their consequences is essential to successful retirement planning. All asset classes do not have the same historical investment returns nor risks. When planning for retirement, it is important to have a historical perspective of investment returns and risks for a wide variety of asset classes. Exhibit 11.11 provides a 74-year perspective on historical investment returns, inflation-adjusted returns, and risk as measured by standard deviation.

EXHIBIT 11.11	HISTORICAL RETURNS, INFLATION-ADJUSTED RETURNS, AND STANDARD DEVIATION OF ASSET CLASSES (1932 - 2006)			

Asset Class	Historical Returns	Inflation-Adjusted Returns	Standard Deviation	Real Return After-Tax and Inflation
Small-Capitalization Stocks	13%	10%	33%	6.1%
Large-Capitalization Stocks	10%	7%	20%	4%
Fixed-Income Securities (Corporate)	6%	3%	9%	1.2%
Treasury	5.5%	2.5%	5.5%	0.9%
Consumer Price Index (CPI)	3%	N/A	3.1%	N/A

Quick Quiz 11.2

Highlight the answer to these questions:

1. Our society tends to save at a rate that is adequate for retirement planning.
   a. True
   b. False

2. Fixed-income securities generally provide the best hedge against inflation and loss of purchasing power.
   a. True
   b. False

3. Individuals must consider the impact of inflation when projecting retirement needs.
   a. True
   b. False

False, False, True.

Exhibit 11.11 illustrates the need to choose investments wisely for inclusion within a portfolio based on the risk and return of the asset class. Notice that after inflation, real economic returns are extremely low for fixed-income securities and Treasuries, and these returns are further reduced by the effects of taxation. This suggests that the only way to have real investment growth in an investment portfolio over a long term is to invest at least some portion of the portfolio in common stocks. Common stocks also provide the best hedge against inflation (the loss of purchasing power).

The risk tolerance and time horizon of the investor, as well as the expected risk and returns from various investment choices is considered in constructing an asset allocation and portfolio. The asset allocation is responsible for the majority of variation in returns within the portfolio and is a critical element in retirement planning.

Appropriate Assets for Tax Advantaged and Taxable Accounts

In addition to the asset allocation decision, investors should consider the appropriateness of assets for the different types of investment accounts. Income earned in a taxable account, such as a brokerage or bank account, is subject to current taxation whereas income earned in a tax-deferred account, such as an IRA, is not subject to current taxation. Because there is a significant difference in the tax rates of capital gains and dividends compared to income from fixed income securities, such as bonds, it is logical to hold fixed income assets in tax-deferred accounts. This decision results in all fixed income securities residing in tax-deferred accounts. However, investors must also consider liquidity needs that are better met through fixed income investments and more easily accessed in taxable accounts. Therefore, there must be a balance between tax efficiency or optimization and the liquidity needs of the investor.

In addition to the asset allocation decision and deciding where to hold fixed income and equity securities, an investor must consider limitations on the types of securities that can be held in various retirement accounts. These issues and limitations are beyond the scope of this textbook. Investors managing assets held in IRAs and qualified plans should also be aware of the rules relating to unrelated business taxable income, discussed below.

Unrelated Business Taxable Income

Unrelated business taxable income (UBTI) is a term used to describe income earned by a tax-exempt entity that is subject to taxation. The tax on unrelated business income applies to most organizations exempt from tax under §501(a). These organizations include charitable, religious, scientific, and other corporations described in §501(c), as well as employees' trusts forming part of pension, profit-sharing, and stock bonus plans described in §401(a). In addition, the following are subject to the tax on unrelated business taxable income:

1. Traditional IRAs
2. Roth IRAs
3. Simplified Employee Pensions (SEP-IRAs)
4. Savings Incentive Match Plans for Employees (SIMPLE IRAs)
5. State and municipal colleges and universities
6. Qualified state tuition programs
7. Medical savings accounts (MSAs)
8. Coverdell savings accounts

Because of the UBTI rules, IRAs and qualified plans, in addition to the other entities listed, are impacted if UBTI is earned within the entity. The impact is that the entity has to pay income tax on the UBTI and file Form 990-T if UBTI exceeds $1,000. The purpose of these rules is to prevent a tax-exempt entity from unfairly competing against businesses subject to tax. This is reflected in the following excerpt from Treas. Reg. §1.513-1.

> "The primary objective of adoption of the unrelated business income tax was to eliminate a source of unfair competition by placing the unrelated business activities of certain exempt organizations upon the same tax basis as the nonexempt business endeavors with which they compete."

The term "unrelated business taxable income" generally means the gross income derived from any unrelated trade or business regularly carried on by an exempt organization, less the deductions directly connected with carrying on the trade or business. If an organization regularly carries on two or more unrelated business activities, its unrelated business taxable income is the total of gross income from all such activities less the total allowable deductions attributable to all the activities.

Generally, an unrelated trade or business includes one that meets the following three requirements:

1. It is a trade or business,
2. It is regularly carried on, and
3. It is not substantially related to furthering the exempt purpose of the organization.

<table>
<tr><td>**EXAMPLE 11.3**</td><td>BU, an exempt scientific organization, enjoys an excellent reputation in the field of biological research. It exploits this reputation regularly by selling endorsements of various items of laboratory equipment to manufacturers. The endorsing of laboratory equipment does not contribute importantly to the accomplishment of any purpose for which exemption is granted BU. Accordingly, the income derived from the sale of endorsements is gross income from unrelated trade or business.</td></tr>
</table>

Generally, income in the form of dividends, interest, payments with respect to securities loans and annuities are excluded in computing unrelated business taxable income. In addition, royalties and rental income are generally not included in determining UBTI. However, investment income that is generally excluded from UBTI must be included to the extent it is derived from debt-financed property. The amount of income included is generally proportionate to the debt on the property.

Typically, a qualified plan, or an IRA, will be subject to the UBTI rules if it:

- Operates a trade or business,
- Owns an interest in a pass through organization, such as a partnership or S corporation, that is operating a trade or business,
- Owns an interest in a master limited partnership, or
- Uses debt to generate portfolio income, as in the case of margin debt.

<table>
<tr><td>**EXAMPLE 11.4**</td><td>Bob's IRA owns an interest in Sushi & Saki LLC, a restaurant. The LLC is taxed as a partnership. Because the LLC interest is held in an IRA, the IRA's share of income from the LLC will be subject to UBTI tax.</td></tr>
</table>

INFLATION

Inflation causes a loss of purchasing power. If a retiree has a fixed retirement income beginning at age 65 and inflation is three percent, the retiree has a loss of purchasing power of 26 percent in 10 years, 45 percent in 20 years, and 59 percent in 30 years. While Social Security retirement benefits are inflation adjusted, most private pension plans are not. Thus, the financial planner must consider the impact of inflation when projecting retirement needs and advise clients to save accordingly. Exhibit 11.12 illustrates the decline in purchasing power over a 50-year period of a $100,000 fixed income with a three percent inflation rate.

EXHIBIT 11.12

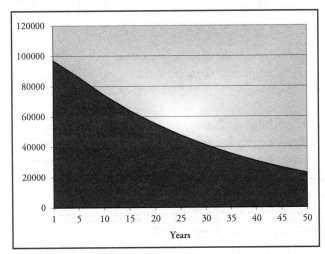

As illustrated, in year 10 the $100,000 has lost 26 percent of its purchasing power. After 10 years, one can only buy $74,409 worth of items using $100,000 of today's dollars. More disturbing is the fact that in year 20, the same person would only be able to purchase $55,368 worth of assets for that same $100,000. Imagine the client that expected to have a carefree retirement in 20 years with the $100,000 income they have today.

MANAGING RETIREMENT DISTRIBUTIONS

There are risks to outliving the retirement accumulation. The risks include taking too large of a distribution in early years either due to underestimating needs, lack of discipline, poor investment performance, unexpected needs, or increasing inflation.

There are many different approaches that can be utilized to reduce the risks of outliving retirement accumulation. Two of the more common approaches are:

1. *4 percent per year approach*: Limit withdrawals from the capital accumulation to four percent per year.
2. *Money-for-life approach*: Divide capital into unequal tranches with each tranche representing five years of retirement. Invest the funds for each tranche in varying asset classes expected to produce inflation adjusted returns of about five to six percent per year.

4 PERCENT OF CAPITAL BALANCE APPROACH

Conceptually, this approach is relatively simple to understand and implement. It provides for distributions equal to four percent of the capital balance each year and generally has a very high success rate, especially when the assets are invested in a balanced portfolio, such as one with 60 percent equities and 40 percent fixed income. Such a portfolio should generally provide a good balance between income, growth and downside protection.

However, one scenario that is a risk for retirees is when the retirement portfolio is subjected to several years of relatively large losses combined with distributions of four percent or more of the portfolio. In this scenario, the portfolio balance may decline so fast that it is irreparably impacted, without the retirees dramatically changing their lifestyle or going back to work.

It should be noted that some planners and clients might choose to use a 3.5 percent model or a 4.5 percent model. Adjustments such as these will provide more confidence or less confidence in the funds lasting through the retirement time period.

A four percent level of withdrawal initially indicates an account balance that is 25 times the income needed and implies a needed earnings rate of only 1.310 percent to pay out at a four percent rate for 30 years, assuming no inflation and annuity due payments. A four percent inflation adjusted withdrawal rate (assume inflation is 3 percent) would require an earnings rate of 4.349 percent annually for 30 years.

	REQUIRED EARNING RATE		
Withdrawal Rate	Fixed Payment Required Earnings Rate	Inflation Adjusted Required Earnings Rate	Portfolio Allocation
4%	1.310%	4.349%	Conservative
5%	3.079%	6.171%	Moderate Conservative
6%	4.696%	7.837%	Moderate
7%	6.218%	9.405%	Moderate Aggressive
8%	7.678%	10.908%	Aggressive

As mentioned above and implicit in the chart above, the investment of the retirement assets is critical to successfully managing the risk of superannuation. The four percent withdrawal rate is an appropriate approach that will likely achieve the objectives of clients as long as the beginning retirement portfolio is large enough.

MONEY-FOR-LIFE APPROACH

This approach divides assets into six five-year tranches and funds each tranche with sufficient money and the correct investment choices to provide retirement income for that period. The schedule below indicates the percent of capital necessary in each tranche, the expected investment return required for that tranche, and the type of asset class necessary to sustain this return.

Years	% of Capital	Rate of Return Required	Investments
1-5	28%	2%	Money Markets
6-10	26%	4%	Treasuries
11-15	20%	6%	Corporate Bonds
16-20	13%	8%	Balanced Fund
21-25	7%	10%	Large Cap & International Stock
26-30	6%	12%	Small Cap & International Stock

This approach is expected to produce a real overall return between five percent and six percent. The goal of this approach is to replenish the first five-year increment (the immediate income) every five years.

It should be noted that this method is not a significant deviation from historical methods of managing assets. In fact, the overall portfolio allocation is similar to that of a moderately allocated portfolio. This model is a different way of accounting for the funds and retirement needs. It should also be noted that the investor and planner might choose to change the percent of capital percentages as well as the number of tranches. For example, seven five-year tranches might be used in lieu of six. This approach helps the client focus on the current needs, which are funded by the most stable types of investments, while longer term investments are invested to provide for growth and future needs.

These two approaches are effective for developing retirement income distribution strategies for clients. It is important to keep in mind that not all models will work with all clients, and clients often have unique goals or needs that must be accounted for specifically.

In addition to the two methods discussed above, it is important to understand that annuitized income reduces the risk of superannuation. Whether from corporate or government pensions, insurance companies, or Social Security, annuities provide a base of cash flow that allows retirees to meet a certain percentage of necessities. There is published research that indicates a positive correlation between annuitized income and happiness. That correlation is not an endorsement for all annuities. Instead, it is a reflection of the risk averse nature of many investors and retirees and the simple fact that annuities reduce one aspect of risk. Those retirees who are extremely risk averse should have a larger portion of their assets annuitized compared to retirees who are less risk averse. While annuities have advantages, they also have disadvantages that must be considered by investors.

RETIREMENT NEEDS ANALYSIS

Key Concepts

Underline/highlight the answers as you read:

1. List the common factors that increase and decrease retirement income needs.

2. What is the wage replacement ratio?

3. Identify the two alternative methods for calculating the wage replacement ratio.

4. How is the WRR calculated utilizing the two applicable methods?

How much money and/or income does a person need to be financially independent? Most people entering retirement intend to maintain the same lifestyle they had immediately prior to retirement. People do not generally reduce their expenses radically during retirement unless it is necessary. When preparing a retirement budget, the budget should have similar expense categories and amounts as the pre-retirement budget with a few adjustments. There are expenses that may increase and there are expenses that may decrease as a person moves into the retirement phase of life. Expenses that may decline in retirement include: (1) costs associated with employment (certain clothing costs, parking, some meal costs); (2) mortgage costs if the mortgage debt is scheduled to be repaid by retirement; (3) costs of children (tuition, clothes); (4) payroll costs (e.g., FICA); and (5) the cost of savings because the plan will require the use of accumulated savings. For some people, retirement can bring increased spending on travel and other lifestyle changes. Some retirees are also at risk for increases in health care costs. Exhibit 11.13 presents lists of potential decreasing and increasing costs when entering retirement.

| EXHIBIT 11.13 | BALANCING INCREASING AND DECREASING RETIREMENT INCOME NEEDS |

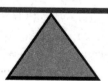

DECREASING INCOME NEEDS:

- Reduced Social Security payments
- Reduced need to save
- Reduced work-related expenses
- House mortgage may be paid off
- Automobile insurance may be reduced
- Possible lifestyle adjustments (less cars, less entertainment, etc.)

INCREASING INCOME NEEDS:

- Rising cost of health care and increased medical expenses
- Increasing expenditures and/or gifts to relatives
- Rising property taxes (due to inflation)
- Possible lifestyle changes (more travel, second home, clubs, hobbies, activities, etc.)

PLANNING FOR RETIREMENT - PRETAX OR AFTER-TAX

It is possible to plan for retirement needs either on a pretax or an after-tax basis. Most financial planners who are not certified public accountants (CPAs) plan in pretax dollars believing that a pretax approach is what their clients best understand. The implicit assumption associated with the pretax approach is that clients are more likely to know their gross income rather than to know their net after-tax cash flow. Therefore, planners establish retirement plans pretax with the expectation that the clients will simply pay whatever income taxes they have out of their gross retirement income, similar to what clients do during pre-retirement years. Many CPAs think in terms of after-tax dollars and, therefore, plan for retirement on an after-tax basis. After-tax planning assumes that income taxes are paid before other retirement needs. Planning can be effective either way as long as the client and the planner understand the pretax or after-tax planning choice. Throughout the text, we generally use a pretax approach.

WAGE REPLACEMENT RATIO (WRR)

The **wage replacement ratio (WRR)** is an estimate of the percent of annual income needed during retirement compared to income earned prior to retirement. The wage replacement ratio or percentage is calculated by dividing the amount of money needed on an annual basis in retirement by the pre-retirement income. For example, if a client in the last year of work (prior to retirement) makes $100,000, and that client needs $80,000 in the first retirement year to maintain the same pre-retirement lifestyle, the wage replacement ratio (WRR) is 80 percent ($80,000 ÷ $100,000).

CALCULATING THE WAGE REPLACEMENT RATIO

There are two alternative methods to calculate the wage replacement ratio: the top-down approach and the bottom-up approach (also called the budgeting approach).

Top-Down Approach

The top-down approach is frequently used with younger clients where income and expenditure patterns are unlikely to remain constant over time. As clients approach retirement age, a more precise wage replacement ratio should be calculated using a budgeting approach. The top-down approach estimates the wage replacement ratio using common sense and percentages.

> To illustrate the top-down approach, assume a 40-year-old client earns $50,000 a year, pays 7.65 percent of his gross pay in Social Security payroll taxes, and saves 10 percent of his gross income. If we assume that any work-related savings resulting from retirement are expected to be completely offset by additional spending adjustments during retirement and that the client wants to maintain his exact pre-retirement lifestyle, we would expect that

EXAMPLE 11.5

the client would need a wage replacement ratio of 82.35% (100% - 7.65% - 10%).

$50,000	=	100.00%	of salary in % terms
(5,000)	=	(10.00%)	less: current savings in % terms
(3,825)	=	(7.65%)	less: payroll taxes in % terms (not paid in retirement)
$41,175	=	82.35%	wage replacement ratio in % terms

The client is currently living on 82.35 percent of his gross pay. The remaining 17.65 percent is paid to FICA taxes and savings. Therefore, the 82.35 percent is a reasonable estimate, or proxy, of the amount necessary, as a percentage of current income, to maintain the (current) pre-retirement lifestyle.

Bottom-Up (Budgeting) Approach

The bottom-up approach used to calculate the wage replacement ratio is also called the budgeting approach. It is often used with older clients because as a person nears retirement age, it is possible to examine the actual current expenditure patterns of the person and to more accurately forecast the retirement expenditure patterns. Working with the client, the planner can determine the costs in the current (pre-retirement) budget that will change (increase or decrease) in the retirement budget, allowing the planner to determine a wage replacement ratio with greater precision than the top-down approach of estimating retirement needs.

Quick Quiz 11.3

Highlight the answer to these questions:

1. The WRR is an estimate of the percentage of annual income needed during retirement compared to income earned prior to retirement.
   a. True
   b. False

2. The two methods for calculating WRR are the top-down approach and the budgeting approach.
   a. True
   b. False

True, True.

EXAMPLE 11.6

Assume you had two clients, Anna and Bart, who had identical income and expenses each year. Anna and Bart each make $120,000 in pre-retirement income. Anna has arranged her financial affairs in such a way that she will have no mortgage payment or car payment while in retirement. Bart, on the other hand, expects to continue to have both a mortgage payment and a car payment throughout the majority of his retirement years. Both of them expect some expenses to decrease during retirement. The following chart illustrates that, while Anna will need a 64.75 percent WRR, Bart will need a 84.75 percent WRR. The difference is due to Bart's $18,000 annual mortgage payments and $6,000 annual car payments.

	CLIENT ANNA & BART	CLIENT ANNA	CLIENT BART
	Current Budget	Retirement Budget	Retirement Budget
Income (Current) Budget	$120,000	***	***
Expenses:	Current	Retirement	Retirement
Income Taxes (28%)	$33,600*	$33,600	$33,600
Food	5,400	5,400	5,400
Utilities/Phone	6,000	6,000	6,000
Mortgage	18,000**	0	18,000
Social Security Taxes	2,500	0	0
Health Insurance	2,000	2,000	2,000
Auto Insurance	1,200	1,200	1,200
Entertainment	6,000	6,000	6,000
Clothing	4,000	2,500	2,500
Auto Maintenance/Operation	1,000	750	750
Auto Payment	6,000	0	6,000
Church	2,400	2,400	2,400
Savings	12,000	0	0
Miscellaneous	19,900	17,850	17,850
Total Expenses (Needs)	$120,000	$77,700	$101,700
Wage Replacement Ratio (WRR)		64.75%	84.75%

*Assume for this example that Anna and Bart's income tax liability remains the same during retirement.
**Note that the mortgage of both is 15% of current income before retirement, but 0% for Anna and 18% of needs for Bart after retirement.
*** The current budget at retirement will be equal to the needs.

Does a person really need the same wage replacement percentage dollar amount or purchasing power amount throughout the entire retirement period? The answer is generally no. There are indications that consumption slows somewhat as people age. The 70 to 80 percent wage replacement ratio is probably most appropriate from the beginning of retirement (regardless of age) until the retiree reaches his or her late 70s. It appears that a person's consumption past the age of 80 declines primarily due to lessened mobility. While this may be correct for society at large, certain individuals will incur dramatic medical costs during the latter part of their retirement period. Therefore, while most people who study retirement expenditures would suggest a consumption function similar to the one provided in Exhibit 11.14 that follows, such a model may or may not apply to a particular individual.

EXHIBIT 11.14 **AVERAGE ANNUAL EXPENDITURES BY AGE**

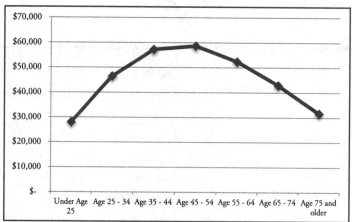

Bureau of Labor Statistics: Consumer Expenditures Study 2009

Many expert financial planners conclude that most clients need approximately 70 to 80 percent of their pre-retirement current income to retire and maintain their pre-retirement lifestyle. While many clients would fall into this range, there are also those particularly frugal clients who may need as little as 40 percent of their pre-retirement income and others who may need substantially more than the 80 percent wage replacement ratio (usually due to corporate perks that are no longer received during retirement).

EXHIBIT 11.15 **ADJUSTMENTS FROM PRE-RETIREMENT INCOME TO RETIREMENT INCOME NEEDS**

From Pre-retirement Income to Retirement Income Needs Adjustments to Expenditures	
Adjustments which decrease income needs:	Amount or Percent Saved
• No longer pay Social Security taxes	7.65% to 15.3%
• No longer need to save	10% to 15%
• No longer pay house mortgage	Maybe
• No longer pay work-related expenses	*
• Auto insurance may be reduced	*
• Possible lifestyle adjustments	*
Adjustments which may increase income needs:	
• Increasing cost of health care	*
• Lifestyle changes	*
• Increase in travel	*
• Second home	*
• Clubs and activities	*
• Expenditures on family/gifts/grandchildren	*
• Increased property taxes	*
*Amounts must be estimated for each individual	

Exhibit 11.15 presents common adjustments from pre-retirement to retirement in terms of estimated percentages. Notice that most of the adjustments in Exhibit 11.15 are client-specific.

SOURCES OF RETIREMENT INCOME

Most retirees rely on a combination of funds to finance retirement, including Social Security, private and company-sponsored retirement plans, income from personal retirement plans, and income from personal savings. These sources of funds are intended to complement each other to provide adequate retirement income. Exhibit 11.16 illustrates the average percent of income for the average retiree in 2008 from each of these sources.

RETIREMENT INCOME SOURCES FOR THE ELDERLY

EXHIBIT 11.16

Other
2%

Earnings
27%

Social Security
41%

Income and
Assets
11%

Pensions and
Annuities
19%

Source: Employee Benefit Research Institute 2009

Notice that the average retiree receives approximately 40 percent of retirement income from Social Security. Social Security will only provide a wage replacement ratio of 14 to 21 percent for a worker with income of $200,000 (see Exhibit 11.18). Therefore, such a worker will need to look to other sources of funds to make up the amount of short-fall in wage replacement to maintain the worker's desired lifestyle.

SOCIAL SECURITY

Social Security provides a foundation of retirement income. Social Security covers almost all occupational groups (except 25 percent of state and local government employees) with retirement benefits adjusted for inflation. It is considered the safety net of a secure income, but for most income levels, it is an insufficient source of income replacement during retirement. According to the Social

> **Key Concepts**
>
> **Underline/highlight the answers as you read:**
>
> 1. Identify the main sources of retirement income.
>
> 2. How does Social Security factor into retirement income?
>
> 3. Discuss the importance of personal savings to an individual's retirement income needs.

Security Administration, 90 percent of individuals aged 65 or older received Social Security benefits in 2010. As Exhibit 11.17 illustrates, Social Security was the major source of income for retired individuals. Historically, Social Security was the only source of income for approximately 21 percent of retirees.

EXHIBIT 11.17 **PERCENTAGE OF RETIRED INDIVIDUALS RECEIVING SOCIAL SECURITY BENEFITS BY RELATIVE IMPORTANCE TO TOTAL RETIREMENT INCOME**

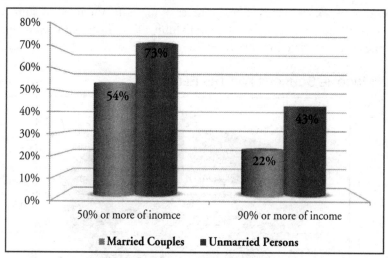

Source: Social Security Administration, Social Security Basic Facts 2010

Most middle to higher income individuals planning for retirement should, therefore, consider Social Security as a foundation rather than depending on Social Security as their main source of retirement income. Social Security retirement benefits provide a wage replacement ratio ranging from less than 20 percent (for high-income earners) to approximately 80 percent (for low-income earners who have a same age, nonworking spouse). As illustrated in Exhibit 11.18, Social Security is an adequate wage replacement for lower wage earners but is clearly inadequate to provide sufficient replacement income for middle-to-higher-wage earners. Keep in mind that Social Security was never intended to be the only source of income upon retirement.

SOCIAL SECURITY AS A WAGE REPLACEMENT PERCENTAGE (FOR INDIVIDUALS HAVING VARIOUS EARNINGS)

EXHIBIT 11.18

Current Earnings	Worker Benefit %*	Worker with Same Age, Nonworking Spouse Total Benefit %	Comment
$13,100	59%	89%	Low Income
$20,000	47%	71%	(WRR Good)
$25,000	41%	62%	
$30,000	38%	57%	Middle Income
$35,000	36%	54%	(WRR Adequate)
$50,000	31%	47%	
$75,000	28%	42%	
$100,000	24%	36%	High Income
$200,000	14%	21%	(WRR Poor)

Estimated based on single person at normal retirement age (2011).
At same age, nonworking spouse would receive 50 percent of the benefits of the covered worker.
The official website of the U.S. Social Security Administration - www.ssa.gov.

PRIVATE PENSION AND COMPANY-SPONSORED RETIREMENT PLANS

Private pension plans are the second source of retirement income. According to a 2007 report by the U.S. Bureau of Labor Statistics, 61 percent of workers age 16 or older worked for an employer or union that sponsored a pension or retirement plan, and almost 51 percent of workers participated in the plans. Qualified retirement plans have dramatically changed over the last few decades from employer-sponsored funded plans to employer-sponsored employee self-reliant plans, increasing the emphasis on personal savings as the primary source of retirement income for middle-to-upper-wage workers.

PERSONAL ASSETS AND SAVINGS

Personal assets and savings is the third source of retirement income and is the one source that has traditionally been the most influenced by the individual. This is a more difficult way to accumulate savings for retirement because of the lack of tax

Quick Quiz 11.4

Highlight the answer to these questions:

1. Retirees generally rely on Social Security, private pension plans, and personal savings to fund their retirement income.
   a. True
   b. False

2. Social Security is an adequate wage replacement for most individuals.
   a. True
   b. False

3. Personal savings is the source of retirement income most influenced by the individual.
   a. True
   b. False

True, False, True.

deductions or tax deferrals on earnings. However, personal savings can be a significant source of retirement income, as the more personal savings put aside for retirement, the larger the accumulation at retirement and the larger the retirement income for the individual.

Exhibit 11.8 illustrates the significant decrease in the personal savings rate since 1990. As illustrated, the savings rate fell from 1990 to 2005, with the trend reversing since then.

Whenever a retiree has income from invested assets, it can mean a substantially higher overall retirement income. The median income of those retirees with asset income is more than twice as large as the income of retirees with no asset income. As the two charts in Exhibit 11.19 illustrate, retirees without personal asset income are concentrated in the lowest income categories. Notice in Exhibit 11.19 that, of retirees having income from personal assets and savings, 33 percent have income of $30,000 or more, whereas for those retirees without personal assets and savings, only six percent have income of $30,000 or more in retirement. There is a noticeable difference between retirees who have income from personal assets and those that do not.

| EXHIBIT 11.19 | INCOME OF RETIREES WITH AND WITHOUT INCOME FROM PERSONAL ASSETS |

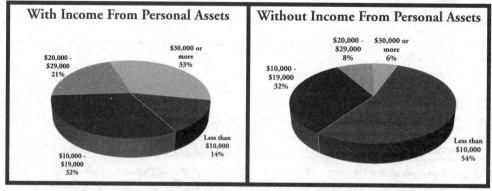

Source: Social Security Administration

QUALITATIVE FACTORS IN RETIREMENT – ADVISING CLIENTS

Qualitative factors associated with retirement may be more important than the financial or quantitative factors. Qualitative factors include involuntary versus voluntary retirement; emotional and psychological factors, such as loss of esteem with loss of job and boredom in retirement; and the decision to relocate or to do things that were postponed during the work life (i.e., travel or pursue another vocation).

The best overall advice financial planners can give their clients is for the client to have a strong support system, a well-planned qualitative side to retirement, and a system in place to maintain ego and self-esteem. Many persons in our culture define themselves by what they do at work. The mere act of going to work may be a ritual or habit that provides that person with a sense of self-worth and reason to live. A trusted colleague at the workplace may be a source of support and personal gratification. Voluntary retirement, even when well-planned, means change - and change can be difficult.

Involuntary retirement, if perceived as undesirable, can have a devastating emotional impact on an individual including shock, anger, and denial. Financial planning professionals need to recognize the emotional state of clients and realize that when someone is emotionally troubled, major decisions (financial or otherwise) are sometimes best delayed. Rather than abruptly making important financial decisions, it may be better to do the minimum financial maneuvering necessary during a grieving period. Such grieving may last for a period of a year or longer. Trying to optimize the financial situation when the client is emotionally unable to determine goals or priorities is probably counterproductive and may add stress to the situation.

Key Concepts

Underline/highlight the answers as you read:

1. Why are qualitative factors important considerations in retirement planning?

2. What are some of the common factors that negatively affect retirement planning and what impact do they have on the planning process?

A client's decision to relocate after retirement (for example, move to another state) should be carefully considered over a long period of planning. Some retirees do not realize that when they move, they will have a completely new environment to adjust to, as well as a substantial loss of their former support system of friends and family. Someone considering moving should conduct a trial transition over a number of years, spending increasingly longer periods at the desired location. This gradual adjustment can help determine if the potential permanent relocation will actually enhance retirement. People considering retiring abroad will encounter even more change, thereby necessitating even more detailed planning.

SUMMARY OF FACTORS AFFECTING RETIREMENT PLANNING

Financial planners may encounter clients who subjectively "feel" they are financially secure because they have a good job and/or a good net worth. If a good job is lost through premature death, disability, lay off, job termination, unexpected illness, etc., or if net worth decreases dramatically, the client's financial security is impaired. Thus, the actual determination of financial security is objective rather than subjective. Regardless of how people feel subjectively, in the real, objective world, there is a certain quantitative percentage of people who will become disabled, die untimely, or become unemployed.

Other complications that affect the retirement planning process include at least two societal issues. Our society has become more mobile with the deterioration of the traditional family unit. Having lost the close connection to family, older persons may not be able to depend on family to provide retirement assistance. Thus, there is a greater need for financial independence for each individual. Additionally, because our society seems to place more value on youth than on age and wisdom in the workplace, retirees have less chance of being hired for part-time employment, which could supplement retirement income.

Many people begin planning for retirement too late in life and save too little to effectively meet retirement capital accumulation needs. Some people do not give retirement funding any thought until they are well into their forties. Even when people do save, many of them make poor investment choices and, therefore, have poor investment returns and insufficient accumulations.

Inflation reduces an individual's purchasing power. To recipients of fixed incomes, inflation is like a progressive tax which causes declining purchasing power.

Exhibit 11.20 lists the factors that frustrate effective retirement planning and the negative impact associated with each factor.

Quick Quiz 11.5

Highlight the answer to these questions:

1. Qualitative factors associated with retirement are of less importance than the financial or quantitative factors.
   a. True
   b. False

2. Many people begin planning too late in life and save too little to effectively meet their retirement income needs.
   a. True
   b. False

3. Factors that positively impact retirement planning include reduced WLE and increased RLE.
   a. True
   b. False

False, True, False.

EXHIBIT 11.20 | **FACTORS THAT NEGATIVELY AFFECT RETIREMENT PLANNING AND THEIR IMPACT ON THE PLANNING PROCESS**

Factors	Impact
Reduced WLE	Insufficient savings period
Increased RLE	Increases capital needs
Reduced family reliance	Fewer alternatives in retirement
Reduced ability to work	Fewer alternatives in retirement
Planned too late	Fewer compounding periods
Low savings rate	Unable to meet capital requirements
Inflation	Reduces purchasing power
Poor earnings rate and asset allocation	Unable to meet capital requirements

Long-term financial security does not happen automatically. It requires careful planning, a clear understanding of the quantification of the goal, and identification and management of the risks that are present. Retirement planning requires the collection and projection of data and must be conducted meticulously and conservatively.

RISKS TO FINANCIAL INDEPENDENCE

There are many risks on the way to achieving financial independence. Selected risks are identified in Exhibit 11.21. It is a wise idea to save early, save a sufficient amount, invest prudently, and not underestimate retirement needs or the impact of inflation.

SUMMARY OF SELECTED FACTORS AFFECTING RETIREMENT PLANNING EXHIBIT 11.21

FACTOR	RISK	MITIGATOR
Work Life Expectancy (WLE)	Shortened due to untimely death, disability, health, unemployment	Life insurance, disability insurance, health insurance, education, training, experience
Retirement Life Expectancy (RLE)	Lengthened	Adequate capital accumulation
Savings rate, amount, and timing	Too low and too late	Save enough; start early
Inflation	Greater than expected	Conservatively estimate inflation and needs
Retirement needs	Underestimated	Use wage replacement estimators; don't include Social Security benefits in the calculation
Investment returns	Inadequate to create necessary retirement capital	Knowledge of and investments in broad portfolio of diversified investments and proper asset allocation
Sources of retirement income	Overestimation of Social Security benefits, private pension plans, or personal income (or adverse changes in taxation of such income)	Conservatively estimate and plan for such income, as well as monitor income projections and tax policy

RETIREMENT FUNDING (CAPITAL NEEDS ANALYSIS)

Capital needs analysis is the process of calculating the amount of investment capital needed at retirement to maintain the pre-retirement lifestyle and mitigate the impact of inflation during the retirement years. It uses both objective and subjective criteria to determine retirement income needs. There are three methods for analyzing capital needs: the basic annuity method, the capital preservation model, and the purchasing power preservation model.

 *Key Concepts*

Underline/highlight the answers as you read:

1. What is capital needs analysis and why is it important in retirement planning?

2. What are the three most common methods for analyzing capital needs?

3. How do each of these methods differ?

4. What assumptions must be made in capital needs analysis?

ACCURATE ASSUMPTIONS

Before calculating the capital needs analysis, the financial planner must first make several assumptions. Assumptions are made for the wage replacement ratio, work life expectancy, retirement life expectancy, inflation, earnings, Social Security, and any other benefits. If these assumptions are inaccurate, the projection using those assumptions will be flawed. The wage replacement ratio should be calculated carefully, especially for a client near retirement. Estimating life expectancy usually begins with the IRS tables and is conservatively estimated at age 90 to 93, due to the risk of outliving retirement money. Where family history indicates a particularly long life expectancy, that age should be increased. The estimate of the work life expectancy is critical, as one less year of work means one less year of saving and one more year of retirement funding. Conversely, working one additional year may make an otherwise unworkable retirement plan work quite nicely due to the additional year of savings, the additional year of compounding, and one less year of consumption.

The assumptions regarding inflation and earnings rates are essential ingredients in capital needs analysis. Historical data is available for inflation; however, future inflation is difficult to predict. Perhaps the best estimate is the long run inflation rate for a period equal to the remaining WLE plus the RLE. Earnings rates are dependent on the client's asset allocation and the markets; however, returns can be estimated for a well-diversified portfolio over a long period. It is wise to conservatively estimate inflation (up a little) and conservatively estimate earnings (down a little). Such estimation provides conservatism in case one or more of the assumptions are not realized. Social Security benefits and pension benefits that are inflation protected should be carefully determined and documented. The retirement plan and capital needs analysis can be adjusted on an annual basis as information becomes more certain.

BASIC PLANNING – CAPITAL NEEDS ANALYSIS / ANNUITY METHOD

The **annuity method** is the simplest way to determine retirement needs. The annuity method assumes the individual saves for a period of time, begins taking distributions at retirement, and then dies with a zero accumulation balance on the projected life expectancy date. The following steps are used to determine the capital necessary at the beginning of retirement to fund the retirement period:

1. **Calculate the WRR.** Determine the wage replacement ratio (WRR) today using one of the two methods identified earlier (top-down or budgeting).

2. **Determine the gross dollar needs.** Determine the wage replacement amount in today's dollars from the first step.

3. **Determine the net dollar needs.** Reduce the result from Step 2 by any expected Social Security benefits in today's dollars or other benefits that are indexed to inflation.

4. **Calculate the inflated pre-retirement dollar needs.** Inflate the result from Step 3 to the retirement age at the CPI rate to determine the first annual retirement payment.

5. **Calculate the capital needed at retirement age.** Calculate the present value at retirement of an annuity due for an annual payment equal to the result from Step 4 over the full retirement life expectancy (estimate life expectancy conservatively at age 90 to 93) and use the inflation-adjusted earnings rate. It is important to note that a conservative approach should be used when estimating the life expectancy, as this will allay any shortfall in funding.

To determine the amount to save during the work life expectancy, discount the capital needed at retirement using the savings rate, being mindful as to whether the client is expected to save annually or more frequently and whether the client is expected to save under an annuity due or an ordinary annuity scheme.

Quick Quiz 11.6

Highlight the answer to these questions:

1. Capital needs analysis is the process of calculating the amount of investment capital needed at retirement to maintain the pre-retirement lifestyle.
   a. True
   b. False

2. The annuity method assumes that the individual will die at the expected life expectancy with a retirement account balance of zero.
   a. True
   b. False

3. The capital preservation model and the purchasing power preservation model are used to mitigate the risk of outliving retirement funds.
   a. True
   b. False

True, True, True.

Jordan, age 42, currently makes $70,000. Her wage replacement ratio is determined to be 80 percent. She expects that inflation will average 3 percent for her entire life expectancy. She expects to earn 9.5 percent on her investments and retire at age 62, possibly living to	**EXAMPLE 11.7**

age 90. She has sent for and received her Social Security benefit statement, which indicated that her Social Security retirement benefit in today's dollars adjusted for early retirement is $15,000 per year. It is reasonable to subtract the Social Security benefit from today's needs because it is inflation adjusted.

1. Calculate Jordan's capital needed at retirement at age 62.

Step 1	80% WRR		
Step 2	($70,000 x 0.80)	=	$56,000 Total needs in today's dollars
Step 3			- 15,000 Less Social Security in today's dollars
			$41,000 Annual amount needed in today's dollars
Step 4	N	=	20 (62 - 42) Work Life Expectancy
	i	=	3% (inflation)
	PV	=	$41,000 (Step 3) Retirement needs in today's dollars
	PMT	=	0
	FV	=	74,050.56 (Step 4) First year needs for retirement
Step 5	N	=	28 (90 – 62) Retirement Life Expectancy
	i	=	6.3107 [(1 + earnings rate ÷1 + inflation rate) – 1] x 100 [(1.095 ÷ 1.03) – 1] x 100
	FV	=	0 Annuity model is 0 at life expectancy
	PMT_{AD}	=	$74,050.56 (from Step 4) this is also an annuity due
	$PV_{AD@62}$	=	$1,022,625.84 (Step 5 - amount needed at age 62)

Note: The math in this example assumes unrounded numbers are used throughout the calculation. If the calculator is cleared at each step and a rounded number for i is used, the results will be slightly lower.

2. Calculate the amount Jordan must save monthly, at month end (an ordinary annuity), assuming she has no current savings to accumulate the capital needed for retirement at age 62.

$FV_{@62}$	=	$1,022,625.84 (from Step 5)
N	=	240 (20 years x 12 months)
i	=	0.79167 (9.5% ÷ 12)
PV	=	0
PMT_{OA}	=	$1,436.43 (monthly savings necessary) at month end

3. Calculate the amount she must save monthly, at month end, assuming she presently has $50,000 in current retirement savings.

$FV_{@62}$	=	$1,022,625.84
N	=	240
i	=	0.79167
PV	=	- $50,000
PMT_{OA}	=	$970.36 (monthly savings necessary) at month end

ASSET ACCUMULATION AND DISTRIBUTION (USING DATA FROM EXAMPLE 11.7)

EXHIBIT 11.22

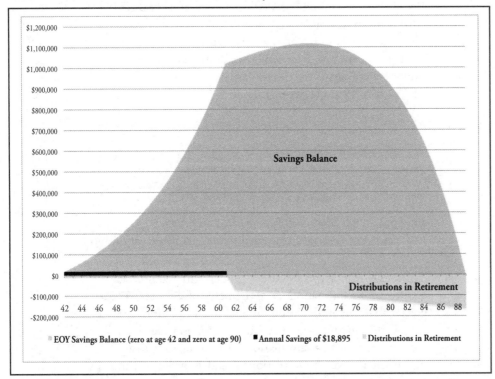

To mitigate against the risk of the assumptions being overly optimistic, the planner can adjust inflation upward, the earnings rate downwards, or make use of a capital preservation model or a purchasing power preservation model rather than a simple annuity model to determine capital needs. These two additional models help to overcome the risks of the pure annuity model (primarily the risk of running out of money).

ADVANCED FINANCIAL PLANNING – CAPITAL PRESERVATION MODEL (CP)

The basic capital needs analysis is a **pure annuity concept**, generally prepared on a pretax basis. The annuity concept means that if all assumptions happen exactly as expected, the person will die exactly at the assumed life expectancy with a retirement account balance of zero. There is some risk that clients could outlive their assets under the annuity approach.

Therefore, they may actually need greater accumulations at retirement. Two models used to mitigate the risk of outliving money are the capital preservation model and the purchasing power preservation model. The **capital preservation model** assumes that at life expectancy, as estimated in the annuity model, the client has exactly the same account balance as started with at retirement. The purchasing power preservation model assumes that the client will have a capital balance of equal purchasing power at life expectancy as he did at retirement. In spite of any conservatism that the planner may have built into the annuity model, it is always possible that one or more assumptions will be unrealized. Therefore, there is the need to consider one of the alternative models.

The capital preservation model maintains the original capital balance needed at retirement for the entire retirement life expectancy.

EXAMPLE 11.8

Recall that the amount needed for Jordan at age 62 calculated from Example 11.7 was $1,022,625.84. If we discount that amount at the expected earnings rate of 9.5 percent, we can determine the additional amount of capital necessary to leave an estate of exactly $1,022,625.84 at life expectancy.

N	=	28
i	=	9.5
$FV_{@90}$	=	$1,022,625.84 (amount at life expectancy)
PMT	=	0
$PV_{@62}$	=	$80,560.37
$1,103,186.21	=	$80,560.37 + $1,022,625.84
		(amount needed for capital preservation model)

Thus, the capital preservation model will require an additional accumulation at retirement of $80,560.37 greater than the pure annuity model but will reduce the risk of running out of money (superannuation). Such an increase in capital accumulation also requires that savings be increased for calculations 2 and 3 in the Jordan example (Example 11.7).

The following chart compares the capital preservation model with the annuity model for our example.

	Capital Preservation Model		Annuity Model	
	Beginning Balance of Zero Savings Calculation 2	Beginning Balance of $50,000 Calculation 3	Beginning Balance of Zero Savings Calculation 2	Beginning Balance of $50,000 Calculation 3
$FV_{@62}$	$1,103,186.21	$1,103,186.21	$1,022,625.84	$1,022,625.84
N	240	240	240	240
i	0.79167	0.79167	0.79167	0.79167
PV	0	- $50,000	0	- $50,000
PMT_{OA}	$1,549.59	$1,083.52	$1,436.43	$970.36

The capital preservation model requires additional savings of $113 per month, but mitigates against many of the risks in the traditional capital needs annuity approach.

ADVANCED PLANNING – PURCHASING POWER PRESERVATION MODEL (PPP)

An even more conservative approach to capital needs analysis is the **purchasing power preservation model**. This model essentially maintains the purchasing power of the original capital balance at retirement.

EXAMPLE 11.9

Again recall Example 11.7. The capital balance of $1,022,625.84 is used as the future value, and then the entire calculation made in the original capital preservation model is repeated. By doing this, the $1,022,625.84 is simultaneously inflated at the rate of inflation and discounted at the earnings rate.

N	=	28
i	=	6.3107
FV	=	$1,022,625.84
PMT_{AD}	=	$74,050.56 (amount needed the first year of retirement)
$PV_{@62}$	=	$1,206,939.24 (if i is not rounded, it will be $3 more)
		capital needed for purchasing power preservation model

The additional accumulation at retirement using a purchasing power model is $184,313.40 greater than the pure annuity approach.

The answers to calculation 2 and 3 in the Jordan example would again change. The chart below compares the purchasing power model with the annuity model for our example.

	Purchasing Power Model		Annuity Model	
	Beginning Balance of Zero Savings Calculation 2	Beginning Balance of $50,000 Calculation 3	Beginning Balance of Zero Savings Calculation 2	Beginning Balance of $50,000 Calculation 3
$FV_{@62}$	$1,206,939.24	$1,206,939.24	$1,022,625.84	$1,022,625.84
N	240	240	240	240
i	0.79167	0.79167	0.79167	0.79167
PV	0	- $50,000	0	- $50,000
PMT_{OA}	$1,695.33	$1,229.25	$1,436.43	$970.36

EXHIBIT 11.23 **CAPITAL NEEDS ANALYSIS COMPARISON FOR JORDAN EXAMPLE[4]**

	Annuity Model	Capital Preservation Model	Purchasing Power Preservation Model
Capital needed at retirement (calculation 1)	$1,022,625.84	$1,103,186.21	$1,206,939.24
Monthly savings with no initial balance (calculation 2)	$1,436.43	$1,549.59	$1,695.33
Monthly savings with $50,000 initial balance (calculation 3)	$970.36	$1,083.52	$1,229.25

---

4. Although we concentrate on the Annuity Model, Capital Preservation Model, and Purchasing Power Model in this textbook, the capital needed at retirement can also be calculated based on complex actuarial assumptions. In order to verify our results in the Jordan example, we sought the advice of an actuary who used a different approach (but one that we verified was competent), which assumed no particular start balance. He calculated the capital needed at retirement to be approximately $1,245,000. We do not present the details of this calculation due to the complexity of the assumptions and calculations. Suffice it to say that the capital needed is $1,200,000 to $1,250,000 regardless of the assumptions. If you are looking for a rule of thumb, it is 10% more for the Capital Preservation Model and 20% more for the Purchasing Power Preservation Model as long as you have similar factors (e.g., 28 years and 3% inflation), but there is no substitution for exact calculations.

RANGE ESTIMATES, SENSITIVITY ANALYSIS, SIMULATIONS, AND MONTE CARLO ANALYSIS

As one might expect, small changes in the assumptions regarding earnings, inflation, life expectancy, and retirement funding needs can have a dramatic impact on the retirement plan. One of the problems with traditional capital needs analysis is that financial planners use deterministic estimates (i.e., the estimate is predetermined as opposed to a probability estimate) for each of the variables (needs, inflation, portfolio returns, life expectancies, etc.). While point estimates help the financial planner create a plan for the client, it is unrealistic to think

Key Concepts

Underline/highlight the answers as you read:

1. Explain how sensitivity analysis is used.

2. What is a Monte Carlo Analysis?

that these variables are really predictable to an exact deterministic point (given) and instead may vary. Generally, point estimates used in deterministic models are the mean expectancy. For example, 2.4 percent on large capitalization common stocks is the mean expected return. While it is true that over the last 78 years large-cap stocks' average returns were 10.4 percent, there were only six years out of 78 when the actual return was close to the mean expected return. In 41 years it was greater and in 31 years it was less by a considerable margin. It is unlikely that for any period going forward the investment return will replicate the historical return. A plan that only uses deterministic assumptions is likely to produce results that may range far from the original forecast. The planner can employ various techniques to help begin to understand the effect of the range of probable outcomes for each variable in a plan. These techniques include range estimates, sensitivity analysis, and simulations such as Monte Carlo Analysis.

Range Estimates

Using range estimates allows the planner to project what outcome will occur if we use a range of assumptions (e.g., 2.5% to 3.5% inflation) for a variable as opposed to a single mean expectation (three percent inflation). A range estimate approach produces multiple outcomes that allow us to gain insight into the impact of a change in one variable or changes in a set of variables. Range estimate assumptions are usually conducted around the mean estimate, both lower and higher than the mean point estimates. If a planner wanted to rotate the assumed coefficient of the variable toward the risk of an adverse outcome (e.g., an investor who is more concerned with down side losses than upside potential returns may use semivariance analysis or alternatively, the number of months returns that were less than T-bill returns), the technique to employ is sensitivity analysis rather than range estimating.

Sensitivity Analysis

Sensitivity analysis consists of rotating each variable assumption toward the undesirable side of the risk to determine the impact of a small change in that variable on not achieving the overall plan. Small deviations in one variable may significantly impact the entire plan.

For example:
1. One additional year of employment often makes the retirement plan work because there is one more year of savings, one more year of earnings accumulation, and one less year of consumption. The opposite is also true; one less year of work may destroy an otherwise achievable plan.
2. Small changes in the spread between the earnings rate and the inflation rate can have a significant impact on a plan, both positively and negatively.
3. A small increase in inflation can have a significant negative impact on an otherwise achievable retirement funding plan.

Understanding the importance of each individual variable and the risk involved if there is a change from the assumed number to a more conservative number allows the planner to use sensitivity analysis to build a slightly worse case scenario and then determine the impact of these more conservative assumptions on the overall plan.

EXAMPLE 11.10

Recall the assumptions given in the Jordan annuity calculation (Example 11.7). The left columns below identify the given variables while the right columns below identify alternative variables that could be used.

Deterministic Example 11.5 Selected Assumptions		Sensitivity Analysis Conservative Assumptions
N	20 years to retirement	• Try 19 years
i	3% inflation	• Try 3.5% inflation
PV	$41,000 current needs	• Try $42,000 needs
PMT	$0	
FV	$74,050.56 future needs	

Deterministic Example 11.6 Selected Assumptions		Sensitivity Analysis Conservative Assumptions
N	28 years in retirement	• Use 30 years in retirement instead of 28
i	$[(1.095 \div 1.03) - 1] \times 100 = 6.3$	• Use a real rate of 5.75 instead of 6.3
PMT_{AD}	$74,050.56 future needs	• Use $80,745 as future needs rather than $74,050.56
$PV_{@62}$	$1,022,625.84 needed at retirement	
FV	$0	

Notice that slightly more conservative assumptions were used for the sensitivity analysis than were used in the original example in order to determine the robustness, or alternatively the sensitivity, of the previously calculated solution. If the retirement plan was recalculated using all of the sensitivity analysis assumptions previously identified, Jordan would need $200,000 more at retirement than originally expected, an increase of 20% just for the annuity model.

Annuity Model Solution with Conservative Assumptions Using Sensitivity Analysis	
N	19 years to retirement
i	3.5 inflation
PV	$42,000 current needs
PMT	$0
FV	$80,745 future needs
N	30 years in retirement
i	5.75 real rate of return
PMT_{AD}	$80,745 real payment (future dollars)
$PV_{@62}$	$1,207,472 (compared to $1,022,625) needed at age 62
FV	$0

Approximately $160,000 of the $200,000 change was caused by the inflation assumption being 3.5% instead of 3%.

Approximate Cause of Change		Explanation
1. Inflation 3.0 to 3.5	$158,916	1. Drive up future needs and drives down real return.
2. Change years 20 to 19	$15,857	2. Drives future needs higher, but over a shorter term.
3. Change years 28 to 30	$25,902	3. Makes more annuity payments.
Total	$200,676	4. The reconciliation cannot be exact because of the changes in terms and rates.
Actual Change	$184,847	

Simulations and Monte Carlo Analysis

There is uncertainty associated with any retirement funding projection. The assumptions can be analyzed using the latest retirement planning software packages that incorporate simulations, such as Monte Carlo Analysis (MCA). As illustrated below, most retirement projections are based on fixed (deterministic) assumptions. While useful during retirement planning, deterministic projections do not account for variations. A **Monte Carlo Analysis** is a mathematical tool that can be used to illustrate the unpredictability of the "real" world and its effects on an individual's retirement plan. MCA uses a random number generator for inputs into a software package that will provide an output with specific probabilities of outcomes. MCA provides insight into the most likely outcome, but also provides other possible outcomes. It allows for a variety of alternative assumptions, such as changes in investment rates of return, the variability of inflation, adjustments to life expectancy,

Quick Quiz 11.7

Highlight the answer to these questions:

1. Sensitivity analysis eliminates the risk of retirement planning.
   a. True
   b. False

2. Monte Carlo analysis predicts particular events.
   a. True
   b. False

3. Simulations allow for an unlimited number of simultaneous ranging variables.
   a. True
   b. False

False, False, True.

and many other market-condition scenarios. Such a method is invaluable to the planner, as it allows the planner to observe a large number of projections illustrating a potential range of future outcomes based on changing variables. Various software programs are available that allow the planner to run simulations projecting various scenarios, thereby increasing the probability that the individual's retirement plan will be successful.

A simulation calculates multiple scenarios of a model by repeatedly sampling values from probability distributions for uncertain variables. Traditional range estimates calculate outcomes on a best case, expected case, and worst case basis. Sensitivity analysis allows the model user to manipulate variables usually one at a time or one set of variables at a time. Simulations allow for an unlimited (or very large) number of simultaneous ranging of variables, possibly leading to more insight into the problem and into the impact of interacting variables.

Because retirement is frequently 20 to 30 years or longer and there are many historical patterns of investment returns for selected 20 to 30 year periods, the planner simply does not know what the market conditions will be when the client retires, nor does the planner know the pattern of market returns that will follow a particular retirement date. Monte Carlo Analysis helps the planner to understand the possibilities and probabilities. However, Monte Carlo Analysis cannot predict particular events. An excellent discussion of the problems with Monte Carlo Analysis was written in the Journal of Financial Planning by David Rawrocki (November 2001, Article 12) and is summarized in Exhibit 11.24.

EXHIBIT 11.24

- Assumes normal distributions, serial independence, and linear relationships for investment returns (none of which are true).
- Stock returns are not normally distributed - kurtosis is higher than expected. (Stock returns are actually **lepto-kurtic**, meaning that they do not have a normal distribution.)
- Means and standard deviations for stock returns vary over time rather than remain static.
- Many Monte Carlo Analysis ignore income tax consequences.

Monte Carlo Analysis is a valuable tool and an interesting exercise. However, as with any analytical tool, it should not be used in a vacuum. It is useful to provide insight, but should not take the place of professional judgment. As with most financial planning, retirement planning is a process that includes regular monitoring and adjustments to the plan as needed. Clients should visit their planner regularly (at least annually) to modify and update their retirement plan to adjust for changes in the preselected variables so that their retirement objectives can be met.

ALTERNATIVES TO COMPENSATE FOR PROJECTED CASH-FLOW SHORTFALLS

There are times when a retirement projection simply works. Occasionally, a person's assets are significantly greater than their needs, and they may actually need encouragement to spend some of the money they have or they may need assistance transferring it to loved ones or donating it to charity. These situations are generally easier to deal with than those involving unrealistic expectations and shortfalls.

Situations can be challenging where the required annual savings amount is unrealistically high or the expressed needs of a client greatly exceed the assets available. In these situations, the plan simply does not work. There are several alternatives to consider, some of which have already been discussed briefly in this chapter. However, many of these alternatives are closely linked to the variables that are quite sensitive in the capital budgeting model. These include the amount of retirement needs, the amount of the required savings, the length of the WLE, the length of the RLE, the earnings rate, and the rate of inflation. With that in mind, the plan may work if one or more of the following adjustments can occur:

1. The annual or monthly retirement needs are reduced
2. The annual or monthly savings amount is increased
3. Expected investment earnings are increased
4. Expected inflation is reduced
5. The WLE is increased
6. The RLE is decreased

Obviously, there are implications and limitations to each of the possibilities listed above. However, there is often a combination of these adjustments that may help to resolve the budget shortfall. For example, a solution might entail refining the needs a bit more precisely, resulting in a decrease in what is actually needed combined with working a few additional years and increasing the portfolio risk slightly, assuming of course that the portfolio is not already heavily weighted toward equities. This solution reduces needs, increases the years of savings, decreases the years of needs, and increases the expected return from the portfolio.

Caution should be taken when adjusting the expected investment returns and inflation. The expected investment return should be based on reasonable expectations about the returns from risky assets and should generally be an output from an asset allocation model that incorporates the investor's risk tolerance and time horizon. Capital budgeting models are extremely sensitive to changes in expected return and inflation and care should be taken when adjusting these input variables.

EXAMPLE 11.11

BJ is 45 years old and plans on retiring at age 65 and living until age 95. Assume that he currently earns $100,000 and his wage replacement ratio is 70 percent and Social Security will provide $20,000 (in today's dollars) in retirement benefits. Also assume that he expects inflation to be 3 percent and expects that he can earn 6 percent on his investments.

Scenario 1: Step 1 of this problem is to determine the needs to be funded in today's dollars. His current income adjusted for the WRR and Social Security result in a funding need of $50,000 ($100,000 x 70% - $20,000) in today's dollars. Step 2 inflates this need until retirement. Based on inflation and when he is retiring, he will need $90,306 his first year of retirement. Step 3 determines the balance he needs in his investment accounts at retirement, which is $1,842,331. Finally, Step 4 calculates the required annual savings of $50,083. The annual funding is problematic because it is 50 percent of his income.

As would likely be the case, assume that Scenario 1 does not work for BJ. Scenarios 2, 3, 4 and 5 illustrate how changing the assumptions will impact the annual funding requirements:

Scenario 2: Requires BJ to work an additional three years. This adjustment increases his savings by three years and decreases his needs by three years.

Scenario 3: Requires a greater investment return from his portfolio increasing the return during his savings years from 6 percent to 9 percent. It does not change the return during retirement.

Scenario 4: Combines Scenarios 2 and 3.

Scenario 5: Combines Scenarios 2 and 3 and requires that he sell an asset, such as land or a boat, for $75,000 and uses the proceeds as the initial fund for his retirement plan.

		Scenario 1 (original projection)	Scenario 2 (work 3 more years)	Scenario 3 (increase investment return)	Scenario 4 (Scenarios 2 & 3 combined)	Scenario 5 (Scenarios 4 & sale of asset)
Step 2: Inflate funds to retirement age	PV	($50,000)	($50,000)	($50,000)	($50,000)	($50,000)
	N	20	23	20	23	23
	i	3.00%	3.00%	3.00%	3.00%	3.00%
	PMT	0	0	0	0	0
	FV	$90,305.56	$98,679.33	$90,305.56	$98,679.33	$98,679.33
Step 3: PV of retirement annuity	PMT	$90,305.56	$98,679.33	$90,305.56	$98,679.33	$98,679.33
	N	30	27	30	27	27
	i	2.9126%	2.9126%	2.9126%	2.9126%	2.9126%
	FV	0	0	0	0	0
	PV	($1,842,330.85)	($1,880,625.32)	($1,842,330.85)	($1,880,625.32)	($1,880,625.32)
Step 4: Annual funding amount	FV	$1,842,330.85	$1,880,625.32	$1,842,330.85	$1,880,625.32	$1,880,625.32
	N	20	23	20	23	23
	i	6.00%	6.00%	9.00%	9.00%	9.00%
	PV	$0.00	$0.00	$0.00	$0.00	($75,000.00)
	PMT	($50,082.95)	($40,016.86)	($36,011.07)	($27,046.93)	($19,218.29)

The impact of these changes is that his annual savings requirement decreases from $50,083 in Scenario 1 to $19,218 in Scenario 5, which is certainly more reasonable based on his income. These changes may or may not be acceptable to BJ, nor are they necessarily the best choices. However, they illustrate how a plan can be adjusted to more realistically achieve the level of funding desired. One obvious choice that was not included was to decrease the annual needs, which would result in a lower savings requirement. Another alternative is to maintain the same 9 percent investment assumption throughout his life. This adjustment combined with Scenario 5 results in an annual savings amount of $15,905.

There are numerous other ways one might adjust a plan to help with its viability. Other considerations might include potential inheritances that would offset future costs or reduce spending needs toward the later part of retirement, which is consistent with the spending patterns of many retirees (see Exhibit 11.14). Part time work may also be a desire or possibility for those who are in good health. Finally, paying off mortgage debt (which often represents 20 percent of a budget) prior to retirement can significantly reduce required expenses during retirement. The examples above are not an exhaustive list. Instead, they should be considered as a starting point for situations in which a retirement plan initially does not work. Investors will generally have to make a choice of sacrificing today, working longer, or sacrificing during retirement when there are projected shortfalls.

IMPLICATIONS OF CAPITAL NEEDS ANALYSIS

Once the question of how much money will be needed at retirement is determined, consideration must be given to how that goal will be achieved. Individuals have several sources of funding for retirement including personal savings, retirement plans from work Social Security, and working while in retirement. Personal savings can be accomplished through banks and brokerage accounts. However, these accounts are not "tax-advantaged," meaning that income earned on accumulated assets will be subject to current taxation. It is generally accepted that in most cases, deferral of taxation is beneficial to the taxpayer. Taxpayers with earned income may be able to fund individual retirement accounts (IRAs) with pre-tax dollars up to $5,500 ($6,500 for those over age 50) for 2013. IRAs are beneficial because they defer taxation until retirement. However, the IRA contribution limit is relatively small compared to what may need to be saved on an annual basis.

The other method to save on a pre-tax basis is through employer-sponsored retirement plans that permit employee salary deferrals, such as 401(k) plans, 403(b) plans, SARSEPs, 457 plans and SIMPLEs, which each permit employees to defer significantly more than can be contributed to an IRA. These plans, pension plans and other qualified plans are discussed in Money Education's *Retirement Planning and Employee Benefits for Financial Planners* textbook.

Key Terms

Annuity Method - Determines how much a client needs to fund their retirement based on the assumption that the person will die exactly at the assumed life expectancy with a retirement account balance of zero.

Capital Needs Analysis - The process of calculating the amount of investment capital needed at retirement to maintain the pre-retirement lifestyle and mitigate the impact of inflation during the retirement years.

Capital Preservation Model (CP) - A capital needs analysis method that assumes that at client's life expectancy, the client has exactly the same account balance as he did at the beginning of retirement.

Lepto-Kurtic - A distribution that appears to be normal but has more area under the two tails than a normal distribution (i.e., fat tails).

Monte Carlo Analysis - A mathematical tool used to calculate the success of an individual's retirement portfolio using changing variables.

Purchasing Power Preservation Model (PPP) - A capital needs analysis method that assumes that at a client's life expectancy, the client will have a capital balance with purchasing power equal to the purchasing power at the beginning of retirement.

Pure Annuity Concept - The basic capital needs analysis approach, generally prepared on a pretax basis.

Remaining Work Life Expectancy (RWLE) - The work period that remains at a given point in time before retirement.

Retirement Life Expectancy (RLE) - The time period beginning at retirement and extending until death; the RLE is the period of retirement that must be funded.

Savings Rate - The average savings amount in the U.S. based on consumption.

Sensitivity Analysis - A tool used to understand the range of outcomes for each variable in a retirement plan by rotating each variable toward the undesirable side of the risk to determine the impact of a small change in that variable on an overall plan.

Suitability - Having a reasonable basis to believe that a recommended transaction or investment strategy is appropriate for a client, after considering the client's age, other investments, financial situation and needs, tax status, investment objectives, investment experience, investment time horizon, liquidity needs, risk tolerance and other relevant issues. See FINRA Rule 2111

Superannuation - The risk of running out of money due to a retired individual living longer than planned.

Key Terms

Wage Replacement Ratio (WRR) - An estimate of the percent of income needed at retirement compared to earnings prior to retirement.

Work Life Expectancy (WLE) - The period of time a person is expected to be in the work force, generally 30-40 years.

1. List the major factors affecting retirement planning.

2. Define work life expectancy.

3. Define retirement life expectancy.

4. What is the median retirement age for individuals in the U.S.?

5. Explain the work life expectancy/retirement life expectancy dilemma.

6. List the major savings and investment concepts that are important to retirement planning.

7. Explain the importance of beginning a retirement savings plan early.

8. Explain the importance of understanding investment decisions and their consequences in retirement planning.

9. How is inflation relevant to a retirement plan?

10. Why do an individual's needs increase or decrease during retirement?

11. List some of the common factors that increase an individual's retirement income needs.

12. List some of the common factors that decrease an individual's retirement income needs.

13. Define the wage replacement ratio.

14. What is the most common estimate range (in percentage terms) for the wage replacement ratio?

15. Describe why a person may or may not need the same wage replacement percentage dollar amount or purchasing power amount throughout their entire retirement period.

16. List the two alternative methods for calculating an individual's wage replacement ratio.

17. How is the WRR calculated utilizing the top-down approach?

18. How is the WRR calculated utilizing the budgeting approach?

19. List the three most common sources of an individual's retirement income.

20. Explain how Social Security affects an individual's retirement income.

21. Describe the importance of personal savings to an individual's retirement income needs.

22. List some of the qualitative considerations that are important in retirement planning.

23. List some of the common factors that negatively affect retirement planning.

24. Explain capital needs analysis and its importance to retirement planning.

25. List the three most common methods for analyzing an individual's capital needs.

26. Identify the main assumptions necessary for capital needs analysis.

27. Describe how Monte Carlo Analysis can be used in retirement planning.

28. Explain how the annuity model calculates retirement needs.

29. What assumption does the capital preservation model make to mitigate the risk of an individual outliving their retirement savings?

30. Why is sensitivity analysis important to retirement planning?

1. Which of the following expenditures will most likely increase during retirement?

    a. Clothing costs.

    b. Travel.

    c. FICA.

    d. Savings.

2. Margaret, a 35-year-old client who earns $45,000 a year, pays 7.65% of her gross pay in Social Security payroll taxes, and saves 8% of her annual gross income. Assume that Margaret wants to maintain her exact pre-retirement lifestyle. Calculate Margaret's wage replacement ratio using the top-down approach (round to the nearest %) and using pre-tax dollars.

    a. 70%.

    b. 80%.

    c. 84%.

    d. 90%.

3. Danny would like to determine his financial needs during retirement. All of the following are expenditures he might eliminate in his retirement needs calculation except:

    a. The $200 per month he spends on drying cleaning for his work suits.

    b. The $1,500 mortgage payment he makes that is scheduled to end five years into retirement.

    c. The FICA taxes he pays each year.

    d. The $2,000 per month he puts into savings.

4. Susie has the following expenditures during the current year:

EXPENSE	AMOUNT
1. Health Care	$800
2. Savings	$4,000
3. Travel	$500
4. Gifts to Grandchildren	$1,000

    Which of these expenditures would you expect to decrease during Susie's retirement?

    a. 2 only.

    b. 1 and 3.

    c. 2 and 4.

    d. 1, 2, 3, and 4.

5. Tiffany, a self-employed dentist, currently earns $100,000 per year. Tiffany has always been a self proclaimed saver, and saves 25% per year of her Schedule C net income. Assume Tiffany paid $13,000 in Social Security taxes. Tiffany plans to pay off her home mortgage at retirement and live debt free. She currently spends $25,000 per year on her mortgage. What do you expect Tiffany's wage replacement ratio to be at retirement based on the above information?

    a. 37.00%.

    b. 59.70%.

    c. 65.30%.

    d. 84.70%.

6. Which factors may affect an individual's retirement plan?

    1. Work life expectancy.

    2. Retirement life expectancy.

    3. Savings rate.

    4. Investment returns.

    5. Inflation.

        a. 1 and 2.

        b. 1, 2, and 3.

        c. 1, 2, 3, and 4.

        d. All of the above.

7. Contributing $1,500 to his retirement fund at the end of each year beginning at age 18 through age 50, with an average annual return of 12%, how much does Juan have in his retirement account at this time to use toward a possible early retirement?

    a. $346,766.42.

    b. $399,987.65.

    c. $457,271.58.

    d. $541,890.55.

8. When Steve and Roslyn retire together they wish to receive $40,000 additional income (in the equivalent of today's dollars) at the beginning of each year. They assume inflation will be 4% and they expect to realize an after tax return of 8%. Based on life expectancies, they estimate their retirement period to be about 30 years. They want to know how much they will need to have in their fund at the time of their retirement.

    a. $698,457.24.

    b. $728,299.37.

    c. $731,894.20.

    d. $813,529.88.

9. Tyrone, age 25, expects to retire at age 60. He expects to live until age 90. He anticipates needing $45,000 per year in today's dollars during retirement. Tyrone can earn a 12% rate of return and he expects inflation to be 4%. How much must Tyrone save, at the beginning of each year, to meet his retirement goal?

    a. $3,980.76.
    b. $4,585.46.
    c. $4,879.29.
    d. $5,132.33.

10. Roy and Barbara are near retirement. They have a joint life expectancy of 25 years in retirement. Barbara anticipates their annual income in retirement will need to increase each year at the rate of inflation, which they assume is 4%. Based on the assumption that their first year retirement need, beginning on the first day of retirement, for annual income will be $85,000, of which they have $37,500 available from other sources, and an annual after-tax rate of return of 6.5%, calculate the total amount that needs to be in place when Roy and Barbara begin their retirement.

    a. $743,590.43.
    b. $859,906.74.
    c. $892,478.21.
    d. $906,131.31.

11. Cathy and her twin sister Carley, both age 25, each believe they have the superior savings plan. Cathy saved $5,000 at the end of each year for ten years then let her money grow for 30 years. Carley on the other hand waited 10 years then began saving $5,000 at the end of each year for 30 years. They both earned 9% on their investment and are 65 years old today and ready to retire. Which of the following statements is correct?

    a. Both strategies are equal as they have equal account balances at age 65.
    b. Cathy's strategy is better because she has a greater account balance at age 65.
    c. Carley's strategy is better because she has a greater account balance at age 65.
    d. Neither strategy is better because Carley has a greater account balance but Cathy contributed less.

12. Shelley saves $3,000 per year, for ten years, at the end of each year starting at age 26 and ending at age 35. She invests the funds in an account earning 10% annually. Shelley stops investing at age 35, but continues to earn 10% annually until she reaches the age of 65. In contrast, Kevin saves $3,000 per year at the end of the year between the ages of 36 and 65 inclusively and invests in a similar account to Shelley, earning 10% annually. What is the value of Shelley's and Kevin's separate accounts at age 65?

	Shelley	Kevin
a.	$710,861	$387,212
b.	$710,861	$493,482
c.	$834,296	$387,212
d.	$834,296	$493,482

13. Kwame and Omarosa, both age 40, have $80,000 of combined retirement assets. They both expect to retire at the age of 65 with a life expectancy of 100 years old. They expect to earn 10% on the assets within their retirement accounts before retirement and 8% during their retirement. If they did not make any additional contributions to their account and they receive a fixed monthly annuity benefit for life, what is the monthly benefit (annuity due) amount they will receive during retirement?

   a. $4,775.30.

   b. $4,984.20.

   c. $6,115.60.

   d. $6,156.37.

14. Charlie would like to retire in 11 years at the age of 66. He would like to have sufficient retirement assets to allow him to withdraw 90% of his current income, less Social Security, at the beginning of each year. He expects to receive $24,000 per year from Social Security in today's dollars. Charlie is conservative and assumes that he will only earn 9% on his investments, that inflation will be 4% per year and that he will live to be 106 years old. If Charlie currently earns $150,000, how much does he need at retirement?

   a. $1,955,893.

   b. $2,049,927.

   c. $3,011,008.

   d. $3,155,768.

15. Bowie, age 52, has come to you for help in planning his retirement. He works for a bank, where he earns $60,000. Bowie would like to retire at age 62. He has consistently earned 8% on his investments and inflation has averaged 3%. Assuming he is expected to live until age 95 and he has a wage replacement ratio of 80%, how much will Bowie need to have accumulated as of the day he retires to adequately provide for his retirement lifestyle?

    a. $726,217.09.

    b. $784,314.45.

    c. $1,050,813.28.

    d. $1,101,823.40.

16. Assuming the same facts as Question 15, approximately how much must Bowie save at the end of each year, from now until retirement, to provide him with the necessary capital balance assuming he has a zero balance today?

    a. $67,163.98.

    b. $70,424.36.

    c. $72,537.10.

    d. $76,058.31.

17. Utilizing the facts given in Question 15, how much more will Bowie need at retirement to have the same amount at his death as he will have (calculated in #15) at his retirement?

    a. $82,897.54.

    b. $86,921.67.

    c. $109,496.29.

    d. $230,545.40.

18. Utilizing the facts given in Question 15, how much more will Bowie need at retirement to have the same amount at his death with an equal purchasing power as he will have (calculated in #16) at his retirement?

    a. $82,897.54.

    b. $86,921.69.

    c. $109,496.29.

    d. $230,545.41.

19. Robin is planning for her retirement. She is currently 35 years old and plans to retire at age 60 and live until age 95. Robin currently earns $100,000 per year and anticipates needing 80% of her income during retirement. She anticipates Social Security will provide her with $15,000 per year leaving her with required savings to provide $65,000 ($100,000 x 0.80 - $15,000) annually during retirement. She believes she can earn 11% on her investments and inflation will be 2% per year. How much must Robin save at the end of each year, if she wants to make her last savings payment at age 60 to meet her retirement goal?

    a. $10,846.78.

    b. $10,899.37.

    c. $11,861.07.

    d. $13,414.60.

20. Assume the same facts as in question 20 except that Robin would like to have the same amount in retirement savings at age 95, as she does at age 60, when she retires. How much must Robin save at the end of each year, if she wants to make her last savings payment at age 60, and maintain the original account balance needed at retirement for the entire retirement life expectancy?

    a. $2,379.57.

    b. $10,899.37.

    c. $11,181.92.

    d. $11,280.51.

21. Assume the same facts as in question 20 except that Robin would like to have the same purchasing power in retirement savings at age 95, as she does at age 60, when she retires. How much must Robin save at the end of each year, if she wants to make her last savings payment at age 60 to meet her retirement goal, assuming she wants to maintain the original purchasing power of her capital balance?

    a. $4,758.88.

    b. $10,899.37.

    c. $11,464.44.

    d. $11,565.52.

22. Which of the following statements is false?

    a. To be more conservative in planning for an individual's retirement, extend the individual's life expectancy.

    b. A Monte Carlo Analysis uses a random number generator to provide the financial planner with an array of possible outcomes utilizing the same fact pattern.

    c. A sensitivity analysis helps the financial planner determine the single most effective factor in a retirement plan.

    d. The capital preservation model assumes that at life expectancy the client will have exactly the same account balance as he did at retirement.

Quick Quiz Explanations

Quick Quiz 11.1
1. False. Approximately 93% of individuals retire between the ages of 62 and 65, not between the ages of 60 and 70.
2. True.
3. True.

Quick Quiz 11.2
1. False. Given that a savings rate of 10% to 13% of gross pay over a long period of time is necessary to meet the retirement goal, the savings rate in the U.S. is insufficient for retirement planning.
2. False. Common stocks provide the best hedge against inflation. The real economic returns for fixed-income securities are low and are not a good hedge against inflation.
3. True.

Quick Quiz 11.3
1. True.
2. True.

Quick Quiz 11.4
1. True.
2. False. Social Security is not a sufficient source of income replacement during retirement for most income levels. Social Security provides 100% of income to only 20% of individuals aged 65 or older receiving Social Security benefits.
3. True.

Quick Quiz 11.5
1. False. Qualitative factors associated with retirement may be more important than the financial or quantitative factors.
2. True.
3. False. A reduced WLE and an increased RLE will negatively impact retirement planning because a reduced WLE will result in an insufficient savings period and an increased RLE will result in an increased capital need.

Quick Quiz 11.6
1. True.
2. True.
3. True.

Quick Quiz Explanations

Quick Quiz 11.7

1. False. While sensitivity analysis does not eliminate all risk associated with retirement planning, it does allow the planner to build a slightly worse case scenario and to determine the impact of more conservative assumptions on the overall plan.

2. False. Monte Carlo Analysis does not predict particular events. Rather, it provides insight into the most likely outcome while also providing other possible outcomes, both good and bad.

3. True.

Income Tax Planning

LEARNING OBJECTIVES

After reading this chapter, you should be able to:

- Describe the three tax systems.
- Describe the three types of income.
- Describe the three types of tax accounting.
- Describe three key tax principles.
- Identify the sources of tax law.
- Describe the interest and penalties for noncompliance.
- Identify the preparer penalties.
- Summarize the failure to pay, failure to file, accuracy related, and fraud penalties.
- Describe the tax formula for individual taxpayers.
- Determine what is included and excluded in gross income.
- List deductions for adjusted gross income.
- List itemized deductions.
- Determine which type of deduction is better above or below the line.
- Understand what is adjusted gross income.
- Determine the standard deduction and additional standard deduction for varying filing statuses.
- Determine the number of personal and dependency exemptions.
- Determine the appropriate tax filing status.
- Identify various tax credits.
- Compare tax credits to deductions.
- Understand basis and how it is determined and the various adjustments to basis.
- Understand capital gain holding periods and tax rates.
- Describe the sale of a personal residence and its tax exemption.

INCOME TAXES AND THE IRS

THE THREE TAX SYSTEMS

In the United States, there are three separate and distinct tax systems that are relevant to financial planning: (1) the income tax system, (2) the estate and gift tax system, and (3) the generation skipping transfer tax system. While many individuals assume that the Internal Revenue Code is one set of rules that all work together, this is not the case. There are three tax systems, and those systems do not always fit together perfectly. It is important for tax professionals and financial planners to understand which tax system they are dealing with when engaging in a transaction. It is possible, for example, for one single transaction to be treated as a gift for income tax purposes and as a sale for estate and gift tax purposes. The tax consequences for income tax purposes and for estate/gift tax purposes will, therefore, differ. This chapter covers fundamental income tax rules.

THREE TYPES OF INCOME

In the U.S. income tax system, there are three types of income: (1) active (ordinary) income, (2) portfolio income, and (3) passive income. Every bit of income earned by a taxpayer must be classified into one of these three categories.

Active income is income derived from labor and income connected with the active conduct of a trade or business. Portfolio income is income derived from investments, such as interest, dividends, and capital gains. Passive income is income derived from dealings in real estate and from the conduct of a trade or business in which the taxpayer does not actively participate.

Categorization of income is important for two reasons: (1) different tax consequences apply to each type of income; and (2) the "bucket rule" limits a taxpayer's ability to write off losses in one income bucket only to the gains in that same bucket.

Active income (and loss) is subject to ordinary income tax rates, which are the highest tax rates in our system. Some types of portfolio income are subject to favorable income tax rates, such as the 15 percent rate that applies to long-term capital gains and qualified dividends. Passive income is subject to a host of anti-abuse rules, and therefore constitutes a separate category of income.

The "bucket rule" limits losses in one bucket to gains in the same bucket. For example, if a taxpayer incurred $5,000 in investment gains and $20,000 in investment losses, $5,000 of the loss could offset the investment gain but could not, under the bucket rule, be used to offset other types of income (such as ordinary or passive income). As in all other areas of tax law, there are exceptions to this rule. In the case of portfolio losses, up to $3,000 of net losses in the portfolio bucket can be used to offset either active or passive income.

THREE TYPES OF TAX ACCOUNTING

For income to be reported properly, taxpayers must follow some method to account for income. There are three methods of accounting that are used for federal income tax purposes: (1) the cash method, (2) the accrual method, and (3) the hybrid method.

The cash method of accounting is the method used by most individuals and small businesses. Under the cash method, income is taxed when it is received, and allowable deductions are claimed when they are paid. Understanding the cash method is particularly important for financial planners, who are typically providing financial advice and planning to individuals and small businesses.

The accrual method of accounting is the method frequently used by larger businesses. Under the accrual method of accounting, income is taxed when it is earned (whether or not it has been received), and deductions are claimed when they are incurred (whether or not they have been paid).

Any method of accounting other than the cash method or accrual method that is approved by the IRS is referred to, collectively, as the hybrid method. The hybrid method is used by some businesses to better reflect their economic income on their income tax returns.

THREE KEY TAX PRINCIPLES

Three key tax principles underlie personal income taxation. They are: (1) the doctrine of constructive receipt, (2) the economic benefit doctrine, and (3) the doctrine of the fruit and the tree.

While most individuals account for their income using the cash method, certain circumstances may arise that will subject income that has not yet been received to current taxation. The doctrine of constructive receipt states that if income is permanently set aside in an account for the benefit of a taxpayer, or if a taxpayer is given the choice to receive income now or defer it to the future, that income will be taxed to the taxpayer currently even if he does not receive it until sometime in the future. For example, consider interest that is earned on a three-year certificate of deposit. Even though a taxpayer does not receive the interest until the certificate of deposit matures, he is taxed on the earned interest currently, since the interest earnings are permanently set aside in an account for the taxpayer's benefit.

Key Concepts

Underline/highlight the answers as you read:

1. Identify the three primary sources of tax law.

2. Describe the legal basis for the modern income tax.

3. Identify how statutory tax law is established.

4. Identify the sources of administrative tax law.

The **doctrine of constructive receipt** (income that is permanently set aside in an account for the taxpayer's benefit) is a special exception to the cash-basis method of income tax accounting. The doctrine states that even if you have not actually received the income, if you have constructively received it, then it is income. For example, if a taxpayer goes to his mailbox on December 31st and sees a check made out to that taxpayer for work he performed, immediately closes the mailbox, and comes back to get the check on January 1st, the income is reported as of December 31st. In fact, the doctrine of constructive receipt is at the cornerstone of retirement planning, and constructive receipt must be avoided if a taxpayer wishes to defer income and taxes into the future to fund his or her retirement.

You may recall from our discussion above that all income received by a taxpayer, in any form, is subject to income tax. The economic benefit doctrine simply states that if a taxpayer receives an economic benefit as income, the value of that benefit will be subject to tax. For example, if a taxpayer is provided group term life insurance by an employer, the value of that group term insurance is subject to income tax, since it is an economic benefit received in return for labor. Congress has, however, for public policy reasons, exempted part of the value of group term life insurance from income tax, but excess amounts are taxable under the economic benefit doctrine.

The third key principal of income taxation is that income is taxed to either: (1) the person who earns it, or (2) the person who owns the asset that produced the income. This principle is referred to as the doctrine of the fruit and the tree. He who owns the tree pays income tax on the fruit that the tree produces. This doctrine is really an anti-abuse provision. It is designed to prevent taxpayers from assigning income to a family member in a lower income tax bracket while retaining the asset that produces the income.

SOURCES OF TAX LAW

There are three primary sources of tax law: statutory sources, administrative sources, and judicial sources. These sources of law reflect the structure of our political system.

Before we elaborate on the direct sources of tax law, however, it is important to understand the origin of our income tax system. As originally adopted, the U.S. Constitution did not give the federal government the ability to collect a tax on income. At the founding of our nation, there was a great deal of suspicion surrounding the new, federal, centralized government, and the states did not want the power of the federal government to get out of hand. Consequently, they imposed limitations on the federal government's ability to impose taxes. As time went on, however, and as the federal government began to assume a more active governance role, a source of revenue was needed to fund the cost of these activities. While Congress had enacted an income tax on several previous occasions, these taxes were either temporary, or were declared unconstitutional by the Supreme Court. With the obvious need for revenue, and the Supreme Court's decree that a federal income tax was unconstitutional, it became clear that a constitutional amendment would be needed to grant the Congress the power to lay and collect taxes on income.

On February 25, 1913, the **16th Amendment** to the U.S. Constitution was adopted. This short amendment stated, "The Congress shall have power to lay and collect taxes on income, from whatever source derived, without apportionment among the several States, and without regard to any census or enumeration."

The Constitution, through enactment of the 16th Amendment, became the foundation for of income tax law in the United States. Two clauses of the 16th Amendment are particularly important in developing an understanding of our income tax system: (1) the "power to lay and collect taxes on income," and (2) the clause "from whatever source derived."

The term "income" is not as easily interpreted as it may first seem. Generally, any accretion to an individual's wealth is income, and is therefore subject to taxation. However, when certain proposals seem to have gone too far, limitations on the definition of income have been imposed by various branches of the government. Exemptions and exclusions also allow some accretions to wealth to avoid income taxes altogether.

As the second important clause from the 16th Amendment indicates, a U.S. citizen is subject to income tax on income "from whatever source derived." In other words, the worldwide income of U.S. citizens from any source is subject to taxation by the U.S.

EXHIBIT 12.1   SOURCES OF TAX LAW

SOURCE	AUTHORITY	LAW
Statutory	Congressionally derived law through legislative power provided by the 16th Amendment to the U.S. Constitution.	Internal Revenue Code of 1986, as amended.
Administrative	• **Treasury Department:** Executive authority of law enforcement delegated to the Treasury Department. • **Internal Revenue Service:** Tax collection authority delegated by the Treasury Department to the Internal Revenue Service.	• **Treasury Regulations:** 　a. Proposed Regulations 　b. Temporary Regulations 　c. Final Regulations • **IRS Determinations:** 　a. Revenue Rulings 　b. Private Letter Rulings 　c. Determination Letters 　d. Revenue Procedures
Judicial	Judicial authority to determine if tax laws enacted by Congress and enforced by the President are constitutional. Also, decides whether a regulation or IRS position follows the intent of Congress.	**Case Law:** Usually a case or controversy between a taxpayer and the IRS resulting in case law expressed in the opinion of a court.

INTEREST AND PENALTIES FOR NONCOMPLIANCE

Taxpayers who choose not to comply with the filing requirements are subject to a series of penalties, including the failure to file penalty, the failure to pay penalty, and the accuracy related penalty.

If a taxpayer fails to file his income tax return on time, the **failure to file penalty** under Section 6651 applies. If a taxpayer fails to pay the tax due on the due date, Section 6651 also imposes a **failure to pay penalty**. Section 6662 imposes an **accuracy-related penalty** on taxpayers who file incorrect returns as a result of: (1) a failure to make a good faith effort to comply with the tax law, (2) a substantial understatement of tax liability (generally more than 10 percent of the correct tax liability and at least a $5,000 deficiency), (3) a substantial valuation understatement, or (4) a substantial estate or gift tax valuation understatement.

The stakes are even higher for those who commit fraud while failing to file or pay, and those who intentionally understate their tax liability. A fraud penalty of 75 percent of the underpayment of tax may be imposed under Section 6663. If a frivolous or incomplete income tax return has been filed, a $500 penalty may be imposed under Section 6702 regardless of tax liability.   Intentional actions constituting fraud, or a willful failure to file or pay the tax liability that is due can rise to the level of criminal offenses. For obvious reasons, taxpayers should properly report their income and deductions on their tax returns, file them in a timely fashion, and pay the tax liability when due.

PREPARER PENALTIES

In addition to tax penalties that may be assessed on taxpayers, tax preparers may also be subject to penalties. IRC Section 6694(a) states that if a tax preparer takes an unrealistic position on a tax return and the preparer knew or reasonably should have known of the position, then the penalty is the greater of $1,000 or 50 percent of the income derived by the preparer for preparing the return. If the understatement was due to willful or reckless conduct, the penalty is the greater of $5,000 or 50 percent of income derived by the preparer for the return.

Other penalties may also be assessed, including penalties for failure to sign a return prepared by the tax preparer (IRC Section 6695(b)), failure to provide a copy of the tax return to the taxpayer (IRC Section 6695(a), failure to keep a copy of the return (IRC Section 6695(d)) and a client list, and failure to comply with due diligence requirements when claiming the earned income credit (IRC Section 6695(g)).

Quick Quiz 12.1

Highlight the answer to these questions:

1. The three top sources of tax law includes statutory, agency, and judicial.
   a. True
   b. False

2. Statutory tax law is established through legislative authority.
   a. True
   b. False

3. The legal basis for the modern income tax is the 16th Amendment to the U.S. Constitution.
   a. True
   b. False

False, True, True.

SUMMARY OF PENALTIES

EXHIBIT 12.2

Failure to File	5% per month or part thereof to 25% maximum
Failure to Pay	0.5% per month or part thereof to 25% maximum
Accuracy Related	20% of underpayment to 30%*
Fraud	15% per month up to 75% of underpayment

*40% if due to substantial valuation misstatement, substantial overstatement of pension liabilities, or substantial estate or gift tax valuation understatement.

TAX FORMULA FOR INDIVIDUAL TAXPAYERS

In very general terms, a taxpayer is required to pay a federal income tax on taxable income. **Taxable income** is determined by subtracting allowable deductions from income:

$$\text{Income} - \text{Deductions} = \text{Taxable Income}$$

Taxable income is multiplied by the income tax rate to determine the tax liability:

$$\text{Taxable Income} \times \text{Tax Rate} = \text{Tax Liability}$$

There is a more extensive tax formula for individual taxpayers than the simple tax calculation presented above. The more complete formula includes exclusions from income, different types of deductions, and tax credits. In addition, there are intermediate calculations (such as adjusted gross income) that can be important considerations in tax planning. Each of these items will be discussed in this chapter and throughout the remainder of the textbook.

Income Broadly Defined	**$xx,xxx**
Less: Exclusions	(x,xxx)
Gross Income	**$xx,xxx**
Less: Deductions for Adjusted Gross Income (*above-the-line deductions*)	(x,xxx)
Adjusted Gross Income	**$xx,xxx**
Less: Deductions from Adjusted Gross Income: Greater of Standard or Itemized Deductions (*below-the-line deductions*)	(xx,xxx)
Less: Personal and Dependency Exemptions	(xx,xxx)
Taxable Income	**$xx,xxx**
Tax on Taxable Income	$x,xxx
Less: Credit for Taxes Withheld	(x,xxx)
Less: Credit for Estimated Tax Payments	(x,xxx)
Less: Other Tax Credits	(x,xxx)
Tax Due or (Refund Due)	**$xxx**

Individuals report their income, deductions, exemptions, and other information required for the calculation of the federal tax liability on one of the following three forms:

- Form 1040EZ,
- Form 1040A, or
- Form 1040.

Form 1040EZ may be used by single or married taxpayers filing jointly who do not have any dependents and whose taxable income is less than $100,000 for 2012. Note that Form 1040EZ may not be used by individuals claiming Head of Household status or by married individuals who file separately. Form 1040A may be used by taxpayers of any filing status, but the taxpayer's taxable income must be less than $100,000 for 2012, the taxpayer must not itemize his deductions, and the taxpayer must only take certain tax credits. Taxpayers must also meet other requirements in order to use Form 1040EZ or Form 1040A. Form 1040, which is the most complex form of the three, can be used by any taxpayer.

Key Concepts

Underline/highlight the answers as you read:

1. Explain the basic tax formula.

2. Define income.

3. Identify items excluded from gross income.

4. Identify items included in gross income.

INCOME

Income, broadly defined, means the gross amount of money and the fair market value of property, services, or other accretion to wealth received, but it does not include borrowed money or a return of invested dollars (sometimes referred to as return of capital or return of adjusted taxable basis).

GROSS INCOME

Gross income includes all income items that must be reported on the federal income tax return and that are subject to the federal income tax. It includes all income as broadly defined, less exclusions. Some of the most common gross income items are listed in Exhibit 12.3.

ITEMS INCLUDED IN GROSS INCOME

EXHIBIT 12.3

• Gains from the sale of assets	• Compensation (salaries and wages, etc.)
• Distributions from retirement plans	• Interest income
• Rental income	• Dividend income
• Unemployment compensation benefits	• Alimony received
• Royalty income	• Gross income from self-employment

EXCLUSIONS

Exclusions are income items that are not subject to income tax. Each exclusion must be specifically authorized by Congress and set forth in the Internal Revenue Code (IRC) or must be determined by the courts to be outside the definition of income as it is used in the 16th Amendment to the U.S. Constitution. Most exclusions from gross income are allowed by IRC Sections 101 through 150. Some of the more common exclusions permitted by the Code are listed in Exhibit 12.4.

PARTIAL LIST OF EXCLUSIONS

EXHIBIT 12.4

• Interest income from municipal bonds	• Cash or property received by gift
• Child support payments received from a former spouse	• Deferral contributions to certain retirement plans
• Cash or property received by inheritance	• Gain on the sale of a principal residence
• Specified employee fringe benefits	• Scholarship or fellowship
• Qualifying distributions from a Roth IRA during retirement	• Life insurance proceeds received because of the death of the insured

DEDUCTIONS

Deductions are subtracted from gross income in arriving at taxable income. For individual taxpayers, deductions are divided into two categories: Deductions *for* (before) adjusted gross income and deductions *from* (after) adjusted gross income. Deductions for adjusted gross income are called **above-the-line deductions**, and deductions from adjusted gross income are called **below-the-line deductions**, itemized deductions, or Schedule A deductions. A small sample of deductions for adjusted gross income (above-the-line deductions) is listed in Exhibit 12.5.

EXHIBIT 12.5	PARTIAL LIST OF DEDUCTIONS FOR ADJUSTED GROSS INCOME

• Alimony paid	• Business expenses
• Contributions to traditional IRAs	• Rental or royalty income expenses
• Tuition for higher education	• Losses from the sale of business property
• Interest paid on student loans	• Moving expenses

Note that the "line," for income tax purposes, is adjusted gross income (AGI). AGI sets many of the phase-outs and thresholds that will have to be met to take advantage of certain deductions and tax planning tools. Understanding where deductions are taken in the tax formula, therefore, is important when considering tax planning alternatives for clients.

When considering income tax deductions and their planning implications for clients, it is helpful to recall the income tax formula.

	Gross Income
-	Exclusions
-	Adjustments (Above-the-line deductions)
=	**Adjusted Gross Income (AGI)**
-	The greater of the Standard Deduction or Itemized Deductions (Below-the-line deductions)
-	Personal and Dependency Exemptions
=	**Taxable Income**

FORM 1040 ADJUSTMENTS SECTION

Adjusted Gross Income	23	Educator expenses	23				
	24	Certain business expenses of reservists, performing artists, and fee-basis government officials. Attach Form 2106 or 2106-EZ	24				
	25	Health savings account deduction. Attach Form 8889 .	25				
	26	Moving expenses. Attach Form 3903	26				
	27	Deductible part of self-employment tax. Attach Schedule SE .	27				
	28	Self-employed SEP, SIMPLE, and qualified plans . .	28				
	29	Self-employed health insurance deduction	29				
	30	Penalty on early withdrawal of savings	30				
	31a	Alimony paid b Recipient's SSN ▶	31a				
	32	IRA deduction	32				
	33	Student loan interest deduction	33				
	34	Tuition and fees. Attach Form 8917	34				
	35	Domestic production activities deduction. Attach Form 8903	35				
	36	Add lines 23 through 35				36	
	37	Subtract line 36 from line 22. This is your **adjusted gross income** . . . . . . ▶				37	

DEDUCTIONS FOR AGI (ABOVE-THE-LINE)

Adjustments, or above-the-line deductions, reduce a taxpayer's adjusted gross income (AGI). Most above-the-line deductions relate to expenses for business and production of income activities (from investment activities) by taxpayers, but there are some deductions permitted for individual taxpayers as well (such as IRA deductions, student loan interest, and educator expenses, to name a few). Above-the-line deductions are listed in IRC Section 62, and they can be claimed by the taxpayer even if the taxpayer does not itemize deductions.

Whenever expenses are associated with a business activity, they are above-the-line deductions. Only the net income of the business (gross receipts from the business less expenses incurred in producing that income) is included in the taxpayer's gross income for the year. For example, if a taxpayer operates a sole proprietorship, the financial results will be reported on Schedule C of the taxpayer's individual tax return. If, instead of operating a business, a taxpayer engages in rental real estate activities, the gross receipts from the rental activity less expenses associated with the rental activity will be reported on Schedule E of the income tax return, and only the net income from the activity will be reported in the taxpayer's gross income for the year. Schedules C and E are essentially income statements for the business and production of income activities, detailing the gross receipts and expenditures incurred in the activity. Since business related and production of income related expenses directly reduce gross income, they are effectively treated as above-the-line deductions.

Quick Quiz 12.2

Highlight the answer to these questions:

1. The basic tax formula is Income - Credits = Taxable Income.
   a. True
   b. False

2. Income includes a return of invested capital.
   a. True
   b. False

3. Property obtained by inheritance is not included in gross income.
   a. True
   b. False

4. Alimony received is included in gross income.
   a. True
   b. False

False, False, True, True.

All other above-the-line deductions are found in the adjustments section on the front page of Form 1040 and are discussed below.

ITEMIZED DEDUCTIONS (BELOW-THE-LINE)

When most taxpayers think of deductions, they usually think of itemized deductions. Itemized, or below-the-line, deductions are deductions that are allowed for personal expenses and losses that are not typically associated with the conduct of a business or with production of income activities. While there are fewer itemized deductions (there are only six categories of itemized deductions) than above-the line deductions, itemized deductions are sometimes more important when planning for individual clients.

Taxpayers may take the greater of their itemized deductions or the standard deduction in determining taxable income. In order to achieve a tax benefit, the taxpayer will need his total itemized deductions to be greater than the standard deduction.

EXHIBIT 12.6 **PARTIAL LIST OF ITEMIZED DEDUCTIONS**

• Miscellaneous expenses that exceed 2% of AGI	• Medical and dental expenses in excess of 7.5% of AGI
• Charitable contributions	• State and local income taxes
• Tax return preparation fees	• Real property taxes on home
• Home mortgage interest	• Property taxes based on the value of a car
• Unreimbursed employee expenses	• Certain investment expenses
• Investment interest expense	• Casualty losses in excess of 10% of AGI

EXAMPLE 12.1

Corbin (age 52) and Maria (age 50) have no dependents. During this year, they paid $5,000 in state income taxes, $2,000 in charitable contributions, $8,000 in home mortgage interest, and $1,500 in property taxes on their home. The total of their itemized deductions is $16,500, which exceeds their standard deduction. Therefore, they should itemize deductions rather than use the standard deduction.

In three situations, a taxpayer is not allowed to use the standard deduction and *must* itemize deductions:

1. A married individual who files a separate return (married filing separately filing status) cannot use a standard deduction if that person's spouse itemizes deductions.
2. A nonresident alien and a dual-status alien is not allowed to use a standard deduction.
3. An individual who files a tax return for less than 12 months because of a change in annual accounting period is not allowed to use a standard deduction (not common for individual taxpayers).

Which Type of Deduction is Better – Above or Below-the-Line Deductions?

Due to the limitation imposed on itemized deductions by the standard deduction (a taxpayer can only take the greater of the two), various deduction floors and ceilings, as well as phase-outs associated with below-the-line deductions, above-the-line deductions are usually considered to be more favorable to the taxpayer on a dollar-for-dollar basis.

Adjusted Gross Income (AGI)

Adjusted gross income (AGI) is gross income reduced by above-the-line deductions. When determining whether deductions are taken above-the-line (for AGI) or below-the-line (from AGI), "the line" is AGI. Adjusted gross income is also used to determine limitations on several below-the-line deductions, on several income tax credits (discussed later in this chapter), and on a few other items on the tax return. Adjusted gross income is a concept that applies to individual tax returns; it does not apply to corporate or other entity tax returns.

Key Concepts

Underline/highlight the answers as you read:

1. Define adjusted gross income.

2. Identify the difference between the standard deduction and itemized deductions.

3. Identify when a taxpayer is not permitted to use the standard deduction.

Deductions from Adjusted Gross Income

Deductions from adjusted gross income (below-the-line deductions) are those deductions that are subtracted from AGI. They consist of the greater of the standard deduction or certain allowable itemized deductions and the deduction for personal and dependency exemptions.

Standard Deduction

An individual taxpayer is allowed to deduct the greater of the standard deduction or allowable itemized deductions. In recent years, approximately 70 percent of individual taxpayers have used the standard deduction. The **standard deduction** is a standard amount used to offset AGI that is specified by Congress. The standard deduction is adjusted for inflation on an annual basis. The total standard deduction includes a basic standard deduction plus additional standard deduction amounts for taxpayers age 65 or older and for taxpayers who are blind. The basic standard deduction amounts depend on the taxpayer's filing status (discussed below). The standard deduction amounts for nondependents are listed in Exhibit 12.7. The standard deduction for a dependent is different and is discussed below.

EXHIBIT 12.7 STANDARD DEDUCTION

Filing Status	2012
Married Filing Jointly	$11,900
Married Filing Separately	$5,950
Surviving Spouse	$11,900
Head of Household	$8,700
Single	$5,950

Additional Standard Deduction

An additional standard deduction is allowed for a taxpayer or spouse (not for a dependent) who is 65 years of age or older or blind. The age of the taxpayer is determined as of the end of the year. It is therefore possible for an unmarried taxpayer to receive one or two additional standard deductions and for a married couple to receive up to four additional standard deductions. The amounts allowed for each additional standard deduction are adjusted for inflation and depend upon the filing status of the taxpayer. The additional standard deduction amounts are listed in Exhibit 12.8.

EXHIBIT 12.8 ADDITIONAL STANDARD DEDUCTION

Filing Status	2012
Married Filing Jointly	$1,500
Married Filing Separately	$1,500
Surviving Spouse	$1,500
Head of Household	$1,450
Single	$1,450

CALCULATION OF THE STANDARD DEDUCTION FOR A DEPENDENT

An individual who can be claimed as a dependent by someone else cannot use the regular basic standard deduction, as discussed above. The basic standard deduction for someone who can be claimed as a dependent by another taxpayer is determined using a three-step process:

- The minimum basic standard deduction is $950 for 2012;
- If larger, the basic standard deduction is equal to the earned income (wages, salary, self-employment income, or taxable scholarships or fellowships) of the taxpayer plus $300 for 2012; and
- The maximum basic standard deduction is equal to the normal basic standard deduction for the taxpayer's filing status. Any additional standard deductions for age or blindness are added to the basic standard deduction.

Quick Quiz 12.3

Highlight the answer to these questions:

1. Adjusted gross income is gross income reduced by below-the-line deductions.
   a. True
   b. False

2. The standard deduction is an amount specified by Congress that is used to off-set adjusted gross income.
   a. True
   b. False

3. Nonresident aliens and dual-status aliens are allowed to use a standard deduction.
   a. True
   b. False

False, True, False.

PERSONAL AND DEPENDENCY EXEMPTIONS

Personal and dependency exemption amounts are also deductions from adjusted gross income. A **personal exemption** is allowed for the taxpayer and the taxpayer's spouse on a tax return. A **dependency exemption** is allowed for each person who qualifies as a dependent of the taxpayer. Normally, the child of a taxpayer qualifies as the taxpayer's dependent, but many other people may qualify as dependents and in some cases the taxpayer's own child does not qualify as a dependent. The inflation-adjusted amount allowed as a deduction for each personal and dependency exemption is $3,800 for 2012.

TAX ON TAXABLE INCOME

The income tax on taxable income is determined by applying certain tax rates to taxable income. The tax rates currently range from 10 percent to 35 percent. The amount of taxable income subject to tax at each rate (each tax bracket) depends on the filing status of the taxpayer.

Although the tax can be determined by directly applying the tax rates from the tax rate schedules to taxable income, taxpayers are required to determine the tax using tax tables provided by the Internal Revenue Service, if possible. These tax tables, published by the Internal Revenue Service in the instructions for individual income tax returns, show small ranges of taxable income and the amount of tax for taxable income within each range. These tax tables are available, as released by the IRS, on our website, money-education.com.

Key Concepts

Underline/highlight the answers as you read:

1. Define personal and dependency exemptions.

2. Identify how the tax on taxable income is calculated.

3. Identify various tax credits.

TAX RATE SCHEDULES

2012 SINGLE - SCHEDULE X

If taxable income is over--	But not over--	The tax is:
$0	$8,700	10% of the amount over $0
$8,700	$35,350	$870 plus 15% of the amount over $8,700
$35,350	$85,650	$4,867.50 plus 25% of the amount over $35,350
$85,650	$178,650	$17,442.50 plus 28% of the amount over $85,650
$178,650	$388,350	$43,482.50 plus 33% of the amount over $178,650
$388,350	no limit	$112,683.50 plus 35% of the amount over $388,350

2012 MARRIED FILING JOINTLY OR SURVIVING SPOUSE - SCHEDULE Y-1

If taxable income is over--	But not over--	The tax is:
$0	$17,400	10% of the amount over $0
$17,400	$70,700	$1,740 plus 15% of the amount over $17,400
$70,700	$142,700	$9,735 plus 25% of the amount over $70,700
$142,700	$217,450	$27,735 plus 28% of the amount over $142,700
$217,450	$388,350	$48,665 plus 33% of the amount over $217,450
$388,350	no limit	$105,062 plus 35% of the amount over $388,350

2012 HEAD OF HOUSEHOLD - SCHEDULE Z

If taxable income is over--	But not over--	The tax is:
$0	$12,400	10% of the amount over $0
$12,400	$47,350	$1,240 plus 15% of the amount over $12,400
$47,350	$122,300	$6,482.50 plus 25% of the amount over $47,350
$122,300	$198,050	$25,220 plus 28% of the amount over $122,300
$198,050	$388,350	$46,430 plus 33% of the amount over $198,050
$388,350	no limit	$109,229 plus 35% of the amount over $388,350

2012 MARRIED FILING SEPARATELY - SCHEDULE Y-2

If taxable income is over--	But not over--	The tax is:
$0	$8,700	10% of the amount over $0
$8,700	$35,350	$870 plus 15% of the amount over $8,700
$35,350	$71,350	$4,867.50 plus 25% of the amount over $35,350
$71,350	$108,725	$13,867.50 plus 28% of the amount over $71,350
$108,725	$194,175	$24,332.50 plus 33% of the amount over $108,725
$194,175	no limit	$52,531 plus 35% of the amount over $194,175

2012 ESTATES AND TRUSTS

If taxable income is over--	But not over--	The tax is:
$0	$2,400	15% of the amount over $0
$2,400	$5,600	$360 plus 25% of the amount over $2,400
$5,600	$8,500	$1,160 plus 28% of the amount over $5,600
$8,500	$11,650	$1,972 plus 33% of the amount over $8,500
$11,650	no limit	$3,011.50 plus 35% of the amount over $11,650

FILING STATUS

The filing status of a taxpayer is used to determine the amount of the taxpayer's standard deduction, the tax rate schedule (or tax table) to be used, and the eligibility of the taxpayer to use various tax benefits. A list of filing statuses is presented in Exhibit 12.9.

FILING STATUS FOR INDIVIDUALS

EXHIBIT 12.9

Married Filing Jointly
Married Filing Separately
Surviving Spouse
Head of Household (Including an Abandoned Spouse)
Single

Marital Status

The determination of whether a taxpayer is married is normally made as of the close (the last day) of the tax year. However, if a taxpayer's spouse dies during the year, the marital status of the taxpayer is determined on the date of the spouse's death. A married person normally has two filing status options: married filing jointly or married filing separately.

If a person is not married, then he or she may qualify for the surviving spouse, head of household, or single filing status. A very rare situation is discussed below which may allow a married person to file as a single taxpayer. A taxpayer who is legally separated from his spouse under a decree of divorce or of separate maintenance is not considered to be married for federal income tax purposes.

Married Filing Jointly

Married taxpayers are allowed to choose either married filing jointly or **married filing separately filing status**. Most married taxpayers use the **married filing jointly filing status**. This filing status allows a married couple to combine their gross income and deductions. If they do not itemize deductions, the basic standard deduction when filing jointly is double the size of the basic standard deduction for a married taxpayer filing separately. Each tax bracket (the 15 percent tax bracket, for example) for joint filers is twice as broad as for a married taxpayer filing separately, subjecting twice as much income to the lower rates. In addition, a married couple is required to file jointly in order to be eligible for certain benefits such as the earned income credit.

Married Filing Separately

A married taxpayer can elect to file separately for any reason. This may be necessary if the husband and wife are separated at the end of the year, or if the taxpayer is not sure that his spouse is accurately reporting income. It may also be used for tax minimization purposes, by permitting one spouse to deduct more of his unusually large medical expenses or employee business expenses for the tax year.

For a taxpayer whose spouse dies during the year, a joint return can be filed. The joint return will include the income and deductions of the taxpayer for the full year and the income and deductions of the spouse for the part of the year that the spouse lived. If the surviving taxpayer remarries before the end of the year, she will be able to file a joint return with the new spouse but not with the deceased spouse. In this situation, the final income tax return for the deceased spouse must use the married filing separately filing status.

Abandoned Spouse

There is one situation in which a legally married taxpayer will be allowed to use a filing status (head of household) generally reserved for unmarried taxpayers. As discussed below, the head of household status is more favorable than filing as married filing separately and when an individual cannot locate his spouse, and does not want to file a tax return with him, it may be available. To be eligible to file as an abandoned spouse (and therefore use the head of household filing status), the taxpayer must meet *all* of the following requirements:

- The taxpayer must be married;
- Must file a separate tax return from the spouse;
- Must maintain as his/her home a household which for more than one-half of the taxable year is the principal place of abode of a child who can be claimed as a dependent;
- Must furnish over one-half of the cost of maintaining the household; *and*
- The spouse must not be a member of the household during the last six months of the tax year.

Unmarried Taxpayers

A taxpayer who is not married on the final day of the tax year may be able to file as surviving spouse, head of household, or single. The tax benefits for the surviving spouse filing status are most favorable, those for head of household are next, and those for the single filing status are the least favorable.

Surviving Spouse

The **surviving spouse filing status** affords the same basic standard deduction and tax rates as the married filing jointly filing status. However, eligibility for this filing status is not something that most people desire. To be eligible, the spouse of the taxpayer must have died within the two preceding tax years of the taxpayer. Specifically, a taxpayer must meet all of the following requirements to qualify:

- The taxpayer's spouse must have died during either of the two preceding tax years;

- The taxpayer must maintain (pay more than half the cost of) a household as his home which is also the principal place of residence of a dependent child (son, step-son, daughter, or stepdaughter);
- The taxpayer has not remarried; and
- The taxpayer and spouse were eligible to file a joint return for the spouse's year of death.

It should be noted that the filing status called surviving spouse in the Internal Revenue Code and Treasury Regulations is referred to as the qualifying widow(er) filing status in IRS publications. Surviving spouse and qualifying widow(er) are alternate names for the same filing status.

Head of Household

The **head of household filing status** provides a basic standard deduction and tax bracket sizes that are less favorable to the taxpayer than those for the surviving spouse, but more favorable than those for the single filing status. Head of household filing status can be used by an unmarried taxpayer who is not a surviving spouse and who meets the following requirements:

- The taxpayer must maintain (pay more than half the cost of) a household as his home, which is also the principal place of residence for more than half the year for:
  - a qualifying child of the taxpayer who is claimed as a dependent (discussed later in this chapter) of the taxpayer,
  - an unmarried qualifying child who lives with the taxpayer but is not a dependent of the taxpayer (e.g., a taxpayer's child or grandchild who lives in the taxpayer's household but is claimed as the dependent of another person), or
  - a qualifying relative (discussed later in this chapter) who is: (1) claimed as a dependent of the taxpayer, and (2) actually related to the taxpayer.

If a married child of the taxpayer lives with the taxpayer but cannot be claimed as a dependent of the taxpayer either because the child: (1) files a joint return (married filing jointly) with her spouse, or (2) fails to meet a citizenship or residency test, the taxpayer is not allowed to use the head of household filing status.

Special Rule for the Father or Mother of the Taxpayer

In order to use the head of household filing status, a qualifying child or a qualifying relative must normally live with the taxpayer. However, a taxpayer may also qualify for the head of household status by maintaining a separate household for the father or mother of the taxpayer who qualifies as the taxpayer's dependent.

Single

The **single filing status** must be used by an unmarried taxpayer who is not eligible to use the surviving spouse nor head of household filing status. It provides the least desirable basic standard deduction and tax brackets for an unmarried taxpayer.

CREDIT FOR TAXES WITHHELD

Although income taxes could (in theory) all be paid at the time the tax return is filed, Congress has decided that federal income taxes should be withheld by an employer from the employee's wages or salary and sent to the government during the year. This not only provides the government with revenues throughout the year, but it also taxes the employee when the employee has the wherewithal (the cash) to pay. This withholding is merely a prepayment of income tax. Therefore, the employee is allowed to subtract any federal income taxes withheld during the year from the tax on taxable income when a tax return is filed. When an amount is subtracted from a tax, it is called a credit or a **tax credit**.

FICA

The Federal Insurance Contributions Act (FICA) provides for old-age, survivors, disability, and hospital insurance. This coverage is financed by Social Security and Medicare taxes. Employers are required to withhold Social Security and Medicare tax from an employee's wages with the employer paying a matching amount of tax. The Social Security tax has a wage base limit of $113,700 for 2013. Employers are required to contribute 6.2 percent of each employee's income up to the Social Security wage base for 2013. The required Medicare tax is collected from an employee at a rate of 1.45 percent of their salary or wages, with a matching tax of 1.45 percent collected from the employer (2.9% total).[1] The Medicare tax is not subject to a wage base limit.[2]

Employers who are required to withhold income tax and FICA tax must file a federal return each quarter on Form 941. This form must be filed by the last day of the month that follows the end of the previous quarter.

FUTA

The Federal Unemployment Tax Act (FUTA) exists in concert with state unemployment systems to pay unemployment compensation to employees who have become unemployed. This tax is paid by the employer only and is taxed at a rate of 6.0 percent (historically) on the first $7,000 that an employer pays in each employee's wages (note: the state wage base may be different). FUTA tax is reported annually on federal Form 940. A credit is allowed for unemployment taxes paid to states.

Self-Employment Tax

A self-employed individual pays income tax, as well as self-employment FICA taxes of 15.3 percent (12.4% for Social Security and 2.9% for Medicare), on his earnings up to the wage base of $113,700 (2013) and 2.9 percent beyond the wage base for Medicare.[3] However, the self-employed worker is not required to pay FUTA tax on himself. In addition, a self-

---

1. During 2011 and 2012, the 6.2% rate was decreased as part of the Payroll Tax Holiday. This tax break is scheduled to expire at 12/31/2012 but could be extended into 2013.
2. Beginning in 2013, the Additional Medicare Tax (IRC §1401(b)(2) and §3101(b)(2)), which is part of the Affordable Care Act, of 0.9 percent (above the 1.45% or 2.9%) applies to individuals' wages, other compensation, and self-employment income over certain thresholds. The additional medicare tax of 0.9 percent applies to income over $200,000 for individuals and to income over $250,000 for couples filing jointly.
3. During 2011 and 2012, the 12.4% rate was decreased as part of the Payroll Tax Holiday. This tax break is scheduled to expire at 12/31/2012 but could be extended into 2013.

employed person can take a FICA deduction for adjusted gross income on his own tax return, in the amount of one-half of his total FICA taxes paid.

TAX CREDITS

A **tax credit** is an amount that is subtracted from calculated tax. Tax credits can reduce the tax on taxable income to zero, and some tax credits can also generate a tax refund in excess of tax pre-payment. Tax credits come in two forms; nonrefundable or refundable. Nonrefundable credits may only apply to the current year or, in some cases, they may be carried back to an earlier year, carried forward to future years, or both. Refundable tax credits can be used to reduce or eliminate the current year's tax, but can also generate a refund.

Nonrefundable Tax Credits

Nonrefundable tax credits can reduce the tax on taxable income to zero, but they cannot generate a tax refund, an excess withholding, estimated payments, amounts applied from prior years tax refunds to this year's tax liability, and excess Social Security tax contributions. Nonrefundable tax credits include:

- Foreign Tax Credit
- Credit for Child and Dependent Care
- Credit for the Elderly or Disabled
- Education Credits: Lifetime Learning, and part or all of the American Opportunity Tax Credit
- Retirement Savings Contributions Credit
- Child Tax Credit
- Residential Energy Efficient Property Credit
- Nonbusiness Alternative Motor Vehicle Credit
- Nonbusiness Alternative Fuel Vehicle Refueling Property Credit
- General Business Credit

> Monica's tax on taxable income is $600. She is eligible for a nonrefundable tax credit of $700. Monica is allowed to use the credit to reduce her tax to $0 for the year, but she is not allowed to use the remaining $100 of the credit to generate a refund.

EXAMPLE 12.2

Carryback or Carryforward of a Credit

If a nonrefundable credit exceeds the tax on taxable income for a tax year, the excess credit is normally lost. With certain credits, however, the excess can be carried back and/or carried forward to be offset against the tax on taxable income for the years to which the excess credit is carried.

Refundable Tax Credits

Refundable tax credits can be used not only to reduce or eliminate the current year's tax, but also to generate a tax refund in excess of tax pre-payment.

Tax on Taxable Income – Refundable Credits = Tax Due (or Refund Due)

For federal income tax purposes, nonrefundable credits are used before refundable credits. A more complete presentation of the use of tax credits is presented by the following formula:

Tax on Taxable Income − Nonrefundable Credits − Refundable Credits = Tax Due (or Refund Due)

EXAMPLE 12.3

The tax calculated on the taxable income of Johnny and Jennifer Johnson is $3,000. They are eligible to claim a $1,000 nonrefundable credit and a refundable credit of $2,800. They can claim a tax refund of $800 ($3,000 - $1,000 - $2,800) even if they had no withholding or other tax prepayments for the year.

EXHIBIT 12.10 **REFUNDABLE TAX CREDITS**

Item	IRC §	IRS Publication	Reported on Form
Qualified Adoption Expense Credit	23	17	8839
American Opportunity Tax Credit (formerly the Hope Scholarship Credit)	25A(i)(6)	970	1040
Federal Income Tax Withheld from Forms W-2 & 1099	31	17/505	1040
Estimated Tax Payments	6402	17/505	1040
Federal Income Tax Refunds Applied from Prior Years	6402	17	1040
Excess Social Security Taxes Withheld	31(b)	17/505	1040
Earned Income Credit	32	17/596	Sched. EIC
Additional Child Tax Credit	24(d)	17/972	8812
Credit for Tax on Undistributed Capital Gain From:			
A Mutual Fund	852(b)(3)(D)(ii)	17/564/550	2439
A Real Estate Investment Trust (REIT)	857(b)(3)(D)(ii)	17/550	2439
Health Coverage Tax Credit	35	17/502	8885
Credit for Excise Taxes on Gasoline and Special Fuels	34	510	4136

TAX CREDITS VS. TAX DEDUCTIONS

The benefit received by a taxpayer from a tax credit is not dependent on the taxpayer's marginal tax rate (tax bracket). A tax credit of $1,000 provides the same $1,000 tax reduction for a taxpayer in the 15 percent tax bracket or the 35 percent tax bracket. On the other hand, the tax reduction received by a taxpayer for a tax deduction is entirely dependent on the marginal tax rate of the taxpayer. A tax deduction of $1,000 generates a tax reduction of $150 ($1,000 x 0.15) for a taxpayer in the 15 percent bracket and a tax reduction of $350 ($1,000 x 0.35) for a taxpayer in the 35 percent tax bracket.

TAX CREDIT REQUIREMENTS

In order to claim a tax credit, a taxpayer must normally do the following:

- Meet eligibility requirements;
- Determine the amount of the credit by multiplying a base by an applicable rate(s);
- Apply any specified limitations to the credit;
- Subtract the allowable credits from the tax in the proper sequence; and
- Carryback or carryforward any amounts disallowed for the current tax year, if permitted.

Quick Quiz 12.4

Highlight the answer to these questions:

1. A personal exemption is allowed for each person who qualifies as a dependent of the taxpayer.
   a. True
   b. False

2. Nonrefundable tax credits can reduce the tax on taxable income to zero and can generate a tax refund.
   a. True
   b. False

3. For federal income tax purposes, nonrefundable credits are used before refundable credits.
   a. True
   b. False

False, False, True

INTRODUCTION TO BASIS

Basis represents capital (or after-tax income) that a taxpayer uses to purchase an investment. Taxpayers keep track of the capital that was used to purchase the investment, or basis, so that the capital can be recovered without the imposition of a second income tax.

USES OF BASIS

Basis is the income tax system's method of keeping track of capital in an investment, and is used in several different ways. First, basis is used to determine gain or loss on an investment when it is sold. An investor would subtract his or her basis from the sales proceeds of the investment to determine the taxable gain or loss. Second, basis is used to determine depreciation deductions that an investor can take on an investment. Third, basis is used to determine the amount an investor has "at risk" which limits loss deductions for income tax purposes under the at risk and passive activity loss rules.

Key Concepts

Underline/highlight the answers as you read:

1. Define the purpose of basis.

2. Identify the uses of basis.

3. Define the cost basis of an asset.

4. Identify items that increase basis.

5. Identify items that decrease basis.

DETERMINING BASIS

Cost Basis

Cost basis is the initial basis an investor acquires in an asset by using capital to purchase an investment. As explained above, it represents the amount of after-tax dollars that the investor has dedicated to purchasing an investment. For most investments, the initial basis in an investment is the cost basis.

The amount paid for an asset includes not only its purchase price, but also any amounts paid for sales tax, freight, installation and testing of the asset and any other costs necessary to acquire the asset and get it into operations. All of the items below are included in the cost basis of the asset.

Items Included in Basis
Purchase Price
Sales Tax
Freight
Installation and Testing Costs
"All costs to get the asset into operations"

For example, if Tom has acquired construction equipment, his basis in the property can be determined as follows:

Acquisition Method	Affect on Basis
Purchase	Tom's basis is the price he paid for the equipment, plus other costs associated with making the equipment operational.
Gift	Tom's basis is the donor's basis plus any gift tax the donor has paid.
Inheritance	Tom's basis is the equipment's fair market value at the decedent's date of death (or alternative valuation date for federal estate tax purposes).

ADJUSTMENTS TO BASIS

Once an asset is acquired and it's initial cost basis is established, that basis may be adjusted over the holding period of the asset, resulting in an adjusted basis for income tax purposes.

Increases in Basis

The first and most frequently encountered adjustment to basis is an upward adjustment to cost basis for additions to the investment. If additional capital is added to the investment, the cost basis must be increased to reflect this so that upon sale, the investor receives all of his or her capital back income tax-free. Examples of capital infusions that increase a taxpayer's basis in an investment include subsequent investments in the same vehicle, additions to the investment, or changes to the investment.

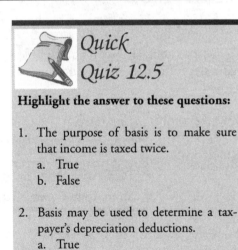

Quick Quiz 12.5

Highlight the answer to these questions:

1. The purpose of basis is to make sure that income is taxed twice.
   a. True
   b. False

2. Basis may be used to determine a taxpayer's depreciation deductions.
   a. True
   b. False

False, True.

Decreases in Basis

If an individual's basis in an investment increases when capital is added to the investment, the opposite will happen when capital is removed from an investment. When capital is removed from an investment, a basis reduction must occur because the taxpayer has received a refund of some of his or her capital. Capital can be taken out of an investment in several ways. Two of the most common methods of removing capital from an investment are: (1) distributions from business entities that have pass-through tax treatment (such as partnerships, LLCs, and S corporations), and (2) claiming depreciation deductions.

REALIZATION AND RECOGNITION

Unlike ordinary income, which is subject to income tax when earned, gains on capital assets are subject to tax only when there has been both a **realization event** (implying that the asset has been sold or exchanged) and a **recognition event** for federal income tax purposes. Recognition occurs when a realized gain is required to be included on a taxpayer's income tax return. Generally, all realized gains are recognized (that is, all realized gains are subject to current taxation) unless a provision can be found in the Code that either exempts the gain from taxation, or defers the gain to a future tax period.

CAPITAL GAIN HOLDING PERIODS AND TAX RATES

HOLDING PERIODS

The **holding period** for an asset can be either short-term or long-term.

If a taxpayer holds an asset for a year or less, the taxpayer has a short-term holding period for that asset. If the holding period is more than one year, it is said to be a long-term holding period.

EXHIBIT 12.11 **HOLDING PERIOD SUMMARY**

Capital Gain/Loss	Holding Period
Long-Term Capital Gain/Loss	> 1 Year
Short-Term Capital Gain/Loss	≤ 1 Year

Property Acquired by Inheritance

There are a few special rules concerning holding periods that are worth noting. First, whenever property is received from a decedent's estate, it is deemed to have a long-term holding period, regardless of when the asset was acquired by the decedent. An easy way to remember this rule is to recall that "death is long-term."

Gifted Property

The second special rule concerning holding periods applies to gifted property. When gifted property has a fair market value in excess of the donor's basis in the property on the date of the gift, the donee's holding period will tack on to the donor's holding period. In other words, the donee's holding period begins on the date the donor acquired the property.

CAPITAL GAINS TAX RATES

The capital gains tax rate that applies to a particular transaction is a function of the holding period of the asset.

Short-term gains and losses are subject to tax at the taxpayer's ordinary marginal income tax rate. There is no tax benefit afforded to assets held for a short-term holding period.

If the asset sold was held for a long-term holding period, the gain or loss will be subject to long-term capital gains tax rates, which are lower than the taxpayer's ordinary marginal income tax rate. Generally speaking, if the transaction results in a gain, this is a good result since the taxpayer will pay less tax on the gain. If the transaction results in a loss, however, the taxpayer will receive less of a tax benefit. As discussed in our review of asset categorization, capital gains are good, but capital losses are bad for the taxpayer.

The maximum long-term capital gains tax rate is 15 percent. This rate applies for anyone in the 25 percent or higher ordinary marginal income tax brackets. For those taxpayers in the 10 or 15 percent ordinary marginal income tax bracket, the capital gain rate is zero. If lower capital gains rates were not available to taxpayers in these tax brackets, there would be no benefit to long-term capital gains for those in the 15 percent tax bracket, and those in the 10 percent marginal ordinary income tax bracket would have to pay a higher tax rate on their capital gains than on their ordinary income. To ensure that all taxpayers would receive a tax break for long-term capital gains, Congress eliminated the long-term capital gains tax rate for lower income taxpayers.

SALE OF PERSONAL RESIDENCE (SECTION 121)

Perhaps the most widely used type of nontaxable exchange occurs when an individual sells his or her principal residence. IRC Section 121 excludes up to $500,000 of the gain from the sale of a principal residence from income tax if certain requirements are met.

The amount of the available exclusion will depend on the filing status of the individual who claims the exemption. For married couples filing jointly, up to $500,000 of the gain is excluded from income tax. All other individuals may exclude up to $250,000 of the gain from income tax. Any gain on the sale of a principal residence in excess of this amount is subject to income tax, typically long-term capital gains.

Qualifications

To qualify for the exclusion of gain under IRC Section 121, two requirements must be met. First, the taxpayer must have owned and used the home as his principal residence for two out of the last five years (the ownership and use test). Ownership implies that the taxpayer holds title to the home outright, or the home is owned by a grantor trust (see Ltr. Rul. 199912026). If the home is owned by a partnership, family limited partnership, or irrevocable trust, the taxpayer is not deemed to own the home for purposes of claiming the Section 121 exclusion (see Ltr. Rul. 200029046 and Ltr. Rul. 200104005). Second, to claim the exemption, the taxpayer must not have excluded gain on the sale of a principal residence within the last two years. An individual will qualify for this exclusion as often as the individual can meet these two requirements.

Married couples who wish to claim up to the $500,000 exclusion must meet conditions in addition to the two requirements set forth above. For the $500,000 exclusion to apply for a married couple, they must file a joint tax return for the year (filing status must be married filing jointly), and both spouses must have used the residence for two out of the previous five years as a principal residence (referred to as the use test). Only one of the spouses must have owned the residence for two out of the previous five years (the ownership test). Furthermore, if either spouse claimed the Section 121 exclusion within the previous two years, the gain cannot be excluded from income taxation.

If, however, a couple is getting divorced and are filing separate returns, and a principal residence is sold, both spouses can exclude up to $250,000 of gain from the sale if the ownership and use tests are otherwise met.

Proration of the Exclusion

If a principal residence is sold before the two-year ownership and use test is met, or if the exclusion was used during the last two years, it may be possible to qualify for a reduced exclusion. A reduced exclusion will be available when the sale of the principal residence is caused by: (1) a change of employment, (2) a change of health, or (3) an unforeseen circumstance. When one of these exceptions apply, the amount of the exclusion is determined by dividing the number of months the taxpayer used the home as a principal residence, or the number of months since the exclusion was used last, by 24 (the number of months in a two year period), and multiplying that result by the otherwise applicable exclusion. The formula for calculating the partial exclusion may be expressed as:

$$\frac{\text{\# of months of use (or last exclusion)}}{24} \times \text{Applicable Exclusion (\$250,000 or \$500,000)}$$

Key Terms

16th Amendment - Amendment to the U.S. Constitution adopted on February 25, 1913 that gave Congress the power to lay and collect taxes on income.

Above-the-Line Deductions - Deductions for adjusted gross income, also known as adjustments to income.

Accuracy-Related Penalty - A penalty of 20 percent of the underpayment amount imposed on taxpayers who file incorrect tax returns in certain situations.

Adjusted Gross Income - Gross income less above-the-line deductions.

Basis - Represents the total capital or after-tax income used by a taxpayer to purchase an investment.

Below-the-Line Deductions - Deductions from adjusted gross income. Also known as itemized deductions.

Cost Basis - Initial basis an investor acquires in an asset by using capital to purchase the investment.

Deductions - Items that are subtracted from gross income, either below or above-the-line, in order to arrive at taxable income.

Dependency Exemption - A deduction from adjusted gross income that is allowed for each person who is a qualifying child or qualifying relative of the taxpayer.

Doctrine of Constructive Receipt - A cash method taxpayer must report income when it is credited to the taxpayer's account or when it is made available without restriction.

Exclusions - Income items that are specifically exempted from income tax.

Failure to File Penalty - A five percent penalty of the unpaid tax balance for each month or part thereof that a tax return is late.

Failure to Pay Penalty - A penalty of 0.5 percent per month or part thereof that a taxpayer fails to pay tax that is owed.

Gross Income - All income from whatever source derived unless it is specifically excluded by some provision of the Internal Revenue Code.

Head of Household Filing Status - A filing status that provides a basic standard deduction and tax bracket sizes that are less favorable to the taxpayer than those for the surviving spouse status, but more favorable than those for the single filing status.

Key Terms

Holding Period - The period for which a taxpayer owns an asset.

Income - Broadly defined as the gross amount of money, property, services, or other accretion to wealth received, but it does not include borrowed money or a return of invested dollars.

Married Filing Jointly Filing Status - A filing status that allows married couples to combine their gross incomes and deductions.

Married Filing Separately Filing Status - A filing status used when married couples do not choose to file a joint return.

Nonrefundable Tax Credits – Tax credits that can reduce the tax on taxable income to zero, but cannot generate a tax refund.

Personal Exemption - A deduction from adjusted gross income that is allowed for the taxpayer and the taxpayer's spouse.

Realization Event - Generally occurs when an asset has been sold or exchanged. Gains on capital assets are subject to tax only when there has been both a realization event and a recognition event.

Recognition Event - Occurs when a realized gain is included on a taxpayer's income tax return. All realized gains are generally recognized unless a provision in the Code provides otherwise.

Refundable Tax Credits – Tax credits that can be used not only to reduce or eliminate the current year's tax, but also to generate a tax refund.

Single Filing Status - A filing status used by an unmarried taxpayer who does not qualify as a surviving spouse or head of household.

Standard Deduction - A standard amount that is specified by Congress and includes inflation adjustments. Taxpayers may deduct the greater of the standard deduction or allowable itemized deductions.

Surviving Spouse Filing Status - A filing status for a surviving spouse with a dependent child that affords the same basic standard deduction and tax rates as the married filing jointly status.

Tax Credit - An amount that reduces the calculated tax liability of the taxpayer.

Taxable Income - Determined by subtracting allowable deductions from income.

DISCUSSION QUESTIONS

1. What are the three primary sources of tax law?

2. What is the legal basis for today's income tax?

3. What are the statutory sources of tax law?

4. What are the administrative sources of tax law?

5. How is income defined?

6. What are exclusions and where do they come from?

7. Define gross income.

8. List some examples of items that would be included in gross income.

9. What are the two types of deductions?

10. What is adjusted gross income and what is its significance?

11. Under what circumstances may a taxpayer be entitled to an additional standard deduction?

12. What are the different filing statuses available to taxpayers?

13. Compare and contrast nonrefundable and refundable tax credits.

14. Why is a tax credit generally more beneficial than a tax deduction of the same amount?

15. What is basis and what is the purpose of basis?

16. Describe three uses of basis.

17. What is cost basis?

18. Name several items that increase basis.

19. Name several items that decrease basis.

20. What is the amount realized?

21. What is the difference between a short-term and long-term holding period?

22. How is the holding period determined for property received from a decedent's estate?

23. What is the difference between the tax rate for short-term capital gains and long-term capital gains?

MULTIPLE-CHOICE PROBLEMS

1. Amy filed her tax return on April 15. At that time, she owed $800 on a total tax liability of $10,000 and she submitted a check for $800 with her tax return. Which of the following penalties will apply to Amy?

    a. Failure to file.

    b. Failure to pay.

    c. Underpayment of estimated tax.

    d. None of the above.

2. Arturo, a consultant, uses the cash method of accounting for his business. Arturo recently provided consulting services to his best customer Sergio. When should Arturo recognize income from this service?

    a. When Sergio writes a check, made out to Arturo.

    b. When Arturo deposits Sergio's check.

    c. When Sergio gives the check to Arturo.

    d. When Sergio receives an invoice from Arturo for the service.

3. Angie and Patrick were married on September 1 of this year. Following a honeymoon in Hawaii, Patrick died of a heart attack. Neither Angie nor Patrick had any dependents. What filing status can Angie use this year?

    a. Angie must use the single filing status because she was not married as of the end of the year.

    b. Angie will be able to file as married filing jointly as long as she would have qualified for this filing status if Patrick had survived.

    c. Angie may use the head of household filing status.

    d. Angie will be eligible to file as a surviving spouse.

4. Which of the following is not an itemized deduction from adjusted gross income?

    a. Alimony paid.

    b. Medical expenses in excess of 7.5% of AGI.

    c. Charitable contributions.

    d. Home mortgage interest.

5. Under which of the following circumstances must a taxpayer itemize his deductions?

   1. When the taxpayer has been married for less than one year.
   2. When the taxpayer is married and files a separate return and the taxpayer's spouse itemizes his or her deductions.
   3. When the taxpayer is a nonresident alien.

   a. 1 and 2.
   b. 1 and 3.
   c. 2 and 3.
   d. 1, 2, and 3.

6. Which of the following is not an available filing status?

   a. Qualified dependent child.
   b. Married filing jointly.
   c. Head of household.
   d. Surviving spouse.

7. Which of the following is not excluded from gross income?

   a. Gifts.
   b. Scholarships.
   c. Interest income from municipal bonds.
   d. Dividend income.

8. Which of the following statements is true regarding refundable tax credits?

   a. There are more refundable tax credits than nonrefundable credits.
   b. Refundable tax credits can be used only to reduce or eliminate the current year's tax.
   c. Refundable tax credits can generate a tax refund.
   d. For federal income tax purposes, refundable credits are used before nonrefundable credits.

9. On September 20 of Year 1, Sean purchased 1,000 shares of Austin Enterprises, Inc. common stock for $25,000. He sold the shares for $35,000 on September 20 of Year 2. Which of the following statements correctly identifies the tax consequences of this transaction?

   a. Sean will recognize a $10,000 ordinary gain on the sale.
   b. Sean will recognize a $10,000 short-term capital gain on the sale.
   c. Sean will recognize a $10,000 long-term capital gain on the sale.
   d. Sean will not be required to recognize the gain on the transaction.

10. Trina gave her nephew Roy 100 shares of HLM Corporation stock that she purchased 6 months ago for $10,000. At the time of the gift, the fair market value of the stock was $12,000. Which of the following statements concerning the stock is correct?

    a. If Trina sold the stock, she would have realized a long- term capital gain.

    b. Roy's basis in the stock is $10,000.

    c. Roy's basis in the stock is $12,000.

    d. If Roy sells the stock immediately after the gift, he will realize a long-term capital gain.

11. Bruce, a single taxpayer, has been transferred by his company to Philadelphia. He sold his house for $650,000 and he had an adjusted basis of $330,000. He owned and lived in the home for 18 months. What is his capital gain from the sale of the personal residence?

    a. $0.

    b. $132,500 LTCG.

    c. $187,500 LTCG.

    d. $320,000 LTCG.

12. Isaac is a middle school teacher with gross income this year of $35,000. Based on the following, what is Isaac's adjusted gross income?

    1. $4,000 qualified education interest expense.

    2. $2,000 alimony received.

    3. $1,000 contribution to a traditional IRA.

    4. $750 in educator expenses.

        a. $27,250.

        b. $28,750.

        c. $29,500.

        d. $31,250.

13. Aurora had the following cash inflows during the current taxable year:

    1. Wages: $45,000

    2. Loan Proceeds: $2,000

    3. Child Support: $5,000

    4. Stock Sale Proceeds: $3,000

    5. U.S. Government Bond Interest: $1,000

What is her gross income for income tax purposes if her adjusted tax basis in the stock was $2,000?

    a. $45,000.

    b. $47,000.

    c. $49,000.

    d. $51,000.

14. Sammy failed to file his tax return from a few years ago and pay the $5,000 tax liability that was owed at the time. Sammy's new tax advisor prepares and files the return in the current year, 21 and half months late. How much is his:

    1. Failure to pay penalty,

    2. Failure to file penalty, and

    3. Total penalty?

        a. (1) $550; (2) $1,125; (3) $1,675.

        b. (1) $425; (2) $1,250; (3) $1,675.

        c. (1) $550; (2) $700; (3) $1,250.

        d. (1) $1,250; (2) $550; (3) $1,800.

15. Contributions to charity are limited to a certain percentage of income. How long is the carry-over period for individuals to use any excess current charitable deduction?

    a. One year.

    b. Five years.

    c. Seven years.

    d. Fifteen years.

16. Ima Clipper, a well-known artists, donated one of her original bronze creations to a local charity, which auctioned the piece for $3,000. Ima totaled her costs as follows:

- Bronze = $425
- Other materials = $150
- Pro-rata overhead = $125
- Furnace/casting fees = $200
- Artistic contribution = $2,100

Assuming this is Ima's only charitable contribution, based on an annual income of $150,000, what is the maximum amount of charitable deduction available to her?

a. $3,000.

b. $2,100.

c. $775.

d. $900.

17. Jason has three capital transactions for the current year:

- Short-term capital loss of $5,000
- Short-term capital gain of $3,000
- Long-term capital loss of $2,000

What is the net effect on Jason's taxes if he is in the 35% tax bracket?

a. $1,400 tax reduction.

b. $1,050 tax reduction.

c. $850 tax reduction.

d. $450 tax reduction.

18. Sam's Turbo Repair, Inc. (STR) purchased a new machine for cleaning and retooling the turbo blades on semi-trucks. The machine cost was $30,000, 10% sales tax, and $1,000 delivery and setup fee. What is STR's basis in the new machine?

a. $30,000.

b. $31,000.

c. $33,000.

d. $34,000.

19. Lucy, a single mother, has four children, ages 4, 8, 12, and 17. How much will her child tax credit be for the current tax year assuming she is under the AGI threshold?

a. $1,000.

b. $2,000.

c. $3,000.

d. $4,000.

20. Kim and Warren are both 67 years old and healthy. They are filing their tax return and want to know how many personal exemptions they may take. You correctly inform them that they can take:

    a. 1.

    b. 2.

    c. 3.

    d. 4.

21. Lauren has purchased a home worth $1.5 million with an interest-only mortgage of $1.2 million. She is currently only paying interest on the mortgage in the amount of $60,000 per year. What amount may she deduct as home mortgage interest on Schedule A of her individual income tax return?

    a. $45,000.

    b. $50,000.

    c. $55,000.

    d. $60,000.

22. Income to U.S. taxpayers is taxed in the year it is derived in which of the following situations?

    1. Interest earned but reinvested in a savings account in an FDIC savings bank.

    2. Unrealized long-term capital gains on stocks.

    3. Income directly earned on most municipal bonds.

    4. Short-term gains realized within a qualified plan.

    5. Increased value of personal residence.

        a. 1 only.

        b. 1 and 3.

        c. 2, 3, and 4.

        d. 2, 3, 4, and 5.

23. Greg just received his student loan statement that indicates he paid $3,000 of interest on his student loan during the tax year. How much of the loan may he deduct?

    a. None of the interest is deductible since it is consumer debt.

    b. $3,000 as an itemized deduction.

    c. $2,500 as an itemized deduction.

    d. $2,500 as an adjustment to income.

Quick Quiz Explanations

Quick Quiz 12.1
1. False. The three top sources of tax law includes statutory, administrative (Treasury Department and Internal Revenue Service), and judicial.
2. True.
3. True.

Quick Quiz 12.2
1. False. The basic tax formula is Income - Deductions = Taxable Income.
2. False. Income, broadly defined, means the gross amount received, but it does not include borrowed money or a return of invested dollars.
3. True.
4. True.

Quick Quiz 12.3
1. False. Adjusted gross income is gross income reduced by above-the-line deductions.
2. True.
3. False. Nonresident aliens and dual-status aliens are not allowed to use a standard deduction and must itemize deductions.

Quick Quiz 12.4
1. False. A dependency exemption is allowed for each person who qualifies as a dependent of the taxpayer. A personal exemption is allowed for the taxpayer and the taxpayer's spouse.
2. False. Nonrefundable tax credits cannot generate a tax refund.
3. True.

Quick Quiz 12.5
1. False. The purpose of basis is to keep track of after-tax dollars an individual invests so that upon the sale of the investment, income is not taxed twice.
2. True.

Business Entity Selection and Taxation

LEARNING OBJECTIVES

After reading this chapter, you should be able to:
- Understand the issue of personal liability in the selection of entities.
- Differentiate between the organizational form and the tax treatment of income, expenses, payroll and wage taxes for sole proprietorships, partnerships, LLPs, LLCs, S-corps and C-corps.*
- Compare the income and payroll tax effects of wage versus ownership income.*
- Identify adjustments, deductions and exclusions that may be available to sole proprietors, partners, LLPs, LLCs, S-corp and C-corp owners.*
- Describe the calculation of the deduction for retirement plan contributions by self-employed individuals.
- Understand the basics involved in protecting owners from each other.

* CFP Board Resource Document - Student-Centered Learning Objectives based upon CFP Board Principal Topics.

INTRODUCTION

One of the most important decisions new business owners will make is the selection of the entity type to be used for conducting the business activities of the enterprise.

The most common legal forms of business (entity types) used in the United States are the sole proprietorship, general and limited partnerships, including limited liability partnerships (LLPs) and family limited partnerships (FLPs), the limited liability company (LLC), the regular C corporation, and the S corporation.

The selection process includes consideration of the following factors:
1. Ease and cost of formation,
2. Complexity of management and governance,
3. How transferability and dissolution are achieved,
4. Liability protection for owners' personal assets, and
5. Reporting requirements and taxation.

EASE AND COST OF FORMATION

Proprietorships and general partnerships are less complex, inexpensive, and easy to form, while the other entity types are more complex and expensive to form. Entities are almost always formed under state law. Therefore, the state itself will dictate the requirements for formation and the formalities that must be followed to maintain the entity's status.

COMPLEXITY OF MANAGEMENT AND GOVERNANCE

Proprietorships are the least complex in terms of management and governance. In addition, the administrative requirements and formalities dictated by state law are the least burdensome for sole proprietorships. Proprietorships and general partnerships do not typically require an initial filing registration with the state and have fewer state-imposed annual filing requirements. Furthermore, proprietorships and general partnerships have fewer state-imposed operational requirements that must be met to assure continuation of the entity's status and the benefits that the status brings.

TRANSFERABILITY AND DISSOLUTION

Transferability of an ownership interest is easiest with a proprietorship and becomes increasingly more difficult as we move along a spectrum of business entities to the C corporation. Transferability is most difficult with a publicly traded C corporation that has stock listed on an exchange. Partnerships, limited partnerships, LLPs, FLPs, LLCs, S corporations, and smaller C corporations generally have limited or restricted transferability rights. Unlike other business forms, proprietorships can be dissolved at the election of the owner and do not require formal steps for dissolution.

Key Concepts

Underline/highlight the answers as you read:

1. Name the most common legal entities.

2. Identify the factors to be considered during the entity selection process.

3. Define "piercing the veil."

LIABILITY PROTECTION FOR OWNERS' PERSONAL ASSETS

Some business forms offer liability protection for investors. If liability protection is available, the investors in such business ventures or entities will not have their personal assets exposed to business (entity) debts or obligations. This protection, which may be the most important factor in entity choice, is not available to proprietorships or general partnerships, nor to general partners of a limited partnership and only to a limited extent for limited liability partnerships (LLP). We refer to this protection as limited liability.

There are situations in which an entity that has limited liability protection for its owners under state law can lose that protection. The state requires that for such protection to continue, the entity must alert the public to its status in a clear and identifiable manner so as to put business creditors on notice that the entity has such protection. Entities do this through markings on business correspondence such as invoices, letterhead, business cards, and through markings on vehicles (with the name and LLC or Inc. designated), which signals the limited liability status to the public. The entities receiving such protection usually are required to maintain a reasonable amount of liability insurance to protect the public (e.g., vehicle liability insurance) and are required to be vigilant in meeting any annual formalities to maintain the state-granted entity status.

General Liability Issues

Relying on the entity as the primary source of liability protection is dependent on it maintaining a clear and consistent identity of the entity as a corporation, limited partnership, or limited liability company. Failure to maintain that identity in contracts and correspondence could result in a court "**piercing the veil**" of liability protection, which may result in personal liability for the owner(s). Piercing the veil means disregarding the status of the entity that gives the owners limited liability. A secondary source of protection is liability insurance, which must be sufficient in amount and sufficiently comprehensive in risk coverage, to cover the claims of creditors.

To avoid piercing the veil, the entity should keep its books and records separate from the personal books and records of the owners, segregate activities of business from personal affairs, follow corporate formalities such as meeting requirements and filings, and address all content in contracts and correspondence from the view point of the business entity (rather than the owners').

REPORTING REQUIREMENTS AND TAXATION

States individually require annual filings and other types of reporting. All entities that have employees will have payroll reporting at both the state and federal level. All entities that have retail sales will have sales tax returns to prepare in states that impose sales taxes.

However, there are few, if any, other state reporting requirements for proprietorships and general partnerships. However, for all other types of entities there will be annual reporting requirements that are state-imposed to maintain the entity's status.

For federal income tax purposes, the income of a proprietorship or a single-member LLC is reported on the Schedule C of the individual owner's Form 1040. For all other types of entities, an entity-level tax return is filed. A partnership files Form 1065, an S corporation files Form 1120S, and a C corporation files Form 1120. All of the returns other than the C corporation return are informational returns because there is no tax at the entity level. The income and losses of such entities "flow through" to the individual owners. Each owner's share of the entity's income or loss is reported to the owner on a Schedule K-1.

Quick Quiz 13.1

Highlight the answer to these questions:

1. Not all entities are separate legal entities for the purposes of taxation.
   a. True
   b. False

2. "Piercing the veil" may occur if business owners fail to keep their personal records with their business records.
   a. True
   b. False

True, False.

The C corporation is a separate entity for taxation and its income is taxed at the entity level. However, it does have the advantage of being able to accumulate profits at the corporate level without the owners having to pay income taxes on those profits until they are distributed to the owners by the corporation.

Choosing the correct entity type requires an understanding of each type of the entity, its advantages and disadvantages, competing considerations including each of the factors above, and business loss considerations.

In general, the most important factors in entity selection are ease of formation, liability protection, and the manner of taxation. However, serious thought should be given to all of the factors to make the right choice for the nature of the business and the objectives of the owners.

It is also important to periodically review the choice of legal form (entity) to determine whether changes in circumstances may suggest a change in entity type.

SOLE PROPRIETORSHIPS

Sole proprietorships are business ventures owned and operated by a single individual. A sole proprietorship arises when an individual engages in a business for profit. A sole proprietorship can operate under the name of the owner or it can conduct business under a trade or fictitious name such as "The Corner Pocket." No filings are required with the Secretary of State and no annual filing fees are required. There is no transfer of assets to the entity because the entity is considered a legal extension of the proprietor.

FORMATION

Formation is easy and inexpensive, although the proprietorship may be required to obtain a local business license. In addition, if the proprietorship will be collecting sales taxes, it must register with the state or local taxing authority. Operation is easy in that all decisions are made by the proprietor. Any trade names or assets are owned by the individual proprietor.

INTEREST, DISPOSAL OF INTEREST, AND DISSOLUTION

A proprietor has a 100 percent interest in the proprietorship assets and income. It is relatively easy to sell assets of a proprietorship, but it does require finding a buyer. Dissolution is achieved by simply discontinuing business operations and paying creditors or by the death of the proprietor.

 *Key Concepts*

Underline/highlight the answers as you read:

1. Describe the formation and operation of a sole proprietorship.

2. Describe the liability issues associated with a sole proprietorship.

3. Explain how a sole proprietorship can raise capital.

4. Explain the tax attributes of a sole proprietorship.

CAPITAL

Capital for a proprietorship is limited to the resources of the proprietor including the proprietor's ability to borrow.

LIABILITY

One of the major disadvantages of a sole proprietorship is the potential legal liability. The sole proprietor is personally legally liable for the debts and torts of his sole proprietorship business. There is no separate legal entity under which limited liability protection for personal assets may be claimed.

MANAGEMENT/OPERATIONS

The proprietor has the day-to-day management and decision-making responsibilities, including the hiring and firing of employees. There is no guarantee of continuity beyond the proprietor.

INCOME TAXATION AND PAYROLL (SOCIAL SECURITY) TAXES

The cost of tax compliance is low because the proprietor simply adds a Schedule C to his Form 1040 (See Exhibit 13.1) and generally does not even obtain a separate federal taxpayer tax identification number (unless the proprietor hires employees, in which case an Employer Identification Number (EIN) must be obtained). Rather, the proprietor conducts business under his own Social Security number. There is no ability to allocate income to other taxpayers since there is only one owner. A sole proprietor does not have to pay unemployment taxes on himself, but he must pay unemployment taxes for his employees. However, the proprietor does pay self-employment tax (up to 15.3 percent) on his own earnings (see Schedule SE, Exhibit 13.2) and one-half of Social Security taxes for his employees.

Taking Deductions

The proprietor can deduct all ordinary and necessary business expenses from gross income. The business deductions are in Part II of Schedule C, lines 8-27 (Exhibit 13.1). The net profit or loss from line 31 of Schedule C is then carried over to line 12 of Form 1040 (identified by the arrow in Exhibit 13.1 and the first arrow in Exhibit 13.3). The proprietor may also make deductible contributions to a qualified or other retirement plan, but these contributions are reported on his Form 1040 as a deduction for AGI on line 28 of the 1040 (identified by the second arrow in Exhibit 13.3).

Employer Deduction for Retirement Plans

The proprietor can usually deduct, subject to certain limitations, contributions made to a qualified plan for employees, including those made for the proprietor. The contributions (and the attributable earnings and gains) are generally not taxed to the employee until distributed by the plan. The deduction limit for contributions to a qualified plan depends on the type of plan.

The deduction for contributions to a defined contribution plan cannot exceed 25 percent of the compensation paid or accrued during the year to eligible employees participating in the plan. The proprietor must reduce this limit in figuring the deduction for contributions made to his own account. The maximum compensation that can be taken into account when calculating plan funding for each employee is the covered compensation limit, $255,000 for 2013.

The deduction for contributions to a defined benefit plan is based on actuarial assumptions and computations. Consequently, an actuary must calculate the appropriate amount of mandatory funding.

In the case of an employer who maintains both a defined benefit plan and a defined contribution plan, the funding limit set forth is combined. The maximum deductible amount is the greater of:
- 25 percent of the aggregate covered compensation of employees; or
- The required minimum funding standard of the defined benefit plan.

This limit does not apply if the contributions to the defined contribution plan consist entirely of employee elective deferrals (elective contributions to the plan by employees). In other words, employee elective deferrals do not count against the plan limit.

FORM 1040 SCHEDULE C

EXHIBIT 13.1

The 2011 form was the latest available at the time of printing. Please visit our website at money-education.com for updates.

SCHEDULE C (Form 1040)	**Profit or Loss From Business** (Sole Proprietorship)	OMB No. 1545-0074
Department of the Treasury Internal Revenue Service (99)	▶ For information on Schedule C and its instructions, go to *www.irs.gov/schedulec* ▶ Attach to Form 1040, 1040NR, or 1041; partnerships generally must file Form 1065.	**2011** Attachment Sequence No. **09**

Name of proprietor | Social security number (SSN)

A Principal business or profession, including product or service (see instructions) | **B** Enter code from instructions ▶

C Business name. If no separate business name, leave blank. | **D** Employer ID number (EIN), (see instr.)

E Business address (including suite or room no.) ▶ -----------------------------
City, town or post office, state, and ZIP code

F Accounting method: **(1)** ☐ Cash **(2)** ☐ Accrual **(3)** ☐ Other (specify) ▶ -------------------

G Did you "materially participate" in the operation of this business during 2011? If "No," see instructions for limit on losses . ☐ Yes ☐ No

H If you started or acquired this business during 2011, check here . . . . ▶ ☐

I Did you make any payments in 2011 that would require you to file Form(s) 1099? (see instructions) . . . . ☐ Yes ☐ No

J If "Yes," did you or will you file all required Forms 1099? . . . . ☐ Yes ☐ No

Part I Income

1a	Merchant card and third party payments. For 2011, enter -0- . . .	1a	
b	Gross receipts or sales not entered on line 1a (see instructions) . .	1b	
c	Income reported to you on Form W-2 if the "Statutory Employee" box on that form was checked. **Caution.** See instr. before completing this line	1c	
d	**Total gross receipts.** Add lines 1a through 1c	1d	
2	Returns and allowances plus any other adjustments (see instructions)	2	
3	Subtract line 2 from line 1d	3	
4	Cost of goods sold (from line 42)	4	
5	**Gross profit.** Subtract line 4 from line 3	5	
6	Other income, including federal and state gasoline or fuel tax credit or refund (see instructions) . . .	6	
7	**Gross income.** Add lines 5 and 6 . . . . ▶	7	

Part II Expenses — Enter expenses for business use of your home only on line 30.

8	Advertising	8		**18**	Office expense (see instructions) .	18
9	Car and truck expenses (see instructions).	9		**19**	Pension and profit-sharing plans .	19
10	Commissions and fees .	10		**20**	Rent or lease (see instructions):	
11	Contract labor (see instructions)	11		**a**	Vehicles, machinery, and equipment	20a
12	Depletion	12		**b**	Other business property . . .	20b
13	Depreciation and section 179 expense deduction (not included in Part III) (see instructions).	13		**21**	Repairs and maintenance . . .	21
				22	Supplies (not included in Part III) .	22
				23	Taxes and licenses	23
				24	Travel, meals, and entertainment:	
14	Employee benefit programs (other than on line 19) . .	14		**a**	Travel	24a
15	Insurance (other than health)	15		**b**	Deductible meals and entertainment (see instructions) .	24b
16	Interest:			**25**	Utilities	25
a	Mortgage (paid to banks, etc.)	16a		**26**	Wages (less employment credits) .	26
b	Other	16b		**27a**	Other expenses (from line 48) . .	27a
17	Legal and professional services	17		**b**	**Reserved for future use** . . .	27b

28	**Total expenses** before expenses for business use of home. Add lines 8 through 27a . . . . . . ▶	28	
29	Tentative profit or (loss). Subtract line 28 from line 7	29	
30	Expenses for business use of your home. Attach **Form 8829**. Do **not** report such expenses elsewhere . .	30	
31	**Net profit or (loss).** Subtract line 30 from line 29.		

* If a profit, enter on both **Form 1040, line 12** (or **Form 1040NR, line 13**) and on **Schedule SE, line 2.**
If you entered an amount on line 1c, see instr. Estates and trusts, enter on **Form 1041, line 3.**

* If a loss, you **must** go to line 32. | **31** |

32 If you have a loss, check the box that describes your investment in this activity (see instructions).

* If you checked 32a, enter the loss on both **Form 1040, line 12,** (or **Form 1040NR, line 13**) and on **Schedule SE, line 2.** If you entered an amount on line 1c, see the instructions for line 31. Estates and trusts, enter on **Form 1041, line 3.**

* If you checked 32b, you **must** attach **Form 6198.** Your loss may be limited.

32a ☐ All investment is at risk.
32b ☐ Some investment is not at risk.

For Paperwork Reduction Act Notice, see your tax return instructions. Cat. No. 11334P Schedule C (Form 1040) 2011

EXHIBIT 13.2 | FORM 1040 SCHEDULE SE

The 2012 form was the latest available at the time of printing. Please visit our website at money-education.com for updates.

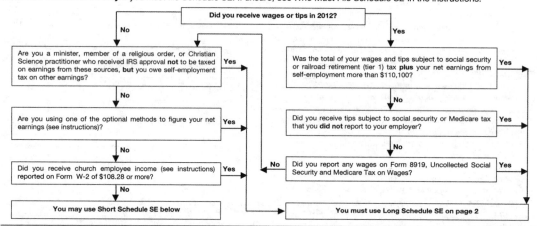

SCHEDULE SE
(Form 1040)

Department of the Treasury
Internal Revenue Service (99)

Self-Employment Tax

▶ Information about Schedule SE and its separate instructions is at *www.irs.gov/form1040.*
▶ Attach to Form 1040 or Form 1040NR.

OMB No. 1545-0074

2012

Attachment
Sequence No. **17**

Name of person with **self-employment** income (as shown on Form 1040) | Social security number of person with **self-employment** income ▶

Before you begin: To determine if you must file Schedule SE, see the instructions.

May I Use Short Schedule SE or Must I Use Long Schedule SE?

Note. Use this flowchart **only if** you must file Schedule SE. If unsure, see *Who Must File Schedule SE* in the instructions.

Did you receive wages or tips in 2012?

No → Are you a minister, member of a religious order, or Christian Science practitioner who received IRS approval **not** to be taxed on earnings from these sources, **but** you owe self-employment tax on other earnings? — Yes →

No ↓

Are you using one of the optional methods to figure your net earnings (see instructions)? — Yes →

No ↓

Did you receive church employee income (see instructions) reported on Form W-2 of $108.28 or more? — Yes →

No ↓

You may use Short Schedule SE below

Yes → Was the total of your wages and tips subject to social security or railroad retirement (tier 1) tax **plus** your net earnings from self-employment more than $110,100? — Yes →

No ↓

Did you receive tips subject to social security or Medicare tax that you **did not** report to your employer? — Yes →

No ↓

No ← Did you report any wages on Form 8919, Uncollected Social Security and Medicare Tax on Wages? — Yes →

You must use Long Schedule SE on page 2

Section A—Short Schedule SE. Caution. Read above to see if you can use Short Schedule SE.

1a Net farm profit or (loss) from Schedule F, line 34, and farm partnerships, Schedule K-1 (Form 1065), box 14, code A	**1a**	
b If you received social security retirement or disability benefits, enter the amount of Conservation Reserve Program payments included on Schedule F, line 4b, or listed on Schedule K-1 (Form 1065), box 20, code Y	**1b**	( )
2 Net profit or (loss) from Schedule C, line 31; Schedule C-EZ, line 3; Schedule K-1 (Form 1065), box 14, code A (other than farming); and Schedule K-1 (Form 1065-B), box 9, code J1. Ministers and members of religious orders, see instructions for types of income to report on this line. See instructions for other income to report	**2**	
3 Combine lines 1a, 1b, and 2	**3**	
4 Multiply line 3 by 92.35% (.9235). If less than $400, you do not owe self-employment tax; **do not** file this schedule unless you have an amount on line 1b . . . . ▶	**4**	
Note. If line 4 is less than $400 due to Conservation Reserve Program payments on line 1b, see instructions.		
5 **Self-employment tax.** If the amount on line 4 is: • $110,100 or less, multiply line 4 by 13.3% (.133). Enter the result here and on **Form 1040, line 56,** or **Form 1040NR, line 54** • More than $110,100, multiply line 4 by 2.9% (.029). Then, add $11,450.40 to the result. Enter the total here and on **Form 1040, line 56,** or **Form 1040NR, line 54**	**5**	
6 **Deduction for employer-equivalent portion of self-employment tax.** If the amount on line 5 is: • $14,643.30 or less, multiply line 5 by 57.51% (.5751) • More than $14,643.30, multiply line 5 by 50% (.50) and add $1,100 to the result. Enter the result here and on **Form 1040, line 27,** or **Form 1040NR, line 27**	**6**	

For Paperwork Reduction Act Notice, see your tax return instructions.   Cat. No. 11358Z   Schedule SE (Form 1040) 2012

NOTE: The normal self-employment rate is 15.3%. The "Payroll Tax Holiday" has reduced it by 2 percentage points to 13.3%. This reduction is scheduled to expire on 12/31/2012, but could be extended.

FORM 1040

EXHIBIT 13.3

The 2011 form was the latest available at the time of printing. Please visit our website at money-education.com for updates.

Form **1040**	Department of the Treasury—Internal Revenue Service (99) **U.S. Individual Income Tax Return**	20**12**	OMB No. 1545-0074	IRS Use Only—Do not write or staple in this space.

For the year Jan. 1–Dec. 31, 2012, or other tax year beginning	, 2012, ending	, 20	See separate instructions.

Your first name and initial | Last name | **Your social security number**

If a joint return, spouse's first name and initial | Last name | **Spouse's social security number**

Home address (number and street). If you have a P.O. box, see instructions. | Apt. no. | ▲ Make sure the SSN(s) above and on line 6c are correct.

City, town or post office, state, and ZIP code. If you have a foreign address, also complete spaces below (see instructions).

Presidential Election Campaign
Check here if you, or your spouse if filing jointly, want $3 to go to this fund. Checking a box below will not change your tax or refund. ☐ You ☐ Spouse

Foreign country name | Foreign province/state/county | Foreign postal code

Filing Status

Check only one box.

1 ☐ Single
2 ☐ Married filing jointly (even if only one had income)
3 ☐ Married filing separately. Enter spouse's SSN above and full name here. ▶
4 ☐ Head of household (with qualifying person). (See instructions.) If the qualifying person is a child but not your dependent, enter this child's name here. ▶
5 ☐ Qualifying widow(er) with dependent child

Exemptions

6a ☐ **Yourself.** If someone can claim you as a dependent, **do not** check box 6a . . . . . .
b ☐ **Spouse** . . . .
c Dependents:

(1) First name Last name	(2) Dependent's social security number	(3) Dependent's relationship to you	(4) ✓ if child under age 17 qualifying for child tax credit (see instructions)
			☐
			☐
			☐
			☐

If more than four dependents, see instructions and check here ▶ ☐

Boxes checked on 6a and 6b
No. of children on 6c who:
• lived with you
• did not live with you due to divorce or separation (see instructions)
Dependents on 6c not entered above
Add numbers on lines above ▶

d Total number of exemptions claimed . . . .

Income

Attach Form(s) W-2 here. Also attach Forms W-2G and 1099-R if tax was withheld.

If you did not get a W-2, see instructions.

Enclose, but do not attach, any payment. Also, please use Form 1040-V.

7 Wages, salaries, tips, etc. Attach Form(s) W-2 . . . . | 7
8a Taxable interest. Attach Schedule B if required . . . . | 8a
b Tax-exempt interest. **Do not** include on line 8a . . | 8b
9a Ordinary dividends. Attach Schedule B if required . . . . | 9a
b Qualified dividends . . . . | 9b
10 Taxable refunds, credits, or offsets of state and local income taxes | 10
11 Alimony received . . . . | 11
12 Business income or (loss). Attach Schedule C or C-EZ . . . . . . | 12
13 Capital gain or (loss). Attach Schedule D if required. If not required, check here ▶ ☐ | 13
14 Other gains or (losses). Attach Form 4797 . . . . | 14
15a IRA distributions . | 15a | b Taxable amount . . . | 15b
16a Pensions and annuities | 16a | b Taxable amount . . . | 16b
17 Rental real estate, royalties, partnerships, S corporations, trusts, etc. Attach Schedule E | 17
18 Farm income or (loss). Attach Schedule F . . . . | 18
19 Unemployment compensation . . . . | 19
20a Social security benefits | 20a | b Taxable amount . . . | 20b
21 Other income. List type and amount _____ | 21
22 Combine the amounts in the far right column for lines 7 through 21. This is your **total income** ▶ | 22

Adjusted Gross Income

23 Reserved . . . . | 23
24 Certain business expenses of reservists, performing artists, and fee-basis government officials. Attach Form 2106 or 2106-EZ | 24
25 Health savings account deduction. Attach Form 8889 . | 25
26 Moving expenses. Attach Form 3903 . . . . . | 26
27 Deductible part of self-employment tax. Attach Schedule SE . | 27
28 Self-employed SEP, SIMPLE, and qualified plans . . | 28
29 Self-employed health insurance deduction . . . . | 29
30 Penalty on early withdrawal of savings . . . . . | 30
31a Alimony paid   b Recipient's SSN ▶ | 31a
32 IRA deduction . . . . | 32
33 Student loan interest deduction . . . . | 33
34 Reserved . . . . | 34
35 Domestic production activities deduction. Attach Form 8903 | 35
36 Add lines 23 through 35 . . . . | 36
37 Subtract line 36 from line 22. This is your **adjusted gross income** . . . . . ▶ | 37

For Disclosure, Privacy Act, and Paperwork Reduction Act Notice, see separate instructions. | Cat. No. 11320B | Form **1040** (2012)

Deduction Limit for Self-Employed Individuals (Keogh Plans)

Sole proprietors who file a Schedule C, partners of a partnership, and members of an LLC are generally treated as self-employed individuals for tax purposes. In contrast, owners of C corporations or S corporations may also be employees of those entities. While self-employed individuals may adopt almost any qualified plan, they cannot normally choose a stock bonus plan or an employee stock ownership plan (ESOP) because there is no stock involved with sole proprietorships, partnerships, or LLCs. A qualified retirement plan selected by a self-employed individual is referred to as a **Keogh plan**. A Keogh plan is simply a qualified plan for a self-employed person usually structured as a profit sharing plan, a money purchase pension plan (MPPP), or a combination of both. (Note that self-employed individuals may also be able to establish a 401(k) plan.)An important characteristic of a Keogh plan is the reduced contribution that can be made on behalf of the self-employed individual. The employees of a firm that maintains a Keogh plan will generally be treated in the same manner as if the plan were not a Keogh plan. Employees will generally receive a benefit based on their W-2 income. The reason for the distinction is that self-employed individuals do not receive a W-2 form and will instead file a Schedule C or receive a K-1 which details the owner's earnings.

There is a special computation needed to calculate the maximum contribution and tax deduction for a Keogh plan on behalf of a self-employed individual. Since self-employed individuals do not have W-2s, the IRC uses the term "earned income" to denote the amount of compensation that is earned by the self-employed individual.

Earned income is defined as net earnings from self-employment less one-half of self-employment tax less the deduction for contributions to the qualified plan on behalf of the self-employed person. Through this process, the IRC attempts to treat self-employed individuals as if they were corporations instead of self-employed individuals. An employer and an employee each pays one-half of the employee's Social Security taxes; however, in the case of self-employed individuals, they are required to pay both halves. If the company was a corporation, then it would deduct one half of the self employment taxes paid on behalf of the individual in arriving at net income. Therefore, earned income for self-employed individuals is the self-employment income reduced by one-half of self-employment tax. Similarly, a corporation would deduct the contribution made to a qualified retirement plan

Quick Quiz 13.2

Highlight the answer to these questions:

1. Sole proprietorships are never required to register with the state in which they do business.
    a. True
    b. False

2. One of the major disadvantages of a sole proprietorship is the potential legal liability.
    a. True
    b. False

3. The ordinary and necessary expenses of a sole proprietorship are reported on Schedule C of the owner's Form 1040.
    a. True
    b. False

False, True, True.

in arriving at net income. Therefore, calculating earned income for a self-employed individual also requires a reduction for the amount of the contribution to the Keogh plan.

The two primary parts of the Social Security system are OASDI (Old Age Survivor Disability Insurance) and Medicare. Both employers and employees contribute to the system through FICA payments that generally consists of 6.2 percent for OASDI and 1.45 percent for Medicare.[1] The OASDI portion of 6.2 percent applies to income up to the Social Security wage base ($113,700 for 2013) while the Medicare portion applies to all income with no limit.

The deduction for the self-employed person's own plan contribution and his net earnings are interrelated. For this reason, the self-employed person must determine the deduction for his own contributions by using simultaneous equations or a circular calculation or by using the simpler method described below that adjusts the plan contribution rate for the self-employed person.

To calculate the self-employed individual's 2013 contribution to the Keogh plan, utilize the following formulas:

1. Calculate the self-employed individual's contribution rate:

$$\text{Self-Employed Contribution Rate} = \left(\frac{\text{Contribution Rate to Other Participants}}{1 + \text{Contribution Rate to Other Participants}} \right)$$

2. Calculate Self-Employment Tax:

Net Self-Employment Income

Times: 92.35%

Net Earnings subject to Self Employment Tax

Times: 15.3% up to $113,700 + 2.9% over $113,700

Equals: Self-Employment Tax

3. Calculate the self-employed individual's contribution:

Net Self-Employment Income

Less: ½ of Self-Employment Taxes

Equals: Adjusted Net Self-Employment Income (Earned Income)

Times: Self-Employed Contribution Rate

Equals: Self-Employed Individual's Qualified Plan Contribution

---

1. The "Payroll Tax Holiday" reduced the 6.2% rate to 4.2% during 2011 and 2012. In addition, the normal self-employment rate is 15.3%. The "Payroll Tax Holiday" has reduced it by 2 percentage points to 13.3%. This reduction is scheduled to expire on 12/31/2012, but could be extended.

<table>
<tr><td>**EXAMPLE 13.1**</td><td>Alex has Schedule C net income of $200,000 and wants to know the maximum amount he can contribute to a Keogh profit sharing plan. In this instance Alex can contribute $38,054 to the plan. The contribution is calculated as follows:</td></tr>
</table>

1. Calculate the self-employed individual's contribution rate:

$$\text{Self-Employed Contribution Rate} = \left(\frac{25\%}{1 + 25\%} \right)$$

Self-Employed Contribution Rate = 20%

2. Calculate Self-Employment Tax:

2013

$200,000	Net Self-Employment Income
x 0.9235	Times: 92.35%
$184,700	**Net Earnings subject to Self-Employment Tax**
x 15.3%/2.9%	Times: 15.3% up to $113,700 + 2.9% over $113,700
$19,455.10	**Equals: Self-Employment Tax ($17,396.10 + $2,059) *Rounded**

3. Calculate the self-employed individual's contribution:

2013

$200,000	Net Self-Employment Income
$9,728	Less: ½ of Self-Employment Taxes (50% x $19,455.10)
$190,272	**Equals: Adjusted Net Self-Employment Income**
x 0.20	Times: Self-Employed Contribution Rate
$38,054	**Equals: Self-Employed Individual's Qualified Plan Contribution**

Check figure:

2013

$$\frac{\$38,054}{\$190,272 - \$38,054} = 25\%$$

When solving the Keogh contribution calculation, it is important to understand that while 25 percent of compensation is the limit for deductible employee contributions, the self-employed individual maximum contribution is 25 percent of the self-employed individual's earned income. The 25 percent of earned income effectively translates to 20 percent of net self-employed income less one-half of self employment tax.

In the previous example, Alex's earned income is calculated as follows:

EXAMPLE 13.2

2013

$200,000	Schedule C net income
- $9,728	Less: ½ self-employment taxes
- $38,054	Less: Keogh contribution
$152,218	Earned income
X 0.25	Times: 25% to determine Keogh contribution
$38,054	**Total Keogh contribution**

Notice that the maximum Keogh contribution for each year is exactly 25% of the earned income.

Cargile Co., a sole proprietorship, employs B, C, D, and E as well as the sole proprietor, A, who files a Schedule C 1040 for his business.

EXAMPLE 13.3

	Compensation	Contributions
A*	$150,000	See note below
B	$100,000	$15,000
C	$80,000	$12,000
D	$50,000	$7,500
E	$20,000	$3,000

*A's compensation is Schedule C net income

Cargile maintains a Keogh profit sharing plan with a 15% contribution to each employee (not the owner). In spite of the fact that each employee receives exactly 15%, A is limited to receiving 13.04% (0.15/1.15) of $150,000 less one-half of the self-employment taxes due on his earnings.

$150,000	Schedule C net income
$6,000	Less: ½ self-employment taxes ($12,000 assumed for ease of calculation)
$144,000	Self-employment income
X 0.1304	Contribution rate (0.15/1.15)
$18,782.61	**Contribution on behalf of A** *

Rounding was not utilized when applying the contribution rate.

The special calculation is required because Schedule C net income must be reduced by both the self-employed person's qualified plan contribution and one-half of his self-employment tax before the reduced contribution rate is applied. For all of the other employees, their contribution is calculated based upon 15% of their compensation.

EXHIBIT 13.4

A SUMMARY OF ADVANTAGES AND DISADVANTAGES OF SOLE PROPRIETORSHIPS

Advantages
• Easy to form.
• Simple to operate.
• Easy to sell business assets.
• Few administrative burdens.
• Income is generally passed through to the owner on Schedule C of Form 1040.
Disadvantages
• Generally have limited sources of capital.
• Unlimited liability.
• No guarantee of continuity beyond the proprietor.
• Business income is subject to self-employment tax.

GENERAL PARTNERSHIPS

Partnerships are joint business ventures among two or more persons or entities to conduct a business as co-owners under their names or under a trade or fictitious name. A partnership is automatically created when two or more individuals conduct business for a profit. There are different types of partnerships and we will examine each type, including general partnerships and limited partnerships. Typically, **general partnerships** are not required to be registered with the Secretary of State in the state of formation, but limited partnerships are required to register.

FORMATION

Although partnerships are easy to form, state law will govern the relative rights and obligations of the partners (including equal sharing of profits and losses regardless of contributions of property or effort), unless there is a contrary agreement among the partners. Ownership of a general partnership may be in the form of partnership units, shares, or percentages.

Key Concepts

Underline/highlight the answers as you read:

1. Discuss the formation and operation of a general partnership.

2. Explain why disposing of a general partnership interest may be difficult.

3. Describe the sources of liability for a general partnership.

4. Explain the tax attributes of a general partnership.

INTEREST, DISPOSAL OF INTEREST, AND DISSOLUTION

A partner's interest in a partnership is frequently referred to as his partnership percentage interest. The partners usually have voting power in proportion to their ownership interest. Thus, majority voting rules generally apply.

It is generally difficult to dispose of a partnership interest because any buyer will not only have to evaluate the business, but also the other partners. In addition, partnership agreements often require the approval of non-selling partners before a partner's share can be sold to an outside party.

Partnership dissolution is either voluntary or judicial (ordered by a court). Partners usually vote for voluntary dissolution and, if affirmed, pay creditors and then distribute remaining assets to partners in accordance with either the partnership agreement or in proportion to their individual partnership interests. Judicial dissolution may be necessary when the partners cannot agree on how to conduct the business or whether to dissolve the entity. This situation is most likely to arise when partnership votes are required to be unanimous.

CAPITAL

The amount of capital contributed usually determines the ownership interest of a partner in a partnership. However, sometimes partners allocate ownership interest differently from capital contributed. Such a situation could occur when one partner brings ideas and talent and the other brings money. Whenever partners are deviating from ownership based on capital contributed, there should be a written partnership agreement that clarifies partnership interests and each partner's distributive share of partnership profits and losses. If a partnership wants to divide profits and/or losses in a proportion that does not equal partnership interest, it will be considered a special allocation. There must be a sound business purpose for a special allocation and partners are well advised to seek the counsel of an attorney or CPA.

LIABILITY

The co-owner partners share the risks and rewards of the business. Each partner is jointly and severally liable for partnership obligations. Like a sole proprietorship, a partner's personal assets can be seized to satisfy partnership obligations.

A principal disadvantage of the general partnership arrangement is that all general partners in a partnership are subject to joint and several liability for the debts and obligations of the partnership. These liabilities can arise from:
1. Negligence and acts of employees,
2. Negligence of other partners,
3. Commercial liabilities (e.g., loans) to the partnership, and
4. Commercial obligations to other trade creditors.

MANAGEMENT/OPERATIONS

Partnerships are generally managed equally by all partners. It is possible to name a "**managing partner**" to have responsibilities for some specific task or day-to-day operations. Partnerships can even appoint presidents and vice presidents as officers. If so, these should be spelled out in the written partnership agreement. Partnerships are not required to have annual meetings of partners, but rather have a relatively relaxed set of rules regarding formalities.

Employees of general partnerships are eligible to receive a wide variety of tax-free fringe benefits provided by the employer such as health care. This is not so for partners since partners are not considered to be employees for most employee fringe benefit purposes. However, partners can participate in company-sponsored retirement plans, but they have the same limitations as proprietors in terms of calculations (see discussion under proprietorships).

Quick Quiz 13.3

Highlight the answer to these questions:

1. General partnerships are governed by federal law.
   a. True
   b. False

2. The owners of a general partnership have limited liability from the debts and obligations of the partnership.
   a. True
   b. False

3. General partnerships are pass-through entities for tax purposes.
   a. True
   b. False

False, False, True.

INCOME TAXATION AND PAYROLL (SOCIAL SECURITY) TAXATION

Partnerships are not subject to entity level taxation. Partnerships file a Form 1065 (See Exhibit 13.6), including Schedule K (Exhibit 13.7), which is the summary of all distributive items to individual partners. Income and losses are then "passed through" to the individual partners in proportion to their partnership interests on Form 1065 Schedule K-1 (see Exhibit 13.8) regardless of whether the income is distributed to partners in the form of cash. However, partnership taxation may be complex because of the tax rules related to basis. All partnership business net income is subject to self-employment tax up to 15.3 percent. Partnerships are legal entities and thus are required to obtain a Federal Employer Identification Number (FEIN). The year-end for tax purposes is usually the calendar year-end.

Partnerships can deduct all "ordinary and necessary" business expenses from their income. Partners can deduct partnership losses against other ordinary income to the extent of their investment. However, passive partners (those not actively involved in the enterprise) may not be able to deduct losses due to passive activity rules even if they are at-risk. Limited partners may not be subject to self-employment tax.

EXHIBIT 13.5

Advantages
• More sources of initial capital than proprietorships.
• Usually have more management resources available than proprietorships.
• Have fewer administrative burdens than corporations.
• Income and losses are generally passed through to the partners for tax purposes.

Disadvantages
• Transfer of interests is more difficult than for proprietorships.
• Unlimited liability - each partner is liable for partnership debts and obligations.
• Partnership income tax and basis adjustment rules can be complex.
• Business net income is subject to self-employment tax.
• Partners are entitled to few tax-free fringe benefits that are generally available to employees.

EXHIBIT 13.6 FORM 1065

The 2011 form was the latest available at the time of printing. Please visit our website at money-education.com for updates.

Form 1065
Department of the Treasury
Internal Revenue Service

U.S. Return of Partnership Income

For calendar year 2011, or tax year beginning _____ , 2011, ending _____ , 20 _____ .
▶ See separate instructions.

OMB No. 1545-0099

2011

A Principal business activity	Name of partnership	D Employer identification number
B Principal product or service	**Print or type.** Number, street, and room or suite no. If a P.O. box, see the instructions.	E Date business started
C Business code number	City or town, state, and ZIP code	F Total assets (see the instructions) $

G Check applicable boxes: **(1)** ☐ Initial return **(2)** ☐ Final return **(3)** ☐ Name change **(4)** ☐ Address change **(5)** ☐ Amended return
(6) ☐ Technical termination - also check (1) or (2)
H Check accounting method: **(1)** ☐ Cash **(2)** ☐ Accrual **(3)** ☐ Other (specify) ▶ _____
I Number of Schedules K-1. Attach one for each person who was a partner at any time during the tax year ▶ _____
J Check if Schedules C and M-3 are attached . . . . ☐

Caution. Include **only** trade or business income and expenses on lines 1a through 22 below. See the instructions for more information.

Income	**1a** Merchant card and third-party payments (including amounts reported on Form(s) 1099-K). For 2011, enter -0-	**1a**	
	b Gross receipts or sales not reported on line 1a (see instructions)	**1b**	
	c Total. Add lines 1a and 1b	**1c**	
	d Returns and allowances plus any other adjustments to line 1a (see instructions)	**1d**	
	e Subtract line 1d from line 1c	**1e**	
	2 Cost of goods sold (attach Form 1125-A)	**2**	
	3 Gross profit. Subtract line 2 from line 1e		**3**
	4 Ordinary income (loss) from other partnerships, estates, and trusts (attach statement) . .		**4**
	5 Net farm profit (loss) (attach Schedule F (Form 1040))		**5**
	6 Net gain (loss) from Form 4797, Part II, line 17 (attach Form 4797)		**6**
	7 Other income (loss) (attach statement)		**7**
	8 **Total income (loss).** Combine lines 3 through 7		**8**
Deductions (see the instructions for limitations)	**9** Salaries and wages (other than to partners) (less employment credits)		**9**
	10 Guaranteed payments to partners		**10**
	11 Repairs and maintenance		**11**
	12 Bad debts		**12**
	13 Rent		**13**
	14 Taxes and licenses		**14**
	15 Interest		**15**
	16a Depreciation (if required, attach Form 4562) **16a**		
	b Less depreciation reported on Form 1125-A and elsewhere on return **16b**		**16c**
	17 Depletion (**Do not deduct oil and gas depletion.**)		**17**
	18 Retirement plans, etc.		**18**
	19 Employee benefit programs		**19**
	20 Other deductions (attach statement)		**20**
	21 **Total deductions.** Add the amounts shown in the far right column for lines 9 through 20 .		**21**
	22 **Ordinary business income (loss).** Subtract line 21 from line 8		**22**

Sign Here

Under penalties of perjury, I declare that I have examined this return, including accompanying schedules and statements, and to the best of my knowledge and belief, it is true, correct, and complete. Declaration of preparer (other than general partner or limited liability company member manager) is based on all information of which preparer has any knowledge.

▶ _____
Signature of general partner or limited liability company member manager

▶ _____
Date

May the IRS discuss this return with the preparer shown below (see instructions)? ☐ **Yes** ☐ **No**

Paid Preparer Use Only

Print/Type preparer's name	Preparer's signature	Date	Check ☐ if self- employed	PTIN
Firm's name ▶			Firm's EIN ▶	
Firm's address ▶			Phone no.	

For Paperwork Reduction Act Notice, see separate instructions.   Cat. No. 11390Z   Form **1065** (2011)

FORM 1065 SCHEDULE K

EXHIBIT 13.7

The 2011 form was the latest available at the time of printing. Please visit our website at money-education.com for updates.

Form 1065 (2011)   Page **4**

Schedule K		Partners' Distributive Share Items			Total amount	
Income (Loss)	1	Ordinary business income (loss) (page 1, line 22)		1		
	2	Net rental real estate income (loss) (attach Form 8825)		2		
	3a	Other gross rental income (loss)	3a			
	b	Expenses from other rental activities (attach statement)	3b			
	c	Other net rental income (loss). Subtract line 3b from line 3a		3c		
	4	Guaranteed payments		4		
	5	Interest income		5		
	6	Dividends: a Ordinary dividends		6a		
		b Qualified dividends	6b			
	7	Royalties		7		
	8	Net short-term capital gain (loss) (attach Schedule D (Form 1065)) . . .		8		
	9a	Net long-term capital gain (loss) (attach Schedule D (Form 1065))		9a		
	b	Collectibles (28%) gain (loss)	9b			
	c	Unrecaptured section 1250 gain (attach statement) . .	9c			
	10	Net section 1231 gain (loss) (attach Form 4797)		10		
	11	Other income (loss) (see instructions) Type ▶		11		
Deductions	12	Section 179 deduction (attach Form 4562)		12		
	13a	Contributions		13a		
	b	Investment interest expense		13b		
	c	Section 59(e)(2) expenditures: **(1)** Type ▶ _____ **(2)** Amount ▶		13c(2)		
	d	Other deductions (see instructions) Type ▶		13d		
Self-Employ-ment	14a	Net earnings (loss) from self-employment		14a		
	b	Gross farming or fishing income		14b		
	c	Gross nonfarm income		14c		
Credits	15a	Low-income housing credit (section 42(j)(5))		15a		
	b	Low-income housing credit (other)		15b		
	c	Qualified rehabilitation expenditures (rental real estate) (attach Form 3468)		15c		
	d	Other rental real estate credits (see instructions) Type ▶		15d		
	e	Other rental credits (see instructions) Type ▶		15e		
	f	Other credits (see instructions) Type ▶		15f		
Foreign Transactions	16a	Name of country or U.S. possession ▶				
	b	Gross income from all sources		16b		
	c	Gross income sourced at partner level		16c		
		Foreign gross income sourced at partnership level				
	d	Passive category ▶ _____ **e** General category ▶ _____ **f** Other ▶		16f		
		Deductions allocated and apportioned at partner level				
	g	Interest expense ▶ _____ **h** Other . . . . ▶		16h		
		Deductions allocated and apportioned at partnership level to foreign source income				
	i	Passive category ▶ _____ **j** General category ▶ _____ **k** Other ▶		16k		
	l	Total foreign taxes (check one): ▶ Paid ☐ Accrued ☐		16l		
	m	Reduction in taxes available for credit (attach statement)		16m		
	n	Other foreign tax information (attach statement)				
Alternative Minimum Tax (AMT) Items	17a	Post-1986 depreciation adjustment		17a		
	b	Adjusted gain or loss		17b		
	c	Depletion (other than oil and gas)		17c		
	d	Oil, gas, and geothermal properties—gross income		17d		
	e	Oil, gas, and geothermal properties—deductions		17e		
	f	Other AMT items (attach statement)		17f		
Other Information	18a	Tax-exempt interest income		18a		
	b	Other tax-exempt income		18b		
	c	Nondeductible expenses		18c		
	19a	Distributions of cash and marketable securities		19a		
	b	Distributions of other property		19b		
	20a	Investment income		20a		
	b	Investment expenses		20b		
	c	Other items and amounts (attach statement)				

Form **1065** (2011)

EXHIBIT 13.8 **FORM 1065 SCHEDULE K-1**

The 2011 form was the latest available at the time of printing. Please visit our website at money-education.com for updates.

651111

☐ Final K-1   ☐ Amended K-1   OMB No. 1545-0099

Schedule K-1
(Form 1065)

20**11**

Department of the Treasury
Internal Revenue Service

For calendar year 2011, or tax
year beginning _____, 2011
ending _____, 20 _____

**Partner's Share of Income, Deductions,
Credits, etc.**   ► **See back of form and separate instructions.**

Part I	**Information About the Partnership**
A	Partnership's employer identification number
B	Partnership's name, address, city, state, and ZIP code
C	IRS Center where partnership filed return
D	☐ Check if this is a publicly traded partnership (PTP)

Part II	**Information About the Partner**
E	Partner's identifying number
F	Partner's name, address, city, state, and ZIP code

G ☐ General partner or LLC member-manager   ☐ Limited partner or other LLC member

H ☐ Domestic partner   ☐ Foreign partner

I What type of entity is this partner? _____

J Partner's share of profit, loss, and capital (see instructions):

	Beginning	**Ending**
Profit	%	%
Loss	%	%
Capital	%	%

K Partner's share of liabilities at year end:

Nonrecourse . . . . . . $ _____
Qualified nonrecourse financing . $ _____
Recourse . . . . $ _____

L Partner's capital account analysis:

Beginning capital account . . . $ _____
Capital contributed during the year $ _____
Current year increase (decrease) . $ _____
Withdrawals & distributions . . $ (_____)
Ending capital account . . . . $ _____

☐ Tax basis   ☐ GAAP   ☐ Section 704(b) book
☐ Other (explain)

M Did the partner contribute property with a built-in gain or loss?
☐ Yes   ☐ No
If "Yes," attach statement (see instructions)

Part III	**Partner's Share of Current Year Income, Deductions, Credits, and Other Items**	
1	Ordinary business income (loss)	15 Credits
2	Net rental real estate income (loss)	
3	Other net rental income (loss)	16 Foreign transactions
4	Guaranteed payments	
5	Interest income	
6a	Ordinary dividends	
6b	Qualified dividends	
7	Royalties	
8	Net short-term capital gain (loss)	
9a	Net long-term capital gain (loss)	17 Alternative minimum tax (AMT) items
9b	Collectibles (28%) gain (loss)	
9c	Unrecaptured section 1250 gain	
10	Net section 1231 gain (loss)	18 Tax-exempt income and nondeductible expenses
11	Other income (loss)	
		19 Distributions
12	Section 179 deduction	
13	Other deductions	20 Other information
14	Self-employment earnings (loss)	

*See attached statement for additional information.

For IRS Use Only

For Paperwork Reduction Act Notice, see Instructions for Form 1065.   Cat. No. 11394R   Schedule K-1 (Form 1065) 2011

LIMITED PARTNERSHIPS (LP)

Limited partnerships are associations of two or more persons as co-owners to carry on a business for profit except that one or more of the partners have limited participation in the management of the venture and thus limited risk exposure. If the limited partners participate in the management of the enterprise, they become general partners for liability purposes. In the normal limited partnership, there is at least one general partner. Because limited partners are passive investors in the enterprise, their liability is normally limited to the amount of their investment. A limited partner's personal assets cannot normally be seized to satisfy partnership obligations.

 Key Concepts

Underline/highlight the answers as you read:

1. Describe the ways in which a limited partnership is different from a general partnership.

2. Explain the advantages and disadvantages of a limited partnership.

FORMATION

Limited partnerships are generally required to file a partnership agreement or any other required documentation with the domiciliary state to establish the limited partnership. Those states that require initial filings also require annual filings to maintain the entity status. The written partnership agreement specifies which partners are limited partners and which partners are general partners.

INTEREST, DISPOSAL OF INTEREST, AND DISSOLUTION

The dissolution and transfer of an interest in a limited partnership is essentially the same as for a general partnership. Although the limited liability feature might attract more buyers, the inability for limited partners to have a say in the day-to-day operations of the company is likely to make the transfer of a limited partnership share very difficult.

CAPITAL

It is easier to raise capital in a limited partnership than in a general partnership because of the availability of the liability shield for the non-managing limited partners. However, the limited liability may negatively affect the partnership's ability to obtain outside financing. Third party lenders may desire personal guarantees from the partners (which would partially defeat the benefits associated with the limited liability feature).

LIABILITY

Liability for limited partners is limited as long as they refrain from participating in the management of the enterprise. The general partners, who are responsible for the day-to-day operations in a limited partnership, have unlimited liability for enterprise debts and obligations.

Quick Quiz 13.4

Highlight the answer to these questions:

1. Limited partnerships are generally required to register with the state.
   a. True
   b. False

2. Limited partnerships offer limited liability for all partners.
   a. True
   b. False

True, False.

MANAGEMENT/OPERATIONS

A limited partnership is somewhat of a hybrid entity. The general partners run the business and are exposed to personal liability. The limited partners must avoid making management decisions to protect their limited liability status.

INCOME TAXATION AND PAYROLL (SOCIAL SECURITY) TAXES

Limited partners are not usually subject to self-employment tax since they are passive investors who do not participate in management. The general partners in a limited partnership have self-employment income. As with the general partnership, the entity files a Form 1065 and issues Schedule K-1s to both its general and limited partners.

EXHIBIT 13.9 **A SUMMARY OF ADVANTAGES AND DISADVANTAGES OF LIMITED PARTNERSHIPS**

Advantages
• Favorable pass-through partnership taxation status.
• Flexibility in structuring ownership interests.
• Limited partners are not personally liable for the debts and obligations of the limited partnership as long as they do not engage in management.

Disadvantages
• Must file with the state to register.
• In most states, general partners are liable for debts and other obligations of the limited partnership.
• Losses for limited partners are generally passive losses.

LIMITED LIABILITY PARTNERSHIPS (LLP)

A **limited liability partnership (LLP)** is a hybrid entity that provides partial liability protection to its members and may be taxed as either a corporation or partnership. LLPs are similar to LLCs, but may not offer complete liability protection. The limited liability partnership is generally one comprised of licensed professionals such as accountants, attorneys, and doctors who practice together. The partners may enjoy liability protection from the acts of their other partners, but each partner remains personally liable for his own acts with respect to malpractice.

FORMATION

Limited liability partnerships are generally required to file with the domiciliary state to establish the limited liability partnership. Those states that require initial filings also require annual filings to maintain the entity status.

INTEREST, DISPOSAL OF INTEREST, AND DISSOLUTION

The dissolution and transfer of an interest in a limited partnership is essentially the same as for a general partnership. If the LLP is comprised of licensed professionals, however, transfer of an interest will usually be more difficult because such interest may only be transferred to another similarly licensed professional.

Key Concepts

Underline/highlight the answers as you read:

1. Explain who can form a limited liability partnership.

2. Explain the ways in which an LLP differs from a general partnership.

CAPITAL

The amount of capital contributed usually determines the ownership interest in a partnership. However, sometimes partners allocate ownership interest differently from capital contributed. Such a situation could occur when one partner brings ideas and talent and the other brings money. Whenever partners are deviating from ownership, based on capital contributed, there should be a written partnership agreement that clarifies partnership interests and each partner's distributive share of the profits and losses. If a partnership divides profits and/or losses in a proportion that does not reflect partnership interests, the arrangement is considered to be a special allocation. There must be a sound business purpose for special allocations and partners are well advised to seek the counsel of an attorney or CPA.

LIABILITY

A principal disadvantage of the general partnership arrangement is that all general partners in a partnership are subject to joint and several liability for the debts and obligations of the partnership. These liabilities can arise from:
1. liability for the negligence and acts of employees,
2. negligence of other partners,

3. commercial liabilities (e.g., loans) to the partnership, and
4. commercial obligations to other trade creditors.

However, general partners of an LLP can insulate themselves from liabilities arising from the acts of other partners. General partners of an LLP will not be personally liable for the debts and obligations arising from errors, omissions, negligence, incompetence, or acts committed by another partner or representative of the partnership who is not under the supervision or direction of the first partner. It is important to note that general partners remain personally liable for commercial and trade obligations. If the partners wish to insulate themselves from these obligations, they should consider an LLC and once formed, they should not personally guarantee commercial obligations.

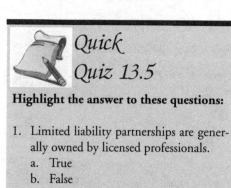

Quick Quiz 13.5

Highlight the answer to these questions:

1. Limited liability partnerships are generally owned by licensed professionals.
   a. True
   b. False

2. The transferability of an interest in an LLP is the same as for any other type of partnership.
   a. True
   b. False

True, False.

MANAGEMENT/OPERATIONS

The management of an LLP is generally the same as for any general partnership. Note that unlike a limited partnership, the LLP confers limited liability status on all partners, not just limited partners.

INCOME TAXATION AND PAYROLL (SOCIAL SECURITY) TAXES

For federal income tax purposes, the entity may elect to file as a corporation or as a partnership. This choice is known as "**checking the box**." Choosing to be taxed as a C corporation allows owners to take advantage of tax-free fringe benefits which may be provided by C corporations. Operating as a partnership has the disadvantages of subjecting income to employment taxes and limited fringe benefits for owners. If the entity files as a partnership it will file Form 1065. If it files as a corporation, it will file either the Form 1120S (if it elects S corporation status) or Form 1120 (if it files as a C corporation).

A Summary of Advantages and Disadvantages of Limited Liability Partnerships

EXHIBIT 13.10

Advantages
• Favorable pass-through partnership taxation status available.
• Flexibility in structuring ownership interests.
• Partners can insulate themselves from the acts of other partners.
Disadvantages
• Required to file with the state to register.
• Unlimited liability for own acts of malpractice.

FAMILY LIMITED PARTNERSHIPS (FLP)

A **family limited partnership** (FLP) is a special type of limited partnership created under state law with the primary purpose of transferring assets to younger generations using annual exclusions and valuation discounts for minority interests and lack of marketability.

FORMATION

Usually, one or more family members transfer highly appreciated property that is expected to continue to appreciate to a limited partnership in return for both a small (one percent, for example) general and a large (99 percent, for example) limited partnership

Key Concepts

Underline/highlight the answers as you read:

1. Describe how the tax attributes of an FLP can be useful in other areas of financial planning.

2. Explain the advantages of using an FLP to protect family assets.

interest. In a limited partnership, the general partner has unlimited liability and the sole management rights of the partnership, while the limited partners are passive interest holders with limited liability and no management rights.

EXHIBIT 13.11 FAMILY LIMITED PARTNERSHIP

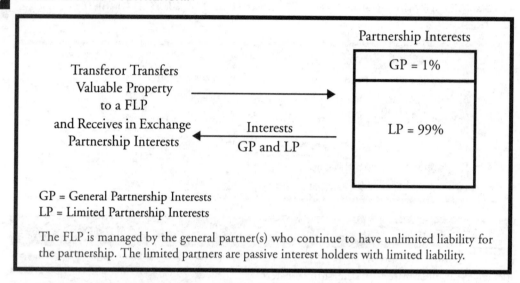

Transferor Transfers Valuable Property to a FLP and Receives in Exchange Partnership Interests

Interests GP and LP

Partnership Interests

GP = 1%

LP = 99%

GP = General Partnership Interests
LP = Limited Partnership Interests

The FLP is managed by the general partner(s) who continue to have unlimited liability for the partnership. The limited partners are passive interest holders with limited liability.

INTEREST, DISPOSAL OF INTEREST, AND DISSOLUTION

Upon creation of the partnership (FLP), there are neither income nor gift tax consequences because the entity created (the limited partnership and all of its interests, both general and limited) is owned by the same person, or persons, who owned it before the transfer.

Once the FLP is created, the owner of the general and limited partnership interests values the limited partnership interests. Since there are usually transferability restrictions on the limited partnership interests (lack of marketability), and since the limited partners have little control of the management of the partnership (lack of control), limited partnership interests are usually valued at a substantial discount from their fair market values. It is not uncommon for the discount of such interests to range between 20 and 40 percent for the purpose of calculating gift taxes payable by the transferor. The original transferor (grantor) then begins an annual gifting program utilizing the discounts, the gift tax annual exclusions, and gift-splitting (where applicable) to transfer limited partnership interests to younger generation family members at reduced transfer costs.

EXAMPLE 13.4	Charles, age 52, is married to Debbie, and they have three children and nine grandchildren. The three children are happily married and Charles and Debbie think of their children's spouses as their own children. Charles transfers a 100% interest in a business with a fair market value of $3,200,000 to a family limited partnership. Charles, in return, receives a general partnership interest of one percent and 162 units of limited partnership interests representing 99 percent, at $19,555 (($3,200,000 x 99%) / 162) per unit. Charles then transfers two limited partnership units to each child, the spouse of each child, and each grandchild using a 33.52

percent discount, the annual exclusion, and the gift-splitting election.

$19,555 x 0.6648 (1.00 - 0.3352) = $13,000 x 2 = $26,000 per donee x 15 donees (three children, three spouses, nine grandchildren) = 30 units valued at $586,650 ($19,555 x 30) total but discounted to $390,000 in total and $13,000 each.

In this scenario, Charles does not pay any gift tax. It will take six years with this level of gifting for Charles to transfer his entire limited partnership interest to his children, their spouses, and his grandchildren without paying any gift taxes.

CAPITAL

One of the unique features of the FLP, and perhaps its most important non-tax benefit, is that the original owner/transferor can maintain control of the property transferred to the limited partnership by only retaining a small general partnership interest. If the FLP is funded with a business interest, the general partner could remain president of the business, direct the company's strategic plan, receive reasonable compensation and fringe benefits, hire and fire employees, receive executive perks, and generally control the limited partners' interests. As with all limited partnerships, the limited partners have no control over any of these enumerated management decisions.

The FLP is often undertaken as a series of transfers, including an initial nontaxable contribution of property to the partnership followed by annual exclusion gifts of limited partnership interests. While a general partner has control over partnership affairs, an individual who transfers his property to an FLP needs to be financially secure without the transferred property, both from a net worth and cash flow perspective.

LIABILITY

The use of the FLP structure can also help protect family assets. By placing the assets in the FLP and only making gifts of limited partnership interests to heirs, judgments or liens entered against a donee (limited partner) will not jeopardize the assets of the partnership. A donee's creditor would not be able to force the donee to liquidate his interest, since the donee does not have the right to force the liquidation of a limited partnership interest.

Transferring limited partnership interests to children and children's spouses can also help protect assets from divorce claims. If the child and his spouse divorce, even if the divorced spouse received a limited partnership interest, he or she could not force distributions from the partnership, participate in management, require his or her interest to be redeemed, or force a liquidation of the partnership.

TAXATION

The creation of family limited partnerships and the use of discounts to transfer value at a lower gift tax cost has been regularly contested by the IRS. However, in several cases, the courts have ruled in favor of the taxpayer and upheld discounts on the valuation of limited partnership interests in the range of 10 percent to 40 percent, as long as the FLP was operated like a separate business. The IRS has won, and the valuation discounts have not been allowed, in cases where the family withdrew money from the business at leisure, shared checking accounts with the business, had the FLP pay medical or other ordinary living expenses for the family, and when other non-business transactions were prevalent within the FLP.

The estate planning benefits of the FLP are lost and expenses are increased (as the result of legal fees) when the IRS successfully contests the use of the FLP arrangement. To mitigate against this risk and to ensure the use of the favorable discounts, the FLP should possess economic substance by having its own checking accounts, tax identification number, payroll (including payment of reasonable compensation to the general partner if he is managing the business), and should not allow family members to withdraw funds at will, nor should the FLP pay for personal expenses of its owners.

Quick Quiz 13.6

Highlight the answer to these questions:

1. Only a limited partner can manage a family limited partnership.
   a. True
   b. False

2. At formation of a family limited partnership, the founder is subject to gift tax on the transfer of the property interest to the family limited partnership.
   a. True
   b. False

False, False.

A FLP is taxed as a partnership and, the entity files a Form 1065 and issues Schedule K-1s to both general and limited partners. The general partner may be a corporation or an individual. The treatment of payroll taxes will be determined by whether the general partner is an individual or a corporation. The limited partners are passive and not subject to employment tax.

Advantages
• Control retained by senior family member.
• Valuation discounts are available for minority interests.
• Annual exclusion gifts are generally used to transfer interests to family members.
• Some creditor protection.
• Restrictions can be placed on transferability of limited partnership interests of junior family members.
• FLP is commonly used as an estate planning strategy.

Disadvantages
• Attorney setup fees and costs.
• Periodic valuation costs.
• Operational requirements.
• Potential IRS challenges regarding valuations and discounts.

LIMITED LIABILITY COMPANIES (LLC)

Limited Liability Companies are separate legal entities formed by one or more individuals by meeting state statutory requirements necessary for the formation of an LLC.

FORMATION

LLCs are formed in much the same way as corporations. They are chartered entities registered with the Secretary of State in the state of organization. The charter document is called **Articles of Organization** and the state requires the entity to have a resident agent. In addition, the state will require annual filings.

INTEREST, DISPOSAL OF INTEREST, AND DISSOLUTION

Usually, owners' contributions determine the ownership percentage of an LLC. However, sometimes the organization will want to divide the ownership interests in an amount differently than the initial contributions. They can do this in a variety of ways, including revaluing assets or issuing units for some obligation.

Disposal or transferability of interests may be difficult and may be restricted to transferring only to named parties. Such restrictions are clarified in the operating agreement.

 **Key Concepts**

Underline/highlight the answers as you read:

1. Discuss the formation and operation of an LLC.

2. Discuss the liability protection offered by an LLC.

3. Explain the tax attributes of an LLC.

CAPITAL

Capital is easier to raise in an LLC than in a proprietorship. Ease of raising capital in an LLC is similar to the ease of raising capital in a partnership.

Capital Structure

There is no limitation on the number of members or the types of members in an LLC. Members may include foreign (nonresident aliens) individuals, estate, trusts, corporations, etc. LLCs may allocate items of income and gains in any manner agreed to by the members in the operating agreement and can also create different classes of ownership interests which have different rights.

LIABILITY

The most important feature of an LLC is that the LLC's individual owners are protected from personal liability for the LLC's debts and obligations unless they personally guarantee such obligations.

The liability protection is not absolute. Piercing the veil and alter ego concepts give courts the power to disregard the LLC liability protection in extraordinary cases of owner/manager abuse or failure to maintain a clear and continuing identity.

MANAGEMENT/OPERATIONS

An LLC usually is managed by virtue of an **operating agreement**. The operating agreement is similar to corporate bylaws and may be amended from time to time. The agreement specifies how and who will manage the LLC, how interests may be transferred, etc. Operating agreements are not filed with the state. Operating agreements sometimes specify simple majority rules for some decisions, super majority rules for other decisions (e.g., 2/3 or 3/4 to take on debt in excess of certain amounts) and unanimous votes for special situations (e.g., changing the operating agreement). Caution should be used with unanimous agreement provisions because they essentially give a minority owner (member) a veto power over all other members.

Note that an LLC is not legally required to have an operating agreement. If an LLC does not have an operating agreement, it will (by default) be governed by the state laws regarding LLCs. Although this might be sufficient for some LLCs, it is generally best to have a written operating agreement signed by all members that specifies the rules and regulations pertinent to the LLC.

INCOME TAXATION AND PAYROLL (SOCIAL SECURITY) TAXES

A single member/LLC is a disregarded entity for federal income tax purposes. The owner must file a Schedule C of Form 1040 for the LLC, the same as for a proprietorship. Single member LLC owners have the same issues as proprietors with respect to self-employment tax, unemployment compensation, and fringe benefits.

An LLC with two or more members can elect to be taxed for federal income tax purposes as a partnership (Form 1065 with Schedule K-1s), an S corporation (Form 1120S with Schedule K-1s), or a C corporation (Form 1120 with W-2 income to the owners).

Taxation of Income

The LLC is not taxed at the entity level if it is taxed as a partnership. As a pass-through entity, an LLC's income is taxed to members at their personal rates. LLC losses are deductible on personal income tax returns to the extent of basis and may be limited by the passive activity rules. A unique characteristic of LLCs is that no gain or loss is recognized upon the distribution of appreciated property from an LLC to an LLC member. Gain will only be recognized to the extent that cash received exceeds the members adjusted basis.

Fringe Benefits

LLCs are usually taxed as partnerships. Therefore, members are not generally allowed to exclude from gross income the value of fringe benefits paid on their behalf by the LLC.

Employment Tax on Income

LLCs are usually taxed as partnerships. Income earned by the LLC members is normally subject to self-employment tax on the tax returns of individual members. There are exceptions: (1) for LLC income derived from rental real estate, and (2) for LLC members who are not the managing member and are the equivalent of limited partners.

Once elected, the tax status (partnership, S corporation, or C corporation) will dictate the handling of self-employment tax and fringe benefits.

Quick Quiz 13.7

Highlight the answer to these questions:

1. There is no limitation on the number of members of a LLC.
   a. True
   b. False

2. A written operating agreement is an important element of the management of a LLC.
   a. True
   b. False

True, True.

EXHIBIT 13.13 **A SUMMARY OF ADVANTAGES AND DISADVANTAGES OF LLCs**

Advantages
• Members have limited liability.
• Number of members is unlimited but a single member LLC is a disregarded entity for tax purposes (File Form 1040 Schedule C).
• Members may be individuals, corporations, trusts, other LLCs, and other entities.
• Income is passed through to the members, usually on Schedule K-1.
• Double taxation affecting most C corporations is avoided if partnership tax status is elected.
• Members can participate in managing the LLC.
• Distributions to members do not have to be directly proportional to the members' ownership interests as they do for S corporations.
• Can have multiple classes of ownership.
• Entity may elect to be taxed as a partnership, an S corporation, or a C corporation.

Disadvantages
• May have limited life (often by termination on the death or bankruptcy of a member).
• Transfer of interests is difficult and sometimes limited by operating agreement.
• Some industries or professions may not be permitted to use LLC status.
• Laws vary from state to state regarding LLCs.
• Laws are relatively new for LLCs; therefore, precedent from prior court cases are limited.
• For tax purposes, the complex partnership rules generally apply.
• Members not meeting exceptions are subject to self-employment tax on all earned income if partnership status is elected.

C CORPORATIONS

Corporations are chartered legal entities formed by one or more individuals by meeting state statutory requirements necessary for the formation of a corporation. There are two types of corporations: the C corporation and the S corporation. For tax purposes, S corporations are simply C corporations with a special tax election and will be discussed in the next section.

Key Concepts

Underline/highlight the answers as you read:

1. Describe the formation and operation of a corporation.

2. Discuss the tax attributes of a corporation.

3. Discuss the ability of a corporation to raise capital.

FORMATION

Corporations can only be created by filing a charter document with the state of incorporation (called **articles of incorporation**). The articles of incorporation generally require a corporation to disclose its name, number of shares, and the purpose of the corporation. The corporation's purpose may be broad (e.g., to engage in any lawful activity) or specific (e.g., to sell textbooks). In addition, the corporation will be required to name a registered agent located in the state of incorporation.

INTEREST, DISPOSAL OF INTEREST, AND DISSOLUTION

Ownership interests in a corporation are held by a shareholder and are evidenced by shares of stock certificates. Shares may be easy to transfer if there is a market, but certain small corporations restrict the transfer of shares through a shareholder agreement. The shares of stock issued by the corporation may be all one class or several classes. Different classes of stock generally have different values and/or voting rights.

CAPITAL

Corporations can raise capital more easily than a proprietorship or partnership. The limited liability status appeals to outside non-employee owner/investors.

LIABILITY

Liability in corporations is limited to the invested capital. Individual shareholders of the corporation have limited liability, presuming the corporation behaves in such a way as to clearly and consistently maintain its identity and complies with state-mandated requirements.

MANAGEMENT/OPERATIONS

Corporations are managed by one or more officers appointed by the board of directors. The board of directors is the governing body of a corporation. The board of directors appoints various officers to run the corporation (usually includes president, chief financial officer, secretary, treasurer). The board of directors acts, or should act, in a very formal way and is required under the corporate charter to meet and follow certain formalities. Observing corporate formalities, and maintaining good standing with the Secretary of State in the state of incorporation, is an ongoing requirement.

INCOME TAXATION AND PAYROLL (SOCIAL SECURITY) TAXES

A corporation is taxed as a C corporation unless S corporation status is elected. C corporations must file Form 1120 (Exhibit 13.17) and pay taxes on their own income on a calendar or fiscal year basis. The owner/employees of both C corporations and S corporations are treated as employees for payroll tax purposes. Therefore, the entity withholds 7.65 percent of the employee's pay for Social Security taxes and matches such withholding for Social Security taxes. The owner/employee's compensation is not considered to be self-employment income.

Distributions of cash and other assets to a shareholder/employee in his capacity as a shareholder rather than as an employee are considered to be dividends. A C corporation is not allowed to take a tax deduction for

Quick Quiz 13.8

Highlight the answer to these questions:

1. A corporation's purpose must be narrowly defined in the articles of incorporation.
   a. True
   b. False

2. In-kind distributions of appreciated assets by a C corporation are treated as a deemed sale by the corporation.
   a. True
   b. False

False, True.

dividends distributed to shareholders, but shareholders must include the dividends in gross income. Therefore, the income of a C corporation can be taxed two times, once at the corporation level and a second time at the shareholder level when dividends are distributed. In a closely-held corporation, careful tax planning can minimize or even eliminate this double taxation.

When noncash distributions of appreciated property are made to shareholder/employees, gain must be recognized at the corporate level as though the property had been sold and the cash proceeds distributed. For a C corporation, this gain must be recognized at the corporation level. For an S corporation, the gain is passed through to shareholders and taxed on their individual income tax returns based on their ownership interests in the S corporation. Unlike this corporation treatment, appreciated assets can be distributed by an LLC or by any entity taxed as a partnership without any gain recognition at the time of the distribution.

TAX FORMULA FOR C CORPORATION

EXHIBIT 13.14

Total Income (From Whatever Source Derived)	$XX,XXX
Less: Exclusions From Gross Income	(X,XXX)
Gross Income	$XX,XXX
Less: Deductions	(X,XXX)
Taxable Income	$XX,XXX

CORPORATION INCOME TAX RATES

EXHIBIT 13.15

2011 Effective Tax Rate	Taxable Income	
	Over	Not Over
15%	$0	$50,000
$7,500 + 25% over $50,000	$50,000	$75,000
$13,750 + 34% over $75,000	$75,000	$100,000
$22,250 + 39% over $100,000	$100,000	$335,000
$113,900 + 34% over $335,000	$335,000	$10,000,000
$3,400,000 + 35% over $10,000,000	$10,000,000	$15,000,000
$5,150,000 + 38% over $15,000,000	$15,000,000	$18,333,333
35%	$18,333,333	....

| EXHIBIT 13.16 | ADVANTAGES AND DISADVANTAGES OF C CORPORATIONS |

Advantages
• Relative ease of raising capital.
• Limited liability of shareholders.
• Unlimited life of entity.
• Ease of transfer of ownership interests.
• Generally more management resources.
• Shareholder/employees may receive the full array of employer-provided tax-free fringe benefits.

Disadvantages
• Potential for double taxation due to entity level taxation.
• Administrative burdens (e.g., filings).
• More difficult to form and dissolution can cause taxable gains.
• Borrowing may be difficult without stockholder personal guarantees, which negates part of the advantage of limited liability.
• Requires a registered agent.
• Requires a federal tax ID number.

FORM 1120

EXHIBIT 13.17

The 2011 form was the latest available at the time of printing. Please visit our website at money-education.com for updates.

Form 1120
Department of the Treasury
Internal Revenue Service

U.S. Corporation Income Tax Return

For calendar year 2011 or tax year beginning _____ , 2011, ending _____ , 20 ____

► See separate instructions.

OMB No. 1545-0123

2011

A Check if:
1a Consolidated return (attach Form 851) ☐
b Life/nonlife consolidated return ☐
2 Personal holding co. (attach Sch. PH) ☐
3 Personal service corp. (see instructions) ☐
4 Schedule M-3 attached ☐

TYPE OR PRINT

Name

Number, street, and room or suite no. If a P.O. box, see instructions.

City or town, state, and ZIP code

B Employer identification number

C Date incorporated

D Total assets (see instructions)
$

E Check if: (1) ☐ Initial return (2) ☐ Final return (3) ☐ Name change (4) ☐ Address change

Income	1a	Merchant card and third-party payments. For 2011, enter -0-	1a
	b	Gross receipts or sales not reported on line 1a (see instructions)	1b
	c	Total. Add lines 1a and 1b	1c
	d	Returns and allowances plus any other adjustments (see instructions)	1d
	e	Subtract line 1d from line 1c	1e
	2	Cost of goods sold from Form 1125-A, line 8 (attach Form 1125-A)	2
	3	Gross profit. Subtract line 2 from line 1e	3
	4	Dividends (Schedule C, line 19)	4
	5	Interest	5
	6	Gross rents	6
	7	Gross royalties	7
	8	Capital gain net income (attach Schedule D (Form 1120))	8
	9	Net gain or (loss) from Form 4797, Part II, line 17 (attach Form 4797)	9
	10	Other income (see instructions—attach schedule)	10
	11	**Total income.** Add lines 3 through 10	11

Deductions (See instructions for limitations on deductions.)	12	Compensation of officers from Form 1125-E, line 4 (attach Form 1125-E)	12
	13	Salaries and wages (less employment credits)	13
	14	Repairs and maintenance	14
	15	Bad debts	15
	16	Rents	16
	17	Taxes and licenses	17
	18	Interest	18
	19	Charitable contributions	19
	20	Depreciation from Form 4562 not claimed on Form 1125-A or elsewhere on return (attach Form 4562)	20
	21	Depletion	21
	22	Advertising	22
	23	Pension, profit-sharing, etc., plans	23
	24	Employee benefit programs	24
	25	Domestic production activities deduction (attach Form 8903)	25
	26	Other deductions (attach schedule)	26
	27	**Total deductions.** Add lines 12 through 26	27
	28	Taxable income before net operating loss deduction and special deductions. Subtract line 27 from line 11	28
	29a	Net operating loss deduction (see instructions)	29a
	b	Special deductions (Schedule C, line 20)	29b
	c	Add lines 29a and 29b	29c

Tax, Refundable Credits, and Payments	30	**Taxable income.** Subtract line 29c from line 28 (see instructions)	30
	31	Total tax (Schedule J, Part I, line 11)	31
	32	Total payments and refundable credits (Schedule J, Part II, line 21)	32
	33	Estimated tax penalty (see instructions). Check if Form 2220 is attached ► ☐	33
	34	**Amount owed.** If line 32 is smaller than the total of lines 31 and 33, enter amount owed	34
	35	**Overpayment.** If line 32 is larger than the total of lines 31 and 33, enter amount overpaid	35
	36	Enter amount from line 35 you want: **Credited to 2012 estimated tax** ► _____ **Refunded** ►	36

Sign Here

Under penalties of perjury, I declare that I have examined this return, including accompanying schedules and statements, and to the best of my knowledge and belief, it is true, correct, and complete. Declaration of preparer (other than taxpayer) is based on all information of which preparer has any knowledge.

► Signature of officer _____ Date _____

► Title _____

May the IRS discuss this return with the preparer shown below (see instructions)? ☐ Yes ☐ No

Paid Preparer Use Only

Print/Type preparer's name	Preparer's signature	Date	Check ☐ if self-employed	PTIN

Firm's name ► _____ Firm's EIN ►
Firm's address ► _____ Phone no.

For Paperwork Reduction Act Notice, see separate instructions.   Cat. No. 11450Q   Form **1120** (2011)

S CORPORATIONS

An **S corporation** is normally created under state law by first forming a C corporation and then filing an "S" election with the IRS. The incorporation is normally the same as for a C corporation. There are, however, significant ways in which an S corporation differs from a C corporation.

INTEREST, DISPOSAL OF INTEREST, AND DISSOLUTION

Like a C corporation, the ownership interests in an S corporation are held by shareholders and are evidenced by shares of stock. Transferability of shares may be restricted by shareholders agreement.

CAPITAL

It is easier to raise capital in an S corporation than in a proprietorship or partnership because of the limited liability protection. However, the limited number of allowable shareholders may have a negative affect on the ability to raise capital. Recent changes in the IRC allow close family members to be treated as a single shareholder.

Key Concepts

Underline/highlight the answers as you read:

1. Explain how an S corporation differs from a C corporation.

2. Discuss the advantages and disadvantages of an S corporation.

LIABILITY

An S corporation offers the same limited liability protection as a C corporation or an LLC.

MANAGEMENT/OPERATIONS

Corporations are managed by one or more officers appointed by the board of directors. The board of directors is the governing body of a corporation. The board of directors appoints various officers to run the corporation. The board of directors acts, or should act, in a very formal way and is required under the corporate charter to meet and follow certain formalities. Observing corporate formalities and maintaining good standing with the Secretary of State in the state of incorporation is an ongoing requirement.

The number of shareholders of an S corporation is limited to 100 and the S corporation can only have one class of stock. LLCs, partnerships, and other corporations are prohibited from becoming S corporation shareholders. Additionally, non-resident aliens and most trusts may not be S corporation shareholders.

Quick Quiz 13.9

Highlight the answer to these questions:

1. The number of S corporation shareholders is limited to 100.
   a. True
   b. False

2. All payments from an S corporation to an S corporation shareholder will be treated as income subject to payroll taxes.
   a. True
   b. False

True, False.

INCOME TAXATION AND PAYROLL (SOCIAL SECURITY) TAXES

The income of an S corporation is passed through to shareholders and is not taxed at the corporation level. Therefore, an S corporation provides many of the benefits of a corporation without any double taxation of income earned by the corporation.

The owner/employees of S corporations are employees for payroll tax purposes. Therefore, the entity withholds 7.65 percent of the employees' pay for Social Security taxes and matches such withholding for Social Security taxes. The owner/employee compensation is not considered self-employment income. Additional distributions to shareholders beyond reasonable compensation are treated as dividends not subject to payroll tax.

Since the income of an S corporation is taxed to the shareholders for the year in which it is earned, dividend distributions to shareholders are normally not subject to income tax at the time they are distributed. Stated differently, S corporation dividends normally represent the distribution of income that has previously been taxed to the shareholder.

As indicated in the C corporation discussion, in-kind distributions of appreciated assets will be treated as a deemed sale; thus, such distributions will generate a capital gain in the case of an S corporation to all shareholders in proportion to their ownership even if the asset was only distributed to one shareholder.

Generally, S corporations file Form 1120S (Exhibit 13.19) on a calendar year basis and provide each shareholder with a Form 1120S Schedule K-1 (Exhibit 13.20).

EXHIBIT 13.18 **ADVANTAGES AND DISADVANTAGES OF S CORPORATIONS**

Advantages
• Income is passed through to the shareholders for federal income tax purposes.
• Income is taxed at the individual level which may be a lower tax rate than the applicable corporate rate.
• Shareholders have limited liability.
• Distributions from S corporations are exempt from the payroll tax system, assuming the corporation provides adequate compensation to those shareholders who are employees of the corporation.

Disadvantages
• Limited to 100 shareholders.
• Only one class of stock is permitted.
• Cannot have corporate, partnership, certain trust, or nonresident alien shareholders.
• Shareholder employees owning more than two percent of the company must pay taxes on a range of employee fringe benefits that would be tax-free to a shareholder/employee of a C corporation.
• The tax rate of the individual shareholder may be higher than the corporate tax rate.
• Borrowing may be difficult without stockholder personal guarantees, which negates part of the advantage of limited liability.

FORM 1120S

The 2011 form was the latest available at the time of printing. Please visit our website at money-education.com for updates.

EXHIBIT 13.19

Form **1120S**

Department of the Treasury
Internal Revenue Service

U.S. Income Tax Return for an S Corporation

▶ Do not file this form unless the corporation has filed or is attaching Form 2553 to elect to be an S corporation.
▶ See separate instructions.

OMB No. 1545-0130

20**11**

For calendar year 2011 or tax year beginning _____ , 2011, ending _____ , 20 ____

A S election effective date		Name	D Employer identification number
	TYPE		
B Business activity code number *(see instructions)*	OR	Number, street, and room or suite no. If a P.O. box, see instructions.	E Date incorporated
	PRINT	City or town, state, and ZIP code	F Total assets *(see instructions)*
C Check if Sch. M-3 attached ☐			$

G Is the corporation electing to be an S corporation beginning with this tax year? ☐ Yes ☐ No   If "Yes," attach Form 2553 if not already filed

H Check if: **(1)** ☐ Final return **(2)** ☐ Name change **(3)** ☐ Address change **(4)** ☐ Amended return **(5)** ☐ S election termination or revocation

I Enter the number of shareholders who were shareholders during any part of the tax year . . . . ▶

Caution. Include **only** trade or business income and expenses on lines 1a through 21. See the instructions for more information.

Income

1a	Merchant card and third-party payments. For 2011, enter -0- . . .	**1a**		
b	Gross receipts or sales not reported on line 1a (see instructions) .	**1b**		
c	Total. Add lines 1a and 1b	**1c**		
d	Returns and allowances plus any other adjustments (see instructions)	**1d**		
e	Subtract line 1d from line 1c		**1e**	
2	Cost of goods sold (attach Form 1125-A)		**2**	
3	Gross profit. Subtract line 2 from line 1e		**3**	
4	Net gain (loss) from Form 4797, Part II, line 17 *(attach Form 4797)* . . .		**4**	
5	Other income (loss) *(see instructions—attach statement)*		**5**	
6	**Total income (loss).** Add lines 3 through 5 . . . . ▶		**6**	

Deductions (see instructions for limitations)

7	Compensation of officers	**7**	
8	Salaries and wages (less employment credits)	**8**	
9	Repairs and maintenance	**9**	
10	Bad debts	**10**	
11	Rents	**11**	
12	Taxes and licenses	**12**	
13	Interest	**13**	
14	Depreciation not claimed on Form 1125-A or elsewhere on return *(attach Form 4562)* . . .	**14**	
15	Depletion **(Do not deduct oil and gas depletion.)**	**15**	
16	Advertising	**16**	
17	Pension, profit-sharing, etc., plans	**17**	
18	Employee benefit programs	**18**	
19	Other deductions *(attach statement)*	**19**	
20	**Total deductions.** Add lines 7 through 19 . . . . ▶	**20**	
21	**Ordinary business income (loss).** Subtract line 20 from line 6	**21**	

Tax and Payments

22a	Excess net passive income or LIFO recapture tax (see instructions) . .	**22a**		
b	Tax from Schedule D (Form 1120S)	**22b**		
c	Add lines 22a and 22b (see instructions for additional taxes)		**22c**	
23a	2011 estimated tax payments and 2010 overpayment credited to 2011	**23a**		
b	Tax deposited with Form 7004	**23b**		
c	Credit for federal tax paid on fuels *(attach Form 4136)*	**23c**		
d	Add lines 23a through 23c		**23d**	
24	Estimated tax penalty (see instructions). Check if Form 2220 is attached . . . . . ▶ ☐		**24**	
25	**Amount owed.** If line 23d is smaller than the total of lines 22c and 24, enter amount owed . . .		**25**	
26	**Overpayment.** If line 23d is larger than the total of lines 22c and 24, enter amount overpaid . .		**26**	
27	Enter amount from line 26 **Credited to 2012 estimated tax** ▶		Refunded ▶	**27**

Sign Here

Under penalties of perjury, I declare that I have examined this return, including accompanying schedules and statements, and to the best of my knowledge and belief, it is true, correct, and complete. Declaration of preparer (other than taxpayer) is based on all information of which preparer has any knowledge.

▶ _____   _____   ▶ _____
Signature of officer   Date   Title

May the IRS discuss this return with the preparer shown below (see instructions)? ☐ Yes ☐ No

Paid Preparer Use Only

Print/Type preparer's name	Preparer's signature	Date	Check ☐ if self-employed	PTIN
Firm's name ▶			Firm's EIN ▶	
Firm's address ▶			Phone no.	

For Paperwork Reduction Act Notice, see separate instructions.   Cat. No. 11510H   Form **1120S** (2011)

EXHIBIT 13.20 FORM 1120S SCHEDULE K-1

The 2011 form was the latest available at the time of printing. Please visit our website at money-education.com for updates.

671111

| ☐ Final K-1 | ☐ Amended K-1 | OMB No. 1545-0130 |

Schedule K-1 (Form 1120S)
Department of the Treasury
Internal Revenue Service

2011

For calendar year 2011, or tax
year beginning _____, 2011
ending _____, 20_____

Shareholder's Share of Income, Deductions, Credits, etc. ► See back of form and separate instructions.

Part I Information About the Corporation

A Corporation's employer identification number

B Corporation's name, address, city, state, and ZIP code

C IRS Center where corporation filed return

Part II Information About the Shareholder

D Shareholder's identifying number

E Shareholder's name, address, city, state, and ZIP code

F Shareholder's percentage of stock ownership for tax year . . . . _____ %

For IRS Use Only

Part III Shareholder's Share of Current Year Income, Deductions, Credits, and Other Items

1	Ordinary business income (loss)	13	Credits
2	Net rental real estate income (loss)		
3	Other net rental income (loss)		
4	Interest income		
5a	Ordinary dividends		
5b	Qualified dividends	14	Foreign transactions
6	Royalties		
7	Net short-term capital gain (loss)		
8a	Net long-term capital gain (loss)		
8b	Collectibles (28%) gain (loss)		
8c	Unrecaptured section 1250 gain		
9	Net section 1231 gain (loss)		
10	Other income (loss)	15	Alternative minimum tax (AMT) items
11	Section 179 deduction	16	Items affecting shareholder basis
12	Other deductions		
		17	Other information

* See attached statement for additional information.

For Paperwork Reduction Act Notice, see Instructions for Form 1120S.   Cat. No. 11520D   Schedule K-1 (Form 1120S) 2011

COMPARISON OF S CORPORATIONS AND LLCs

Many business owners know that they want limited liability and a flow through tax entity, but cannot distinguish between an S corporation and a LLC (taxed as a partnership). Below is a side-by-side comparison of these two very important entity types.

COMPARISON OF S CORPORATIONS AND LLCs (TAXED AS A PARTNERSHIP)   EXHIBIT 13.21

	S Corporation	LLC / Partnership
Double taxation	No	No
Pass through tax losses	Yes	Yes
Availability of preferred return for certain investors (1 class of stock in S)	No	Yes
Partnerships, corporations, and trusts can be entity owners	No	Yes
Foreign investors	No	Yes
Distribute in-kind appreciated assets to owners without gain recognition	No	Yes
Ability to transfer interest to trust for estate planning	No	Yes
Low filing fees	Yes (Generally)	No
Self employment tax on all income for owner/employees	No	Yes (Generally)
Limited number of owners	Yes (100)	No
Owner's basis for deductibility of losses includes pro-rata share of loans to entity by third parties	No	Yes
The law is well settled pertaining to the entity	Yes	No
Filing date with extensions	October 15th	September 15th

EXHIBIT 13.22 ENTITY COMPARISON

	Proprietorship	General Partnership	Limited Partnership	LLP	FLP	LLC	S Corp.	C Corp.
Cost to create (money & time)	Low	Medium	Medium–High	High	High	High	High	High
Personal liability of investors for enterprise debt	Yes	Yes	No (if limited partner)	Yes	Yes	No	No	No
Annual state filing requirement	No	Generally Not	Yes	Yes	Yes	Yes	Yes	Yes
Maximum owners	One	Unlimited	Unlimited	Unlimited	Unlimited	Unlimited	100	Unlimited
Owners are known as	Owner	Partner	Partner or Limited Partner	Partner or Limited Partner	Partner or Limited Partner	Member	Shareholder	Shareholder
Tax filing alternatives	Schedule C 1040	Form 1065 K-1 flows to Schedule E of Form 1040	Form 1065 K-1 flows to Schedule E of Form 1040	May file as corporation or partnership	Form 1065 K-1 flows to Schedule E of Form 1040	If one member, entity is disregarded and owner files Schedule C of Form 1040. If two or more members, choice of Form 1065 (Partnership), Form 1120-S (S Corporation), or Form 1120 (C Corporation)	Form 1120S K-1 to shareholders	Form 1120
Federal Tax ID required	No	Yes	Yes	Yes	Yes	No, if one member Yes, if two or more members	Yes	Yes
Taxation concept	Individual	Flow Through	Flow Through	Flow Through	Flow Through	Flow Through	Flow Through	Entity
Owners income	Self Employment	Self employment but limited partners/members are not subject to Soc. Sec. tax unless they perform personal services for the entity	Self employment but limited partners/members are not subject to Soc. Sec. tax unless they perform personal services for the entity	Self employment but limited partners/members are not subject to Soc. Sec. tax unless they perform personal services for the entity	Self employment but limited partners/members are not subject to Soc. Sec. tax unless they perform personal services for the entity	Depends on filing choice, but limited partners/members are not subject to Soc. Sec. tax unless they perform personal services for the entity	W-2 and ordinary income Excess profits distributed are not subject to Soc. Sec. tax	W-2 and dividend income

PROTECTING OWNERS FROM EACH OTHER

As the old saying goes "there is risk in the future." The choice of entity provides certain advantages and disadvantages to the partner, member, or shareholder. However, there are certain recurring situations where a little forethought could have prevented a bad result. Some of these situations are unexpected events like death or disability of an owner, divorce, bankruptcy, retirement, or a voluntary or involuntary disassociation with the entity.

Each owner faces the above risks. In entities where there are multiple owners, a written shareholder agreement, partnership agreement, or operating agreement addressing the listed issues and any others that are of concern should be considered.

PROTECTING MINORITY SHAREHOLDERS/MEMBERS

A minority shareholder or member who is also an employee should have two different types of protection from termination by having an employment agreement (rather than being an employee at will) and should also have a shareholder agreement with a buyout provision in the event of termination.

ELEMENTS OF SHAREHOLDER/PARTNERSHIP AGREEMENTS

For each risk there should be a method provided for valuing the entity and funding the departing owner's interest. For example:
- For the first five years, the departing owner gets nothing.
- After five years, the departing owner is entitled to his proportional share. The company shall be valued at 1.5 times the average revenues for the three previous years.
- If the departing owner is terminated for cause, the company shall be valued at 50 percent of the average revenues for the last three years.

It is not enough to identify the risk and calculate the valuation; a funding method must also be provided. While cross purchase or entity life insurance may work for untimely death, life insurance does not work for voluntary termination. A payout over time that will not burden the remaining owners and entity may be a solution. Whatever the solution, it needs to be clearly articulated in the shareholder agreement, the operating agreement, or the partnership agreement. In addition, the funding mechanism must be real.

ISSUES REGARDING ADDITIONAL CAPITAL REQUIRED

In the situation where multiple owners have made a certain initial investment into a business enterprise, there is always the chance that additional capital will be needed. What happens if one of the investors refuses to pay his proportional share of such new capital? Can the partners, or shareholders compel the unwilling owner to pay? At the outset of an entity the initial owners should prepare an analysis of the risks of needing additional capital (e.g., debt service is certain). If additional capital is likely or even possibly needed, the joint owners should prepare for it. One way to do so is to have all owners put up a negotiable letter of credit for a reasonable period of time to assure cash calls will be met. Additionally, a provision should be put in the partnership agreement, shareholder agreement, or operating agreement to the effect that any owner who defaults on a cash call obligation automatically forfeits his original investment and such default makes the letter of credit immediately due and payable.

Key Terms

Articles of Incorporation - The charter document for a corporation that must be filed with the Secretary of State in the state of organization.

Articles of Organization - The charter document of an LLC that must be filed with the Secretary of State in the state of organization.

Checking the Box - When an eligible entity chooses to be taxed as either a corporation or a partnership.

Corporations - Chartered legal entities formed by one or more individuals by meeting state statutory requirements necessary for the formation of a corporation.

Family Limited Partnership - A special type of limited partnership created under state law with the primary purpose of transferring assets to younger generations using annual exclusions and valuation discounts for minority interests and lack of marketability.

General Partnership - A joint business venture among two or more persons/entities to conduct business as co-owners in which all owners have unlimited liability with regard to the debts and obligations of the partnership.

Keogh Plan - A qualified plan for a self-employed person. An important distinction of Keogh plans is the reduced contribution that can be made on behalf of the self-employed individual.

Limited Liability Company - Separate legal entity formed by one or more individuals by meeting state statutory requirements necessary for the formation of an LLC that may be taxed as a sole proprietorship, partnership, or corporation.

Limited Liability Partnership - A hybrid entity generally comprised of licensed professionals that provides partial liability protection to its members and may be taxed as either a corporation or partnership.

Limited Partnerships - Associations of two or more persons as co-owners to carry on a business for profit except that one or more of the partners have limited participation in the management of the venture and thus limited risk exposure.

Managing Partner - A partner named to have responsibilities for specific tasks or for day-to-day operations.

Operating Agreement - A written agreement similar to corporate bylaws that specify the rules and regulations for the operation of an LLC.

Piercing the Veil - Occurs when a court disregards the status of the entity that gives the owners limited liability because the owners failed to maintain a clear and consistent identity for the entity.

Key Terms

S Corporation - A corporation formed under state law that elects to be taxed under Subchapter S of the Internal Revenue Code.

Sole Proprietorship - A business venture owned and operated by a single individual.

1. What are the different types of legal entities from which a business owner can conduct business?

2. How is a general partnership taxed?

3. What are the differences between a a general and a limited partnership?

4. How do different types of business entities differ from each other with regard to the personal liability of owners for business obligation?

5. How is a C corporation taxed?

6. What type of business entity should be chosen if the owners expect losses in the first few years and the owners want limited personal liability?

7. How is a limited liability company taxed if it has one or more owners?

8. Compare an S corporation to a limited liability company.

9. How can an entity avoid having a court "pierce the veil?"

10. Why is it often difficult to dispose of an interest in a partnership?

11. What is the principal disadvantage of the general partnership arrangement?

12. How does the limited partnership arrangement affect an entity's ability to raise capital?

13. Define "checking the box."

14. How is a family limited partnership usually formed?

15. What are the risks associated with the taxation of an FLP?

16. What is an operating agreement and why is it important to have this document?

17. What are some of the advantages of a corporation?

18. What are some of the disadvantages of an S corporation?

MULTIPLE CHOICE PROBLEMS

1. An architect performed services for Bill and Sue and, in lieu of her normal fee, accepted a 10 percent interest in a partnership with a fair market value of $10,000. How much income from this arrangement should the architect report on her income tax return?

    a. The architect does not have any currently taxable income.
    b. The architect has realized $10,000 in capital gains.
    c. The architect must recognize $10,000 in compensation income.
    d. The architect has realized $10,000 in compensation income, but does not have to recognize it until she sells her interest in the partnership.

2. An S corporation has the following information for the taxable year:

Net Income before the items below	$90,000
Bill's Salary	($38,000)
Other Income	$29,000
Other Expenses	($14,000)
Net Income	$67,000

    Bill is a 20 percent owner of the S corporation and he performs services for the business as an employee. What is Bill's self-employment income?

    a. $0.
    b. $52,000.
    c. $67,000.
    d. $90,000.

3. On August 1, 2013, Jack bought a 5 percent interest (5 shares) in XYZ, an S corporation that files as a calendar-year taxpayer. In 2013, the S corporation income was $160,000. How much will be reported to Jack on his 2013 1120S Schedule K-1?

    a. $0.
    b. $3,333.
    c. $3,353.
    d. $8,000.

4. At the beginning of the current year, Donna's basis in her partnership interest was $100,000. At the end of the year, Donna received a K-1 from the partnership that showed the following information:

Cash Withdrawn	$31,000
Partnership Taxable Income	$60,000
Charitable Contribution	$1,000

What is Donna's basis in her partnership interest at year-end?

    a. $128,000.

    b. $129,000.

    c. $159,000.

    d. $160,000.

5. Cobalt, a calendar-year S corporation, was incorporated in 2010. The company had the following taxable income and distributions each year:

	Taxable Income	Distributions
2010	($20,000)	$0
2011	($30,000)	$0
2012	$150,000	$60,000
2013	$400,000	$175,000

Cobalt has a single shareholder. His original basis in the stock was $150,000. What is the shareholder's basis at the end of 2013?

    a. $150,000.

    b. $250,000.

    c. $415,000.

    d. $650,000.

6. Which of the following statements is/are true?

    1. Partnerships offer limited liability protection to partners.

    2. LLCs offer limited liability protection to members.

    a. 1 only.

    b. 2 only.

    c. Both 1 and 2.

    d. Neither 1 nor 2.

7. Which of the following statements is/are true?

  1. LLCs offer limited liability protection to members.
  2. S corporations offer limited liability protection to owners.
     a. 1 only.
     b. 2 only.
     c. Both 1 and 2.
     d. Neither 1 nor 2.

8. Which of the following statements is/are true?

  1. It is necessary to register with the state when forming a proprietorship.
  2. It is necessary to register with the state when forming a partnership.
     a. 1 only.
     b. 2 only.
     c. Both 1 and 2.
     d. Neither 1 nor 2.

9. Which of the following statements is/are true?

  1. Partnerships require registration with the state.
  2. Limited partnerships require registration with the state.
     a. 1 only.
     b. 2 only.
     c. Both 1 and 2.
     d. Neither 1 nor 2.

10. Which entity does not have all of the following characteristics?

  1. Limited liability.
  2. Ability to distribute in-kind appreciated assets to owners without gain recognition.
  3. Can have foreign investors.
     a. LLC.
     b. S corporation.
     c. Limited partnership.
     d. LLP.

11. Which type of entity could possibly file any of the following forms?

    1. Form 1040.

    2. Form 1065.

    3. Form 1120S.

        a. Partnership.

        b. Limited partnership.

        c. Proprietorship.

        d. LLC.

12. Which entity will meet the following requirements?

    1. Flow-through entity.

    2. Limited liability.

    3. Can have foreign investors.

        a. Proprietorship.

        b. Partnership.

        c. LLC.

        d. S corporation.

13. Which entity will meet the following requirements?

    1. Disregarded entity.

    2. Limited liability.

    3. Self-employment tax on all income.

        a. Partnership.

        b. Single-member LLC.

        c. S corporation.

        d. Proprietorship.

14. Which entity will meet the following requirements?

    1. Unlimited number of owners.

    2. Limited liability.

    3. Self-employment tax on all income.

        a. Proprietorship.

        b. Partnership.

        c. LLC.

        d. S corporation.

15. Which entity will meet the following requirements?

    1. Availability of preferred returns for certain investors.

    2. Considers loans from third parties in basis of owners.

    3. Limited liability.

       a. Partnership.

       b. LLC.

       c. S corporation.

       d. C corporation.

16. Which of the following can file as a corporation or partnership?

       a. LLC and LLP.

       b. LLC only.

       c. LLP only.

       d. LLC and S corporation.

17. Excess distributed income over reasonable compensation:

    1. is treated as self-employment income in a LLC.

    2. is treated as dividend income in a S corporation.

       a. 1 only.

       b. 2 only.

       c. Both 1 and 2.

       d. Neither 1 nor 2.

Quick Quiz Explanations

Quick Quiz 13.1
1. True.
2. False. To avoid piercing the veil, the entity should keep books and records separate from the personal books and records of the owners, segregate activities of business from personal affairs, follow corporate formalities such as meeting requirements and filings, and address all content in contracts and correspondence from the viewpoint of the business entity (rather than the viewpoint of the owners).

Quick Quiz 13.2
1. False. A proprietorship may be required to obtain a local business license or register with the state or local taxing authority if it will be collecting sales tax.
2. True.
3. True.

Quick Quiz 13.3
1. False. General partnerships are governed by the laws of the state in which they are formed.
2. False. A principal disadvantage of the general partnership arrangement is that all general partners in a partnership are jointly and severally liable for the debts and obligations of the partnership.
3. True.

Quick Quiz 13.4
1. True.
2. False. Limited partnerships offer limited liability for the limited partners. The general partners run the business and are exposed for personal liability.

Quick Quiz 13.5
1. True.
2. False. If the LLP is comprised of only licensed professionals, transfer of an interest will usually be more difficult because such interest may only be transferred to another similarly licensed professional.

Quick Quiz 13.6
1. False. Only a general partner can manage a family limited partnership.
2. False. Upon creation of the partnership (FLP), there are neither income nor gift tax consequences because the entity created (the limited partnership and all of its interests, both general and limited) is owned by the same person, or persons, who owned it before the transfer.

Quick Quiz Explanations

Quick Quiz 13.7
1. True.
2. True.

Quick Quiz 13.8
1. False. The corporation's purpose may be broad (e.g., to engage in any lawful activity) or specific (e.g., to sell textbooks).
2. True.

Quick Quiz 13.9
1. True.
2. False. Additional distributions to shareholders beyond reasonable compensation are treated as dividends not subject to payroll tax. In-kind distributions of appreciated assets will be treated as a deemed sale; thus, such distributions will generate a capital gain in the case of an S corporation to all shareholders in proportion to their ownership even if the asset was only distributed to one shareholder.

Estate Planning

LEARNING OBJECTIVES

After reading this chapter, you should be able to:

- Define estate planning.
- List and discuss the goals, objectives, and risks of estate planning.
- Describe the estate planning process.
- Identify the basic documents included an estate plan including wills, side letters, powers of attorney and appointment, and directives regarding healthcare.
- Clearly differentiate between limited and general powers.
- Describe the various types of property interests including fee simple, tenants-in-common, joint tenancy with right of survivorship, tenants by the entirety, and community property.
- Define and describe the probate process and its purposes.
- Understand the difference between testate and intestate succession.
- Identify the common duties of an executor and/or administrator.
- Describe the use of trusts in estate landing.
- Describe the federal estate and gift tax system.
- Describe the characteristics of a gift, the valuation of gifts, and exclusions and exemptions associated with gifts.
- Discuss a basic understanding of the estate tax system.

INTRODUCTION

Many philosophers and great thinkers have contemplated the inevitability of death and taxes. Benjamin Franklin is known for his famous saying that "in this world nothing is certain but death and taxes." Despite Mr. Franklin's words of wisdom, there is often uncertainty when it comes to both death and taxes. While no one likes to plan for death, the fact remains that no one lives forever. Unless we prepare for our deaths, there is uncertainty as to where our assets and liabilities will end up when we die. The best way to eliminate some of that uncertainty is through a properly prepared estate plan that incorporates planning for the accumulation, protection, and disposition of wealth.

Estate planning is complex. Among other things, it is about planning for risks, including the risks of untimely death, ill health, artificially sustaining life, inability to manage property, immaturity of heirs, and application of state intestacy rules that may be totally inconsistent with a person's wishes. In large measure, estate planning is about the transfer of property, either during life or at death, the methods of effecting those transfers, and the risks associated with those transfers. It is also about the process of growing old, or not, and the planning for financial consequences of each possible outcome, as well as providing the greatest assistance (financial and otherwise) for loved ones left behind.

If we knew exactly what we would face in the future, we would arrange our financial affairs, prepare our families and loved ones, get our financial records in order, identify who is to receive what property, advise our relatives what to do if we are unable to make our own decisions, select someone to make critical healthcare decisions for us, confide in someone about our funeral and burial wishes, select someone to care for our children, provide for our children's education, and provide for our spouse. We would evaluate whether we could, in good conscience, leave money or property outright to particular heirs or whether we need to have someone else protect them from themselves and others.

ESTATE PLANNING DEFINED

Estate planning may be broadly defined as the process of accumulation, management, conservation, and transfer of wealth considering legal, tax, and personal objectives. Estate planning is financial planning in anticipation of a client's inevitable death. The goal of estate planning is the effective and efficient transfer of assets. An **effective transfer** occurs when a person's assets are transferred to the person or institution intended by that person. An **efficient transfer** occurs when transfer costs are minimized consistent with the greatest assurance of effectiveness. Some estate planning experts define estate planning more narrowly to include only conservation and transfer, ignoring the accumulation factor in the broader definition above.

Key Concepts

Underline/highlight the answers as you read:

1. What is estate planning?

2. Explain the differences between an efficient and effective transfer.

3. What are the common goals of estate planning?

GOALS, OBJECTIVES, AND RISKS OF ESTATE PLANNING

Common goals and objectives of estate planning include transferring (distributing) property to particular persons or entities consistent with client wishes; minimizing taxes (income, gift, estate, state inheritance, and generation-skipping transfer taxes); minimizing transaction costs associated with the transfer (costs of documents, lawyers, accountants, and the probate process - the legal process of changing title to the decedent's assets from the decedent to the heirs and legatees); maximizing the transfer of assets to heirs; providing for guardianship; and providing the estate of the decedent with sufficient liquidity to pay for costs that commonly arise upon or around one's death, such as taxes, funeral expenses, and final medical costs. An **heir** is a person who inherits under state law whereas a **legatee** is a person named in a will.

EXHIBIT 14.1

ESTATE PLANNING GOALS AND OBJECTIVES

- Fulfill client's property transfer wishes.
- Minimize transfer taxes.
- Minimize transfer costs.
- Maximize net assets to heirs.
- Provide for guardianship.
- Provide needed liquidity at death.
- Fulfill client's healthcare decisions.

Everyone needs a basic estate plan to address health care issues, property management, and the ultimate transfer of property according to their wishes. Typically, the most important estate planning objective is to assure that the decedent's property is transferred to the person, persons, or entities consistent with the decedent's wishes.

The risks associated with failing to plan for an estate transfer include the transfer of property contrary to the client's wishes, insufficient financial provision for the client's family, and the emergence of liquidity problems at the time of death. Any one of these risks could be catastrophic for the decedent's heirs and family.

EXHIBIT 14.2

RISKS IN FAILING TO PLAN AN ESTATE

- Client's property transfer wishes go unfulfilled.
- Transfer taxes are excessive.
- Transfer costs are excessive.
- Client's family not properly provided for financially.
- Insufficient liquidity to cover client's debts, taxes, and costs at death.

THE ESTATE PLANNING PROCESS

THE SIX BASIC STEPS

There are six basic steps in the estate planning process:

1. Establish the client/planner relationship.
2. Gather client information, including the client's current financial statements and establish the client's transfer objectives, including family and charitable objectives.
3. Determine the client's financial status.
4. Develop a comprehensive plan of transfers consistent with all information and objectives.
5. Implement the estate plan.
6. Review the estate plan periodically and update the plan when necessary (especially for changes in family situations).

The first two steps will be discussed in this chapter and the remaining steps generally follow the financial planning process covered earlier in the text.

ESTABLISH THE CLIENT/PLANNER RELATIONSHIP

The client / planner relationship may arise in several different ways, but clients are often reluctant to seek out a planner to plan their estate. This reluctance may stem from several causes including concern about the expense associated with estate planning, the belief that estate planning is only for the extremely wealthy, or the desire to avoid the inevitability of the client's own mortality. Therefore, the opportunity to discuss the issue of estate planning generally arises when the planner is meeting with the client for financial planning matters other than estate planning.

Key Concepts

Underline/highlight the answers as you read:

1. Identify the risks associated with failing to plan for estate transfer.

2. Identify the six basic steps of the estate planning process.

3. What is usually the most important estate planning client objective?

The estate planning engagement is the same as any other financial planning engagement. The planner should meet with the client, detail the services to be provided and the expectations of both the client and the planner. The financial planner should then send an engagement letter to the client detailing the information discussed in the meeting.

COLLECTING CLIENT INFORMATION AND DEFINING TRANSFER OBJECTIVES

Collecting a client's information is essential to gain a complete financial and family picture of the client and to assist the client in identifying their financial risks. Information about prospective heirs and legatees needs to be collected to properly arrange for any transfer that the client wants to make.

To begin the estate planning process, the planner should collect:
- Current financial statements (Statement of Financial Position and Income Statement).
- A detailed list of assets and liabilities, including, for each asset, the fair market value, adjusted basis, expected growth rate, how title is being held, and the date acquired.
- Family information - information about parents and children, including the age and health of each family member.
- Copies of medical, disability, and long-term care insurance policies.
- Copies of all current life insurance policies identifying the owner of each policy, the named insured, and the designated beneficiaries.
- Copies of annuity contracts.
- Copies of wills and trusts.
- Identification of powers of attorney and general powers of appointment.
- Copies of all previously filed income tax, gift tax, and estate tax returns.

- Identification of assets previously transferred to loved ones.

After collecting the client and family information, the client's transfer objectives must be determined. Usually the client's most important objective is to transfer his assets as he wishes (an effective transfer). Next, the client generally wishes to maximize the net transfers to his heirs while minimizing the reduction in his or her estate due to taxes and transfer cash. Exhibit 14.3 provides a list of common transfer objectives.

COMMON TRANSFER OBJECTIVES

EXHIBIT 14.3

1. Transfer property as desired and minimize estate and transfer taxes to maximize the assets received by heirs.
2. Avoid the probate process.
3. Use lifetime transfers – gifts.
4. Meet liquidity needs at death.
5. Plan for children.
6. Plan for the incapacity of the transferor.
7. Provide for the needs of the transferor's surviving spouse.
8. Fulfill the transferor's charitable intentions.

BASIC DOCUMENTS INCLUDED IN AN ESTATE PLAN

Effective estate planning usually requires the execution of some basic estate planning documents. These documents effectuate the transfer of property at the death of the testator, grant powers to others for both property and health care decisions, and direct doctors and hospitals on matters concerning the artificial sustenance of life. The basic documents that are used in estate planning include:

- wills,
- side letters of instruction,
- powers of attorney for property,
- durable powers of attorney for health care,
- living wills or advance medical directives, and
- do not resuscitate orders.

WILLS

A **will** is an essential part of any estate plan. A will is a legal document that gives the **testator** (will-maker) the opportunity to control the distribution of his property at death and thus avoid his state's intestacy laws (the distribution scheme provided by each state for those individuals that die without a valid will). A will may be amended or revoked by the testator at any time prior to his death provided that the testator is competent. In addition, the provisions of a will are not invoked until the death of the testator. Any assets that do not automatically transfer upon the testator's death under state contract laws, state property titling law, or state trust law (such as retirement benefits with a designated beneficiary, jointly owned property, and life insurance policies) will become part of the probate estate, which is normally distributed according to the will. The will is the voice of the decedent directing how probate assets should be administered and distributed through the probate process.

Types of Wills

In most states, the only requirements necessary to execute a valid will are:

1. the will must be in writing, and
2. the will must be signed at its logical end by the testator.

The three basic forms of wills include statutory, holographic, and nuncupative. While most wills are statutory wills (professionally drafted by an attorney), some states continue to recognize the other two types of wills.

- **Statutory wills** are drawn by an attorney, and comply with the statutes for wills of the domiciliary state. Statutory wills are generally witnessed and attested. Statutory wills must be typed or be in writing, be signed by the testator (generally in front of witnesses), and be signed by the witnesses. Typically, a statutory will includes a self-proving affidavit which aids in the institution of probate proceedings when the testator dies.
- **Holographic wills** are handwritten (not typed) by the testator and include the material provisions of a will. The holographic will must be dated and signed by the testator, but most states do not require a witness. Holographic wills are valid in most states.
- **Nuncupative wills** are oral, dying declarations made before a sufficient number of witnesses. In some states, nuncupative wills may only be effective to pass personal property, not real property, and the dollar amount transferred by this method may be limited. The use of nuncupative wills is restrictive and is not valid in most states. In states where such wills are permitted, the witnesses must generally submit an affidavit declaring the testator's final wishes.

SIDE INSTRUCTION LETTER

Another separate document from the will, the **side instruction letter**, or personal instruction letter, details the testator's wishes regarding the disposition of specific tangible possessions (such as household goods), as well as funeral and burial wishes. The side instruction letter exists separately from the will, to avoid cluttering the will with small details that may create conflicts among heirs and is not binding in the probate process. In many states, burial is required before probate can begin, and the side letter of instruction gives specific instructions to the heirs. This letter, which is given to the executor, may contain information regarding the location of important personal documents, safe deposit boxes, outstanding loans, and other personal and financial information that the executor will use to administer the decedent's estate. While the letter has no legal standing, the executor will generally carry out the wishes of the decedent.

Quick Quiz 14.1

Highlight the answer to these questions:

1. Estate planning is the process of accumulation, management, conservation, and transfer of wealth considering only the estate tax consequences.
   a. True
   b. False

2. An effective transfer occurs when a person's assets are transferred to the person or institution intended by that person.
   a. True
   b. False

False, True.

POWERS OF ATTORNEY AND POWERS OF APPOINTMENT

Power of Attorney

People frequently need a trusted person to make decisions or sign papers for them regarding their property or health. A **power of attorney** is a legal document that authorizes a trusted person to act on one's behalf. It grants a right to one person, the **attorney-in-fact** (sometimes called the power holder or agent), to act in the place of the other person, the **principal** (the grantor of the power). Generally, any person who is legally capable to act for himself may act as an attorney-in-fact for another. The principal must have reached the age of majority, defined in most states as 18 years old, and be legally competent in order to grant the power. All powers are revocable by the principal and all powers granted cease at the principal's death.

General Power of Attorney

The broadest power a person can give another is a general power of attorney. The person who is given the power of attorney will be able to act in the principal's place as though he is the principal. Essentially the general power of attorney gives the agent the power to do anything that the principal could do. The general power of attorney may be revoked by the principal by giving notice, usually with a revocation form, to the agent and is automatically revoked at the principal's death.

Limited Power of Attorney

A limited power of attorney, also referred to as a special power of attorney, gives the agent very specific, detailed powers. The power granted in a limited power of attorney may be extremely narrow, only authorizing the agent to act on a specific matter. For

Key Concepts

Underline/highlight the answers as you read:

1. What is a power of attorney?

2. Identify and discuss the parties to a power of attorney.

3. What is a durable power of attorney for health care and why are they used?

4. What is a living will and why are they used?

5. What is a DNR and why are they used?

example, if the principal were purchasing a new home and was unable to attend the actual closing because he was out of the country, he can give a power of attorney to someone else specifically authorizing them to sign his name at the act of sale. Other uses for a limited power of attorney include situations where a principal gives an agent the authority to act on his behalf to pay his bills, or handle a specific business transaction.

| EXHIBIT 14.4 | GRAPHICAL DEPICTION OF POWERS OF ATTORNEY |

Powers of Attorney

Special/Limited Powers		General Powers
Narrow Broad		
"Pay my Bills" "Anything I can do except…"		"Anything I can do without exception" Generally should only be given to spouse
Does not cause inclusion of assets under the power in the agent's gross estate		Causes inclusion of the assets that are under the power in the agent's gross estate in the event the agent dies before the principal

Power of Appointment

A power of appointment is sometimes included in a power of attorney. A **power of appointment** is a power to appoint the assets of one person to another and may be either general or limited.

General Power of Appointment

If the agent dies before the principal and is holding a general power of appointment over assets of the principal, the agent's gross estate will include the fair market value of the principal's assets over which the agent held the power of appointment regardless of whether the power has been invoked. Therefore, a general power of appointment should be granted sparingly and with forethought.

Limited Power of Appointment

Like a general power of appointment, a limited power of appointment is the power to affect the beneficial enjoyment of property. Unlike a general power of appointment, a limited power of appointment is limited in some way. One of the ways in which a power of appointment can be limited is by the application of an ascertainable standard. According to the Internal Revenue Code, a power is limited by such a standard if the extent of the holder's duty to exercise and not to exercise the power is reasonably measurable in terms of his needs for health, education, maintenance, or support (or any combination of them). If a power of appointment is limited by an ascertainable standard, then the property subject to the power will not be includible in the gross estate of the power holder. Furthermore, the use of an ascertainable standard allows the principal to give the power holder the ability to appoint assets to himself without creating a general power of appointment.

EXAMPLE 14.1	Jack gives Bonnie the power to appoint the $1,000,000 in his bank account to herself or her mother. Jack has given Bonnie a general power of appointment. If Bonnie dies while holding the power of appointment, the $1,000,000 bank account will be included in her gross estate.

EXAMPLE 14.2

Jack gives Bonnie the power to appoint the $1,000,000 in his bank account to herself or to her mother, but only for educational expenses. Even though Bonnie can appoint the assets to herself (which would usually create a general power of appointment), she has a limited power of appointment because she is limited by the fact that the assets can only be used for educational expenses. Therefore, if Bonnie dies while holding the power, the value of Jack's bank account will not be included in her gross estate.

GRAPHICAL DEPICTION OF POWERS OF APPOINTMENT

EXHIBIT 14.5

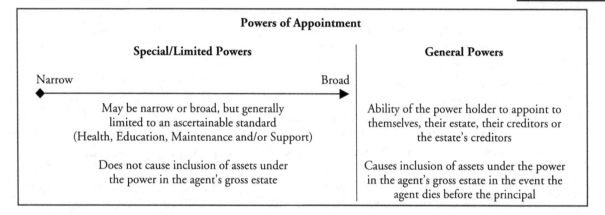

Powers of Appointment	
Special/Limited Powers	**General Powers**
Narrow ——————————————→ Broad	
May be narrow or broad, but generally limited to an ascertainable standard (Health, Education, Maintenance and/or Support)	Ability of the power holder to appoint to themselves, their estate, their creditors or the estate's creditors
Does not cause inclusion of assets under the power in the agent's gross estate	Causes inclusion of assets under the power in the agent's gross estate in the event the agent dies before the principal

POWER OF ATTORNEY VS. POWER OF APPOINTMENT

EXHIBIT 14.6

POWER OF ATTORNEY	POWER OF APPOINTMENT
• A stand alone document that allows an agent to act for the principal and may include the power to appoint assets	• A power, usually included in a trust or power of attorney, allowing the power holder to direct assets to another
• Power to act	• Power to transfer assets
• Ends at the death of the principal	• May survive the death of the grantor
• May be general or limited	• May be general or limited
• May be revoked at any time by the principal	• May be revoked by the principal during life or at death (via last will and testament)

DIRECTIVES REGARDING HEALTH CARE

Directives regarding health care are probably the most controversial and difficult documents to discuss with your client. Individuals tend to have strong feelings regarding their health care and the ability of others to make health care decisions for them. This section discusses some of the alternative documents available in most states.

Durable Power of Attorney for Health Care

A **durable power of attorney for health care**, also called a medical power of attorney or health care proxy, is a legal document that appoints an agent (someone with authority to act on behalf of another) to make health care decisions on behalf of a principal who is unable to make those decisions for him/herself. Unlike the living will, which states the person's wishes regarding the sustainment of life, the durable power of attorney for health care puts health care decision making in the hands of a third person.

The durable power of attorney for health care may provide direction in terminal and nonterminal situations, such as disclosure of medical records, blood transfusions, cardiac resuscitation, organ transplants, and selection of medical support staff, but generally does not provide the right to end life-sustaining treatment. (Note that in some states a power of attorney for health care may provide the right to withhold or end life-sustaining treatment.) The durable power of attorney for health care eliminates the necessity of petitioning a local court to appoint a guardian to make health care decisions for a person who is incapacitated or disabled.

Living Wills/Advance Medical Directives

A **living will**, also known as an **advance medical directive** or in some states, a Natural Death Declaration or Instruction Directive, is not a will at all, but rather a legal document expressing an individual's last wishes regarding sustainment of life under specific circumstances. The living will establishes the medical situations and circumstances in which the individual no longer desires life-sustaining treatment in the event he is no longer capable of making those decisions. The document only covers a narrow range of situations, and is usually limited to decisions concerning administering artificial life support treatments when there is no reasonable expectation of recovery from extreme physical or mental disability. Almost every state has legislation in place that disregards the living will if the patient is pregnant.

Quick Quiz 14.2

Highlight the answer to these questions:

1. A durable power of attorney for health care typically directs the termination of life-sustaining treatment.
   a. True
   b. False

2. A living will acts to transfer property during life.
   a. True
   b. False

False, False.

The purpose of the living will is to allow individuals who are terminally ill to die on their own terms, or as it has been coined, "die with dignity." Many states have adopted Natural Death Acts stating that the withholding or discontinuance of any extraordinary means of keeping a patient alive, or the withholding or discontinuance of artificial nutrition and hydration, shall not be considered the cause of death for any civil or criminal purpose, nor shall it be considered unprofessional conduct, thus allowing terminal individuals the right to choose the healthcare provided to them.

The living will is also used to avoid the expense of sustaining life artificially and thus to preserve assets for the decedent's heirs. The living will is prepared in advance of an illness to: (1) explicitly state the client's wishes, and (2) avoid the necessity for heirs to seek court approval for life-sustaining or termination decisions. The document, though authorized in all states, must meet the specific requirements of the individual's state statute. If the document is not drafted by a competent attorney, problems may arise with vagueness or ambiguities in drafting. Some states have developed a computerized registry of those who have filed living wills so if a person is alive solely because of life-sustaining treatments, the institution providing care can determine if the document exists, and thus comply with the wishes of the registrants. In addition, privately administered national registries have also increased in popularity in the wake of the highly publicized case of Terri Schiavo in 2005. Schiavo's case highlights the importance of having a living will regardless of age or current health.

Do Not Resuscitate Order (DNRs)

Individuals may also have a document called a "DNR" which stands for **Do Not Resuscitate**. These documents declare the principals wish to avoid having cardiopulmonary resuscitation (CPR) performed in the event their heart stops beating. This is not generally prepared as part of an overall estate plan unless the individual is already terminally ill. These types of orders are generally prepared once an individual has already been admitted to the hospital and is near death, and are commonly used by patients with advanced cancer or kidney damage, or patients suffering from significant ailments relating to old age.

DNRs are generally executed on a form provided by the state and may be filed with the patient's medical records. Some states also provide statewide registries allowing these documents to be placed on file for easy access. Some states provide medical bracelets to patients with DNRs that have been sent home to spend their remaining days. The bracelet notifies emergency personnel of the individual's wish to decline CPR.

It is crucial to understand that DNRs only apply to CPR and do not apply to any other medical treatment. DNRs are not sufficient to avoid other life sustaining treatment. As the application of DNRs vary by state, a thorough understanding of the individual state law is imperative when working with DNRs.

TYPES OF PROPERTY INTEREST

OWNERSHIP AND TRANSFER OF PROPERTY

In our legal system, all property interests are classified into one of three categories: (1) real property, (2) tangible personal property, or (3) intangible personal property. **Real property** (realty) includes land and anything permanently attached to the land (such as buildings, trees, and items permanently affixed to buildings, called fixtures). **Tangible personal property** consists of all property that is not realty (not affixed to the land and generally movable) and that has physical substance. **Intangible personal property** is property that is not real property and is without physical substance (such as stocks, bonds, patents, and copyrights). Some types of property require a state title as proof of ownership. Examples of titled property include real estate, automobiles (assuming the state has a motor vehicle title law), stocks, bonds, bank accounts, and retirement accounts. Other property, such as household goods, may not have a specific title. State law determines the forms of ownership interest available as well as the ways in which property interests can be transferred from one person to another during lifetime or at death.

Key Concepts

Underline/highlight the answers as you read:

1. Identify the three types of property and examples of each.

2. Identify the characteristics of fee simple ownership.

3. Identify the characteristics of tenancy in common ownership.

4. Identify the characteristics of joint tenancy with right of survivorship.

5. Identify the characteristics of tenancy by the entirety.

6. Identify the characteristics of community property.

SOLE OWNERSHIP - FEE SIMPLE

Fee simple ownership is the complete ownership of property by one individual who possesses all ownership rights associated with the property, including the right to use, sell, gift, alienate, convey, or bequeath the property. The key characteristic of fee simple ownership is that the owner has the unfettered right to transfer his ownership interest in the property during lifetime (gift, sale) or at death (will). Fee simple ownership is the most common way to own property interests today.

When someone owns property in fee simple, he can mortgage that property and use it in any way he desires. Of course, jurisdictional restrictions may place reasonable limits on the use of property. For example, if someone owns land in the middle of an urban area, certain zoning laws may prohibit the owner from using the land to hunt, conduct outdoor concerts, or engage in other types of activities that could endanger others or interfere with the rights other people have to the quiet enjoyment of their own property.

EXHIBIT 14.7	FEE SIMPLE OWNERSHIP SUMMARY
Number of Owners	Only 1
Right to Transfer	Freely
Automatic Survivorship Feature	No, transfers at death via will or intestacy laws
Included in the Gross Estate	Yes, 100%
Included in the Probate Estate	Yes, 100%

Quick Quiz 14.3

Highlight the answer to these questions:

1. Examples of real property are land, automobiles, and stocks.
   a. True
   b. False

2. In a fee simple ownership, the joint tenants must agree to sever.
   a. True
   b. False

3. Fee simple property owned by a decedent is included in the owner's gross estate for federal estate tax purposes.
   a. True
   b. False

False, False, True.

TENANCY IN COMMON (TIC)

Tenancy in common is an interest in property held by two or more related or unrelated persons. Each owner is referred to as a tenant in common. Tenancy in common is the most common type of joint ownership between nonspouses. Each person holds an undivided, but not necessarily equal, interest in the entire property. Each co-owner does not own a designated portion of the property, instead he owns an interest in the entire property. For example, if Jim and Bill own a two story home together, Jim does not own the top floor and Bill does not own the bottom floor. Instead, they each own a percentage of the entire house, and both are entitled to use the entire property.

TENANCY IN COMMON OWNERSHIP SUMMARY

EXHIBIT 14.8

Number of Owners	2 or more
Right to Transfer	Freely without the consent of other co-tenants
Automatic Survivorship Feature	No, transfers at death via will or intestacy laws
Included in the Gross Estate	Usually the FMV of ownership percentage
Included in the Probate Estate	Yes, fair market value of interest
Partitionable	Yes, with or without consent of joint owner

JOINT TENANCY WITH RIGHT OF SURVIVORSHIP (JTWROS)

Joint tenancy is an interest in property held by two or more related or unrelated persons called joint tenants. Each person holds an undivided, equal interest in the whole property. Each joint tenant shares equally in the income and expenses of the property in proportion to his interest.

A right of survivorship is normally implied with this form of ownership, and at the death of the first joint tenant, the decedent's interest transfers to the other joint tenants outside of the probate process according to state titling law. Because of this right of survivorship, joint tenancy is often called joint tenancy with right of survivorship (JTWROS).

EXHIBIT 14.9

JOINT TENANCY WITH RIGHT OF SURVIVORSHIP OWNERSHIP SUMMARY

Number of Owners	2 or more
Right to Transfer	Freely without consent
Automatic Survivorship Feature	Yes, transfers at death to other owners
Included in the Gross Estate	Yes, FMV times the % contributed
Included in the Probate Estate	No
Partitionable	Yes, with or without consent of joint owner

TENANCY BY THE ENTIRETY (TE)

Tenancy by the entirety is very similar to joint tenancy between a husband and wife. To understand this form of ownership it is important to remember the following four key components:

1. tenancy by the entirety applies to joint ownership only between married couples,
2. neither tenant is able to sever their interest without the consent of the other tenant (spouse),
3. property ownership interest is automatically transferred to the surviving spouse upon death, and
4. it may involve the ownership interest of either real or personal property.

Quick Quiz 14.4

Highlight the answer to these questions:

1. Tenancy by the entirety is a tenancy in common that can only occur between a husband and wife.
   a. True
   b. False

2. Property owned as tenancy by the entirety does not pass through probate because of the automatic right of survivorship.
   a. True
   b. False

False, True.

In most respects, tenancy by the entirety is simply a JTWROS that can only occur between a husband and wife. Tenancy by the entirety exists throughout the length of the marriage and terminates upon divorce or death. Upon divorce, the tenancy by the entirety form of ownership ceases to exist, thus transforming the ownership interests of both parties to some form of joint ownership, usually tenants in common.

In most states, neither tenant (spouse) is able to sever their interest in property titled tenancy by the entirety without the consent of the other tenant (spouse). If either husband or wife wishes to transfer their share of interest in the property to a third party (through sale or gift), both parties must join (or consent) in a mutual transfer of the property. This stipulation helps to prevent any termination of the other spouse's right of survivorship by transfer of property to a third party. In such cases, the interest in the property between the remaining tenant (spouse) and the new third party owner becomes a joint tenancy or tenancy in common. Spouses may choose to convert their tenancy by the entirety ownership into a tenancy in common or a joint tenancy. The form of property ownership is simply changed without triggering any gift tax consequences.

EXHIBIT 14.10

Number of Owners	2 - spouses only
Right to Transfer	Need consent of other spouse
Automatic Survivorship Feature	Yes, transfers at death to other spouse
Included in the Gross Estate	Yes, always 50% of FMV
Included in the Probate Estate	No
Partitionable	Not without consent of spouse / joint owner

COMMUNITY PROPERTY AND SEPARATE PROPERTY IN COMMUNITY REGIMES

Community property is a civil law originating statutory regime under which married individuals own an equal undivided interest in all property accumulated during their marriage. During marriage, the income of each spouse is considered community property. Property acquired before the marriage and property received by gift or inheritance during the marriage retains its status as separate property. However, if any separate property is commingled with community property, it is often assumed to be community property. The states following the community property regime are Arizona, California, Idaho, Louisiana, Nevada, New Mexico, Texas, Washington, and Wisconsin. In addition, Alaska allows residents and nonresidents to enter into community property agreements permitting in-state property to be treated as community property. Community property regimes may vary slightly from state to state; thus, a thorough understanding of a client's state laws is needed for proper planning.

Key Concepts

Underline/highlight the answers as you read:

1. Define the probate process.

2. List the elements of a gift.

3. How much can an individual transfer, gift tax-free, each year?

4. What is the lifetime gift tax applicable exclusion amount?

EXHIBIT 14.11   COMMUNITY-PROPERTY STATES

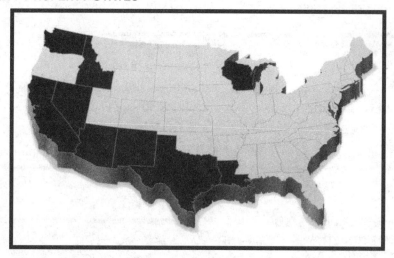

Community property does not usually have an automatic right of survivorship feature although some states, including Texas and California, have a survivorship option. When the first spouse dies, one half of the value of the property will pass through the probate process for retitling per the direction of the decedent's will or the state intestacy law. Each spouse's one-half interest will also be included in their own federal gross estate.

THE PROBATE PROCESS DEFINED

When a person dies, there are many things the survivors must do. Relatives and friends must be notified, funeral and burial arrangements must be made, and the survivors must begin to rebuild their lives without the decedent. After facing the emotional distress that naturally occurs upon the death of a loved one, the survivors must evaluate their financial security and the process of transferring the decedent's assets from the decedent's estate to the heirs. Surviving heirs need a method to obtain clear legal title to property inherited from the decedent. The **probate process** is the legal process through which the decedent's assets that are not automatically transferred to their heirs by contract or law are retitled in the name of the heirs. The probate process can be defined as the legal proceeding that serves to prove the validity of an existing will, supervise the orderly distribution of a decedent's assets to the heirs, assure heirs that they receive clear title, and protect creditors by insuring that valid debts of the estate are paid prior to distribution of assets to heirs.

TESTATE VS. INTESTATE SUCCESSION

The preparation of the will is often considered the first step in an overall estate plan, since it expresses some or all of the decedent's transfer wishes regarding property. In theory, every person who dies has an estate plan. If the decedent did not establish his own estate plan by executing a will, the state in which he is domiciled has created one for him under the state intestacy laws. The state intestacy laws specify to whom assets will be transferred for a person who does not validly transfer assets by will, contract law, state titling law, or trust law.

A person who dies with a valid will is said to die testate, whereas a person who dies without a valid will is said to die intestate. A person named in a will to receive property is referred to as a legatee, while a person who receives property under the state intestacy laws is called an heir. In addition, the term devisee is used to refer to a person who inherits real property under the will. Historically, the term heir was reserved only for those individuals who received property under the intestacy laws, but the term is now used more loosely and may refer to any individual who inherits property from the decedent, even under a will. A planner should understand these distinctions since there are legal differences in some states, but realize that clients and non professionals may not use the terminology appropriately in practice.

ADVANTAGES OF PROBATE

Transferring assets through the probate process has several advantages over transferring assets outside of probate. The central advantage to the probate process is the protection of the individuals involved in the probate process. The advantaged parties include the decedent, the decedent's legatees and creditors. The following is a discussion of the more common advantages of the probate process.

ADVANTAGES OF PROBATE (SUMMARY)

EXHIBIT 14.12

1.	Implements disposition objectives of testator.
2.	Provides for an orderly administration of assets.
3.	Provides clean title to heirs or legatees.
4.	Increases the chance that parties of interest have notice of proceedings and, therefore, a right to be heard.
5.	Protects creditors by insuring that debts of the decedent are paid.

DISADVANTAGES OF THE PROBATE PROCESS

The probate process also has certain disadvantages. While the advantages of probate center around protecting individuals, the disadvantages center around the losses individuals may face. The losses include time (delays), money (costs), and privacy (publicity).

DISADVANTAGES OF PROBATE (SUMMARY)

EXHIBIT 14.13

1.	Can be complex and excruciatingly slow - Delays
2.	Can result in substantial monetary costs - Costs
3.	The process is open to public scrutiny - Publicity

PROPERTY PASSING THROUGH PROBATE

Property passing through probate includes property that can be disposed of by a will, such as fee simple property, the decedent's share of property held as tenancy in common, the decedent's share of community property.

PROPERTY PASSING OUTSIDE OF THE PROBATE PROCESS

Property that passes outside of the probate process includes property that passes by state contract law, state property titling law, and state trust law. All of these transfers reduce the probate estate and therefore reduce probate transaction costs, reduce the time it takes for property to pass through probate, and may improve liquidity for the named heirs and legatees.

EXHIBIT 14.14 **COMMON DUTIES OF EXECUTOR AND/OR ADMINISTRATOR**

When the Decedent Dies Testate (with a will)	When the Decedent Dies Intestate (without a will)
The Executor: • Locates and proves the will. • Locates witnesses to the will. • Receives letters testamentary from court.	The Administrator: • Petitions court for his or her own appointment. • Receives letters of administration. • Posts the required bond.
Duties of the Executor or Administrator	
• Locates and assembles all of the decedent's property. • Safeguards, manages, and invests property. • Advertises in legal newspapers that the person has died and that creditors and other interested parties are on notice of the death and opening of probate. • Locates and communicates with potential beneficiaries of the decedent. • Pays the expenses of the decedent. • Pays the debts of the decedent. • Files both federal and state income, fiduciary, gift tax, and estate tax returns (such as Forms 1040, 1041, 709, and 706 for federal tax purposes) and makes any required tax payments. • Distributes remaining assets to beneficiaries according to the will or to the laws of intestacy. • Closes the estate formally or informally.	

TRUST PROPERTY

Trusts are used in estate planning to provide for the management of assets and flexibility in the operation of the plan. Most trusts, other than charitable trusts, provide great flexibility by allowing the trustee to make decisions based on criteria set forth in the trust document by the grantor. This flexibility can be particularly important when the trust arrangement will last for an extended period of time.

The basic structure of a trust is depicted by the following diagram:

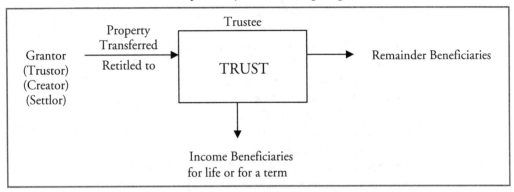

A **trust** is a structure that vests legal title to assets in one party, the trustee, who manages those assets for the benefit of others, the beneficiaries of the trust. The beneficiaries hold the beneficial, or equitable, interest in the trust. By dividing the ownership rights into two parts (legal and equitable), a trust can be a useful tool in managing both the property and the tax consequences attached to the transfer of property.

To form a trust, a grantor of a trust transfers (retitles) money or other property to the trustee. The money or property transferred is referred to as the trust principal, corpus, res, or fund. The trust principal will be managed by the trustee to accomplish the grantor's objectives as expressed in the detailed provisions of the trust document.

PARTIES

The three parties to a trust agreement are the grantor, the trustee, and the beneficiaries. The **grantor** is the person who creates and initially funds the trust. The **trustee** is the individual or entity responsible for managing the trust assets and carrying out the directions of the grantor that are formally expressed in the trust instrument. The **beneficiary** is the person (or persons) who holds the beneficial title to the trust assets. While the beneficiary's name does not appear on the deed to the trust assets, the trustee must manage the assets in the best interests of the beneficiary and is upheld to a fiduciary standard.

Key Concepts

Underline/highlight the answers as you read:

1. Identify the parties to a trust.

2. Identify at least three reasons to use a trust.

WHY USE A TRUST?

Management

In addition to using a trust to avoid probate, a principal reason for establishing a trust is to provide for the management of the trust property. Not everyone is adept at managing assets. A person not experienced in handling wealth may squander it or invest imprudently. A trust can be used to provide professional management of assets for individuals who are not suited, by training or experience, to manage assets for themselves.

EXAMPLE 14.3

Charlotte thinks of herself as the world's foremost expert in the fields of financial planning and money management. Her husband and children have relied on her to manage all of the family finances. Instead of leaving her property outright to her family when she dies, Charlotte can transfer the property into a trust, name professional money managers as trustees, and they will manage the money for her husband and children based on the investment guidelines intended in the trust documents.

Creditor Protection

When asked, most individuals would say they would rather receive an outright transfer of money than a transfer in trust. This statement is often based on the belief that with an outright transfer, they will have complete control over the assets and can use the assets in a way that will maximize their utility. If, however, an outright transfer of assets is made, creditors of the recipient (judgment creditors or otherwise) will have access to those funds to satisfy outstanding obligations.

If property is placed in a trust with appropriate spendthrift protection provisions instead of being transferred outright, the creditors of the beneficiary will not be able to access the funds in the trust to satisfy outstanding creditor claims. A spendthrift clause, coupled with a provision that allows the trustee to make distributions solely on a discretionary basis, is a very strong and effective asset protection tool. The

Quick Quiz 14.5

Highlight the answer to these questions:

1. The grantor is the individual who contributes property to a trust.
   a. True
   b. False

2. A trust cannot provide for creditor protection.
   a. True
   b. False

3. Including a spendthrift clause in a trust allows a trustee to use trust assets for administration expenses.
   a. True
   b. False

True, False, False.

spendthrift clause simply states that the beneficiary may not anticipate distributions from the trust, and may not assign, pledge, hypothecate, or otherwise promise to give distributions from the trust to anyone and, if such a promise is made, it is void and may not be enforced against the trust. Most states enforce spendthrift clauses, since the property in trust never belonged to the beneficiary and the beneficiary cannot be sure that he will ever receive discretionary distributions from the trustee. In some states, claims for spousal or child support can be obtained from a trust despite the presence of a spendthrift clause.

EXAMPLE 14.4

Samantha, a registered nurse, always wanted her children to enter the medical profession. None of her children became physicians, but her grandson, Kurt, decided to go to medical school. Understanding the malpractice dilemma faced by physicians, Samantha decided she wanted to protect any property that would pass during her lifetime, or at her death, to Kurt from Kurt's creditors. She created a trust that named Kurt as the discretionary income beneficiary for life and upon Kurt's death, would distribute the trust corpus to Kurt's children in equal shares, per stirpes. The trust included a spendthrift clause. If a malpractice claim is filed against Kurt, the assets in the trust will not be available to satisfy those claims. If the trust purchases assets for Kurt's use instead of making distributions to Kurt, those assets will also be protected. Note that if Samantha had not used a trust, any assets that she transferred to Kurt directly would be subject to malpractice claims.

FEDERAL ESTATE AND GIFT TAXES

The federal government uses a linked set of taxes on estates, gifts, and generation-skipping transfers to tax transfers of wealth from one generation to the next and to limit the extent to which wealth can be given away during life to avoid taxation at death. Federal taxes on transfers of wealth at death have been enacted in various forms since 1797, initially to raise revenue during crisis or war, and have been modified periodically over time.[1] The United States has collected revenues from the current form of the tax, an estate tax, since 1916. A gift tax, first introduced in 1924, prevents wealthy individuals from avoiding the estate tax by transferring wealth while they are alive.

Federal transfer taxes have historically made up a relatively small share of total federal revenues, accounting for one percent to two percent of total revenues in most of the past 60 years. The Congressional Budget Office (CBO) projects that, under current law, federal revenues from estate and gift taxes will be $420 billion, or 1.2 percent of total revenues, over the 2010–2019 period.

THE GIFT TAX SYSTEM

HISTORICAL BACKGROUND AND PURPOSE

The **gift tax** is an excise tax on the right to transfer assets gratuitously to another person during life. Like the federal estate tax, the gift tax exists as a method of raising revenue for the federal government and functions as a method of social reallocation of wealth by taxing wealth transferred from one generation to subsequent generations. The gift tax is paid from

---

1. Congressional Budget Office December 18, 2009 Economic and Budget Issue Brief.

the taxpayer's wealth to the federal government and thus is reallocated to other members of society through social programs and other expenditures of the federal government.

INTRODUCTION TO GIFTS

While the gift tax system is replete with rules, exceptions, and exemptions, the overall scheme of gift taxation can be understood by asking four basic questions:
1. Disregarding all other factors, is the transfer a taxable gift?
2. Is the gift nontaxable because of an available exemption, exclusion, or due to legislative grace?
3. If the gift is taxable, what is the tax due and how is it reported?
4. Is the gift appropriate considering the objectives and goals of donor and donee?

CHARACTERISTICS OF A GIFT

The first step in the gift tax system is to determine if a transfer is a gift. This section covers the elements and types of gifts.

Parties

There are two parties involved in a gift transfer. The **donor** is the person who makes the gift. The **donee** is the person who receives the gift.

Definition of a Gift

A **gift** is a voluntary transfer, for less than full consideration, of property from one person (a donor) to another person or entity (a donee).

Elements of a Gift

In general, the elements of a gift are:
1. The donor must have the intent to make a voluntary transfer.
2. The donor must be competent to make the gift.
3. The donee must be capable of receiving the gift.
4. The donee must take delivery.
5. The donor must actually part with dominion and control over the gifted property.

VALUATION OF A GIFT

The value of a gift for gift tax purposes is equal to the fair market value of the gifted property on the date of the gift. For real estate and closely-held businesses, an appraisal is usually necessary to determine the fair market value of the property. Publicly-traded securities are valued at the average of the high and low trading price for the day.

EXCLUSIONS AND EXEMPTIONS

Once a transfer is determined to be a gift, the donor should determine whether an exclusion or exemption applies making the transfer a nontaxable transfer.

The Annual Exclusion

All individuals may gift transfer-tax-free, up to $14,000 for 2013 ($13,000 for 2012) per donee per year to a related or unrelated party, under an exemption known as the **annual exclusion**. The annual exclusion is an effective wealth transfer tool that can be used to reduce a person's taxable estate over several or many years. It can be used to transfer many types of property, including interests in real property, trusts, and family limited partnerships.

There is a special annual exclusion for noncitizen spouses equal to $143,000 (as indexed) for 2013. In addition to the annual exclusion, each person has a $5,120,000 lifetime applicable gift tax exclusion (2012). The $5,120,000 exclusion can be used to transfer wealth during life or upon death.[2] Transfers during life that are taxable gifts are reported to the IRS on Form 709.

ESTATE TAX

When a citizen of the United States dies, his estate may be subject to the estate tax if it is sizable enough. As mentioned above, the lifetime exemption is currently $5,120,000 (2012). Therefore, an individual is permitted to transfer up to $5,120,000 during life and death without incurring transfer tax. Transfers above the $5,120,000 level will incur a transfer tax, whether during life or at death.

The estate tax is imposed when the sum of the decedent's taxable estate and lifetime gifts exceeds the $5,120,000 level. The decedent's taxable estate is the difference between the gross estate (all property owned by the decedent at death) and various deductions. Lifetime gifts are added to the taxable estate in the determination of the estate tax.

The estate tax applies to both citizens and residents of the United States and to nonresidents of the United States. For U.S. citizens and residents, estate tax is imposed on worldwide assets. Non-U.S. citizens and non-U.S. residents only pay estate tax on assets located within the United States.

Generation skipping transfer tax (GSTT) is an additional transfer tax that is imposed on transfers that skip a generation. The purpose of this tax is to prevent a transfer from the first generation to the third generation allowing for transfer tax to be avoided at the second generation.

As with gift tax and estate tax, there is a lifetime GST exemption of $5,120,000 (2012) that allows a taxpayer to transfer up to $5,120,000 to a third or fourth generation person without incurring the additional transfer tax. In addition, the annual exclusion also applies to generation skipping transfers. Therefore, a gifting strategy can be implemented to transfer wealth to "skip persons" using the annual exclusion and thereby avoiding both gift tax and GST tax.

A "skip person" is either a natural person assigned to a generation that is two or more generations below the generation assignment of the transferor, or a trust, if all the interests in the trust are held by skip persons.[3]

2.At the time this textbook went to print, it was uncertain what the 2013 lifetime exemptions would be for estates, gifts, and generation lifetime skipping transfer taxes.
3.IRC Section 2613.

GSTT is imposed at a flat rate equal to the highest federal estate tax rate, currently 35% and is added to the value of a gift in determining the gift tax calculation.

EXAMPLE 14.5

Martin wants to transfer $5,120,000 in 2012 to Ashley, who is Martin's great granddaughter. Martin has already used his lifetime GST exemption and already transferred the annual exclusion amount to Ashley earlier in the year, Martin would have to pay $4,211,200 calculated as follows:

GST tax = $5,120,000 x 0.35% = $1,792,000

Gift tax = $6,912,000 x 0.35% = $2,419,200 (GSTT adds to the gift. Martin is assumed to be at the top rate for gift tax.)

Total transfer tax = $4,211,200 (GST tax plus gift tax)

Properly leveraging one's GST lifetime exemption can result is large transfers to lower generations while avoiding a significant amount of transfer tax.

ESTATE PLANNING FOR FINANCIAL PLANNERS

2012, 2013 Update for Estate, Gifts, and GST Tax[4]

- There was no estate or generation skipping transfer (GST) tax for 2010. There is an $5,120,000 exemption for 2012.
- The gift, estate, and GST tax rate is 35%.
- The annual gift tax exclusion is $14,000 per donee, per donor for 2013 ($13,000 for 2012).
- The lifetime gift exemption is $5,120,000 for 2012.
- The credit equivalency for the gift exemption is $1,772,800 for 2012 (see Exhibit 14.15).

4.At the time this textbook went to print, it was uncertain what the 2013 lifetime exemptions would be for estates, gifts, and generation lifetime skipping transfer taxes.

CREDIT EQUIVALENCY AMOUNTS

EXHIBIT 14.15

If the amount with respect to which the tentative tax to be computed is	The tentative gift tax is:
Not over $10,000	18% of such amount
Over $10,000 but not over $20,000	$1,800, plus 20% of the excess over $10,000
Over $20,000 but not over $40,000	$3,800, plus 22% of the excess over $20,000
Over $40,000 but not over $60,000	$8,200 plus 24% of the excess over $40,000
Over $60,000 but not over $80,000	$13,000 plus 26% of the excess over $60,000
Over $80,000 but not over $100,000	$18,200 plus 28% of the excess over $80,000
Over $100,000 but not over $150,000	$23,800 plus 30% of the excess over $100,000
Over $150,000 but not over $250,000	$38,800 plus 32% of the excess over $150,000
Over $250,000 but not over $500,000	$70,800 plus 34% of the excess over $250,000
Over $500,000	$155,800 plus 35% of the excess over $500,000

Key Terms

Annual Exclusion - An exclusion from gift taxes for present interest transfers less than or equal to $14,000 per year per donee.

Attorney-in-Fact - Agent or power holder of a power of attorney.

Beneficiary - The person(s) entitled to receive the death benefit of a life insurance policy at the insured's death. Also, the person(s) who hold(s) the beneficial title to a trust's assets.

Community Property - A regime in which married individuals own an equal undivided interest in all of the property accumulated, utilizing either spouse's earnings, during the marriage.

Donee - The person who receives the gift.

Donor - The person who gives the gift.

Do Not Resuscitate (DNR) - Documents declare the principals wish to avoid having cardiopulmonary resuscitation (CPR) performed in the event their heart stops beating.

Durable Power of Attorney for Health Care - A written document enabling one individual, the principal, to designate another person(s) to act as his "attorney-in-fact." A durable power of attorney survives the incapacity and/or disability of the principal.

Effective Transfer - A transfer of a person's assets to the person or charitable institution intended by that person.

Efficient Transfer - A transfer in which costs of the transfer are minimized consistent with the greatest assurance of effectiveness.

Estate Planning - The process of accumulation, management, conservation, and transfer of wealth considering legal, tax, and personal objectives.

Estate Tax - Imposed on the decedent's right to transfer property to his heirs when a citizen or resident of the United States dies.

Fee Simple Ownership - The complete individual ownership of property with all the rights associated with outright ownership.

Gift - A voluntary transfer, without full consideration, of property from one person (a donor) to another person (a donee) or entity.

Gift Tax - An excise tax on the right to transfer assets gratuitously to another person during life.

Key Terms

Grantor - The person who creates and initially funds a trust. The grantor is also known as the settlor or creator.

Heir - A person who inherits under state law.

Holographic Will - Handwritten will.

Intangible Personal Property - Property that cannot truly be touched such as stocks, bonds, patents, and copyrights.

Joint Tenancy (with right of survivorship) - An undivided interest in property held by two or more related or unrelated persons, generally includes a right of survivorship.

Legatee - A person named in a will.

Living Will / Advance Medical Directive - Legal document expressing an individual's last wishes regarding life sustaining treatment.

Nuncupative Will - Oral will consisting of dying declarations.

Power of Appointment - A power to appoint the assets of one person to another and may be either general or limited.

Power of Attorney - Legal document that authorizes an agent to act on a principal's behalf.

Principal - The grantor giver of a power of attorney.

Probate Process - The legal proceeding that serves to prove the validity of existing wills, supervise the orderly distribution of decedent's assets to the heirs, and protect creditors by insuring that valid debts of the estate are paid.

Real Property - Property that is land and buildings attached to the land.

Side Instruction Letter - Also known as a personal instruction letter, details the testator's wishes regarding the disposition of tangible possessions (household goods), the disposition of the decedent's body, and funeral arrangements. A side instruction letter is not legally binding, but generally followed.

Spendthrift Clause - A clause in a trust document which does not allow the beneficiary to anticipate distributions from the trust, assign, pledge, hypothecate, or otherwise promise to give distributions from the trust to anyone. If such a promise is made, it is void and may not be enforced against the trust.

Statutory Will - A will meeting state statutes generally drawn up by an attorney and signed in the presence of witnesses.

Key Terms

Tangible Personal Property - Property that is not realty and may be touched.

Tenancy by the Entirety - A JTWROS that can only occur between a husband and wife.

Tenancy in Common - An undivided interest in property held by two or more related or unrelated persons.

Testator - Writer of a will.

Trust - A structure that vests legal title (the legal interest) to assets in one party, the trustee, who manages those assets for the benefit of the beneficiaries (who hold the equitable title) of the trust.

Trustee - The individual or entity responsible for managing the trust assets and carrying out the directions of the grantor that are formally expressed in the trust instrument.

Will - A legal document that provides the testator, or will maker, the opportunity to control the distribution of property, appoint an executor and avoid the state's intestacy law distribution scheme.

DISCUSSION QUESTIONS

1. Define estate planning.

2. What is an effective transfer?

3. What is an efficient transfer?

4. List three common goals of estate planning.

5. Discuss some of the risks associated with failing to plan for estate transfer.

6. List the six basic steps of the estate planning process.

7. What is usually the most important client objective?

8. List the basic documents used in estate planning.

9. Briefly define the types of wills.

10. What is a living will?

11. What is a power of attorney?

12. Identify and discuss the parties to a power of attorney.

13. List and define the three major types of property.

14. List at least three types of property ownership.

15. Define fee simple property ownership.

16. Define tenancy in common.

17. Define joint tenancy.

18. Define right of survivorship.

19. Can a joint tenancy by partitioned?

20. Define community property.

21. Which states recognize community property?

22. Describe the probate process.

23. Describe at least three advantages and three disadvantages of the probate process.

24. Why are trusts used in estate planning?

25. What is a trust?

26. List the common parties of a trust.

27. What is a spendthrift clause and why is it included in a trust?

28. List the elements of a gift.

1. Which of the following is included in the definition of estate planning?

    1. Asset management.
    2. Accumulation of wealth.
    3. Asset preservation.
        a. 1 only.
        b. 1 and 2.
        c. 2 and 3.
        d. 1, 2, and 3.

2. Which of the following statements is the best definition of estate planning?

    a. Estate planning is the process of accumulation, management, conservation, and transfer of wealth considering legal, tax, and personal objectives.
    b. Estate planning is the management, conservation, and transfer of wealth considering estate tax transfer costs.
    c. Estate planning is the management, conservation, and transfer of wealth considering legal, tax, and personal objectives.
    d. Estate planning is the process of accumulation, management, conservation, and transfer of wealth considering estate and generation-skipping transfer tax costs.

3. Which of the following does not need estate planning?

    a. Tom, age 30, married with two minor children, and a net worth of $375,000.
    b. Carly, age 35, never been married, one severely disabled son.
    c. Michelle, age 45, single, has a net worth of $450,000 and two dogs.
    d. All of the above need estate planning.

4. The first step in the estate planning process includes:

    a. Meeting with the client and discussing the client's assets, family structure, and desires.
    b. Prioritizing the client's goals.
    c. Developing a formal written estate plan.
    d. Identifying key areas of concern in relation to the client's plan - taxes, cash on hand, etc.

5. Tyrone does not want to write a will. It upsets him to contemplate his own death and he simply desires to avoid the estate planning process. All of the following are risks Tyrone's estate may face due to Tyrone's inaction, except:

    a. Tyrone's property transfers contrary to his wishes.

    b. Tyrone's estate may face liquidity problems.

    c. Tyrone's estate faces increased estate administration fees.

    d. Tyrone's estate faces increased debt payments for outstanding debts at death.

6. Which the following is a risk of failing to plan for the estate?

    1. Property transfers contrary to the client's wishes.

    2. The client's family may not be provided for financially.

    3. The estate suffers liquidity problems at the client's death.

    4. The estate may bear higher transfer costs.

        a. 2 only.

        b. 2 and 3.

        c. 1, 3, and 4.

        d. 1, 2, 3, and 4.

7. Which of the following documents appoints a surrogate decision-maker for health care?

    a. Durable power of attorney for health care.

    b. General power of appointment.

    c. Life insurance beneficiary designation.

    d. All of the above.

8. Which type of will is handwritten and does not generally require a witness?

    a. Holographic.

    b. Oral.

    c. Nuncupative.

    d. Statutory.

9. Which type of will complies with the statutes of the domiciliary state and is drawn by an attorney?

    a. Holographic.

    b. Oral.

    c. Nuncupative.

    d. Statutory.

10. While he was in the hospital, Emile told his wife that if he died he wanted to give his fishing tackle to his son, Joseph; his golf equipment to his son, Joshua; his truck to his daughter, Abigail; and everything else to her (his wife). Emile died the next day without writing anything that he told his wife, but a nurse and another patient were in the room and heard his declarations. What type of will does Emile have, if any?

    a. Holographic.

    b. Nuncupative.

    c. Statutory.

    d. Emile does not have a will.

11. Maxine is terminally ill. Her doctors gave her twenty-four months to live thirty-six months ago. Maxine has decided that she does not want to be placed on life support. Which document will direct Maxine's doctors to refrain from putting her on life support?

    a. Living will.

    b. Power of attorney.

    c. Durable power of attorney.

    d. General power of appointment.

12. Donald agreed to sell his house to his brother, but could not attend the closing date of the sale (act of sale). Of the following options, which would allow Donald's mother to attend the closing and sign the necessary documents on Donald's behalf?

    a. Living will.

    b. Advanced real estate directive.

    c. Power of attorney.

    d. Side instruction letter.

13. Twenty-two years ago, Kyle and John began dating, and 19 years ago, they began living together. Last year, Kyle inherited over $9,000,000 from his grandfather. He wants to ensure that if he dies first, John will be taken care of for the rest of his life. Despite your insistence, Kyle does not have a will, and you have advised him previously that state intestacy laws do not protect same-sex partners. Which of the following asset ownership options would fulfill Kyle's goal of transferring assets to John at his death?

    a. Community property.

    b. Tenancy in common with each other.

    c. Joint tenancy with rights of survivorship.

    d. Tenancy by the entirety.

14. Steve has been married to Louise for six years. They are about to buy their first home and have come to you with some questions that they have regarding titling of the home. In your explanation of the different property ownership arrangements, which of the following titling structures can only be entered into by spouses?

    a. Tenancy by the entirety.

    b. Tenancy in common.

    c. Joint tenancy with rights of survivorship.

    d. Fee simple.

15. Of the following types of ownership, which is available for married couples?

    1. Tenancy by the entirety.

    2. Tenancy in common.

    3. JTWROS.

    4. Tenants by marriage.

        a. 1 only.

        b. 1 and 3.

        c. 1, 2, and 3.

        d. 1, 2, 3, and 4.

16. If Priscilla died with each of the following property interests, which will be excluded from her probate estate?

    a. Property owned as community property.

    b. Property held tenancy in common.

    c. Death proceeds of life insurance payable to a living stranger.

    d. Property owned fee simple.

17. Which of the following is a disadvantage of the probate process?

    a. The decedent's heirs and/or legatees are given clear title to property.

    b. The probate process requires several court filings.

    c. The probate process provides for an orderly distribution of the decedent's assets.

    d. The decedent's creditors are protected.

18. Which of the following is considered an advantage of the probate process?

    a. The probate process creates delays.

    b. The probate process is costly.

    c. Heirs receive property with clear title.

    d. Information that is filed with the court becomes public information.

19. Which of the following is not a party to a trust?

    a. Trustee.

    b. Income beneficiary.

    c. Grantor.

    d. Principal.

20. A spendthrift clause:

    a. Requires the fiduciary of a trust to make small distributions.

    b. Protects the trust assets from the claims of the beneficiary's creditors.

    c. Eliminates the problems associated with multiple beneficiaries.

    d. Prevents the lapse of a general power of appointment and its subsequent estate tax consequences.

21. This estate planning tool will cause assets to be included in non-grantor holder's gross estate:

    a. An intervivos trust.

    b. A special power of attorney.

    c. The exercise of a nuncupative will.

    d. A general power of appointment that is unexercised.

22. Which of the following tasks are the primary responsibilities of the personal representative?

    1. Inventory the estate.

    2. File income tax returns for all beneficiaries.

    3. Contest payment of all debts of the estate.

    4. Probate the will.

        a. 1 and 4.

        b. 2 and 3.

        c. 2 and 4.

        d. 1, 3 and 4.

        e. 1, 2, 3 and 4.

23. Which of the following does NOT relate to a will?

    a. A Codicil.

    b. A Devisee.

    c. A Legatee.

    d. An in terrorem clause.

    e. All of the above.

24. Claude decides to prepare his will, but does not want to seek the help of an attorney. Claude handwrites, signs and dates all of the provisions of the will but does not have it witnessed by anyone. What type of will does Claude have, if any?

    a. None.

    b. Nuncupative.

    c. Self Prepared.

    d. Holographic.

25. A person or entity entitled to act on behalf of another is known as:

    a. A principal.

    b. A curator.

    c. An attorney at law.

    d. An attorney in fact.

26. The unrestricted ability to ultimately name beneficiaries of income and corpus of a trust is known as:

    a. A HEMS power.

    b. A special power of attorney.

    c. A crummey power.

    d. A general power of appointment.

27. A tenancy by the entirety may be terminated in which of the following ways?

    1. Death, whereby the survivor takes the entire tenancy.

    2. Mutual agreement.

    3. Divorce, which converts the tenancy into a tenancy in common or a joint tenancy.

    4. Severance, whereby one tenant transfers his or her interest to a third party with or without the consent of the other tenant.

        a. 1 and 2.

        b. 1 and 3.

        c. 2 and 4.

        d. 1, 2 and 3.

        e. 1,2, 3 and 4.

28. Which of the following is an undivided ownership in the property that, upon death of one owner, automatically passes to the surviving owner?

1. Tenants by the Entirety.
2. Tenants in Common.
3. Community Property.
4. Joint Tenancy with Rights of Survivorship.
    a. 1 and 4.
    b. 1 and 2.
    c. 2 and 4.
    d. 1, 3 and 4.
    e. 3 and 4.

29. A tenancy by the entirety may be terminated in which of the following ways?

1. Death, whereby the survivor takes the entire estate.
2. Mutual agreement.
3. Divorce, which converts the estate into a tenancy in common or a joint tenancy.
4. Severance, whereby one spouse transfers his or her interest to a third party but requires the consent of the other spouse.
    a. 4 only.
    b. 1 and 3.
    c. 2 and 4.
    d. 1, 2, 3 and 4.

30. Which of the following are advantages of allowing property to pass through the probate process?

1. Assets do not need to be retitled if they pass though probate.
2. There are limitations on creditors' time to make claims against the estate.
3. There is stricter supervision of the disposition and management of assets.
4. A will cannot be contested under the probate process.
    a. 1 and 2.
    b. 2 and 3.
    c. 3 and 4.
    d. 1, 2 and 3.

31. Which of the following is/are considered a disadvantage(s) of probate?

    1. The process can result in delays.

    2. The process may be expensive.

    3. The process provides clear title to heirs and legatees.

    4. The process is open to public scrutiny.

      a. 1 only.

      b. 1 and 2.

      c. 1, 2 and 4.

      d. 1, 2, 3, and 4.

32. Which of the following items will be retitled through probate?

      a. A house subject to a mortgage and owned fee simple by the decedent.

      b. 1/2 of real estate held tenancy by the entirety.

      c. Bank accounts with a POD designation.

      d. None of the above will be retitled through probate.

33. Which of the following would meet the requirements for the annual exclusion under the gift tax rules?

      a. A gift to a trust, to be distributed to a beneficiary contingent upon the beneficiary's survivorship.

      b. A gift to a trust that has an ascertainable value at the time of the gift.

      c. A gift to a secular (not a 2503c trust) trust that does not require annual income distribution to be beneficiary.

      d. A gift to a trust where the grantor can benefit from current income.

34. Jose created a joint bank account for himself and his friend, Amparo. At what earliest point has a gift been made to Amparo?

      a. When the account is created.

      b. When Jose notifies Amparo that the account has been created.

      c. When Amparo withdraws money from the account for her benefit.

      d. When Jose dies.

Quick Quiz Explanations

Quick Quiz 14.1
1. False. To result in an effective transfer of assets, estate planning must first consider the goals and objectives of the client. Given the overriding goals of the client, his or her affairs should be arranged to minimize estate taxes and other transfer costs.
2. True.

Quick Quiz 14.2
1. False. A durable power of attorney for health care does not typically direct the termination of life-sustaining treatment, although this is allowed in some states.
2. False. A living will is concerned with the provision or withholding of life-sustaining treatment. It does not direct the transfer of property during life.

Quick Quiz 14.3
1. False. Automobiles and stocks are examples of tangible and intangible personal property. Land is real property.
2. False. If property is held in fee simple, there are no joint owners / joint tenants.
3. True.

Quick Quiz 14.4
1. False. A tenancy by the entirety is essentially a joint tenancy with right of survivorship between spouses that cannot be severed without the consent of both spouses.
2. True.

Quick Quiz 14.5
1. True.
2. False. One of the classic reasons for using a trust is to protect assets from the claims of the beneficiaries' creditors.
3. False. A spendthrift clause provides asset protection by legally restricting a beneficiary's ability to anticipate distributions from the trust. A properly constructed spendthrift clause will prevent creditors from being able to access trust assets unless they are distributed to the beneficiary.

Economics and the External Environment

LEARNING OBJECTIVES

After reading this chapter, you should be able to:

- Describe the external environment and its makeup.
- Define macroeconomics and defined gross national product, gross domestic product, inflation, interest rates, and unemployment.
- Describe the business cycle and summarize the key economic variables.
- Identify the three types of economic indicators that describe the current and future economy and business cycle.
- Explain monetary and fiscal policy and the role of the Federal Reserve including its goals and tools.
- Explain microeconomics, demand and supply, and shifting demand and supply curves.
- Explain price elasticity of demand and the factors that impact alas this today.
- Explain opportunity costs and diminishing returns.
- Explain the external legal environment including bankruptcy laws and other consumer protection laws.
- Explain investor protection laws including SIPC, the Securities Act of 1933, the Security Exchange Act of 1934, the Investment Company Act of 1940, and the Investment Advisers Act of 1940.
- Explain the role of FINRA and the Sarbanes-Oxley Act of 2002.
- Identify worker protection laws and explain the impact of ERISA, workman's compensation, unemployment benefits, and OSHA.
- Explain the economic functions, customer base, products, and regulation of American financial institutions.*
- Compare the secondary market institutions and their regulators for each security (stock, bond, ETFs, real estate, commodities and options exchanges) and of primary market institutions (investment banking firms, mutual funds and hedge funds).*
- Apply the following economic concepts and measures in making financial planning recommendations: (1) Supply and demand, (2) National Income Accounts (includ-

ing GDP), (3) Business cycles (unemployment, recession, fiscal and monetary policy), (4) Interest rates (including its term structure and the yield curve) and inflation, and (5) Exchange rates.*

- Describe and distinguish between the elements of agency, suitability, fiduciary responsibility and the duties of agents to their principals including clients and their employers and the duties of fiduciaries to their clients and employers.*
- Describe the elements of a contract, special issues with oral contracts, and mechanisms for enforcement of contracts.*
- Describe security interests (including buyer-in-due-course) and creditor/debtor rights in the legal process including garnishment and bankruptcy.*
- Describe the nature of professional liability and compare mechanisms for controlling this risk.*
- Describe consumer laws that impact clients, including bankruptcy, banking, credit, privacy regulations, and other relevant laws.

* CFP Board Resource Document - Student-Centered Learning Objectives based upon CFP Board Principal Topics.

INTRODUCTION

Economics is the social science that studies individual and firm behavior and the interrelationship between consumer choices and government decisions that result in the production, distribution, and consumption of wealth. The study of economics is divided into the study of microeconomic and macroeconomic factors. Microeconomics focuses on the decisions of individuals and firms, such as those that affect supply and demand and the resulting pricing of products and services. Macroeconomics is centered on the entire or broader economy and uses measurements such as the Gross Domestic Product, inflation, unemployment, and investment in order to determine the performance of the overall economy. Individuals and firms then use the information derived from studying economic performance in order to make choices. Government uses the economic information to legislate issues such as consumer protection and to make monetary and fiscal decisions in an attempt to positively influence economic results. This chapter covers microeconomic and macroeconomic topics that are important for the financial planner to understand in order to properly guide client recommendations based on current and projected economic data.

External forces such as the economic, political, technological, sociological, and legal environments impact client choices. While all external economic forces are relevant, this chapter covers external economic and legal factors (bringing an equalizing of bargaining power between government, industry, and the individual) including consumer protection, investor protection, and worker protection laws. Exhibit 15.1 portrays some external environmental factors and the impact those factors can have on client finances and decisions. For example, economics impacts the client's cost of borrowing, the rate of taxation, the price of goods and services, overall economic activity, and investment returns.

Clients look to their financial planner for professional, competent, and objective advice related to a wide array of topics including current and future economic conditions and client's rights as consumers, investors, and workers. By having a thorough understanding of current economic conditions and government policies, the planner is better able to forecast future economic conditions and perhaps potential investment returns. After developing an economic forecast, the planner can position the client to achieve appropriate investment returns and mitigate investment risks.

EXTERNAL ENVIRONMENT

EXHIBIT 15.1

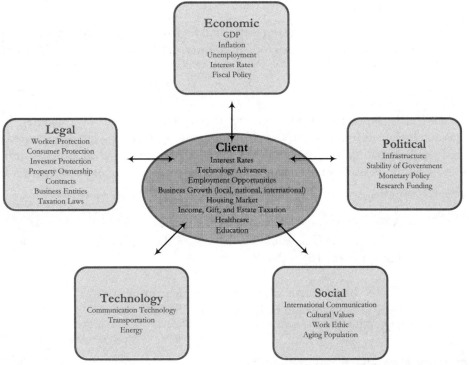

As previously stated, the study of economics can be divided into macroeconomics and microeconomics. **Macroeconomics** is the study of large economic factors that are reflective of the entire economy such as gross domestic product (GDP), the unemployment rate, and the inflation rate. GDP measures the total economic output for a country. The unemployment rate measures the percentage of workers that are unable to find work. The inflation rate measures the rate at which prices are increasing. **Microeconomics** is the study of factors that impact small or individual economies, such as supply and demand for a product. All of these macro and micro economic variables are discussed in this chapter.

Key Concepts

Underline/highlight the answers as you read:

1. Distinguish between microeconomic and macroeconomic factors.

2. Identify the difference between GNP and GDP.

3. Distinguish between inflation, disinflation, and deflation.

ECONOMIC OUTPUT

Gross National Product

Gross National Product (GNP) measures the total final output by the citizens of a country, whether produced domestically or in a foreign country. GNP does not include the output of foreigners in a country.

Gross Domestic Product

Gross Domestic Product (GDP) represents the total final output of a country, by its citizens and foreigners in the country, over a period of time. GDP is typically measured on a quarterly and annual basis. Although comparing GDP between two countries is difficult, GDP is useful for measuring the growth or contraction in the output of a country over time. Historically, the GDP rate has been a three percent real increase.

EXAMPLE 15.1	A Russian national hockey player that plays professional hockey in the U.S. would be included in the U.S. GDP, but not in the U.S. GNP.
EXAMPLE 15.2	A U.S. businessman who owns a manufacturing company in China would be included in U.S. GNP, but not U.S. GDP.

GDP is calculated by the Bureau of Economic Analysis, which is part of the U.S. Department of Commerce. A positive GDP is generally a sign that the economy is expanding, a negative GDP is a sign that the economy is contracting. The following exhibit is a compilation of the United States GDP from 1930 - 2011. The graph reflects the negative GDP of the Great Depression (1930's) as well as the subsequent recovery of output. Other periods of positive and negative output reflect the associated economic stability or instability, including the most recent negative output associated with the period (2007 - 2009) referred to as the Great Recession.

EXHIBIT 15.2

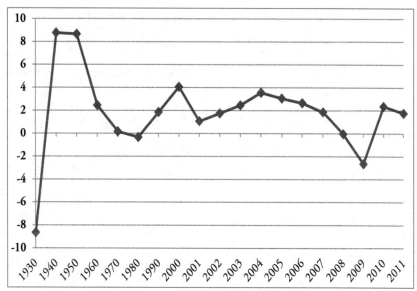

Source: Bureau of Economic Analysis

Nominal GDP measures the value of goods and services in current prices. The disadvantage of nominal GDP is that if the price of goods and services increases, nominal GDP will increase even though there was not an increase in the amount of goods and services produced. If the quantity of goods and services produced remains constant but the price increases, nominal GDP may be misleading because it reflects inflation rather than a quantitative increase in goods and services.

Real GDP measures the value of goods and services at a base year price. Real GDP only changes when the quantity of goods and services produced changes, not when prices change. Real GDP is a better measure of economic output than nominal GDP since prices are held constant when calculating real GDP. A recession is characterized by a decline in real GDP for at least six months (two quarters).

The **GDP deflator** measures the current price of goods and services (nominal GDP) relative to a base year (real GDP). The formula for the GDP deflator is:

$$\text{GDP Deflator} = \frac{\text{Nominal GDP}}{\text{Real GDP}}$$

Alternatively, we could take $\frac{\text{Nominal GDP}}{\text{GDP Deflator}}$ to determine the real GDP, therefore stating the nominal GDP in real terms. The GDP deflator could also be thought of as a measure of price increases or decreases.

INFLATION

Inflation represents an increase in the general level of prices of goods and services representing the economy as a whole over a period of time and without a corresponding increase in productivity. The biggest risks inflation presents are the loss of purchasing power and price instability. Individuals on fixed incomes are impacted the most by a loss of purchasing power, such as a retiree on a fixed pension while income remains constant, the cost of goods and services increase.

Inflation causes a decline in the real value of money, as consumers holding cash are priced out of goods and services because prices for those items increase. A primary cause of inflation is when the money supply increases faster than the growth in real GDP. The Federal Reserve is responsible for controlling the money supply to keep inflation at reasonable levels, typically targeted at two to three percent per year.

Key Concepts

Underline/highlight the answers as you read:

1. Identify measures of inflation.

2. What is an interest rate and what influences increases or decreases in the rate?

3. Identify how unemployment is measured and the different types of unemployment.

4. Explain what the business cycle represents and the phases of the business cycle.

5. Identify the three economic indicators.

A financial planner must be aware of the current and future conditions of the economy, including the status of inflation, in order to make proper financial planning recommendations to the client. Inflation's erosion of purchasing power can impact the client's successful implementation of a financial plan. For example, purchases of personal use assets may be negatively impacted due to inflation driving up prices and the cost of borrowing. The planner may choose to recommend that investments are made in stocks in order to hedge inflationary pressure. The planner who understands the impact of inflation and the mechanics of economics will remain informed of inflationary pressures and important government reaction, such as the Federal Reserve raising short-term interest rates in order to decrease the money supply (slowing down inflation). This knowledge will result in better client recommendations and more successful implementation of financial plans.

Disinflation is a slowdown in the rate of inflation or a slowdown in the rate of price increase of goods and services. Inflation is continuing but at a declining rate.

Deflation is a decrease in overall price levels of goods and services. As a result of deflation, there is a transfer of wealth from borrowers (like homeowners) to holders of cash. During periods of deflation, the real value of money increases as the dollars consumers hold are able to buy more goods and services as prices, such as homes, continue to decrease. A deflationary spiral is likely to lead to lower GDP because consumers prefer to hold their money, while waiting for lower prices.

Measures of Inflation

The **Consumer Price Index (CPI)** measures the overall price levels for a basket of goods and services consumers purchase. According to the Bureau of Labor Statistics,[1] items included in the CPI are:

- Food and Beverages: cereal, milk, coffee, snacks, etc.
- Housing: rent, mortgage, etc.
- Transportation: new vehicles, airline fares, gasoline, insurance.
- Medical Care: prescription drugs, physician services, eye care, etc.
- Recreation: televisions, toys, pets and pet products, sports equipment, etc.
- Education and Communication: college tuition, postage, telephone services, computer software and accessories, etc.
- Other Goods and Services: tobacco and smoking products, haircuts and other personal expenses, etc.

The CPI is a measure of prices at the retail level relative to the price levels of the same basket of goods and services in some base year. The **Producer Price Index (PPI)** measures the inflation rate for raw materials used in the manufacturing process. The PPI is an important measure of inflation, since inflation in the manufacturing process will likely lead to inflation at the retail level.

Although the CPI and GDP deflator measure price changes, there are major differences between these two measures. The GDP deflator measures price changes for all goods and services, whereas the CPI measures changes for a fixed basket of goods and services at the retail level only. Another difference is that the GDP deflator only measures the price of goods and services produced domestically. The CPI measures changes in prices of goods manufactured overseas and sold in the U.S., such as cars produced overseas and sold in the U.S. A final difference between the GDP deflator and CPI is that the CPI measures the price changes of a fixed basket of goods and services, whereas the GDP deflator will change over time as the economic output of a country changes.

The CPI is the most widely quoted and relied upon measure of inflation. Social Security benefit increases are tied to the CPI through Cost Of Living Adjustments (COLA) so that retirees receiving Social Security income will not lose purchasing power during their retirement or benefit years.

The inflation rate is calculated as follows:

$$\text{Inflation Rate} = \frac{P_1 - P_0}{P_0}$$

Where:

P_1 = Current prices

P_0 = Prices during a prior period

---

1. Source: http://www.bls.gov/cpi/cpifaq.htm#Question_7

The inflation rate, as measured by the CPI and calculated by the U.S. Bureau of Labor and Statistics for the last six years reported is:

2011: 3.2%
2010: 1.6%
2009: -0.4%
2008: 3.8%
2007: 2.8%
2006: 3.2%

Source: www.bls.gov/cpi/cpi_ds.htm#2011

INTEREST RATES

An **interest rate** is the price that a borrower pays to borrow money. The interest rate is an important factor in decision making by individuals and firms. Individuals make purchasing decisions, such as a home or automobile purchase, that consider the cost of financing as a key factor. Firms make business decisions regarding investment projects where the borrowing interest rate must be exceeded by the yield or return on the project.

The nominal interest rate represents the real rate of return plus an adjustment for anticipated future inflation. When lenders loan funds, the real rate of return represents their income. The real rate of interest is the nominal interest rate less inflation. If the lending interest rate were equal to inflation, there would be no income derived from the loan, so lenders need to lend at the nominal interest rate to earn revenue.

Interest rates are influenced by the demand for and the supply of loanable funds. When the supply of money increases, there is the tendency to temporarily hold more money than necessary. When the excess money is no longer held, interest rates fall and consumers make purchases because the cost of borrowing (the interest rate) has decreased. In addition, interest rates can be influenced by fiscal and monetary policy. If monetary policy is to tighten the supply of money resulting in upward pressure on interest rates, then purchases would likely fall. The fiscal and monetary policy can also include easing the supply of money in order to stimulate the economy in which case downward pressure on interest rates would occur and purchases would rise.

Quick Quiz 15.1

Highlight the answer to these questions:

1. Microeconomics is the study of economic factors that impact the economy as a whole including GDP, unemployment, and inflation.
   a. True
   b. False

2. Inflation results in a transfer of wealth from borrowers to holders of cash.
   a. True
   b. False

3. CPI measures the overall price levels for a basket of goods and services that consumers purchase.
   a. True
   b. False

False, False, True.

Financial planners need to be aware of economic forecasts of anticipated inflation and corresponding expected changes in interest rates, because this will affect many financial plans. If there is an anticipated rise in inflation, then client purchases or refinancing should be considered earlier rather than later as the cost of borrowing (the interest rate) is currently priced more favorably. If anticipated inflation is expected to fall, then purchases should be delayed to take advantage of the future lower price of borrowing.

UNEMPLOYMENT

The measurement of unemployment is important because aggregate supply and aggregate demand (discussed under the microeconomics section of this chapter) are affected when unemployment increases as output decreases and GNP falls below its potential. On a more personal level, high unemployment can lead to depressed personal income and economic distress for individuals and families.

In order to understand what the measurement of unemployment means, the criteria used to measure unemployment is essential. **Unemployed** refers to those individuals 16 years of age and older who are not working and are making an effort to seek employment. The government measurement of unemployment does not include those individuals who are underemployed (overqualified for a job such as a PhD waiting tables) or those who are discouraged and have discontinued their job search. Some unemployment is consistent with economic efficiency, but prolonged high rates of unemployment are an indication of economic instability. Economists have divided unemployment into three categories as follows:

- **Frictional unemployment** occurs when people are voluntarily unemployed because they are seeking other job opportunities and they haven't found the desired employment yet.
- **Structural unemployment** occurs when there is inequality between the supply of adequately skilled workers and the demand for workers.
- **Cyclical unemployment** occurs when there is an overall downturn in business activity and fewer goods are being produced causing a decrease in the demand for labor (related to changes in the business cycle).

Given that some unemployment is normal, **full employment** is defined as the rate of employment that exists when there is efficiency in the labor market. Full employment can include both frictional and structural unemployment when there is efficiency in the labor market that results in approximately 95 percent employment of the labor force. Conversely, note that high cyclical unemployment is an indication of problematic unemployment economy-wide and can reflect overall economic inefficiencies. Very low unemployment (e.g., 2-3 percent) can also be problematic leading to inflationary issues. Therefore, economic policy is to sustain a **natural rate of unemployment**, being the lowest unemployment rate where labor and product markets are in balance. At the natural rate of unemployment both price and wage inflation is stable.

The following exhibit is a representation of the annual unemployment rate from 1970 – 2011.[2] Recessionary periods are identifiable and associated with periods of high unemployment.

EXHIBIT 15.3 **UNEMPLOYMENT FROM 1970 - 2011 (IN PERCENTAGES)**

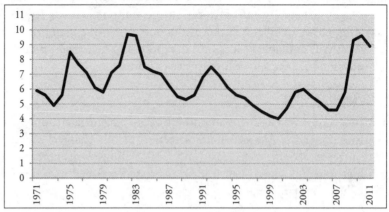

Source: bls.gov/cps/prev_yrs.htm

BUSINESS CYCLE

Both firms and consumers make financial decisions to maximize their utility, based on constraints. The primary constraint for both firms and consumers is limited financial resources. **Utility** is the benefit firms and consumers receive when allocating or spending financial resources. Firms are constrained by the capacity of their workforce, products they offer, and the level of competition. Firms maximize their utility by making decisions on how to best use their resources to maximize profits. Consumers and households maximize their utility by making decisions on employment, spending for today, and saving for tomorrow. Consumers are constantly evaluating how to allocate their limited resource of funds to meet the necessities of life and planning for financial goals of tomorrow. Consumers evaluate how to allocate their scarce resource of funds based on the cost and benefits derived from making decisions to spend today or save for tomorrow. One of the decisions many families face is whether to have both parents work outside of the home. Opportunity cost represents the cost of the highest valued alternative that is forgone. For families that decide one parent will not work outside of the house, the opportunity cost is the income that is forgone. These families value the benefit of having a parent at home as exceeding the cost of the forgone income.

Consumer spending is a key economic variable that drives the U.S. economy and the business cycle. Consumer spending accounts for approximately two-thirds of GDP. The **business cycle** measures economic activity over time. Economic activity is measured by gross domestic product. As consumer spending increases, firms hire more employees and produce more goods and services. When consumer spending slows, firms stop hiring or reduce their workforce and produce less goods and services. These fluctuations in consumer spending and output by firms are reflected in the business cycle.

The business cycle shown in Exhibit 15.4 is characterized by the following phases:
- Expansion
- Peak

---

2. Bureau of Labor Statistics: Annual average unemployment rate, civilian labor force 16 years and over (percent).

- Contraction or Recession
- Trough

BUSINESS LIFE CYCLE

EXHIBIT 15.4

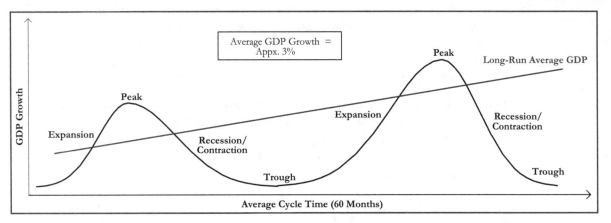

Source: www.bls.gov/cps/prev_yrs.htm

A contraction in the business cycle is characterized by a slow down in consumer spending, which leads to lower output by firms. As the output of firms decreases, GDP decreases and the unemployment rate increases, as firms reduce staff to offset the lower demand for their products and services. As GDP decreases, inflation begins to decrease, as consumers are demanding fewer goods and services, which may lead to lower prices. In an effort to stimulate economic activity, the Federal Reserve will ease monetary policy, by increasing the money supply and lowering interest rates to reduce the cost of borrowing and encourage consumers to begin spending again.

As GDP reaches its lowest levels and unemployment reaches its highest point, the business cycle is entering the trough phase. Generally, the trough phase represents lower GDP, lower inflation, lower interest rates, and higher unemployment.

SUMMARY OF BUSINESS CYCLE AND KEY ECONOMIC VARIABLES

EXHIBIT 15.5

	Expansion	Peak	Contraction	Trough
GDP	Increasing	High	Decreasing	Low
Inflation	Increasing	High	Decreasing	Low
Interest Rates	Increasing	High	Decreasing	Low
Unemployment	Decreasing	Low	Increasing	High

Once the financial planner has an idea of where current economic conditions are in the business cycle and the direction of key economic variables, the planner is in a good position to forecast where the economy may be in the next three to six months. Investment returns are highly correlated to the business cycle and GDP. During periods of expansion, increasing GDP, and low unemployment, consumers have more money to spend. Consumer spending drives corporate earnings and corporate earnings drive equity prices and investment returns. The planner can position a client's investments to take advantage of the likely increasing equity prices and positive investment returns. As the economy is approaching or at the peak, the planner may forecast an upcoming contraction, leading to lower GDP, lower consumer spending, lower interest rates, and higher unemployment. During periods of a contraction, corporate earnings decrease leading to lower equity prices and potentially negative equity returns. However, as interest rates decrease, bond prices will increase which presents an opportunity for the planner to position the client's investments to take advantage of increasing bond prices.

ECONOMIC INDICATORS

There are three types of **economic indicators**[3] that describe the current and future economy and business cycle. The three types of economic indicators are:
- Index of Leading Economic Indicators
- Index of Lagging Economic Indicators
- Index of Coincident Economic Indicators

All three types of indicators incorporate key economic data that is used by economists to predict future economic activity or confirm current assessments of the economy and business cycle.

The Index of Leading Economic Indicators
The index of leading economic indicators is comprised of 10 data points that are relied on to predict changes in the economy. Economists believe the index of leading economic indicators can predict changes to the economy six to nine months before the change actually occurs. The index consists of the following indicators:
- Average weekly hours, manufacturing
- Average weekly initial claims for unemployment insurance
- Manufacturers' new orders, consumer goods and materials
- Index of supplier deliveries – vendor performance
- Manufacturers' new orders, nondefense capital goods
- Building permits, new private housing units
- Stock prices, 500 common stocks
- Money supply, M2
- Interest rate spread, 10-year Treasury bonds less federal funds
- Index of consumer expectations

The Index of Lagging Economic Indicators
The index of lagging economic indicators summarizes past performance. The index of lagging economic indicators does not predict future trends in the economy, instead it validates current assessments of the economy. The index consists of the following indicators:
- Average duration of unemployment
- Inventories to sales ratio, manufacturing and trade
- Labor cost per unit of output, manufacturing
- Average prime rate
- Commercial and industrial loans

---

3. The composite indexes of leading, coincident, and lagging indicators produced by The Conference Board (www.conference-board.org).

- Consumer installment credit to personal income ratio
- Consumer price index for services

The Index of Coincident Indicators

The index of coincident indicators is comprised of economic variables that change along with the business cycle. The index of coincident indicators reflects where the economy is in the business cycle. The index consists of the following indicators:
- Number of employees on non-agricultural payrolls (payroll employment)
- Index of Industrial Production or industrial output
- Level of manufacturing and trade sales which measures total spending in real dollars
- Personal income measured in real dollars, excluding transfer payments (Social Security)

MONETARY POLICY

Monetary policy represents the intended influence on the money supply and interest rates by the central bank of a country. In the United States, the central bank is the Federal Reserve. The Federal Reserve system is composed of the Board of Governors and twelve regional Federal Reserve Banks. Monetary policy is established by:
- The Chairman of the Federal Reserve and the Board of Governors, who are appointed by the President of the United States and confirmed by the U.S. Senate, and
- The Federal Open Market Committee (FOMC), which is comprised of members of the Board of Governors, the president of the Federal Reserve Bank of New York, and four presidents of other Federal Reserve Banks serving on a rotating basis.

Key Concepts

Underline/highlight the answers as you read:

1. What is monetary policy?

2. Identify and define the four tools that are used to implement monetary policy.

3. Distinguish between fiscal policy and monetary policy.

4. Identify the two tools that government can use to implement fiscal policy.

The FOMC meets eight times a year to set monetary policy and make decisions regarding how monetary policy will be implemented.

The Federal Reserve has three primary goals:
- Maintain price levels
- Maintain long-term economic growth
- Maintain full employment

The Federal Reserve accomplishes its goals by influencing money supply and interest rates. If GDP is slowing and unemployment is increasing the Federal Reserve may want to stimulate or expand the economy. In an effort to expand the economy, it may ease monetary policy. The Federal Reserve will take steps to increase the money supply, which will put downward pressure on interest rates. Interest rates represent the cost of borrowing money, so when the money supply is abundant, the cost to borrow will be low and encourage consumers to borrow money to buy houses and cars. Alternatively, if the Federal Reserve believes the economy is growing too quickly and inflation is showing signs of increasing or is actually increasing, the Federal Reserve may **tighten** monetary policy. It will then take steps to decrease the supply of money and ultimately increase short-term interest rates, in an effort to slow down consumer spending.

The Federal Reserve has four tools that it uses to implement monetary policy. The four tools are:
- Reserve Requirement
- Discount Rate / Federal Funds Rate
- Open Market Operations
- Excess Reserve Deposits

Reserve Requirement

The Federal Reserve requires that banks maintain a certain percentage of their deposits on hand, in the form of cash known as their **reserve requirement**. A simplified bank's balance sheet might appear as follows:

Assets	Liabilities
Loans	Deposits
Cash	

Banks receive deposits that are applied to checking accounts, savings accounts, money market accounts, and Certificates of Deposit. Those deposits actually represent liabilities since the bank owes those funds to its' depositors. A bank creates an asset when it uses deposits to lend funds to businesses and consumers for commercial or personal purposes. A bank also maintains a percentage of deposits as available cash for future loans or to meet the reserve requirement. The reserve requirement for banks (as set by the Federal Reserve), is effectively 10 percent.[4] For every $10 in deposits, a bank can lend $9 and keep $1 in cash to meet the reserve requirement.

Banks create money by taking a liability in the form of a deposit and then lending that money to a business or consumer. Bank business models are impacted by the unique risk of being in the business of lending money in order to make a profit. However, during the peak of the business cycle they are lending money to businesses, consumers, and investors who are making purchases when prices and values are at their peak. The reserve requirement is influential in controlling how much leverage and risk banks can undertake. Since banks are able to lend 90 percent of every deposit that they receive, they may undertake significant financial risk during periods of peak prices.

The Federal Reserve can increase or decrease the reserve requirement, which will have a direct impact on the money supply and ultimately influence interest rates. If the Federal Reserve's monetary policy is to tighten the money supply, it can increase the reserve

---

4. Banks with less than $11.5 million in accounts are not required to maintain a minimum reserve level. The reserve requirement for banks over $11.5 million up to $71.0 million is 3 percent. Banks with over $71.0 million are required to maintain a 10 percent reserve. These are effective 12/29/2011.

requirement which causes banks to maintain more deposits in the form of cash and have less funds available for loans. Since there are fewer funds available for loans, the money supply will decrease and interest rates will increase.

Alternatively, if the Federal Reserve's monetary policy is to ease the money supply, it will decrease the reserve requirement. Banks will maintain fewer deposits in the form of cash and will increase the funds available for loans. Since there are more funds available for loans, the money supply will increase and interest rates will decrease.

SUMMARY CHART

Monetary Policy	Reserve Requirement	Money Supply	Interest Rates
Tighten	Increase	Decrease	Increase
Ease	Decrease	Increase	Decrease

Discount Rate

The **discount rate** is the interest rate that the Federal Reserve charges financial institutions for short-term loans. Loan borrowing from the Federal Reserve institutions go to the discount window, which is the term used from when financial institutions would send a representative to the Federal Reserve's bank window to borrow funds. Borrowing is now accomplished electronically, but the term discount window is still used.

The Federal Reserve sets the discount rate and the rate is increased or decreased based on the Federal Reserve's monetary policy. The discount rate represents the overnight borrowing rate that banks are charged for funds used to meet their reserve requirement or other liquidity issues. The discount rate is typically 100 basis points (or 1%) higher than the rate banks charge each other to borrow.

When the Federal Reserve tightens monetary policy, the discount rate increases. If the Fed eases monetary policy, they are going to decrease the discount rate.

Quick Quiz 15.2

Highlight the answer to these questions:

1. An expansion phase in the business cycle is characterized by an increase in consumer spending resulting in higher output by firms.
   a. True
   b. False

2. The index of leading economic indicators summarizes past performance.
   a. True
   b. False

3. Monetary policy represents the government's position on whether to expand or contract the economy by using taxation and government spending.
   a. True
   b. False

True, False, False.

The bank to bank lending rate is the **federal funds rate** (also known as the overnight rate). It is important to be able to differentiate between the discount rate and federal funds rate.

The supply and demand of funds is an important consideration when federal funds rates are negotiated between banks. If a number of banks have reserve deficiencies and a few banks have excess reserves, the federal funds rate is likely to increase, since the demand for funds is higher than the supply. If a number of banks have excess reserves and a few banks have reserve deficiencies, the federal funds rate is likely to decrease. Since the discount rate is usually higher than the federal funds rate, the Federal Reserve is known as the bank of last resort.

Prior to the credit crisis of 2007 to 2009, the discount rate was an overnight interest rate and the funds had to be repaid the next day. Since many banks were facing insolvency (CITI, Bank of America, etc.) during this time period, the terms of the discount rate were temporarily extended for up to 90 days.

The Federal Open Market Committee (FOMC) will set the discount rate and also a target for the federal funds rate. The Federal Reserve does not directly control the federal funds rate, because banks negotiate the federal funds rate between themselves. However, the Federal Reserve will set a target federal funds rate, which is typically very close to the actual rate.

Open Market Operations

Through the Federal Reserve's open market operations, it can directly influence the money supply and interest rates. **Open market operations** is the process by which the Federal Reserve will buy or sell U.S. Treasury securities such as T-bills, notes, and bonds. This process is done electronically with the Federal Reserve crediting or debiting financial institution's transactions. Only about 10 percent of the country's money supply is in the form of bank notes or cash; the rest is maintained electronically.

If the Federal Reserve's monetary policy is to tighten, then it will sell U.S. Treasury securities and reduce the deposits held by banks at the Federal Reserve. When deposits are decreased, the money supply decreases and interest rates are likely to increase.

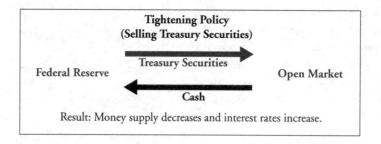

If the Federal Reserve's monetary policy is to ease, then it will buy U.S. Treasury securities and increase the deposits held by banks at the Federal Reserve. When deposits increase, the money supply is increasing and interest rates are likely to decrease.

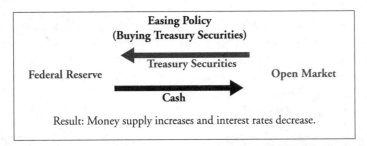

Easing Policy
(Buying Treasury Securities)

Federal Reserve   Treasury Securities   Open Market

Cash

Result: Money supply increases and interest rates decrease.

Excess Reserves

As previously discussed, banks must maintain a minimum level of cash reserves (based on the amount of their deposits), which is determined by the reserve requirement. The cash reserves are on deposit with the Federal Reserve. **Excess reserves** represent the amount of cash or deposits with the Federal Reserve in excess of the minimum amount required. Prior to 2008, it was disadvantageous for financial institutions to keep cash in excess of their reserve requirement on deposit with the Federal Reserve because there was no return on that capital. Institutions were more inclined to keep reserve deposits at minimum levels and instead took risks by lending the excess reserves to generate higher returns.

The Financial Services Regulatory Relief Act of 2006 established that on October 1, 2011, the Federal Reserve could begin paying interest on cash balances financial institutions have on deposit at the Federal Reserve. The Economic Stabilization Act of 2008 changed the effective date from October 1, 2011 to October 1, 2008. The impact of the Federal Reserve paying interest on deposits is that financial institutions have an incentive to keep excess reserves on deposit with the Federal Reserve. The Federal Reserve now has the ability to increase or decrease the interest rate paid on excess reserves to help control the money supply.

If the Federal Reserve's policy is to slow down or contract the economy, it will increase the interest rate paid on excess reserves. This creates an incentive for institutions to keep cash on deposit with the Federal Reserve, as opposed to making risky loans.

If the Federal Reserve's policy is to stimulate or expand the economy, it will decrease the interest rate paid on excess reserves. This creates an incentive for financial institutions to lend money and grow the money supply.

Quick
Quiz 15.3

Highlight the answer to these questions:

1. The discount rate is the interest rate that the Federal Reserve charges financial institutions for short-term loans.
   a. True
   b. False

2. If the Federal Reserve's monetary policy is to tighten the money supply, then it will sell U.S. Treasury securities (open market operations) to reduce the deposits held by banks at the Federal Reserve.
   a. True
   b. False

True, True.

FISCAL POLICY

Fiscal policy is exerted by Congress as a means of expanding or contracting the economy. Congress uses taxes and government spending to implement fiscal policy. Congress has the same three goals that the Federal Reserve has, which are to:

- Maintain price levels,
- Maintain long-term economic growth, and
- Maintain full employment.

Fiscal policy is an attempt to either stimulate or reduce aggregate demand within a country. Fiscal policy is implemented using three tools: taxes, spending, and deficit management.

Taxes

When taxes decrease, consumers will have more income to spend on products and services. As consumers demand more products and services, consumer spending will increase causing aggregate demand to increase. Congress is likely to decrease taxes when fiscal policy is to expand the economy. Alternatively, when taxes increase, consumers will have less income to spend on products and services. As consumers demand fewer products and services, consumer spending will decrease, causing aggregate demand to decrease or slow down. Congress is likely to increase taxes when fiscal policy is to contract the economy.

FISCAL POLICY TAX IMPACT	
Taxes	**Fiscal Policy**
Decrease	Expand
Increase	Contract

Spending

Spending by the federal government can directly impact aggregate demand. As the federal government spends funds on building more roads, hiring law enforcement, and strengthening national defense, the spending may result in a positive impact on unemployment. In February of 2009, Congress passed the American Recovery and Reinvestment Act which included some of the following benefits in an attempt to increase aggregate demand:

- Making Work Pay Tax Credit – Decreased the amount of taxes withheld from each paycheck to help stimulate consumer spending.
- First-Time Homebuyer Credit – Provided a tax credit for first time and longtime homebuyers.
- Money Back for New Vehicle Purchases - Provided a tax deduction for the purchase of certain new vehicles.
- Education Benefits - Enhanced an education tax credit (American Opportunity Tax Credit) to provide families with additional tax savings.
- Other Savings - Provided funds for projects that are designed to create jobs or keep existing jobs, reduced COBRA insurance premiums, and provided tax-free unemployment benefits.

The Act was a combination of tax credits, cost reduction, and increased spending all designed to increase economic activity and aggregate demand.

A disadvantage of spending to implement fiscal policy occurs when the U.S. government borrows money, which increases the federal deficit. Deficit spending is exaggerated during periods of decreasing or negative GDP because tax revenues are lower and the federal government is spending more to help stimulate the economy. The only way to finance deficit spending is to print more money (which can have serious inflation implications) or to borrow more money. As the federal government borrows more money, it has a crowding out effect where business and consumers are either unable to borrow or they are forced to borrow at higher interest rates. An implication of deficit spending is that it may ultimately lead to lower aggregate demand since businesses and consumers are interest rate sensitive when borrowing. As the cost of borrowing increases, businesses and consumers are less likely to borrow, which can lead to slower economic growth and have the opposite consequences than what was intended by the spending policy.

An expansion is characterized by an increase in consumer spending, which leads to higher output by firms. As the output increases, GDP increases and the unemployment rate decreases, as firms are hiring more employees to meet the demand for the firm's products. If GDP continues to increase, inflation in the form of higher prices for goods and services begins to increase. Higher prices are the result of consumer spending and high demand for a limited supply of products and services. In response, the Federal Reserve is going to take a tightening monetary policy and reduce the money supply and increase interest rates, in an effort to slow consumer spending and GDP growth. A financial planner that is knowledgeable regarding the business life cycle (Exhibit 15.4) can anticipate the direction of the economy and assist the client with informed decisions accordingly.

Deficit Management

Deficit spending is a financial circumstance that is avoided by most consumers, individuals and firms alike, because spending beyond available cash (increasing debt) can be problematic and lead to insolvency. However, the concept of deficit spending and the resulting management and decision making associated with this type of spending must be examined based on need. For example, if a fiscal policy of deficit spending is chosen in an unstable economy, such as a deep recession or depression, the deficit increase can be worth the risk. However, if deficit spending is related to overspending or failure to follow a budget, then the risks associated with deficit spending are not reasonable. In the latter case fiscal policy should include a cut in spending (including a reduction in expenses, if necessary) to meet budget constraints.

MICROECONOMICS

DEMAND

Demand represents the quantity consumers are willing to purchase of a good or service, at a particular price. The quantity consumers are willing to demand is known as the quantity demanded and is inversely related to price, so as price increases, quantity demand decreases. As price decreases, quantity demand will increase. The **aggregate demand curve** is a graphical representation of the quantity of goods and services consumers are willing to buy at any given price level.

EXHIBIT 15.6   THE DEMAND CURVE

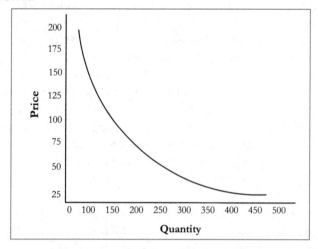

It is important to differentiate between shifts in the demand curve and movements along the demand curve. Anytime something other than price changes, the demand curve will shift, either up and to the right or down and to the left. The easiest way to determine when the demand curve is going to shift, is based on changes to the amount of money in the consumer's pocket. If consumers have more money in their pocket to spend, the demand curve will shift up and to the right. If consumers have less money to spend, the demand curve will shift down and to the left.

The examples below are events that cause the demand curve to shift up and to the right, which means consumers are willing to demand more of a good or service, at a higher price:
- Increase in disposable income
- Decrease in tax rates
- Decrease in unemployment rate
- Decrease in savings rate
- Increase in price of a substitute product
- Decrease in price of a complement product

Key Concepts

Underline/highlight the answers as you read:

1. Explain what demand represents and the difference between a shift in the demand curve and movement along the demand curve.

2. Distinguish between product substitutes and complements.

3. Identify what the price elasticity of demand is and factors that impact elasticity.

4. Explain what supply represents and the difference between a shift in the supply curve and movement along the supply curve.

5. What does equilibrium price represent?

SHIFTING DEMAND CURVE

EXHIBIT 15.7

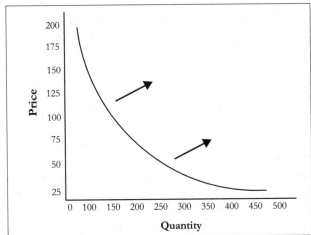

The examples below are events that will cause the demand curve to shift down and to the left, which means consumers are willing to demand less of a good or service, at a lower price:

- Decrease in disposable income
- Increase in tax rate
- Increase in unemployment rate
- Increase in savings rate
- Decrease in price of a substitute product
- Increase in price of a complement product

SHIFTING DEMAND CURVE

EXHIBIT 15.8

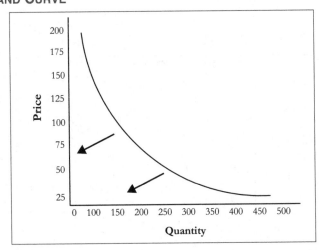

Substitutes and Complements

Substitutes are products that serve a similar purpose, whereas **complements** are products that are consumed jointly. For substitutes and complements, when the price of one product changes, it will impact the quantity demand for both the original product and the substitute or complement product.

EXAMPLE 15.3

If the price of movie tickets increases, the quantity demanded for movie tickets is likely to decrease. However, if DVD rentals are a substitute product, as the price of movie tickets increase, the demand for DVD rentals is likely to increase.

EXAMPLE 15.4

If flashlights and batteries are complements, then if flashlights are on sale, it is likely to increase the demand for batteries.

Price Elasticity of Demand

As discussed, consumer demand will change with price. As price decreases, the quantity demanded will increase. The question is, how much will demand increase, based on changes in price? This question is answered by looking at the price elasticity of demand. For some products, such as gasoline, changes in price will result in a relatively small change in the quantity demanded within a given range of prices. For other products, such as luxury goods, a small change in price may lead to a relatively large change in the quantity demanded.

The elasticity of demand is measured by the following formula:

$$\text{Elasticity} = \frac{\text{Percentage Change in Quantity Demanded}}{\text{Percentage Change in Price}}$$

Demand is elastic if a small percentage change in price, results in a large percentage change in the quantity demanded. Anytime elasticity is greater than 1, demand is considered to be elastic.

EXHIBIT 15.9 **ELASTIC DEMAND (LUXURY CARS)**

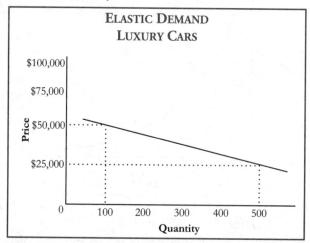

Demand is inelastic if a small percentage change in price results in a small percentage change in the quantity demanded. When elasticity is less than one, demand is relatively inelastic.

INELASTIC DEMAND (GASOLINE)

EXHIBIT 15.10

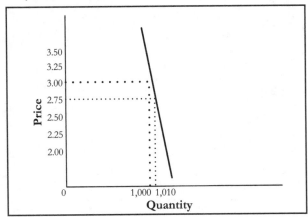

If a one percent change in price leads to a one percent change in quantity demanded, then elasticity is one, which is defined as unit elasticity. If demand is perfectly inelastic, regardless of what happens to price, the quantity demanded will not change. If demand is perfectly elastic, given a small price change, consumers will demand an unlimited amount of the good or service.

Factors that Impact Elasticity

The elasticity of demand is impacted by three primary factors. The first factor is whether there are substitute products. If there are substitute products, then a small price increase for one product will lead to lower demand and increase the demand for the substitute product. Substitute products lead to elastic demand.

EXAMPLE 15.5

> If the price of steak increases and consumers substitute chicken instead of steak, the demand for steak will decrease.

The second factor that impacts elasticity is consumer's income. If prices increase and consumer's income remains constant, then consumer's are going to demand less of the good or service. Whether the demand is elastic or inelastic will depend on the percentage change in the quantity demanded. The third factor that impacts elasticity is time. If consumers don't have a substitute product in the short-term, demand is likely to be inelastic. However, over time as consumer's find substitute products, demand will become more elastic.

SUPPLY

Supply represents the quantity firms are willing to produce and sell of a good or service, at a particular price. The quantity firms are willing to supply is known as the quantity supplied and is directly related to price, such that as price increases, quantity supplied increases. As price decreases, quantity supplied will decrease. The **aggregate supply curve** is a graphical representation between quantity supplied and price.

EXHIBIT 15.11 **THE SUPPLY CURVE**

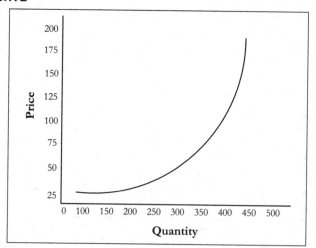

As it was with the demand curve, it is also important to differentiate between shifts in the supply curve and movements along the supply curve. Anytime something other than price changes, the supply curve will shift, either up and to the left or down and to the right. A change in price is movement along the supply curve, impacting the quantity supplied.

The examples below are situations that cause the supply curve to shift up and to the left, which means firms are supplying less of a good or service, at a higher price:
- Decreased competition
- Outdated technologies
- Increased price of an input used in the manufacturing process

EXHIBIT 15.12 **THE SUPPLY CURVE SHIFTING**

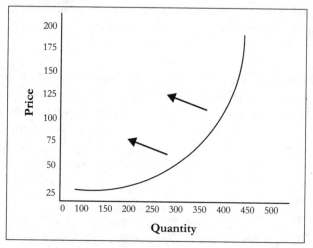

The examples below are situations that cause the supply curve to shift down and to the right, which means firms are willing to supply less of a good or service, at a lower price:
- Increased competition
- Improved technology to increase efficiency
- Decreased price of an input used in the manufacturing process

SHIFT IN SUPPLY CURVE

EXHIBIT 15.13

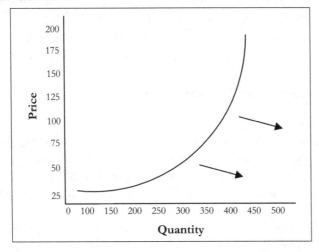

Equilibrium

It is not every day that financial planners work with the concepts of supply and demand. However, it is important to understand these concepts since they help to explain or anticipate how changes in unemployment, taxes, savings, and competition can impact the overall economy as well as the price of goods and services.

When combining supply and demand curves on one graph, the intersection of the supply and demand curve is the equilibrium price. The **equilibrium price** represents the price at which the quantity demanded equals the quantity supplied.

The following is a graph reflecting the money supply, the demand for funds, and the cost for those funds as measured by interest rates (price).

EQUILIBRIUM GRAPH

EXHIBIT 15.14

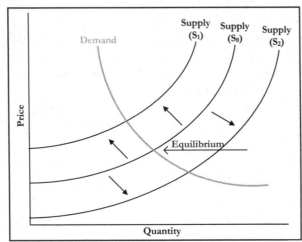

As the money supply shifts up (decreases) from S_0 to S_1, a new equilibrium price will be established, which is higher interest rates. As a result, businesses and consumers will demand less money at the higher interest rates. As the money supply shifts down (increases) from S_0 to S_2, business and consumers will demand more money as the money supply increases and a new equilibrium price is established, which is lower interest rates.

OPPORTUNITY COSTS AND DIMINISHING RETURNS

Opportunity Costs

Opportunity cost represents the value of the best foregone alternative. What is the significance of opportunity cost to the financial planner? The planner will evaluate the client's financial opportunities together with personal goals and objectives to make recommendations that require a review of alternative choices. A recommendation may be to pay off a high balance, high interest rate credit card by selling a client's favorite recreational vehicle (e.g., a boat). However, the client may find such value in the recreational vehicle that he is not willing to lose the opportunity of that enjoyment. So instead the client might choose another opportunity, like delaying the purchase of a home (as the best alternative that is foregone) in order to keep the boat and use the savings from the home purchase to pay off the credit card debt. Therefore, it is important for the planner to appreciate that a client's opportunity cost is subjective and should be considered when making financial planning recommendations.

Another important aspect of opportunity cost is considering what a resource could earn using its best alternative use. A financial planner can evaluate the client's use of assets to determine a better alternative asset use leading to an improved financial status.

EXAMPLE 15.6	Sally is a financial planner. Sally's clients, Luis and Mary, own several acres of land that are being used for infrequent family camping trips. Luis and Mary hire a vendor for maintenance of the acreage. Sally recommends that Luis and Mary lease the land for agricultural crop growth. The clients may have to forego the use of the property for camping trips, but this in turn, will eliminate the need for the maintenance vendor and will earn revenue from the asset. Leasing the property may be the better financial use of the property depending on the client's utility curves.

Quick
Quiz 15.4

Highlight the answer to these questions:

1. Demand represents the quantity firms are willing to produce and sell of a good or service, at a particular price.
   a. True
   b. False

2. Complements are products that are consumed jointly and substitutes are products that serve a similar purpose.
   a. True
   b. False

3. Elasticity of demand determines how much demand will change as a result of a change in price.
   a. True
   b. False

4. Anytime there is a change in price there will be a shift in the supply curve.
   a. True
   b. False

False, True, True, False.

Diminishing Returns

The law of diminishing returns is an economic production concept that states, as more and more additional units of a variable input are applied to a fixed input, output will eventually increase by smaller and smaller amounts. For example, a person who has consumed five chocolate bars is unlikely to have the same utility for the last bar consumed as a person who eats his first chocolate bar. The financial planner should have an understanding of this economic concept because it is common sense and applicable to business decisions where resource decisions are made and an evaluation of return on investment occurs. As part of analyzing a client's financial profile, the planner may need to assess the assets available and recommend where an increase in variable inputs should be applied and at what point is there a diminishing return on those inputs.

EXAMPLE 15.7

Continuing with Sally's clients, Luis and Mary, from above. Mary, who has a degree in horticulture, decides that she can manage the crop growth on their land. Mary successfully grows and harvests the crops for a couple of years and refines her method of production by applying more and more fertilizer to increase the harvest output. Eventually, Mary's cost of more and more fertilizer is producing less and less amounts of crop since the land (fixed input) will not support any further production. Mary is experiencing the law of diminishing returns.

Key Concepts

Underline/highlight the answers as you read:

1. Identify the difference between Chapter 7, Chapter 11, and Chapter 13 bankruptcies.

2. What is the purpose and mission of the FTC?

3. Identify important consumer protection laws and their purpose.

4. What are the three goals of the FDIC?

5. Identify the rules regarding FDIC insurance as pertains to account ownership and the amount of insurance coverage.

A financial planner should have an understanding of consumer protection laws, investor protections laws, and worker protection laws. Consumer protection laws are designed to protect the rights of individual consumers while promoting competition and fair business practices. Investor protection laws are designed to promote investor confidence in security markets and protect investors from fraudulent or inappropriate investments. Worker protection laws protect the rights of workers, ensure fair treatment by current employers, provide unemployment and worker insurance benefits, and require safe and healthy working conditions.

CONSUMER PROTECTION

Bankruptcy Laws

The Bankruptcy Reform Act of 1978 defines the law governing all federal bankruptcy cases in the U.S. Over the years, the Act of 1978 has been amended and additional acts have been passed to refine and address current day issues. The bankruptcy laws generally favor the rehabilitation of the debtor rather than punishing the debtor. There are no debtor jails and the bankruptcy process generally does not have criminal consequences. The bankruptcy laws provide the debtor with an opportunity to reorganize, adjust, and repay their debts. The bankruptcy laws are designed to protect both the debtor and creditors. Bankruptcy proceedings allow creditors an opportunity to be heard and to potentially lay claim to nonexempt assets of the debtor.

There are three primary chapters to the bankruptcy law that most individuals and businesses will use when filing for bankruptcy.[5] The three primary chapters are:
- Chapter 8 – For wage earners to discharge debts by liquidation
- Chapter 12 – For companies to reorganize and adjust debts
- Chapter 14 – For wage earners to repay a portion of debts with income over the future 36 to 60 months

---

5. http://www.uscourts.gov/bankruptcycourts/bankruptcybasics.aspx

Chapter 7 Bankruptcy

Chapter 7 bankruptcy allows individuals or businesses to obtain protection from creditors. Under Chapter 7, assets are liquidated to repay all or a portion of the debts. A Chapter 7 bankruptcy can be voluntary or involuntary. Voluntary bankruptcy is when the debtor files a bankruptcy petition with the courts. Involuntary bankruptcy is when the creditors file the petition for bankruptcy and force the debtor into bankruptcy.

To initiate bankruptcy protection, a debtor must file a bankruptcy petition with the federal bankruptcy court in the appropriate federal judicial district. Once the petition is filed, the court notifies creditors and all collection calls, lawsuits, and wage garnishments must stop. Typically within 40 days of filing the bankruptcy petition, the U.S. Trustee or bankruptcy administrator will hold a creditor's meeting with the debtor and creditors. During this meeting, assets are disclosed that may be available to satisfy creditors.

As a result of the Bankruptcy Abuse Prevention and Consumer Protection Act (BAPCPA) of 2005, a "means test" is applied by the bankruptcy court to determine if the debtor's income is above or below the average income for their state. If the debtor's income is below the average income, the debtor is permitted to file bankruptcy under Chapter 7 but may file under Chapter 13. If the debtor's income is above the average income, the debtor is not permitted to file under Chapter 7 and must file under Chapter 13.

TOTAL BANKRUPTCY FILINGS

EXHIBIT 15.15

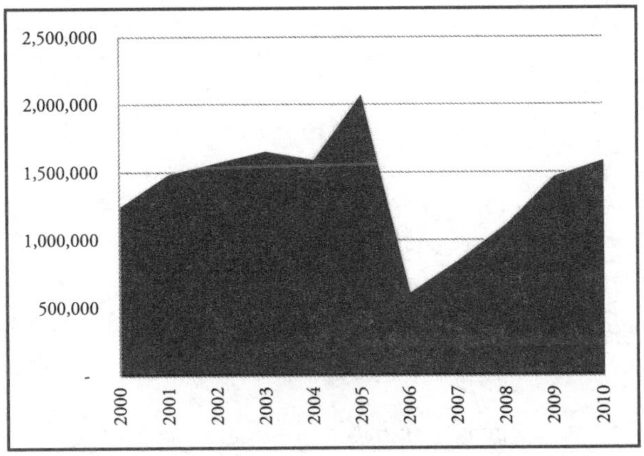

The BAPCPA also requires that before filing for bankruptcy, a debtor must attend a credit counseling program. Once a debtor has filed for bankruptcy, the debtor must attend a personal financial management course before their debts are discharged.

As part of the bankruptcy proceedings under Chapter 7, the court will liquidate nonexempt assets to repay creditors. This may include losing a secured asset, such as a primary residence. This is known as "relief through liquidation."

Some assets and property are exempt from the bankruptcy court and creditors,[6] such as:

- Federal law limits the homestead exemption to $125,000 of equity if the home was purchased within 40 months of filing for bankruptcy. However, if the debtor has resided in the state for longer than 40 months, the state's laws prevail. In states like Florida, a debtor has an unlimited homestead exemption, so they can keep their house on the beach. In Georgia, a debtor is only allowed $10,000 of home equity ($20,000 if married).
- Traditional and Roth IRAs up to $1 million (as indexed).
- Rollover IRAs for an unlimited amount.
- Qualified retirement plans, deferred compensation, and tax–deferred annuities.
- Some personal property including one car, one television, etc.
- Education funds contributed to a qualified tuition plan, although there are limits based on the timing and amounts of the contributions.

The federal bankruptcy law allows a debtor to list their exempt property by following either the federal or their state's bankruptcy law. A debtor may elect either their state or the federal property exemption amounts. Usually, states have more favorable asset exemption amounts and debtors elect to follow their state laws, unless the federal law takes precedence, like the homestead exemption amount.

The bankruptcy court will liquidate assets and use those proceeds to repay creditors. Certain debts are not discharged in bankruptcy, and include:

- All student loans
- Property liens
- Three years of back taxes
- Child support
- Alimony
- Debts obtained through fraud

Another important law revision as a result of BAPCPA is that a debtor must wait eight years before filing again under Chapter 7 bankruptcy. Prior to BAPCPA, the law required a six year waiting period before filing again under Chapter 7.

Note that Chapter 7 bankruptcy is designed to liquidate assets to repay creditors. The debtor may be able to keep a house or an automobile, but will still have a mortgage or automobile loan payment.

Chapter 11 Bankruptcy

Chapter 11 bankruptcy is known as "reorganization bankruptcy" for corporations, sole proprietorships, and partnerships. A Chapter 11 bankruptcy can be voluntary or involuntary.

Under Chapter 11, the debtor is a "debtor in possession" of assets of the company. The debtor in possession is responsible for managing the assets of the company and acting as a fiduciary, which places the interest of the company ahead of the individual.

---

6. www.bankruptcyaction.com/questions.htm#Exemptions

Companies that file under Chapter 11 are required to file a reorganization plan with the courts, which must be approved by the creditors and bankruptcy court. The plan is deemed to be accepted by all creditors, if the plan is accepted by creditors that hold at least two-thirds of the debt and more than one-half the number of claims in the class of creditors. A reorganization plan outlines how the company will restructure contracts, what assets will be liquidated, and to what extent creditors will be repaid. All contracts, debts, and obligations will be discharged once the reorganization plan is approved by the creditors and the court. The company must adhere to any payment schedules agreed to in the reorganization plan.

> **EXAMPLE 15.8**
>
> General Motors (GM) filed for Chapter 11 bankruptcy on June 1, 2009 and emerged as a new company on July 6, 2009. Under terms of the bankruptcy reorganization GM, the U.S. Government, United Auto Workers Union, and debt holders agreed to the following terms:
>
> - The company created a new entity with all remaining assets of the original GM company. The new entity is 61% owned by the U.S. Government, 17% owned by the United Auto Workers Pension Fund, 12% owned by the Canadian government, and 10% by bondholders of the original GM.
> - Much of the debt was forgiven or restructured. GM's debt went from $94 billion to $17 billion under the new entity.
> - Many debtholders were forced to accept equity in the new entity in exchange for giving up their debt position.
>
> The result of GM's chapter 11 bankruptcy is a new company without the burden of significant debt, liabilities, and poor performing product lines.

Chapter 13 Bankruptcy

Chapter 13 bankruptcy, also known as a "wage earners plan," is for individuals or self-employed workers who want to keep their assets and payoff a portion of their debts over time. Corporations and partnerships are not eligible to file Chapter 13.

The BAPCPA requires that before filing for a Chapter 13 bankruptcy, a debtor must attend a credit counseling program. Once a debtor has filed for bankruptcy, the debtor must attend a personal financial management course before their debts are discharged. Similar to Chapter 7, once the debtor files a bankruptcy petition, the court notifies creditors and all collection calls, lawsuits, and wage garnishments must stop.

If a debtor's income is greater than the mean average for their state, the debtor's "applicable commitment period" to repay all or a portion of their debts (as least as much under the plan as the creditor would receive if the debtor's assets were liquidated under Chapter 7) is five years. If the debtor's income is less than the mean average for their state, the debtor's "applicable commitment period" to repay all or a portion of their debts (as least as much under the plan as the creditor would receive if the debtor's assets were liquidated under Chapter 7) is three years. Repayment under a Chapter 13 bankruptcy is made by the debtor to the trustee. The trustee is responsible for allocating the payment to the creditors, according to the terms of the repayment plan.

Generally, any secured creditors are repaid in full. Any unsecured creditors will likely receive less than the full amount owed. If the debtor fails to make payments to the trustee as agreed, the court will dismiss the Chapter 13 bankruptcy filing or force a Chapter 7 liquidation bankruptcy.

Certain debts are not discharged in Chapter 13 (similar to Chapter 7). Those debts that are not discharged include:
- All student loans
- Property liens
- Three years of back taxes
- Child support
- Alimony
- Debts obtained through fraud

There are differences between Chapter 13 and Chapter 7 which may make Chapter 13 more attractive. Note that some debts are dischargeable in Chapter 13, but not in Chapter 7 (a discussion of this topic is beyond the scope of this textbook).

OTHER CONSUMER PROTECTION LAWS AND AGENCIES

Federal Trade Commission (FTC)

The **Federal Trade Commission (FTC)** was created in 1914 and its purpose was to prevent unfair methods of competition in commerce as part of the battle to "bust the trusts."[7] Since then, many consumer protection laws have been passed by Congress, which the FTC is responsible for enforcing. The overriding mission of the FTC is to protect the consumer and prevent unfair, anti-competitive business practices. The FTC works for the consumer to prevent fraudulent, deceptive, and unfair business practices in the marketplace and to provide information to help consumers identify, prevent, and avoid them. Several major consumer protection laws are discussed below.

Fair Packaging and Labeling Act

The purpose of the **Fair Packaging and Labeling Act (FPLA)** is to help consumers compare the value of products and to prevent unfair or deceptive packaging and labeling of many household items. This Act requires manufacturers to disclose the manufacturer's name, address, and contents of the package. The act also prevents deceptive packaging with regards to ingredients, labeling, and misleading presentation of package sizes. This act does not regulate food, drugs, or cosmetics.

---

7. www.ftc.gov/ftc/about.shtm

Equal Credit Opportunity Act

The **Equal Credit Opportunity Act** prohibits discrimination, when evaluating a decision to grant consumer credit. Denying credit as a result of any of the following actions by a creditor **would** constitute discrimination under this Act:

- On the basis of race, color, religion, national origin, sex, marital status, age or receipt of public assistance.
- The consumer's income derives from any public assistance program.
- The consumer exercised a right that is due to him under this Act.

The following actions by a creditor **would not** constitute discrimination:

- For the creditor to ask about the consumer's marital status, as long as the information is used to determine the creditor's recourse if the debt is not satisfied and the information is not used to determine credit-worthiness.
- For the creditor to ask for the consumer's age or if their income is from public assistance if the creditor is ascertaining the probability of the consumer maintaining their current income level.

If an applicant is denied credit (adverse action), this Act requires that the creditor provide the applicant with reasons why the decision was made to deny extending credit.

A good credit history of responsibly managing the amount of your debt and making timely payments will lead to good credit and increase the likelihood of future credit being extended. Women may run into credit issues because they lose their credit history when they marry and begin using their married name, or bills and loans are reported under their husband's credit history. Often, divorced women will decide to keep their married name because they have established good credit. It is highly recommended that women establish a credit history in their name, so they don't lose their credit history upon marriage or divorce.

Credit history is used to determine an individual's credit score. The most popular method of determining a credit score is the Fair Isaac Credit Organization (FICO) method. A FICO score is used to evaluate the creditworthiness of a borrower. The three major credit reporting agencies Equifax, Experian, and TransUnion track an individual's credit history, amount of credit available, amount of credit used, timeliness of payments, credit inquiries and more to determine a credit or FICO score. Although there are other formulas used to derive a credit score, the FICO score is the most widely used credit scoring methodology. A FICO score will range from 300 – 850. The higher the credit score, the more likely a borrower is to qualify for credit, at the lowest interest rates available. FICO does not publish a national average FICO score. The last published report put the national average FICO score at 692.

The best ways to increase a FICO score[8] are to:
- "Pay all bills on time"
- "Keep outstanding balances low on revolving credit accounts"
- "Take on new credit obligations sparingly and only when really needed"

Fair Credit Reporting Act

The **Fair Credit Reporting Act** protects consumer's information collected by the major credit bureaus (Equifax, TransUnion, and Experian). The information contained in a credit report can only be provided to a person who has a specific purpose that is detailed in the Act, such as a potential employer considering making a job offer, a creditor considering extending credit, or an insurance company evaluating an insurance application. Companies that report information to the credit bureaus have a legal duty to investigate any disputed items in a credit report. Credit reporting agencies must correct or remove inaccurate or unverified information within 30 days of being notified. Anyone who relies on information contained in a credit report must notify the consumer of negative items on the credit report that may have led to being denied a job offer, credit, or insurance. Anyone relying on the information in a credit report must notify the consumer of the credit bureau that supplied the information, so the consumer can take the appropriate steps to remedy the negative item. Negative items cannot be reported beyond seven years and bankruptcies cannot be reported beyond 10 years.

The Fair Credit Reporting Act entitles consumers to one free credit report each year from each of the major credit reporting bureaus.[9] In response to many websites promoting "free credit reports" but requiring consumers to enroll in credit monitoring programs, starting April 2, 2010 any websites or advertisements that promote free credit reports must include the following disclosure:

THIS NOTICE IS REQUIRED BY LAW. Read more at FTC.GOV.
You have the right to a free credit report from AnnualCreditReport.com
or 877-322-8228, the **ONLY** authorized source under federal law.[10]

Fair Debt Collection Practices Act

The **Fair Debt Collection Practices Act** prevents third-party debt collectors from using deceptive or abusive methods to collect debts. Examples of deceptive or abusive tactics prevented by this Act include:
- Debt collectors cannot threaten legal action if there is no intention to bring legal action.
- Debt collectors cannot disclose the debt to employers, co-workers, other family members, or anyone else, in an attempt to embarrass the debtor. In addition, the debt collector may not contact the debtor at their place of employment, if they know that the debtor's employer prohibits the contact.

---

8. http://www.fico.com/en/Company/News/Pages/study-findings.aspx
9. http://AnnualCreditReport.com
10. http://www.ftc.gov/opa/2010/02/facta.shtm

- The collectors cannot contact the debtor at unusual hours or make repeated, harassing telephone calls. Appropriate times to contact the debtor are from 8:00 a.m. – 9:00 p.m. Debt collectors are not allowed to contact debtors outside of those hours.
- Debt collectors cannot threaten to use violence as a means of collecting the debt.
- If the debtor informs the collector that they have retained an attorney and the collector should contact the attorney, the debt collector can no longer contact the debtor and must contact the attorney.

Truth in Lending Act

The **Truth in Lending Act** was written to protect consumers so that they fully understand the terms of a loan. Regulation Z of the Truth in Lending Act outlines the specific requirements of lenders. For example, this Act requires creditors to disclose all finance charges and the costs of credit in writing. Lenders must state the interest rate using the annual percentage rate. This Act also requires that debtors be provided with a "three-day out" for loans that are secured by the debtor's primary residence. The Act also regulates how creditor's may advertise loan and financing costs.

Fair Credit Billing Act

This Act amended the Truth in Lending Act. The **Fair Credit Billing Act** requires timely, written verification to a consumer disputing a billing error. The creditor must provide a written acknowledgement of the consumer dispute within 30 days of being notified. This Act also requires that creditors promptly credit consumer's accounts to reflect payment.

Quick Quiz 15.5

Highlight the answer to these questions:

1. Chapter 11 bankruptcy is for individuals and businesses to use for protection from creditors under federal and state bankruptcy laws.
   a. True
   b. False

2. The FTC works for the consumer to prevent fraudulent, deceptive, and unfair business practices in the marketplace.
   a. True
   b. False

3. Denying credit on the basis of race, color, religion, national origin, sex, marital status, age, or receipt of public assistance is a violation of the Equal Credit Opportunity Act.
   a. True
   b. False

False, True, True.

Examples of billing errors that are covered under this Act include:
- Charges posted with a wrong date or dollar amount.
- Charges for goods or services that were never received.
- Failure of the creditor to credit payment to the consumer's account.
- Failure of the creditor to send the bill to the correct address, if the consumer has notified the creditor of the correct address, in writing, with at least 20 days notice prior to the end of a billing period.

Consumers must take the following steps to dispute a billing error:

1. Notify the creditor, in writing within 60 days of receiving the bill, about the disputed item.
2. The creditor must notify the consumer of receiving the dispute, in writing, within 30 days of receiving the notification.
3. The creditor has 90 days to resolve the billing dispute, after receiving notification from the consumer.

During the time period that the error is being investigated, the creditor may not take any legal action to collect the disputed amount and cannot impose finance or penalty related charges. While an item is being disputed, the creditor cannot report the unpaid amount to a credit reporting agency and negatively impact a consumer's credit score. The Act also stipulates that credit card holders are only responsible for the lesser of the charges incurred or $50 for lost or stolen credit cards.

The Fair Credit Billing Act applies to credit cards and revolving charge accounts that are typically issued by big chain stores. This Act does not apply to loans a consumer repays over a period of time or on a fixed repayment schedule, such as automobile payments or installment type payment plans.

Bankruptcy Abuse Prevention and Consumer Protection Act (BAPCPA) of 2005

The **BAPCPA of 2005** amends the Truth in Lending Act in various respects, including requiring certain creditors to disclose on the front of billing statements a minimum monthly payment warning for consumers and a toll-free telephone number, established and maintained by the Commission, for consumers seeking information on the time required to repay specific credit balances.

Credit Card Accountability, Responsibility and Disclosure (CARD) Act of 2009

The **CARD Act of 2009** prevents credit card companies (and banks) from charging hidden fees and extraordinary interest rates as well as promoting easy to understand statements.

The CARD Act of 2009 addressed the following issues:

- **Prevent certain rate increase practices** - credit card companies can no longer increase interest rates on a credit card at any time for any reason, or no reason at all. Prior to the CARD Act a credit card company would raise their interest rate if a consumer missed payments on another card. Alternatively, credit card companies would offer extremely low introductory rates to entice balance transfers, only to later raise the rate. Credit card companies would follow a "universal default" policy, such that if a cardholder would default on one credit card, other credit card companies would raise the interest rate. Credit card companies can no longer penalize cardholders for defaults or missed payments on other credit cards. Credit card companies cannot retroactively increase a promotional interest rate, unless the cardholder is at least 60 days late on their payments. In addition, promotional interest rates must last at least six months and low interest rates for purchases on a new credit card must last at least one year.

- **Prevent hidden fees and confusing payment due dates** - credit card companies can no longer charge for over the limit fees, without consent from the cardholder. In the past, credit card companies would allow a cardholder to go over their credit limit, but charge an over the limit fee. In addition, credit card companies must provide at least 21 days from the date the bill is mailed until the payment is due. Credit card companies may not randomly change the billing due date, or require payments due on a weekend or holiday.

- **Easy to understand disclosures** - All language regarding the terms and conditions of a credit card must be in plain, easy to understand language and no more fine print. Credit terms must be disclosed before an account is opened. On the monthly statements, credit card companies must disclose how long and how much it will cost to pay off the current balance if only the minimum payment is made. Credit card companies must display the total cost if the balance is paid off in 36 months. Credit card companies must now give 45 days notice regarding any changes that will negatively impact the cardholders. Credit card companies must also give cardholders the option of cancelling the card, rather than accepting the changes.

- **Protection for young adults** - credit card companies are not permitted to issue a credit card to anyone under the age of 21, without a co-signer.

Federal Deposit Insurance Corporation (FDIC)

The **Federal Deposit Insurance Corporation (FDIC)** was formed in 1933, as a result of the bank failures that occurred in the 1920's and 1930's. The three goals of the FDIC are to:
- Insure deposits
- Manage receiverships
- Supervise financial institutions for financial stability and consumer protection

In 2008, the FDIC insurance amount for insured deposits was increased from $100,000 to $250,000, as a result of the turmoil experienced in the financial markets in 2008 and 2009. The $250,000 insurance amount is effective until December 31, 2013. Starting on January 1, 2014, the insurance amount will go back to $100,000, except IRA and other retirement accounts, which will continue to be insured up to $250,000.

FDIC insurance only applies to deposit accounts. Deposit accounts include: checking accounts, savings accounts, money market deposit accounts, and certificates of deposit. FDIC insurance does not apply to stocks, bonds, mutual funds, money market mutual funds, insurance products, or annuities. In addition, FDIC insurance does not apply to deposits that are only payable outside the United States.

The FDIC is funded entirely through premiums charged to banks, to insure their deposits, known as deposit insurance. The FDIC insures up to $250,000 per depositor, per legal account ownership, per financial institution. Legal account ownership includes four distinct categories, which are: Individual, Joint, Testamentary, and Retirement accounts. It is possible for a person to have $250,000 of coverage in an individual, joint, testamentary, and retirement account at one financial institution and have a total of $1,000,000 of FDIC coverage.

EXAMPLE 15.9

Homer and Marge are married and have one child, Bart.
They have the following accounts.

Account Title	Account Ownership Category	Owner(s)	Account Balance	Amount Insured Homer	Amount Insured Marge	Amount Insured Bart	Not Insured
CD 1	Single Account	Homer	$75,000	$75,000 (Single)			
Savings	Joint Account	Homer and Marge	$150,000	$75,000 (Joint)	$75,000 (Joint)		
IRA (CD's)	Retirement Account	Husband	$300,000	$250,000 (Retirement)			$50,000 (Retirement)
Checking A	Joint Account	Homer and Marge	$50,000	$25,000 (Joint)	$25,000 (Joint)		
CD 2	Joint Account	Homer, Marge, and Bart	$600,000	$150,000 (Joint)	$150,000 (Joint)	$200,000 (Joint)	$100,000 ($50,000 for Homer and $50,000 for Marge's Joint)
UGMA	Custodian	For Bart, Marge is Custodian	$100,000			$100,000 (Single)	
Checking B	Single Account	Bart	$10,000			$10,000 (Single)	
Trust	Testamentary	Marge	$300,000		$250,000 (Testamentary)		$50,000
Single Totals				$75,000		$110,000	
Joint Totals				$250,000	$250,000	$200,000	
Testamentary Totals					$250,000		
Retirement Totals				$250,000			
Amount Uninsured							$200,000

Summary of Example

Single Account Ownership

All accounts titled as a single account by the same person are combined and insured, up to $250,000. The single account ownerships in the example are Homer's CD for $75,000 and Bart's checking account for $10,000. Both single accounts are fully insured for FDIC purposes.

Joint Account Ownership

The entire balance for accounts titled as joint account ownership are divided evenly by the number of persons on the account. So, if there are two owners on a joint account, the balance is divided 50/50 between the two account owners. If there are three owners on a joint account, the account balance is divided evenly - one-third for each owner. The joint account ownership in the example are Homer and Marge's savings account of $150,000, which is allocated $75,000 to Homer's joint account and $75,000 to Marge's joint account. Checking account A for $50,000 is also a joint account, which is allocated $25,000 to Homer's joint account and $25,000 to Marge's joint account. CD 2 for $600,000 is a joint account and is allocated $200,000 to Homer, $200,000 to Marge and $200,000 to Bart. However, when combining the savings account, plus the checking account A, plus the CD 2, Homer and Marge are each $50,000 over the FDIC limit.

Key Concepts

Underline/highlight the answers as you read:

1. Identify the purpose of the SIPC.

2. Distinguish between the Securities Act of 1933 and the Securities Exchange Act of 1934.

3. What is an investment adviser and what rules must an investment adviser adhere to?

4. What is FINRA?

5. Identify the purpose of the enactment of the Sarbanes-Oxley Act.

Revocable Trust Account Ownership

The amount of FDIC insurance coverage of revocable trust accounts is determined by the amount of the trust's deposits belonging to each owner. For the above example, Marge has a trust with a value of $300,000, however only $250,000 of the $300,000 is insured for FDIC purposes.

INVESTOR PROTECTION

Securities Investor Protection Corporation (SIPC)

The **Securities Investor Protection Corporation (SIPC)** was formed in 1970 as a statutorily created nonprofit membership corporation funded by its member securities broker dealers, with the goal of returning cash and securities to investors, in the event a brokerage firm becomes insolvent. SIPC covers cash, stocks, bonds, and investment company shares (mutual funds). The SIPC does not cover annuity contracts, gold, silver, or futures contracts. The SIPC is not intended to protect investors from poor investment selection or losses arising from bad investments.

The SIPC provides coverage if a broker-dealer becomes insolvent or if there is unauthorized trading in an investor's account. When a broker-dealer becomes insolvent, the SIPC will step in and return the investor's cash and securities, up to $500,000 in securities. The $500,000 limit includes up to $250,000 in cash.

EXAMPLE 15.10

Joe has securities worth $100,000 and cash of $350,000 in his brokerage account. If the brokerage firm becomes insolvent, Joe's securities worth $100,000 would be returned to him but only $250,000 of his $350,000 in cash would be covered.

EXAMPLE 15.11

Mike has 10,000 shares of ABC stock trading at $30 per share, plus $75,000 of cash. SIPC provides coverage of the securities for $300,000 (10,000 shares x $30) and his cash of $75,000.

In the event that Mike's broker-dealer becomes insolvent, the SIPC will either replace the securities or give Mike a check for the amount of his account, up to the $500,000 limit. There is some risk that a broker-dealer could become insolvent when Mike's stock is trading at $30 per share and the broker-dealer is shut down. It may take a few months before the SIPC is appointed as a trustee and the stock price could fall to $20 per share. The SIPC could return the shares to Mike or give him a check for his 10,000 shares at $20 per share. Alternatively, if the stock price increased to $40 per share before the SIPC was appointed as a trustee, then Mike would receive the 10,000 shares or a check for $475,000 ($400,000 in securities + $75,000 in cash). The market risk associated with the stock price increasing or decreasing before the SIPC is appointed trustee is not covered by the SIPC.

Securities Act of 1933

The **Securities Act of 1933** requires that any new security be registered with the Securities and Exchange Commission (SEC) by filing a registration statement with the SEC. Since this Act regulates new securities, it regulates the primary market. This Act requires disclosure of financial and other significant information regarding new securities and prohibits deceit, misrepresentations, and fraud in the sale of new securities.

Registering a security includes the filing of a registration statement and financial statements with the SEC. The registration process discloses information such as a description of the company, the security and information about management. This Act also requires a prospectus that contains information in the registration statement, and is provided to prospective investors. This information allows investors to make well informed investment decisions. After filing registration statements with the SEC, there is a 20-day cooling off period. During this cooling off period, the security's issuer may distribute a red herring prospectus. A red herring prospectus does not include the price of the security or the amount of the security being sold. Once the registration with the SEC is complete, the security can be bought and sold.

Certain securities are exempt from being registered with the SEC. These are some examples of securities that are exempt from the registration requirements:

- Securities of a municipality, state, or federal government.
- Intrastate offerings where the investors and issuers are residents of the same state where the issuer performs most activities.
- Commercial paper with a maturity of 270 days or less.
- Securities issued by a bank, savings institution, common carrier, or farmers' cooperative and subject to other regulatory legislation.
- Stock dividends, stock splits and securities issued in connection with corporate reorganizations.
- Insurance, endowment, and annuity contracts.

Quick Quiz 15.6

Highlight the answer to these questions:

1. The Card Act of 2009 prevents credit card issuers from charging hidden fees and extraordinary interest rates.
   a. True
   b. False

2. The FDIC insures deposit accounts up to $100,000 per depositor, per legal account ownership, per financial institution.
   a. True
   b. False

True, False.

Regulation A is a process for small businesses to sell shares through an initial public offering. Regulation A requires a less stringent registration process for small issues, less than $5,000,000 during a 12 month period. Regulation A also allows shareholders to resell up to $1,500,000 of the security.

Regulation D provides three exemptions to registration for small issues, such as:

- Rule 504: Securities of up to $1,000,000 in a 12 month period to investors who receive restricted securities, that may not be resold without registration or meeting an exemption. Companies may sell non-restricted securities if:
    - The company registers the offering exclusively in one or more states that require a publicly filed registration statement and delivery of a substantive disclosure document to investors;
    - A company registers and sells the offering in a state that requires registration and disclosure delivery and also sells in a state without those requirements, so long as the company delivers the disclosure documents required by the state where the company registered the offering to all purchasers (including those in the state that has no such requirements); or

- The company sells exclusively according to state law exemptions that permit general solicitation and advertising, so long as the company sells only to "accredited investors" (defined below).

- Rule 505: Securities totaling up to $5 million in a 12 month period to:
  - An unlimited number of accredited investors. An accredited investor is:
    - A person who has an individual net worth, or joint net worth with the person's spouse, that exceeds $1 million at the time of the purchase;
    - A person with income exceeding $200,000 in each of the two most recent years or joint income with a spouse exceeding $300,000 for those years and a reasonable expectation of the same income level in the current year;
    - A bank, insurance company, registered investment company, business development company, or small business investment company;
    - A charitable organization, corporation, or partnership with assets exceeding $5 million;
    - A director, executive officer, or general partner of the company selling the securities.
  - Up to 35 unaccredited investors

- Rule 506: Sales of any amount of securities to accredited investors or up to 35 other purchasers that have a sufficient knowledge and experience in financial and business matters to make them capable of evaluating the merits and risks of the prospective investment. The shares must be restricted and cannot freely trade the securities in the secondary markets.

Securities Exchange Act of 1934

The **Securities Exchange Act of 1934** created the Securities and Exchange Commission (SEC) and provides the SEC with the authority to regulate the secondary market. The secondary market includes the subsequent trading of securities, after their initial public offering. The SEC has the power to regulate brokerage firms, stock market exchanges [(New York Stock Exchange, National Association of Securities Dealers Automated Quotations (NASDAQ))] and self regulatory organizations, such as the Financial Industry Regulatory Authority (FINRA).

This Act requires companies with more than 500 shareholders and $10 million in assets to file and disclose financial statements with the SEC. The reporting requirements include quarterly financial statements (10Q) and audited annual financial statements (10k).

This Act requires that information such as shareholder proxy materials soliciting shareholder votes, be filed with the SEC prior to distribution to shareholders. The SEC ensures compliance with disclosure requirements. This Act also requires the disclosure by anyone attempting to purchase more than five percent of a company's securities.

This Act prohibits insider trading, which is the trading of a security while in the possession of material nonpublic information. Basically, if you have information that is not public, you cannot trade on that information. This Act also prohibits price manipulation of a security and making misleading statements about a security. An investment advisor may be liable for an investor's losses under this Act if all of the following conditions are met:

1. There was a material misstatement or omission,
2. The person intended to deceive the investor, and
3. The client relied on the misrepresentation and incurred a loss as a result.

Regulation T under this Act provides the Federal Reserve with the authority to set the margin trading requirements. The Federal Reserve has set the minimum initial margin to 50 percent, which requires investors who borrow from the broker to enter a securities transaction to contribute at least 50 percent equity and borrow up to 50 percent of the transaction total.

Investment Company Act of 1940

The **Investment Company Act of 1940** set standards to regulate investment companies such as open end, closed end, and unit investment trusts. Investment companies are more broadly thought of as mutual funds, which pool investor resources and purchase securities in anticipation of earning a return for the investors.

This Act requires investment companies to register with the SEC. The Act also requires that investment companies disclose the financial statements, investments, costs, objectives, and management of the investment company. These disclosures must be made when the security is initially sold and on an ongoing basis.

Investment Advisers Act of 1940

The **Investment Advisers Act of 1940** requires investment advisers to register with their state or the SEC. Under this Act, an investment adviser is anyone who "receives compensation, engages in the business of advising others, either directly or through publications or writings, as to the value of securities or as to the advisability of investing in, purchasing, or selling securities, or who, for compensation and as part of a regular business, issues or promulgates analyses or reports concerning securities."

The Act can be broken down into a three-pronged test to determine who is an investment adviser. The three-pronged test is:

1. Does the person provide **advice or analysis** regarding securities? Advice or analysis can be as simple as recommending that a client invest in some index mutual funds and providing the client with a list of index funds for the client to choose. Advice does not constitute discussing the current economy or business cycle with a client.
2. Does the person hold themselves out as "**in the business?**" Investment advice regarding securities does not need to be the adviser's primary business. For example, an accounting firm that primarily offers tax preparation and audit services with a

small financial planning division that provides investment advice would meet the "in the business" requirement.

3. Does the person receive **compensation** for their advice? Compensation can be in the form of commissions, flat rate or a fee for a financial plan where investment advice is a part of the overall plan and services provided by the planner.

An adviser who meets all three of the three-pronged test must register as a Registered Investment Adviser (RIA) with their state or the SEC, unless the adviser meets an exception. Investment advisers with assets in excess of $100,000,000 are required to register with the SEC. Advisers with assets below $100,000,000 are required to register with their state.

The Act provides **exceptions** to classification as an investment adviser. Even if an adviser meets the three-pronged test, but meets one of the exceptions, they do not have to register as an investment adviser and is not considered an investment adviser. The following are **exceptions** to registering as an investment adviser:

- A bank, or any bank holding company as defined in the Bank Holding Company Act of 1956, which is not an investment company.
- Any lawyer, accountant, engineer, or teacher whose performance of such services is solely incidental to the practice of his profession.
- Any broker or dealer whose performance of such services is solely incidental to the conduct of his business as a broker or dealer and who receives no special compensation.
- The publisher of any bona fide newspaper, news magazine, or financial publication of general and regular circulation.
- Any person whose advice, analyses, or reports relate to no securities other than securities which are direct obligations of or obligations guaranteed as to principal or interest by the United States.

The Act provides for **exemptions** from registration as an investment adviser, however they are still considered investment advisers. The following are **exemptions**[11] from registering as an investment adviser:

- Any investment adviser who during the course of the preceding twelve months has had fewer than fifteen clients and who neither holds himself out generally to the public as an investment adviser nor acts as an investment adviser to any investment company registered under the Investment Company Act of 1940.
- An adviser whose only clients are insurance companies.
- An adviser whose clients are all residents of the state in which the adviser maintains his, her, or its principal office and place of business and who only gives advice regarding securities that are not listed on any exchange and/or does not have unlisted trading privileges on any national securities exchange.
- Internet Investment Advisers if the adviser provides investment advice to all of its clients exclusively through an interactive website. A limited exception, however, permits an adviser relying on the rule to provide investment advice to fewer than 15 clients through other means during the preceding 12 months.

---

11. http://www.sec.gov/rules/final/ia-2091.htm

Once an adviser is deemed an investment adviser, they have certain duties under the Investment Advisers Act of 1940. Some of the duties include:
- Register as an Investment Adviser
- No Fraudulent Activities
- Disclosure to Prospective and Current Clients (Brochure Rule)
- Prohibits the Assignment of Advisory Contracts
- Proper Use of the Term "Registered Investment Adviser"
- Books and Records to be Maintained

Registering as an Investment Adviser

To file as an investment adviser with the SEC or state, Form ADV must be filed. There are two parts to Form ADV:
- Part 1 contains information about the adviser's education, business, and disciplinary history within the last ten years. Part 1 is filed electronically with the SEC and Part 2 is not required to be filed electronically.
- Part 2 includes information on an adviser's services, fees, and investment strategies.

To withdraw registration as an investment adviser with the SEC, Form ADV-W must be filed.

Representatives of broker-dealers and investment advisers register with their state and the Financial Industry Regulatory Authority (FINRA) by filing Form U-4. Essentially this form is disclosing background information about representatives and investment advisers with the industry's self-regulatory organization, which is FINRA. To withdraw registration, Form U-5 is filed.

No Fraudulent Activities

The Act prohibits fraud by the investment adviser, either directly or indirectly, by:
- Employing any device, scheme, or artifice to defraud any client or prospective client;
- Engaging in any transaction, practice, or course of business which operates as fraud or deceit upon any client or prospective client;
- Acting as principal for his own account, knowingly to sell any security to or purchase any security from a client, or acting as broker for a person other than such client, knowingly to effect any sale or purchase of any security for the account of such client, without disclosing to such client in writing before the completion of such transaction the capacity in which he is acting and obtaining the consent of the client to such transaction;
- Engaging in any act, practice, or course of business which is fraudulent, deceptive, or manipulative.

Disclosure to Prospective and Current Clients (Brochure Rule)

This Act requires a registered investment adviser to provide clients with a written disclosure prior to entering an advisory contract. The requirement is for registered investment advisers to disclose their education background, services provided, fees, business practices and any legal or disciplinary action, within the last 10 years, taken against the adviser. This disclosure requirement is known as the "brochure rule." The registered investment adviser must provide the written disclosure at least 48 hours prior to entering an advisory contract or allow the client five days to terminate the contract, without penalty. The disclosure requirement can be satisfied using Form ADV Part 2 or providing clients with a brochure that at least contains the information on Form ADV Part 2. In addition, the brochure or Form ADV Part 2 must be provided to all clients annually, without charge.

Prohibits the Assignment of Advisory Contracts

Investment advisers who sell their business are prohibited from assigning current investment contracts to the new owner. An investment adviser owes clients the care of a fiduciary, which is the highest professional level of responsibility. The duty of a fiduciary cannot be assigned without the written consent of a client. For a planner that is selling their investment advisory business, they must obtain a written consent from each client in order to transfer that client's contract to the new business owner.

Proper Use of the Term "Registered Investment Adviser"

Advisers who are registered under the Investment Advisers Act of 1940 are Registered Investment Advisers (RIAs). The term Registered Investment Adviser must be spelled out and the adviser is not permitted to use the letters "RIA" after their name, as it may lead clients to believe RIA is a professional designation or credential that required a unique education and/or experience background. Use of the letters RIA may also create unjustified expectations on behalf of the client.

Books and Records to be Maintained

A registered investment advisor is required to maintain accurate and current financial statements, ledgers, journals, copies of instructions from clients regarding purchases and sales of securities, advertisements, reports or other investment advisory services sent to more than 10 persons. The registered investment advisor is generally required to keep records for at least 5 years, even if they leave the business for another career. State laws may be more restrictive and require longer periods of record retention.

Financial Industry Regulatory Authority (FINRA)

The **Financial Industry Regulatory Authority (FINRA)** is a self regulatory organization for all security firms doing business in the United States. FINRA was created in July 2007 by the merging of the National Association of Security Dealers (NASD) and the enforcement functions of the New York Stock Exchange. Any person who sells securities must register with FINRA.[12] Before an individual can sell securities, they must first register with a broker/dealer. After registering with a broker/dealer, they must pass securities licensing exams.

Some of the security licensing exams are listed below.
- Series 3 – Permits an individual to sell futures contracts.
- Series 6 – Permits an individual to sell investment company products such as a mutual fund or unit investment trust and variable life and variable annuities. Note: A person must also have a state insurance license to sell insurance products. Individuals holding a Series 6 license are not permitted to sell corporate or municipal securities.
- Series 7 – General Securities Registered Representative – Permits and individual to sell stocks, bonds, government and municipal bonds, options, REITS and invest-

---

12. http://www.finra.org/Industry/Compliance/Registration/CRD/FilingGuidance/p005419

ment company products. It does not permit the selling of futures. This is the most comprehensive and most common of the registered representative exams.

- Series 24 – General Securities Principal - qualifies individuals required to register as general securities principals in order to manage or supervise the member's investment banking or securities business for corporate securities, direct participation programs, and investment company products/variable contracts.
- Series 26 - Investment Company Products/Variable Contracts Limited Principal - This examination qualifies an individual who will function as a principal for the solicitation, purchase, and/or sale of redeemable securities of companies registered pursuant to the Investment Company Act of 1940; securities of closed-end companies registered pursuant to the Investment Company Act of 1940 during the period of original distribution only; and variable contracts and insurance premium funding programs and other contracts issued by an insurance company.
- Series 63 – Uniform Securities Agent State Law Exam – Most states require an individual to pass the Series 63 exam, before being registered with the state. The Series 63 exam tests primarily state laws and regulations, often referred to as blue sky laws. Blue sky laws prohibit fraud by requiring securities and advisers to be registered with the state. The name blue sky laws is a phrase used to describe an investor being sold a highly speculative investment or nothing more than the big blue sky.
- Series 65 – Uniform Investment Adviser Law Exam – This license is required for an individual to register as an Investment Advisor Representative (IAR) with the state. Most states do not require the Series 65 exam if an individual already passed the Series 7 and Series 66 exams.
- Series 66 – Uniform Combined State Law Exam - This exam combines the Series 63 and 65 exams into one exam. Passing this exam qualifies for registering as an Investment Adviser Representative (IAR) with all 50 states.

Sarbanes-Oxley Act of 2002

The **Sarbanes-Oxley Act of 2002** was passed in response to accounting scandals at firms like Enron and Tyco that ultimately caused those company's stocks to collapse resulting in billions of dollars of losses for investors. The legislation established new or enhanced standards for all U.S. public company boards, management, and public accounting firms. This Act addressed the issues that led to the accounting scandals through the following actions:

- Established the Public Company Accounting Oversight Board, to provide independent oversight of public accounting firms providing audit services.
- Establishes standards for external auditor independence and to limit conflicts of interest. It also addresses new auditor approval requirements, audit partner rotation every five years, and auditor reporting requirements. It restricts auditing companies from providing non-audit services, such as consulting services, for the same clients.
- Mandates that senior executives take individual responsibility for the accuracy and completeness of corporate financial reports. It requires that, typically the CEO and CFO personally certify the integrity of the financial statements.

Quick Quiz 15.7

Highlight the answer to these questions:

1. The SIPC is a statutorily created non-profit membership corporation funded by its member securities broker dealers, with the goal of returning cash and securities to investors, in the event a brokerage firm becomes insolvent.
   a. True
   b. False

2. The Securities Act of 1934 requires that any new security be registered with the SEC by filing a registration statement.
   a. True
   b. False

3. FINRA is a self regulatory organization for all security firms doing business in the United States and requires any person who sells securities to register with the organization.
   a. True
   b. False

True, False, True.

•Requires internal controls for assuring the accuracy of financial reports and disclosures, and mandates both audits and reports on those controls. It also requires timely reporting of material changes in financial condition and specific enhanced reviews by the SEC or its agents of corporate reports.
•Defines the codes of conduct for securities analysts and requires disclosure of knowable conflicts of interest.
•Describes specific criminal penalties for manipulation, destruction or alteration of financial records or other interference with investigations, while providing certain protections for whistle-blowers.
•Increases the criminal penalties associated with white-collar crimes and conspiracies.

Regulation Full Disclosure (FD)

Regulation Full Disclosure (or Regulation FD) was implemented in October 2000 by the SEC to level the playing field between investment analysts and the general public. Prior to Regulation FD, companies would disclose important information about the performance of a company behind closed doors to the investment community, which consisted of mutual fund managers and stock analysts. Regulation FD requires companies to disclose all material information simultaneously to both the investment community and individual investors. Firms comply with Regulation FD by disclosing material information during earnings conference calls and press releases.

DODD-FRANK WALL STREET REFORM AND CONSUMER PROTECTION ACT

The Dodd-Frank Wall Street Reform and Consumer Protection Act, also known as "Dodd-Frank" was signed into law on July 21, 2010 as a result of the Great Recession. The Great Recession was a worldwide economic downturn that started in December 2007 and peaked in September 2008. Many economic conditions contributed to the Great Recession, however some of the most important conditions included risky lending practices by banks, sub-prime mortgage defaults and mortgage backed securities that received high credit ratings, but ultimately resulted in default, high unemployment and sovereign debt concerns in Europe. The Dodd-Frank Act was passed to prevent a collapse of major financial institutions, promote transparency and to protect consumers from abusive financial services practices.

The Dodd-Frank Act consists of sixteen major sections addressing everything from debit card transaction fee limits to preventing firms that are "too big to fail," and much more. Some the more relevant parts for financial panning include FDIC limits and ordering a study to potentially require broker-dealers to abide by a fiduciary duty of care.

The Dodd-Frank Act permanently increased FDIC insurance for interest bearing accounts from $100,000 to $250,000.[13] Prior to Dodd-Frank, the FDIC limit was temporarily increased from $100,000 to $250,000 in response to the Great Recession, to avoid a run on the banks where customers would attempt to withdraw all their deposits at a bank. Banks only maintain 10 percent of deposits in the form of cash, so banks would be unable to meet all withdrawal requests from their depositors if the withdrawal requests occurred over a very short period of time. Raising the FDIC limit was intended to provide reassurances in our banking system that all deposits are safe.

The Dodd-Frank Act also gives the SEC the authority to require broker-dealers to abide by a fiduciary standard duty of care, rather than the current suitability standard. Broker-dealers are required to determine if an investment is suitable for a client, before making an investment recommendation. To fulfill the suitability standard of care, a broker-dealer would require a client to complete a risk tolerance questionnaire. The suitability standard simply requires that an investment is appropriate given an investor's risk tolerance and time horizon, without regard to the overall impact to a client's investment portfolio and other investments. A fiduciary duty of care is required by investment advisors and CFP® professionals which requires both to put their client's interest ahead of their own and to always act in the best interest of the client. A fiduciary duty of care would require the advisor to consider the overall impact to a client's investment portfolio, before recommending an investment. CFP Board, along with the Financial Planning Association and other groups have been advocating the SEC to adopt and enforce the fiduciary duty of care.

WORKER PROTECTION

ERISA

The **Employee Retirement Income Security Act (ERISA)** of 1974 was designed to protect employee retirement savings accounts from creditors and from plan sponsors. Some of the ERISA protection benefits include:
* Anti-alienation protection over all assets within a qualified retirement plan. This anti-alienation protection prohibits any action that may cause the plan assets to be assigned, garnished, levied, or subject to bankruptcy proceedings while the assets remain in the qualified retirement plan.
* Laws, rules and enforcement provisions to protect employees from abuse and misuse of the qualified plan by employers as plan sponsors.

---

13. Source: http://www.fdic.gov/deposit/deposits/changes.html.

EXAMPLE 15.12

O.J. Simpson was found guilty in civil court for the wrongful death of Ronald Goldman and Nicole Simpson. The judgment against O.J. Simpson was for $33.5 million, however because of ERISA protection, his NFL pension and qualified retirement plans cannot be used to satisfy the judgment. Those funds are exempt assets under both federal and Florida law.

Workers' Compensation

Workers' compensation is designed to protect employees if they are injured while at work. Workers' compensation will provide income replacement if the employee is unable to work. It will also provide medical expense coverage if the employee is injured while at work and it can provide a death benefit to an employee's beneficiary. Workers' compensation is an absolute form of liability, which simply means that regardless of why or how the employee is injured, they can collect workers' compensation benefits. So, regardless if an employee's injury is the result of the employer or employee's negligence, they will still collect workers' compensation benefits. Benefits received under workers' compensation are not subject to income tax.

Key Concepts

Underline/highlight the answers as you read:

1. Identify some ERISA protections.

2. Identify the benefits available under Workers' Compensation.

3. What are unemployment benefits and what are conditions associated with receiving benefits?

4. Identify the purpose of OSHA.

EXAMPLE 15.13

Mike works at a winery and is responsible for putting corks in the wine bottles. Mike has a history of drinking a few glasses of wine during his lunch break. Although it is against company policy to drink while on the job and even though Mike's boss, Donna, has repeatedly reprimanded him, he continues to drink wine at lunch. On St. Patrick's Day, Mike decided to celebrate by drinking two bottles of his favorite wine at lunch. After lunch and feeling quite inebriated, Mike proceeds to try and cork a bottle of wine, but instead used his finger instead of a cork. Mike was rushed to the hospital but lost his finger. Even though Mike's injury was his fault because he drank too much wine at lunch, he is still entitled to workers' compensation benefits.

Cynthia, who works in HR, was not very good at using the paper shredder. One day, Cynthia was talking on her cell phone while shredding some documents at work. Unfortunately for Cynthia, she wasn't paying attention and her finger became stuck in the paper shredder and she had to be rushed to the emergency room. Even though Cynthia wasn't paying attention and caused her own injury, workers' compensation will still provide her with benefits.

EXAMPLE 15.14

Unemployment Benefits

Unemployment benefits are designed to provide an unemployed worker with income for a period of time. Unemployment compensation is a program offered jointly by the state and federal governments through unemployment insurance premiums paid by employers. Both the state and federal government have an unemployment tax paid by employers. As a condition of receiving unemployment benefits, the worker must be unemployed and also actively seeking work. Unemployment benefits are taxable income to the recipient. Unemployment benefits do not apply to part-time workers, seasonal workers, or self-employed individuals. To collect unemployment benefits, the worker must be unemployed through no fault of their own, usually as the result of layoffs.

Occupational Safety and Health Administration

OSHA (Occupational Safety and Health Administration) was created by Congress under the Occupational Safety and Health Act of 1970 to promote safe and healthy working conditions for workers by providing training, outreach, education, and assistance. The program covers private employers and employees and is administered federally or by a federally approved state run organization. OSHA establishes rules for employers to follow to protect their employees from hazards. There are differing standards for the worksites of various industries including construction, maritime, and general industry. For example, rules are established to limit hazardous chemical exposure for protection of workers. OSHA also requires employers to keep records of workplace injuries and illnesses.

If a worker believes an employer is not following OSHA standards or if there is a serious hazard at the worksite, the worker can file a complaint with OSHA (confidentiality is provided upon request). The law gives worker protection such that a worker cannot be fired, demoted, transferred, or discriminated against for filing a complaint or otherwise using their OSHA rights.

CONCLUSION

While a financial planner may find that studying economics is less interesting than studying other financial planning topics, the rudiments of this topic must be understood. The planner needs to be able to competently assist clients with making choices potentially involving scarce resources. Financial planning decisions are affected by the business cycle, interest rates, inflation, supply and demand, as well as the concept of opportunity cost which are the basis for making informed client recommendations. Knowledge regarding the external legal environment is also important because laws that protect the consumer, investor, and worker will likely at some point involve a client's financial situation. Currently, changes in product and technology affect economies so quickly that an understanding of economic concepts and relationships is vital for the capable and successful financial planner.

Key Terms

Aggregate Demand Curve - A graphical representation of the quantity of goods and services consumers are willing to buy at any given price level.

Aggregate Supply Curve - A graphical representation between quantity supplied and price.

BAPCPA of 2005 - Amends the Truth in Lending Act in various respects, including requiring certain creditors to disclose on the front of billing statements a minimum monthly payment warning for consumers.

Business Cycle - Measures economic activity over time. The business cycle is characterized by expansion, peak, contraction or recession, and trough.

CARD Act of 2009 - Prevents credit card companies (and banks) from charging hidden fees and extraordinary interest rates as well as promoting easy to understand statements.

Chapter 7 Bankruptcy - For individuals or businesses to use for protection from creditors under federal and state bankruptcy laws.

Chapter 11 Bankruptcy - Known as "reorganization bankruptcy" for corporations, sole proprietorships, and partnerships.

Chapter 13 Bankruptcy - Also known as a "wage earners plan," is for individuals or self-employed workers that want to keep their assets and payoff a portion of their debts over time.

Complements - Products that are consumed jointly.

Consumer Price Index (CPI) - Measures the overall price levels for a basket of goods and services consumers purchase.

Cyclical Unemployment - Occurs when there is an overall downturn in business activity and fewer goods are being produced causing a decrease in the demand for labor.

Deflation - A decrease in the overall price levels of goods and services.

Demand - Represents the quantity consumers are willing to purchase of a good or service, at a particular price.

Discount Rate - The interest rate that the Federal Reserve charges financial institutions for short-term loans.

Disinflation - A slowdown in the rate of inflation or a slowdown in the general price increase of goods and services.

Key Terms

Economic Indicators - Describes the current and future economy and business cycle. The three economic indicators are: Index of Leading Economic Indicators, Index of Lagging Economic Indicators, and Index of Coincident Economic Indicators.

Equal Credit Opportunity Act - Prohibits discrimination, when evaluating a decision to grant consumer credit.

Equilibrium Price - Represents the price at which the quantity demanded equals the quantity supplied.

ERISA (Employee Retirement Income Security Act) - Designed to protect employee retirement savings accounts from creditors and from plan sponsors.

Excess Reserves - Represents the amount of cash or deposits with the Federal Reserve in excess of the minimum amount required.

Fair Credit Billing Act - Requires timely, written verification to a consumer disputing a billing error.

Fair Credit Reporting Act - Protects consumer's information collected by the major credit bureaus (Equifax, TransUnion, and Experian).

Fair Debt Collection Practices Act - Prevents third-party debt collectors from using deceptive or abusive methods to collect debts.

Fair Packaging and Labeling Act (FPLA) - Helps consumers compare the value of products and to prevent unfair or deceptive packaging and labeling of many household items.

Federal Deposit Insurance Corporation (FDIC) - Formed in 1933, as a result of the bank failures that occurred in the 1920's and 1930's. The three goals of the FDIC are to insure deposits, manage receiverships, and supervise financial institutions.

Federal Funds Rate - The bank to bank lending rate.

Federal Trade Commission (FTC) - Works for the consumer to prevent fraudulent, deceptive, and unfair business practices in the marketplace and to provide information to help consumers identify, prevent, and avoid them.

Financial Industry Regulatory Authority (FINRA) - A self regulatory organization for all security firms doing business in the United States.

Fiscal Policy - Represents the government's position on whether to expand or contract the economy. Congress uses taxes and government spending to implement its fiscal policy.

Frictional Unemployment - Occurs when people are voluntarily unemployed because they are seeking other job opportunities.

Key Terms

Full Employment - The rate of employment that exists when there is efficiency in the labor market.

GDP Deflator - Measures the current price of goods and services (nominal GDP) relative to a base year (real GDP).

Gross Domestic Product (GDP) - Represents the total final output of a country, by its citizens and foreigners in the country, over a period of time.

Gross National Product (GNP) - Measures the total final output by the citizens of a country, whether produced domestically or in a foreign country. GNP does not include the output of foreigners in a country.

Inflation - Represents an increase in the price of a basket of goods and services representing the economy as a whole over a period of time.

Interest Rate - The price that a consumer pays to borrow funds.

Investment Advisers Act of 1940 - Requires investment advisers to register with their state or the SEC.

Investment Company Act of 1940 - Set standards to regulate investment companies such as open end, closed end, and unit investment trusts.

Macroeconomics - The study of large economic factors that impact the entire economy such as gross domestic product (GDP), unemployment, and inflation.

Microeconomics - The study of factors that impact small or individual economies, such as supply and demand for a product.

Monetary Policy - Represents the intended influence on the money supply and interest rates by the central bank of a country.

Natural Rate of Unemployment - The lowest unemployment rate where labor and product markets are in balance. At the natural rate of unemployment both price and wage inflation is stable.

Nominal GDP - Measures the value of goods, services, and current prices.

Open Market Operations - The process by which the Federal Reserve will buy or sell U.S. Treasury securities such as T-bills, notes, and bonds.

Opportunity Cost - Represents the value of the best alternative that is foregone.

OSHA (Occupational Safety and Health Administration) - Created by Congress under the Occupational Safety and Health Act of 1970 to promote safe and healthy working conditions for workers by providing training, outreach, education, and assistance.

Key Terms

Producer Price Index (PPI) - Measures the inflation rate for raw materials used in manufacturing.

Real GDP - Measures the value of goods and services at a base year price.

Regulation Full Disclosure (or Regulation FD) - Requires companies to disclose all material information simultaneously to both the investment community and individual investors.

Reserve Requirement - The Federal Reserve requires that banks maintain a certain percentage of their deposits on hand, in the form of cash.

Sarbanes-Oxley Act of 2002 - The legislation established new or enhanced standards for all U.S. public company boards, management, and public accounting firms.

Securities Act of 1933 - Requires that any new security be registered with the Securities and Exchange Commission (SEC) by filing a registration statement with the SEC.

Securities Exchange Act of 1934 - Created the Securities and Exchange Commission (SEC) and provides the SEC with the authority to regulate the secondary market.

Securities Investor Protection Corporation (SIPC) - Formed in 1970 as a statutorily created nonprofit membership corporation funded by its member securities broker dealers, with the goal of returning cash and securities to investors, in the event a brokerage firm becomes insolvent.

Structural Unemployment - Occurs when there is inequality between the supply and demand for workers.

Substitutes - Products that serve a similar purpose.

Supply - Represents the quantity firms are willing to produce and sell of a good or service, at a particular price.

Truth in Lending Act - Protects consumers so that they fully understand the terms of a loan.

Unemployed - Refers to those individuals 16 years of age and older who are not working and are making an effort to seek employment.

Unemployment Benefits - Designed to provide an unemployed worker with income for a period of time. The worker must be unemployed and also actively seeking work.

Utility - The benefit firms and consumers receive when allocating or spending financial resources.

Workers' Compensation - Designed to protect employees when injured at work. It will provide income replacement if the employee is unable to work. It will also provide medical expense coverage if the employee is injured while at work and it can provide a death benefit to an employee's beneficiary.

1. Discuss why a financial planner must understand economic concepts and the direction of the current economy.

2. Discuss the economic measurements associated with the Gross Domestic Product (GDP).

3. What is inflation and how is it measured?

4. Describe the phases of the business cycle.

5. Define the three indexes of economic indicators.

6. What are the goals of the Federal Reserve's monetary policy and how are those goals implemented?

7. Discuss how fiscal policy is implemented.

8. Discuss the factors and relationships associated with measuring demand.

9. Discuss the factors and relationship associated with measuring supply.

10. List and discuss the three types of bankruptcy filings.

11. What is the purpose of the Federal Trade Commission (FTC)?

12. List and describe some major consumer protection laws.

13. What is the function of the Federal Deposit Insurance Corporation (FDIC)?

14. List and describe some major investor protection laws.

15. List and describe some major worker protection laws.

1. During a period of recession /contraction, which of the following would be true?

    1. The supply of goods and services would be decreasing.
    2. Interest rates would be decreasing.
    3. Unemployment would be increasing.
    4. Inflation would be decreasing.

        a. 1 and 2.
        b. 1 and 3.
        c. 1, 2 and 3.
        d. 1, 2 and 4.
        e. 1, 2, 3, and 4.

2. Which of the following is a fiscal policy tool used by Congress that influences the money supply and interest rates?

    a. Prime Lending Rate.
    b. Open Market Operations.
    c. Discount Rate.
    d. Debt Management.

3. Phyllis had three credit cards stolen. Before she realized they were stolen, the following amounts were already fraudulently charged:

American Express	$2,000
VISA	$500
MasterCard	$40

    How much is Phyllis' expected liability for the fraudulent charges?

    a. $50.
    b. $140.
    c. $150.
    d. $2,400.

4. Orenthal James Sampson lost a wrongful death lawsuit and was ordered to pay the plaintiff $5 million dollars. As a result of the lawsuit, Mr. Sampson filed for bankruptcy. Which of the following assets are exempt assets in bankruptcy from his creditors?

    1. A Roth IRA worth $900,000.

    2. A conversion IRA worth $3.5 million.

    3. Football memorabilia worth $1.5 million.

    4. A brokerage account worth $2 million.

        a. 1 only.

        b. 2 only.

        c. 1 and 2.

        d. 3 and 4.

5. All of the following claims will be discharged in bankruptcy except:

        a. Tort claim as a result of personal negligence.

        b. Consumer credit card debt.

        c. A claim arising out of a breach of contract.

        d. Child support.

6. Due to a shortage in supply, the price of corn increases suddenly, causing a decrease in the demand for corn and an increase in the demand for carrots. Which term best describes the relationship between corn and carrots?

        a. Substitute.

        b. Complement.

        c. By-Products.

        d. Fungible.

7. A grocery store puts chocolate chip cookies on sale, which increases the demand for milk. What are the two products?

        a. Substitute.

        b. Complement.

        c. Elastic.

        d. Inelastic.

8. Low interest rates and high unemployment would be characteristic of what phase of the business cycle?

        a. Expansion.

        b. Peak.

        c. Contraction.

        d. Trough.

9. Increasing inflation rates and increasing interest rates would be characteristic of?

    a. Expansion.

    b. Peak.

    c. Contraction.

    d. Trough.

10. Movement along the demand curve represents a change in quantity demanded. Which of the following is the likely cause of a change in quantity demanded?

    a. Increased savings rate.

    b. Decrease tax rate.

    c. Price change.

    d. More suppliers.

11. Which of the following items would cause the demand curve to shift to the right?

    a. Increased savings rate.

    b. Decreased tax rate.

    c. Price change.

    d. More suppliers.

12. If the price of a luxury car decreases by a small amount, and there is a significantly large increase in demand, what can be said about the demand?

    a. Demand is elastic.

    b. Demand is inelastic.

    c. There is a shift in the demand curve.

    d. The demand curve is inverted.

13. If the Federal Reserve wants to increase interest rates, which of the following actions might it take?

    a. Buy government securities.

    b. Sell government securities.

    c. Decrease the reserve requirement.

    d. Decrease federal government spending.

14. All of the following are examples of monetary policy except?

    a. Open market operations.

    b. Discount rate.

    c. Excess Reserves.

    d. Prime Lending Rate.

15. Which of the following is NOT one of the primary responsibilities of the Federal Reserve?

      a.   Maintain price levels supported by the economy.

      b.   Maintain long-term economic growth.

      c.   Maintain full employment.

      d.   Ensure consistent positive returns in the equity markets.

Quick Quiz Explanations

Quick Quiz 15.1
1. False. This is the definition of macroeconomics. Microeconomics is the study of factors that impact small or individual economies, such as supply and demand for a product.
2. False. This is a result of deflation, which is a decrease in the overall price levels of goods and services.
3. True.

Quick Quiz 15.2
1. True.
2. False. This is the definition of the index of trailing economic indicators. The index of leading economic indicators predicts changes in the economy.
3. False. This is the definition of fiscal policy. Monetary policy is the intended influence on the money supply and interest rates by the central bank of a country.

Quick Quiz 15.3
1. True.
2. True.

Quick Quiz 15.4
1. False. This is the definition of supply. Demand represents the quantity consumers are willing to purchase of a good or service, at a particular price.
2. True.
3. True.
4. False. A change in price will cause a movement along the supply curve impacting the quantity supplied whereas a shift in the supply curve is cause by other factors such as decreased competition or outdated technologies.

Quick Quiz 15.5
1. False. This is the definition of Chapter 7 bankruptcy. Chapter 11 bankruptcy is known as "reorganization bankruptcy" for corporations, sole proprietorships, and partnerships.
2. True.
3. True.

Quick Quiz 15.6
4. True.
5. False. The insured amount is currently $250,000 effective until December 31, 2013.

Quick Quiz 15.7
1. True.
2. False. This is the purpose of the Securities Act of 1933 law. The Securities Act of 1934 created the SEC and gives authority to the SEC to regulate the secondary market.
3. True.

Ethics & Standards of Professional Conduct

LEARNING OBJECTIVES

After reading this chapter, you should be able to:
- Describe the standards of professional conduct and the five different categories.
- Identify, list, and describe each of the principles.
- Identify and list the six different categories of the rules of conduct.
- Differentiate what constitutes providing material elements of the financial planning process.
- Discuss the fiduciary requirements that are imposed by Rule 1.4.
- Clearly differentiate the disclosure obligations and whether they must be orally or must be in writing for different types of client engagements.
- List and discuss the practice standards.
- Describe the various disciplinary rules and procedures paying particular attention to the forms of discipline.
- Describe the fitness standards for candidates and registrants.
- Discuss the issues and outcome of the various anonymous case histories.
- Recognize unethical practices in the financial planning profession based on the CFP Board Standards of Professional Conduct.*

* CFP Board Resource Document - Student-Centered Learning Objectives based upon CFP Board Principal Topics.

INTRODUCTION

The **Certified Financial Planner Board of Standards, Inc. ("CFP Board")** maintains professional standards necessary for competency and ethics in the financial planning profession for those professionals who have been granted the right to use their designation. The CFP Board has exclusive authority to determine who may use their markings, including CFP®, CERTIFIED FINANCIAL PLANNER,™ and CFP® certification (hereinafter "CFP®") in the United States. Considering that the CFP Board has this exclusive authority, CFP Board conditions permission, and grants to such individuals the right, to use these marks on their agreement to abide by certain terms and conditions specified by CFP Board. CFP Board also enforces the requirements, including ethics, for CFP® **certificants** and **registrants**[1] through, among other things, a series of professional and ethical standards designed to protect the public and advance professionalism in the financial planning industry. CFP Board's Standards of Professional Conduct ("Standards of Professional Conduct") include the highest level of professional and ethical standards.

The **Standards of Professional Conduct** are comprised of five different categories:
1. Code of Ethics and Professional Responsibility ("Code of Ethics");
2. Rules of Conduct;
3. Financial Planning Practice Standards ("Practice Standards");
4. Disciplinary Rules and Procedures ("Disciplinary Rules"); and
5. Candidate Fitness Standards.

| EXHIBIT 16.1 | STANDARDS OF PROFESSIONAL CONDUCT |

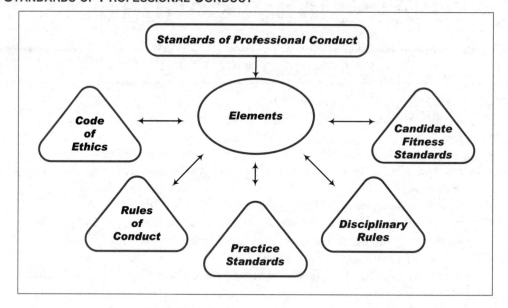

---

1. CFP Board has provided terminology in its booklet as to the Standards of Professional Conduct (hereinafter "Standards of Professional Conduct booklet," available online at www.cfp.net), and included is the definition of a certificant who is an individual currently certified by the CFP Board. A registrant is an individual who, though not currently certified, has been certified by CFP Board in the past and has an entitlement, direct or indirect, to potentially use the CFP® marks. This includes individuals who have relinquished their certification and who are eligible for reinstatement without being required to pass the current CFP certification examination. The Standards of Professional Conduct apply to registrants when the conduct at issue occurred at a time when the registrant was certified, in which case CFP Board has jurisdiction to investigate such conduct. Standards of Professional Conduct booklet, p. 5.

These Standards of Professional Conduct form part of the certification process and create terms and conditions imposed upon certificants and registrants on a continuing basis beyond initial certification.

The first Code of Ethics was introduced in 1985 and in 1988, the Code of Ethics was revised and the first Disciplinary Rules were introduced. In 1993, another major revision occurred which established the principles and rules of the Code of Ethics. The Practice Standards were first published for review and comment in 1999, were finalized in 2002, and became effective starting on July 1, 2008, with amendments in 2009. The Disciplinary Rules were revised and amended with an effective date of June 1, 2012.

Key Concepts

Underline/highlight the answers as you read:

1. Identify the five different categories included in the Standards of Professional Conduct.

2. Determine the purpose of the Code of Ethics and the seven principles included in the Code of Ethics.

The CFP Board has placed the highest ethical and professional standards upon CFP® certificants and registrants. The interrelated and organized set of rules and guidelines encourages sound practices and standards and creates a mechanism to penalize those who do not meet the high professional and ethical standards of conduct. By doing so, the CFP Board has created a streamlined and objective set of standards on par with those applicable to doctors, attorneys, and certified public accountants. The profession benefits from setting high standards and legitimizing its services and process, and importantly the public is the ultimate beneficiary from the establishment and enforcement of the ethics, conduct, practices, procedures, and standards. This chapter will evaluate each of the five categories of CFP Board's Standards of Professional Conduct.

CODE OF ETHICS AND PROFESSIONAL RESPONSIBILITY

The fundamental starting point for establishing these principles and standards is CFP Board's Code of Ethics. The **Code of Ethics** is organized into seven different principles ("Principles") that espouse general statements regarding ethical and professional ideals that certificants and registrants are expected to enact into their professional activities. The Code of Ethics provide principles that are "aspirational in character," meaning they are: (1) basic tenets of fairness and professionalism to which all in this profession should aspire, or (2) examples of how certificants and registrants should act. The Principles may also serve as a guide to certificants and registrants through the various obstacles that are frequently encountered during the financial planning process.[2]

The seven Principles form not only the Code of Ethics, but they form the basis of and are repeated throughout the CFP Board's Rules of Conduct, Practice Standards and Disciplinary Rules. Throughout the Standards of Professional Conduct, there are references and reliance on the responsibilities of certificants and registrants to the public, to clients (actual or prospective), to the profession, and to employers.

The following is the actual Code of Ethics, word-for-word, as promulgated by CFP Board:[3]

PRINCIPLE 1 – INTEGRITY

Provide Professional Services with Integrity.
Integrity demands honesty and candor which must not be subordinated to personal gain and advantage. Certificants are placed in positions of trust by clients, and the ultimate source of that trust is the certificant's personal integrity. Allowance can be made for innocent error and legitimate differences of opinion, but integrity cannot co-exist with deceit or subordination of one's principles.

PRINCIPLE 2 – OBJECTIVITY

Provide Professional Services Objectively.
Objectivity requires intellectual honesty and impartiality. Regardless of the particular service rendered or the capacity in which a certificant functions, certificants should protect the integrity of their work, maintain objectivity and avoid subordination of their judgment.

PRINCIPLE 3 – COMPETENCE

Maintain the Knowledge and Skill Necessary to Provide Professional Services Competently.
Competence means attaining and maintaining an adequate level of knowledge and skill, and application of that knowledge and skill in providing services to clients. Competence also includes the wisdom to recognize the limitations of that knowledge and when consultation with other professionals is appropriate or referral to other professionals necessary. Certificants make a continuing commitment to learning and professional improvement.

PRINCIPLE 4 – FAIRNESS

Be Fair and Reasonable in All Professional Relationships. Disclose Conflicts of Interest.
Fairness requires impartiality, intellectual honesty and disclosure of material conflicts of interest. It involves a subordination of one's own feelings, prejudices and desires so as to achieve a proper balance of conflicting interests. Fairness is treating others in the same fashion that you would want to be treated.

---

2. CFP Board's Standards of Professional Conduct defines a "personal financial planning process" or a "financial planning process" as a process which typically includes establishing and defining the client-planner relationship, gathering client data, including goals, analyzing and evaluating the client's current financial status, developing and presenting recommendations or alternatives, implementing the recommendations, monitoring the recommendations, and some or all of the above. Standards of Professional Conduct booklet, Terminology, p. 5.
3. Standards of Professional Conduct booklet, Code of Ethics, pp. 6-7.

PRINCIPLE 5 – CONFIDENTIALITY

Protect the Confidentiality of All Client Information.

Confidentiality means ensuring that information is accessible only to those authorized to have access. A relationship of trust and confidence with the client can only be built upon the understanding that the client's information will remain confidential.

PRINCIPLE 6 – PROFESSIONALISM

Act in a Manner that Demonstrates Exemplary Professional Conduct.

Professionalism requires behaving with dignity and courtesy to clients, fellow professionals, and others in business-related activities. Certificants cooperate with fellow certificants to enhance and maintain the profession's public image and improve the quality of services.

PRINCIPLE 7 – DILIGENCE

Provide Professional Services Diligently.

Diligence is the provision of services in a reasonably prompt and thorough manner, including the proper planning for, and supervision of, the rendering of professional services.

These Principles provide a framework for the ethical and professional standards and ideals for certificants and registrants. Integrity brings out honesty and candor in the provision of professional services, while Objectivity protects the integrity of work. Objectivity also requires intellectual honesty and impartiality, whereas Competence, requires certificants and registrants to obtain and maintain an adequate level of knowledge and skill, along with the ability to recognize those times when one's knowledge is limited and consultation with, or referral to, other professionals is appropriate. Fairness dictates that certificants and registrants be fair and reasonable in all professional relationships. It is here where disclosure of conflicts of interest is paramount. Confidentiality is a key component in any relationship where clients place things in trust of another. The professional must safeguard that information, which, in turn, will build the relationship of trust and confidence between the client and certificant and registrant.

Quick Quiz 16.1

Highlight the answer to these questions:

1. The Standards of Professional Conduct include the Code of Ethics, Rules of Conduct, Practice Standards, Disciplinary Rules, and the Candidate Fitness Standards.
   a. True
   b. False

2. The Code of Ethics includes tenets of fairness and professionalism which financial professionals should aspire or, are examples of how certificants and registrants should act.
   a. True
   b. False

True, True.

Professionalism, the sixth principle, requires courtesy and dignified activity with not only clients but others in the profession and others in business-related activities. Finally, diligence encourages good old-fashioned hard work provided in a reasonably prompt and thorough manner.

EXAMPLE 16.1

Michael is a CFP certificant and is faced with a potential conflict of interest during his work for a client. Michael asks you which Principles of the Code of Ethics are invoked when actual or potential conflicts of interest arise? What is the most vital action to take when a conflict of interest arises?

While Fairness expressly discusses conflicts of interest, the Principles of Integrity, Objectivity and Professionalism could also be said to address some aspect of conflicts of interest. While some conflicts are unavoidable or only perceived, the vital action that must be taken on the certificant or registrant's behalf is to <u>disclose</u> any actual or perceived conflicts of interest to the client.

RULES OF CONDUCT

The **Rules of Conduct** are not designed to be a foundation of legal liability to third parties. Rather, the Rules of Conduct establish expected high standards and also describe the level of professionalism required. The Rules of Conduct govern all those who have the right to use the CFP® marks, whether or not those marks are actually used. The CFP Board cannot enumerate in the Rules of Conduct every area of service that may be provided by financial planning professionals, and the Rules of Conduct may not apply to every specific activity. It is up to the certificant or registrant to determine whether a specific Rule of Conduct applies to any given activity. Compliance is exhibited by certificant's demonstration of the completed required action.

 *Key Concepts*

Underline/highlight the answers as you read:

1. Identify the six different categories of the Rules of Conduct.

2. Determine the CFP Board definition of a fiduciary.

The Rules of Conduct are organized into six different categories, with those being as follows:
1. Defining the relationship with a prospective client or client;
2. Information disclosed to prospective clients and clients;
3. Prospective client and client information and property;
4. Obligations to prospective clients and clients;
5. Obligation to employers; and
6. Obligations to CFP Board.

FINANCIAL PLANNING[4]

Financial planning is providing "material elements of the financial planning process" i.e., the process of determining whether and how an individual can meet life goals through the proper management of financial resources. When a certificant uses the six step financial planning process (see the Practice Standards) in connection with an engagement involving multiple financial planning subject areas, both the duty of care and disclosure requirements are more stringent than for engagements that do not rise to the definition of financial planning. There are four areas that are considered to make this determination:

1. The client's understanding and intent in engaging the certificant.
2. The degree to which multiple financial planning subject areas are involved (generally, two or more).
3. The comprehensiveness of data gathering.
4. The breadth and depth of recommendations.

Examples of Activities that May Be Considered Financial Planning:
- Conducting detailed data-gathering regarding multiple aspects of a client's financial situation.
- Analyzing a client's data and making wide-ranging recommendations.
- Providing investment advisory services as defined by the SEC.

Examples of Activities that May NOT Be Considered Financial Planning:
- A broker completing paperwork to open an account.
- Acting as an order-taker for brokerage services.
- Engaging solely in sales activity related to insurance products.
- Acting as a mortgage broker without providing any other financial services.
- Completing tax returns without providing any other financial services.
- Teaching a financial class or continuing education program.

The certificant must consider the total client relationship in making this determination, not just any single, limited engagement. Thus, a series of limited engagements which, when combined, meet the criteria above may be considered material elements of the financial planning process. Some engagements, such as a comprehensive retirement plan, may be considered material elements of financial planning even though they involve only one of the financial planning subject areas, if sufficient data gathering and breadth of recommendations are provided.

Because these Rules are not voluminous and explain proper and sound actions for certificants and registrants, the CFP Board's Rules of Conduct are provided below, word-for-word:[5]

1. Defining the Relationship with the Prospective Client or Client

1.1   The certificant and the prospective client or client shall mutually agree upon the services to be provided by the certificant.

---

4. Source: CFP Board Report "Focus on Ethics" 7/2/07
5. Standards of Professional Conduct booklet, Rules of Conduct, pp. 8-12.

1.2 If the certificant's services include financial planning or material elements of financial planning, prior to entering into an agreement, the certificant shall provide written information or discuss with the prospective client or client the following:

    a.   The obligations and responsibilities of each party under the agreement with respect to:

        i.   Defining goals, needs and objectives,

        ii.   Gathering and providing appropriate data,

        iii.   Examining the result of the current course of action without changes,

        iv.   The formulation of any recommended actions,

        v.   Implementation responsibilities, and

        vi.   Monitoring responsibilities.

    b.   Compensation that any party to the agreement or any legal affiliate to a party to the agreement will or could receive under the terms of the agreement; and factors or terms that determine costs, how decisions benefit the certificant and the relative benefit to the certificant.

    c.   Terms under which the agreement permits the certificant to offer proprietary products.

    d.   Terms under which the certificant will use other entities to meet any of the agreement's obligations.

        If the certificant provides the above information in writing, the certificant shall encourage the prospective client or client to review the information and offer to answer any questions that the prospective client or client may have.

1.3 If the services include financial planning or material elements of financial planning, the certificant or the certificant's employer shall enter into a written agreement governing the financial planning services ("Agreement"). The Agreement shall specify:
- The parties to the Agreement,
- The date of the Agreement and its duration,
- How and on what terms each party can terminate the Agreement, and
- The services to be provided as part of the Agreement.

The Agreement may consist of multiple written documents. Written documentation that includes the items above and is used by a certificant or certificant's employer in compliance with state or federal law, or the rules or regulations of any applicable self-regulatory organization, such as the Securities and Exchange Commission's Form ADV or other disclosure documents, shall satisfy the requirements of this Rule.

1.4 A certificant shall at all times place the interest of the client ahead of his or her own. When the certificant provides financial planning or material elements of financial planning, the certificant owes to the client the duty of care of a fiduciary as defined by CFP Board.

2. *Information Disclosed To Prospective Clients and Clients*

2.1 A certificant shall not communicate, directly or indirectly, to clients or prospective clients any false or misleading information directly or indirectly related to the certificant's professional qualifications or services. A certificant shall not mislead any parties about the potential benefits of the certificant's service. A certificant shall not fail to disclose or otherwise omit facts where that disclosure is necessary to avoid misleading clients.

2.2 A certificant shall disclose to a prospective client or client the following information:

    a.   An accurate and understandable description of the compensation arrangements being offered. This description must include:

        i.   Information related to costs and compensation to the certificant and/or the certificant's employer, and

        ii.   Terms under which the certificant and/or the certificant's employer may receive any other sources of compensation, and if so, what the sources of these payments are and on what they are based.

    b.   A general summary of likely conflicts of interest between the client and the certificant, the certificant's employer or any affiliates or third parties, including, but not limited to, information about any familial, contractual or agency relationship of the certificant or the certificant's employer that has a potential to materially affect the relationship.

    c.   Any information about the certificant or the certificant's employer that could reasonably be expected to materially affect the client's decision to engage the certificant that the client might reasonably want to know in establishing the scope and nature of the relationship, including but not limited to information about the certificant's areas of expertise.

    d.   Contact information for the certificant and, if applicable, the certificant's employer.

e. If the services include financial planning or material elements of financial planning, these disclosures must be in writing. The written disclosures may consist of multiple written documents. Written disclosures used by a certificant or certificant's employer that includes the items listed above, and are used in compliance with state or federal laws, or the rules or requirements of any applicable self-regulatory organization, such as the Securities and Exchange Commission's Form ADV or other disclosure documents, shall satisfy the requirements of this Rule.

The certificant shall timely disclose to the client any material changes to the above information.

3. Prospective Client and Client Information and Property

3.1 A certificant shall treat information as confidential except as required in response to proper legal process; as necessitated by obligations to a certificant's employer or partners; as required to defend against charges of wrongdoing; in connection with a civil dispute; or as needed to perform the services.

3.2 A certificant shall take prudent steps to protect the security of information and property, including the security of stored information, whether physically or electronically, that is within the certificant's control.

3.3 A certificant shall obtain the information necessary to fulfill his or her obligations. If a certificant cannot obtain the necessary information, the certificant shall inform the prospective client or client of any and all material deficiencies.

3.4 A certificant shall clearly identify the assets, if any, over which the certificant will take custody, exercise investment discretion, or exercise supervision.

3.5 A certificant shall identify and keep complete records of all funds or other property of a client in the custody, or under the discretionary authority, of the certificant.

3.6 A certificant shall not borrow money from a client. Exceptions to this Rule include:

a. The client is a member of the certificant's immediate family, or

b. The client is an institution in the business of lending money and the borrowing is unrelated to the professional services performed by the certificant.

3.7 A certificant shall not lend money to a client. Exceptions to this Rule include:

a. The client is a member of the certificant's immediate family, or

b.   The certificant is an employee of an institution in the business of lending money and the money lent is that of the institution, not the certificant.

3.8   A certificant shall not commingle a client's property with the property of the certificant or the certificant's employer, unless the commingling is permitted by law or is explicitly authorized and defined in a written agreement between the parties.

3.9   A certificant shall not commingle a client's property with other clients' property unless the commingling is permitted by law or the certificant has both explicit written authorization to do so from each client involved and sufficient record-keeping to track each client's assets accurately.

3.10 A certificant shall return a client's property to the client upon request as soon as practicable or consistent with a time frame specified in an agreement with the client.

4. Obligations to Prospective Clients and Clients

4.1   A certificant shall treat prospective clients and clients fairly and provide professional services with integrity and objectivity.

4.2   A certificant shall offer advice only in those areas in which he or she is competent to do so and shall maintain competence in all areas in which he or she is engaged to provide professional services.

4.3   A certificant shall be in compliance with applicable regulatory requirements governing professional services provided to the client.

4.4   A certificant shall exercise reasonable and prudent professional judgment in providing professional services to clients.

4.5   In addition to the requirements of Rule 1.4, a certificant shall make and/or implement only recommendations that are suitable for the client.

4.6   A certificant shall provide reasonable and prudent professional supervision or direction to any subordinate or third party to whom the certificant assigns responsibility for any client services.

4.7   A certificant shall advise his or her current clients of any certification suspension or revocation he or she receives from CFP Board.

5. Obligations to Employers

5.1   A certificant who is an employee/agent shall perform professional services with dedication to the lawful objectives of the employer/principal and in accordance with CFP Board's Code of Ethics.

5.2 A certificant who is an employee/agent shall advise his or her current employer/principal of any certification suspension or revocation he or she receives from CFP Board.

6. Obligations to CFP Board

6.1 A certificant shall abide by the terms of all agreements with CFP Board, including, but not limited to, using the CFP® marks properly and cooperating fully with CFP Board's trademark and professional review operations and requirements.

6.2 A certificant shall meet all CFP Board requirements, including continuing education requirements, to retain the right to use the CFP® marks.

6.3 A certificant shall notify CFP Board of changes to contact information, including, but not limited to, e-mail address, telephone number(s) and physical address, within forty five (45) days.

6.4 A certificant shall notify CFP Board in writing of any conviction of a crime, except misdemeanor traffic offenses or traffic ordinance violations unless such offense involves the use of alcohol or drugs, or of any professional suspension or bar within thirty (30) calendar days after the date on which the certificant is notified of the conviction, suspension or bar.

6.5 A certificant shall not engage in conduct which reflects adversely on his or her integrity or fitness as a certificant, upon the CFP® marks, or upon the profession.

FIDUCIARY REQUIREMENT

The Rules of Conduct address the fiduciary standard of care applicable to the CFP® financial planning profession. Rule 1.4 provides that a certificant has the duty of care of a fiduciary as defined by the CFP Board when providing financial planning or "material elements" of financial planning.[6] A **fiduciary** is defined as "one who acts in utmost good faith, in a manner he or she reasonably believes to be in the best interest of the client."[7] It is important to note that Rule 1.4 expressly applies only to certificants providing financial planning or material elements of financial planning. Rule 1.4 also requires that a certificant shall at all times place the interests of the client ahead of his or her own interests, which is directly related to the Principles of Integrity, Objectivity, Fairness and Professionalism.

---

6. Standards of Professional Conduct booklet, Rules of Conduct. Rule 1.4.
7. Standards of Professional Conduct booklet, Terminology, p. 4.

SUMMARY OF RULES OF CONDUCT

As a certifying and standards-setting body, the CFP Board has made it clear that violations of the Rules of Conduct may subject a certificant or registrant to discipline. Discipline extends to the rights of registrants and certificants who have the right to use the CFP® marks. Exhibit 16.2 provides a synopsis of certificants' and registrants' various duties and responsibilities found in the CFP Board's Rules of Conduct to the public, clients, the profession, and employers.

SUMMARY OF DISCLOSURE OBLIGATIONS

Disclosure Obligations vary depending upon whether the certificant is providing financial planning or material elements of financial planning. Certificants must disclose either orally or in writing the following information for ALL client engagements (see Rule 2.2 for more specific explanation of each item):

1. An accurate and understandable description of the compensation arrangements.
2. A general summary of likely conflicts of interest.
3. Any information about the certificant or the certificant's employer that could reasonably be expected to materially affect the client's decision to engage the certificant.
4. Contact information for the certificant and, if applicable, the certificant's employer.

If the engagement involves financial planning or material elements of financial planning:
1. The disclosures above must be in writing (Rule 2.2 (e)).

2. A written agreement governing the engagement must include (Rule 1.3):
   a. The parties to the Agreement,

   b. The date of the Agreement and its duration,

   c. How and on what terms each party can terminate the Agreement, and

   d. The services to be provided as part of the Agreement.

Quick Quiz 16.2

Highlight the answer to these questions:

1. The Rules of Conduct are organized into seven different principles of ethics and professional ideals that certificants and registrants are expected to enact into their professional activities.
   a. True
   b. False

2. Rule 1.4 of the Rules of Conduct provides that a certificant has the duty of care of a fiduciary as defined by the CFP Board when providing financial planning or "material elements" of financing planning.
   a. True
   b. False

3. The duty of care of a fiduciary involves acting in a manner that is in the best interest of the client.
   a. True
   b. False

False, True, True.

3. The following disclosures required by Rule 1.2 may be made in writing or through discussions with the client or prospective client:

    a. The obligations and responsibilities of each party under the agreement with respect to:

        i. Defining goals, needs and objectives,

        ii. Gathering and providing appropriate data,

        iii. Examining the result of the current course of action without changes,

        iv. The formulation of any recommended actions,

        v. Implementation responsibilities, and

        vi. Monitoring responsibilities.

    b) Compensation that any party to the agreement or any legal affiliate to a party to the agreement will or could receive under the terms of the agreement; and factors or terms that determine costs, how decisions benefit the certificant and the relative benefit to the certificant.

    c) Terms under which the agreement permits the certificant to offer proprietary products.

    d) Terms under which the certificant will use other entities to meet any of the agreement's obligations.

Note: Rule 2.2 (e) would generally require that items b & c above be made in writing for financial planning engagements even though the wording of this rule allows for oral communication.

| **EXHIBIT 16.2** | **SUMMARY OF DISTINCTIONS** |

	Activities NOT Financial Planning	**Providing Financial Planning or "Material Elements" of Financial Planning**
Duty of Care	Put client's interest first	Fiduciary: Act in the BEST interest of the client.
Disclosure	Rule 2.2(a)-(d), oral or written	Rule 2.2(e): (a)-(d) must be written.
		Rule 1.3 Written agreement covering parties, services, timing and termination conditions.
		Rule 1.2(a)-(d), oral or written covering obligations, compensation, proprietary products and other entities.

EXHIBIT 16.3

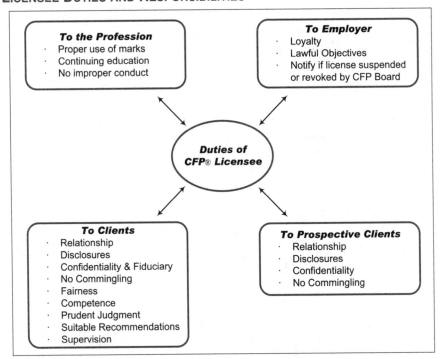

To the Profession
· Proper use of marks
· Continuing education
· No improper conduct

To Employer
· Loyalty
· Lawful Objectives
· Notify if license suspended or revoked by CFP Board

Duties of CFP® Licensee

To Clients
· Relationship
· Disclosures
· Confidentiality & Fiduciary
· No Commingling
· Fairness
· Competence
· Prudent Judgment
· Suitable Recommendations
· Supervision

To Prospective Clients
· Relationship
· Disclosures
· Confidentiality
· No Commingling

FINANCIAL PLANNING PRACTICE STANDARDS

The CFP Board established its Board of Practice Standards in 1995. The Board of Practice Standards is composed exclusively of CFP® practitioners. These practitioners were commissioned to draft Standards of Practice for financial planning. Ultimately, the Board of Practice Standards drafted and revised the Practice Standards by considering input from CFP® certificants, consumers, regulators and other organizations, resulting in the CFP Board adopting the Revised Standards in 2005. The Practice Standards became effective as of July 1, 2008, with amendments in March and July 2009.

Key Concepts

Underline/highlight the answers as you read:

1. Identify the description of the Practice Standards.

2. Identify the six series of the Practice Standards.

DESCRIPTION OF PRACTICE STANDARDS

As with the Rules of Conduct, the Practice Standards are not designed to be a basis for legal liability to any third party. Rather, the **Practice Standards** seek to establish the level of professional practice expected of certificants engaged in financial planning. Regardless of the person's title, job position, type of employment or method of compensation, the Practice Standards are mandatory for all certificants whose services include financial planning or material elements of financial planning. The Practice Standards delineate six different elements of the financial planning process that comprise the best practices of financial planning practitioners. For those financial planning professionals who are not necessarily providing services that include financial planning or material elements of financial planning, they are nonetheless encouraged to use Practice Standards when performing tasks or activities in financial planning that are addressed by the Practice Standards.

Rather than reiterate the Practice Standards, reference is made to CFP Board's website at www.cfp.net/learn/standards.asp, which provides the full text of the Practice Standards. Nonetheless, the highlights and important aspects of the Practice Standards, some of which also correlate to the Code of Ethics and Rules of Conduct, are discussed below.

<table>
<tr><td>EXHIBIT 16.4</td><td>FINANCIAL PLANNING PROCESS[8]</td></tr>
</table>

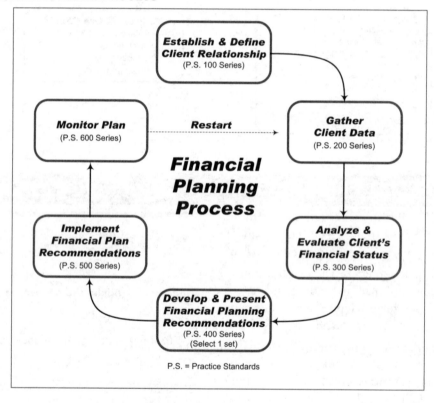

---

8. Abbreviated from Financial Planning Practice Standards.

Practice Standards 100 Series: Establishing and Defining the Relationship with a Client

The Practice Standards 100 Series deals with establishing and defining the relationship with the client.

100-1: Defining the Scope of the Engagement

The financial planning practitioner and the client are required to mutually define the scope of any engagement before any financing planning service is provided. While this is a sound practice for any business, it is especially true in the financial planning process because it is essential that the financial planning practitioner is cognizant of the scope of the engagement and performs those activities that are necessary to further the engagement. In order for the engagement to be fulfilled, the process must be mutually defined and agreed upon by all parties to the engagement. This Practice Standard does not require the scope of the engagement to be in writing, though in subsequent Practice Standards, there are certain disclosures that must be in writing. By mutually defining the scope of the engagement at the outset of the relationship, it is anticipated that the public is best served by a mutual understanding of the engagement. Also, clarifying the scope of the engagement enhances the likelihood of achieving client expectations.

Practice Standards 200 Series: Gathering Client Data

The Practice Standards 200 Series addresses determining a client's personal and financial goals, needs and priorities,[9] as well as obtaining quantitative information and documents[10] from the client.

200-1: Determining a Client's Personal and Financial Goals, Needs, and Priorities

Before making any recommendations to a client, the financial planning practitioner and the client must mutually define the financial goals, needs and priorities of the client. This will require revealing the client's values, attitudes, expectations and time horizons. Here, the role of the practitioner will be to facilitate the goal-setting process and to clarify the client's goals and objectives. It is essential that the practitioner assist the client in recognizing the implications of unrealistic goals and objectives.

200-2: Obtaining Quantitative Information and Documents

Practice Standard 200-2 provides more specific focus, requiring the financial planning practitioner to obtain sufficient quantitative information and documents about a client relative to the scope of the engagement <u>before</u> any recommendation is made or implemented. It could be said that this correlates to Principle 7, Diligence. A practitioner must be diligent in obtaining sufficient and relevant quantitative information and documents pertaining to the client's financial resources, obligations and personal situation. If the practitioner is unable to obtain sufficient and relevant quantitative information and documents to form a recommendation, the practitioner must restrict the scope of the engagement or terminate the engagement.

---

9. Standards of Professional Conduct booklet, Practice Standards 200-1, pp. 18-19.
10. Standards of Professional Conduct booklet, Practice Standards 200-2, p. 19.

While the impact of this Practice Standard increases the chance of achieving a client's goals and objectives, it may also enhance appropriate recommendations by the practitioner and encourage the public to seek services of a practitioner who uses a sound approach like that described in the 200 series.

Practice Standards 300 Series: Analyzing and Evaluating the Client's Financial Status
300-1: Analyzing and Evaluating the Client's Information

Financial planning practitioners are required to analyze and evaluate the client's information to gain an understanding of the client's financial situation and evaluate to what extent the client's goals, needs and priorities can be met by the client's resources and current course of action. Another key component of this Practice Standard is, prior to making a recommendation, the financial planning practitioner must assess the client's financial situation and determine the likelihood of reaching the stated objectives. Personal economic assumptions must be considered in this step of the process, which would include personal assumptions such as retirement age, life expectancy, income needs, risk factors, time horizons and special needs. Economic assumptions must also be made, such as inflation rates, tax rates and investment returns. These activities form the foundation for determining strengths and weaknesses of a client's financial situation and course of action. Objective analyses and evaluation by a financial planning practitioner may result in a client's heightened awareness of specific financial planning issues, which may increase the likelihood of achieving the client's goals and objectives. This is intended to benefit the public and the profession by increasing the public's confidence in the financial planning practitioner.

Practice Standard 400 Series: Developing and Presenting Financial Planning Recommendations
The very heart of financial planning is the moment where the financial planning practitioner, using both science and art, formulates recommendations designed to achieve the goals, needs and priorities of the client. Through these series of distinct but interrelated tasks, the CFP Board has simply described these Practice Standards as "What is Possible?," "What is Recommended?," and "How is it Presented?" [11] The Principles of Competence and Diligence are highly involved with the 400 Series.

400-1: Identifying and Evaluating Financial Planning Alternatives
A financial planning practitioner must identify and consider various alternatives, including continuing the present course of action. The financial planning practitioner must consider sufficient and relative alternatives to the client's current course of action in an effort to reasonably meet the client's goals, needs and priorities. More than one alternative may reasonably meet the goals, needs and priorities of the client, so the subjective nature of the professional judgment of financial planning practitioners is evident. Again, it is imperative that the financial planning practitioner identify alternative actions before presenting recommendations to the client. During this aspect of the process, the practitioner evaluates the effectiveness of actions that would reasonably meet the client's goals.

---

11. *Id.*

400-2: Developing the Financial Planning Recommendation(s)

The financial planning recommendations are developed by the financial planning practitioner based on the selected alternatives and the current course of action in an effort to reasonably meet the client's goals. While different professionals may reasonably meet the client's goals through different alternatives, the recommendations must be consistent with and directly affected by:

- mutually defined scope of the engagement;
- mutually defined client goals, need and priorities;
- quantitative data provided by the client;
- personal and economic assumptions;
- practitioner's analysis and evaluation of client's current situation; and
- alternative(s) selected by the practitioner.

Quick Quiz 16.3

Highlight the answer to these questions:

1. The Practice Standards are designed to be a basis for legal liability to any third party and establishes the level of professional practice expected of certificants engaged in financial planning.
   a. True
   b. False

2. In accordance with Practice Standard 200 Series, the financial planner and client mutually define the scope of engagement.
   a. True
   b. False

3. Facilitating the goal-setting process and clarifying the client's goals and objectives is part of the Practice Standards 200 Series: Gathering Client Data.
   a. True
   b. False

False, False, True.

400-3: Presenting the Financial Planning Recommendations

Though the engagement has been discussed, agreed upon and investigated by the practitioner, recommendations were not made at the onset of the engagement, nor have recommendations been made at this point in the process. Rather, the financial planning practitioner has gone through an internal process and an external process with the client to ensure that it is understood what the client's goals, needs and priorities are. Once these tasks are done and considerations have been addressed, it is time to present the financial planning recommendations in a manner and to an extent reasonably necessary to assist the client in making an informed decision.[12] The practitioner must make a reasonable effort to assist the client in understanding the client's current situation, the recommendation itself, and the impact of the recommendation process on the ability to meet the client's goals. The practitioner must avoid presenting the practitioner's opinion as fact. It should be presented as it is, an opinion. If there are any conflicts of interest that have not been previously disclosed, such conflicts and how they may impact the recommendation should be addressed at this time.

---

12. Standards of Professional Conduct booklet, Practice Standards 400-3, pp. 23-24.

The anticipated impact of the Practice Standards 400 Series is that strategies and objective recommendations will be developed and communicated clearly to meet each client's individual financial planning goals, needs and priorities. Having a commitment to a systematic process for the development and presentation of financial planning recommendations advances the profession as a whole, and aids the practitioner by creating responsive and meaningful solutions for clients. Likewise, customizing strategies and recommendations contributes to client satisfaction.

Practice Standard 500 Series: Implementing Financial Planning Recommendation(s)

500-1: Agreeing on Implementation Responsibilities

The financial planning practitioner and the client must mutually agree on the implementation responsibilities consistent with the scope of the engagement.[13] The practitioner's responsibilities may include identifying activities necessary for implementation, determining division of activities between the practitioner and the client, referring to other professionals, coordinating with other professionals, sharing of information as authorized, and selecting and securing products and services. Also, if there are conflicts of interest, sources of compensation or material relationships with other professionals or advisers that have not been previously been disclosed, then those must be disclosed at this time. If the client is referred to other professionals or advisers, the financial planning practitioner must indicate the basis on which the practitioner believes the other professional or advisor may be qualified. With respect to referrals to other professionals, this correlates to the Principle of Competence where referral to other professionals is appropriate if one's knowledge is limited.

500-2: Selecting Products and Services for Implementation

Under Practice Standard 500-2, the financial planning practitioner must select appropriate products and services that are consistent with the client's goals, needs and priorities. While products and services selected by a practitioner may differ from other practitioners, the practitioner must investigate products or services that reasonably address the client's needs. It is only necessary that the recommendations are suitable to the client's financial situation and consistent with the client's goals.

Through the 500 Series, it is anticipated that the public will benefit from an increase in the likelihood of their goals being achieved, while the profession will have increased credibility. The benefit to the practitioner is a long-term benefit of putting the interests of the client before all others in the selection of products and services. This is in line with the Principle of Fairness and acting as a fiduciary for the client.

Practice Standard 600 Series: Monitoring

600-1: Defining Monitoring Responsibilities

The financial planning practitioner and the client shall mutually define monitoring responsibilities.[14] At this point, recommendations have been made, but once the recommendations are implemented, there must be a monitoring process. By clarifying the

---

13. Standards of Professional Conduct booklet, Practice Standards 500-1, p. 25.
14. Standards of Professional Conduct booklet, Practice Standards 600-1, p. 27.

role of the practitioner in the monitoring process, the client's expectations are more likely to be aligned with the level of monitoring services the practitioner provides. If engaged for monitoring services, the practitioner must make reasonable efforts to define and communicate to the client those monitoring activities the practitioner is able and willing to provide. This Practice Standard may also help ensure that monitoring, or adequate monitoring, does in fact occur. The public is best served when the practitioner and client have similar perceptions and a mutual understanding about monitoring responsibilities, while the profession as a whole benefits because clients are satisfied especially when expectations of a monitoring process are realistic and clear.

SUMMARY AS TO PRACTICE STANDARDS

CFP Board has provided a chart that summarizes the Practice Standards and how they are broken down in the financial planning process:

PRACTICE STANDARDS SUMMARY   EXHIBIT 16.5

Financial Planning Process	Related Practice Standard
1. Establishing and defining the relationship with a client	100-1 Defining the Scope of the Engagement
2. Gathering the client data	200-1 Determining a Client's Personal and Financial Goals, Needs and Priorities
	200-2 Obtaining Quantitative Information and Documents
3. Analyzing and evaluating the client's financial status	300-1 Analyzing and Evaluating the Client's Information
4. Developing and presenting financial planning recommendations	400-1 Identifying and Evaluating Financial Planning Alternative(s)
	400-2 Developing the Financial Planning Recommendation(s)
	400-3 Presenting the Financial Planning Recommendation(s)
5. Implementing the financial planning recommendations	500-1 Agreeing on Implementation Responsibilities
	500-2 Selecting Products and Services for Implementation
6. Monitoring	600-1 Defining Monitoring Responsibilities

The CFP Board embarked upon a monumental effort in creating, developing and establishing the Practice Standards. The Practice Standards were developed and promulgated to benefit clients serviced by CFP® professionals. The purpose of the Practice Standards is to advance professionalism in financial planning,[15] enhance the value of the financial planning practitioner, and assure that CFP® professionals follow established norms of practice. This

---

15. See Principle 6, Professionalism in Standards of Professional Conduct booklet, Code of Ethics, p. 7.

monumental effort was thirteen years in the making, but financial planning practitioners are left with an informative and detailed roadmap for a sound, organized financial planning process.

EXAMPLE 16.2

Patrick, a client, asks Matthew (a CFP® certificant) to draft a financial plan for him. Patrick generally explains his financial situation and his goals and objectives over the telephone to Matthew. Matthew requests quantitative information and documents, but before receiving the quantitative information and documents, Matthew provides Patrick with a thorough and detailed financial plan that matches Patrick's goals, expectations and timeline. Patrick is satisfied. Has Matthew complied with the Practice Standards?

<u>Answer</u>: No. Under Practice Standard 200-2, the financial planning practitioner must obtain sufficient quantitative information and documents from the client relative to the scope of the engagement prior to any recommendations being made or implemented.

DISCIPLINARY RULES AND PROCEDURES

The **Disciplinary Rules** provide detailed procedures followed by the CFP Board in enforcing the Code of Ethics, Rules of Conduct, and Practice Standards. The Disciplinary Rules clearly set out the process whereby certificants and registrants are given notice of potential violations. The process is intended to be fair and allow opportunities for the certificant or registrant to be heard by a panel of other professionals. To promote and maintain the integrity of the marks for the benefit of clients and potential clients of certificants and registrants, the CFP Board has the power to enforce the provisions of the Code of Ethics, Rules of Conduct and the Practice Standards. Those who violate these regulations are subject to discipline or sanctions.

The Disciplinary Rules are lengthy and are organized into 17 different sections entitled "Articles." For a full text of the Disciplinary Rules, go to www.cfp.net/learn/procedures.asp.

The Disciplinary Rules are designed to provide a fair and reasonable process for CFP® certificants and registrants whom allegations of violations of the Code of Ethics, Rules of Conduct or Practice Standards are brought. While the full details of this process are contained in the Disciplinary Rules, the CFP Board's chart, provided in Exhibit 16.5,[16] summarizes the Investigative and Hearing Process.

---

16.   For this online, go to www.cfp.net/Downloads/cfp_board_investigative_and_Hearing_process.pdf

EXHIBIT 16.6

CERTIFIED FINANCIAL PLANNER
BOARD OF STANDARDS, INC.

Investigative and Hearing Process

Full details of this process are contained in CFP Board's *Disciplinary Rules and Procedures*

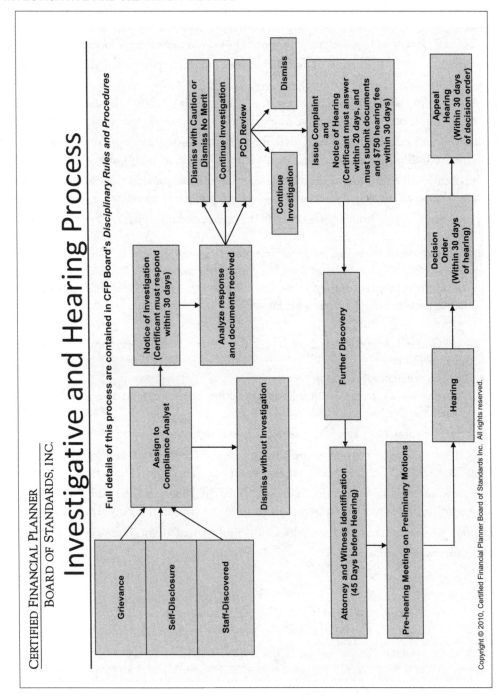

Copyright © 2010, Certified Financial Planner Board of Standards Inc. All rights reserved.

INVESTIGATION

To initiate a review of allegations of a violation of the Code of Ethics, Rules of Conduct or Practice Standards, there must be a written complaint received requesting an investigation. CFP Board, through its Counsel, reviews the allegations to determine if further investigation is warranted.[17] If CFP Board Counsel determines that an investigation is warranted, the CFP® professional is provided with written notice of the investigation containing the general nature of the allegations. The certificant or registrant has 30 calendar days from the date of notice of the investigation to file a written response to the allegations with the Disciplinary and Ethics Commission (hereinafter "Commission").[18] If no timely response is received, a second notice is issued. Failure to respond within an additional 20 calendar days may be deemed an admission of the allegations. [19] Failure to provide requested information may give rise to an adverse inference. An adverse inference is an inference, adverse to the concerned party, drawn from silence or absence of requested information.[20]

If the Commission then issues a formal complaint, a written answer must be submitted within 20 calendar days. A Hearing Panel is convened, and the recommended disciplinary action (if any) is submitted to the Commission for review. Once the Commission issues an order, the Respondent has 30 days to file an appeal.

CFP Board Counsel determines if there is probable cause[21] to believe grounds for discipline exists and shall either:
- dismiss the allegations as not warranted,
- dismiss the allegations with a letter of caution or recommend a remedial action or other appropriate orders, or
- begin processing a complaint against the certificant or registrant.[22]

If probable cause exists, a formal complaint against the CFP® professional and a notice of hearing is provided. The complaint must contain the allegations of misconduct with the potential Code of Ethics or Practice Standards violations, providing the CFP® professional with twenty days from receipt of the complaint to file an answer. If no answer is received, the allegations are deemed admitted, and the CFP® professional's right to use the CFP® marks is administratively revoked.[23]

---

17. Standards of Professional Conduct booklet, Disciplinary Rules, Article 6.1, p. 34.
18. The Commission is responsible for interpreting and applying the Code of Ethics and Practice Standards to specific factual situations involving certificants and imposing appropriate discipline. See www.cfp.net/aboutus/dec.asp.
19. Standards of Professional Conduct booklet, Disciplinary Rules, Article 6.2.
20. Standards of Professional Conduct booklet, Disciplinary Rules, Article 6.2b.
21. There is no formal definition of probable cause in the CFP Board's Standards of Professional Conduct. Generally, "probable cause" in this context could be defined as information sufficient to warrant a reasonable person's belief that Respondent has committed the alleged violation. Probable cause is commonly believed to require more than a reasonable suspicion, but less that what is required for a criminal conviction.
22. See Standards of Professional Conduct booklet, Disciplinary Rules, Article 6.3.
23. Standards of Professional Conduct booklet, Disciplinary Rules, Article 9.1.

Example - Probable Cause

The following is an actual case, referred to by the CFP Board as an Anonymous Case History,[24] dealing with a finding of insufficient evidence to warrant probable cause:

CFP Board received a grievance, alleging unsuitability concerning two "preferred client increases" that Respondent sold his client in conjunction with a life insurance policy after the death of her husband. CFP Board Counsel reviewed the grievance and determined that there was insufficient evidence to warrant a finding of probable cause. Due to Counsel's concern as to previously-dismissed client complaints against Respondent with similar fact patterns, CFP Board dismissed the matter. The CFP Board cautioned Respondent as to the importance of ensuring that clients understand the investments they choose by documenting to them, in writing, the reasons certain investment vehicles have been implemented for them and/or the reasons when changes are made to their investments.

HEARING PROCESS AND FORMS OF DISCIPLINE

When a formal complaint is filed, a hearing takes place before a panel of at least three individuals. The respondent is entitled to appear in person or by telephone, may be represented by counsel at the hearing, may cross-examine witnesses, and may present evidence on his or her behalf.[25] The Hearing Panel submits its findings to a review by the full Disciplinary and Ethics Commission (DEC). After considering all facts and recommendations, the Commission renders a final decision.[26] The DEC reserves the authority to review any determination by the Hearing Panel. Within 45 calendar days of the hearing, the DEC must mail a final order of its findings to the respondent and, if any sanctions are imposed.[27] There is also an Appeals Committee that provides for an appellate process.[28] The Commission may also consider a written Offer of Settlement by the Respondent subject to specific rules and procedure; the Commission has final decision-making authority to accept or reject an Offer of Settlement.[29]

If the Commission finds grounds for discipline, there are various forms of disciplinary actions that the Commission may impose. The Commission may publicly disseminate all disciplinary actions, except for private written censure. As provided in Article 4 of the Disciplinary Rules, the forms of discipline are as follows:

- Article 4.1: Private Censure;
- Article 4.2: Public Letter of Admonition;
- Article 4.3: Suspension;
- Article 4.4: Revocation; and
- Article 4.5: Forms of Discipline Concerning Candidates.

---

24. *See* subsequent discussion in Section VII of this chapter entitled "Anonymous Case Histories" for a more complete discussion of CFP Board's reporting of actual disciplinary cases.
25. Standards of Professional Conduct booklet, Disciplinary Rules, Article 9.1, p. 36.
26. Standards of Professional Conduct booklet, Disciplinary Rules, Articles 10.2 and 10.3, p. 37.
27. Standards of Professional Conduct booklet, Disciplinary Rules, Article 11.2.
28. Standards of Professional Conduct booklet, Disciplinary Rules, Article 11, p. 37.
29. Standards of Professional Conduct booklet, Disciplinary Rules, Articles 13.1-13.4, pp. 38-39.

Private Censure

Private censure is an unpublished written reproach mailed by the Commission to a censored certificant or registrant.

Public Letter of Admonition

A **letter of admonition** is a publishable written reproach of the certificant's or registrant's behavior. The Disciplinary Rules provide that public letters of admonition should have a standard procedure of being published in press releases or other forms of publicity selected by the Commission, but in some cases, the Commission may withhold a public letter of admonition if there are mitigating circumstances.

Suspension

The Commission may also order suspension for up to five years. **Suspension** is for those individuals the Commission deems susceptible to rehabilitation. It is standard procedure to publish suspensions with identification of the certificant or registrant in press releases or other forms of publicity, but the Commission may withhold public notifications for extreme mitigating circumstances.

Revocation

As for **revocation**, the Commission may order permanent revocation of a certificant's or registrant's right to use the marks. While it is standard procedure to publish revocation through press releases or other forms of publicity, the Commission may withhold public notification in extreme mitigating circumstances. However, revocation is **permanent**.

After a suspension or revocation, a respondent must provide CFP Board evidence that the respondent has ceased using the marks within 30 days of receiving the suspension or revocation order. Failure to provide written evidence will result in automatic revocation.[30]

Forms of Discipline as to Candidates

The final form of discipline concerns candidates for the CFP® marks. Under certain circumstances, the Commission may take action in matters involving the conduct of candidates for CFP® certification. Candidates, though not yet certified, are subject to the four forms of discipline described in Articles 4.1 through 4.4 above.

For private censure, if the candidate meets all other requirements of certification, the certification will be accompanied by a private censure in the candidate's record. In the case of a letter of admonition, the candidate's satisfaction of all requirements of certification will result in certification with the issuance of admonition in the candidate's record. In the case of suspension, certification (if any) would be suspended for a specified period not to exceed five years. If the grounds are revocation, then the certification (if any) is simply denied. If there is a suspension or denial of a candidate's certification, the suspension or denial will be published at the discretion of the Committee. A candidate for the CFP® certification who has been subject to an order of suspension may reapply for certification according to the Disciplinary Rules.

---

30. Standards of Professional Conduct booklet, Disciplinary Rules, Article 15.

During the hearings that take place under the Disciplinary Rules, rules of procedure and evidence[31] applicable in a court of law are not required. Proof of misconduct must be established to a standard of a preponderance of the evidence, which is more commonly known as a standard of more probable than not, or more likely than not.

> **EXAMPLE 16.3**
>
> The following is another Anonymous Case History,[32] but this case involves the revocation of a certificant's CFP® license.
>
> CFP Board permanently revoked Respondent's right to use the CFP® marks after Respondent failed to respond to a complaint initiated by CFP Board. CFP Board investigated Respondent's company and asserted that the company's use of a mark was confusing to the public and diluted the CFP® certification marks. The Respondent did not comply with the procedure outlined in the Disciplinary Rules by failing to respond to CFP Board's Complaint. As a result, the allegations in the complaint were deemed admitted, and an order of revocation was issued.

Interim Suspension

Recent amendments to the Disciplinary Rules provide for more abrupt and precise action by CFP Board. Certain conduct by CFP professionals may cause CFP Board to issue an Interim Suspension of the right to use the CFP marks during the pendency of an investigation. The following amendments took effect on June 1, 2012:

- If a CFP® professional's conduct poses an immediate threat to the public, and the gravity of the conduct significantly impinges upon the stature and reputation of the marks, CFP Board may issue an Order to Show Cause why the CFP® professional's right to use the marks should not be suspended during the pendency of the proceedings. If the certificant does not respond within 20 calendar days, the allegations are deemed admitted.
- An interim suspension shall immediately be issued without a hearing when CFP Board Counsel receives evidence of a conviction or a professional discipline for any of the following conduct:
    a. Felony conviction for any crime;
    b. Misdemeanor conviction for fraud, misrepresentation or crimes of moral turpitude; or
    c. Revocation of a financial professional license (securities, insurance, accounting or bank-related license) unless the revocation is administrative in nature, ie. the result of the individual determining to not renew the

---

31. Standards of Professional Conduct booklet, Disciplinary Rules, Article 9.3.
32. See discussion in Section VII of this chapter entitled "Anonymous Case Histories" for a more complete discussion of CFP Board's reporting of actual disciplinary cases.

license by not paying the required fee and/or not completing the required continuing education.

There is one very common theme throughout the Anonymous Case Histories. That theme is failing to cooperate with CFP Board or its disciplinary process will result in severe penalties or discipline. Cooperation with the process is paramount. Stated another way, cooperating does not necessarily mean that one has to admit to the allegations; instead, it means that the Respondent must timely respond within the time frames and procedures outlined in the Disciplinary Rules.

FITNESS STANDARDS FOR CANDIDATES AND REGISTRANTS

The CFP Board has established standards for candidates for certification and registrants. The Fitness Standards for Candidates and Registrants, as they are called, ensure specific character and fitness standards as to an individual's conduct before certification. These rules came into existence through an interesting turn of events, as articulated by CFP Board in its booklet on the Standards of Professional Conduct. In the past, during the certification process, various candidates indicated that, had they known that their prior conduct would bar or delay their certification, they would not have taken the CFP® certification examination.[33] As a result, CFP Board implemented the Fitness Standards for Candidates and Registrants (hereinafter also referred to as "Fitness Standards").

RECENT AMENDMENTS INCLUDING ADDITION OF REGISTRANTS TO FITNESS STANDARDS

In 2007, the Standards of Professional Conduct had, in its fifth category, what was referred to as "Candidate Fitness Standards." CFP Board formed a working group in 2010 to review the Candidate Fitness Standards to improve CFP Board's investigation and hearing processes. This task force came up with three significant amendments that were adopted by CFP Board as follows:

1. The Candidate Fitness Standards were extended to include Registrants, and thus beginning on January 1, 2011, the "Candidate Fitness Standards" were re-titled "Fitness Standards for Candidates and Registrants."
2. The Commission has authority to allow a candidate or registrant to re-apply for CFP® certification at some future date; and
3. Appeals are allowed of decisions of the Commission concerning a candidate's or registrant's fitness to the Appeals Committee of the CFP Board of Directors.

DIFFERING LEVELS OF UNACCEPTABLE CONDUCT

It is clear that any felony conviction, revocation of financial or professional licenses, or two or more personal or business bankruptcies would "always bar an individual from becoming certified." CFP Board's list of unacceptable conduct that will always bar an individual from becoming certified is as follows:[34]

---

33. Standards of Professional Conduct booklet, Fitness Standards, p. 44.
34. Standards of Professional Conduct booklet, Fitness Standards, p. 44.

(i)   Felony conviction for theft, embezzlement or other financially-based crimes;

(ii)   Felony conviction for tax fraud or other tax-related crimes;

(iii) Revocation of a financial professional license, unless revocation was administrative in nature (such as the result of the individual knowingly letting license expire by not paying the required fees);

(iv)   Felony conviction for any degree of murder or of rape;

(v)   Felony conviction for any other violent crime within the last five (5) years.

The above list is also referred to as the "always bar list." CFP Board also provides a specific list of conduct that is presumed to be unacceptable and will bar an individual from becoming certified <u>unless</u> that individual petitions the Commission for reconsideration. The list of presumed unacceptable conduct (also referred to as the "presumption list") requiring a petition from the individual is:

(i) Two or more personal or business bankruptcies;

(ii) Revocation or suspension of a non-financial professional license, unless the revocation is administrative in nature (such as the result of the individual knowingly not renewing the license by not paying the required fees);

(iii) Suspension of a financial professional license unless the suspension is administrative in nature;

(iv) Felony conviction for nonviolent crimes, including perjury, within the last five (5) years; or

(v) Felony conviction for violent crimes (other than murder or rape) that occurred more than five (5) years ago.

When reviewing candidates or registrants for CFP® certification, CFP Board also considers customer complaints, arbitrations and other civil proceedings, felony convictions for non-violent crimes that occurred more than five (5) years ago, misdemeanor convictions and employer reviews and terminations. CFP Board and the Commission will continue to review matters that result in the delay or denial of certification but do not result in an automatic bar (unless one of the always bar list items provides a time frame, as with felony convictions for any violent crime other than any degree of murder or rape, within the last five (5) years). One method by which CFP Board learns of a candidate's or registrant's fitness is through the disclosure of matters on the ethics portion of the initial certification application, also known as the declaration page.

Note: Personal or business bankruptcies were part of the "always bar list" until July 1, 2012. Since July 1, 2012, CFP Board will no longer investigate and the Commission will no longer adjudicate, single bankruptcy-only cases. Instead, all bankruptcies will be disclosed on the CFP® professional's public profile displayed on the CFP Board's website for 10 years, and their names will be included once in a press release issued periodically by the Board.

PETITIONS FOR RECONSIDERATION

The "presumption list" does provide the candidate or registrant with a transgression to petition the Commission for reconsideration. In determining whether a candidate's or registrant's conduct will bar certification, CFP Board has outlined the basic process for such reviews:

- A written petition for reconsideration must be submitted to professional review staff, and the individual requesting reconsideration must sign a form agreeing to CFP Board's jurisdiction.
- Professional review staff must review the request to ensure the transgression is within the "presumption list."
- Professional review staff will notify the individual if the transgression falls within the "presumption list" or the "always bar list."
- If the transgression is within the "presumption list," professional review staff will request all relevant documentation from the individual.
- All relevant information will be provided to the Commission for determination.

The Commission may either: (1) grant the petition after determining the conduct does not reflect adversely on the individual's fitness as a candidate or registrant for CFP certification or upon the profession or upon the CFP® certification marks, and certification should be permitted; or (2) deny the petition after determining the conduct reflects adversely on the individual's fitness as a candidate or registrant for CFP® certification or upon the profession or the CFP® certification marks, whereby certification is barred.

Note: The current Standards of Professional Conduct booklet indicates that the Commission's decision regarding a petition for reconsideration is final and that the decision on a petition for reconsideration may not be appealed unless the underlying, relevant professional revocation or suspension is vacated or the relevant, underlying felony conviction is overturned, at which time the individual may submit a new petition; nonetheless, the recent 2011 Amendments indicate that appeals are allowed of decisions of the Commission concerning a candidate's or registrant's fitness to the Appeals Committee of the CFP Board of Directors. Thus, because the Amendment is the latest publication by CFP Board, it appears that the Commission's decisions as to petitions for reconsideration can be appealed.

ANONYMOUS CASE HISTORIES

As part of its multi-prong effort to improve ethics and standards in the financial planning profession as to CFP® certificants and registrants, the CFP Board publishes a review of misconduct cases processed by the CFP Board and the Commission. These are referred to as "**anonymous case histories,**" which provide a summary of the relevant events in certain cases of misconduct, accompanied by an explanation of any discipline penalty, action by CFP Board, and other information. The intent behind publication of these anonymous case histories is, among other things, to provide an understanding for those using the CFP® marks as to what types of allegations are made and what form of discipline is administered.

Failing to cooperate with the CFP Board or its disciplinary process will result in severe penalties or discipline. The Respondent must timely respond according to the procedures outlined in the Disciplinary Rules. Specifically, Article 7.4 provides that if Respondent does not timely respond to a formal complaint, then the allegations are deemed admitted, and the CFP® professional's right to use the CFP® marks is administratively revoked.[35]

The following are actual anonymous case histories provided by the CFP Board.

ANONYMOUS CASE HISTORY #1

CFP Board received a grievance against Respondent. The allegations were that he solicited a prostitute, failed to notify clients of the outcome of a civil suit, transferred monies from the clients' accounts without written authorization, and "cut and pasted" client signatures from other forms previously executed. CFP Board discovered during its investigation that Respondent was discharged from employment in 1996 and named in a civil suit initiated by the former employer for interference with prospective contractual relations, fraud, and breach of implied duty. Judgment was entered against Respondent for $2,824. After a State Securities Board ("SSB") inquiry about allegations that Respondent's firm conducted

Key Concepts

Underline/highlight the answers as you read:

1. Determine the purpose of the Candidate Fitness Standards.

2. Identify the "always bar list" and the "presumption list."

3. Define anonymous case histories and determine the purpose of publishing them.

unregistered advisory activities, Respondent entered into a consent order with the SSB wherein he was suspended from soliciting new accounts for a period of ten business days and fined $1,000. Respondent further consented with the SSB for a $500 fine for failure to disclose the previous 1996 consent order and failure to disclose he had been held civilly liable for fraud. Respondent had falsely attested on his Renewal Forms in 1997 and 2003. Respondent submitted a settlement offer, admitting to violating the Code of Ethics by

---

35. Standards of Professional Conduct booklet, Disciplinary Rules, Article 7.4.

starting a competing business with his then-current employer and consenting to a private censure. Respondent's offer of settlement was accepted.

While this decision involved the former Code of Ethics, the Principles noted to be involved in the decision were Integrity, Fairness and Professionalism, though arguments could have been made for most or all Principles being involved.

<u>Commission's Decision</u>: Private Censure

ANONYMOUS CASE HISTORY #2

In his Declaration Form to CFP Board, Respondent disclosed that he was named along with his employer and others in four civil suits. He was named solely in his capacity as vice president and partial owner of the company. He disclosed that the lawsuits were consolidated into a global settlement in which his company participated, resulting in a settlement of $14.7 million. Respondent's pro rata share of the settlement was $240,000. The SEC determined not to initiate formal proceedings against him. A probable cause review was conducted by CFP Board. It was determined to dismiss the matter as having no merit, with a reservation to reopen the investigation if any regulatory authority, including the SEC, initiated any further inquiry or took any action against Respondent.

<u>Commission's Decision</u>: Dismiss - No Merit

ANONYMOUS CASE HISTORY #3

CFP Board received a grievance, alleging Respondent sold unsuitable unsecured promissory notes to grievant's elderly parents. Respondent (who was serving a 3 year suspension from a previous disciplinary case) submitted an Offer of Settlement, consenting to violating the Code of Ethics by (1) directing his clients to a company involved in property development, which issued unsecured promissory notes unsuitable for the clients; (2) failing to disclose his conflicts of interest with the company, including his retention as a business consultant for the company, providing occasional bookkeeping for the company, and sharing a business address and fax number with the company; and (3) failing to respond in a timely or open manner in response to the grievant's requests on behalf of her parents that the promissory notes be liquidated and the proceeds delivered to the clients. Respondent consented to a permanent, voluntarily relinquishment of his right to use the CFP® marks, with publication of that fact only on CFP Board's website and via verbal or written inquiry. A Hearing Panel accepted Respondent's offer, so Respondent's right to use the CFP® marks was permanently relinquished. The decision noted that Principles of Objectivity, Fairness and Diligence were violated or involved.[36]

<u>Commission's Decision</u>: Settlement - Relinquish

ANONYMOUS CASE HISTORY #4

CFP Board received a grievance from Respondent's clients, alleging that investments recommended and sold by Respondent were unsuitable for them based on their ages and risk

---

36.   These were cites to the former version of the Code of Ethics, but the Principles have remained similar.

tolerances. CFP Board then discovered that Respondent entered into a consent with the NASD, consenting to the entry of findings that he altered the grievants' listed address on a variable life insurance application. Respondent consented to a one month suspension and a $10,000 fine. Respondent submitted a settlement offer, admitting that he altered an address on an insurance policy in violation of the Code of Ethics and proposing a private censure. A counter-offer was made for a public letter of admonition, which Respondent accepted. The Principles of Integrity and Professionalism were expressed as being involved in the decision.

Commission's Decision: Letter of Admonition

ANONYMOUS CASE HISTORY #5

Respondent disclosed that he was charged with a felony count of attempting to purchase cocaine and a felony count of conspiracy to traffic cocaine after he attempted to purchase one gram of cocaine from an undercover operative. Respondent submitted an offer of settlement, consenting to findings that (1) he pleaded guilty to a misdemeanor of attempting to purchase a gram of cocaine, first offense, for which he was sentenced to two years of probation (which was completed), and ordered to pay a $2,000 fine; and (2) he falsely attested on the applicable renewal form that he had not been a defendant in a criminal proceeding since his last renewal. Respondent proposed a private censure. A counter offer for a public letter of admonition was made, to which Respondent accepted. Integrity and Professionalism were stated to be the Principles from Code of Ethics involved.

Commission's Decision: Letter of Admonition

ANONYMOUS CASE HISTORY #6

Respondent disclosed his involvement in an arbitration filed by his client who claimed unsuitability, breach of contract, negligence and breach of fiduciary duty regarding mutual funds Respondent recommended and sold her. A Hearing Panel found that Respondent violated the Code of Ethics by: (1) knowing she had no source of income, Respondent recommended and sold nearly $1 million of mutual fund B shares to her; (2) knowing she had no source of income, Respondent approved appreciation and speculation as his client's primary investment objectives; (3) failing to implement any source of income for her; (4) providing inaccurate information on the new account forms he helped his client execute; and (5) failing to acknowledge this financial planning relationship even though he claimed to have completed a financial analysis with recommendations, implementation and monitoring of the mutual funds. Respondent's right to use the CFP certification marks for a period of one year and one day. Objectivity, Professionalism and Diligence were stated to be the Principles from the Code of Ethics involved.

In aggravation, the Board considered that (1) the B shares were changed to C shares only upon the client's insistence and not due to the realization that it should be done; (2) Respondent lacked an understanding of the Practice Standards and the scope of his engagement with his client; and (3) as a result of his actions, Respondent's broker/dealer was required to pay a $652,000 arbitration award.

Commission's Decision: Suspension

Quick Quiz 16.4

Highlight the answer to these questions:

1. When the Commission finds grounds for discipline, the following forms of discipline available include private censure, public letter of admonition, suspension, revocation, and discipline concerning candidates.
   a. True
   b. False

2. The CFP publishes a review of misconduct cases processed by the CFP Board and the Commission.
   a. True
   b. False

True, True.

ANONYMOUS CASE HISTORY #7

Respondent was the subject of a related civil action, criminal action, and grievance sent to CFP Board, filed by a former business associate and fellow CFP® certificant. Respondent was also the subject of an NASD inquiry and related customer complaint. The civil action alleged that Respondent transferred information concerning his business associate's clients, including their confidential information, to an "outside computer" and solicited clients for future tax and investment services in a manner that may have led those clients to believe his former business associate was no longer in business. Respondent filed a counterclaim against the plaintiff. During the course of the civil action, the plaintiff filed criminal charges against Respondent, alleging theft and possession of certain property. The criminal case was dismissed, and the civil matter was resolved through a settlement agreement with Respondent paying $35,000 to plaintiff. The customer complaint generally alleged that Respondent had changed broker/dealers without informing the customers and submitted their application for purchase of a Boston Capital Product to Respondent's new broker/dealer without the customer's permission. Respondent reversed his commission, returned the monies to his previous broker/dealer and consented to a $2,000 fine. The NASD initiated an inquiry regarding the customer complaint matter, ending with Respondent consenting to a $5,000 fine. After a probable cause review, CFP Board Staff Counsel dismissed the matters, cautioning Respondent regarding the importance of complying with the laws, rules and regulations of all applicable governing agencies including CFP Board, and of governing oneself in a manner which reflects positively on the financial planning profession.

<u>Commission's Decision</u>: Dismiss with Caution

SUMMARY

The CFP Board requires CFP® certificants and registrants to maintain professional standards and ethics in the financial planning profession. The CFP Board has accomplished this through an interrelated series of professional and ethical standards designed to protect the public and advance professionalism in the financial planning industry. These Standards of Professional Conduct are all connected through the Code of Ethics, Rules of Conduct, Practice Standards, Disciplinary Rules and Fitness Standards.

The CFP Board has placed the highest ethical and professional standards upon CFP® certificants and registrants. The profession as a whole benefits from these standards. More importantly, the public benefits from these procedures and standards. However, these rules should be a mere formality, as all CFP® certificants, registrants and candidates should act and aspire to act towards actual and prospective clients, the public, the profession and employers as described throughout the Standards of Professional Conduct.

Key Terms

Always Bar List - CFP Board's list of unacceptable conduct that will <u>always</u> bar an individual from becoming certified.

Anonymous Case Histories - Summary of the relevant events in certain cases of misconduct, accompanied by an explanation of any discipline penalty, action by CFP Board, and other information.

Certificant - An individual who is currently certified by the CFP Board.

Certified Financial Planner Board of Standards, Inc. ("CFP Board") - Board that maintains professional standards necessary for competency and ethics in the financial planning profession for those professionals who have been granted the right to use their designation.

Code of Ethics - One of the Standards of Professional Conduct. They are organized into seven different principles ("Principles") that certificants and registrants are expected to enact into their professional activities.

Competence - Principle 3. Requires attaining and maintaining an adequate level of knowledge and skill, and application of that knowledge and skill in providing services to clients.

Confidentiality - Principle 5. Ensuring that information is accessible only to those authorized to have access.

Diligence - Principle 7. Requires the provision of services in a reasonably prompt and thorough manner, including the proper planning for, and supervision of, the rendering of professional services.

Disciplinary Rules - Provide detailed procedures followed by the CFP Board in enforcing the Code of Ethics, Rules of Conduct, and Practice Standards.

Fairness - Principle 4. Requires impartiality, intellectual honesty and disclosure of material conflicts of interest.

Fiduciary - Defined by the CFP Board as "one who acts in utmost good faith, in a manner he or she reasonably believes to be in the best interest of the client."

Financial Planning - providing "material elements of the financial planning process" i.e., the process of determining whether and how an individual can meet life goals through the proper management of financial resources.

Fitness Standards - Ensure specific character and fitness standards as to an individual's conduct before certification.

Integrity - Principle 1. Demands honesty and candor which must not be subordinated to personal gain and advantage.

Key Terms

Letter of Admonition - A publishable written reproach of the certificant's or registrant's behavior.

Objectivity - Principle 2. Requires intellectual honesty and impartiality.

Practice Standards - Establish the level of professional practice expected of certificants engaged in financial planning. The Practice Standards are mandatory for all certificants whose services include financial planning or material elements of financial planning.

Presumption List - CFP Board's list of conduct that is presumed to be unacceptable and will bar an individual from becoming certified unless that individual petitions the Commission for reconsideration.

Private Censure - An unpublished written reproach mailed by the Commission to a censored certificant or registrant.

Professionalism - Principle 6. Requires behaving with dignity and courtesy to clients, fellow professionals, and others in business-related activities.

Registrant - An individual who, though not currently certified, has been certified by CFP Board in the past and has an entitlement, direct or indirect, to potentially use the CFP® marks. This includes individuals who have relinquished their certification and who are eligible for reinstatement without being required to pass the current CFP certification examination.

Revocation - Permanent revocation of a certificant's or registrant's right to use the marks.

Rules of Conduct - Establish expected high standards and also describe the level of professionalism required. The Rules of Conduct govern all those who have the right to use the CFP® marks, whether or not those marks are actually used.

Standards of Professional Conduct - CFP Board standards comprised of five different categories: Code of Ethics and Professional Responsibility ("Code of Ethics"); Rules of Conduct; Financial Planning Practice Standards ("Practice Standards"); Disciplinary Rules and Procedures ("Disciplinary Rules"); and Candidate Fitness Standards.

Suspension - Temporary suspension of a certificant's or registrant's right to use the marks for a term of up to five years for those individuals the Commission deems susceptible to rehabilitation.

1. What is the function of the Certified Financial Board of Standards, Inc. (CFP Board)?

2. Discuss the difference between a CFP® certificant and registrant.

3. What areas of ethics are included in the Standards of Professional Conduct?

4. What is the Code of Ethics and Professional Responsibility (Code of Ethics)?

5. Discuss the Rules of Conduct and the six categories within the rules.

6. Define the Financial Planning Practice Standards and the various series that form the standards.

7. Discuss what are the Disciplinary Rules and Procedures.

8. Discuss the investigative process under the Disciplinary Rules and Procedures.

9. Discuss the hearing process and forms of discipline under the Disciplinary Rules and Procedures.

10. Define the five forms of discipline by the Commission.

11. Define the Candidate Fitness Standards and the "always bar list."

12. Discuss the purpose of the publication of anonymous case histories.

MULTIPLE-CHOICE PROBLEMS

1. The CFP Board is a certification and standard-setting organization that:

    a. Establishes and enforces education requirements for CFP certificants.

    b. Establishes and enforces examination requirements for CFP certificants.

    c. Establishes and enforces ethics requirements for CFP certificants.

    d. All of the above.

2. Which of the following is not part of the CFP Board's Standards of Professional Conduct?

    a. Code of Ethics.

    b. Risk Management.

    c. Rules of Conduct.

    d. Candidate Fitness Standards.

3. Which of the following is not a principle in the Code of Ethics?

    a. Frugality.

    b. Integrity.

    c. Competence.

    d. Fairness.

4. Which of the following best describes the intent behind the principles of the CFP Board's Code of Ethics?

    a. To avoid getting sued by clients.

    b. To make more money as a financial planner.

    c. To establish the highest principles and standards that are aspirational in character and provide a source of guidance for certificants and registrants.

    d. To assist candidates in getting certified.

5. Under the CFP Board's Rules of Conduct, violations of the Rules of Conduct may subject a certificant or registrant to discipline. Which of the following is true with respect to any such violations?

    1. Discipline extends to the rights of registrants and certificants to use the CFP marks.

    2. The rules are designed to be a basis for legal liability to any third party.

    3. The CFP Board has the exclusive right to ensure that certificants and registrants meet and continue to meet the CFP Board's initial and ongoing certification requirements.

        a. 1 and 2.

        b. 1 and 3.

        c. 2 and 3.

        d. 1, 2, and 3.

6. Under the CFP Board's Rules of Conduct, which of the following are a category of rules within the CFP Board's Rules of Conduct?

    a. Obligations to prospective clients and clients.

    b. Obligations to employers.

    c. Obligations to the profession.

    d. All of the above.

    e. None of the above.

7. The CFP Board's Practice Standards are intended to:

    a. Assure that the practice of financial planning by CFP certificants and registrants are based on established norms of practice.

    b. Enhance the value of the financial planning process.

    c. Advance professionalism and financial planning.

    d. All of the above.

8. Which of the following are true with respect to the Practice Standards?

    1. Each Practice Standard is a statement regarding one of the steps in the financial planning process or investments planning process.

    2. Includes monitoring responsibilities after a financial plan is implemented.

    3. The scope of the engagement does not have to be in writing.

        a. 3 only.

        b. 1 and 3.

        c. 1, 2, and 3.

        d. None of the above.

9. Which of the following does NOT apply to Practice Standard 500-2, which provides that the financial planning practitioner shall select appropriate products and services that are consistent with the client's _____ ?

    a. Goals.

    b. Desires.

    c. Needs.

    d. Priorities.

10. Which of the following is true with respect to forms of discipline?

    1. If the Disciplinary and Ethics Commission orders revocation of a certificant's or registrant's right to use the marks, the revocation is permanent until after a period after five years, at which time a request for reinstatement can be made.

    2. All revocations issued by the Commission are permanent.

    3. The Commission may order suspension for an unspecified period of time.

    a. 2 only.

    b. 1 and 3.

    c. 1, 2, and 3.

    d. None of the above.

11. Under the Candidate Fitness Standards, the following conduct is unacceptable and will always bar an individual from becoming certified:

    1. Two or more personal or business bankruptcies.

    2. Felony conviction for any degree of murder or rape.

    3. Felony conviction for any other violent crime within the last five years.

    a. 3 only.

    b. 1 and 2.

    c. 2 and 3.

    d. 1, 2, and 3.

12. The Commission may make one of the following decisions regarding a petition for reconsideration by a candidate for certification:

    a. Grant the petition after determining the conduct does not reflect adversely on the individual's fitness as a candidate for CFP certification, or adversely upon the profession or the CFP certification marks (and certification should be permitted).

    b. Deny the petition after determining the conduct does reflect adversely on the individual's fitness as a candidate for CFP certification, or does reflect adversely upon the profession or the CFP certification marks (and certification should be barred).

    c. Both a and b.

    d. Neither a nor b.

13. Which of the following is not a form of discipline under the Disciplinary Rules?

    a. Private censure.

    b. Public letter of admonition.

    c. Suspension.

    d. A monetary fine.

14. Which of the following definitions best defines a fiduciary under the CFP Board's Standards of Professional Conduct?

    a. One who acts in utmost good faith, in a manner he or she reasonably believes to be in the best interest of the client.

    b. One who acts in the best interests of the certified financial planner.

    c. One who acts in the utmost good faith in a manner he or she reasonably believes to be in the best interest of the profession.

    d. One who acts in the best interests of the public.

15. Which of the following is not specifically addressed in the CFP Board's Standards of Professional Conduct?

    a. Conflicts of interest.

    b. Care of a Fiduciary.

    c. Implementing and monitoring a financial plan designed for a client.

    d. Comparing rates of return for exchange traded funds.

16. Bob, a CFP® professional, has developed a comprehensive financial plan for his client, Sue. Based on the CFP Board Practice Standards which of the following should Bob do next?

    a. Review the plan with Sue's CPA.

    b. Implement the financial plan with Sue.

    c. Present the financial plan to Sue.

    d. Develop financial planning recommendations.

17. According to Practice Standard 200-1 Determining a Client's Personal and Financial Goals, Needs and Priorities, which of the following are necessary inputs to determine a client's goals?

    1. Client's attitude.

    2. Client's values.

    3. Client's current income.

    4. Client's expectations.

        a. 1 and 2.

        b. 2, 3, and 4.

        c. 1, 2 and 4.

        d. 1, 2 and 3.

18. Jill is a prospective client, recently approached Mike, a CFP® professional with significant estate planning needs. Mike does not feel like he can adequately fulfill all of Jill's needs so he refers Jill to a colleague who specializes in estate planning. According to the CFP Code of Ethics, what principle did Mike most clearly demonstrate?

        a. Fairness.

        b. Objectivity.

        c. Professionalism.

        d. Competence.

19. Rose is employed as a loan officer at a bank. Rose recently sat down and visited with her financial planner Julie, a CFP® professional. Rose was in need of cash and borrowed $15,000 from Julie. Based on Rule 3.7 of the CFP® Rules of Conduct (A certificant shall not lend money to a client.), which of the following statements is accurate?

        a. Julie is not in violation of the rule because Rose is in the business of lending money.

        b. Julie is in violation of the rule because a CFP® certificant must never lend money to a client.

        c. Julie is not in violation since she loaned Rose less than $20,000.

        d. Julie is in violation of the rule.

20. Bob is a CFP® professional. He recently met with a new client, Jack, that requests a needs analysis concerning Jack's life insurance situation. Jack is 42 years old, married, and has 2 children he plan to send to college. He wants Bob to evaluate how much and what type of insurance he should purchase. Which of the following is required to be provided to Jack according to the Code of Ethics?

    a. A written agreement for Bob's services specifying on what terms the agreement can be terminated.

    b. An accurate and understandable description of the compensation arrangements being offered, in writing.

    c. A written summary of likely conflicts between the client and the certificant.

    d. None of the above is required by the Code of Ethics.

21. Bob, a CFP® professional, performed a needs analysis concerning Jack's life insurance situation last year and sold him a universal life policy under a limited scope engagement. This year, Jack wants Bob to evaluate his retirement allocation and recommend some investments. All of the following are required to be provided to Jack according to the Code of Ethics EXCEPT?

    a. A written agreement for Bob's services specifying on what terms the agreement can be terminated.

    b. An accurate and understandable description of the compensation arrangements being offered, in writing.

    c. A written summary of likely conflicts of interest between the client and the certificant.

    d. A written agreement covering the obligations and responsibilities of each party.

22. John is a client and seems to be suffering from dementia and wants to remove his children from his will and give all of his wealth to Marie, a neighbor who periodically visits John and delivers him groceries. What should the CFP® professional do?

    a. He should contact John's children to let them know.

    b. He should do what John asks.

    c. He should contact the doctor to confirm if he is suffering from dementia or not.

    d. He should contact John's lawyer.

23. A number of years ago Ron was divorced and subsequently had severe financial issues. Two years ago, he filed for bankruptcy. After getting back on his feet financially, he decided to become a CFP® professional. Today, he made his application to CFP Board for certification. Which of the following is correct under the Board's policy regarding bankruptcy?

    a. Ron's bankruptcy falls on the presumed unacceptable list because it is within five years preceding his application. He will be denied the right to use the marks unless he files a successful consideration request with the CFP Board.

    b. Ron's bankruptcy falls on the always bar list because it is within five years preceding his application. He will be denied the right to use the marks.

    c. Ron's bankruptcy is no longer a concern of the CFP Board as long as he discloses it in writing to all potential clients for the five year period following the bankruptcy.

    d. Ron's bankruptcy will not prevent him from becoming a CFP® professional, but it will be disclosed on the CFP® professional's public profile displayed on the CFP Board's website for 10 years.

24. William, a CFP® professional, has been working with his new client Cole. He has completed all required disclosures and provided all written documents required for a financial planning engagement. Cole is 42, divorced, and has one child. William discussed Cole's insurance coverage following a thorough review of Cole's policies and recommended Cole purchase a disability policy and additional term life insurance through his employer. William also performed a retirement needs analysis and developed an investment plan he believes will help Cole achieve his goals. While presenting the retirement and investment plan, Cole mentioned that he was rejected for the life insurance for medical reasons that he does not wish to discuss with William.

To comply with the Practice Standards of the Code of Ethics, William should:

    a. Gather appropriate information from Cole's prior spouse to determine if Cole's condition may affect the retirement and investment plan.

    b. Inform Cole that without more information on his medical condition William will not be able to properly address his situation and he would have to restrict the scope of the engagement to the already completed insurance review.

    c. Inform Cole that without more information on his medical condition William will not be able to properly address his situation and he would have to restrict the scope of the engagement to the already completed insurance review and retirement and investment analyses.

    d. Inform Cole in writing that his medical condition could affect William's conclusions and recommendations.

25. What must be included, in writing, in any engagement letter that involves financial planning?

    a. Conflicts of interest.
    b. Privacy policy.
    c. References.
    d. Compensation amounts.

26. Owen, a CFP® professional, works for a brokerage firm that requires any investment products or loans offered to a client must be proprietary products of the brokerage firm. One of Owen's clients, "Dominic" that he has been providing financial planning services to for the past 10 years asked Owen to recommend a loan. Owen is still engaged in the financial planning process with this client. According to the CFP Code of Ethics, what action is Owen required to take?

    a. The Code of Ethics forbid a CFP® professional from making loans to clients.
    b. Owen has an inherent conflict of interest, since the bank only permits him to offer proprietary products, therefore he cannot make the loan. Owen must discuss this conflict of interest to his client.
    c. Owen may offer a bank loan but the limitations concerning the proprietary products must be disclosed and they must be in writing to Owen.
    d. Owen may make the loan, but must disclose the conflict of interest in writing or verbally to Jack.

27. Sydney is a CFP® professional and recently met with a prospective client, Karen. Karen is the owner of a chain of retail hardware stores throughout the southeast. Karen was referred to Sydney through a mutual friend. Karen is considering rolling out a new 401(k) plan to her employees and has asked Sydney to review her current plan and make a recommendation on improving the plan. Which of the following is required to be provided to Karen according to the Code of Ethics?

    a. No written disclosures are required.
    b. Sydney cannot accept the engagement without gathering comprehensive client data on Karen and the company.
    c. Recommending and implementing a retirement plan for a company does not meet the definition of financial planning, however an accurate and "plain English" description of the compensation arrangements being provided, must be disclosed in writing.
    d. Recommending and implementing a retirement plan for a company meets the definition of financial planning and requires certain written disclosures.

28. Sara is a CFP® professional with her own financial planning practice. Barry was referred to Sara, as Barry was looking to purchase a disability insurance policy. Sara gathers data from Barry to complete an application to submit to the insurance underwriter. Sara also explains, in detail, the tax implications of purchasing a private disability insurance policy. What duty of care does Sara owe Barry, according to the CFP Board of Standard's Code of Ethics?

   a. Sara is required to place Barry's interest ahead of her own interest at all times.

   b. Sara owes Barry the duty of a fiduciary.

   c. Sara is not engaged in the material elements of financial planning and does not owe Barry any duty of care.

   d. Sara must place Barry's interest ahead of her own and she owes him the duty of a fiduciary.

29. What is the client's responsibility during the financial planning process?

   a. To interpret all the information that is gathered.

   b. To provide the professional with all requested information.

   c. To pay their fees.

   d. To implement the financial plan.

30. What do you have to disclose to your financial planning client at the first meeting?

   a. Your areas of expertise.

   b. Your compensation.

   c. Your involvement in community activities.

   d. 10 years of employment history.

Quick Quiz Explanations

Quick Quiz 16.1
1. True.
2. True.

Quick Quiz 16.2
1. False. This is the definition for the Code of Ethics and Professional Responsibility. The Rules of Conduct are organized into six different categories and establish expected high standards and describe the level of professionalism required.
2. True.
3. True.

Quick Quiz 16.3
1. False. The Practice Standards are not designed to be a basis for legal liability to any third party.
2. False. Defining the scope of engagement is including in Practice Standard 100 Series: Establishing and Defining the Relationship with a Client.
3. True.

Quick Quiz 16.4
1. True.
2. True.

Planning for Special Circumstances

17

LEARNING OBJECTIVES

After reading this chapter, you should be able to:

- Identify at least six situations that call for special financial planning needs.
- Understand some of the emotional and all of the financial issues associated with a special needs dependent.
- Describe the typical governmental benefits for special-needs dependents including the special education programs and Social Security benefits.
- List and explain other public benefits that are or may be provided by state and local governments.
- List some examples of not for profit organizations that are funded by states for the support of special needs dependents.
- Describe the steps that a caretaker should take in planning for a special needs dependent.
- Describe special-needs trusts and their elements and the benefits that they can provide.
- Describe a third-party special needs trust (SNT).
- Describe a special-needs trust under 42 U.S.C. Section 1396p (d)(4)(A).
- Describe a pooled trust created under 42 U.S.C. Section 1396p(d)(4)(C).
- List and describe the content of a letter of intent.
- Describe the need for financial planning necessary for divorcing couples.
- Discuss the need for gathering information that is complete and reliable prior to entering into any divorce agreement.
- List the common mistakes with regard to financial planning that divorcing spouses make.
- List the financial planning issues that arise in planning for terminal illness.
- List the financial planning recommendations for terminal illness planning.
- Discuss the issue of financial planning for the nontraditional household.
- Describe civil unions and registered partners.
- Identify the major issues in planning for the death of a partner in a nontraditional household.

- Describe each of the ways that property owned by a decedent passes to heirs or legatees.
- Discuss the issue of job loss or job change with regard to financial planning.
- Identify the factors that weigh on financial planning decisions with regard to job loss or job change.
- Discuss the issues related to financial planning for a financial windfall.
- List and discuss the financial planning recommendations for a windfall recipient.
- Evaluate the need for and recommend financial management strategies for clients with special challenges. Examples of these groups include: single head-of-household families, non-traditional families, pre- and post-divorce planning, pre- and post-mortem planning, remarriage, elderly clients, disabled clients or families with disabled offspring, business owners, and athletes/entertainers.*
- Identify the impact of divorce and/or remarriage on an estate plan including asset titling and distribution, changes in beneficiary status, and selection of heirs.
- Recommend strategies that can be implemented to help ensure the appropriate management and transfer of assets to a same-sex, nontraditional and/or non-married partners.*

* CFP Board Resource Document - Student-Centered Learning Objectives based upon CFP Board Principal Topics.

INTRODUCTION

Many clients consider themselves inimitable and having unique financial circumstances and often they do. Financial planners are trained to approach clients from the perspective of every client being unique and the planning for clients should be individually tailored. However, with hundreds of millions of people in America and millions more around the world, the simple fact is that many people have common goals - retirement, education funding for children, and mitigation of catastrophic risks. These common goals and similar life cycle positioning allows for bucketing or grouping of people into specific profiles. Earlier in Chapter 3 seven different, but frequently seen client profiles, were identified. Using the life cycle approach, the usual risks and goals for each profile were identified. While it is useful to realize that many families fit into one of these seven profiles, it is also true that these seven profiles do not represent all families nor all of their different financial situations.

 Key Concepts

Underline/highlight the answers as you read:

1. Identify the common client profiles and their typical financial risks and goals

2. Identify the statistics regarding the frequency and types of special needs situations.

3. List the types of issues that related to a special needs situation.

4. Understand the key steps and tasks that a caretaker should perform regarding a special needs person.

This chapter presents special financial planning situations that are less common then the seven profiles presented in Chapter 3, but that occur often enough in our society that a well-educated and well-trained financial planner should be able to assist a client with the financial planning needs associated with these unique circumstances.

The special circumstances covered in this chapter include planning for the family that has a special needs dependent, planning for divorce, planning for terminal illness, planning for non-traditional households, planning for job loss and job change, and planning for monetary windfalls. These are clearly not the only special needs situations, but rather represent a large percentage of special needs situations. There are common threads through most of these situations, including emotional as well as financial needs.

Special Financial Planning Situations
Persons with Special Needs Dependent
Planning for Divorce
Planning for Terminal Illness
Planning for the Non-Traditional Household
Planning for Job Loss or Job Change
Planning for Monetary Windfalls

In each of these special financial planning situations, the financial planning issues may not be as immediately important as the emotional issues, nonetheless they need to be addressed sooner or later. A client with such needs should acquaint themselves with the emotional issues related to the particular situation prior to attempting to solve the financial issues. Regardless of the planning situation, the financial planning issues will include planning for cash flows, perhaps legal issues or documents, perhaps government benefits (e.g. Social Security, unemployment, or other), and family support issues.

EXHIBIT 17.1 **COMMON CLIENT PROFILES AND THEIR TYPICAL FINANCIAL RISKS AND GOALS**

Life Cycle Factors							
Age	22-30	25-35	25-35	35-45	45-55	55-65	65-75
Marital Status	Single	Married	Married	Married	Married	Married	Married
Children	No	No	Yes	Yes	Yes	Yes	Yes
Grandchildren	No	No	No	No	No	Yes	Yes
Income	$35-$75k	$35-$75k	$45-$100k	$50-$150k	$75-$200k	$100-$200k	$50-$200k
Net Worth	$10-$20k	$10-$20k	$15-$25k	$20-$40k	$50-$100k	$500-$1,200k	$400-$1,500k
Self Employed	No	No	No	No	Yes	Maybe	No
Typical Risks/Insurance Coverage Needs							
Life Insurance	No	Maybe	Yes	Yes	Yes	Yes	No
Disability	Yes	Yes	Yes	Yes	Yes	Yes	No
Health	Yes	Yes	Yes	Yes	Yes	Yes	Yes
Long-Term Care*	No	No	No	No	No	Maybe Yes	Maybe Yes
Property	Yes	Yes	Yes	Yes	Yes	Yes	Yes
Liability	Yes	Yes	Yes	Yes	Yes	Yes	Yes
Typical Goals							
Retirement Security	Yes	Yes	Yes	Yes	Yes	Yes	In Retirement
Education Funding	No	No	Yes	Yes	Yes	No	No
Gifting	No	No	No	No	No	Yes	Yes
Lump-Sum Expenses	Yes	Yes	Yes	Yes	Yes	Yes	No
Legacy	No	No	No	No	No	Maybe	Maybe

* While younger clients will not typically require long-term care insurance, in some circumstances long-term care may be appropriate.

PLANNING FOR SPECIAL NEEDS DEPENDENT

Many families have one or more special needs dependents. A **special needs dependent** could be an infant, adolescent, or adult. The dependent could have a wide range of challenges from very mild physical, emotional, or psychological, to a situation where around the clock care is required. Consider that:

- One out of nine children (11%) under the age of 18 in the U.S. receives special education services.
- Two out of seven families (29%) reported having at least one family member with a disability.
- One of every 26 (4%) families reported raising children with a disability.
- One of every three families (33%) with a female head of household and no husband present reported members with a disability.
- An estimated 2.8 million families in the U.S. are raising at least one child aged 5 - 17 with a disability.[1]

---

1. The MetLife Center for Special Planning Needs.

Planning for the future of an individual with special needs requires knowledge of federal and state laws; federal, state, and local benefits; legal documents; and legal arrangements (not to mention a lot of love and care). There are both financial and quality of life issues to consider.

Of immediate concern to the parent / guardian is how:

- to provide a good quality of life for the child or dependent;
- to preserve government benefit eligibility for the child or dependent;
- to provide lifetime care for the child or dependent as needed;
- to have appropriate health insurance for the dependent;
- to have sufficient resources to supplement government benefits to provide a good quality of life for that dependent.

For each stage of a special needs dependent's life, from birth to adult, parents will need comprehensive advice and strategies to address each of the following issues:

- *financial issues* - from budgeting to investments;
- *legal issues* - estate planning, guardianship, and other arrangements such as trusts;
- *government benefits* - knowing about and preserving government benefits;
- *family and support factors* - family values, careers, siblings, extended family, and community resources;
- *emotional factors* - dealing with positive and negative emotions of the dependent, siblings, and parents.

Quick Quiz 17.1

Highlight the answer to these questions:

1. The seven common client profiles identified are helpful to understand the general population but do not address special needs situations.
   a. True
   b. False

2. An estimated 2.8 million families are raising at least one child aged 5 to 17 with a disability in the US.
   a. True
   b. False

3. The only relevant issues that a financial planner should be aware of for a special needs situation are the financial issues.
   a. True
   b. False

4. It is important that the special needs person have less than $100,000 to ensure that they retain their eligibility for governmental programs.
   a. True
   b. False

True, True, False, False.

TYPICAL GOVERNMENT BENEFITS

The Federal government does not provide adequate funding for every need of a special needs dependent. The federal system with budget constraints is inadequate to provide full funding to an increasing population of persons with special needs. Thus, the need to plan for the financial future of the dependent is critical.

Key Current Programs at the Federal and State Level:
Federal

- *Special Education Programs* - supported by Individuals with Disability Education Improvement Act 2004.
- *Social Security Benefits* - including disability, SSI, and Medicaid. Social Security has a booklet on its website that provides helpful information for these situations, entitled, *Benefits For Children With Disabilities SSA Publication No. 05-10026, June 2012, ICN 455360.*
- The website, childwelfare.gov, provides great information for special needs families. It also provides links to other national organizations that may provide assistance to those with special needs situations.

State and Local

- *Other Public Benefits* - state and local services may include:
  - Residential services
  - Transportation services
  - Respite Care Services
  - Family Support Services
  - Day Program Services
  - Employment Services

There are many state based and local based organizations that provide assistance and information for these situations. There are also parent groups that can be easily located through social media or an Internet based search.

NON-PROFIT ORGANIZATIONS

Each state has different support services which it funds. Eligibility must be determined and the amount and type of benefits provided must be determined. Some examples of non-profit support organizations are:

- The Arc
- United Health Care Children Foundation
- National Autism Foundation
- Easter Seals

WHAT SHOULD A CARETAKER DO

- Have a vision and plan for how the dependent will live after the initial caretaker is no longer able to serve as caretaker;
- Identify and name a guardian, and possibly a trustee for the dependent. This guardian may have general or limited powers. The caretaker / guardian must specify the types of powers for the trustee.
- Have a complete and documented understanding of Social Security disability (SSDI), Supplemental Social Security Income (SSI) government benefits, and Medicaid benefits.
- Set aside money for the dependent in a special needs trust. This trust could take the form of an irrevocable life insurance trust (ILIT) or an irrevocable secular trust with special needs provisions. (A description will be presented later in this material).
- Prepare a letter of intent (see Exhibit 17.3 for content).

- Prepare a will and do not leave assets directly to a special needs dependent. Rather, leave assets for special needs dependents in a special needs trust that preserves government benefits.
- Remove all assets from the name of any special needs dependent that are in excess of the $2,000 federal limit for benefits.
- Make sure the special needs dependent has adequate health insurance.

SPECIAL NEEDS TRUSTS

Trusts are a general tool that are beneficial in many financial planning situations. Many trust benefits, such as asset protection and control, are appropriate considerations for a family with a special needs person. A special needs trust is a specific type of trust that is used to provide benefits to persons or beneficiaries with special needs. Typically, these trusts are established to ensure that benefits available from federal and state agencies are preserved and maintained. Federal benefits include available funds and healthcare, such as provided by Social Security disability, Medicaid and the SSI (Supplemental Security Income) program through Social Security. Many of these programs will not pay benefits if the person has even limited resources. For example, to qualify for SSI, an individual cannot have more than $2,000 and a couple cannot have more than $3,000.

Key Concepts

Underline/highlight the answers as you read:

1. Explain the benefits for special needs trusts.

2. Identify and explain the three types of special needs trusts.

3. Identify the key elements to a letter of intent.

While special needs trusts are used to improve the quality of life and to provide additional resources to the special needs person without interfering with available governmental resources, there are several types of special needs trusts that should be considered. While there are more than three, the more common special trusts are discussed here and include the Third Party Special Needs Trust, the self settled type trust that is established and exempt under 42 U.S.C. Sec. 1396p(d)(4)(A), and what is referred to as a pooled trust.

Third Party (Family) Special Needs Trust (SNT)

A **third party** SNT is sometimes referred to as a family trust because the trust is a receptacle for funds from a parent, guardian or other family member. The assets of these trusts, if properly structured, are not counted or considered for purposes of available benefits for the beneficiary, thus making possible federal, state, and local funds.

These trusts can be funded by a parent or guardian during life or at death and are sometimes funded through the proceeds from a life insurance policy. The funds are contributed to a trust by the grantor or settlor for the benefit of the person with the special needs (beneficiary). The assets were never the property of or owned by the beneficiary and are therefore not counted as assets for purposes of federal benefits.

The provisions trust must be established so as to not provide food, shelter or any asset that could be converted into food or shelter, such as cash. It may provide for other benefits, such as medical treatment, therapy, education, travel, computer equipment, etc. These types of benefits can improve the lifestyle of the beneficiary and not interfere with governmental benefits.

For example, on the website for Social Security, under SSI, it states that "Money paid directly to someone to provide you with items other than food and shelter does not reduce your SSI benefits. (Items that are not "food or shelter" include medical care, telephone bills, education, entertainment, etc.)."

Assets exceeding $2,000 owned by or distributed to a person with a disability may jeopardize federal government benefits. A common way to structure assets either during life or at death that are intended to provide benefits for a disabled dependent is through the use of a special needs trust.

A special needs trust, created to hold contributed or inherited assets, or its trustee is the legal owner of the trust property. The dependent special needs person is not the owner of these trust assets, but rather the beneficiary of such a trust. Special needs trusts are irrevocable. However, an irrevocable life insurance trust with a second-to-die life insurance policy insuring parents of a special needs dependant may satisfy this need. Also, a revocable living trust (inter vivos) may also satisfy this need as it will become irrevocable upon the death of the grantor (parent). In any case, the special needs trust may provide benefits for education, transportation, insurance, rehabilitation, and other life enhancing benefits. The trustee needs to have discretion over the distribution and management of income and assets, but should be explicitly prevented by trust provision from any action that would jeopardize eligibility for government benefits. The remainder beneficiaries can be other children, grandchildren, or charities.

| EXHIBIT 17.2 | THIRD PARTY (FAMILY) SPECIAL NEEDS TRUST |

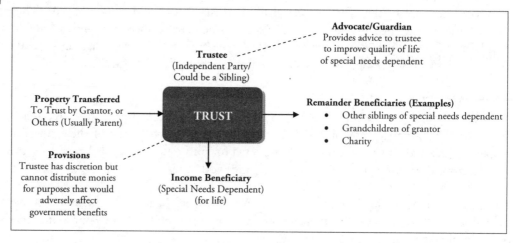

It is a good idea for the grantor of such a trust (generally the parent) to name an advocate (the advocate could be the guardian) for the dependent. The advocate is usually someone close to the dependent who understands both the grantor's wishes and the beneficiary's needs. The advocate works closely with the trustee in determining appropriate distributions that will maintain or improve the quality of life for the beneficiary without jeopardizing government benefits.

The grantor of a special needs trust can write a set of instructions to the advocate and to the trustee. This set of instructions frequently takes the form of a "letter of intent." While not legally enforceable, much like a side letter to a will, the letter of intent expresses the wishes of the grantor. Assuming that the guardian, advocate, and trustee are carefully selected these wishes are likely to be followed.

Special Needs Trusts Under 42 U.S.C. Sec. 1396p(d)(4)(A)

Special needs trusts under 42 U.S.C. Sec. 1396p(d)(4)(A), which are considered to be self-settled in nature, are typically established by the special needs person's parent, grandparent, legal guardian or by a court and will avoid disqualification of Medicaid and SSI benefits. This law was effective with Omnibus Budget and Reconciliation Act of 1993 and permits individuals with special needs or disabilities to establish a trust on their behalf or to direct settlement proceeds from a personal injury case be protected in a trust for their benefit and still qualify for benefits under Medicaid and SSI. Their statutory language for this section is:

> A trust containing the assets of an individual under age 65 who is disabled ... and which is established for the benefit of such individual by a parent, grandparent, legal guardian of the individual, or a court if the State will receive all amounts remaining in the trust upon the death of such individual up to an amount equal to the total medical assistance paid on behalf of the individual under a State plan under this subchapter.

The funds can be contributed to the trust and they can still qualify, but the assets remaining at the death of the beneficiary must be paid to the State to the extent funds and assistance from the State have been paid to or for the beneficiary.

It should be obvious that it would be better if the trust were not self-settled. However, in some cases, a beneficiary may receive an award from a litigation settlement or from proceeds from a life insurance policy or from an inheritance. If a financial planner were involved, the last two should be able to be paid into a third party trust. However, these funds, which are the property of the beneficiary, can be contributed to a trust as described above.

Pooled Trust (42 U.S.C. Sec. 1396p(d)(4)(C))

The other exception that resulted from the Omnibus Budget and Reconciliation Act of 1993 is a **pooled trust** that is managed by a nonprofit association. While each beneficiary will have their own account, the assets will generally be pooled and managed together. This type of trust can be funded by a parent, grandparent, legal guardian of the individual, or even by the beneficiary. These accounts must be established solely for the benefit of individuals who are disabled. To the extent that amounts remaining in the beneficiary's account upon the death of the beneficiary are not retained by the trust, the trust pays to the State from such remaining amounts in the account an amount equal to the total amount of medical assistance paid on behalf of the beneficiary under the State plan. In other words, the assets remaining at the death of the beneficiary will either go to the nonprofit association or to the State.

LETTER OF INTENT

The **letter of intent** is a "life plan" document. It describes the family of the special needs dependent and the special needs dependent's wishes for the future once the initial caregiver is no longer able to provide care. It should include pertinent information about the special needs dependent's history, medical needs, living arrangement preferences, hobbies, and contact persons (doctor, lawyer, accountant, guardians, etc).

Quick Quiz 17.2

Highlight the answer to these questions:

1. A special needs trust allows family members to provide for a special needs person without adversely effecting government benefits.
   a. True
   b. False

2. The three types of special needs trusts identified in the chapter are the Third Party SNT, the SNT created from the Omnibus Budget Reconciliation Act of 1993 and the Pooled Trust.
   a. True
   b. False

3. One of the key elements to a letter of intent is medical history.
   a. True
   b. False

True, True, True.

SAMPLE LETTER OF INTENT

EXHIBIT 17.3

This sample gives you an idea of what should be covered in a letter of intent. An actual letter would contain far more details than what is indicated here.

To Whom It May Concern:
Re: Our daughter, Lori X

1. **Contact the following people if anything should happen to us:** *Names, addresses, mail and e-mail addresses of other children, extended family, case manager, and a close family friend.*

2. **Current situation and family life:** Lori is a thirteen-year-old with autism who lives with her brother and parents. At home, she enjoys reading, playing computer games, cooking, and helping with chores. She enjoys family outings such as hiking, swimming, visiting friends, and going to restaurants and movies. At least once a week, she goes out with her support worker *(name and contact info) to* outings in the community such as swimming and basketball at the YMCA. She is a happy, engaging, and highly verbal child who enjoys the chance to socialize. In addition, she loves animals and spending time with her family cat.

3. **Education:** Lori is included in a regular class at James Madison Middle School with one-to-one support. Her strengths are reading, memory, and music. Since she is unable to print by hand, she uses a laptop computer. When class lessons are too complicated, her assistant allows her to access related computer games and programs instead. In the future, she could attend (with support) a high school that offers vocational opportunities such as cooking or animal care. Alternatively, she could attend a self-contained class at the high school level with students who have high functioning autism or a mild intellectual disability.

4. **Future Residence:** Lori would like to someday share an apartment with a roommate. She will likely need a support worker to check in with her daily (or less frequently) to help with activities of daily living, banking, or general support. Lori's name is already on a waiting list for the Supported Independent Living Apartment Program, offered through Name *of Agency.* Contact our case manager *(name and contact)* for details. Alternatively, she could move in with her brother, who plans on having a basement apartment for Lori in his home.

5. **Employment:** Lori has a keen interest in animals and cooking, and is skilled with computers. She would probably enjoy working or volunteering at an animal shelter, a pet store, or in the food service industry. Perhaps she could also find work requiring some computer expertise.

6. **Medical Care:** Lori has no medical challenges. She is seen for a yearly check up by Dr. Smith *(contact information),* who is familiar with Lori's strengths and challenges. In addition, she sees an eye doctor *(name and contact information)* and dentist *(name and contact information)* with special needs expertise. Lori is not allergic to any medications. However, in the past, she has experienced adverse side effects from the following medications, which should be avoided in the future: *(list drugs and adverse reactions).*

7. **Behavior Management:** Lori occasionally pinches and gets teary when she is anxious. The best strategy is to provide her with a written schedule or calendar of what will be happening in the day. Also, she has been seen by a behavior therapist at the *Name of Clinic (contact info).* They have agreed to consult on any future behavioral issues that may arise.

8. **Social:** Lori participates in several community programs, including YMCA sports for kids *(day, time, location),* a community cooking class *(day, time, location),* and therapeutic horseback riding *(day, time, location).* She also greatly enjoys visiting our close family friends *(name and contact info) at* least once per week.

9. **Religious/Spiritual Life:** Most Sundays, Lori attends services with us at *(Name) Church.* In addition, she occasionally attends youth group social programs for pre-teens.

10. **Guardian and Trustee:** Guardians and trustees have been assigned in our wills, which were last updated on *(insert date) and* are on file with *(attorney name, contact info).*

Both parents' signatures.

A detailed and comprehensive letter of intent will generally serve the special needs dependent better than one that is brief or less comprehensive. A whole notebook of information, pictures, and documents about the special needs dependent can provide assistance to the many persons who may be involved in providing care to the special needs dependent. Sensitive information such as Social Security numbers, account numbers, and account access should be encrypted / redacted or otherwise made secure.

| EXHIBIT 17.4 | LETTER OF INTENT - SAMPLE CONTENTS (NOT EXHAUSTIVE) |

- **Contacts** - including advocates, siblings, other family members, trustee, and/or case worker, including names, addresses, email addresses, phone numbers.
- **Dependent Description** - including likes, dislikes, current living arrangement, relationships with others, etc.
- **Medical History** - including primary doctor, specialists, medications, medications to be avoided,
- **Education** - including current education level, any ongoing education, copies of diplomas, plans and aspirations for the future.
- **Employment** - including any past and current jobs and any future job interests and abilities.
- **Religion** - including any services or programs usually attended.
- **Future Residential Possibilities** - including contacts, facilities, etc.
- **Social** - including any interests, programs, extra curricular activities.
- **Behavior** - including any behavioral issues that may need special care or attention.
- **Tax Information** - including any tax returns with Social Security numbers redacted.

PLANNING FOR DIVORCE

Financial planners regularly assist clients post-divorce. However, they can also be valuable resources for those who are planning for or are in the middle of a divorce.

Property settlements, child support, and alimony are major factors in divorce and are generally financial in nature. Often, the financial data that divorcing couples have is incomplete and/or unreliable. It is not uncommon that one or both parties are unaware of retirement benefits, asset values, projected cash flows, and or tax basis of assets, just to mention a few issues.

 *Key Concepts*

Underline/highlight the answers as you read:

1. Identify the recommendations for couples that are going through a divorce.

2. Identify the common mistakes that are made in a divorce.

3. List the recommendations for a terminally ill planning situation.

FINANCIAL PLANNING RECOMMENDATIONS FOR DIVORCING COUPLES

Gather, compare, verify, prepare, analyze, estimate, and project!

- Gather data to get a clear and complete understanding of the current and projected financial situation.
- Properly compile current investment and banking statements, organizing, and valuing all assets (e.g., businesses).
- Clearly analyze all liabilities. Determine if there are joint obligations that cannot be severed. For each liability, determine the monthly obligation, term of indebtedness, value of the corresponding asset, interest rate, and any other applicable information.
- Make a projection of future needs.
- Prepare both a current and projected Statement of Financial Position and Income Statement complete with explanatory footnotes.
- Gather five years of income tax returns. The information in the tax returns along with bank statements and investment statements will help to reduce the risk of overlooked or hidden assets.
- Collect any monthly, quarterly, or annual financial statements of an owned business plus five years of business tax returns. In addition, if the business has any debt, or has ever had any debt, financial statements provided to any such lender will yield useful information as will financial statements and loan applications for any personal credit (e.g., mortgages, auto loans, credit cards) that has been obtained by either party within the last five years.
- Analyze post divorce insurance needs.
- Analyze post divorce emergency fund requirements.
- Analyze post divorce retirement and education needs.
- Be sure to know the tax basis of each asset.
- Estimate any post divorce job training costs.
- Consider the built-in tax cost associated with assets in the property settlement.

All of this information, once collected, or prepared should be thoroughly reviewed by a competent party to get a clear and complete picture of the current financial situation. Cash flow and ongoing access to credit are important as both parties may be required to pay legal retainers and at least one party may find it necessary to set up a new household.

There are other factors to consider in financial planning for the person getting a divorce. While there may be an equitable distribution of assets (or even a 50% split of community property) that does not necessarily speak to the future income of each party or to future obligations that are beyond the legal term requirements of child support (commonly age 18), namely college education of children. These are issues that should be addressed and resolved in any divorce planning situation.

COMMON MISTAKES IN DIVORCE

Some of the most common financial planning mistakes that divorcing couples make are:

- Failure to adequately obtain individual credit prior to the divorce.
- Failure to differentiate between separate property, gifted or inherited property, and property acquired during marriage.
- Failure to discover hidden assets.

- Failure to resolve joint obligations, thus causing credit problems, especially where the party assigned the obligation is unreliable or irresponsible. This situation can have serious credit implications.
- Failure to make good choices regarding the property settlement of pension plans and other qualified plans where each spouse has a federal property right.
- Failure to be clear on the tax basis and thus tax implications of assets divided by agreement.
- Failure to provide a complete and contractually binding agreement regarding college education support for children.
- Failure to change beneficiary designations on insurance contracts and retirement plans, including qualified plans, IRAs, SEPs, and SIMPLEs.
- Failure to insure the support agreement from the risk of death, disability, inability, refusal of/by the payor. For example, if the husband is to provide child support to age 18 and college support to age 22 and he dies prematurely, did the she spouse own a life insurance policy on his life that would replace the support income? What about the disability of an ex-spouse or just plain laziness? What about bankruptcy of an ex-spouse? Could a spouse bankrupt against assigned joint obligations, thus transferring the obligation for them back to the other spouse, and causing a financial catastrophe for the non-bankrupt spouse?
- Failure to follow through, prior to the financial settlement, on paperwork to change the titling of assets and to account for assets to be transferred in the divorce property settlement.
- Failure to know the Social Security benefits of a spouse married for 10 or more years to a covered worker?

Even after proper planning and after avoiding common mistakes, it is important for spouses to prepare and maintain a budget so as to avoid financial troubles. There may be additional expenses setting up a new household and it is easy to spend more than the amount budgeted.

PLANNING FOR TERMINAL ILLNESS

At birth we have an approximate life expectancy of about 78 years. This means that for any given birth day, half of those persons born on that date are expected to live less than and half are expected to live longer than 78 years. The sad reality is that of the half who die before age 78, some die each year and the number of deaths usually forms a graph that is an upward sloping exponential function.

It is common that when people are in their 50s, 60s, and 70s, they begin to develop a comprehensive estate plan answering such questions as to whom, and how, will assets pass? Other questions to be answered are: (1) What are my thoughts on funeral and burial arrangements? (2) How will I provide for myself in the interim and for those I love after I pass? (3)Who will I empower to make my health care decisions? (4) What arrangements do I want with regard to the artificial sustainment of my life?

If people do not plan for those eventualities, usually the state of residence legislates the answers. The legislature passes these kinds of laws because many people fail to plan for their succession.

For a client diagnosed with a terminal illness, the above questions are relevant but the remaining time to begin to finalize a plan is compressed. In addition to dealing with the medical and emotional issues associated with being diagnosed as terminal, the client will frequently want to "get their financial house in order."

FINANCIAL PLANNING RECOMMENDATIONS FOR TERMINAL ILLNESS PLANNING

- Prepare or update personal financial statements.
- Prepare up-to-date estate documents (will, durable power of attorney for healthcare, advance medical directives, and do not resuscitate orders.
- Review all property titling arrangements to make sure they are as desired.
- Review all named beneficiaries of life insurance, qualified plans, other tax advantaged plans (IRAs, SEPs, SIMPLEs).
- Review all funeral and burial arrangements, including selection of location, minister, eulogizer, music, flower, determination of announcement in paper, etc.
- Determine whether there are viatical settlement considerations or accelerated benefits provisions in any life insurance policy.
- Consider home health care and Hospice services.
- Identify Social Security benefits to survivors.
- Inform the executor of accounts, account access, online accounts, and passwords.
- Consider organ donation.
- Do not forget income, estate, and gift tax consequences.

Quick Quiz 17.3

Highlight the answer to these questions:

1. There are few steps that need to be undertaken with a client who is going through a divorce.
   a. True
   b. False

2. One of the common mistakes that are made in a divorce is to not identify the types of property, such as separate or inherited property.
   a. True
   b. False

3. In addition to the recommendations for a terminally ill person, the financial planner should consider the emotional issues.
   a. True
   b. False

False, True, True.

The above recommendations are certainly sound, but the person with the terminal illness and the family and caregivers must also deal with the emotional issues. In some cases, the relationship may change or the person with the terminal illness may be in denial. The emotional issues will certainly impact the success of the financial objectives.

PLANNING FOR THE NON-TRADITIONAL HOUSEHOLD

While many financial planners will think of their prospective clients as married with children, the percentage of the population that is getting married in the United States is declining and the age at which individuals get married is increasing. The chart below depicts the percent of young adults who are married from the year 2000 to the year 2009.

MARITAL STATUS AMONG YOUNG ADULTS AGES 25-34 (PERCENT)

	2000	2006	2007	2008	2009
Married	55.1	48.9	48.2	46.9	44.9
Never Married	34.5	41.4	42.6	43.9	46.3

Source: U.S. Census Bureau, 2000 Census and American Community Survey.

As the chart indicates, the percent of younger people that are married is going down. In addition, the number of non-traditional households is on the rise.

The so-called **"non-traditional household"** is a broad phrase that may include any household other than the traditional husband, wife, and children. It could be heterosexual or homosexual couples living together with or without children. The adults may or may not be romantically involved, but may wish to include each other and their respective descendants in their estate plan.

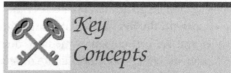

Key Concepts

Underline/highlight the answers as you read:

1. Explain what is meant by non-traditional household.

2. Explain how the Defense of Marriage Act impacts federal law with respect to the definition of marriage.

3. Identify the four ways property passes to heirs or legatees.

There are many federal and state laws that provide a surviving spouse of a married couple with certain rights. Examples include Social Security survivor benefits, rights under the state intestacy laws, rights to decide funeral and burial arrangements, tax filing choices, and the unlimited marital deduction to name a few.

In general, there are few, if any, laws which govern property division, support payments, or other rights for non-married couples. Unmarried couples must take great care to avoid intestacy laws that do not provide for non-married partners. Also, unmarried couples should carefully consider and prepare wills, durable powers of attorney for health care, and advance medical directives. Frequently, and especially in the case of same-sex couples, legal difficulties arise regarding funeral and burial wishes for deceased partners.

CIVIL UNIONS AND REGISTERED PARTNERS

A civil union is a separate legal status conveying to the partners most of, if not all, the rights available to married couples under state (but not federal) law. Civil unions are currently available in Vermont, Connecticut, New Jersey, and New Hampshire. Some other states have domestic partnership registries. These states include California, Maine, New Jersey, Oregon, Washington, and the District of Columbia. Rights and responsibilities vary among jurisdictions.

California's Domestic Partner Rights and Responsibilities Act of 2003 expanded previous rights to include almost all rights and responsibilities of spouses under state law. These rights include hospital visitation, a right to be appointed a conservator and make medical decisions, inheritance rights, joint responsibilities for debts, and the right to seek financial support from each other upon the dissolution of the relationship for "registered" domestic partners. These persons can even file the state income tax return as married filing jointly or separately.

The **Defense of Marriage Act (DOMA)** was signed into law on September 21, 1996 and was "to define and protect the institution of marriage." Under Section 7, Definition of 'marriage' and 'spouse' the law states, "In determining the meaning of any Act of Congress, or of any ruling, regulation, or interpretation of the various administrative bureaus and agencies of the United States, the word 'marriage' means only a legal union between one man and one woman as husband and wife, and the word 'spouse' refers only to a person of the opposite sex who is a husband or a wife." Since the Internal Revenue Code is an act of Congress, the definitions of marriage and spouse are largely dictated by DOMA.

The important point here is that the financial planning client in a non-traditional relationship must understand the state law of the state in which they reside, as will as Federal law.

PROPERTY TRANSFERS AT DEATH

In general, all property owned by a decedent passes to the heirs or legatees in one of four alternative ways:
1. by state contract law (e.g., life insurance, annuities, TODs, PODs),
2. by state titling law where there is a survivorship feature (e.g., JTWROS, TE),
3. by state trust law, or
4. by state probate or succession law including both testate and intestate successions.

Forms of testamentary transfers such as beneficiary designations on contracts (life insurance, annuities, qualified plans, IRAs, SEPs, SIMPLEs, Pay on Death bank accounts (PODs), and transfer on death investments accounts (TODs), may be used as a will substitute. Other will substitutes include real property titling joint tenancy with rights of survivorship (JTWROS) and revocable trusts that become irrevocable at the death of the grantor. These will substitutes used to pass assets are much more difficult arrangements to challenge than a will in probate court.

Wills are presented in the probate count and are frequently problematic for same-sex couples as they may get challenged by the decedent's relatives. However, it may be advantageous to have a will that while not passing assets does confer powers such as the power to name an executor, to appoint a guardian for children, and for the making of gifts of personal property by virtue of a side letter.

Quick Quiz 17.4

Highlight the answer to these questions:

1. Traditional marriage has been on the rise over the last decade.
   a. True
   b. False

2. The Defense of Marriage Act defines what a marriage is for federal law.
   a. True
   b. False

3. All property must pass through probate.
   a. True
   b. False

False, True, False.

It is also a wise idea to even restate beneficiary designations and titling with survivorship rights in the will even though the asset is passing out of probate so as to provide additional evidence of the decedent's wishes for the probate court.

Generally, for non-married persons wishing to provide for the surviving partners, it is preferred to avoid probate due to the public nature and openness of the process. Whether assets will be passed by contract, titling, or trust will depend on the concerns and reservations the party with the assets has toward the surviving partner. In general, "if you don't trust 'em, trust 'em," (i.e. create a trust to hold assets).

PLANNING FOR JOB LOSS OR JOB CHANGE

Financial planners regularly suggest that clients have an emergency fund of three to six times their nondiscretionary monthly cash flows. However, this rule of thumb is potentially misguided even though it may be the average of all averages. The reality is there are a variety of risks that might require the use of an emergency fund that includes but are not limited to job loss.

In a poor labor market, it will take longer on average to find a replacement job than for a similar job in a vibrant labor market. Some workers are highly specialized and do not have adaptable skill sets to generalized employment, so it may take those workers much longer than six months to find a replacement job especially in a poor labor market.

EXHIBIT 17.5

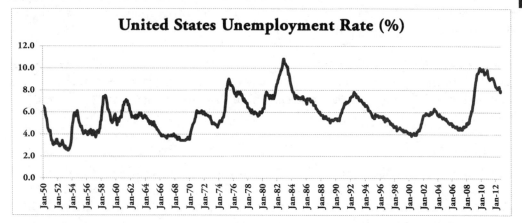

Questions to ask include:
- Is the market for the client's type of job a national market or a local market?
- Is the client willing to relocate?
- How long does the client think it would take to replace his job if lost? (Clients are more likely to have a better idea about how long it would take to replace a lost job in the client's field than the planner.)

Once these things are considered, a new emergency fund ratio should be established for this client (e.g., it could be 1-2 months for a tenured faculty member and it could be 18 months for a specialized position at a local market).

CASH FLOWS

Job loss that is unplanned causes significant cash flow consequences, including no income, no savings, and continued nondiscretionary expenses. There cannot be enough emphasis on cash flow planning including the use of debt, sale of assets, cutting expenses, and taking funds from retirement accounts if absolutely necessary.

Key Concepts

Underline/highlight the answers as you read:

1. Explain the general rule of thumb regarding the amount of money necessary for an emergency fund.

2. Explain the recommendations for a windfall recipient.

AGE AS A FACTOR

Age is a significant factor in finding work. During 2011, those unemployed over age 55 took, an average, 52.2 weeks to find work and 10 percent of those age 55 and older simply quit looking for work.[2] This is twice as long as the average 30 year old required to replace a job. Keep in mind that the replacement job may or may not, and often does not, offer the same salary and benefits as the job that was lost.

When job loss happens, it may be an ideal time to try self-employment or a second career in an area of interest or return to school to retool. Each of these options also has cash flow implications that must be considered.

Those workers age 62 or older, or if a survivor age 60 or older should determine Social Security benefits especially if previously married. To claim benefits on a divorced spouse's work record will not preclude the beneficiary from claiming on their own work record at a later date.

HEALTH INSURANCE

Health insurance becomes a major issue for the unemployed. COBRA, if available, will provide benefits from 18 months to 36 months, but the premiums are expensive. It is very likely that the former employer was paying part of the insurance premiums. With COBRA, the individual is responsible for 100 percent of the premiums and may even be charged an administrative premium. An unemployed client may want to consider a high deductible plan to provide health benefits. Clients should request that the former employer keep the client on health insurance for a transition period.

FINANCIAL PLANNING ADVICE

The financial planner should recommend that the client who has just lost a job should immediately start looking for work. Recent skills and recent contracts are critical to finding a replacement job. The planner should recommend that the client try competitors of the former employer. The client should be advised to immediately file for unemployment benefits and for any employer severance if possible. The planner should also recommend that the client network with people in the same field and also make it clear to friends and family that the client is looking for a new job.

A client may want to reassess their career objectives but the key to planning when job loss occurs is very precise budgeting and managing of cash flows. From a portfolio perspective, it may make sense to evaluate the portfolio to determine the amount of

Quick Quiz 17.5

Highlight the answer to these questions:

1. Clients only need savings equal to 3 to 6 months of income as an emergency fund.
   a. True
   b. False

2. A windfall recipient, in addition to often being ecstatic, has a lot of work to do to help ensure that the unexpected wealth is not squandered.
   a. True
   b. False

False, True.

liquid assets that are available to the client to use in the event of an extended period of

---

2. U.S. Labor Department (December 2011).

unemployment. It might make more sense to make small adjustments in the portfolio sooner rather than when there is little or no alternative.

PLANNING FOR A FINANCIAL WINDFALL

A financial **windfall** is often treated by the recipient as quite different than earned money. Windfalls can include lottery winnings, an unexpected inheritance, stock options, IPOs, sometimes marrying into money, or the sale of a business. Once someone has sudden wealth, especially if the information about that wealth is public information, there will be scores of people willing to give the recipient suggestions. Most of these are likely to be bad, or at least suspect.

Financial planners who assist clients with new found or sudden wealth do not just provide financial advice and education, but provide assistance to the client in the transition from one set of economic circumstances to another. Planners should keep in mind that the windfall recipient is often under great emotional stress for a wide variety of reasons, most likely caused by the uncertain future as to what to do.

The curious fact is that there is story after story of lottery winners subsequently going broke. Why? The answer may lie in the fact that before the windfall they had a support, advice, and money knowledge system consistent with their then economic situation and lifestyle. The realization is that people who have always been wealthy have experience with wealth and also with the management of spending, using debt, investing, and wealth transfer. Many of those who experience a financial windfall do not have such experiences.

The worst course of action for a windfall recipient to do after receiving a windfall is to spend freely in an attempt to change to an unsustainable lifestyle. One of the best things they could do is to do nothing. They should take time to carefully consider goals of debt payoff, funding education, and funding and planning for retirement. The client should proceed very slowly and should seek expert financial advice and get many opinions. They should use as a guide "the first principle of financial planning is to protect the principal!"

FINANCIAL PLANNING RECOMMENDATIONS FOR A FINANCIAL WINDFALL RECIPIENT

- Get educated - learn about investments, your risk tolerance, etc.
- Take time (18-36 months) to decide what to do, "protect the principal."
- Find at least one competent CPA, financial advisor, and legal advisor (be efficient with their time, particularly those that charge by the hour).
- Do not quit your job.
- Do not invest in a new business.
- Do not invest in illiquid assets.
- Do not give others discretion over your money.
- Do not forget the tax consequences, if any.
- Do not incur debt or sign personal guarantees, for anyone.

Key Terms

Defense of Marriage Act (DOMA) - Signed into law on September 21, 1996 and was "to define and protect the institution of marriage." Under Section 7, Definition of 'marriage' and 'spouse' the law states, "In determining the meaning of any Act of Congress, or of any ruling, regulation, or interpretation of the various administrative bureaus and agencies of the United States, the word 'marriage' means only a legal union between one man and one woman as husband and wife, and the word 'spouse' refers only to a person of the opposite sex who is a husband or a wife."

Letter of Intent - a "life plan" document that describes the family of the special needs dependent and the special needs dependent's wishes for the future once the initial caregiver is no longer able to provide care. It should include pertinent information about the special needs dependent's history, medical needs, living arrangement preferences, hobbies, and contact persons (doctor, lawyer, accountant, guardians, etc).

Non-traditional Household - a broad phrase that may include any household other than the traditional husband, wife, and children. It could be heterosexual or homosexual couples living together with or without children. The adults may or may not be romantically involved, but may wish to include each other and their respective descendants in their estate plan.

Pooled Trust - An exception that resulted from the Omnibus Budget and Reconciliation Act of 1993; managed by a nonprofit association. While each beneficiary will have their own account, the assets will generally be pooled and managed together.

Special Needs Dependent - could be an infant, adolescent, or adult. The dependent could have a wide range of challenges from very mild physical, emotional, or psychological, to a situation where around the clock care is required.

Special Needs Trusts Under 42 U.S.C. Sec. 1396p(d)(4)(A) - considered to be self-settled in nature, are typically established by the special needs person's parent, grandparent, legal guardian or by a court and will avoid disqualification of Medicaid and SSI benefits.

Third Party SNT - sometimes referred to as a family trust because the trust is a receptacle for funds from a parent, guardian or other family member. The assets of these trusts, if properly structured, are not counted or considered for purposes of available benefits for the beneficiary, thus making possible federal, state, and local funds.

Windfall - often treated by the recipient as quite different than earned money. Windfalls can include lottery winnings, an unexpected inheritance, stock options, IPOs, sometimes marrying into money, or the sale of a business.

DISCUSSION QUESTIONS

1. List six special circumstances outside a normal financial planning engagement.

2. How prevalent are special needs dependents?

3. What are some of the important concerns of a parent or guardian regarding a special needs dependent?

4. Where can parents or guardians obtain information about benefits for special needs dependents?

5. What are some of the tasks that should be completed by a caretaker of a special need dependent?

6. What are the three types of special needs trusts?

7. Describe a third party special needs trust.

8. What are some of the requirement for a special needs trust under 42 U.S.C. Sec. 1396p(d)(4)(A)?

9. List several topics that might be included in a letter of intent.

10. List the recommendations for divorcing couples.

11. What are some of the common mistakes that are made in a divorce?

12. What are the recommendations for someone with a terminal illness?

13. What are the trends regarding married status in the United States?

14. Why is it important to understand federal and state law regarding the definition of marriage?

15. What are the four ways property can transfer at death?

16. How many months of income is the recommended amount to be accumulated as an emergency fund?

17. What are the general recommendations for someone who has a financial windfall, such as winning the lottery or received a substantial inheritance?

1. Which of the following is not an example of a special needs situation?

    a. Planning for Candice, who has a daughter that is autistic.

    b. Planning for the Smith family with three boys ages 2, 3 and 4.

    c. Planning for Sam and Pat, who live together but are not married.

    d. Planning for Joe the plumber, who just won the powerball jackpot for $823 million.

2. Approximately how any families are raising one or more children with a disability?

    a. Less than half a million.

    b. Between half a million and a million

    c. Between a million and 2 million

    d. More than two million.

3. Providing a good home and maintaining a family is challenging enough without a special needs dependent. However, it becomes much more complicated with a child who is disabled or who has special needs. Which of the following is not correct?

    a. A parent or guardian should attempt to provide a good quality of life for the child.

    b. A parent or guardian should attempt to help the child accumulate assets in the child's name to be sure the child can be cared for.

    c. A parent or guardian should attempt to provide health insurance for the child.

    d. A parent or guardian should attempt to preserve government benefits for the child.

4. Trusts are a general tool that are beneficial in many financial planning situations. Many trust benefits, such as asset protection and control, are appropriate considerations for a family with a special needs person. Which of the following is not generally associated with planning for a special needs situation?

    a. Family trust or third party trust.

    b. A trust under 42 U.S.C. Sec. 1396p(d)(4)(A).

    c. A pooled trust.

    d. A special general advocate trust.

5. Trusts are a general tool that are beneficial in many financial planning situations. Many trust benefits, such as asset protection and control, are appropriate considerations for a family with a special needs person. Which of the following is generally correct regarding special needs trusts?

    a. Family trusts can be established but will likely cause the child to lose federal benefits.

    b. A special needs trust under 42 U.S.C. Sec. 1396p(d)(4)(A) will permit a family member to contribute to the trust for the benefit of the special needs child without adversely effecting government benefits if funds are paid back to the State to the extent of the benefit at the death of the child.

    c. A pooled trust can be established. Banks and brokerage firms establish many of these trusts.

    d. A life insurance trust is prohibited from to assist with the needs of a special needs child.

6. The statement, "Adam is a very pleasant young man who is interested in animals and is generally skilled with computers" might be found in what document?

    a. Family trust or third party trust.

    b. A will.

    c. A letter of intent.

    d. A dossier.

7. Divorce is a very emotional time for those who are going through it and assistance from a financial advisor is generally helpful. Which of the following are common mistakes that are made by those going through divorce?

    a. Obtaining individual credit.

    b. Establishing the tax basis of assets that are separated.

    c. Failure to change beneficiary designations on retirement plans.

    d. All of the above are common mistakes.

8. Terminal illness can be devastating for a family. Which of the following is not correct?

    a. The emotional issues are not relevant to the financial advisor.

    b. Estate documents should be reviewed and updated as necessary.

    c. Funeral arrangements should be considered.

    d. Titling of property should be reviewed to ensure that issues do not arise in the future.

9. Some studies have suggested that up to 70% of lottery winners lose their winnings within as short as a seven-year period. What are some of the reasons that might cause this or cause others who have come into a wind fall to lose it?

    a. Some will invest in businesses without requisite knowledge or experience.

    b. Some will purchase assets that have high maintenance costs combined with other lavish spending.

    c. Some will fail to obtain professional advice on managing the money.

    d. All of the above.

Quick Quiz Explanation

Quick Quiz 17.1
1. True.
2. True.
3. False. A financial planner should be aware of financial issues, but also other issues, such as the emotional issues.
4. False. Generally, to qualify for federal benefits, a person should not have more than about $2,000.

Quick Quiz 17.2
1. True.
2. True.
3. True.

Quick Quiz 17.3
1. False. There are a lot of documents that must be reviewed for a person going through a divorce and there are a lot of task that must be completed.
2. True.
3. True.

Quick Quiz 17.4
1. False. Traditional marriage has been decreasing not increasing over the last decade.
2. True.
3. False. Property may pass through probate or by way of law or contracts.

Quick Quiz 17.5
1. False. They may need more or less depending on their individual situation.
2. True.

David and Amy Rudolph Case & Case Analysis Part 2

LEARNING OBJECTIVES

After reading this chapter, you should be able to:

- Describe an initial meeting and summarize data and draw conclusions for the lifecycle approach.
- Prepare a comprehensive engagement letter.
- Gather internal and external data and prepare financial statements.
- Create the pie chart approach.
- Prepare financial statement analysis using a ratio analysis approach.
- Prepare each of the ratios and compare them to the benchmark.
- Prepare the two-step, three panel, metrics approach with schedules.
- Prepare the cash flow approach.
- Prepare the tax analysis approach.
- Prepare the strategic approach.
- Prepare the present value of all goals approach.
- Make a presentation to the client using current and projected financial statements and ratios.
- Prepare a closing engagement letter that includes the responsibility for implementation and monitoring.

INTRODUCTION

The Rudolphs have returned to continue their financial planning engagement one year later with additional objectives to achieve in the current year. They have accomplished many of their financial planning objectives since their last meeting with their financial planner. Given that the Rudolphs are established clients, it is not necessary for the planner to use all of the financial planning approaches (including the complete life cycle approach, two-step/three-panel approach, and strategic approach) in order to arrive at current recommendations.

DAVID & AMY RUDOLPH CASE - INTERNAL DATA

David Rudolph (age 52, born on December 4th) is the owner of an office furniture company, DR Office Furniture Inc., (DRI) and is married to Amy Rudolph (age 36, born on February 14th) who is a self-employed real estate broker. David's salary is $283,250. The client's net worth is $3.8 million; of which $2.75 million consists of the value of his business, DRI, as per a recent valuation.

This is both David and Amy's second marriage. David has a 31-year-old son, Trevor, from his first marriage to Joyce. Trevor is married and has one child, Trevor Jr. (age 3). Trevor is experiencing financial difficulty because he lost his job in the recent economic downturn and has been unsuccessful in his employment search. Trevor Jr. is now living with David and Amy because Trevor is constantly traveling seeking employment. David and Amy have become very close to Trevor Jr., who they have discovered is extremely intelligent. David and Amy are so taken with Trevor Jr. that they want to explore fully funding his college education, given their affection for him and his high potential for academic success.

Amy has a child from her former marriage, Madelyn (age 15, born on March 31st), who still resides with Amy's former husband, George (age 36, born on October 23rd), who is her legal guardian. Madelyn has become quiet the spender as she progresses into her teenage years, much to the concern of David and Amy. Madelyn has obtained her learner's permit to drive and will be licensed to drive when she becomes age 16.

David and Amy have one child of their own, Danny (age 2). Unfortunately, Danny has been recently diagnosed as autistic. David and Amy are concerned for Danny's future and also that he may be permanently dependent upon them or other caretakers.

Amy was divorced from George three years ago and they continue to have a very contentious relationship.

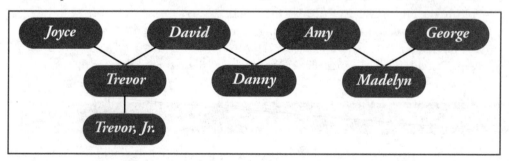

Amy is self-employed as a realtor and has Schedule C net income of $150,000 per year before self-employment tax or any deduction for any qualified or tax advantaged retirement plan.

PERSONAL AND FINANCIAL OBJECTIVES (ACHIEVED WITHIN THE LAST YEAR)

1. The Rudolphs' risk management portfolio is now appropriate (see Insurance - with the exception of long-term care insurance).
2. The Rudolphs refinanced their lake house.
3. The Rudolphs paid off their boat loan.
4. The Rudolphs paid credit cards down to $5,000.
5. The Rudolphs had an attorney prepare basic estate planning documents (durable power of attorneys for healthcare, advance medical directives, and wills).

PERSONAL AND FINANCIAL OBJECTIVES (CURRENT)

1. The Rudolphs want to determine the amount of money to fully fund Trevor Jr.'s college education today using a 529 Savings Plan. The Rudolphs realize that as grandparents to Trevor Jr., they can reclaim amounts in the education savings plan should they need the funds in the future. They are planning for Madelyn's education, but not Danny's education.
2. David has decided to currently sell 32.7229 percent of his 75 percent interest in DRI for $900,000 cash with a put option to sell the remainder of his interest in 10 years for $1,850,000 increased by 3 percent per year. This will leave David with a controlling interest of 50.46 percent (75 x 0.67277) David and Amy have inherited a piece of artwork that they will sell to fund the taxes owed on the current sale of DRI stock.
3. David still has a goal to retire at age 62. Capital needs analysis is required (annuity model and capital preservation model) to know how much funding is needed. Any funding deficit of David's retirement needs will create the need for current annual year-end funding.
4. The Rudolphs want recommendations to revise their estate planning to avoid probate and to provide for Madelyn and Danny in the event of David and Amy's death.
5. The Rudolphs want to consider the advantages and disadvantages of each possible entity form that Amy might use for her business. They were audited last year and the CPA and IRS agent told them that tax returns with Schedule C income get audited more than tax returns with income from flow-through entities.
6. The Rudolphs want a full review of their investment portfolio.
7. David and Amy want to consider purchasing long-term care insurance.

UPDATED SUMMARY OF INITIAL DATA COLLECTED - LIFE CYCLE APPROACH

Using the approaches learned in Chapter 3, the financial planner will initially prepare the life cycle characteristics approach. This approach seeks to efficiently establish which phase or phases of the life cycle the client is in and to then deduce from that assessment the likely client goals and risks. The life cycle approach, while easy and efficient, lacks sufficient detail to permit the financial planner to prepare a complete financial plan.

Based on recent client communications, the information collected is as follows:

Updated Summary of Data Collected - Life Cycle Approach	
Ages	• David (age 52). • Amy (age 36).
Marital Status	• Married (MFJ income tax filing status).
Children & Grandchildren	• Trevor (age 31) - From David's previous marriage with one child Trevor Jr. (age 3) - Trevor is unemployed. • Madelyn (age 15) - From Amy's previous marriage; lives with George (former husband) - learner's permit to drive; spending issue. • Danny - Child of David and Amy (age 2) - Special Needs.
Net Worth	• Approximately $3.8 million (DRI dependent) - based on valuation.
Income	• Amy $150,000 self employed (Schedule C) - proprietorship. • David owner of DRI / employer salary $283,250.
Self-Employed	• Amy is self employed and has no employees. • David is the owner / employer of a C corporation (DRI) with 31 employees.

The financial planner has chosen to update the summary of data collected, but preliminary conclusions are not necessary for an established client.

EXTERNAL DATA

ECONOMIC INFORMATION

- The Rudolphs expect salary increases of 2.5 percent annually in keeping with inflation.
- Inflation is expected to average 2.5 percent annually for the foreseeable future.
- Education inflation is expected to be six percent annually.
- Real GDP has been 2.75 percent and is expected to continue to be 2.75 percent for the next several years.
- It is expected that the S&P 500 will return approximately nine percent this year and annually for the foreseeable future.
- T-bills are considered the appropriate proxy for the risk-free rate of return and are currently earning 3.5 percent.
- The Rudolphs expect that Trevor Jr. and Madelyn will spend $20,000 a year in today's dollars for four years of college education beginning at his age 18. They expect to earn 8 percent annually in his 529 Savings Plan that they plan to implement.
- The Rudolphs have the same risk tolerance (as reflected in Part 1) and want to use 8 percent as their expected portfolio return.

Bank Lending Rates

- 15-year mortgage is 4.75 percent.
- 30-year mortgage is 5.0 percent.
- Any closing costs associated with refinance are an additional three percent of the amount mortgaged.
- Secured personal loan is 8.0 percent.
- Credit card rates are 18 percent.

ECONOMIC OUTLOOK - INVESTMENTS

	Return	Standard Deviation
Small Company Stocks	12%	18%
Large Company Stocks (Actively Managed)	10%	16%
S&P 500	9%	14%
Corporate Bonds	7%	5%
Long-term Treasury Bonds	6%	4%
T-bills	3.5%	2%

The internal data on the Rudolphs are all updated for the client's current circumstances and include:

- Insurance information (life, health, long-term disability, long-term care, property and liability, automobile, and boat);
- Financial statements (1/1/2014 and 1/1/2015);
- Information related to investment assets;
- Information related to personal use assets; and
- Other financial profile data, including income tax, savings and retirement, and estate information.

INSURANCE INFORMATION

Life Insurance

	Policy 1	Policy 2	Policy 3
Insured	David Rudolph	David Rudolph	Amy Rudolph
Face Amount	$2,000,000	2 x Salary = $550,000	$250,000
Type	Whole Life Policy	Group Term - Employer Provided	Term Policy Ten Year Level Term
Cash Value	$120,000	$0	$0
Annual Premium	$10,000	$700	$500
Beneficiary	Amy/Contingent Beneficiary is Danny	Amy/Contingent Beneficiary is Danny	Madelyn/Contingent Beneficiary is David
Owner	David Rudolph	David Rudolph	Amy Rudolph

Health Insurance

David currently has an indemnity group health and major medical hospitalization plan through his company. Amy, David, Danny, and Madelyn are currently covered by his health insurance plan. DRI pays the entire premium for the health insurance policy. Madelyn is covered under both David and George's health insurance plans. David's plan has the following characteristics:

- $500 per individual deductible.
- $1,000 total family deductible.
- 80% co-insurance clause for major medical.
- $3,000 annual family stop loss limit.

Long-Term Disability Insurance

Disability Policies	David's Policy	Amy's Policy
Type	Own Occupation	Own Occupation
Insured	David	Amy
Guaranteed Renewable	Yes	Yes
Benefit	60% of Gross Pay	60% of Gross Pay
Premium Paid By	Employer	Amy
Residual Benefits Clause	Yes	Yes
Elimination Period	90 Days	90 Days
Annual Premium	$2,000	$2,000

Long-Term Care Insurance
Neither David nor Amy have long-term care insurance, but want to consider it now.

Property and Liability Insurance
Homeowners Insurance

	Personal Residence	Lake House
Type	HO3 with endorsements	HO3 with endorsements
Dwelling	$800,000	$450,000
Other Structures	$80,000	$45,000
Personal Property	$400,000	$100,000
Personal Liability	$100,000	$100,000
Medical Payments	$10,000	$10,000
Deductible	$2,000	$2,000
Co-Insurance %	80 / 20	80 / 20
Annual Premium	$3,000	$3,800

There is no flood insurance on the personal residence or the lake house.
Note that the HO3 policies were endorsed, the coverage was reduced for the personal residence,
increased for the lake house, and deductibles were raised on both policies in the last year.

Auto Insurance

	Auto #1 David's Car	Auto # 2 Amy's Car
Type	PAP	PAP
Liability (Bodily Injury)	$100,000/$300,000/$50,000	$100,000/$300,000/$50,000
Medical Payments	$10,000	$10,000
Uninsured Motorist	$100,000/$300,000	$100,000/$300,000
Collision Deductible	$2,000	$2,000
Comprehensive Deductible	$2,000	$2,000
Annual Premium	$750	$1,000

Boat Insurance

Boat	
Type	Personal Boat
Personal Property	$70,000
Personal Liability	$100,000/$300,000/$50,000
Deductible	$2,000
Annual Premium	$1,000

Liability Insurance

The Rudolphs own a personal liability insurance policy (PLUP) with $3 million of coverage at an annual cost of $1,350.

EXHIBIT 18.1	SUMMARY OF RISK MANAGEMENT DATA

	Coverage	Benchmark	Comments / Recommendations
Life Insurance			
Policy 1 - David	$2,000,000	$2,750,000	Adequate coverage Ownership issue for estate tax Beneficiary Changed
Policy 2 - David	$550,000		Group Term - adequate Changed beneficiary
Policy 3 - Amy	$250,000	$1,500,000	Depends on risk tolerance and priorities Changed owner Consider trust for Madelyn
Health Insurance	Yes	Ok	Adequate coverage DRI provided
Disability Insurance			
David	60% Gross Pay / Guaranteed Renewable	60 - 70%	Adequate coverage DRI provided - Taxable
Amy	60% Gross Pay / Guaranteed Renewable	60 - 70%	Added disability insurance adequate
Long-Term Care Insurance	None	36-60 months of savings	Currently considering
Property & Liability Insurance			
Personal Residence	$800,000	≤ FMV	Reduced coverage to FMV Endorsed HO3
Lake House	$450,000	≤ FMV	Raised coverage to FMV Endorsed HO3
Automobile # 1 and # 2	100 / 300	100 / 300	Adequate coverage Raised deductibles
Boat	100 / 300	≤ FMV	Purchased adequate coverage
Liability Insurance	$3 million	$1 - 4 million	Purchased adequate coverage

FINANCIAL STATEMENTS

Balance sheets (Statement of Financial Position) for the year beginning (1/1/2014) and year end (12/31/2014) are presented. In addition, an income statement (Statement of Income and Expenses) is presented for last year (2014) and projected next year income (2015). A reconciliation of the decline in net worth from 1/1/2014 to 1/1/2015 is provided.

EXHIBIT 18.2 **FINANCIAL STATEMENTS: STATEMENT OF FINANCIAL POSITION (1/1/2014 - PREVIOUS YEAR)**

Statement of Financial Position			
David and Amy Rudolph			
Balance Sheet as of 1/1/2014			

ASSETS[1]			LIABILITIES AND NET WORTH		
Current Assets			**Current Liabilities[2]**		
JT Cash & Checking	$25,000		W Credit Cards	$15,000	
JT Money Market	$270,000		**Total Current Liabilities**		$15,000
Total Current Assets		$295,000			
Investment Assets			**Long-Term Liabilities[2]**		
H DR Office Furniture, Inc[3]	$3,325,000		JT Principal Residence	$1,169,619	
H Brokerage Account 1	$500,000		H Lake House	$148,038	
H Education Account[4](529)	$46,000		H Boat	$70,276	
H 401(k) Plan w/ Roth	$50,000		**Total Long-Term Liabilities**		$1,387,933
W Traditional IRA	$15,000				
W Roth IRA	$20,000				
Total Investment Assets		$3,956,000	**Total Liabilities**		$1,402,933
Personal Use Assets					
JT Principal Residence	$800,000				
H Lake House	$450,000				
JT Furniture, Clothing	$100,000		**Total Net Worth**		$4,313,067
H Car # 1	$25,000				
W Car # 2	$35,000				
H Boat	$55,000				
Total Personal Use Assets		$1,465,000			
Total Assets		$5,716,000	**Total Liabilities & Net Worth**		$5,716,000

1. Assets are stated at fair market value.
2. Liabilities are stated at principal only as of January 1, 2014 before January payments.
3. This is David's 75% interest and the value is based on his estimate.
4. This is for Madelyn and Danny. David currently saves $6,000 per year into his account (see portfolio).

Title Designations:
H = Husband (Sole Owner)
W = Wife (Sole Owner)
JT = Joint Tenancy with Survivorship Rights

Statement of Financial Position
David and Amy Rudolph
Balance Sheet as of 12/31/2014 (and 1/1/2015)

ASSETS[1]			LIABILITIES AND NET WORTH		
Current Assets			**Current Liabilities[2]**		
JT Cash & Checking	$20,000		W Credit Cards	$5,000	
JT Money Market	$170,000		**Total Current Liabilities**		$5,000
Total Current Assets		$190,000			
Investment Assets			**Long-Term Liabilities[2]**		
H DR Office Furniture, Inc[3]	$2,750,000		JT Principal Residence	$1,153,009	
H Brokerage Account 1	$600,000		H Lake House	$145,335	
H Education Account[4](529)	$50,000		H Boat	$0	
H 401(k) Plan w/ Roth	$65,076		**Total Long-Term Liabilities**		$1,298,344
W Traditional IRA	$12,000				
W Roth IRA	$16,280				
W Amy 401(k) Plan	$33,000				
Total Investment Assets		$3,526,356	**Total Liabilities**		$1,303,344
Personal Use Assets					
JT Principal Residence	$800,000				
H Lake House	$450,000				
JT Furniture, Clothing	$100,000		**Total Net Worth**		$3,878,012
H Car # 1	$25,000				
W Car # 2	$35,000				
H Boat	$55,000				
Total Personal Use Assets		$1,465,000			
Total Assets		$5,181,356	**Total Liabilities & Net Worth**		$5,181,356

1. Assets are stated at fair market value.
2. Liabilities are stated at principal only as of January 1, 2015 before January payments.
3. This is David's 75% interest and the value is based on a professional appraisal for $3,666,667 for the entire company.
4. This is for Madelyn and Danny. David currently saves $6,000 per year into this account (see portfolio).

Title Designations:
H = Husband (Sole Owner)
W = Wife (Sole Owner)
JT = Joint Tenancy with Survivorship Rights

EXHIBIT 18.4

FINANCIAL STATEMENTS: INCOME STATEMENT
(ADJUSTED FOR RECOMMENDATIONS MADE IN 2014 AND EXPECTED FOR 2015)

Statement of Income and Expenses
David and Amy Rudolph
Statement of Income and Expenses
Expected (Approximate) For This Year (2015)

			Totals
Cash Inflows			
David's Salary		$283,250	
Amy's Salary		$150,000	
Total Cash Inflows			$433,250
Cash Outflows			
Savings			
Money Market		$1,000	
401(k) Plan		$22,000	
401(k) Plan Amy		$16,500	
Education (529 Plan)		$6,000	
Total Savings			$45,500
Taxes			
Federal Income Taxes Withheld		$64,800	
State Income Taxes Withheld		$22,000	
David's Social Security Taxes		$10,729	
Amy's Social Security Taxes Estimated & Estimated Payments		$17,593	
Property Tax Principal Residence		$4,000 ND	
Property Tax Vacation Home		$4,000 ND	
Total Taxes			$123,122
Debt Payments (Principal & Interest)			
Principal Residence		$86,335 ND	
Lake House		$14,232 ND	
Boat		$0	
Credit Cards		$10,000 ND	
Total Debt Payments			$110,567
Living Expenses			
Utilities Principal Residence		$5,000 ND	
Lake House Expenses (net of rental income of $5,000)		$15,000 ND	
Gasoline for Autos		$5,000 ND	
Lawn Service		$2,000 ND	
Entertainment		$15,000	
Vacations		$25,000	
Church Donations		$10,000 ND	
Clothing		$18,000 ND	
Auto Maintenance		$2,000 ND	
Satellite TV		$1,800 ND	
Food		$8,000 ND	
Miscellaneous		$10,000 ND	
Total Living Expenses			$116,800
Insurance Payments			
HO Insurance Principal Residence		$3,000 ND	
HO Insurance Lake House		$3,800 ND	
Boat Insurance		$1,000 ND	
Auto Insurance		$1,750 ND	
Disability Insurance Amy		$2,000 ND	
PLUP		$1,350 ND	
Life Insurance #1		$10,000 ND	
Life Insurance #3		$500 ND	
Total Insurance Payments			$23,400
Total Cash Outflows			$419,389
Net Discretionary Cash Flows			$13,861

ND - Non-discretionary cash flow per mutual understanding between financial planner and client.

CHANGE IN NET WORTH - RECONCILIATION (FROM 2014 TO 2015)

	Change in Net Worth
$4,313,067	Before Recommendations
$3,878,012	After Recommendations
($435,055)	Net Reduction (decline)
	Reconciliation
($575,000)	DRI Valuation Decline Adjustment
($105,000)	Cash and Cash Equivalents Adjustment
$145,356	Other Investments Increases
$99,589	Change in Liabilities Reduction
($435,055)	Reconciled Decline in Net Worth

INVESTMENT ASSETS

General Information

- The Rudolphs have an overall required rate of return of eight percent on their overall portfolio and eight percent for the 529 Savings Plan for Trevor Jr.
- They have a moderate risk tolerance.
- David expects to be able to sell his interest in DRI to partially fund his retirement.
- Their emergency fund is primarily invested in a taxable money market account earning 0.75 percent annually.

DR Office Furniture, Inc. (DRI)

David started working DR Office Furniture, Inc. over 20 years ago when he inherited the business from his father. The fair market value of DRI at the time of David's inheritance was $1 million (and the tax law at that time created a basis for David that was equal to the fair market value at the date of his father's death). Today, it is one of the largest office furniture companies in the southeast and David previously sold 25 percent of the equity in his company to his top employees and value of the business is expected to grow at three percent each year. Paul Carter, Brian Conner, and Sally Walker (the top employees) have agreed to buy the business in 10 years. David insists that this sale will provide an adequate capital balance upon which to retire. DR Office Furniture, Inc. has traditionally offered employees health insurance, group term life insurance, a 401(k) plan with a Roth component and an integrated profit sharing plan. The profit sharing plan requires age 21 and one year of service for participation. David usually receives the maximum allowed for the combination of the profit sharing plan and 401(k) plan deferrals, including matching and catch-ups.

Originally, when attempting to value his business, David's accountant advised him to use a multiple of revenue approach. David's accountant suggested using a multiple of 2.5 times revenue to value the business. David had estimated the value of the business based on revenues for 2013 for his initial valuation. An expert appraiser was recently hired and the company was valued at $3,666,667. David's interest is 75 percent. The Rudolph's balance sheet has been updated accordingly.

Brokerage Account 1

Immediately after his meeting with the financial planner last year, David decided to sell all of his mutual funds and invest the proceeds into four stocks. The brokerage account 1 consists of the stocks indicated below. Any interest and dividends earned on investment are is reflected in the account balance and is not counted or separately stated in the income statement. The investment portfolio is illustrated at the beginning of the year and at the end of the year.

INVESTMENT PORTFOLIO (BROKERAGE ACCOUNT 1) - STOCKS AS OF 1/1/2014

				Stocks							
Name	Shares	Cost per Share	FMV per Share	Beta	P/E Ratio	Div. Yield	Annual Div.	Standard Deviation	Expected Return	Total FMV	
A	500	$50	$35	0.79	5	2.4%	$0.84*	0.12	8%	$17,500	
B	1,000	$80	$99	0.97	15	3.2%*	$3.17	0.14	10%	$99,000	
C	500	$100	$10	1.5	9	0.1%	$0	0.16	9%	$5,000	
D	7,570	$10	$50	1.2	22	0.4%	$0.20	0.19	12.3%	$378,500	
									Totals	$500,000	

* The dividend is expected to grow at 6% per year.

INVESTMENT PORTFOLIO (BROKERAGE ACCOUNT 1) - STOCKS AS OF 1/1/2015

				Stocks							
Name	Shares	Cost per Share	FMV per Share	Beta	P/E Ratio	Div. Yield	Annual Div.	Standard Deviation	Expected Return	Total FMV	
A	500	$50	$46	0.79	5	2.4%	$0.84*	0.12	8%	$23,000	
B	1,000	$80	$117.70	0.97	15	3.2%*	$3.17	0.14	10%	$117,700	
C	500	$100	$10.20	1.5	9	0.1%	$0	0.16	9%	$5,100	
D	7,570	$10	$60	1.2	22	0.4%	$0.20	0.19	12.3%	$454,200	
									Totals	$600,000	

* The dividend is expected to grow at 6% per year.

Education Account 1 (529 Plan)

The contributions to this account are invested in a diversified portfolio of mutual funds based on the age of the youngest beneficiary. David selected an overall investment strategy that resulted in "moderate risk" investments. This savings account is for Madelyn and any remaining funds will be used for Trevor, Jr. by changing the beneficiary on the account to Trevor, Jr. when Madelyn finishes college.

DRI 401(k) Plan with Roth Account

After his financial planning meeting last year, David reallocated 100 percent of this account from cash to a balanced mutual fund consisting of 50 percent equities and 50 percent fixed investments. His expected return of eight percent is equal to the required rate of return. David made his first contribution to this account in 2013.

Traditional IRA

The Traditional IRA is invested in a series of zero coupon bonds. The investment returns in this account over the past six years have been:

	Year	Returns
2009	1	6.50%
2010	2	4.75%
2011	3	- 3.25%
2012	4	- 2.5%
2013	5	5.25%
2014	6	9.09%

David is uncertain what his compound rate of return has been and whether these bonds are appropriate for his goals.

Roth IRA

The Roth IRA is currently invested in a tax-free municipal bond mutual fund, earning 1.75 percent per year. The income is reinvested and not reflected on the income statement.

Amy's 401(k) Plan

Amy has 60 percent of her contributions invested in an equity index mutual fund and 40 percent of her contributions invested in a corporate bond mutual fund.

PERSONAL USE ASSETS

Personal Residence

The Rudolphs purchased their personal residence for $1,500,000 three years ago on January 1, 2012. Their mortgage payment is $7,195 per month. They borrowed $1,200,000 over 30 years at six percent. They were considering refinancing the house but decided not to refinance when the appraised value came in at only $800,000 due to market conditions. They pay their homeowner's insurance premiums and property taxes separately from their mortgage. The Rudolphs contested their property taxes, which lowered to $4,000 annually.

Lake House

The lake house was formerly David's personal residence for the last 15 years (2000). He purchased the lake house for $250,000, by putting down 20 percent and borrowing the rest at seven percent for 30 years. His payment was $15,967 per year. He refinanced at 4.75 percent for 15 years (total amount refinanced is $152,479.14 with payments of $14,232 per year). The lake house is rented for 14 days per year to one of David's key customers for $5,000. The $5,000 is used against expenses and is included in the income statement. The property taxes are $4,000 a year and homeowners insurance is $3,800 per year. Both taxes and insurance are paid separately.

Boat

The Rudolph's purchased their boat for $125,000 four years ago in January 2010. It is a 54' Hatterus with twin inboard motors. Their boat payment was $1,267 per month. They borrowed $100,000 over 10 years at nine percent on a signature loan to finance the purchase of the boat. The Rudolphs have paid off this loan and have also purchased a boat insurance policy at a cost of $1,000 per year.

OTHER FINANCIAL PROFILE INFORMATION

Income Tax Information
The Rudolphs are in the 35 percent marginal income tax bracket for federal income tax purposes and their state income tax rate is five percent. Capital gains are taxed at 15 percent at the federal level and five percent at the state level.

Savings and Retirement Information
David has a safe harbor 401(k) plan through his company (DRI). He contributes the maximum of his salary each year, plus any permissible catch-up contribution. His company matches dollar for dollar on the first three percent of salary and then $0.50 on the dollar on the next two percent of salary to a maximum contribution of four percent of his covered compensation. David also has an integrated profit sharing plan through his company (DRI). The company adds the amount necessary to the profit sharing plan to maximize the overall defined contribution limit of $49,000 (currently). This limit does not include the $5,500 catchup provision to the 401(k) plan. Amy is self-employed and is currently contributing $16,500 to a 401(k) retirement plan. David's total savings, including the employer match, is $54,500 per year.

The Rudolphs define adequate retirement income as 80 percent of pre-retirement income. They both plan to live until age 95 after retiring at David's age 62.

David recently received a notice from Social Security that his full normal age retirement benefit in today's dollars would be $2,200 per month. Normal age retirement for David is 67, so he will receive 70 percent of those benefits at age 62. For capital needs analysis, they want the financial planner to consider David's age only and ignore the age disparity between the spouses.

Estate Information
The Rudolphs have wills, durable power of attorneys for healthcare, and advance medical directives. However, they have serious concerns about avoiding probate and providing for both Madelyn and Danny.

FINANCIAL STATEMENT ANALYSIS - RATIO ANALYSIS APPROACH

INTRODUCTION

As discussed in Chapter 3, the financial statement analysis - ratio analysis approach utilizes ratios to gain insight into the client's financial situation. The approach assesses:

1. the client's ability to pay short-term obligations and fund an emergency,
2. the client's ability to manage debt,
3. whether the client is committed financially to all of his goals,
4. the progress of the client in achieving the goal of financial security based on the client's age and income, and
5. how well the investment assets have performed to benchmarks.

The ratios should be compared to appropriate benchmarks to provide a more meaningful analysis.

EXHIBIT 18.5 RATIO ANALYSIS

LIQUIDITY RATIOS BASED ON 1/1/2015 FINANCIAL STATEMENTS

Ratio	Formula		Comment	Benchmark
Emergency Fund Ratio*	Cash & Cash Equivalents / Monthly Non-Discretionary Cash Flows	$\frac{\$190,000}{\$18,231} = 10.4$	Very Strong	3 - 6:1
Current Ratio	Cash & Cash Equivalents / Current Liabilities	$\frac{\$190,000}{\$5,000} = 38:1$	Very Strong	0.5:1

Monthly non-discretionary cash flows are $18,231 as indicated on the Statement of Income and Expenses - ND ($218,767 ÷ 12).

DEBT RATIOS BASED ON 1/1/2015 FINANCIAL STATEMENTS

Ratio	Formula		Comment	Benchmark
Housing Ratio 1 (HR 1) (Includes both homes.)	Housing Costs / Gross Pay	$\frac{\$115,367}{\$433,250} = 26.6\%$	Okay	≤ 28%
Housing Ratio 2 (HR 2) (Includes both homes.)	Housing Costs + Other Debt Payments / Gross Pay	$\frac{\$125,367}{\$433,250} = 28.9\%$	Good	≤ 36%
Debt to Total Assets	Total Debt / Total Assets	$\frac{\$1,303,344}{\$5,181,356} = 25.15\%$	Very Strong	Age Dependent
Net Worth to Total Assets	Net Worth / Total Assets	$\frac{\$3,878,012}{\$5,181,356} = 74.84\%$	Very Strong	Age Dependent

RATIOS FOR FINANCIAL SECURITY GOALS BASED ON 1/1/2015 FINANCIAL STATEMENTS

Ratio	Formula		Comment	Benchmark
Savings Rate (Overall)	Savings + Reinvestments + Employer Match / Gross Pay	$\frac{\$78,000}{\$433,250} = 18.0\%$	Very Strong	Goal Driven At Least 10-13%
Savings Rate (Retirement)	Employee Contributions + Employer Contributions / Gross Pay	$\frac{\$72,000}{\$433,250} = 16.6\%$	Very Strong	At Least 10-13%
Investment Assets to Gross Pay (Does not include education savings.)	Investment Assets + Cash & Cash Equivalents / Gross Pay	$\frac{\$3,476,356 + \$190,000}{\$433,250} = 8.5:1$	Very Strong	Approx. 4:1 at Age 50

PERFORMANCE RATIOS BASED ON 1/1/2014 AND 1/1/2015 FINANCIAL STATEMENTS				
Return on Investments	$\dfrac{I_1 - (I_0 + \text{Savings})}{I_0}$	= -12.8% (See calculation below)	Very Poor	8 - 10%
Return on Assets	$\dfrac{A_1 - (A_0 + \text{Savings})}{A_0}$	= -10.7% (See calculation below)	Very Poor**	2 - 4%
Return on Net Worth	$\dfrac{NW_1 - (NW_0 + \text{Savings})}{NW_0}$	= -11.9% (See calculation below)	Very Poor**	The higher the better. This ratio is likely to become smaller as the client's net worth increases.

** *The substantial change in the value of DRI because of the expert appraisal has resulted in a negative return on total assets and a negative return on net worth.*

PERFORMANCE RATIOS CALCULATIONS***	
Return on Investments = (Excludes cash and cash equivalents.)	$\dfrac{\$3,526,356 - (\$3,956,000 + \$45,500 + \$32,500)}{\$3,956,000} = -12.8\%$
Return on Assets =	$\dfrac{\$5,181,356 - (\$5,716,000 + \$45,500 + \$32,500)}{\$5,716,000} = -10.7\%$
Return on Net Worth =	$\dfrac{\$3,878,012 - (\$4,313,067 + \$45,500 + \$32,500)}{\$4,313,067} = -11.9\%$

*** *\$32,500 of savings is derived from the employer match of 4% of \$245,000 (covered compensation for qualified plans) which equals \$9,800 plus \$22,700 from the profit sharing plan. (See Schedule C Part 2.)*

Observations

The short-term liquidity and ability to pay ratios are excellent. The housing and debt ratios are good. The Rudolph's savings rate is excellent (18.0 percent) as is the investment assets to gross pay ratio (8.5:1) for his age.

Once again, the issue is the credibility of the valuation of DRI. David says it grows in value at an annual rate of three percent This valuation should be demonstrated by net after-tax cash flows growing year over year by at least three percent.

The investment performance ratios are very poor, but are heavily skewed because of the change in the balance sheet value of DRI and the decline in the value of the principal residence. The performance ratios need to be compared to market returns for the year. However, investment returns are best measured over a longer time period (five years) and then compared to market benchmarks.

The performance ratios suggest the financial planner should take a much closer look at the investment portfolios and the valuation of DRI.

LIQUIDITY AND DEBT RATIOS 1/1/2015 - SCHEDULE A

	Actual	Metric	Comments
Emergency Fund	10.4 x	3 - 6 month	More than adequate.
Housing Ratio:			
1 - Combined	26.6%	≤ 28%	These are high at age 51 / 35 but do not exceed the metric.
2 - Combined	28.9%	≤ 36%	
Evaluation of Debt			On personal residence there continues to be a loan to value issue.

Observations

The Rudolph's emergency fund is substantial at 10.4 times monthly non-discretionary cash flows. The housing ratios are within the metric limits.

Informational Inputs for Liquidity and Debt Ratios		
Non-Discretionary Cash Flows*	$18,230.58 per month $218,767 annually	Income Statement
Cash and Cash Equivalents	$190,000	Balance Sheet
Principal Residence**	P&I & T&I = $93,335	Income Statement
Lake House***	P&I & T&I = $22,032	Income Statement
Credit Card Payments	$5,000	Income Statement
Gross Pay	$433,250	Income Statement

*Monthly non-discretionary cash flows are $18,230 as indicated on the Statement of Income and Expenses - ND
($218,767 ÷ 12).
**$86,335 + $4,000 + $3,000 = $93,335
***$14,232 + $4,000 + $3,800 = $22,032

LONG-TERM SAVINGS AND INVESTMENTS - SCHEDULE B

To achieve financial security (retirement) requires persistent savings of 10 to 13 percent of gross pay and investment assets appropriate for the age of the client and the client's gross pay. Many clients have multiple goals such as retirement, education funding, lump-sum expenditures, and legacy aspirations. The more goals a client has, the greater the need for an increased savings rate.

SCHEDULE B - PART 1

	Actual	Metric	Comments
Retirement Security Goal			
Overall Savings Rate	18.0%	At least 10% - 13% of gross pay	Excellent
Retirement Savings Rate	16.6%	10 - 13% of gross pay	The total savings rate is consistent with the retirement goal.
Investment Assets as % of Gross Pay (Excludes education savings)	8.5 x	8 x	They currently exceed the necessary investment assets for retirement (for their age). Education assets are excluded. Valuation of DRI remains critical.
Educational Funding	$6,000 per year	$6,000 per year	Adequate
Lump-Sum Goals	None	None	Okay
Estate Planning	Documents	Documents	Estate planning issues remain: (1) avoid probate, and (2) provide for minors.

SCHEDULE B - PART 2

David	401(k) Plan (EE) Deferral	$16,500	
	Over 50 Catch-Up	$5,500	
	ER Match	$9,800	
	Profit Sharing (ER)	$22,700	
	David Total	$54,500	(See Retirement Information)
	Education	$6,000	
	Money Market	$1,000	
Amy	401(k) Plan (EE) Deferral	$16,500	
	Combined Total	$78,000	

New Savings Rate: $\frac{\$78,000}{\$433,250}$ = 18.00% Excellent

Observations

The Rudolphs have an excellent savings rate of 18.0 percent [($71,000 + $6,000 + $1,000) ÷ $433,250)] overall and have investment assets equal to 8.5 x their gross pay which, using David's age, the benchmark or metric is 8 x. The only problem is the ownership of the business. DRI makes up 78 percent of the investment assets. There is a serious issue regarding valuation and concern over whether the employees will be willing and able to buy the business in eleven years at David's retirement. This issue is central to the overall plan and alternatives need to be addressed.

IMMEDIATE AND LONG-TERM OBJECTIVES AND ANALYSIS

PERSONAL AND FINANCIAL OBJECTIVES (CURRENT)

1. The Rudolphs want to determine the amount of money to fully fund Trevor Jr.'s college education today using a 529 Savings Plan. The Rudolphs realize that as grandparents to Trevor Jr., they can reclaim amounts in the education savings plan should they need the funds in the future.

2. David has decided to currently sell 32.7229 percent of his 75 percent interest in DRI for $900,000 cash with a put option to sell the remainder of his interest in 10 years for $1,850,000 increased by three percent per year. David and Amy have inherited a piece of artwork that they will sell to fund the taxes owed on the current sale of DRI stock.

3. David still has a goal to retire at age 62. Capital needs analysis is required (annuity model, capital preservation model, and purchasing power preservation model) to know how much funding is needed. Any funding deficit of David's retirement needs will create the need for current annual year-end funding.

4. The Rudolphs want recommendations to revise their estate planning to avoid probate and to provide for Madelyn and Danny in the event of David and Amy's demise.

5. The Rudolphs want to consider the advantages and disadvantages of each possible entity form that Amy might use for her business. They were audited last year and the CPA and IRS agent told them that Schedule C income tax returns get audited more than other entity forms.

6. The Rudolphs want a full review of their investment portfolio.

7. David and Amy want to consider purchasing long-term care insurance.

8. The Rudolphs plan to name a special needs trust for Danny as the contingent beneficiary of Life Insurance Policy 1. Amy's will, if she survives David, will also provide for funding the special needs trust for Danny.

OBJECTIVE 1: EDUCATION FUNDING - 529 SAVINGS PLAN 2 FOR TREVOR JR.

- Objective: The Rudolphs want to determine the amount of money to fully fund Trevor Jr.'s college education today using a 529 Savings Plan.
- The planner needs to provide an analysis of the funding option required for the 529 Savings Plan for Trevor Jr.

Risk Tolerance:

- The Rudolphs have a moderate risk tolerance but expect to earn nine percent in this particular investment account.

Trevor 529 Savings Plan Funding

Informational Inputs	
Present Value of Education in Today's Dollars	$20,000
Expected Education Inflation Rate	5%
Expected Years of College Education	4 years
Beginning Year of College Education (age 18)	15 years from now
Investment Portfolio Expected Return	8%

Calculation Method: Traditional Method - in real dollars

Step 1: Determine the present value of the cost of five years of college education at age 18 using real dollars with the $25,000 payment being made at the beginning of each year of Trevor Jr.'s college.

10BII Keystrokes	12C Keystrokes
[**ORANGE**] [BEG/END]	[g] [BEG]
4 [N]	4 [n]
1.09 [÷] 1.05 – 1 x 100 = [I/YR]	1.09 [ENTER] 1.05 [÷] 1 [-] 100 [x] [i]
20,000 [PMT]$_{AD}$	20,000 [PMT]$_{AD}$
0 [FV]	0 [FV]
[PV]	[PV]
Answer: <76,727.97>	**Answer: <76,727.97>**

Step 2: Determine the present value today (at Trevor Jr.'s age 3) using real dollars, of the lump-sum amount needed to deposit now to fully fund Trevor Jr.'s education.

10BII Keystrokes	12C Keystrokes
[**ORANGE**] [BEG/END]	[g] [BEG]
15 [N]	15 [n]
1.09 [÷] 1.05 – 1 x 100 = [I/YR]	1.09 [ENTER] 1.05 [÷] 1 [-] 100 [x] [i]
0 [PMT]	0 [PMT]
76,727.97 [FV]	76,727.97 [FV]
[PV]	[PV]
Answer: <50,284.81>	**Answer: <50,284.81>**

Given the funding requirement of $50,284.81 today to fully fund Trevor Jr.'s college education, David and Amy could each contribute half ($25,142.41) to the 529 Plan. The $25,142.41 contribution each is well below the annual gift exclusion limit for 529 Savings Plans of $70,000 (5 x $14,000 for 2013) per donor per beneficiary.

OBJECTIVE 2: SALE OF DRI

- Objective: David has decided to currently sell 32.7229 percent of his 75 percent interest in DRI for $900,000 cash with a put option to sell the remainder of his interest in 10 years for $1,850,000 increased by three percent per year. David and Amy have inherited a piece of artwork that they will sell to fund the taxes owed on the current sale of DRI stock.
- The planner needs to provide an analysis of the impact of the sale of DRI.

If David sells 32.72229 percent of his current 75 percent interest in DRI to other executives for $900,000 cash, then he can retain $1,850,000 of stock representing 50.4545 percent ownership (a controlling interest). Then David can receive a put option to put 50.4545 percent of DRI at $1,850,000 (at his age 62) plus a three percent inflationary increase per year.

Tax Implications of the Sale of DRI Stock

Amount of Sale	$900,000	
Less Basis in Stock	$245,454	24.54% of whole (32.72727 of 75% interest)
Gain	$654,546	from sale of DRI (subject to capital gains taxation)
Estimated Federal Tax (15%)	$98,182	($654,546 x 0.15)
Estimated State Tax (5%)	$32,727	($654,546 x 0.05)
	$130,909	

Artwork (Payment of Taxes)

David and Amy inherited a piece of art from Amy's Uncle George Freeman who recently died. While the client appreciates being thought of by Uncle George, the artwork is not particularly aesthetically pleasing to them. The fair market value was $150,000 at Uncle George's death, but his tax basis was only $25,000. The executor of Uncle George's estate has indicated that he will apply $125,000 of adjustment to this asset so that Amy's basis is $150,000. Therefore, considering their funding goals, Amy and David agree to immediately sell the art to pay the taxes on the sale of DRI.

OBJECTIVE 3: RETIREMENT CAPITAL NEEDS ANALYSIS

- Objective: David still has a goal to retire at age 62. Capital needs analysis is required (annuity model, capital preservation model, and purchasing power preservation model) to know how much funding is needed.
- Objective: Any funding deficit of David's retirement needs will create the need for current annual year-end funding.
- The planner needs to provide an analysis of David's capital needs analysis for retirement funding along with an analysis of any additional required funding.
- His latest estimate for Social Security benefits is $2,200 per month in today's dollars at normal age retirement of 67. He will retire at 62, and therefore, receive 70 percent of the full benefit from Social Security.

Retirement Needs Analysis:

David and Amy Current Income	$433,250	
80% Wage Replacement	0.80	
Subtotal	**$346,600**	(See Retirement Chapter for calculation)
Less: Social Security	$18,480	($2,200 x 12) x 0.70
Total	**$328,120**	First year retirement income in today's dollars.

When calculating David's retirement needs analysis, inflation of 2.5 percent is used as well as the required investment rate of return of 8 percent.

Step 1: Calculate the future value of $328,120 in 10 years (David's age 52 to his age 62) using the inflation rate.

10BII Keystrokes	*12C Keystrokes*
10 [N]	10 [n]
2.5 (inflation) [I/YR]	2.5 (inflation) [i]
0 [PMT]	0 [PMT]
328,120 [PV]	328,120 [PV]
[FV]	[FV]
Answer: <420,021.34>	**Answer: <420,021.34>**

Step 2: Calculate the amount needed at retirement, based on the annual income need of $420,021.34 being withdrawn for 33 periods (62 - 95), using the two alternative methods of capital needs analysis.

Annuity Model to Capital Needs Analysis

10BII Keystrokes	*12C Keystrokes*
[ORANGE] [BEG/END]	[g] [BEG]
33 [N]	33 [n]
1.08 [÷] 1.025 – 1 x 100 = [I/YR]	1.08 [ENTER] 1.025 [÷] 1 [-] 100 [x] [i]
420,021.34 [PMT]$_{AD}$	420,021.34 [PMT]$_{AD}$
0 [FV]	0 [FV]
[PV]	[PV]
Answer: <6,777,966.85>	**Answer: <6,777,966.85>**

Capital Preservation Model to Capital Need Analysis

10BII Keystrokes	12C Keystrokes
33 [N]	33 [n]
8 [I/YR]	8 [i]
0 [PMT]	0 [PMT]
6,777,966.85 [FV]	6,777,966.85 [FV]
[PV]	[PV]
Answer: <534,706.55>	**Answer: <534,706.55>**

This model adds $534,706.55 to capital needs of $6,777,966.85 for a total of $7,312,673.40.

<table>
<tr><td>EXHIBIT 18.6</td><td colspan="3">SUMMARY OF CAPITAL NEEDS MODELS</td></tr>
</table>

	Annuity Model	Capital Preservation Model
Capital Needed at Retirement (age 62)	$6,777,966.85	$7,312,673.40

An evaluation of whether the Rudolphs have or will have sufficient money to fund their retirement needs is required. The Rudolphs are subject to single asset risk (DRI). Therefore, the financial planner considers the current sale of a portion of DRI stock to fund retirement in the analysis.

Retirement Assets Available Today (considering sale of DRI stock)

Cash and Cash Equivalents	$123,704
Brokerage Account #1	$600,000
Brokerage Account #2	$900,000 **from sale of DRI**
Roth 401(k) Plan	$65,076
IRA	$12,000
Roth IRA	$16,280
Amy 401(k) Plan	$33,000
	$1,750,060

Given the $1,750,000 in assets available today to invest for retirement funding, the following calculations are made to assess the adequacy of current retirement funding.

Calculate the future value of $1,750,000 invested today plus the ongoing annual retirement savings ($78,000) at the client's required rate of return (8%) until David's age 62.

10BII Keystrokes	12C Keystrokes
10 [N]	10 [n]
8 [I/YR]	8 [i]
78,000 [PMT]$_{OA}$	78,000 [PMT]$_{OA}$
1,750,000 [PV]	1,750,000 [PV]
[FV]$_{@62}$	[FV]$_{@62}$
Answer: <4,908,070.61>	**Answer: <4,908,070.61>**

At age 62, David will have $4,908,070 saved for retirement funding, plus his 50.4545% ownership in DRI. The expected value of his ownership in DRI at age 62 is as follows:

10BII Keystrokes	12C Keystrokes
10 [N]	10 [n]
3 [I/YR]	3 [i]
0 [PMT]	0 [PMT]
1,850,000 [PV]	1,850,000 [PV]
[FV]$_{@62}$	[FV]$_{@62}$
Answer: <2,486,245.30>	**Answer: <2,486,245.30>**

Retirement Funds Available at David's Age 62

Value at David's Age 62 of Current Funding	$4,908,070
Value at David's Age 62 of DRI Stock	$2,486,245 **50.4545% ownership interest**
	$7,394,315

Observations

Based on the previous capital needs analysis, the $7,394,315 in retirement funding exceeds the annuity model requirement ($6,777,967) and the capital preservation model requirement ($7,312,673). Current Income Utilization Compound to Wage Replacement in Today's Dollars

Client's current income	$433,250
Less: Social Security	($28,322)
Savings, not including employer match	($45,500)
Lake house loan will be paid off	($14,232)
Result is close to 80% wage replacement ratio	$345,196 *

* This is very close to their estimated needs.

OBJECTIVE 4: ESTATE PLANNING

- Objective: The client wants recommendations to revise their estate planning to avoid probate and to provide for Madelyn and Danny in the event of David and Amy's death.
- The planner needs to recommend the establishment of trusts to avoid probate and provide for Madelyn and Danny.

Life Insurance Policy 1 should be transferred to a Life Insurance Trust (LIT#1) for the benefit of income to Amy for her life and the remainder to Danny. The initial trustee is Amy, but successor trustees need to be named to ultimately provide a lifetime of care for Danny. This trust could have provisions that it will only pay for expenses that are not paid by a state agency to create a special needs trust. Another benefit of this trust is that it will avoid probate.

Life Insurance Policy 2 should name as its beneficiary Life Insurance Trust #1 (LIT#1). It will avoid probate and will be managed during Amy's life by Amy.

Life Insurance Policy 3 should be transferred to Life Insurance Trust #2 with David as both Trustee and income beneficiary and Madelyn having the remainder interest upon David's death. Provisions can be made to accumulate earnings until such time as Madelyn is financially mature (for example, she receives 25 percent at age 35 and 25 percent at age 45 and the balance at age 55).

The professional costs of creating the two trusts will be approximately $3,000 and will be paid from their current income statement on a non-recurring basis.

OBJECTIVE 5: BUSINESS ENTITY CHANGE FOR AMY'S SOLE PROPRIETORSHIP

- Objective: The client wants to consider the advantages and disadvantages of each possible entity form that Amy might use for her business. They were audited last year and the CPA and IRS agent told them that Schedule C income tax returns get audited more than other entity forms.
- The planner needs to analyze business entity forms to establish a recommendation of business type for Amy.

Amy is a sole proprietor with Schedule C income. She wants to explore other business entity options to avoid future IRS audits (due to Schedule C income risk for audit) and to obtain personal liability protection. Amy is seeking a form of business entity where the cost of formation and maintenance of the organization is not excessive.

Partnerships

Being a sole proprietor, Amy would need a partner in order to form her business as a partnership. David could become a minimal ownership partner (1%) in order to form the entity, which has medium to high costs of formation dependent upon the type of partnership. However, the general, limited, and limited liability partnerships would not give Amy the personal liability protection she seeks. Amy has not indicated interest in transferring assets to younger family members, therefore the family limited partnership is not being considered.

Limited Liability Companies (LLC)

An LLC is a viable option for Amy's business. She may want to bring David in as a member since single member / owner LLCs are disregarded as an entity for federal income tax purposes and she would in that case still be filing her income under Schedule C. If David is brought in as a member of the entity, she could file as a partnership, S corporation, or C corporation for federal income tax purposes avoiding Schedule C income. The cost of formation of an LLC can be high, but the benefit of protection from personal liability may be worth making the transition from sole proprietorship. It would be important for Amy to maintain the entity separately to keep her liability protection.

Corporations

C corporations are state chartered legal entities formed by one or more individuals and owned by corporate shareholder(s). The cost of formation can be high, but liability is limited to shareholder investment as long as the entity follows corporate formalities and is maintained as a separate entity from the shareholder(s) / owner(s). A C corporation is taxed separately from shareholders (double taxation issue), unless S corporation status is elected. The owner/employee's compensation is not considered to be self-employment income, which fulfills Amy's requirement to avoid Schedule C income.

S corporations are state chartered legal entities (same formation as C corporations). The cost of formation can be high. An S corporation is limited to 100 shareholders with one class of stock.[1] To obtain the income tax benefit of being an S corporation, the C corporation files an "S" election with the IRS. The "S" election avoids the double taxation issue of a C corporation and allows the income of the S corporation to be passed through to shareholders. As with a C corporation, corporate formalities must be followed to maintain the corporation as a separate entity from the shareholder(s) / owner(s) in order to limit liability. The S corporation entity is a viable option for Amy's needs.

Recommendation

An LLC or S corporation is likely the best options for Amy's business needs. Both forms of entity can avoid Schedule C income and offer the personal liability protection she desires. Amy can seek the services of an attorney to make her final decision as to entity form and for the creation of the entity itself.

OBJECTIVE 6: INVESTMENT ANALYSIS

- Objective: The client wants a full review of their investment portfolio.
- The planner needs to provide an analysis of the client's entire investment portfolio including:
  1. Brokerage Accounts 1 and 2,
  2. Education Funding Accounts,
  3. 401(k) plan with Roth,
  4. Traditional IRA,
  5. Roth IRA, and
  6. Amy's 401(k) plan.

---

1. IRC Section 1361.

Investment Portfolio of Stock (Brokerage Account 1)

The Rudolph's investment policy statement is as follows:

Rudolph's Investment Policy Statement As of January 1, 2015	
Retirement Goals	• Generate adequate retirement capital. • Retire debt free.
Education Goals	• Provide for Danny and Madelyn's education.
Return Requirements	• They require an 8% return on their overall portfolio. • They require a 9% return on their education portfolio.
Risk Tolerance	• They have a moderate risk tolerance.
Time Horizon	• Retirement for David is 10 years away. • Retirement for Amy is 6 years away. • Education for Danny is 16 years away. • Education for Madelyn is 3 years away.
Constraints	• They still have liquidity issues with a majority of their net worth being in a small business that they are planning to sell and then use the proceeds for retirement. The value of this business will increase at least by 3% per year based on the current sale arrangement. • They have a very short time horizon to fund Madelyn's education, which is only three years away.

INVESTMENT PORTFOLIO ANALYSIS

The Rudolph's investments are compared to their investment policy statement for an analysis of their progress towards accomplishing their goals.

Overall Investment Growth

The Rudolph's investment assets declined by 12.8 percent from $3,956,000 (2014) to $3,526,356 (2015) which is net of savings contributions and is also due to the revaluing of DRI (a decline of 17.3%).

This decline in the portfolio value is not an immediate concern as the restated value is still sufficient to meet their retirement goals and given their current savings rate of 18 percent. Since the Rudolphs have an overall required rate of return of eight percent and the remaining value of DRI is $1,850,000 ($2,750,000 - $900,000) with growth at three percent (or more) per year, the financial planner must revisit the Rudolph's asset allocation and expected return for their overall portfolio.

	Expected Return	Amount Invested	Weighting	Weighted Expected Return
DRI	3.00%	$1,850,000	53.2%	1.6%
Brokerage Account 1	11.66%	$600,000	17.3%	2.0%
Brokerage Account 2	8.00%	$900,000	25.9%	2.1%
401(k) Plan w Roth	8.20%	$65,076	1.9%	0.2%
Traditional IRA	3.20%	$12,000	0.3%	0.0%
Roth IRA	1.75%	$16,280	0.5%	0.0%
Amy 401(k) Plan	8.20%	$33,000	0.9%	0.1%
Total		**$3,476,356**		**5.9%**

Note: The expected return for each investment is calculated in the subsequent sections. The portfolio expected return is 5.9 percent, which is below the Rudolph's overall required rate of return of eight percent.

DRI Stock

One of the major investment concerns last year was the liquidity and valuation of DRI stock. The liquidity risk has partially been addressed, since David has decided to sell 32.7229 percent of DRI stock for $900,000. The most recent valuation of DRI stock resulted in restating the business value to $2,750,000 from $3,325,000. The valuation concerns from last year have been appropriately addressed by the new valuation.

David has also "locked in" his price on DRI stock by using a put option as part of the buy/ sell agreement. As the owner of the put option, David has the right to sell his remaining interest in DRI stock in 10 years, at $1,850,000 with an annual growth rate of three percent (or more). Assuming the value of DRI stock increases by three percent over the next 10 years, the value of David's interest in DRI stock will be $2,486,245:

N	=	10
i	=	3
PV	=	<$1,850,000>
PMT	=	0
FV	=	?
Answer	=	**$2,486,245.30**

Although David's interest in DRI has decreased, 47 percent ($1,850,000 ÷ $3,963,399[2]) of his net worth is still invested in DRI stock, which is extremely high. The put option helps to reduce the Rudolph's risk of losing a substantial amount of their net worth if the value of DRI declines.

Another issue to consider is the financial ability of DRI key employees to fund the remaining purchase of David's stock in 10 years. If the key employees are unable to fund the purchase,

---

2. From revised Statement of Financial Position.

it may delay David's retirement goal. David may have to find a different buyer or the sale price may be different than the current agreement under the put option.

Recommendation

A thorough review of the buy/sell agreement is required to evaluate the riskiness and likelihood of David's key employees' ability to purchase the business in 10 years if the value grows at three percent or more each year.

Brokerage Account 1 ($600,000 Stock Portfolio)

Although the financial planner was surprised to learn that David sold his mutual fund portfolio and invested in stocks, an evaluation of the riskiness, expected return, and impact on the Rudolph's overall asset allocation is required.

The expected return of his stock portfolio is:

Name	Expected Return	Amount Invested	Weighting	Expected Return for the Portfolio
A	8%	$23,000	($23,000 ÷ $600,000) = 0.0383	0.0031
B	10%	$117,700	($117,700 ÷ $600,000) = 0.1962	0.0196
C	9%	$5,100	($5,100 ÷ $600,000) = 0.0085	0.0008
D	12.3%	$454,200	($454,200 ÷ $600,000) = 0.7570	0.0931
				0.1166 or 11.66%

The expected return of 11.66 percent for this portfolio is appropriate given the Rudolph's required rate of return of eight percent.

Based on the information provided by the Rudolphs for their stock portfolio, there is an issue with the risk return relationship between two of their stocks.

Name	Standard Deviation	Expected Return
A	0.12	8%
B	0.14	10%
C	0.16	9%
D	0.19	12.3%

Stock B has a standard deviation of 14 percent and an expected return of 10 percent and Stock C has a standard deviation of 16 percent and an expected return of nine percent. Stock C is considered "inefficient" because it provides less return and is more risky than Stock B.

It is likely that after reviewing the buy / sell agreement, the planner may decide to recommend that David allocate this portfolio to well diversified stock and bond mutual funds.

Recommendations

- David should keep the stock portfolio until a more thorough analysis of his buy/sell arrangement with his key employees is completed.
- A determination of the standard deviation of the portfolio using financial software to make sure the portfolio is appropriate given their moderate risk tolerance is required.
- The Rudolphs should sell Stock C and invest in a stock that has a more appropriate risk/return relationship.
- The stock portfolio is not well diversified, as 75.7 percent of the portfolio is invested in Stock D. Since the client is going to keep the stock portfolio in the short term, the Rudolphs should sell at least 50 percent to 75 percent of Stock D and allocate it across industries not currently represented in their portfolio. Generally, a stock portfolio of 15 stocks is considered relatively diversified, so the Rudolphs should purchase 10 to 12 more stocks. More information is required on the current stocks to evaluate which industries are currently represented and not represented in the portfolio.
- The Rudolphs should also sell about 50 percent of Stock B and allocate the proceeds equally to each new stock purchased.

Brokerage Account 2 ($900,000 Proceeds from DRI Sale)

Prior to the sale of 32.7229 percent of DRI, the Rudolph's asset allocation was:

EQUITIES IN PORTFOLIO
• DRI: $2,750,000
• Brokerage Account 1: $600,000
• 401(k) Plan with Roth – balanced fund: $32,538 ($65,076 total with ½ in equities and ½ in bonds)
• Amy 401(k) Plan: $19,800 (33,000 x 60% in a stock index fund)
Total Equities = $3,402,338
BONDS IN PORTFOLIO
• 401(k) Plan with Roth – balanced fund: $32,538 ($65,076 total with ½ in equities and ½ in bonds)
• Traditional IRA: $12,000
• Roth IRA: $16,280
• Amy 401(k) Plan: $13,200 ($33,000 x 40% in a corporate bond fund)
Total Bonds = $74,018
Allocation is 97.9% Equities / 2.1% Bonds

David should invest the $900,000 proceeds into balanced mutual funds, which have an equal weighting of both equity and fixed income investments.

His new asset allocation will be:

EQUITIES IN PORTFOLIO
• DRI: $2,750,000 - $900,000 = $1,850,000
• Brokerage Account 1: $600,000
• Brokerage Account 2: $450,000 ($900,000 in balanced mutual fund with ½ in equities and ½ in bonds)
• 401(k) Plan with Roth – balanced fund: $32,538 ($65,076 total with ½ in equities and ½ in bonds)
• Amy 401(k) Plan: $19,800 (33,000 x 60% in a stock index fund)
Total Equities = $2,952,338
BONDS IN PORTFOLIO
• Brokerage Account 2: $450,000 ($900,000 in balanced mutual fund ½ equities and ½ bonds)
• 401(k) Plan with Roth – balanced fund: $32,538 ($65,076 total with ½ in equities and ½ in bonds)
• Traditional IRA: $12,000
• Roth IRA: $16,280
• Amy 401(k) Plan: $13,200 ($33,000 x 40% in a corporate bond fund)
Total Bonds = $524,018
Allocation is 84.9% Equities / 15.1% Bonds

The asset allocation is heavily weighted to equities, which is due to the client's investment in his company (DRI) stock. This is not uncommon for entrepreneurs and presents challenges for the planner to overcome. An analysis of the buy/sell agreement is needed to make an evaluation regarding the likelihood and financial ability of the key employees to fulfill the agreement. Once the buy/sell agreement has been evaluated, the planner may recommend the allocation of Brokerage Account #1 to a mutual fund or bond portfolio.

Assume that a balanced mutual fund invests 50 percent in stocks that match the performance of the market (S&P 500) of nine percent and 50 percent of the portfolio will match the performance of corporate bonds of seven percent. The expected return for the balanced mutual fund below is eight percent, which is appropriate given the client's required rate of return of eight percent on their overall portfolio.

S&P 500	50% x 9%	Expected Return =	4.5%
Corporate Bond Fund	50% x 7%	Expected Return =	3.5%
	4.5% + 3.5%	**Total Expected Return =**	**8.0%**

Recommendation:

- Invest the $900,000 proceeds in a balanced mutual fund (50/50 equities and fixed income) with an overall expected rate of return of eight percent.

Education Account

The 529 Savings Plan balance for Madelyn (and Danny) was $46,000 as of 1/1/2014 and was $50,000 the following year (1/1/2015), but the Rudolph's contributed $6,000 to the fund during 2014. Therefore the account declined 4.3 percent for the year.

With a 529 Savings Plan, the investment options may be limited based on the age of the children and their time horizon until they enter college. Some 529 Savings Plans have the option of aggressive allocation or moderate allocation based on the child's age. In the Rudolph's case, there is not enough information to determine the riskiness of the investments held. However, since some 529 Savings Plans become more conservative as the beneficiary approaches 18, it is likely that the Rudolph's education investments are appropriate. The client and planner agree to investigate.

The Rudolphs are considering establishing a 529 Savings Plan for Trevor Jr. given their affection for him and his high potential for academic success. When this account is established it will be Education Account #2 and likely be invested appropriately based on the age of Trevor, Jr., and time until he attends college.

401(k) Plan with Roth Account

One year ago, this account was invested 100 percent in cash. Since that time, David has reallocated the account to a balanced mutual fund, which provides an equal weighting investment in equities and bonds. Since his expected return of eight percent is expected to equal his required rate of return, no further recommendations are needed at this time.

Traditional IRA

This portfolio continues to be invested in a series of zero coupon bonds. Amy's compounded rate of return on the bond investments in the Traditional IRA is 3.2 percent:

$$GM = \sqrt[6]{(1.065)(1.0475)(0.9675)(0.975)(1.0525)(1.0909)} - 1 \times 100$$

$$GM = \sqrt[6]{1.2083} - 1 \times 100$$

$$GM = 1.0320 - 1 \times 100 = 3.2\%$$

Although the 3.2 percent return is less than the Rudolph's overall required rate of return, zero coupon bond investments are appropriate in this account, because zero coupon bonds in a traditional IRA avoid the phantom income tax issue. Amy still needs to provide information on the actual investments in this portfolio so the bonds can be evaluated on their riskiness and expected returns.

Recommendation

- Provide a detailed list of the securities held in this account.

Roth IRA

During the last meeting with the Rudolphs, the financial planner recommended that Amy change the Roth IRA investment into a higher growth investment, rather than tax-free municipal bonds. Amy and David have been focused on negotiating the terms of selling DRI and have not reallocated the investments in Amy's Roth IRA. Currently, the planner is still recommending that Amy sell the Municipal bonds and invest in higher growth investments, like a balanced mutual fund. This account balance is small and the planner is not immediately concerned about the asset allocation implications of changing into a balanced mutual fund.

If Amy reallocates this portfolio into a balanced mutual fund, her expected return would be eight percent, whereas if she continues to leave the account invested in Municipal bonds, her expected return is 1.75 percent.

Recommendation
- Reallocate the Municipal bond investments into a balanced mutual fund.

Amy's 401(k) Plan

Amy's current allocation for her 401(k) plan contributions is 60 percent in an index mutual fund and 40 percent in a corporate bond mutual fund. Her allocation seems appropriate given her retirement time horizon of 30+ years.

Index Fund	60% x 9%	Expected Return =	5.4%
Corporate Bond Fund	40% x 7%	Expected Return =	2.8%
	5.4% + 2.8%	**Total Expected Return =**	**8.2%**

The expected rate of return of 8.2 percent is appropriate given their required rate of return of eight percent on their overall portfolio.

Recommendation
- None at this time.

OBJECTIVE 7: LONG-TERM CARE INSURANCE
- Objective: David and Amy want to consider purchasing long-term care insurance.
- The planner needs to provide an analysis of long-term care options and costs.

The client has indicated they will consider this objective during the next six months.

TAX ANALYSIS

Tax Analysis
(using 2012 tax numbers)

Tax Analysis	Amount
	Amount
Amy's Schedule C	$150,000
David's Salary	$283,250
401(k) Deferrals	($22,000)
401(k) Deferrals	($16,500)
Total Income	**$394,750**
Adjustments:	
Less 1/2 SE Tax	($8,835)
AGI	**$385,915**
Less Personal Exemptions	
David	($3,800)
Amy	($3,800)
Trevor	($3,800)
Danny	($3,800)
Less Itemized Deductions	($100,000)
Taxable Income	**$270,715**
Income Tax (2012 MFJ bracket)	$66,242.51
Self Employment Tax	$17,669.63
Total	**$83,912.14**
Withholding & Est. Payments	$82,393.00
Refund (Due to IRS)	**($1,519.14)**

Self Employment Tax

Self Employment Income		$150,000
Times 92.35%		$138,525 **A**
Max Social Security Wage Base (2012)	$110,100	
Less Wages For	$0	
Net	$110,100 **B**	
Smaller of A or B		$110,100
OASDI (amount above times 12.4%)		$13,652.40
A times 2.9%		$4,017.23
Total		**$17,669.63**
1/2 SE Tax		$8,834.81

Itemized Deductions

	2012
Taxes	$8,000.00
Mortgage interest (limited to $1 million of mortgage debt)	$60,000.00
Income taxes for State	$22,000.00
Church	$10,000.00
Itemized Deductions	**$100,000.00**

Conclusion: The Rudolphs' federal tax is calcualted using 2012 numbers. Their tax may increase depending on what happens to future tax rates. However, there is not much of a difference between what is withheld / estimated and what they owe the IRS.

IMPLEMENTATION

The Rudolphs have decided to implement the following recommendations:
1. 529 Savings Plan for Trevor Jr.
2. David selling 32.7229 percent of his 75 percent interest in DRI for $900,000 cash with a put option to sell the remainder of his interest in 10 years for $1,850,000 increased by 3 percent per year. David and Amy will use the proceeds from the sale of the inherited piece of artwork to fund the taxes owed on the current sale of DRI stock.
3. David will use savings and the sale of DRI stock to implement the retirement funding goal. At this time, the Rudolphs have decided to fund any deficit of David's retirement needs with either a modification in retirement withdrawals (decrease in amount) or a delay in retirement.

4. David and Amy have decided to have the trusts created to avoid probate and provide for Madelyn and Danny.
5. Amy has decided to change her business entity form from sole proprietor to either an LLC or S corporation to avoid the higher risk of an IRS audit as a Schedule C filer and for personal liability protection. She will seek the services of an attorney to implement this recommendation.
6. David has agreed to sell 75 percent of stock D and purchase 50 percent of Stock B. He will purchase 10 more stocks across multiple industries, allocating an equal amount to each new stock (Brokerage Account 1).
7. David has agreed to invest the $900,000 proceeds from DRI (Brokerage Account 2) into balanced mutual funds.
8. Amy has agreed to reallocate her Roth IRA into a balanced mutual fund.

THE CASH FLOW APPROACH

The cash flow approach adjusts the cash flows on the income statement as projected after implementing all of the financial planner's recommendations. The approach starts with the discretionary cash flows at the bottom of the income statement and accounts for the recommendations in the order of priority by charging the cost of the expense against the discretionary cash flows regardless of any negative cash flow impact. The cash flow approach is discussed in detail in Chapter 3. The analysis is prepared carefully to differentiate between recurring cash flows and non-recurring cash flows.

CASH FLOW APPROACH WITH RECOMMENDATIONS

Rudolph Cash Flow Approach with Implementation of 1/2/2015 Recommendations			
	Income Statement Recurring Impact	Balance Statement Non-Recurring Impact	Comments/Explanations
Beginning Cash Flow (Income Statement)	$13,681		
Recommendations:			
Risk Management:	None	None	
• Life Insurance -Change Owner to Trusts	0	0	
Debt Management:	None	None	
Education Funding		($50,284.81)	Fund 529 #2 for Trevor Jr.
Retirement Savings:			
• DRI - Sell 32.7229 percent		$900,000	Creates Brokerage Account #2
• Receive and Sell Art		$150,000	Listed as Asset
Tax on Sale of DRI		($130,909)	Listed as Liability
Estate Planning:			
• Create ILIT Trusts	($3,000)		Legal Costs of $3,000
TOTALS	$10,681	$868,806.19	

( ) indicates a negative impact on cash flow and + indicates a positive impact on cash flow.

RESTATED FINANCIAL STATEMENTS

The revised Balance Sheet is presented for 1/2/2015, as if all of the recommendations have been implemented. Other than the long-term care issue, the Rudolph's are in excellent position from a financial planning perspective. The Rudolph's financial planner and attorney will want to monitor any legislation regarding estate tax that may affect their client.

FINANCIAL STATEMENTS: STATEMENT OF FINANCIAL POSITION (END OF YEAR-REVISED AFTER IMPLEMENTATION OF RECOMMENDATIONS)

EXHIBIT 18.7

Statement of Financial Position (With Adjustments for Recommendations) David and Amy Rudolph Balance Sheet as of 1/2/2015					
ASSETS[1]			**LIABILITIES AND NET WORTH**		
Current Assets			**Current Liabilities[2]**		
JT Cash & Checking	$20,000		JT Taxes-Sale of DRI	$130,909	
JT Money Market	$170,000		W Credit Cards	$5,000	
JT Cash from Art (inherited)[6]	$150,000		**Total Current Liabilities**		$135,909
Total Current Assets		$340,000			
Investment Assets			**Long-Term Liabilities[2]**		
H DR Office Furniture, Inc[3]	$1,850,000		JT Principal Residence[5]	$1,153,009	
H Brokerage Account #1	$600,000		H Lake House[5]	$145,335	
H Brokerage Account #2[3]	$900,000		H Boat[5]	$0	
H Education Account #1[4](529)	$50,000		**Total Long-Term Liabilities**		$1,298,344
JT Education Account #2 (529)	$66,296				
H 401(k) Plan w/ Roth	$65,076				
W Traditional IRA	$12,000				
W Roth IRA	$16,280				
W Amy 401(k) Plan	$33,000				
Total Investment Assets		$3,592,652	**Total Liabilities**		$1,434,253
Personal Use Assets					
JT Principal Residence	$800,000				
H Lake House	$450,000				
JT Furniture, Clothing	$100,000		**Total Net Worth**		$3,963,399
H Car # 1	$25,000				
W Car # 2	$35,000				
H Boat	$55,000				
Total Personal Use Assets		$1,465,000			
Total Assets		$5,397,652	**Total Liabilities & Net Worth**		$5,397,652

1. Assets are stated at fair market value.
2. Liabilities are stated at principal only as of January 1, 2015 before January payments.
3. This is David's remaining 50.4545% interest after selling stock in DRI to other executives. Brokerage account #2 has the $900,000 from the sale of DRI.
4. This is for Madelyn and Danny. David currently saves $6,000 per year into this account (see portfolio).
5. Current portion of long-term liabilities is $17,635 and $7,490, respectively. Paid off boat 1/2/2014.
6. David and Amy inherited artwork from her Uncle George and subsequently sold the artwork.

Balance Sheet Adjustments:

Sold DRI Stock	$900,000
Funded 529 for Trevor Jr.	$66,296
Inherited Artwork and Sold It	$150,000
Tax Liability on Sale of DRI	$130,909

SUMMARY

When the Rudolphs returned to the financial planner this year for additional services they had the following strengths and weaknesses:

STRENGTHS

1. Income $433,250 annually.
2. Savings rate of 18.0%.
3. Net Worth of $3.878 million.
4. Investment assets of $3.526 million.
5. Adequate life insurance coverage on David.
6. Adequate health insurance coverage.
7. Adequate disability insurance coverage on David and Amy.
8. Adequate homeowners insurance coverage on the principal residence and the lake house.
9. Adequate automobile insurance coverage.
10. Excellent financial ratios, except investment performance ratios.
11. Improved net discretionary cash flows ($13,861).
12. Adequate insurance coverage on the boat.
13. Adequate coverage under their personal liability umbrella policy.
14. Some estate planning documents prepared.
15. Reduced property taxes on their principal residence.

WEAKNESSES (AND RESPONSES)

1. Questionable life insurance coverage on Amy. *(Remains unresolved.)*
2. No long-term care insurance coverage on David or Amy. *(Remains unresolved.)*
3. Poor investment returns. *(Repositioned investments; should perform as expected.)*
4. Need additional estate planning to avoid probate and provide for minors. *(Corrected.)*
5. Negative equity on the client's principal residence. *(Unresolved due to market.)*
6. The debt rates of the lake house is too high. *(Resolved.)*
7. DRI. *(Sold portion of client interest and now has put option.)*
8. Amy's business remains as a sole proprietorship. *(Proper entity recommended; client will implement this year.)*
9. Need to set up a special needs trust for Danny.

RECOMMENDATIONS - IMPLEMENTED

The financial planner solved the client's weaknesses as follows:

- The 529 Savings Plan funding amount for Trevor Jr. has been calculated and funded.
- The Rudolphs' capital needs (annuity method and capital preservation method) for retirement funding has been calculated and is adequate.
- Any deficit in retirement capital needs has been determined with recommendations for solving any potential shortage. Calculated, but the Rudolphs think it is unnecessary.
- The Rudolphs have implemented two ILITs for estate planning (to avoid probate and provide for Madelyn and Danny).
- The financial planner is continuing to work on the investment returns and is encouraging the clients to consider long-term care policies for both David and Amy.
- The ongoing valuation of DRI remains critical to the plan.

UNMET GOALS

The goal to be debt free at David's age 62 (retirement) is questionable given the mortgage on the principal residence.

Expected investment returns remain an issue that will require periodic monitoring and reevaluation.

Glossary

A

Above-the-Line Deductions - Deductions for adjusted gross income, also known as adjustments to income.

Academic Competitiveness Grant (ACG) - A grant for students graduating from a rigorous secondary school program of study. Rigorous secondary school programs are designated by stated education agencies and recognized by the secretary of education.

Accuracy-Related Penalty - A penalty of 20 percent of the underpayment amount imposed on taxpayers who file incorrect tax returns in certain situations.

Active Listening - Requires the listener's undivided attention. Active listening involves concentration of what the speaker is saying. The listener must put aside irrelevant thoughts.

Adjusted Gross Income - Gross income less above-the-line deductions.

Affect Heuristic - Deals with judging something, whether it is good or bad.

Aggregate Demand Curve - A graphical representation of the quantity of goods and services consumers are willing to buy at any given price level.

Aggregate Supply Curve - A graphical representation between quantity supplied and price.

Aggressive Growth Funds - Typically invest in small cap stocks, where price appreciation is the primary objective.

Alpha - The difference between the actual return generated by the fund relative to the expected return give the level of riskiness of the fund, as measured by beta.

Always Bar List - CFP Board's list of unacceptable conduct that will always bar an individual from becoming certified.

American Opportunity Tax Credit (AOTC) - Created by the American Recovery and Reinvestment Act of 2009. The new legislation increased the amount of the tax credit and provided other benefits. The AOTC provides a tax credit of up to $2,500 (2011) per student for the first four years of qualified education expenses for postsecondary education.

Amortization Schedule - Illustrates the repayment of debt, over time. Each debt payment consists of both interest expense and principal repayment.

Anchoring - Attaching or anchoring one's thoughts to a reference point even though there may be no logical relevance or is not pertinent to the issue in question. Anchoring is also known as conservatism or belief perseverance.

Annual Exclusion - An exclusion from gift taxes for present interest transfers less than or equal to $13,000 per year per donee.

Annuity - A recurring cash flow, of an equal amount that occurs at periodic (but regular) intervals.

Annuity Due - Occurs when the timing of the first payment is at the beginning of the first period. The period may be the beginning of a month, quarter, or year.

Annuity Due Payment from a Lump-Sum Deposit - The payment that can be generated at the beginning of each period, based on a lump-sum amount deposited today.

Annuity Method - Determines how much a client needs to fund their retirement based on the assumption that the person will die exactly at the assumed life expectancy with a retirement account balance of zero.

Anonymous Case Histories - Summary of the relevant events in certain cases of misconduct, accompanied by an explanation of any discipline penalty, action by CFP Board, and other information.

Arithmetic or Average Return - The sum of all returns divided by the number of periods.

Articles of Incorporation - The charter document for a corporation that must be filed with the Secretary of State in the state of organization.

Articles of Organization - The charter document of an LLC that must be filed with the Secretary of State in the state of organization.

Asset Accumulation Phase - This phase is usually from the early 20s to late 50s when additional cash flow for investing is low and debt to net worth is high.

Asset Allocation - The dividing of a portfolio into various asset classes.

Assets - A balance sheet category that represents anything of economic value that can ultimately be converted to cash.

Attorney-in-Fact - Agent or power holder of a power of attorney.

Availability Heuristic - When a decision maker relies upon knowledge that is readily available in his or her memory, the cognitive heuristic known as "availability" is invoked.

B

Balance Sheet - A statement of financial position that represents the accounting for items the client "owns" (assets) and items that are "owed" (liabilities). The balance sheet provides a snapshot of the client's assets, liabilities, and net worth as of a stated date.

Balanced Funds - Typically invest in both fixed income securities and equity securities.

BAPCPA of 2005 - Amends the Truth in Lending Act in various respects, including requiring certain creditors to disclose on the front of billing statements a minimum monthly payment warning for consumers.

Basis - Represents the total capital or after-tax income used by a taxpayer to purchase an investment.

Behavioral Finance - Contains much of the scientific framework and lessons learned from Traditional Finance, amends some of it with basic assumptions based on normal, more human-like behavior, and supplements other aspects of it with notions from psychology and sociology.

Below-the-Line Deductions - Deductions from adjusted gross income. Also known as itemized deductions.

Beneficiary - The person(s) entitled to receive the death benefit of a life insurance policy at the insured's death. Also, the person(s) who hold(s) the beneficial title to a trust's assets.

Beta - A measure of systematic risk and provides the correlation of the volatility of a portfolio as compared to the market benchmark.

Bonds - A debt issuance where the bond issuer makes a promise to make periodic coupon payments (interest) and repayment of the par value (principal) at maturity.

Business Cycle - Measures economic activity over time. The business cycle is characterized by expansion, peak, contraction or recession, and trough.

Business Risk - The inherent risk of doing business in a particular industry.

C

Call Risk - The risk that a bond will be retired early by the issuing company.

Calls - Gives the holder the right to buy the underlying security at a certain price by a certain date.

Candidate Fitness Standards - Ensure specific character and fitness standards as to an individual's conduct before certification.

Capital Asset Pricing Model (CAPM) - Calculates the relationship of risk and return for an individual security using Beta (ß) as its measure of risk.

Capital Market Line (CML) - The macro aspect of the Capital Asset Pricing Model (CAPM). It specifies the relationship between risk and return in all possible portfolios.

Capital Needs Analysis - The process of calculating the amount of investment capital needed at retirement to maintain the pre-retirement lifestyle and mitigate the impact of inflation during the retirement years.

Capital Preservation Model (CP) - A capital needs analysis method that assumes that at client's life expectancy, the client has exactly the same account balance as he did at the beginning of retirement.

Capitalization of Earnings Method - A method that uses a numerator and denominator to determine life insurance needs.

CARD Act of 2009 - Prevents credit card companies (and banks) from charging hidden fees and extraordinary interest rates as well as promoting easy to understand statements.

Cash and Cash Equivalents - A balance sheet category that represents assets that are highly liquid, which means they are either cash or can be converted to cash (within the next 12 months) with little to no price concession from their current value.

Cash Flow Approach - This approach takes an income statement approach to recommendations. It uses the three-panel approach and uses a pro forma approach (as if) "to purchase" the recommendations thus driving down the discretionary cash flow. Next, positive cash flows or the sale of assets are identified to finance the recommendations which were purchased.

Cash Flow Statement - Explains how cash and cash equivalents were used or generated between two balance sheets.

Certificant - An individual who is currently certified by the CFP Board.

Certified Financial Planner Board of Standards, Inc. ("CFP Board") - Board that maintains professional standards necessary for competency and ethics in the financial planning profession for those professionals who have been granted the right to use their designation.

Chapter 7 Bankruptcy - For individuals or businesses to use for protection from creditors under federal and state bankruptcy laws.

Chapter 11 Bankruptcy - Known as "reorganization bankruptcy" for corporations, sole proprietorships, and partnerships.

Chapter 13 Bankruptcy - Also known as a "wage earners plan," is for individuals or self-employed workers that want to keep their assets and payoff a portion of their debts over time.

Checking the Box - When an eligible entity chooses to be taxed as either a corporation or a partnership.

Closed-End Investment Companies - Another type of investment company that trade on stock market exchanges. Closed-end funds do not generally issue additional shares after their initial offering.

Closed Questions - Seeks a response that is very specific and commonly involves an answer that can be accomplished with a single word or two. Closed questions lead with is, are, do, did, could, would, have, or "is it not true that..."

Code of Ethics - One of the Standards of Professional Conduct. They are organized into seven different principles ("Principles") that certificants and registrants are expected to enact into their professional activities.

Coefficient of Determination - A measure of how much return is a result of the correlation to the market or what percentage of a security's return is a result of the market.

Cognitive-Behavioral Paradigm (Cognitive-Behavior School of Thought) - Humans are beings are subject to the same learning principles that were established in animal research. The basic principles of classical and operant conditioning are assumed to account for an individuals' behavior and understandings throughout their lives.

College Savings Plans (529 Savings Plans) - A plan that allows for college saving on a tax-deferred basis with attendance at any eligible education institution. Distributions from a College Savings Plan are federal and state income tax-free, as long as they are used to pay for qualified education expenses.

Community Property - A civil law originating statutory regime under which married individuals own an equal undivided interest in all property accumulated during their marriage. Property acquired before the marriage and property received by gift or inheritance during the marriage retains its status as separate property.

Competence - Principle 3. Requires attaining and maintaining an adequate level of knowledge and skill, and application of that knowledge and skill in providing services to clients.

Complements - Products that are consumed jointly.

Confidentiality - Principle 5. Ensuring that information is accessible only to those authorized to have access.

Confirmation Bias - A commonly used and popular phrase is that "you do not get a second chance at a first impression." People tend to filter information and focus on information supporting their opinions.

Conservation (Risk Management) Phase - This phase is from late 20s to early 70s, where cash flow assets and net worth have increased and debt has decreased somewhat. In addition, risk management of events like employment, disability due to illness or accident, and untimely death become a priority.

Constant Growth Dividend Discount Model - Values a company's stock by discounting the future stream of cash flows or dividends.

Consumer Price Index (CPI) - Measures the overall price levels for a basket of goods and services consumers purchase.

Corporate Bonds - Bonds issued by firms to raise capital to fund ongoing operations, retire debt, fund capital projects or acquisitions.

Corporations - Chartered legal entities formed by one or more individuals by meeting state statutory requirements necessary for the formation of a corporation.

Correlation Coefficient - Measures the movement of one security relative to that of another security.

Cost Basis - Initial basis an investor acquires in an asset by using capital to purchase the investment.

Country Risk - The risk of political and economic stability of a country that a company faces when doing business in a particular country.

Covariance - The measure of two securities when combined and their interactive risk (relative risk).

Coverdell Education Savings Account (ESA) - A tax deferred trust or custodial account established to pay for qualified higher education or qualified elementary / secondary school expenses.

Current Ratio - This ratio provides insight as to the client's ability to meet short-term obligations should this debt all come due immediately.

Cyclical Unemployment - Occurs when there is an overall downturn in business activity and fewer goods are being produced causing a decrease in the demand for labor.

D

Debt - The lending of funds in return for periodic interest payments and the repayment of the principal debt obligation.

Debt Management - The analysis of debt because clients can have too much debt, debt that has high interest rates, and debt that is generally not well managed. The analysis of debt includes calculating housing ratios 1 and 2 and comparing those to well established benchmarks (metrics) of 28% / 36%. In addition, the financial planner will evaluate the quality and the cost of each client's individual debt.

Debt Ratios - Measures how well the client is managing their overall debt structure.

Debt to Total Assets Ratio - Indicates what percentage of assets is being provided by creditors. The lower this ratio the better, as it indicates that the assets owned have a low amount of debt owed.

Deductions - Items that are subtracted from gross income, either below or above-the-line, in order to arrive at taxable income.

Default Risk - The risk that a company may not be able to repay its debt obligations.

Defense of Marriage Act (DOMA) - Signed into law on September 21, 1996 and was "to define and protect the institution of marriage." Under Section 7, Definition of 'marriage' and 'spouse' the law states, "In determining the meaning of any Act of Congress, or of any ruling, regulation, or interpretation of the various administrative bureaus and agencies of the United States, the word 'marriage' means only a legal union between one man and one woman as husband and wife, and the word 'spouse' refers only to a person of the opposite sex who is a husband or a wife."

Deflation - A decrease in the overall price levels of goods and services.

Demand - Represents the quantity consumers are willing to purchase of a good or service, at a particular price.

Dependency Exemption - A deduction from adjusted gross income that is allowed for each person who is a qualifying child or qualifying relative of the taxpayer.

Derivatives - Financial securities that derive their value from some underlying asset.

Developmental Paradigm ("Developmental" School of Thought) - Believes that human development occurs in stages over time. Relationships that are formed early in life become a template for establishing relationships in adulthood. As to emotions, the Developmental Paradigm assumes that all humans develop and progress in a predictable sequence.

Diligence - Principle 7. Requires the provision of services in a reasonably prompt and thorough manner, including the proper planning for, and supervision of, the rendering of professional services.

Disability Insurance - Insurance that provides replacement income to the insured while the insured is unable to work because of sickness (illness) or injury (accident).

Disciplinary Rules - Provide detailed procedures followed by the CFP Board in enforcing the Code of Ethics, Rules of Conduct, and Practice Standards.

Discount Rate - The interest rate that the Federal Reserve charges financial institutions for short-term loans.

Discretionary Cash Flows - Expenses which can be avoided in the event of loss of income.

Disinflation - A slowdown in the rate of inflation or a slowdown in the general price increase of goods and services.

Disposition Effect - The cognitive bias was "faulty framing" where normal investors do not mark their stocks to market prices. Investors create mental accounts when they purchase stocks and continue to mark their value to purchase prices even after market prices have changed.

Distribution (Gifting) Phase - This phase is from the late 40s to end of life and occurs when the individual has high additional cash flow, low debt, and high net worth.

Do Not Resuscitate (DNR) - Documents declare the principals wish to avoid having cardiopulmonary resuscitation (CPR) performed in the event their heart stops beating.

Doctrine of Constructive Receipt - A cash method taxpayer must report income when it is credited to the taxpayer's account or when it is made available without restriction.

Donee - The person who receives the gift.

Donor - The person who gives the gift.

Durable Power of Attorney for Health Care - A written document enabling one individual, the principal, to designate another person(s) to act as his "attorney-in-fact." A durable power of attorney survives the incapacity and/or disability of the principal.

Economic Indicators - Describes the current and future economy and business cycle. The three economic indicators are: Index of Leading Economic Indicators, Index of Lagging Economic Indicators, and Index of Coincident Economic Indicators.

Education Funding - Determination of the lump sum or annual savings required to pay for college.

Effective Transfer - A transfer of a person's assets to the person or charitable institution intended by that person.

Efficient Frontier - Compares various portfolios based on their risk-return relationship.

Efficient Transfer - A transfer in which costs of the transfer are minimized consistent with the greatest assurance of effectiveness.

Emergency Fund Ratio - Measures how many months of non-discretionary expenses the client has in the form of cash and cash equivalents or current assets.

Employer Provided Education Assistance Program - A program established by an employer to reimburse employees for education expenses. The education expenses may or may not be directly related to the employee's current job duties; it depends on the employer's policy.

Engagement Letter - A legal agreement between a professional organization and a client that defines their business relationship.

Equal Credit Opportunity Act - Prohibits discrimination, when evaluating a decision to grant consumer credit.

Equilibrium Price - Represents the price at which the quantity demanded equals the quantity supplied.

Equity - Represents ownership in a business or property.

Equity Mutual Funds - Typically invest in equity securities.

ERISA (Employee Retirement Income Security Act) - Designed to protect employee retirement savings accounts from creditors and from plan sponsors.

Estate Planning - The process of accumulation, management, conservation, and transfer of wealth considering legal, tax, and personal objectives.

Estate Tax - Imposed on the decedent's right to transfer property to his heirs when a citizen or resident of the United States dies.

Excess Reserves - Represents the amount of cash or deposits with the Federal Reserve in excess of the minimum amount required.

Exchange Rate Risk - The risk that international investments and domestic companies that import or export goods are subject to changes in relationship to the price of a dollar, relative to foreign currencies.

Exchange Traded Funds (ETF's) - Another form of an investment company. An ETF invests in securities that are included in a particular index.

Exclusions - Income items that are specifically exempted from income tax.

Executive Risk - The risk of moral character of the executives running the company. The extent to which executives break laws, regulations, or ethical standards that may negatively impact a company.

Expected Return - The rate of return expected for an asset or investment portfolio.

Expenses - An income statement category. Expenses represent those items that are paid regularly by the client during the time period being presented. Examples of expenses include mortgage principal and interest, utilities, taxes, insurance, telephone, water, cable or satellite, internet, and cell phone.

External Data - The external data, also known as the external environment includes the current economic, legal, political, sociological, tax, and technology environments. Examples of external data are the current interest rates, status of the housing, job, insurance and investment markets, the local cost of living, and the expected inflation rate.

Failure to File Penalty - A five percent penalty of the unpaid tax balance for each month or part thereof that a tax return is late.

Failure to Pay Penalty - A penalty of 0.5 percent per month or part thereof that a taxpayer fails to pay tax that is owed.

Fair Credit Billing Act - Requires timely, written verification to a consumer disputing a billing error.

Fair Credit Reporting Act - Protects consumer's information collected by the major credit bureaus (Equifax, TransUnion, and Experian).

Fair Debt Collection Practices Act - Prevents third-party debt collectors from using deceptive or abusive methods to collect debts.

Fair Packaging and Labeling Act (FPLA) - Helps consumers compare the value of products and to prevent unfair or deceptive packaging and labeling of many household items.

Fairness - Principle 4. Requires impartiality, intellectual honesty and disclosure of material conflicts of interest.

Family Limited Partnership - A special type of limited partnership created under state law with the primary purpose of transferring assets to younger generations using annual exclusions and valuation discounts for minority interests and lack of marketability.

Federal Deposit Insurance Corporation (FDIC) - Formed in 1933, as a result of the bank failures that occurred in the 1920's and 1930's. The three goals of the FDIC are to insure deposits, manage receiverships, and supervise financial institutions.

Federal Funds Rate - The bank to bank lending rate.

Federal Pell Grant - Need based financial aid for students that have not earned an undergraduate degree or a professional degree. A Pell Grant does not have to be repaid. Pell Grants are awarded based on financial need.

Federal Perkins Loan - A program for undergraduate and graduate students with exceptional financial need. The Perkins Loan is a low interest rate loan (5%), which is offered through a university's financial aid office. The university serves as the lender and the federal government provides the funds.

Federal Supplemental Educational Opportunity Grant (FSEOG) - A grant awarded to students with exceptional financial need. Pell Grant recipients with the lowest EFC are considered first for a FSEOG.

Federal Trade Commission (FTC) - Works for the consumer to prevent fraudulent, deceptive, and unfair business practices in the marketplace and to provide information to help consumers identify, prevent, and avoid them.

Federal Work Study (FWS) - Jobs on campus or off campus for undergraduate or graduate students to help students pay for their education expenses. To be eligible students must have financial need.

Fee Simple Ownership - The complete ownership of property by one individual who possesses all ownership rights associated with the property, including the right to use, sell, gift, alienate, convey, or bequeath the property.

Fellowships - Paid to students for work, such as teaching while studying for a Master's degree or conducting research while working towards a Doctorate of Philosophy degree (Ph.D.). Fellowships can last anywhere from a few weeks to a few years, depending on the depth and level of work involved.

Fiduciary - Defined by the CFP Board as "one who acts in utmost good faith, in a manner he or she reasonably believes to be in the best interest of the client."

Financial Industry Regulatory Authority (FINRA) - A self regulatory organization for all security firms doing business in the United States.

Financial Needs Method - A method that evaluates the income replacement and lump-sum needs of survivors in the event of an income producer's untimely death.

Financial Plan - A written document that generally sets out a list of recommendations to achieve a set of goals and objections based on an understanding of a client's current financial situation.

Financial Risk - The amount of leverage the company is using in its capital structure. Leverage is a measure of the amount of debt a company uses to capitalize the business.

Financial Statement Analysis - The process of calculating financial ratios and comparing the actual ratios to industry established benchmarks.

Financial Statement and Ratio Analysis Approach - The ratio analysis provides an opportunity to assess the client's strengths, weaknesses, and deficiencies when the client's ratios are compared to benchmark metrics. The ratio approach usually follows the pie chart approach and provides the planner with the actual ratios with which to compare the benchmarks in the metrics approach.

Fiscal Policy - Represents the government's position on whether to expand or contract the economy. Congress uses taxes and government spending to implement its fiscal policy.

Fixed Expenses - Those expenses that are due and payable regardless of whether income is available to cover the cost. There is less discretion over fixed expenses in the short term. Examples of fixed expenses include mortgage payment, car payment, boat payment, student loan payment, property taxes, and insurance premiums.

Fixed Income or Bond Funds - Typically invest in bonds of various maturities.

Free Application for Federal Student Aid (FAFSA) - A form used to determine a student's eligibility for all types of financial aid, including grants, work study, and loans. The FAFSA is used to determine the Expected Family Contribution amount (EFC).

Frictional Unemployment - Occurs when people are voluntarily unemployed because they are seeking other job opportunities.

Full Employment - The rate of employment that exists when there is efficiency in the labor market.

Future Contract - A commitment to deliver an amount of a certain item at a specified date at an agreed upon price.

Future Value - The value at some point in the future of a present amount or amounts after earning a rate of return, for a period of time.

Future Value of an Annuity Due -The future value of equal periodic deposits, made at the beginning of the period.

Future Value of an Ordinary Annuity - The value of equal periodic payments or deposits, at some point in the future. The future value of an ordinary annuity assumes that deposits are made at the end of a period or end of a year.

G

Gambler's Fallacy - One of the incorrect assumptions from the world of probabilities; in the realm of probabilities, misconceptions can lead to faulty predictions as to occurrences of events.

GDP Deflator - Measures the current price of goods and services (nominal GDP) relative to a base year (real GDP).

General Obligation Bonds - Bonds backed by the taxing authority that issued the bonds. The bonds are repaid through taxes that are collected by the municipality.

General Partnership - A joint business venture among two or more persons/entities to conduct business as co-owners in which all owners have unlimited liability with regard to the debts and obligations of the partnership.

Geometric Return - A time-weighted compounded rate of return.

Gift - A voluntary transfer, without full consideration, of property from one person (a donor) to another person (a donee) or entity.

Gift Tax - An excise tax on the right to transfer assets gratuitously to another person during life.

Global Funds - Not only invest in foreign securities and markets, but also in U.S. domestic securities.

Government or Regulation Risk - The potential risk that a country may pass a law or regulation that negatively impacts a particular industry.

Graduate PLUS Loans - Loans for student's seeking graduate and professional degrees. A Graduate PLUS Loan is based on the parent's credit history and is not based on financial need.

Grantor - The person who creates and initially funds a trust. The grantor is also known as the settlor or creator.

Grants - Money provided to students for postsecondary education that does not require repayment.

Gross Domestic Product (GDP) - Represents the total final output of a country, by its citizens and foreigners in the country, over a period of time.

Gross Income - All income from whatever source derived unless it is specifically excluded by some provision of the Internal Revenue Code.

Gross National Product (GNP) - Measures the total final output by the citizens of a country, whether produced domestically or in a foreign country. GNP does not include the output of foreigners in a country.

Growth and Income Funds - Invest in both equities and fixed income securities. However, a much larger percentage of the fund is allocated to equities.

Growth Mutual Funds -Typically invest in large and mid cap stocks, where price appreciation is the primary objective.

Hazard - A condition that creates or increases the likelihood of a loss occurring.

Head of Household Filing Status - A filing status that provides a basic standard deduction and tax bracket sizes that are less favorable to the taxpayer than those for the surviving spouse status, but more favorable than those for the single filing status.

Heir - A person who inherits under state law.

Herding - This cognitive bias is explained just by looking at the word. People tend to follow the masses or the "herd."

Hindsight Bias - Another potential bias for an investor. Hindsight is looking back after the fact is known.

Holding Period - The period for which a taxpayer owns an asset.

Holding Period Return - Represents the time period an investment return is measured by an investor.

Holographic Will - Handwritten will.

Homeowners Insurance Coverage - A package policy covering dwelling, dwelling extensions (garage), personal property, loss of use, medical payments for others, and liability.

Horizontal Analysis - Lists each financial statement item as a percentage of a base year and creates a trend over time.

Housing Ratio 1 - This ratio reflects the proportion of gross pay on an annual or monthly basis that is devoted to housing (principal, interest, taxes, and insurance). It does not include utilities, lawn care, maintenance, etc. The benchmark for housing ratio 1 is less than or equal to 28 percent.

Housing Ratio 2 - This ratio combines basic housing costs (principal, interest, taxes, and insurance) with all other monthly debt payments, including automobile loans, student loans, bank loans, revolving consumer loans, credit card payments, and any other debt payments made on a recurring basis. The benchmark for housing ratio 2 should be less than or equal to 36 percent of gross pay on a monthly or annual basis.

Human Communications - Comprised of fundamental elements. Societal groups use a system of signs in their communication process. A sign could be a word, object, gesture, tone, quality, image, substance or other reference according to a code of shared meaning among those who use that sign for communication purposes.

Human Life Value (HLV) Method - A method that uses projected future earnings as the basis for measuring life insurance needs.

Humanistic Paradigm (The "Humanistic" School of Thought) - Dominated by theorists whose models have their origins from a shared philosophical approach. For a client to grow, the relationship requires a transparent and genuine counselor. The advisor needs a philosophical stance that humankind is basically good and that people have the inherent capability of self-direction and growth under the right set of circumstances.

Income - Broadly defined as the gross amount of money, property, services, or other accretion to wealth received, but it does not include borrowed money or a return of invested dollars.

Income Funds - Typically invest in corporate and government bonds.

Index Fund - Purchases a basket of stocks to match or replicate the performance of a particular industry.

Inflation - Represents an increase in the price of a basket of goods and services representing the economy as a whole over a period of time.

Inflation Adjusted Rate of Return - The nominal rate of return adjusted for inflation. The real (after inflation) rate of return equals $[(1+Rn) \div (1 + i) - 1] \times 100$, where Rn is the nominal return and i is the inflation rate.

Information Ratio - Measures the excess return above a benchmark, such as the S&P 500, per unit of risk.

Intangible Personal Property - Property that cannot truly be touched such as stocks, bonds, patents, and copyrights.

Integrity - Principle 1. Demands honesty and candor which must not be subordinated to personal gain and advantage.

Interest Rate - The price that a consumer pays to borrow funds.

Interest Rate Risk - The risk that changes in interest rates will inversely impact both equities (stocks) and bonds.

Internal Data - The client's internal data has both quantitative and qualitative elements. Some quantitative data includes family specifics, insurance, banking, investment, tax, retirement, and estate planning information. Some qualitative data includes the client's values, attitudes, expectations, goals, needs, and priorities.

Internal Rate of Return (IRR) - A compounded annual rate of return. IRR allows for the comparison of projects or investments with differing costs and cash flows. The rate that equates the PV of a series of cash flows to an initial investment.

International Funds - Invest in securities and firms that are outside of the U.S. domestic market.

Intrinsic Value - The underlying value of a security, when considering future cash flows and the riskiness of the security.

Investing - The process where capital resources are allocated and committed by investors with the expectation of earning a future positive economic return.

Investment Advisers Act of 1940 - Requires investment advisers to register with their state or the SEC.

Investment Assets - A balance sheet category that includes appreciating assets or those assets being held to accomplish one or more financial goals.

Investment Assets to Gross Pay Ratio - Measures progress towards a client's retirement goal, based on the client's age and income.

Investment Companies - Financial services companies that sell shares of stock to the public and use the proceeds to buy portfolios of securities. Mutual funds are one type of investment company where investors buy shares in a fund and own a pro rata portion of the investment portfolio, entitling them to a share of capital gains, interest and dividend income.

Investment Company Act of 1940 - Set standards to regulate investment companies such as open end, closed end, and unit investment trusts.

Investment Planning Process - Comprised of steps the financial planner and client follow to build an investment portfolio designed to accomplish the client's investment goals.

Investment Policy Statement - A written document that specifically identifies an investor's investment goals.

J

Jensen's Alpha - Absolute risk adjusted performance measurement.

Joint Tenancy with Right of Survivorship (JTWROS) - Typically how a husband and wife own joint property. Joint tenancy is an interest in property held by two or more related or unrelated persons called joint tenants. Each person holds an undivided, equal interest in the whole property. A right of survivorship is normally implied with this form of ownership, and at the death of the first joint tenant, the decedent's interest transfers to the other joint tenants outside of the probate process according to state titling law.

K

Keogh Plan - A qualified plan for a self-employed person. An important distinction of Keogh plans is the reduced contribution that can be made on behalf of the self-employed individual.

L

Legatee - A person named in a will.

Lepto-Kurtic - A distribution that appears to be normal but has more area under the two tails than a normal distribution (i.e., fat tails).

Letter of Admonition - A publishable written reproach of the certificant's or registrant's behavior.

Letter of Intent - A "life plan" document that describes the family of the special needs dependent and the special needs dependent's wishes for the future once the initial caregiver is no longer able to provide care. It should include pertinent information about the special needs dependent's history, medical needs, living arrangement preferences, hobbies, and contact persons (doctor, lawyer, accountant, guardians, etc).

Liabilities - A balance sheet category that represents client financial obligations that are owed to creditors.

Liability Risk - A risk that may cause financial loss (injury to another for which the client is determined to be financially responsible).

Life Cycle Approach - This approach provides the planner with a brief overview of the client's financial profile which permits the planner to have a relatively focused conversation with the client. It is used very early in the engagement.

Life Insurance - At its most basic is income replacement insurance.

Lifetime Learning Credit - Provides a tax credit of up to $2,000 (2011) per family for an unlimited number of years of qualified education expenses. The qualified education expenses must be related to a postsecondary degree program or to acquire or improve job skills.

Limited Liability Company - Separate legal entity formed by one or more individuals by meeting state statutory requirements necessary for the formation of an LLC that may be taxed as a sole proprietorship, partnership, or corporation.

Limited Liability Partnership - A hybrid entity generally comprised of licensed professionals that provides partial liability protection to its members and may be taxed as either a corporation or partnership.

Limited Partnerships - Associations of two or more persons as co-owners to carry on a business for profit except that one or more of the partners have limited participation in the management of the venture and thus limited risk exposure.

Liquidity Ratios - Measures the amount of cash and cash equivalents relative to short-term liabilities.

Living Will / Advance Medical Directive - Legal document expressing an individual's last wishes regarding life sustaining treatment.

Long-Term Liabilities - Financial obligations owed that are due beyond the next 12 months. Long-term liabilities are usually the result of major financial purchases and resulting obligations that are being paid off over multiple years (house, vacation, boat, student loan).

Loss Frequency - The expected number of losses that will occur within a given period of time.

Loss Severity - The potential size or financial damage of a loss.

M

Macroeconomics - The study of large economic factors that impact the entire economy such as gross domestic product (GDP), unemployment, and inflation.

Managing Partner - A partner named to have responsibilities for specific tasks or for day-to-day operations.

Market Risk - The risk that in the short term, the daily fluctuations of the market tend to bring all securities in the same direction.

Married Filing Jointly Filing Status - A filing status that allows married couples to combine their gross incomes and deductions.

Married Filing Separately Filing Status - A filing status used when married couples do not choose to file a joint return.

Metrics Approach - This approach uses qualitative benchmarks for a measurement of where a client's financial profile should be. When combined with the two-step/three-panel approach, metrics help establish objectives that are measurable compared to ratio analysis.

Microeconomics - The study of factors that impact small or individual economies, such as supply and demand for a product.

Modern Portfolio Theory - An approach to plan and construct a portfolio.

Monetary Policy - Represents the intended influence on the money supply and interest rates by the central bank of a country.

Money Market Mutual Funds - Invests in short-term government securities, certificates of deposit, commercial paper and bankers acceptance.

Monte Carlo Analysis - A mathematical simulation to determine the probability of success of a given plan. Monte Carlo analysis is useful for financial planners to help measure the probability of assumptions being true or false.

Moral Hazard - A character flaw or level of dishonesty an individual possesses that causes or increases the chance for a loss.

Morale Hazard - Indifference to losses based on the existence of insurance.

Municipal Bonds - Bonds issued to fund projects and spending for state or local governments. The three primary types of municipal bonds are general obligation bonds, revenue bonds, and private activity bonds.

Named-Perils Policy - A policy that provides protection against losses caused by the perils that are specifically listed as covered in the policy.

National Science and Mathematics Access to Retain Talent (SMART) Grant - A grant available during the third and fourth years of undergraduate studies. The National SMART Grant pays up to $4,000 per year and is paid in addition to the Pell Grant.

Natural Rate of Unemployment - The lowest unemployment rate where labor and product markets are in balance. At the natural rate of unemployment both price and wage inflation is stable.

Net Discretionary Cash Flow - Represents the amount of cash flow available after all savings, expenses, and taxes have been paid.

Net Present Value (NPV) - Measures the excess or shortfall of cash flows based on the discounted present value of the future cash flows, less the initial cost or investment. NPV uses the investor's required rate of return for similar projects as the discount rate.

Net Worth - A balance sheet category that represents the amount of total equity (assets - liabilities = net worth) a client has accumulated.

Net Worth to Total Assets Ratio - The compliment of the debt to assets ratio. These two should add up to one. This provides the planner with the percentage of total assets owned or paid for by the client.

Nominal GDP - Measures the value of goods, services, and current prices.

Nominal Interest Rates - The actual rate of return earned on an investment.

Non-Discretionary Cash Flows - Mostly fixed expenses which are required to be met monthly or annually regardless of loss of income.

Nonrefundable Tax Credits - Tax credits that can reduce the tax on taxable income to zero, but cannot generate a tax refund.

Non-Traditional Household - A broad phrase that may include any household other than the traditional husband, wife, and children. It could be heterosexual or homosexual couples living together with or without children. The adults may or may not be romantically involved, but may wish to include each other and their respective descendants in their estate plan.

Nonverbal Behaviors - Nonverbal cues, or body language, can communicate feelings and attitudes from the client to the financial advisor and are mainly provided from the body and the voice. Body position and body movement are important, while voice tone and voice pitch are also telling.

Normal Distribution - Describes how returns are dispersed around the average return.

Nuncupative Will - Oral will consisting of dying declarations.

Objectivity - Principle 2. Requires intellectual honesty and impartiality.

Open Market Operations - The process by which the Federal Reserve will buy or sell U.S. Treasury securities such as T-bills, notes, and bonds.

Open-end Investment Company - Also referred to as a mutual fund, is an investment company where investors purchase their shares from and sell them back to the mutual fund itself.

Open-Perils Policies - Policies that are called "all-risks" policies, because they cover all risks of loss (perils) that are not specifically excluded from the contract.

Open Questions - Result in a person answering with a lengthy response that usually begin with words such as how, what, when, where, who and why.

Operating Agreement - A written agreement similar to corporate bylaws that specify the rules and regulations for the operation of an LLC.

Opportunity Cost - Represents the value of the best alternative that is foregone.

Options - Includes both calls and puts.

Ordinary Annuity - Occurs when the timing of the first payment is at the end of a period. The period may be, for example, the end of a month or the end of a year.

Ordinary Annuity Payment from a Lump-Sum Deposit - The payment that can be generated at the end of each period, based on a lump-sum amount deposited today.

OSHA (Occupational Safety and Health Administration) - Created by Congress under the Occupational Safety and Health Act of 1970 to promote safe and healthy working conditions for workers by providing training, outreach, education, and assistance.

Overconfidence Bias - Usually concerns an investor that listens mostly to himself or herself, overconfident investors mostly rely on their skills and capabilities to do their own homework or make their own decisions.

Overreaction - A common emotion towards the receipt of news or information.

P

Passive Listening - Described as listening in the normal or usual conversation or conversational setting to which most people are accustomed at seminars, in class, at social gatherings, or at sermons.

Performance Ratios - These ratios determine the adequacy of returns on investments, given the risks taken.

Perils - The proximate or actual cause of a loss, such as fire, liability, or accidental death.

Personal Automobile Policy (PAP) - A package policy that protects against loss due to damage to the owned automobile, damage to the property of others, and bodily injury to the insured, family members, and others.

Personal Exemption - A deduction from adjusted gross income that is allowed for the taxpayer and the taxpayer's spouse.

Personal Financial Planning - The process of formulating, implementing, and monitoring financial decisions integrated into a plan that guides an individual or a family to achieve their financial goals.

Personal Liability Umbrella Policy (PLUP) - A policy usually sold in millions of dollars coverage (e.g., $1M, $3M, $5M) and provides excess liability coverage and legal defense for claims that may arise and that exceed the limits of the underlying homeowners and automobile policies.

Personal Risk - A risk that may cause the loss of income (untimely death, disability, health issues), or alternatively cause an increase in the cost of living (disability, health issues).

Personal Risk Management - A systematic process for identifying, evaluating, and managing pure risk exposures faced by an individual.

Personal Use Assets - A balance sheet category that includes those assets that help to maintain the client's lifestyle.

Physical Hazard - A tangible condition or circumstance that increases the probability of a peril occurring and/or the severity of damages that result from a peril.

Pie Chart Approach - This approach is a visual presentation of how the client spends money. It provides a broad perspective on the client's financial status and it is generally used after the collection of internal data and the preparation of financial statements.

Piercing the Veil - Occurs when a court disregards the status of the entity that gives the owners limited liability because the owners failed to maintain a clear and consistent identity for the entity.

PLUS Loans - Loans for parents to borrow to help pay for a dependent's undergraduate education expenses. PLUS Loans are not based on financial need, but are instead based on the parent's credit history.

Pooled Trust - An exception that resulted from the Omnibus Budget and Reconciliation Act of 1993; managed by a nonprofit association. While each beneficiary will have their own account, the assets will generally be pooled and managed together.

Power of Appointment - A power to appoint the assets of one person to another and may be either general or limited.

Power of Attorney - Legal document that authorizes an agent to act on a principal's behalf.

Practice Standards - Establish the level of professional practice expected of certificants engaged in financial planning. The Practice Standards are mandatory for all certificants whose services include financial planning or material elements of financial planning.

Prepaid Tuition Plan - A plan that will allow a parent to purchase college credits today and use those credits when the child attends college.

Present Value - The value today of one or more future cash payments discounted at an interest rate.

Present Value of a Future Amount - The current value today of a future amount. The future amount is discounted over time using a discount rate (an interest rate that reflects the individual's risk or opportunity cost that could be earned on a similar project or investment) to arrive at the present value.

Present Value of an Annuity Due - The timing of the first payment is at the beginning of a time period (today) representing today's value of that even cash flow stream. On a timeline, the first payment occurs at time period zero (now).

Present Value of an Ordinary Annuity - Today's value of an even cash flow stream received or paid over time. The present value of an ordinary annuity assumes that the first annuity payment is made at the end of a period.

Present Value of Goals Approach - This approach considers each short-term, intermediate-term, and long-term goal, determines their respective present value, then sums all of these together and treats the sum as an obligation (liability) that is then reduced by current resources of investment assets and cash and cash equivalents.

Presumption List - CFP Board's list of conduct that is presumed to be unacceptable and will bar an individual from becoming certified unless that individual petitions the Commission for reconsideration.

Price Earnings (P/E) Approach - Valuing equity securities is an earnings based valuation model that places a premium on the amount investors are willing to pay for each dollar of earnings.

Principal - The grantor giver of a power of attorney.

Privacy Activity Bonds - Bonds issued to finance a joint project between the private sector and a municipality. Private activity bonds are often issued to fund the building of professional sports stadiums.

Private Censure - An unpublished written reproach mailed by the Commission to a censored certificant or registrant.

Probate Process - The legal proceeding that serves to prove the validity of existing wills, supervise the orderly distribution of decedent's assets to the heirs, and protect creditors by insuring that valid debts of the estate are paid.

Process of Financial Planning - The process of financial planning includes: (1) establishing and defining the client relationship, (2) gathering client data, (3) analyzing and evaluating the client's financial status, (4) developing and presenting financial plan recommendations, (5) implementing financial plan recommendations, and (6) monitoring the plan.

Producer Price Index (PPI) - Measures the inflation rate for raw materials used in manufacturing.

Professionalism - Principle 6. Requires behaving with dignity and courtesy to clients, fellow professionals, and others in business-related activities.

Property Risk - A risk that may cause the loss of property (automobile, home, or other asset).

Prospect Theory - Provides that people value gains and losses differently and will base their decisions on perceived gains rather than perceived losses.

Purchasing Power Preservation Model (PPP) - A capital needs analysis method that assumes that at a client's life expectancy, the client will have a capital balance with purchasing power equal to the purchasing power at the beginning of retirement.

Purchasing Power Risk - The risk that inflation will cause prices to increase and a dollar today will not be able to purchase the same amount of goods and services tomorrow.

Pure Annuity Concept - The basic capital needs analysis approach, which is generally prepared on a pretax basis.

Pure Risk - A risk for which there is a possibility of loss, but no possibility of gain. The possibility of a home being damaged or destroyed by a fire is an example of a pure risk. Most pure risks are insurable.

Puts - Gives the holder the right to sell the underlying security at a certain price by a certain date.

Q

Qualified Tuition Plans (Savings Plans) - A plan that allows families to save for education expenses on a tax-deferred basis. Section 529 of the Internal Revenue Code authorized states to adopt qualified tuition plans. The two types of qualified tuition plans are prepaid tuition and college savings plans.

R

Ratio Analysis - The process of calculating key financial ratios for a client, comparing those metrics to industry benchmarks and then making an evaluation regarding any deficiencies.

Ratios for Financial Security Goals - These ratios assess the progress that the client is making toward achieving long-term financial security goals.

Real Estate Investment Trusts (REITs) - A type of mutual fund that pools investor contributions to purchase real estate or make construction or mortgage loans.

Real GDP - Measures the value of goods and services at a base year price.

Real Property - Property that is land and buildings attached to the land.

Realization Event - Generally occurs when an asset has been sold or exchanged. Gains on capital assets are subject to tax only when there has been both a realization event and a recognition event.

Recognition Event - Occurs when a realized gain is included on a taxpayer's income tax return. All realized gains are generally recognized unless a provision in the Code provides otherwise.

Refundable Tax Credits - Tax credits that can be used not only to reduce or eliminate the current year's tax, but also to generate a tax refund.

Registrant - An individual who, though not currently certified, has been certified by CFP Board in the past and has an entitlement, direct or indirect, to potentially use the CFP® marks. This includes individuals who have relinquished their certification and who are eligible for reinstatement without being required to pass the current CFP certification examination.

Regulation Full Disclosure (or Regulation FD) - Requires companies to disclose all material information simultaneously to both the investment community and individual investors.

Reinvestment Rate Risk - The risk that an investor will not be able to reinvest income received from current investments at the same rate of return as the current investment return.

Remaining Work Life Expectancy (RWLE) - The work period that remains at a given point in time before retirement.

Reserve Requirement - The Federal Reserve requires that banks maintain a certain percentage of their deposits on hand, in the form of cash.

Retirement Life Expectancy (RLE) - The time period beginning at retirement and extending until death; the RLE is the period of retirement that must be funded.

Return on Assets (ROA) Ratio - This ratio measures total asset returns. This ratio must be used cautiously when the client is adding assets that are leveraged with debt.

Return on Investments (ROI) Ratio - A critical performance ratio, as it measures the compounded rate of return on a client's investments.

Return on Net Worth (RONW) Ratio - This ratio further refines the performance set of ratios to calculate the rate of return on net worth.

Revenue Bonds - Bonds issued to raise capital to fund a particular revenue generating project. The revenue generated by the project will be used to repay the bond issuance.

Revocation - Permanent revocation of a certificant's or registrant's right to use the marks.

Risk - The uncertainty associated with investment returns. It is the possibility that actual returns will be different from what is expected.

Risk Adjusted Performance Measures - Sharpe, Treynor and Jensen's Alpha, which can be used to measure the performance of any type of investment including stocks, bonds and mutual funds.

Risk Avoidance - Avoiding an activity so that a financial loss cannot be incurred.

Risk Management - Recommendations usually are related to the insurance portfolio because perils (the cause of a loss) are event driven (e.g., untimely death) or unpredictable, and can occur at any time.

Risk Reduction - Implementing activities that will result in the reduction of the frequency and severity of losses.

Risk Retention - The state of being exposed to a risk and personally retaining the potential for loss.

Risk Tolerance Questionnaire - Evaluates a client's willingness to take risk by addressing risk issues.

Risk Transfer - Transferring or shifting the risk of loss through means such as insurance or a warranty.

Rules of Conduct - Establish expected high standards and also describe the level of professionalism required. The Rules of Conduct govern all those who have the right to use the CFP® marks, whether or not those marks are actually used.

S

S Corporation - A corporation formed under state law that elects to be taxed under Subchapter S of the Internal Revenue Code.

Sarbanes-Oxley Act of 2002 - The legislation established new or enhanced standards for all U.S. public company boards, management, and public accounting firms.

Savings and Investing Management - Management that results in recommendations that require both an increase in savings and an increase in the emergency fund. The savings rate (savings and reinvestment of dividends, interest, and capital gains, plus an employer match/gross pay) should equal 10 - 13 percent if the client only has one goal, that being financial security. If the client and family have multiple goals including retirement, college education, and lump-sum goals (e.g., new house or second home) the savings rate must be increased.

Savings Contributions - An income statement category. Examples of savings contributions include 401(k) plan, 403(b) plan, IRA (traditional or Roth), education savings, any other type of savings account, and reinvested dividends, interest, or capital gains.

Savings Rate - A rate calculated by taking gross savings in dollars (including reinvestment of interest dividends, distributed (realized) capital gains, employee elective deferrals into 401(k), 403(b), and 457 plans plus any employer match), and any other savings divided by gross pay.

Scholarships - A grant of financial assistance made available to students to assist with the payment of education related expenses. Scholarships are available for academic or athletic achievement. Scholarships can be provided to undergraduate or graduate students.

Sector Fund - Restricts investments to a particular segment of the market. For example, there are technology, healthcare, telecommunications, financial, and pharmaceutical.

Securities Act of 1933 - Requires that any new security be registered with the Securities and Exchange Commission (SEC) by filing a registration statement with the SEC.

Securities Exchange Act of 1934 - Created the Securities and Exchange Commission (SEC) and provides the SEC with the authority to regulate the secondary market.

Securities Investor Protection Corporation (SIPC) - Formed in 1970 as a statutorily created nonprofit membership corporation funded by its member securities broker dealers, with the goal of returning cash and securities to investors, in the event a brokerage firm becomes insolvent.

Security Market Line (SML) - The relationship between risk and return as defined by the CAPM (when graphically plotted).

Semivariance - Measures the possibility of returns below the average. Therefore, semivariance is a measure of downside risk.

Sensitivity Analysis - The process of changing key variables in planning assumptions, to determine the overall impact of those changes.

Serial Payments - Payments that are adjusted upward periodically throughout the payment period at a constant rate, in order to adjust for inflation's impact.

Sharpe Ratio - A relative risk adjusted performance indicator, meaning the ratio by itself does not provide any insight. A Sharpe ratio for one fund needs to be compared to the Sharpe ratio for another fund to take on meaning.

Short-Term Liabilities - Represent those obligations that are "current" in nature or due within the next 12 months ($\leq$ 12 months).

Side Instruction Letter - Also known as a personal instruction letter, details the testator's wishes regarding the disposition of tangible possessions (household goods), the disposition of the decedent's body, and funeral arrangements. A side instruction letter is not legally binding, but generally followed.

Similarity Heuristic - Used when a decision or judgment is made when a similar situation occurs.

Single Filing Status - A filing status used by an unmarried taxpayer who does not qualify as a surviving spouse or head of household.

Small, Mid, and Large Cap Funds - May have an objective regarding the size of a firm's market capitalization.

Sole Proprietorship - A business venture owned and operated by a single individual.

Special Needs Dependent - Could be an infant, adolescent, or adult. The dependent could have a wide range of challenges from very mild physical, emotional, or psychological, to a situation where around the clock care is required.

Special Needs Trusts Under 42 U.S.C. Sec. 1396p(d)(4)(A) - Considered to be self-settled in nature, are typically established by the special needs person's parent, grandparent, legal guardian or by a court and will avoid disqualification of Medicaid and SSI benefits.

Specialty Funds - Restrict their investments to firms that are good corporate citizens and do not operate in industries such as alcohol, gambling, or tobacco and are considered socially responsible funds.

Spendthrift Clause - A clause in a trust document which does not allow the beneficiary to anticipate distributions from the trust, assign, pledge, hypothecate, or otherwise promise to give distributions from the trust to anyone. If such a promise is made, it is void and may not be enforced against the trust.

Stafford Loans - Student loans administered by the U.S. Department of Education.

Standard Deduction - A standard amount that is specified by Congress and includes inflation adjustments. Taxpayers may deduct the greater of the standard deduction or allowable itemized deductions.

Standard Deviation - Measures the total risk of an investment.

Standards of Professional Conduct - CFP Board standards comprised of five different categories: Code of Ethics and Professional Responsibility ("Code of Ethics"); Rules of Conduct; Financial Planning Practice Standards ("Practice Standards"); Disciplinary Rules and Procedures ("Disciplinary Rules"); and Candidate Fitness Standards.

Statement of Income and Expenses - A financial statement that represents all income earned or expected to be earned by the client, less all expenses incurred or expected to be incurred during the time period being covered.

Statement of Net Worth - Explains changes in net worth between two balance sheets by reporting financial transactions that are not reported on the income statement or other financial statements.

Statutory Will - A will meeting state statutes generally drawn up by an attorney and signed in the presence of witnesses.

Strategic Approach - This approach uses a mission, goal, and objective approach considering the internal and external environment and may be used with other approaches.

Structural Unemployment - Occurs when there is inequality between the supply and demand for workers.

Substitutes - Products that serve a similar purpose.

Supply - Represents the quantity firms are willing to produce and sell of a good or service, at a particular price.

Surviving Spouse Filing Status - A filing status for a surviving spouse with a dependent child that affords the same basic standard deduction and tax rates as the married filing jointly status.

Suspension - Temporary suspension of a certificant's or registrant's right to use the marks for a term of up to five years for those individuals the Commission deems susceptible to rehabilitation.

Systematic Risk - Represents the risk that is inherent in the "system" and cannot be eliminated through diversification. The system represents U.S. market risk.

T

Tangible Personal Property - Property that is not realty and may be touched.

Tax Credit - An amount that reduces the calculated tax liability of the taxpayer.

Taxable Income - Determined by subtracting allowable deductions from income.

Teacher Education Assistance for College and Higher Education (TEACH) Grant - A grant that provides up to $4,000 per year for students that intend to teach in a public or private elementary, middle, or high school that serves a community of low-income families.

Tenancy by the Entirety - Similar to property owned JTWROS between a husband and wife because property ownership is automatically transferred to the surviving spouse upon death.

Tenancy in Common - An interest in property held by two or more related or unrelated persons. Each owner is referred to as a tenant in common. Tenancy in common is the most common type of joint ownership between nonspouses.

Third Party SNT - Sometimes referred to as a family trust because the trust is a receptacle for funds from a parent, guardian or other family member. The assets of these trusts, if properly structured, are not counted or considered for purposes of available benefits for the beneficiary, thus making possible federal, state, and local funds.

Time Value of Money (TVM) - A mathematical concept that determines the value of money, over a period of time, at a given rate of interest.

Traditional Finance (Modern Portfolio Theory) - Also described in the literature as though some of the concepts of the theory are not necessarily modern and have been subject to much debate and change over recent decades. Traditional finance is premised on four basic premises: (1) Investors are Rational; (2) Markets are Efficient; (3) The Mean-Variance Portfolio Theory Governs; and (4) Returns are Determined by Risk (Beta).

Treynor Ratio - A relative risk adjusted performance indicator. A Treynor ratio for one fund requires comparison to the Treynor ratio for another fund.

Trust - A structure that vests legal title (the legal interest) to assets in one party, the trustee, who manages those assets for the benefit of the beneficiaries (who hold the equitable title) of the trust.

Trustee - The individual or entity responsible for managing the trust assets and carrying out the directions of the grantor that are formally expressed in the trust instrument.

Truth in Lending Act - Protects consumers so that they fully understand the terms of a loan.

Two-step / Three-panel Approach - A step-by-step approach where the client's actual financial situation is compared against benchmark criteria. It stresses the management of risk, seeks to avoid financial dependence, and promotes savings and investing to achieve financial independence.

U

U.S. Government Bonds - Bonds issued by the U.S. government to finance the national debt and to fund deficit spending. The three primary types of bonds issued by the U.S. government are Treasury Bills, Treasury Notes, and Treasury Bonds.

U.S. Government Series EE (issued after 1989) and Series I Bonds - Bonds that can be redeemed to pay for qualified education expenses and the interest earned on the bonds is excluded from taxable income. For purposes of excluding interest income using U.S. Government savings bonds, qualified education expenses include tuition and fees, but do not include room and board.

Unemployed - Refers to those individuals 16 years of age and older who are not working and are making an effort to seek employment.

Unemployment Benefits - Designed to provide an unemployed worker with income for a period of time. The worker must be unemployed and also actively seeking work.

Uneven Cash Flow - An investment or project that has periodic cash flows that are not the same dollar amount.

Uniform Gift to Minors Act (UGMA) - Allows minors to own cash or securities. The UGMA/UTMA accounts are governed by state law that requires the custodian of the account, usually a parent or grandparent, to manage the account for the benefit of the minor child.

Uniform Transfer to Minors Act (UTMA) - Allows minors to own cash, securities, and real estate. The UGMA/UTMA accounts are governed by state law that requires the custodian of the account, usually a parent or grandparent, to manage the account for the benefit of the minor child.

Unit Investment Trust (UIT) - An investment company that passively manages a portfolio of either stocks or bonds, known as a bond or equity UIT.

Unsystematic Risk - Represents the risk that can be diversified away, by combining multiple stocks, from multiple industries, into one portfolio.

Utility - The benefit firms and consumers receive when allocating or spending financial resources.

V

Value Funds - Typically invest in securities that are deemed to be out of favor or extremely under-valued.

Variable Expenses - Those expenses that can be dispensed with and are more discretionary over the short term. Examples of variable expenses include entertainment expenses, vacation expenses, travel expenses, and charitable contributions.

Vertical Analysis - Lists each line item on the income statement as a percentage of total income and presents each line item on the balance sheet as a percentage of total assets. The restated percentage is known as a common size income statement or balance sheet.

W

Wage Replacement Ratio (WRR) - An estimate of the percent of income needed at retirement compared to earnings prior to retirement.

Warrant - A long-term option that gives the holder the right to buy a certain number of shares of stocks in a particular company by a certain date.

Weighted Average Return - Based on the dollar amount or percentage of a portfolio invested in each asset. Investments with a larger allocation or weighting will contribute more to the overall return of the portfolio.

Will - A legal document that provides the testator, or will maker, the opportunity to control the distribution of property, appoint an executor and avoid the state's intestacy law distribution scheme.

Windfall - Often treated by the recipient as quite different than earned money. Windfalls can include lottery winnings, an unexpected inheritance, stock options, IPOs, sometimes marrying into money, or the sale of a business.

Work Life Expectancy (WLE) - The period of time a person is expected to be in the work force, generally 30-40 years.

Workers' Compensation - Designed to protect employees when injured at work. It will provide income replacement if the employee is unable to work. It will also provide medical expense coverage if the employee is injured while at work and it can provide a death benefit to an employee's beneficiary.

Z

Zero Coupon Bonds - Bonds sold at a deep discount to par value and do not pay periodic interest payments. Instead, the bonds increase in value each year, so that at maturity the bonds are worth their par value.

Zero Growth Dividend Model - Values a security based on the stock's capitalized amount of the annual dividends.

Index

F

G